Oxford
STUDEN
Atlas

Editorial Adviser
Dr Patrick Wiegand

OXFORD
UNIVERSITY PRESS

Great Clarendon Street, Oxford OX2 6DP

Oxford University Press is a department of the University of Oxford.
It furthers the University's objective of excellence in research, scholarship,
and education by publishing worldwide in

Oxford   New York

Auckland Cape Town Dar es Salaam Hong Kong Karachi
Kuala Lumpur Madrid Melbourne Mexico City Nairobi
New Delhi Shanghai Taipei Toronto

With offices in

Argentina Austria Brazil Chile Czech Republic France Greece
Guatemala Hungary Italy Japan Poland Portugal Singapore
South Korea Switzerland Thailand Turkey Ukraine Vietnam

Oxford is a registered trade mark of Oxford University Press
in the UK and in certain other countries

ISBN 978 019 913698 8 (hardback)

ISBN 978 019 913699 5 (paperback)

1 3 5 7 9 10 8 6 4 2

Printed in Singapore by KHL Printing Co. Pte Ltd

Paper used in the production of this book is a natural, recyclable productmade from wood
grown in sustainable forests. The manufacturing process conforms to the environmental
regulations of the country of origin.

Acknowledgements

The publishers would like to thank the following for permission to reproduce photographs:

Cover: David Tipling/GettyImages; **p.9**: Planet Observer/Science Photo Library; **p.47**: Planet Observer/Science Photo Library; **p.65**: Planet Observer/Science Photo Library; **p.69**: Joseph Calev/Shutterstock; **p.75**: CNES, 1990 Distribution Spot Image/Science Photo Library; **p.82**: Planet Observer/Science Photo Library; **p.85**: Planet Observer/Science Photo Library; **p.95**: Planet Observer/Science Photo Library; **p.99**: NASA Visible Earth; **p.109**: Planet Observer/Science Photo Library; **p.113**: Celso Pupo/Shutterstock; Amy Nichole Harris/Shutterstock; **p.115**: NASA Visible Earth; **p.122-123**: NASA Visible Earth; **p.124**: NASA Visible Earth; **p.131**: Noaa/Science Photo Library; **p.132tr**: Simon Fraser/Science Photo Library; **p.132 bottom left to right**: Horst Mahr/Photolibrary.com; Jim Steinberg/Photolibrary.com; mediacolor's/Alamy; David Litschel/Alamy; **p.133 top left to right**: blickwinkel/Alamy; Andrew Woodacre/Alamy; Staffan Widstrand/Corbis; Egmont Strigl/Photolibrary.com; **p.133 bottom left to right**: Visions LLC/Photolibrary.com; Dave G. HouserEncyclopedia/Corbis; Charles & Josette Lenars/Corbis; **p.145**: Nasa/Goddard Space Flight Center/Science Photo Library

The page design is by Adrian Smith.

The publishers are grateful to the following .... rice during the development stages of this atlas:
Pam Boardman, Graham Butt, Kathryn Clayton .... y Field, Martyn Gill, Joel Griffiths, Matthew Gunn,
Gareth Huws, Kathryn Jones, Irfon Morris .... a, Liz Roodhouse, John Sadler, Toni Schiavone,
Na .... Yates.

The .... ocieties,

Contents

page

Types of maps _____ 4
Understanding topographic maps _____ 5
Location, scale and direction _____ 6
Map projections _____ 7
GIS _____ 8
Satellite images _____ 9

British Isles   Topographic maps

British Isles _____ 10
Orkney and Shetland Islands _____ 11
Scottish Highlands and Islands _____ 12–13
Northern Ireland   Southern Scotland _____ 14–15
Northern England _____ 16–17
Wales   West and East Midlands _____ 18–19
South East England _____ 20–21
South West England _____ 22–23
Ireland _____ 24–25

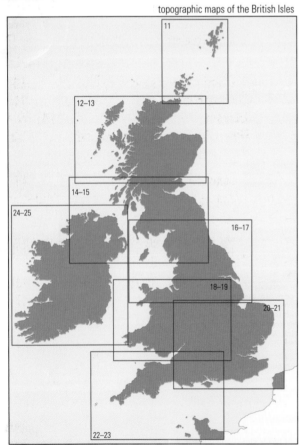

topographic maps of the British Isles

British Isles   Thematic maps

Political	26–27	Employment	37
Physical	28	Population	38–39
Geology	29	Sport	40
Climate	30–31	Quality of life	41
Land use	32	Conservation	
Farming	33	Tourism	42
Water	34	Pollution	43
Energy	35	Transport	44
Manufacturing industry	36	Trade	45

Europe   Thematic maps

Physical _____ 46
Satellite image _____ 47
Political _____ 48
The European Union _____ 49
Population   Wealth _____ 50
Economy _____ 51
Climate   Ecosystems _____ 52
Tourism _____ 53

Europe   Topographic maps

Benelux and the Ruhr _____ 54
Scandinavia and Iceland _____ 55
France _____ 56
Spain and Portugal _____ 57
Middle Europe _____ 58–59
Italy and the Balkans _____ 60–61
East Europe and Turkey _____ 62–63

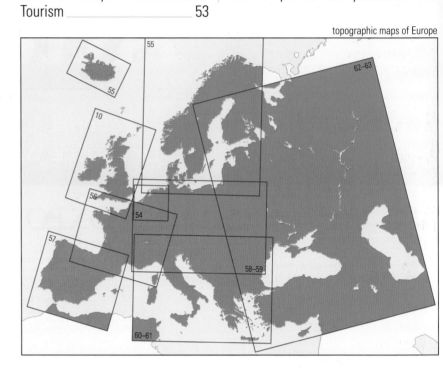

topographic maps of Europe

Asia   Thematic maps

Physical _____ 64
Satellite image _____ 65
Political _____ 66
Economy   Population _____ 67
Climate   Ecosystems _____ 68
Tourism _____ 69

Asia   Topographic maps

Northern Eurasia _____ 70–71
Middle East _____ 72–73
South Asia _____ 74–75
China _____ 76–77
Japan _____ 78
South East Asia _____ 79

topographic maps of Asia

Oceania   Topographic map

Australia and New Zealand _____ 80–81

Oceania   Thematic maps

Physical   Satellite image _____ 82
Climate   Ecosystems
Population   Economy _____ 83

topographic map of Oceania

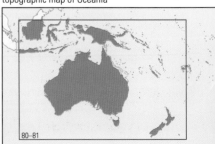

© Oxford University Press

Contents

Africa Thematic maps

Physical ____ 84
Satellite image ____ 85
Political ____ 86
Economy Population ____ 87
Climate Ecosystems ____ 88
Tourism ____ 89

Africa Topographic maps

Northern Africa ____ 90–91
Southern Africa ____ 92
East Africa ____ 93

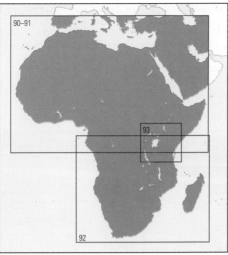

topographic maps of Africa

North America Thematic maps

Physical ____ 94
Satellite image ____ 95
Political ____ 96
Economy Population ____ 97
Climate Ecosystems ____ 98
Tourism ____ 99

North America Topographic maps

Canada ____ 100–101
United States of America ____ 102–103
Great Lakes ____ 104–105
Mexico, Central America
  and the Caribbean ____ 106–107

topographic maps of North America

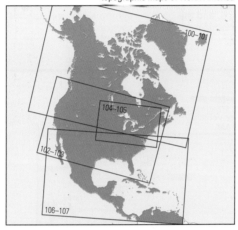

South America Thematic maps

Physical ____ 108
Satellite image ____ 109
Political ____ 110
Economy Population ____ 111
Climate Ecosystems ____ 112
Tourism ____ 113

South America Topographic map

South America ____ 114–115

topographic map of South America

Oceans and Poles Topographic maps

Pacific Ocean ____ 116
Arctic Ocean Antarctica ____ 117

World Thematic maps page

Political ____ 118–119
Physical ____ 120–121
Satellite image ____ 122–123
Earthquakes and volcanoes ____ 124–125

Temperature and ocean currents ____ 126
Pressure, winds and precipitation ____ 127
Climate regions ____ 128–129
Climate data ____ 130

Climate hazards ____ 131
Ecosystems ____ 132–133
Population ____ 134–135
Population trends ____ 136–137

Quality of life ____ 138–139
Economic development ____ 140–141
Energy ____ 142
Trade Transport ____ 143

Environmental issues ____ 144
Climate change ____ 145
Tourism ____ 146–147
Time, distance and cyberspace ____ 148

Globalisation ____ 149
Datasets ____ 150–157

Index

How to use the index ____ 158
Index ____ 159–176

topographic maps of the Poles

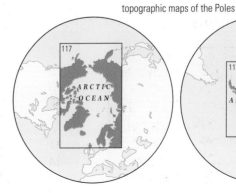

topographic map of the Pacific Ocean

© Oxford University Press

Types of maps

Maps are representations of the Earth's surface on a flat piece of paper. Maps can include such diverse information as the location of places, the depiction of economic and social data, the type and location of transportation routes, and the portrayal of change through time. Maps are everywhere; we come across them in everyday situations such as shopping centres, schools, road atlases, and increasingly on the Internet. These pictures of the Earth's surface find many ways to attract our attention, orient our inquiries, and ultimately help direct our lives. An effective map is like a narrative — an open-ended and dynamic story that creates a dialogue between it and the user. It is not a straightforward text to be read; rather, it is a series of questions to be asked, ideas to be explored, and preconceptions to be challenged.

The two principal kinds of maps used in this atlas are topographic and thematic maps. Examples of these are shown below. In addition to these types of map, other devices can be used to show information about the Earth. These include globes (a spherical model of the Earth), plans (showing small areas), cross-sections (vertical views), and charts (navigational maps). Satellite imagery has also become an increasingly important means of understanding phenomena on the Earth's surface, and examples can be seen throughout the atlas.

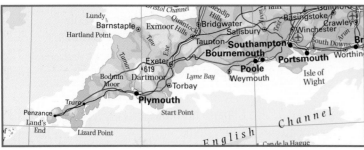

Topographic maps, also known as physical-political maps, are the general purpose maps in most atlases and provide a variety of information such as political boundaries, roads and railways, cities and towns, and the features of the physical landscape. Legends for the topographic maps in this atlas are expained on the opposite page.

Thematic maps provide information about a variety of specific topics such as agriculture, climate, trade, and quality of life. Many different kinds of symbols are used for this purpose; the main ones are detailed in the section below.

Symbols on thematic maps

Point symbols

Dot map
Each blue dot represents 100 000 sheep.
From p33

Economic map
Blue squares represent a main centre of the motor vehicle industry.
From p36

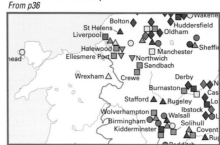

Proportional symbols
The size of the blue circles is proportional to the amount of cargo handled at each port.
From p44

Line symbols

Isopleth map
Lines join places with equal amounts of sunshine.
From p31

Isotherm map
Some isopleths have special names. Isotherms join places with equal temperature.
From p30

Line map
The lines represent major transport routes.
From p143

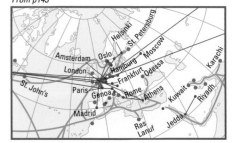

Area symbols

Choropleth map
Darker colours show areas with a higher percentage of land used for growing potatoes.
From p33

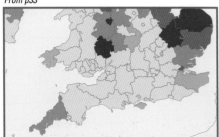

Environmental map
Each colour represents an ecosystem. Purple stands for mountains.
From p133

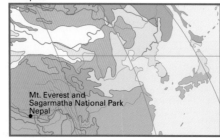

Political map
Colours have no meaning but are simply used to show where one country ends and another begins.
From p118

Topographic maps show the main features of the physical landscape as well as settlements, communications, and boundaries. Background colours show the height of the land.

British Isles maps

boundaries
━━━ international
━━━ national
─── internal
─── national park

communications
━━━ motorway
━━━ primary road
─── A road
─── railway
┼┼┼┼ canal
- - - major ferry route
⊕ major airport
✈ other airport

settlements
⬡ built-up area
■ over 1 million inhabitants
● more than 100 000 inhabitants
◉ 25 000 – 100 000 inhabitants
• smaller towns

Non-British Isles maps

boundaries
━━━ international
▬ ▬ ▬ disputed
─── internal

communications
━━━ motorway
─── major road
─── railway
┼┼┼┼ canal
✈ major airport

settlements
⬡ built-up area
■ over 1 million inhabitants
● more than 100 000 inhabitants
• smaller towns

physical features
⌒ river, lake
⌒ seasonal river
⬭ seasonal lake
▨ marsh
⬭ salt lake
⬭ salt pan
⬭ ice cap
⬭ sand dunes

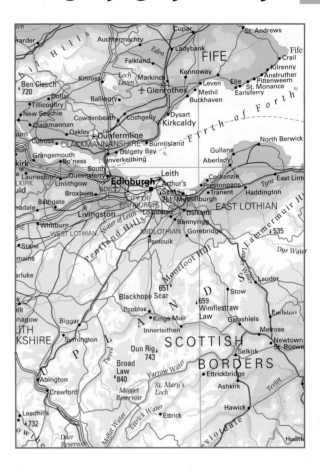

Place names
Anglicized spellings are used. Former names (where places have recently changed their names), and alternative spellings are shown in brackets.

This atlas has been designed for English speaking readers and so all places have been named using the Roman alphabet.

Type style
Contrasting type styles are used to show the difference between physical features, settlements, and administrative areas.

Physical features are separated into two categories, land and water. Land features are shown as roman type:

e.g.   Pentland Hills

Water features are shown in italics:

e.g.   *Firth of Forth*

Peaks are shown in condensed type:

e.g.   Broad Law 840

Settlement names are shown in upper and lower case:

e.g.   Leith

Administrative areas are shown in capital letters:

e.g.   MIDLOTHIAN

The importance of places is shown by the size of the type and whether the type face is bold or medium:

e.g.   **Edinburgh**   Livingston   Broxburn

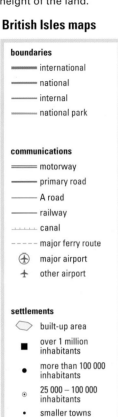

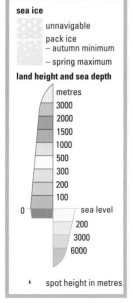

sea ice
▦ unnavigable
▨ pack ice
– autumn minimum
– spring maximum

land height and sea depth
metres
3000
2000
1500
1000
500
300
200
100
0   sea level
200
3000
6000
▲ spot height in metres

Sea ice
White stipple patterns over the sea colour show the seasonal extent of sea ice.

Land height and sea depth
Colours on topographic maps refer only to the height of the land or the depth of the sea. They do not give information about land use or other aspects of the environment.

An imaginary grid is used to pinpoint the position of any place on Earth.

The grid consists of lines running east and west which are called parallels of latitude, and those extending north and south are called meridians of longitude. Both are measured in degrees.

When used together, lines of latitude and longitude form a grid. The position of places on the surface of the Earth can be located accurately using this grid.

Latitude

Parallels of latitude measure distance north or south of the Equator. The Equator is at latitude 0°. The Poles are at latitudes 90°N and 90°S.

Longitude

Meridians of longitude measure distance east and west of the Prime Meridian. The Prime (or Greenwich) Meridian is at longitude 0°. The 180° meridian of longitude, on the opposite side of the Earth is the International Date Line.

The Equator divides the Earth into halves: the Northern Hemisphere and the Southern Hemisphere.

The Prime Meridian and the 180° meridian together also divide the Earth into halves: the Western Hemisphere and the Eastern Hemisphere.

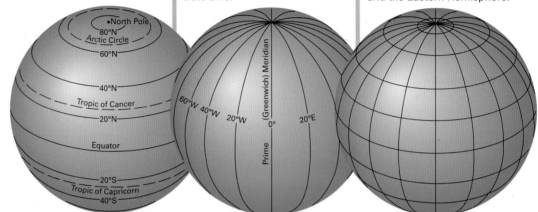

Scale

Maps are much, much smaller than the areas they show. A few centimetres on the map stand for very many kilometres on the ground.

This map has a ratio (also called a representative fraction) of 1: 1 000 000. The map is one million times smaller than the area it shows.

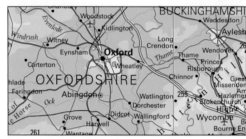

Each division on the scale line is one centimetre.

The scale line shows how many kilometres are represented by one centimetre.

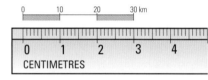

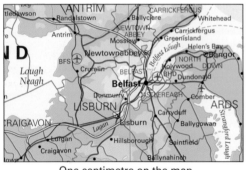

One centimetre on the map represents **10 kilometres** on the ground.

Scale 1: 1 000 000

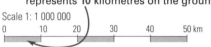

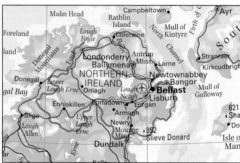

One centimetre on the map represents **45 kilometres** on the ground.

Scale 1: 4 500 000

One centimetre on the map represents **220 kilometres** on the ground.

Scale 1: 22 000 000

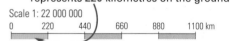

Larger scale
smaller area more detail

Smaller scale
larger area less detail

Compass rose

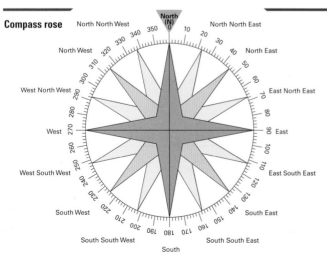

Direction

A direction can be expressed in two ways:

1. In terms of north, east, south, and west (the cardinal points of the compass) and various points between, such as east south east or north west (the intermediate points). These are shown on the diagram of the compass rose.

2. In terms of degrees (as a bearing), ranging through the values of the compass from 0° (north), 90° (east), 180° (south) to 359° (one degree west of north). These are also shown on the compass rose diagram.

The North Pole, is referred to as true or geographic north. Likewise, the South Pole is known as the true or geographic south. By convention, most maps are oriented so that true (geographic) north occurs toward the top of the map. Thus, when we refer to north and south on most maps, we are speaking of these poles.

There are also magnetic north and south poles. The magnetic north pole is presently located to the northwest of Ellesmere Island in the Canadian Arctic (see page 117) and is moving about 24 km a year in a north-easterly direction.

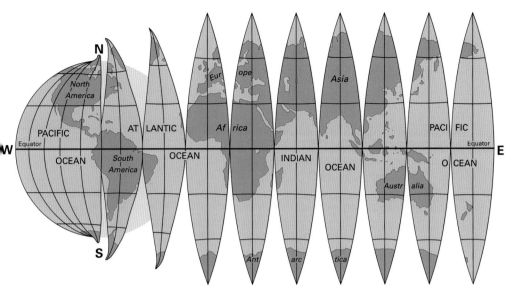

The most accurate way of looking at the Earth's land and sea areas is to use a globe. Globes, however, are not always available and are seldom large enough to show much detail. Thus, for most uses, maps are more convenient. To create a map it is necessary to transfer the surface of the globe on to a flat surface. In theory, as the diagram shows, it is necessary to unpeel strips (also known as gores) from the globe's surface, but such a method has obvious drawbacks. Since it is impossible to flatten the curved surface of the Earth without stretching or cutting part of it, it is necessary to employ other methods in order to produce an orderly system of parallels and meridians on which a map can be drawn. Such systems are referred to as **map projections**.

There are two main types of projections: **equal area projections**, where the area of any territory is shown in correct size proportion to other areas, and **conformal projections**, where the emphasis is on showing the shape correctly. No map can be both equal area and conformal, though some projections are designed to minimize distortions in both area and shape.

lar projections give a good view of the [pol]es. Most other projections do not show [An]tarctica or the Arctic Ocean accurately.

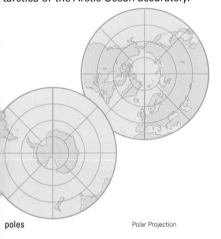

poles   Polar Projection

[Th]e **Oblique Aitoff projection**, created by David [Ait]off in 1889, is an equal area projection. The [arr]angement of the land masses allows a good [vie]w of routes in the northern hemisphere. The [po]sition of North America and Asia on either [sid]e of the Arctic is shown clearly.

——— major air routes

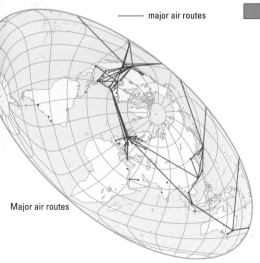

Major air routes   Oblique Aitoff Projection

Mercator's projection is a conformal projection and was initially designed by Gerhardus Mercator in 1569 to be used for navigation. Any straight line on the map is a line of constant compass bearing. Straight lines are not the shortest routes, however. Shape is accurate on a Mercator projection but the size of the land masses is distorted. Land is shown larger the further away it is from the equator. (For example, Alaska is shown four times larger than its actual size).

——— line of constant compass bearing

- - - - - shortest route

Eckert IV projection was designed by the German cartographer Max Eckert (1868–1938). It is an equal area projection, showing the true area of places in relation to each other. This projection is often used in this atlas, the maps permitting fair comparisons to be made between areas of the world.

 tropical forest

Gall's projection represents a compromise between equal area and conformal. This map shows plate boundaries.

——— plate boundaries

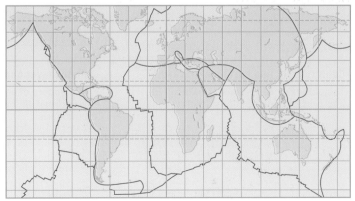

Navigation chart   Mercator's Projection

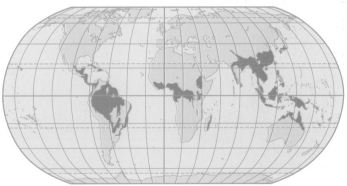

Tropical forest   Eckert IV Projection

Plate boundaries   Gall's Projection

Geographical Information Systems

Increasingly, maps are made using Geographic Information Systems (GIS). These are powerful combinations of databases and mapping software.

A GIS user can decide what information they want to show and how to show it. Information is selected from a database and is arranged in map layers made up of points, lines and polygons. Each of these items has a hidden geographical component, such as an address, city, country or latitude and longitude coordinates. These layers can be turned on and off. Symbols for points, lines and polygons can be selected and changed to meet the user's needs. Patterns on the map can be analysed to show new relationships.

GIS is widely used for scientific investigations, resource management, environmental impact assessment, urban planning, law enforcement, emergency response planning and habitat management.

In the example on this page, GIS is used to investigate characteristics of the Earth's plate boundaries in and around South America.

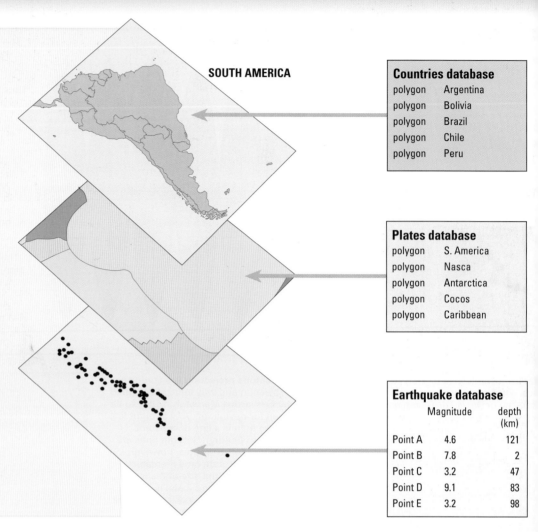

SOUTH AMERICA

Countries database

polygon	Argentina
polygon	Bolivia
polygon	Brazil
polygon	Chile
polygon	Peru

Plates database

polygon	S. America
polygon	Nasca
polygon	Antarctica
polygon	Cocos
polygon	Caribbean

Earthquake database

	Magnitude	depth (km)
Point A	4.6	121
Point B	7.8	2
Point C	3.2	47
Point D	9.1	83
Point E	3.2	98

SOUTH AMERICA

Country layer and earthquakes layer
The pattern of earthquakes is difficult to interpret without additional information.

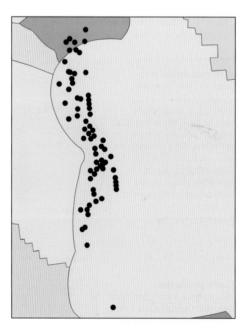

Plates layer and earthquakes layer
The pattern of earthquakes is clearly associated with the pattern of plate boundaries.

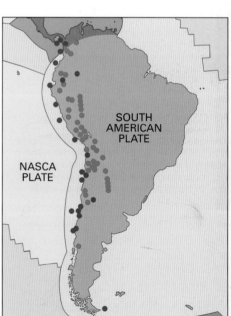

SOUTH AMERICAN PLATE

NASCA PLATE

Plate boundary layer and selection of the largest and deepest earthquakes from the earthquakes database.
The pattern of earthquakes shows the boundary between the Nasca Plate and the South American Plate is a destructive one. The largest earthquakes (●) occur at the plate boundary whilst the deepest earthquakes (●) occur to the east as the Nasca Plate slides below the South American Plate.

Remote sensing
Sensors on spacecraft such as *Landsat* detect and measure radiation from the earth's surface. The radiation can be interpreted to provide information about land cover, the oceans and atmosphere.

Scale 1 : 4 500 000

ATLANTIC OCEAN

NORTH SEA

IRISH SEA

English Channel

St. George's Channel

Bristol Channel

Shetland Islands
Unst
Yell
Fetlar
Mainland
Foula
Lerwick
Sumburgh Head
Fair Isle

Westray
Sanday
Stronsay
Mainland
Kirkwall
Hoy
Orkney Islands
Pentland Firth
Duncansby Head

Rona

Cape Wrath
Thurso
Wick

Butt of Lewis
Lewis
Stornoway

Outer Hebrides

St. Kilda
Harris

North Uist
Benbecula

Ullapool
Ben Wyvis ▲1046
Dingwall
Moray Firth
Elgin
Fraserburgh
Peterhead

Little Minch
The Minch

South Uist

Skye
Kyle of Lochalsh
▲1009
Loch Shin
Dornoch Firth

Northwest Highlands
Loch Ness
Inverness
Monadhliath Mountains
Cairngorms ▲1310
Ben Macdhui
Aberdeen

Barra

Rhum
Eigg
Mallaig
▲1183

SCOTLAND

Fort William ▲1344
Ben Nevis

Grampian Mountains

Coll
Tiree
Iona
Mull
Oban
Loch Linnhe
Loch Lomond

Sidlaw Hills
Perth
Dundee
St. Andrews
Arbroath

Colonsay
Jura
Islay
Sound of Jura
Firth of Lorn

Loch Tay
Stirling
Alloa
Kirkcaldy
Dunfermline
Firth of Forth

Edinburgh
Falkirk
Cumbernauld
St. Abb's Head

Bute
Greenock
Clydebank
Glasgow
Paisley
East Kilbride
Motherwell
Kilmarnock

Berwick-upon-Tweed
Holy Island

Arran
Ayr
▲840
Lammermuir Hills
Galashiels
Hawick
Cheviot Hills

Southern Uplands

Malin Head
Bloody Foreland
Aran Island

Rathlin Island
Campbeltown
Mull of Kintyre

North Channel

UNITED KINGDOM

Dumfries
Blyth
Newcastle upon Tyne
Sunderland

Stranraer
Kirkcudbright
Solway Firth
Gateshead
Durham
Hartlepool
Middlesbrough

Lough Foyle
Londonderry
Ballymena
Antrim Mtns.
Larne
Coleraine
Newtownabbey

Donegal Mountains
Lough Swilly

Carlisle
Penrith
▲893
Eden
Stockton-on-Tees
Darlington
North York Moors
Scarborough

Donegal
Lower Lough Erne
Upper Lough Erne
Omagh

NORTHERN IRELAND
Enniskillen
Portadown
Armagh
Newry
Lough Neagh
Lurgan
Lisburn
Belfast
Bangor

Workington
Whitehaven
Cumbrian Mtns.
St. Bees Head
▲978
Scafell Pike
Kendal

Flamborough Head
Yorkshire Wolds

Donegal Bay
Erris Head

Sligo
Lough Erne
Mourne Mtns.
▲852
Slieve Donard

▲621
Snaefell
Douglas
Barrow-in-Furness
Lancaster

Harrogate
York
Kingston upon Hull

Achill Island
Westport
Castlebar
Lough Conn
Lough Mask

Lough Allen
Dundalk
Kells
Drogheda
IRISH SEA
Isle of Man

Blackpool
Preston
Leeds
Bradford
Huddersfield
Scunthorpe
Spurn Head

Slyne Head

Longford
Mullingar

Blackburn
Bolton
Oldham
Doncaster
Grimsby
Humber

Liverpool
Southport
Wigan
Manchester
Stockport
Sheffield
Lincoln Wolds

Clare
Lough Ree
Athlone
Lough Corrib
Galway
Galway Bay

REPUBLIC OF IRELAND

Tullamore
Dublin
Dún Laoghaire
Bray

Anglesey
Holyhead
Holy Island
Caernarfon
Birkenhead
Colwyn Bay
Bangor
Chester
Crewe
St. Helens
Chesterfield
Stoke-on-Trent
Lincoln
Boston
Skegness

Aran Islands

Naas
Wicklow Mtns.
▲926

▲1085
Snowdon
Wrexham
Derby
Nottingham
The Wash

Loop Head

Portlaoise
Shannon
Barrow
Nore
Kilkenny

Cardigan Bay
Aberystwyth

Shrewsbury
Telford
Stafford
Walsall
Leicester
Peterborough
King's Lynn
Great Yarmouth
Wensum

Limerick
Galty Mtns.
Clonmel

Cambrian Mtns.
▲892

Wolverhampton
Dudley
Birmingham
Coventry
Rugby
Northampton
The Fens
Norwich
Lowestoft
Waveney

Tralee
Kilarney
▲1041
Carrauntoohill
Suir
Blackwater
Waterford
Wexford
Rosslare
Carnsore Point

WALES
Hereford
Worcester
Solihull
Banbury
Bedford
Cambridge
Ipswich
Felixstowe
Harwich

Dingle Bay
Lee
Youghal
Fishguard
St. David's Head
Teifi
Teme
Cheltenham
Cotswold Hills
Oxford
Chiltern Hills
Milton Keynes
Luton
Colchester
Stour
Chelmsford

Cork
Old Head of Kinsale

Carmarthen
Brecon Beacons
Milford Haven
Llanelli
Neath
Merthyr Tydfil
Rhondda
Cwmbran
Black Mtns.
Gloucester
Swindon
Slough
St. Albans
London
Southend-on-Sea

Caha Mtns.
Mizen Head
Cape Clear
Bantry Bay

Swansea
Newport
Cardiff
Barry
Bristol
Bath
Mendip Hills
Reading
Basildon
Guildford
Maidstone
Gillingham
Margate
Canterbury
Dover

Lundy
Barnstaple
Exmoor Hills
Bridgwater
Salisbury Plain
Salisbury
Winchester
Basingstoke
Crawley
The Weald
Folkestone
Hastings

Hartland Point
Taunton
Quantock Hills
Southampton
Bournemouth
Portsmouth
Worthing
Brighton
Eastbourne
Beachy Head

Exeter
▲619
Dartmoor
Torbay
Poole
Weymouth
Isle of Wight

Bodmin Moor
Lyme Bay
Start Point

Truro
Plymouth
Penzance
Land's End
Lizard Point
Isles of Scilly

FRANCE
Cap de la Hague
Alderney
Guernsey
Channel Islands
St. Peter Port
Sark
Jersey
St. Helier
Cherbourg
Baie de la Seine
Caen
le Havre
le Tréport
Dieppe
Boulogne-sur-Mer
le Touquet-Paris-Plage
Calais
Strait of Dover

English Channel

60°N
58°N
56°N
54°N
52°N
50°N

12°W 10°W 8°W 6°W 4°W 2°E

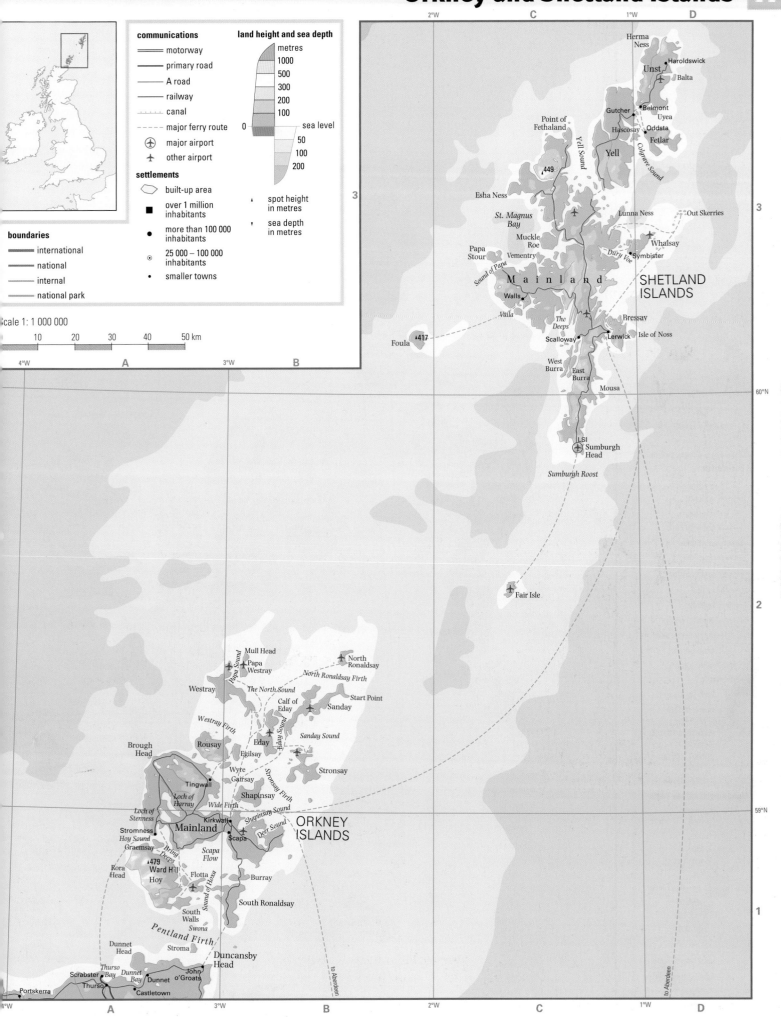

communications
- motorway
- primary road
- A road
- railway
- canal
- major ferry route
- ✈ major airport
- ✈ other airport

settlements
- ⬡ built-up area
- ■ over 1 million inhabitants
- ● more than 100 000 inhabitants
- ◉ 25 000 – 100 000 inhabitants
- • smaller towns

land height and sea depth

metres
1000
500
300
200
100
0 — sea level
50
100
200

- ▲ spot height in metres
- ▼ sea depth in metres

boundaries
- international
- national
- internal
- national park

Scale 1: 1 000 000

0 10 20 30 40 50 km

© Oxford University Press   Transverse Mercator Projection

SHETLAND ISLANDS

Herma Ness
Unst
Haroldswick
Balta
Point of Fethaland
Gutcher
Belmont
Uyea
Hascosay
Oddsta
Fetlar
Yell
Yell Sound
Colgrave Sound
▲449
Esha Ness
Lunna Ness
Out Skerries
St. Magnus Bay
Whalsay
Muckle Roe
Dury Voe
Symbister
Papa Stour
Vementry
Mainland
Sound of Papa
Walls
Bressay
Vaila
The Deeps
Lerwick
Isle of Noss
Foula ▲417
Scalloway
West Burra
East Burra
Mousa
60°N
Sumburgh Head
LSI
Sumburgh Roost

Fair Isle
2

ORKNEY ISLANDS

Mull Head
Papa Westray
North Ronaldsay
North Ronaldsay Firth
Westray
The North Sound
Start Point
Calf of Eday
Sanday
Westray Firth
Sanday Sound
Rousay
Eday
Eday Sound
Brough Head
Egilsay
Stronsay
Wyre
Gairsay
Stronsay Firth
Tingwall
Shapinsay
Loch of Harray
Wide Firth
Shapinsay Sound
Loch of Stenness
Kirkwall
Deer Sound
Stromness
Mainland
Scapa
59°N
Hoy Sound
Graemsay
Bring Deeps
Scapa Flow
Burray
▲479
Ward Hill
Flotta
Hoy
Sound of Hoxa
South Ronaldsay
Rora Head
South Walls
Swona
Pentland Firth
Stroma
Dunnet Head
Duncansby Head
Thurso Bay
Dunnet Bay
John o'Groats
Scrabster
Dunnet
Portskerra
Thurso
Castletown
to Aberdeen
1

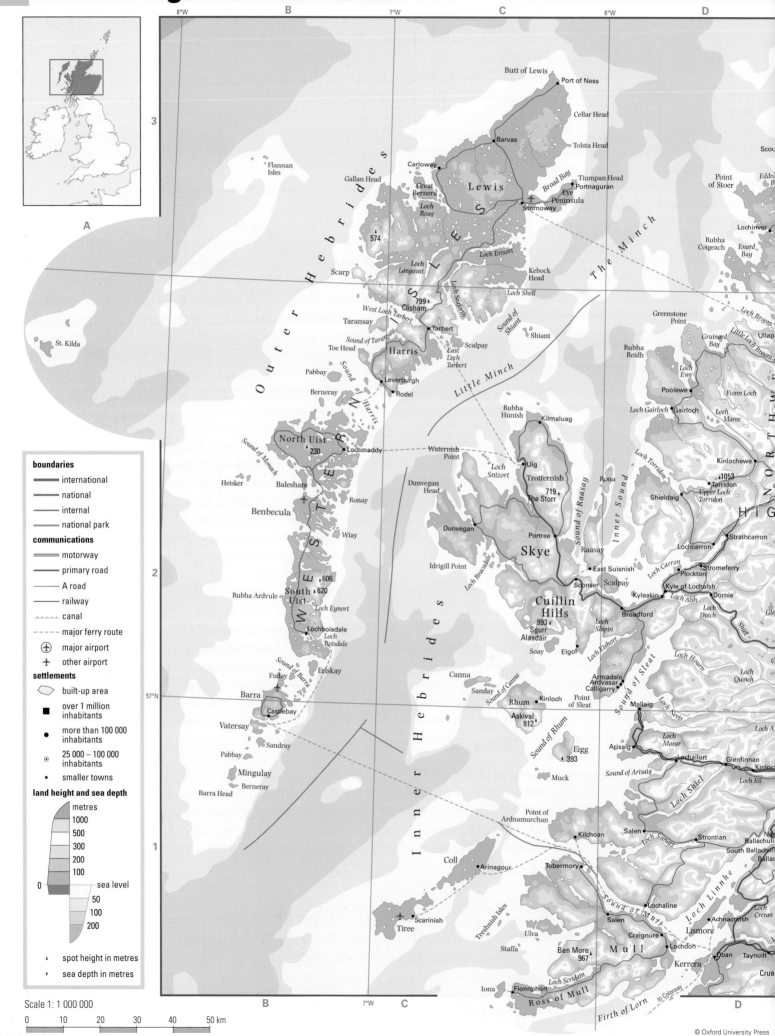

boundaries

▬▬▬	international
▬▬▬	national
▬▬▬	internal
▬▬▬	national park

communications

═══	motorway
───	primary road
───	A road
───	railway
┼┼┼	canal
─ ─ ─	major ferry route
✈	major airport
✈	other airport

settlements

⬡	built-up area
■	over 1 million inhabitants
●	more than 100 000 inhabitants
⊙	25 000 – 100 000 inhabitants
•	smaller towns

land height and sea depth

metres
1000
500
300
200
100
0 — sea level
50
100
200

▲ spot height in metres
▼ sea depth in metres

Scale 1: 1 000 000

0   10   20   30   40   50 km

© Oxford University Press

Pentland Firth

Dunnet Head
Stroma
Duncansby Head
Duncansby
Head

to Kirkwall

Wrath

Durness
Whiten Head
Strathy Point
Scrabster
Thurso Bay
Dunnet Bay
Dunnet
Castletown
John o'Groats
Kyle of Durness
Loch Triboll
Kyle of Tongue
Thurso
Strathy
Portskerra
Halkirk
Loch Watten
Sinclair's Bay
Loch Hope
Ben Loyal 764
Tongue
Melvich
Noss Head
Ben Hope 927
Loch Loyal
Bettyhill
Mybster
Wick
Reay Forest
Loch Meadie
Loch nan Clàr
Wick
Altnaharra
Lybster
Unapool
Ben Klibreck 961
Kinbrace
Morven 705
Latheron
Loch Assynt
Loch Naver
Dunbeath Water
Dunbeath
Camsp 347
Ben More Assynt 998
Loch Shin
Berriedale Water
Berriedale
Ledmore
Helmsdale
Helmsdale

3

Lairg
Brora
Brora
Beinn Dearg 1081
Golspie
Dornoch
58°N
Sgurr Mòr 1109
Ben Wyvis 1046
Bonar Bridge
Dornoch Firth
Tarbat Ness
Loch Fannich
Loch Glass
Alness
Nigg Bay
Tain
Portmahomack
Garve
Loch Luichart
Strathpeffer
Dingwall
Invergordon
Cromarty
Black Isle
Moray Firth
Lossiemouth
Findochty
Portknockie
Portsoy
Whitehills
Troup Head
Rosehearty
Kinnaird Head
Muir of Ord
Conon Bridge
Forttose
Nairn
Burghead Bay
Burghead
Buckie
Cullen
Banff
Gardenstown
Fraserburgh
Beauly
Tore
Fort George
Forres
Elgin
Fochabers
Maeduff
Loch of Strathbeg
Inverness
North Kessock
MORAY
Spey
Aberchirder
Turriff
New Deer
Mintlaw
Rattray Head
Cannich
Drumnadrochit
Beauly Firth
Rothes
Keith
Deveron
Peterhead
Buchan Ness
Loch Ness
Tomatin
Dufftown
Huntly
Boddam
Grantown-on-Spey
Bogie
Rhynie
Oldmeldrum
Ellen
Hatton
Carrbridge
Avon
Don
518
Inverurie
Pitmedden
Monadhliath Mountains
Aviemore
Tomintoul
Alford
Kemnay
Kintore
Dyce
Invermoriston
CAIRNGORMS
Don
Kincardine
ABZ
Bridge of Don
Fort Augustus
Cairn Gorm 1244
CAIRNGORMS NATIONAL PARK
ABERDEENSHIRE
Westhill
Aberdeen
Ben Macdui 1310
Peterculter
Cove Bay
Invergarry
Kingussie
Balmoral
Crathie
Aboyne
Banchory
Portlethen
935
Newtonmore
Braemar
Ballater
Water of Feugh
57°N
Spean Bridge
Dalwhinnie
Bridge of Dee
Lochnagar 1155
Cowie Water
Stonehaven
Ben Alder 1148
Glas Maol 1068
North Esk
Fettercairn
Inverbervie
Ben Nevis 1344
South Esk
Laurencekirk
Milton Ness
Blair Atholl
Glen Shee
Prosen Water
ANGUS
Blackwater Reservoir
Tummel Bridge
Pitlochry
Brechin
Montrose Basin
Montrose
Kinlochleven
Rannoch Station
Bridge of Ericht
Kinloch Rannoch
Dunalastair Reservoir
Loch Tummel
Isla
Inverquharity
South Esk
Lunan Bay
Rannoch Moor
Loch Rannoch
Aberfeldy
Ardle
Kirriemuir
Forfar
Lunan Water
Glen Etive 1108
Alyth
Rattray
Arbroath
Loch Tulla
Ben Lawers 1214
Dunkeld
Blairgowrie
Coupar Angus
Carnoustie
Bridge of Orchy
Loch Tay
Killin
Sidlaw Hills
DUNDEE CITY
Monifieth
Broughty Ferry
Buddon Ness
PERTH AND KINROSS
Dundee
Crianlarich
Ben More 1174
Loch Earn
Comrie
Crieff
New Scone
Perth
Tayport
Newport-on-Tay
Leuchars
Eden Mouth
St. Andrews Bay
Newburgh
Cupar
St. Andrews

1

to Lerwick

communications
motorway
primary road
A road
railway
canal
major ferry route
major airport
other airport

land height and sea depth
metres
1000
500
300
200
100
0 — sea level
50
100
200

settlements
built-up area
over 1 million inhabitants
more than 100 000 inhabitants
25 000 – 100 000 inhabitants
smaller towns

spot height in metres
sea depth in metres

boundaries
international
national
internal
national park

Scale 1: 1 000 000

0 10 20 30 40 50 km

NORTHERN IRELAND

Malin Head
Glengad Head
Fanad Head
Dunaff Head
Horn Head
Clonmany
Culdaff
Cardonagh
Inishowen Head
Ramore Head
Bull Point
Rathlin Island
Benbane Head
Rue Point
Giants Causeway
Fair Head
Sheep Haven
Mulroy Bay
Lough Swilly
Inishowen Peninsula
615 Slieve Snaght
Moville
Magilligan Point
Portrush
Portstewart
Bushmills
Ballycastle
MOYLE
Cushendun
Cushendall
Red Bay
554
Garron Point
Horn Head
Ballymore
Creeslough
Millford
Inch Island
Muff
Quigley's Point
Coleraine
Ballymoney
Antrim Mountains
Falcarragh
Errigal Mountain 752
Kilmacrenan
Rathmelton
Lough Foyle
Eglinton
Limavady
LIMAVADY
COLERAINE
BALLYMONEY
Carnlough Bay
Carnlough
Corsewall Point
DONEGAL
Letterkenny
Newtown Cunningham
Londonderry
LONDONDERRY
New Buildings
Roe
Dungiven
Kilrea
Cullybackey
BALLYMENA
Broughshane
Ballymena
Ballygalley Head
Fintown
St. Johnstown
Raphoe
Lifford
Faughan
Portglenone
Maghera
Ahoghill
Larne
Larne Lough
Island Magee
Kirkcolm
Strabane
Sion Mills
Castlefinn
Sperrin Mountains
683 Sawel
MAGHERAFELT
Tobermore
Draperstown
Magherafelt
Castledawson
Lough Beg
Main
ANTRIM
Randalstown
LARNE
CARRICKFERGUS
Whitehead
Ballybofey
Ballintra
Blue Stack Mountains
Lough Eske
Castlederg
Newtownstewart
Owenkillew
Moneymore
Cookstown
COOKSTOWN
Stewartstown
Antrim
Ballyclare
NEWTOWN ABBEY
Mossley
Carrickfergus
Greenisland
Helen's Bay
Copeland Island
Mew Island
Ballyshannon
Kesh
OMAGH
Dromore
Fintona
Dungannon
Coalisland
Lough Neagh
Newtownabbey
Crumlin
BELFAST
NORTH DOWN
Holywood
Bangor
Donaghadee
Millisle
Lough Melvin
Garrison
FERMANAGH
Lough Macnean Upper
Enniskillen
Lisbellaw
Lisnaskea
Irvinestown
Ballinderry
Camowen
Dungannon
DUNGANNON AND SOUTH TYRONE
Moygashel
Moy
Coalisland
CRAIGAVON
Lurgan
Portadown
Craigavon
Dromore
Lagan
Lisburn
LISBURN
Dunmurry
CASTLEREAGH
Comber
Ballygowan
Kircubbin
Portavogie
ARDS
Ards Peninsula
Strangford Lough
Newtownards
Dundonald
Carryduff
Hillsborough
Saintfield
Ballynahinch
Crossgar
Killyleagh
Portaferry
Ballyquintin Point
Manorhamilton
Lough Macnean Lower
Upper Lough Erne
Lower Lough Erne
Blackwater
Clogher
Augher
Aughnacloy
Emyvale
Armagh
ARMAGH
Richhill
Tandragee
Gilford
Banbridge
Dromore
BANBRIDGE
DOWN
Downpatrick
Ardglass
St. John's Point
Dowra
Ballinagleragh
Swanlinbar
Belturbet
Butlers Bridge
Clones
MONAGHAN
Ballybay
Castleblayney
Muckno Lough
Crossmaglen
Newtownhamilton
Keady
Markethill
Bessbrook
NEWRY AND MOURNE
Newry
Rathfriland
Castlewellan
Newcastle
Mourne Mtns
852 Slieve Donard
Dundrum Bay
Ballykinler
LEITRIM
Drumshanbo
Ballinamore
Garadice Lough
Lough Oughter
Cootehill
Ballyconnell
Annalee
Shannon
Erne
Lough Allen
Warrenpoint
Omeath
Rostrevor
Carlingford Lough
Greenore
Greencastle
Kilkeel
Annalong
Ballagan Point
Dundalk
Carlingford

North Channel

Iona
Fionnphort
Ross of Mull
Firth of Lorn
to Oban
Loch Avich
Loch Melfort
Lochan Shira
Loch Awe
S
Inveraray
Strachur
ARGYLL AND BUTE
Furnace
Loch Fyne
Dunoon
Colintraive
Colonsay
Scalasaig
Loch Craignish
Crinan
Loch Tarbert
Lochgilphead
Scarba
Oronsay
Jura
Rubh' a' Mhail
Loch Gruinart
Loch Gorm
Islay
Port Askaig
Feolin Ferry
785
Craighouse
Sound of Jura
Knapdale
Kilmory
Loch Caolisport
Loch Sween
West Loch Tarbert
Tighnabruaich
Kames
Tarbert
Rhubodach
Toward
Rothesay
Kennacraig
Claonaig
Clachan
Skipness Point
Sound of Bute
Lochranza
Sannox
Goat Fell 874
Brodick
Lamlash
Arran
512
Blackwaterfoot
Portnahaven
Port Wemyss
Laggan Bay
Bowmore
491
Ardmore Point
Gigha
Ardminish
Sound of Gigha
Kilbrannan Sound
Ardbeg
Port Ellen
Mull of Oa
Kintyre
Lussa Loch
Machrihanish
Campbeltown
446
Southend
Sanda Island
Mull of Kintyre
Ailsa Craig
Corsewall Point
Ballantrae
Stranraer
Loch Ryan
Leswalt
The Rhins
Portpatrick
Kirkcolm
Carnryan
Castle Kenne

Transverse Mercator Projection © Oxford University Press

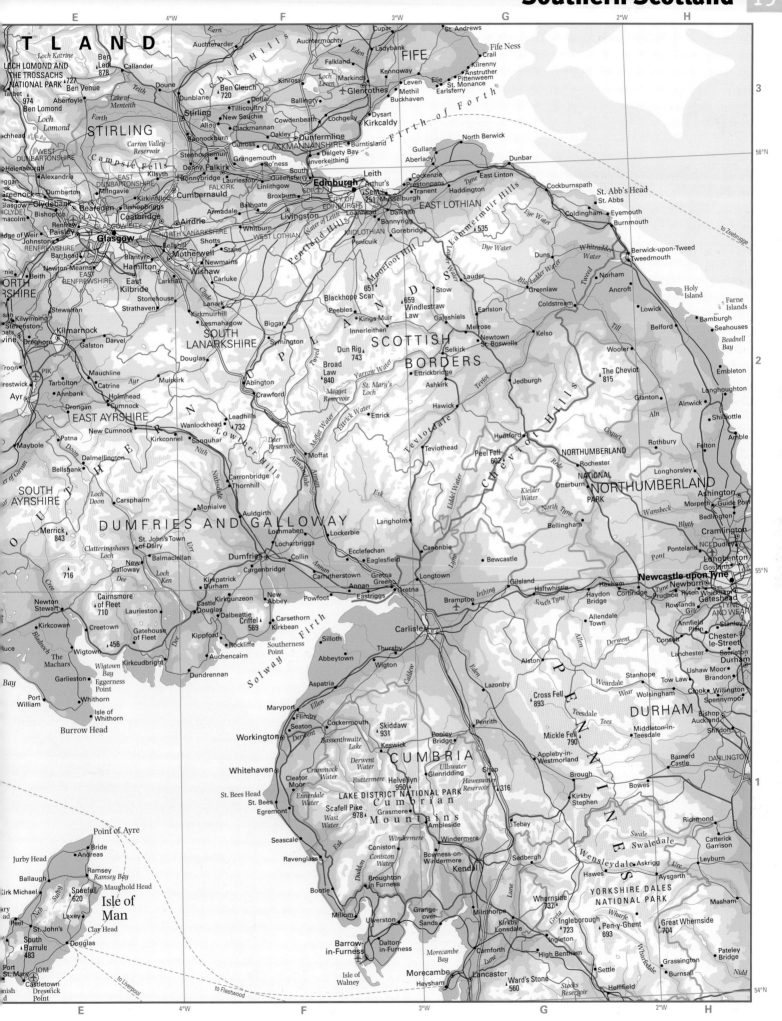

Transverse Mercator Projection   © Oxford University Press

Scale 1: 1 000 000

0   10   20   30   40   50 km

A · B · C

5°W · 4°W · 3°W

to Dublin
to Dublin
to Belfast
to Douglas

Southport
Rufford
Formby
Burscough Bridge
Ormskirk
Skelmersdale
Maghull
Kirkby
Crosby
Liverpool Bay
Liverpool
Bootle
Wallasey
Moreton
Hoylake
West Kirby
Bebington
Birkenhead
Neston
Ellesmere Port

3

Carmel Head
Cemaes
Amlwch
Holyhead
Holy Island
Valley
Rhosneigr
Aberffraw
Llyn Alaw
ISLE OF ANGLESEY
Anglesey
Moelfre
Benllech
Llanerchymedd
Llangefni
Beaumaris
Menai Bridge
Bangor
Bethesda
Great Ormes Head
Llandudno
Conwy
Penmaenmawr
Llanfairfechan
Colwyn Bay
Abergele
Rhyl
Prestatyn
St. Asaph
Holywell
Flint
Connah's Quay
Shotton
Hawarden
Buckley
Mold
Hope
Brymbo
Broughton
CONWY
FLINTSHIRE
Denbigh
Ruthin
Clwydian Range
Llyn Brenig
Alwen Reservoir
DENBIGHSHIRE
Wrexham
WREXHAM
Rhosllanerchrugog
Cefn-mawr
Ruabon
Overton
Ellesmere

Caernarfon
1062 Carnedd Llewelyn
Glyder Fawr 999
Llanberis
Snowdon 1085
Penygroes
Caernarfon Bay
Moel Hebog 782
Blaenau Ffestiniog
Ffestiniog
Betws-y-Coed
Llanrwst
Trawsfynydd
Bala
Llyn Tegid
Corwen
Llangollen
Chirk
Llangollen
Whittington

Nefyn
Criccieth
Tudweiliog
Pwllheli
Porthmadog
Penrhyndeudraeth
Tremadog Bay
Harlech
Llyn Trawsfynydd
SNOWDONIA NATIONAL PARK
GWYNEDD
Llanuwchllyn
Aran Fawddwy 905
Foel Wen 690
Llangynog
West Felton
Oswestry

Lleyn Peninsula
Aberdaron
Abersoch
Bardsey Island

Barmouth
Fairbourne
Cadair Idris 892
Dolgellau
Dinas Mawddwy
Llanfair Caereinion
Welshpool
Llangadfan
Llyn Efyrnwy
Llanfyllin
Shrewsbury

2

Cardigan Bay

Tywyn
Machynlleth
WALES
Caersws
Newtown
Montgomery
Church Stoke
Bishop's Castle
Long Mynd 517

Aberdyfi
Borth
Tal-y-bont
Plynlimon 752
Nant-y-moch Reservoir
Ponterwyd
Llyn Clywedog
Llanidloes
Cambrian Mountains
Clun Forest

Aberystwyth
Rheidol
Devil's Bridge
Ystwyth
Llangurig
Llanbister
Knighton

Llanrhystud
Craig Goch Reservoir
Rhayader
Radnor Forest
Presteigne

Aberaeron
CEREDIGION
Caerwen Reservoir
Caban-coch Reservoir
New Radnor
Pembridge
Leominster

New Quay
Aeron
Tregaron
Newbridge-on-Wye
Llandrindod Wells
Kington

Ystrad Aeron
Llyn Brianne Reservoir
POWYS
Garth
Builth Wells
HEREFORD

Cemaes Head
Aberporth
Lampeter
Teifi
Pumsaint
Garth
Irfon
Mynydd Eppynt
Hay-on-Wye

Cardigan
Newcastle Emlyn
Llanybydder
Llandysul
Llanwrtyd Wells
Wye

Strumble Head
Goodwick
Newport
Teifi
Ffostrasol
Llandovery
Talgarth
Black Mountains 811

52°N

to Rosslare
to Rosslare

Fishguard
Mynydd Preseli
Crymych
Llangadog
Brecon
Sennybridge
Usk
Crickhowell
Abergavenny

St. David's Head
Ramsey Island
St. David's
CARMARTHENSHIRE
Carmarthen
Llandeilo
1802
Black Mountain
Fforest Fawr
886
BRECON BEACONS NATIONAL PARK
Talybont Reservoir
MONMOUTHSHIRE

PEMBROKESHIRE
St. Brides Bay
Skomer Island
Skokholm Island
St. Ann's Head
Haverfordwest
Whitland
St. Clears
Laugharne
Ammanford
Cross Hands
Brynamman
Glanaman
Ystradgynlais
Glyn Neath
Hirwaun
BLAENAU GWENT
Brynmawr
Ebbw Vale
Blaenavon
Abertillery
Pontypool
Mon

PEMBROKESHIRE COAST NATIONAL PARK
Narberth
Kilgetty
Pendine
Kidwelly
Ystalyfera
Pontardawe
Clydach
NEATH PORT TALBOT
MERTHYR TYDFIL
Merthyr Tydfil
Rhymney
Tredegar
New Tredegar
Bargoed
Blackwood
Newbridge
Cwmbran

Milford Haven
Neyland
Pembroke Dock
Pembroke
Saundersfoot
Tenby
Burry Port
Llanelli
Gorseinon
Loughor
Pontardulais
Glynneath
Glyncorrwg
Aberdare
Mountain Ash
Rhondda
CAERPHILLY
Gelligaer
Bedwas
Risca
Caerleon
Newport
NEWPORT

Angle
St. Govan's Head
Caldey Island
Carmarthen Bay
Gower
Burry Port
Loughor
SWANSEA
Swansea
Neath
Briton Ferry
Port Talbot
Maesteg
Margam
Pontypridd
Llantrisant
Llanharan
Pencoed
Caerphilly
Rumney
CARDIFF
Cardiff
Penarth

Rhossili
Worms Head
Port-Eynon
The Mumbles
Swansea Bay
Bishopston
Llanrhidian
Pyle
Porthcawl
Bridgend
BRIDGEND
Pencoed
THE VALE OF GLAMORGAN
Cowbridge
Llantwit Major
Barry
Dinas Powys
Rhoose
Flat Holm

1

to Cork
Gilfach Goch
Tonyrefail
Llanharan

Bristol Channel

St. George's Channel

Weston-super-Mare

Transverse Mercator Projection   © Oxford University Press

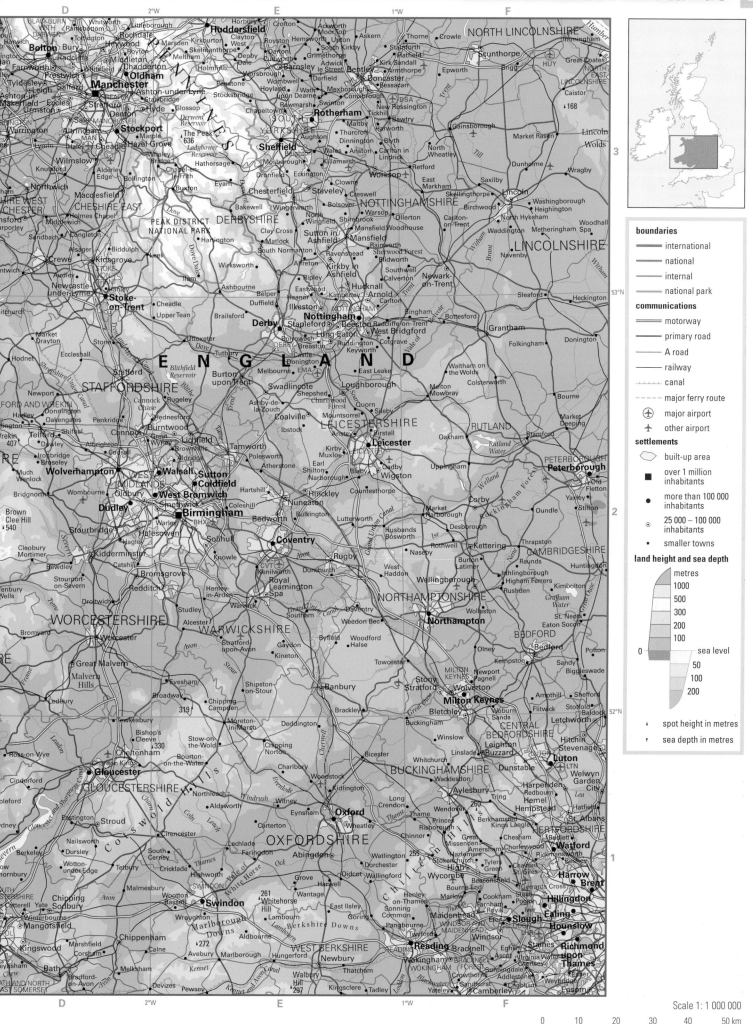

© Oxford University Press

Scale 1: 1 000 000

0 10 20 30 40 50 km

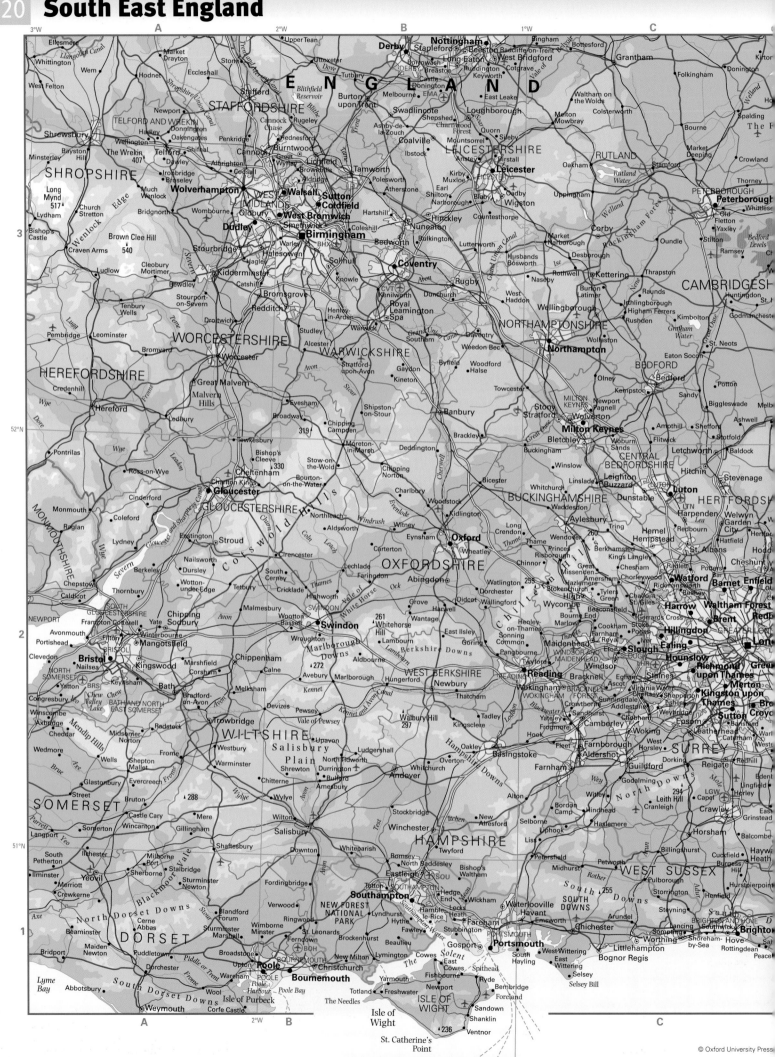

© Oxford University Press

to Esbjerg

The Wash

Burnham
Market
Wells-next-
the-Sea
Hunstanton
Heacham
Blakeney
Point
Sheringham
Cromer
Holt
Docking
Mundesley
Dersingham
Sandringham
Saxthorpe
North
Walsham
Fakenham
King's Lynn
Aylsham
Winterton-
on-Sea
Reepham
Coltishall
Wisbech
Nar
East
Dereham
Taverham
Bure
NWI
Wroxham
Acle
Caister-
on-Sea
Norwich
THE
BROADS
Great
Yarmouth
NORFOLK
Swaffham
Watton
Wensum
Wymondham
Belton
Downham
Market
Attleborough
Loddon
Hopton on Sea
Breckland
Yare
Feltwell
Little Ouse
Bungay
Lowestoft
Littleport
Brandon
Thetford
Beccles
Ely
Lakenheath
Harleston
Kessingland
Lark
Isleham
Mildenhall
Diss
Waveney
Soham
Fordham
Eye
Southwold
Burwell
Kentford
Ixworth
Blyth
Halesworth
Yoxford
Newmarket
Debenham
Leiston
bridge
Bury
St. Edmunds
Alde
Saxmundham
Great Shelford
Stowmarket
Framlingham
sawston
Needham Market
SUFFOLK
Wickham
Market
Aldeburgh
Deben
Linton
Lavenham
Claydon
Orford
Haverhill
Long
Melford
Stour
Orwell
Woodbridge
Orford Ness
Great
Chesterford
Sudbury
Hadleigh
Ipswich
Saffron
Walden
Sible
Hedingham
Bawdsey
Newport
Halstead
Earls Colne
Manningtree
Felixstowe
Thaxted
Great
Bardfield
Colne
Stour
Harwich
ffichet
Braintree
Coggeshall
Thorpe-
le-Soken
The Naze
Walton-on-
the-Naze
STN
Bishop's
stortford
Great
Dunmow
Kelvedon
Wivenhoe
Colchester
Frinton-on-Sea
Abberton
Reservoir
Tiptree
Brightlingsea
wbridgeworth
Witham
Clacton-on-Sea
West Mersea
Mersea Island
Chipping
Ongar
ESSEX
Writtle
Chelmsford
Blackwater
Bradwell-
on-Sea
Ingatestone
Maldon
Danbury
Hanningfield
Reservoir
South Woodham
Ferrers
Southminster
Brentwood
Billericay
Hullbridge
Foulness
Point
Havering
Wickford
Hockley
Burnham-
on-Crouch
Foulness
Island
Rayleigh
Rochford
ng
South
Ockendon
Basildon
Hadleigh
SOUTHEND
THURROCK
South Benfleet
Southend-on-Sea
Aveley
West Thurrock
Canvey
Island
Shoeburyness
exley
Grays
Tilbury
Thames
Grain
artford
Swanscombe
MEDWAY
Sheerness
Swanley
Hoo
Minster
New Ash
Green
Queenborough
Isle of
Sheppey
Leysdown
on Sea
Foreness
Point
Otford
Gravesend
Strood
Rochester
Herne
Bay
Margate
Sevenoaks
Snodland
Gillingham
Chatham
The Swale
Whitstable
MSE
North Foreland
Broadstairs
Aylesford
Sittingbourne
Faversham
Minster
Ramsgate
Tonbridge
Bearsted
Maidstone
Canterbury
Ash
Sandwich
KENT
North
Charing
Wye
Ash
Aylesham
Deal
Paddock Wood
Merden
Great Stour
Downs
Stour
Whitfield
St. Margaret's at Cliffe
Royal
Pembury
Staplehurst
Ashford
Kennington
Brabourne
Lees
Lyminge
South Foreland
Tunbridge Wells
Bethersden
Dover
Cranbrook
Tenterden
Romney
Marsh
Hythe
Wadhurst
Hamstreet
Folkestone
Hawkhurst
Dymchurch
Bewl
Water
Rother
Northiam
New Romney
ield
Heathfield
Rye
Lydd
EAST SUSSEX
Battle
Winchelsea
Dungeness
Hailsham
Fairlight
Polegate
Hastings
Pevensey
Bexhill
Eastbourne
Beachy Head

to Europoort and Hook of Holland

to Vlaardingen

to Oostende

Bray-Dunes
Malo-les-Bains
Dunkerque
Grand Fort-
Philippe
Gravelines
Bergues
Strait of Dover
(Pas de Calais)
Calais
Marck
Bourbourg
Canal de Calais
Cap
Gris-Nez
Guînes
Marck
Esquelbecq
Wormhout
Slack
Ardres
Audruica
Aa
Watten
Cassel
Marquise
NORD-PAS-DE-CALAIS
St-Omer
Wimereux
Boulogne-sur-Mer
Liane
Desvres
Lumbres
Hazebrouck
FRANCE
Hardelot-Plage
Samer
Lys
Aire-
sur-la-Lys
Thérouanne

51°N

52°N

© Oxford University Press   Transverse Mercator Projection

boundaries
— international
— national
— internal
— national park

communications
— motorway
— primary road
— A road
— railway
⋯⋯ canal
– – – major ferry route
⊕ major airport
✈ other airport

settlements
⬡ built-up area
■ over 1 million inhabitants
● more than 100 000 inhabitants
◉ 25 000 – 100 000 inhabitants
• smaller towns

land height and sea depth
metres
1000
500
300
200
100
0 sea level
50
100
200

▴ spot height in metres
▾ sea depth in metres

Scale 1: 1 000 000

0 10 20 30 40 50 km

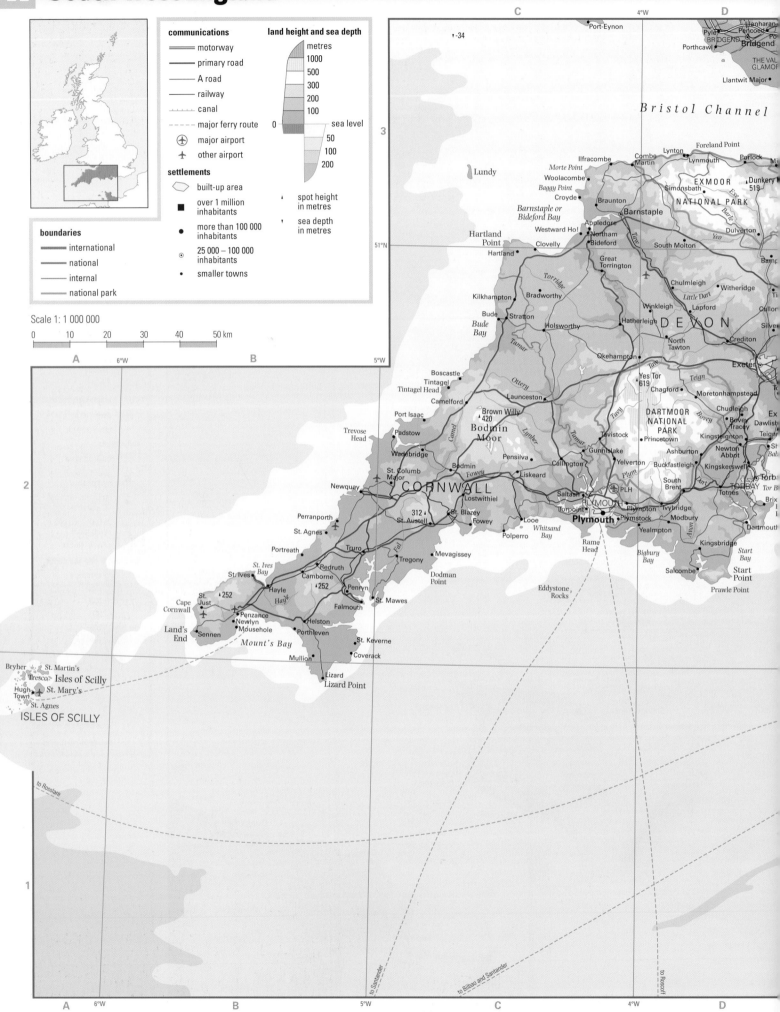

Transverse Mercator Projection © Oxford University Press

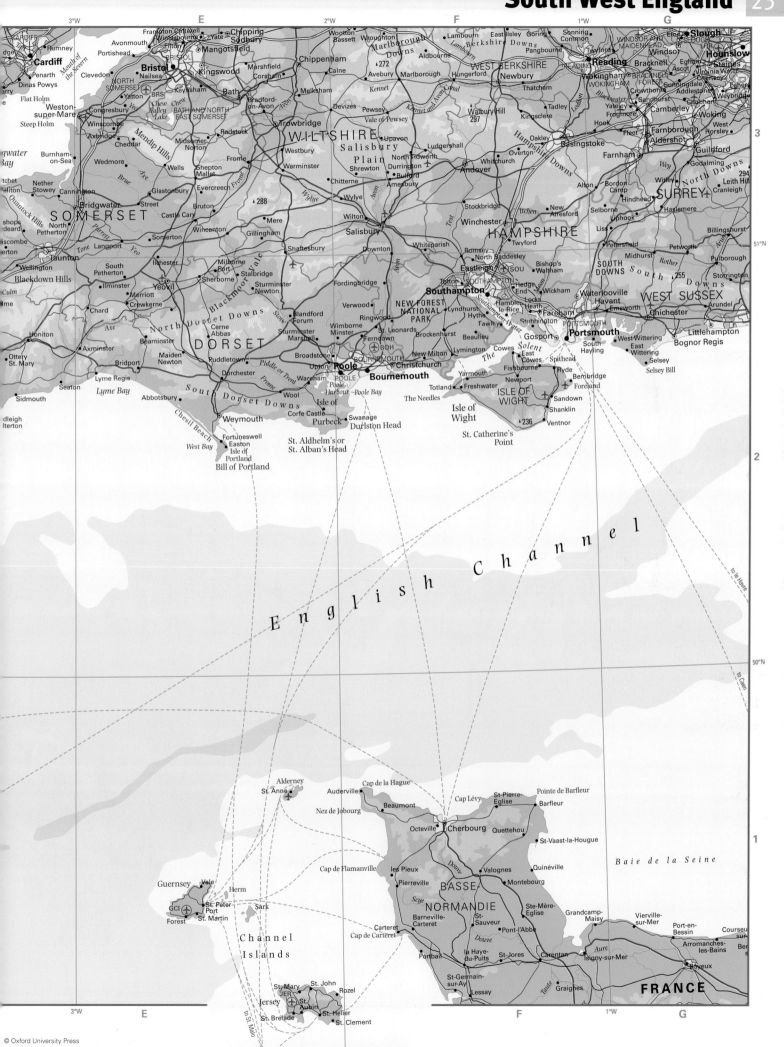

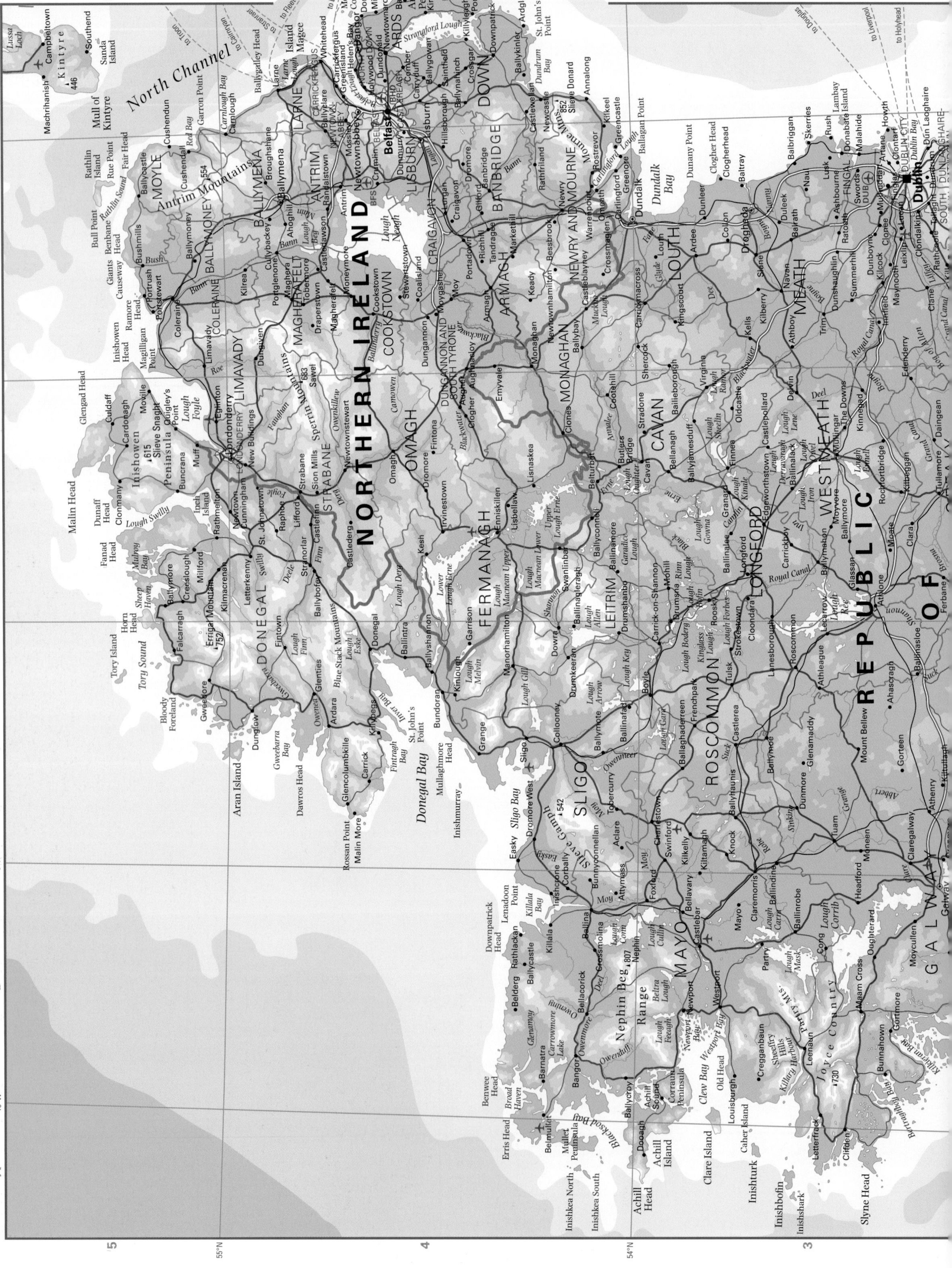

NORTHERN IRELAND

REPUBLIC OF

North Channel

Belfast

Dublin
DUBLIN CITY

Counties and regions: MOYLE, BALLYMONEY, BALLYMENA, ANTRIM, LARNE, COLERAINE, LIMAVADY, MAGHERAFELT, COOKSTOWN, STRABANE, OMAGH, DUNGANNON AND SOUTH TYRONE, CRAIGAVON, ARMAGH, BANBRIDGE, DOWN, ARDS, NEWRY AND MOURNE, FERMANAGH, DONEGAL, SLIGO, LEITRIM, CAVAN, MONAGHAN, LOUTH, MEATH, WESTMEATH, LONGFORD, ROSCOMMON, MAYO, GALWAY, FINGAL, SOUTH DUBLIN

Physical features and places: Malin Head, Fanad Head, Horn Head, Bloody Foreland, Tory Island, Tory Sound, Aran Island, Dawros Head, Slieve Snaght 615, Errigal 752, Blue Stack Mountains, Donegal Bay, Benwee Head, Broad Haven, Erris Head, Mullet Peninsula, Achill Head, Achill Island, Clare Island, Inishturk, Inishbofin, Inishshark, Slyne Head, Clew Bay, Nephin Beg Range, Nephin 807, Lough Conn, Lough Mask, Lough Corrib, Joyce Country, Killary Harbour, Antrim Mountains, Giants Causeway, Rathlin Island, Rathlin Sound, Benbane Head, Rue Point, Fair Head, Lough Neagh, Lough Foyle, Lough Swilly, Sperrin Mountains, Sawel 683, Camowen, Upper Lough Erne, Lower Lough Erne, Lough Gill, Sligo Bay, Slieve Gamph, Lough Allen, Lough Key, Lough Ree, Shannon, Royal Canal, Grand Canal, Carlingford Lough, Slieve Donard 852, Strangford Lough, Dundalk Bay, Lambay Island, Ireland's Eye, Howth, Dún Laoghaire

Kintyre 446, Mull of Kintyre, Sanda Island, Campbeltown, Machrihanish, Lussa Loch, Southend

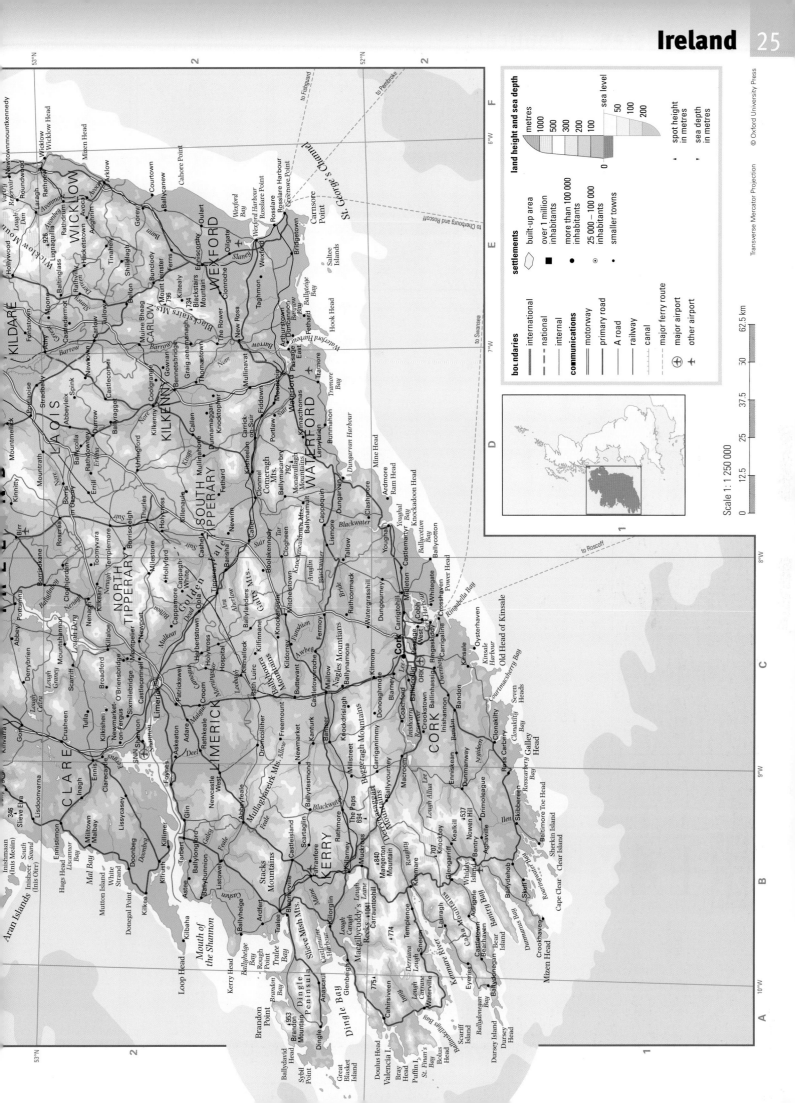

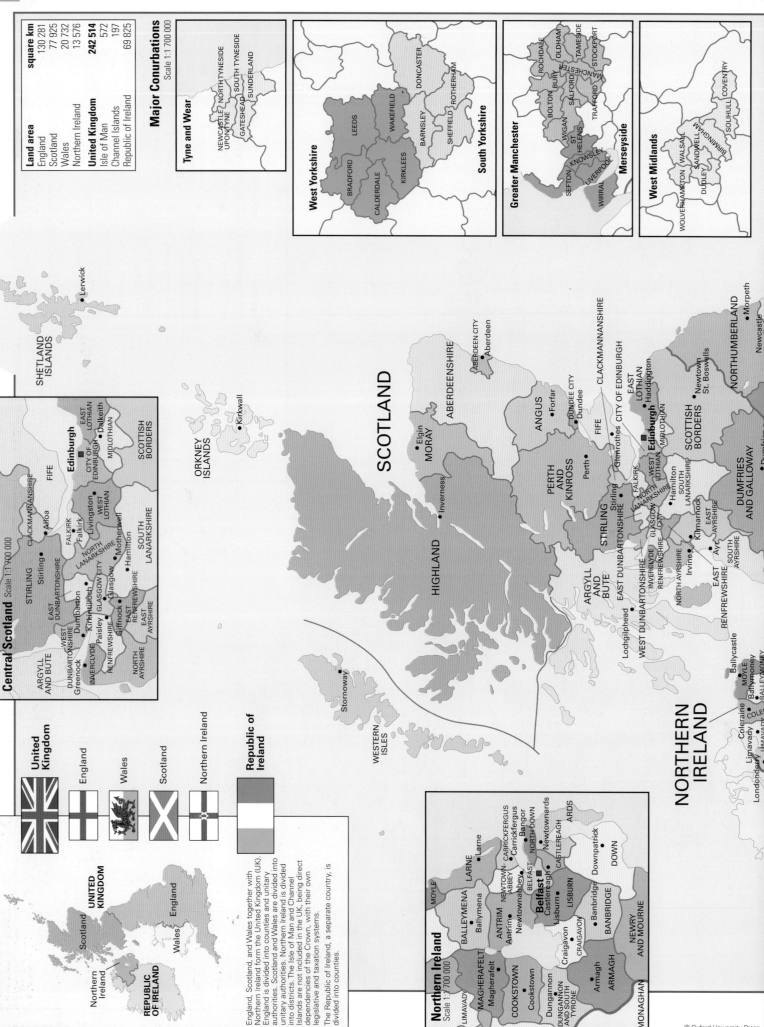

Major Conurbations
Scale 1:1 700 000

Land area	square km
England	130 281
Scotland	77 925
Wales	20 732
Northern Ireland	13 576
United Kingdom	**242 514**
Isle of Man	572
Channel Islands	197
Republic of Ireland	69 825

Tyne and Wear

West Yorkshire — LEEDS, WAKEFIELD, BRADFORD, CALDERDALE, KIRKLEES

South Yorkshire — DONCASTER, BARNSLEY, ROTHERHAM, SHEFFIELD

Greater Manchester — ROCHDALE, OLDHAM, BURY, TAMESIDE, BOLTON, STOCKPORT, MANCHESTER, SALFORD, WIGAN, TRAFFORD, ST HELENS, SEFTON, KNOWSLEY, LIVERPOOL, WIRRAL

Merseyside

West Midlands — COVENTRY, WALSALL, BIRMINGHAM, SANDWELL, SOLIHULL, WOLVERHAMPTON, DUDLEY

Central Scotland
Scale 1:1 700 000

Northern Ireland
Scale 1:1 700 000

United Kingdom

England

Wales

Scotland

Northern Ireland

Republic of Ireland

England, Scotland, and Wales together with Northern Ireland form the United Kingdom (UK). England is divided into counties and unitary authorities. Scotland and Wales are divided into unitary authorities. Northern Ireland is divided into districts. The Isle of Man and Channel Islands are not included in the UK, being direct dependencies of the Crown, with their own legislative and taxation systems.

The Republic of Ireland, a separate country, is divided into counties.

SCOTLAND

NORTHERN IRELAND

© Oxford University Press

Teesside
Scale 1:1 700 000

Hartlepool • HARTLEPOOL
• Durham
DURHAM
Stockton-on-Tees
Darlington • DARLINGTON
STOCKTON-ON-TEES
Redcar • REDCAR & CLEVELAND
Middlesbrough • MIDDLESBROUGH
NORTH YORKSHIRE

ENGLAND

NORFOLK • Norwich
SUFFOLK • Ipswich
CAMBRIDGESHIRE • Cambridge
ESSEX • Chelmsford
THURROCK • Grays • Southend-on-Sea SOUTHEND
KENT • Maidstone
• Chatham MEDWAY
EAST SUSSEX • Lewes
• Brighton BRIGHTON AND HOVE
Hove

international boundary
national boundary
administrative boundary
capital city
administrative centre

Thames Valley
Scale 1:1 700 000

BUCKINGHAMSHIRE • Slough SLOUGH
• Maidenhead WINDSOR AND MAIDENHEAD
BRACKNELL FOREST • Bracknell
• Reading READING
WEST BERKSHIRE • Newbury • Wokingham WOKINGHAM
SURREY
WILTSHIRE HAMPSHIRE

NORTH EAST LINCOLNSHIRE
EAST RIDING OF YORKSHIRE • Beverley
KINGSTON UPON HULL • Kingston upon Hull
NORTH LINCOLNSHIRE • Scunthorpe
• Grimsby
LINCOLNSHIRE • Lincoln
York • YORK
NORTH YORKSHIRE
• Leeds
WEST YORKSHIRE
SOUTH YORKSHIRE • Sheffield
DERBYSHIRE • Matlock
NOTTINGHAMSHIRE • Nottingham NOTTINGHAM
• West Bridgford
RUTLAND • Oakham
LEICESTERSHIRE • Leicester LEICESTER
• Glenfield
NORTHAMPTONSHIRE • Northampton
PETERBOROUGH • Peterborough
BEDFORD • Bedford
CENTRAL BEDFORDSHIRE • Chicksands
LUTON • Luton
MILTON KEYNES • Milton Keynes
HERTFORDSHIRE • Hertford
• Aylesbury
GREATER LONDON • London
• Kingston upon Thames
SURREY
WEST SUSSEX • Chichester
PORTSMOUTH • Portsmouth
ISLE OF WIGHT • Newport

CUMBRIA
NORTH YORKSHIRE
DURHAM
STOCKTON-ON-TEES
DARLINGTON
HARTLEPOOL
REDCAR AND CLEVELAND
MIDDLESBROUGH
Northallerton

LANCASHIRE • Preston
• Blackpool BLACKPOOL
Blackburn • BLACKBURN WITH DARWEN
GREATER MANCHESTER • Manchester
MERSEYSIDE • Liverpool
Warrington • WARRINGTON
HALTON • Widnes
CHESHIRE WEST AND CHESTER • Chester
CHESHIRE EAST • Sandbach
STOKE-ON-TRENT • Stoke-on-Trent
STAFFORDSHIRE • Stafford
DERBY • Derby
WEST MIDLANDS • Birmingham
TELFORD AND WREKIN • Telford
SHROPSHIRE • Shrewsbury
WARWICKSHIRE • Warwick
WORCESTERSHIRE • Worcester
HEREFORDSHIRE • Hereford
GLOUCESTERSHIRE • Gloucester
SOUTH GLOUCESTERSHIRE • Thornbury
BRISTOL • Bristol
BATH & NORTH EAST SOMERSET • Bath
NORTH SOMERSET • Weston-super-Mare
MONMOUTHSHIRE
TORFAEN
NEWPORT
OXFORDSHIRE • Oxford
SWINDON • Swindon
WEST BERKSHIRE
WOKINGHAM
HAMPSHIRE • Winchester
SOUTHAMPTON • Southampton
WILTSHIRE • Trowbridge
SOMERSET • Taunton
DORSET • Dorchester
POOLE • Poole
BOURNEMOUTH • Bournemouth
Newbury

CHANNEL ISLANDS

UNITED KINGDOM

ISLE OF MAN
■ Douglas

WALES
GWYNEDD
ISLE OF ANGLESEY
CONWY • Conwy
• Llangefni
• Caernarfon
CEREDIGION • Aberaeron
POWYS • Llandrindod Wells
DENBIGHSHIRE • Rhyl
FLINTSHIRE • Mold
WREXHAM • Wrexham
MERTHYR TYDFIL
RHONDDA CYNON TAFF
BLAENAU GWENT
CAERPHILLY
BRIDGEND
THE VALE OF GLAMORGAN
CARDIFF • Cardiff
NEATH PORT TALBOT
SWANSEA • Swansea
CARMARTHENSHIRE • Carmarthen
PEMBROKESHIRE • Haverfordwest

DEVON • Exeter
TORBAY • Torquay
PLYMOUTH • Plymouth
CORNWALL • Truro
St. Mary's
ISLES OF SCILLY

REPUBLIC OF IRELAND

■ Dublin DUBLIN CITY
DÚN LAOGHAIRE-RATHDOWN
SOUTH DUBLIN
FINGAL
WICKLOW • Wicklow
WEXFORD • Wexford
CARLOW • Carlow
KILKENNY • Kilkenny
KILDARE • Naas
LAOIS • Portlaoise
OFFALY • Tullamore
WEST MEATH • Mullingar
MEATH • Navan
LOUTH • Dundalk
LONGFORD • Longford
ROSCOMMON • Roscommon
CAVAN • Cavan
MONAGHAN • Monaghan
LEITRIM • Carrick-on-Shannon
SLIGO • Sligo
MAYO • Castlebar
GALWAY • Galway
CLARE • Ennis
NORTH TIPPERARY • Nenagh
SOUTH TIPPERARY • Clonmel
LIMERICK • Limerick
KERRY • Tralee
CORK • Cork
WATERFORD • Dungarvan

BELFAST ■ Belfast
LISBURN
CASTLEREAGH
NORTH DOWN
ARDS
DOWN
BANBRIDGE
NEWRY AND MOURNE
ARMAGH • Armagh
CRAIGAVON
DUNGANNON AND SOUTH TYRONE • Dungannon
COOKSTOWN • Cookstown
OMAGH • Omagh
FERMANAGH • Enniskillen
STRABANE

South Wales
Scale 1:1 700 000

MONMOUTHSHIRE
Ebbw Vale
Blaenau Gwent
TORFAEN • Pontypool • Cwmbran
CAERPHILLY • Hengoed
NEWPORT • Newport
NORTH SOMERSET
MERTHYR TYDFIL • Merthyr Tydfil
RHONDDA CYNON TAFF
BRIDGEND • Bridgend
THE VALE OF GLAMORGAN
CARDIFF • Cardiff
• Barry
NEATH PORT TALBOT
SWANSEA • Swansea
• Port Talbot
• Pontypridd

1 MERTHYR TYDFIL
2 BLAENAU GWENT

Greater London
Scale 1:850 000

ENFIELD
BARNET
HARINGEY
WALTHAM FOREST
REDBRIDGE
HAVERING
BARKING AND DAGENHAM
NEWHAM
HARROW
BRENT
CAMDEN
ISLINGTON
HACKNEY
CITY OF LONDON
TOWER HAMLETS
GREENWICH
BEXLEY
HILLINGDON
EALING
HOUNSLOW
HAMMERSMITH AND FULHAM
KENSINGTON AND CHELSEA
CITY OF WESTMINSTER
SOUTHWARK
LAMBETH
LEWISHAM
BROMLEY
CROYDON
SUTTON
MERTON
WANDSWORTH
RICHMOND UPON THAMES
KINGSTON UPON THAMES

1 KENSINGTON AND CHELSEA
2 CITY OF WESTMINSTER
3 HAMMERSMITH AND FULHAM
4 TOWER HAMLETS

UK Government website
www.direct.gov.uk

National Statistics Online
www.statistics.gov.uk

Scale 1: 4 500 000

Land height and sea depth

metres
1000
500
300
200
100
0 — sea level
50
100
200

▴ spot height in metres

The British Isles consists of the two large islands of Great Britain and Ireland and a number of smaller islands.

Ireland

Great Britain

Shetland Islands
Herma Ness
Yell
Unst
Fetlar
Mainland
Whalsay
Foula
Bressay
Sumburgh Head
Fair Isle

Orkney Islands
Mull Head
Westray
North Ronaldsay
Rousay
Sanday
Mainland
Stronsay
Shapinsay
Hoy
South Ronaldsay
Pentland Firth
Duncansby Head

Rona
Cape Wrath
Thurso

Northwest Highlands
Butt of Lewis
The Minch
Lewis
Loch Shin
Dornoch Firth
Harris
▴799 Clisham
Ben Wyvis ▴1046
Kinnairds Head
St. Kilda
North Uist
Little Minch
Skye
Carn Eige ▴1183
Loch Ness
Moray Firth
Buchan Ness
Benbecula
Cuillin Hills ▴1009
Monadhliath Mountains
Spey
Deveron
South Uist
Great Glen
Cairngorms
Don
Barra
Mallaig
▴1310 Ben Macdhui
Dee
Rhum
Eigg
▴1344 Ben Nevis
N. Esk
Coll
Loch Linnhe
Tay
S. Esk
Tiree
Mull
Loch Awe
Earn
Sidlaw Hills
Firth of Tay
Iona
Loch Tay
Firth of Forth
Colonsay
Firth of Lorn
Loch Fyne
Forth
Ochil Hills
Fife Ness
Jura
Loch Lomond
Central Lowlands
St. Abb's Head
Islay
Sound of Jura
Bute
Lammermuir Hills
Holy Island
Arran
Ayr
Tweed

Grampian Mountains

Southern Uplands
Firth of Clyde
Clyde
Nith
The Cheviot ▴815
Malin Head
Rathlin Island
North Channel
Merrick ▴843
Broad Law ▴840
Cheviot Hills
Coquet
Bloody Foreland
Lough Foyle
Mull of Kintyre
Teviot
Esk
Tyne
Aran Island
Errigal Mt. ▴752
Foyle
▴554
Dee
Annan
Cross Fell ▴893
Wear
Donegal Mountains
Sawel ▴683
Bann
Antrim Mtns.
Solway Firth
Eden
Tees
Sperrin Mountains
Mourne
Mull of Galloway
St. Bees Head
Cumbrian Mtns.
▴978 Scafell Pike
Yorkshire Dales
Swale
▴454
Donegal Bay
Lower Lough Erne
Blackwater
Lough Neagh
Belfast Lough
Strangford Lough
▴621 Snaefell
North York Moors
Erris Head
Upper Lough Erne
Mourne Mtns.
▴852 Slieve Donard
Isle of Man
Lune
Ribble
Nidd
Wharfe
Yorkshire Wolds
Flamborough Head
Rossan Point
Achill Island
Lough Conn
Lough Mask
Lough Allen
Erne
Dundalk Bay
Morecambe Bay
Aire
Ouse
Holderness
Spurn Head
Humber

IRISH SEA

Central Plain
Slyne Head
Lough Corrib
Clare
Lough Ree
Boyne
Anglesey
Liverpool Bay
Mersey
Don
Lincoln Wolds
Aran Islands
Galway Bay
Bog of Allen
Dublin Bay
Holy Island
Caernarfon Bay
Wirral
Cheshire Plain
▴636 The Peak
Trent
Derwent
Lough Derg
Barrow
Wicklow Mtns.
Snowdon ▴1085
Conwy
Dee
The Wash
Loop Head
Shannon
Nore
Wicklow Head
▴926 Lugnaquilla
Cardigan Bay
Cader Idris ▴892
Witham
Wensum
Norfolk Broads
Tralee Bay
Galty Mtns. ▴920
Suir
Wexford Bay
▴690
▴517
Cambrian Mtns.
Severn
Welland
The Fens
Breckland
Waveney
▴953
Blackwater
Lee
Carnsore Point
Teifi
Tywi
Black Mtns.
Wye
Teme
Avon
▴1 Great Ouse
Orford Ness
Dingle Bay
▴1041 Carrauntoohill
St. George's Channel
St. David's Head
St. Bride's Bay
Brecon Beacons ▴886
Usk
▴330
Cotswold Hills
Nene
Lea
The Naze
Caha Mtns.
Bantry Bay
Mizen Head
Cape Clear
Old Head of Kinsale
Carmarthen Bay
Gower
Swansea Bay
Teme
Avon
Thames
Chiltern Hills
Stour
North Foreland
Bristol Channel
Mendip Hills
▴519 Exmoor Hills
Quantock Hills
Parrett
Salisbury Plain ▴297
Hampshire Downs
Test
Itchen
▴294
North Downs
Medway
The Weald
Romney Marsh
Dungeness
Frome
South Downs ▴255
Strait of Dover

CELTIC SEA
Lundy
Hartland Point
Taw
Exe
Frome
Bodmin Moor ▴619
Dartmoor
Lyme Bay
Isle of Wight
Portland Bill
Beachy Head

ATLANTIC OCEAN
Isles of Scilly
Land's End
Lizard Point
Start Point

NORTH SEA

English Channel
Cap de la Hague
Alderney
FRANCE
Guernsey
Channel Islands
Baie de la Seine
Sark
Jersey

Coordinates
2°E, 60°N, 58°N, 56°N, 54°N, 52°N, 50°N
8°W, 6°W, 4°W, 10°W

Transverse Mercator Projection

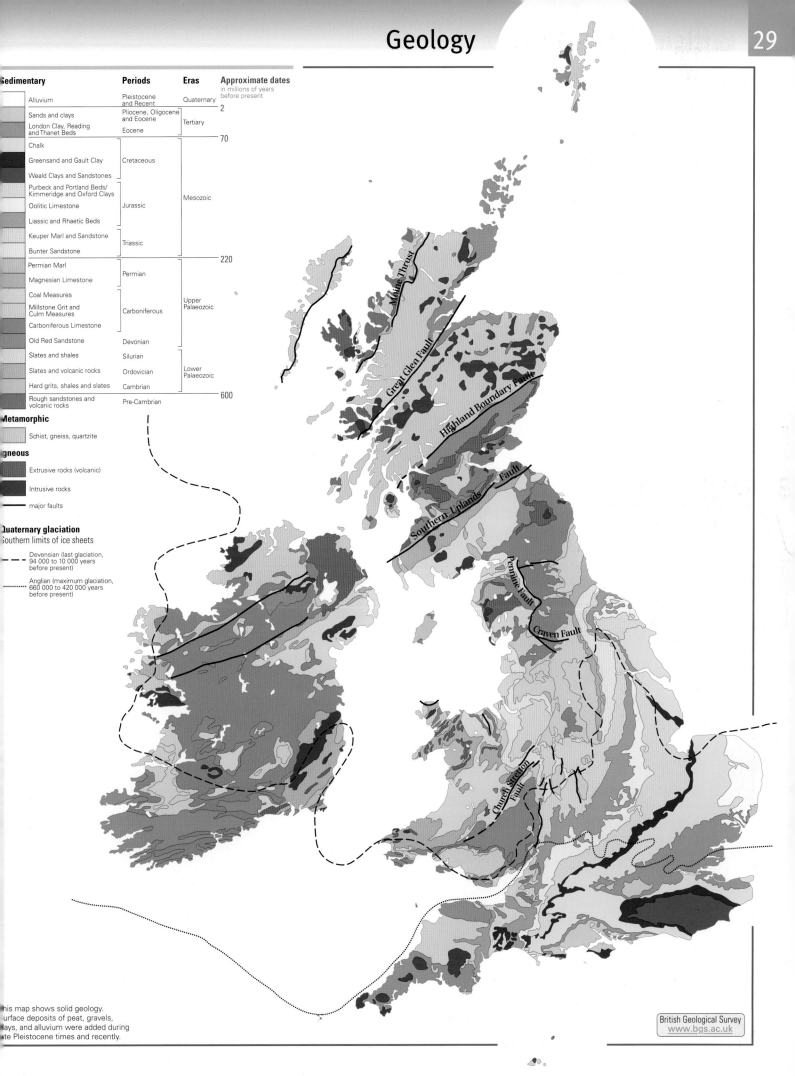

Sedimentary	Periods	Eras	Approximate dates in millions of years before present
Alluvium	Pleistocene and Recent	Quaternary	2
Sands and clays	Pliocene, Oligocene and Eocene	Tertiary	
London Clay, Reading and Thanet Beds	Eocene		70
Chalk			
Greensand and Gault Clay	Cretaceous		
Weald Clays and Sandstones			
Purbeck and Portland Beds/ Kimmeridge and Oxford Clays		Mesozoic	
Oolitic Limestone	Jurassic		
Liassic and Rhaetic Beds			
Keuper Marl and Sandstone	Triassic		
Bunter Sandstone			220
Permian Marl	Permian		
Magnesian Limestone			
Coal Measures		Upper Palaeozoic	
Millstone Grit and Culm Measures	Carboniferous		
Carboniferous Limestone			
Old Red Sandstone	Devonian		
Slates and shales	Silurian		
Slates and volcanic rocks	Ordovician	Lower Palaeozoic	
Hard grits, shales and slates	Cambrian		600
Rough sandstones and volcanic rocks	Pre-Cambrian		

Metamorphic

Schist, gneiss, quartzite

Igneous

Extrusive rocks (volcanic)

Intrusive rocks

— major faults

Quaternary glaciation
Southern limits of ice sheets

– – – Devensian (last glaciation, 94 000 to 10 000 years before present)

········ Anglian (maximum glaciation, 660 000 to 420 000 years before present)

This map shows solid geology. Surface deposits of peat, gravels, clays, and alluvium were added during late Pleistocene times and recently.

Moine Thrust

Great Glen Fault

Highland Boundary Fault

Southern Uplands Fault

Pennine Fault

Craven Fault

Church Stretton Fault

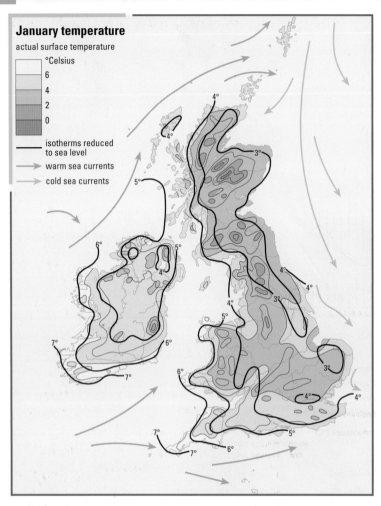

January temperature

actual surface temperature

°Celsius
- 6
- 4
- 2
- 0

— isotherms reduced to sea level
→ warm sea currents
→ cold sea currents

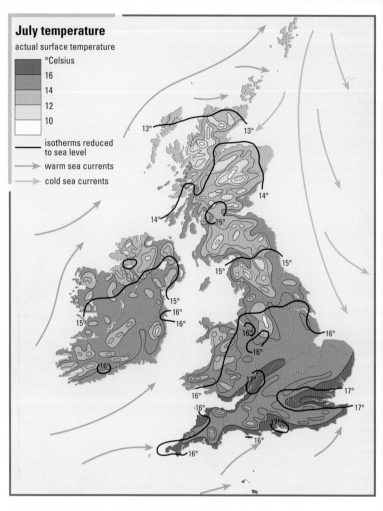

July temperature

actual surface temperature

°Celsius
- 16
- 14
- 12
- 10

— isotherms reduced to sea level
→ warm sea currents
→ cold sea currents

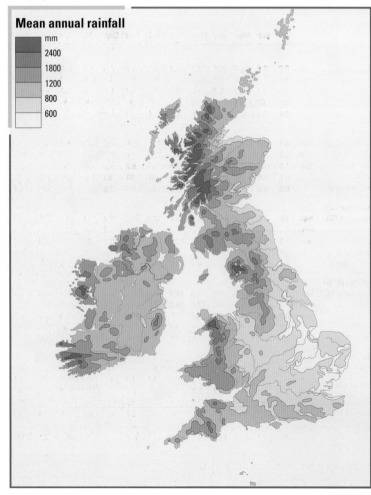

Mean annual rainfall

mm
- 2400
- 1800
- 1200
- 800
- 600

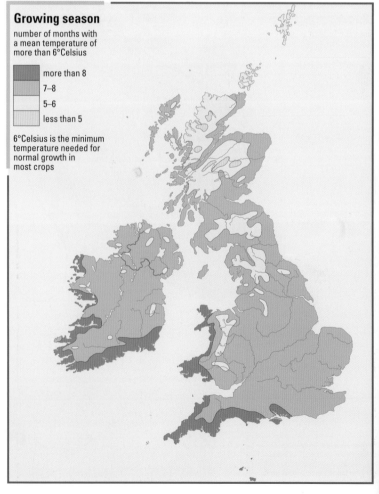

Growing season

number of months with a mean temperature of more than 6°Celsius

- more than 8
- 7–8
- 5–6
- less than 5

6°Celsius is the minimum temperature needed for normal growth in most crops

Snow

average number of
mornings per year with
snow cover

- more than 60
- 40–60
- 30–40
- 20–30
- 10–20
- less than 10
- no data

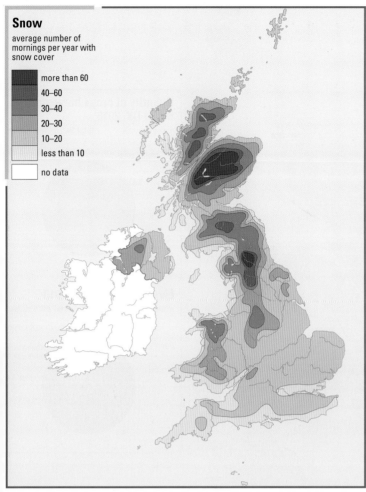

Sunshine

average daily duration of
bright sunshine, in hours

- more than 5.0
- 4.5–5.0
- 4.0–4.5
- 3.5–4.0
- 3.0–3.5
- less than 3.0

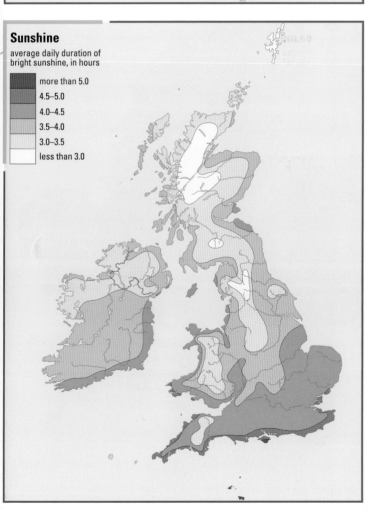

Climate graphs for selected British stations

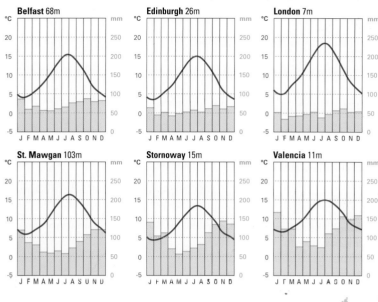

Climate stations

Climate data

averages are for 1971–2000

Anglesey (Valley) 10m — climate station and its height above sea level

Temperature (°C)
- **high** — average daily maximum temperature
- **mean** — average monthly temperature
- **low** — average daily minimum temperature

Rainfall (mm) — average monthly precipitation

Sunshine (hours) — average daily duration of bright sunshine

		Jan	Feb	Mar	Apr	May	Jun	Jul	Aug	Sep	Oct	Nov	Dec	YEAR
Anglesey (Valley) 10m														
Temperature (°C)	high	8.0	8.0	9.4	11.6	14.7	16.8	18.8	18.9	16.9	14.0	10.8	8.9	13.1
	mean	5.8	5.6	6.9	8.5	11.3	13.6	15.7	15.8	14.0	11.4	8.4	6.7	10.3
	low	3.5	3.1	4.3	5.3	7.8	10.3	12.5	12.6	11.1	8.8	6.0	4.4	7.5
Rainfall (mm)		82	60	67	52	45	51	49	68	73	90	101	92	828
Sunshine (hours)		1.9	2.9	3.7	5.9	7.4	6.8	6.6	6.2	4.8	3.5	2.1	1.5	4.4
Braemar 339m														
Temperature (°C)	high	4.1	4.4	6.4	9.3	13.1	15.9	18.1	17.4	14.2	10.6	6.8	4.8	10.5
	mean	1.2	1.3	3.0	5.2	8.3	11.2	13.4	12.8	10.2	7.2	3.8	2.0	6.7
	low	-1.8	-1.8	-0.4	1.0	3.5	6.5	8.7	8.2	6.2	3.7	0.7	-0.9	2.8
Rainfall (mm)		113	68	77	55	59	56	54	61	83	102	92	95	913
Sunshine (hours)		0.9	2.0	3.1	4.4	5.6	5.6	5.4	4.9	3.8	2.2	1.2	0.6	3.3
Cambridge 26m														
Temperature (°C)	high	7.0	7.4	10.2	12.6	16.5	19.4	22.2	22.3	18.9	14.6	9.9	7.8	14.1
	mean	4.2	4.3	6.6	8.3	11.6	14.6	17.1	17.1	14.5	10.9	6.8	5.1	10.1
	low	1.3	1.1	2.9	4.0	6.7	9.8	12.0	11.9	10.1	7.1	3.7	2.3	6.1
Rainfall (mm)		45	33	42	43	45	54	38	49	51	54	51	50	554
Sunshine (hours)		1.8	2.6	3.5	4.9	6.1	6.0	6.2	6.0	4.7	3.7	2.3	1.5	4.1
Teignmouth 3m														
Temperature (°C)	high	9.0	8.9	10.5	12.2	15.3	18.2	20.6	20.4	18.1	14.8	11.7	9.9	14.2
	mean	6.4	6.2	7.6	9.0	12.0	14.7	17.1	16.9	14.8	11.9	8.9	7.4	11.1
	low	3.7	3.5	4.6	5.7	8.6	11.2	13.5	13.4	11.4	8.9	6.0	4.8	8.0
Rainfall (mm)		102	83	68	55	52	51	36	57	67	83	84	113	850
Sunshine (hours)		2.0	2.7	3.8	6.0	7.0	7.1	7.4	6.9	5.3	3.5	2.8	1.8	4.7
Tiree 9m														
Temperature (°C)	high	7.6	7.4	8.5	10.1	12.8	14.5	16.1	16.3	14.7	12.4	9.8	8.3	11.6
	mean	5.4	5.2	6.0	7.4	9.8	11.8	13.6	13.8	12.2	10.2	7.5	6.2	9.1
	low	3.1	3.0	3.6	4.7	6.8	9.1	11.1	11.2	9.7	7.9	5.2	4.0	6.6
Rainfall (mm)		143	98	105	67	54	62	78	99	119	143	137	135	1236
Sunshine (hours)		1.2	2.3	3.3	5.5	7.3	6.6	5.2	5.2	4.1	2.7	1.6	1.0	3.8
		Jan	Feb	Mar	Apr	May	Jun	Jul	Aug	Sep	Oct	Nov	Dec	YEAR

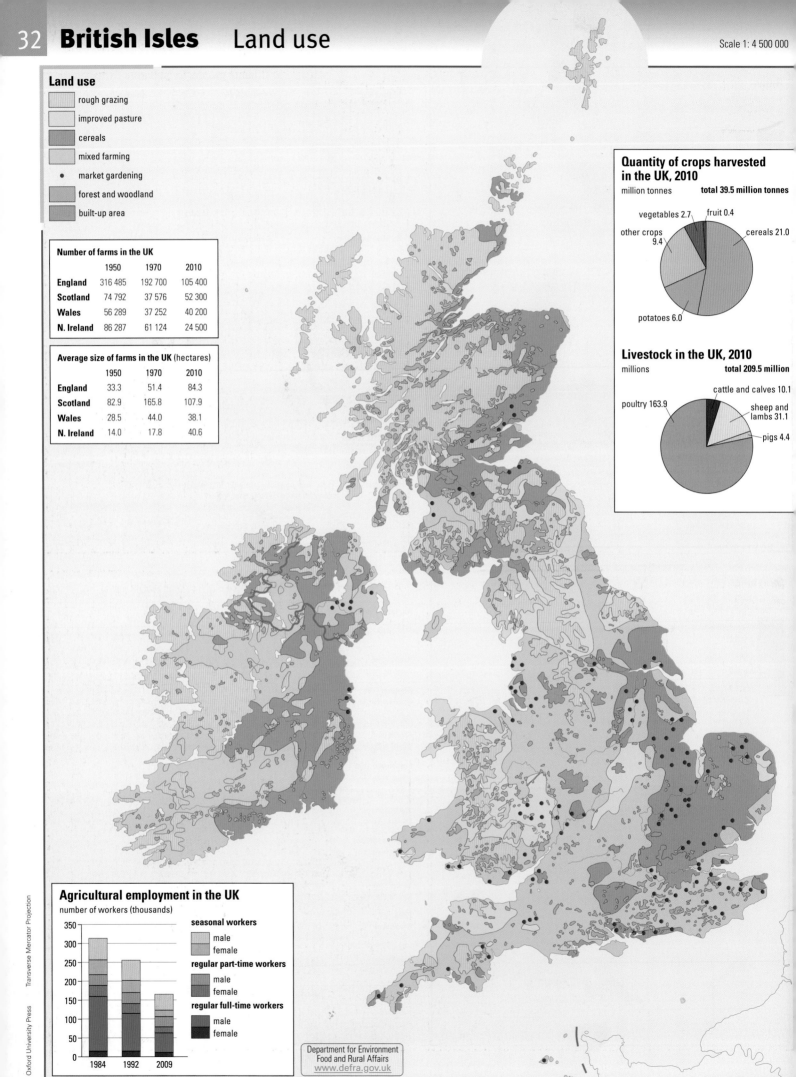

Land use

- rough grazing
- improved pasture
- cereals
- mixed farming
- • market gardening
- forest and woodland
- built-up area

Number of farms in the UK

	1950	1970	2010
England	316 485	192 700	105 400
Scotland	74 792	37 576	52 300
Wales	56 289	37 252	40 200
N. Ireland	86 287	61 124	24 500

Average size of farms in the UK (hectares)

	1950	1970	2010
England	33.3	51.4	84.3
Scotland	82.9	165.8	107.9
Wales	28.5	44.0	38.1
N. Ireland	14.0	17.8	40.6

Quantity of crops harvested in the UK, 2010

million tonnes **total 39.5 million tonnes**

vegetables 2.7
fruit 0.4
other crops 9.4
cereals 21.0
potatoes 6.0

Livestock in the UK, 2010

millions **total 209.5 million**

cattle and calves 10.1
poultry 163.9
sheep and lambs 31.1
pigs 4.4

Agricultural employment in the UK

number of workers (thousands)

seasonal workers
- male
- female

regular part-time workers
- male
- female

regular full-time workers
- male
- female

(bar chart: 1984, 1992, 2009; vertical axis 0–350)

Department for Environment
Food and Rural Affairs
www.defra.gov.uk

© Oxford University Press

Transverse Mercator Projection

Wheat, 2010

percentage of farmland
used for wheat

- over 40%
- 30–40%
- 20–30%
- 10–20%
- 0–10%

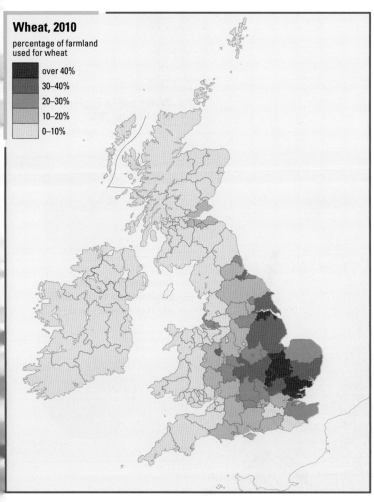

Potatoes, 2010

percentage of farmland
used for potatoes

- over 3%
- 2–3%
- 1–2%
- 0.5–1%
- 0–0.5%

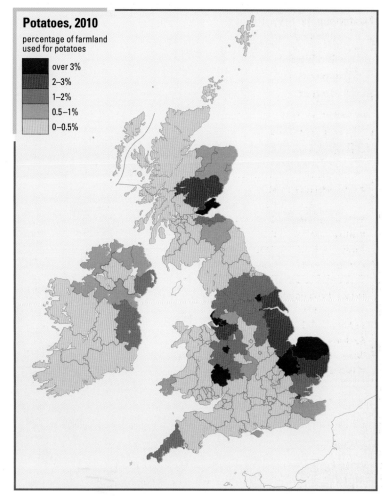

Market gardening, 2010

percentage of farmland used
for market gardening

- over 4%
- 3–4%
- 2–3%
- 1–2%
- under 1%

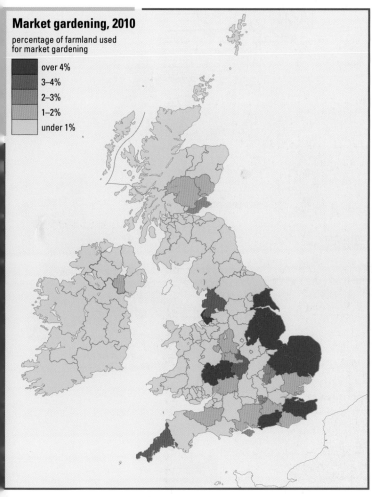

Sheep, dairy and beef cattle, 2010

one dot represents 100 000 animals

- sheep

one dot represents 10 000 animals

- dairy cattle
- beef cattle

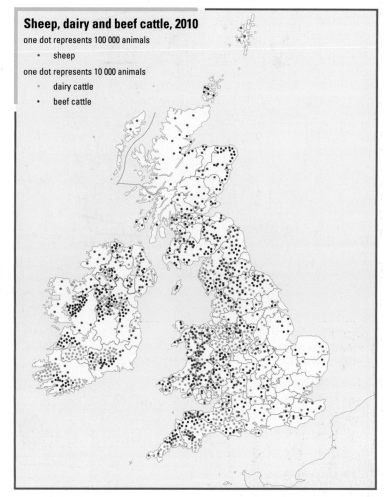

Transverse Mercator Projection

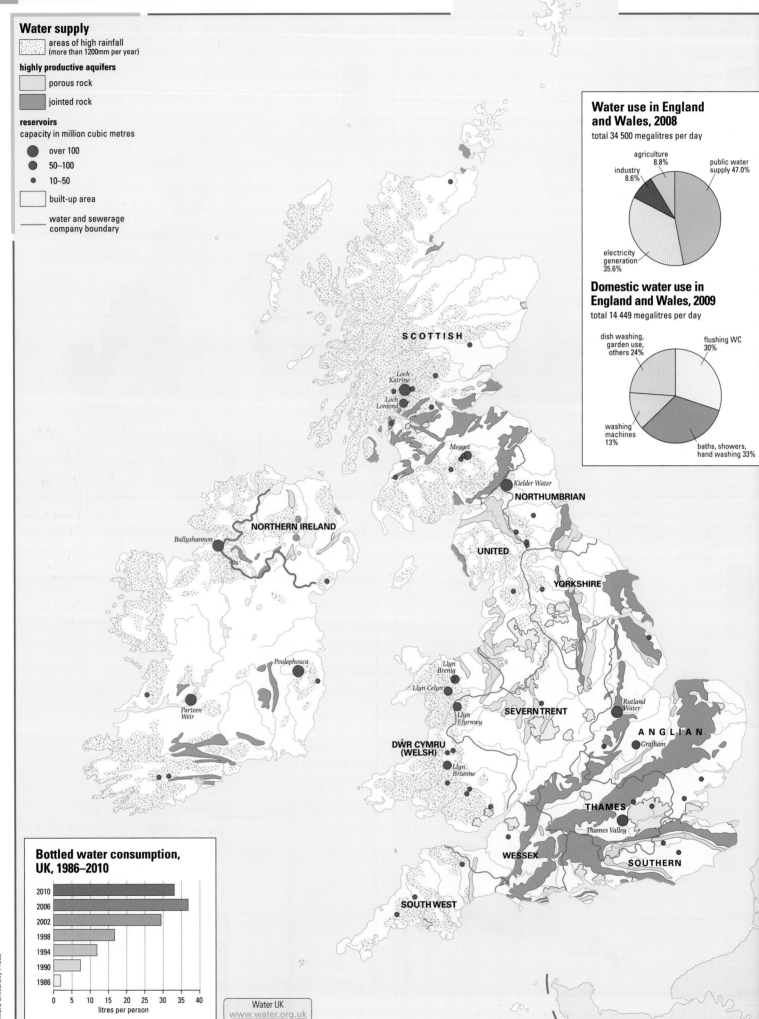

Water supply

areas of high rainfall
(more than 1200mm per year)

highly productive aquifers

porous rock

jointed rock

reservoirs
capacity in million cubic metres

- over 100
- 50–100
- 10–50

built-up area

water and sewerage
company boundary

Water use in England and Wales, 2008
total 34 500 megalitres per day

- agriculture 8.8%
- industry 8.6%
- public water supply 47.0%
- electricity generation 35.6%

Domestic water use in England and Wales, 2009
total 14 449 megalitres per day

- dish washing, garden use, others 24%
- flushing WC 30%
- washing machines 13%
- baths, showers, hand washing 33%

Bottled water consumption, UK, 1986–2010

litres per person

2010, 2006, 2002, 1998, 1994, 1990, 1986

0 5 10 15 20 25 30 35 40

SCOTTISH

Loch Katrine

Loch Lomond

Megget

Kielder Water

NORTHUMBRIAN

NORTHERN IRELAND

Ballyshannon

UNITED

YORKSHIRE

Poulaphouca

Parteen Weir

Llyn Brenig

Llyn Celyn

Llyn Efyrnwy

SEVERN TRENT

Rutland Water

ANGLIAN

DŴR CYMRU (WELSH)

Llyn Brianne

Grafham

THAMES

Thames Valley

WESSEX

SOUTHERN

SOUTH WEST

Water UK
www.water.org.uk

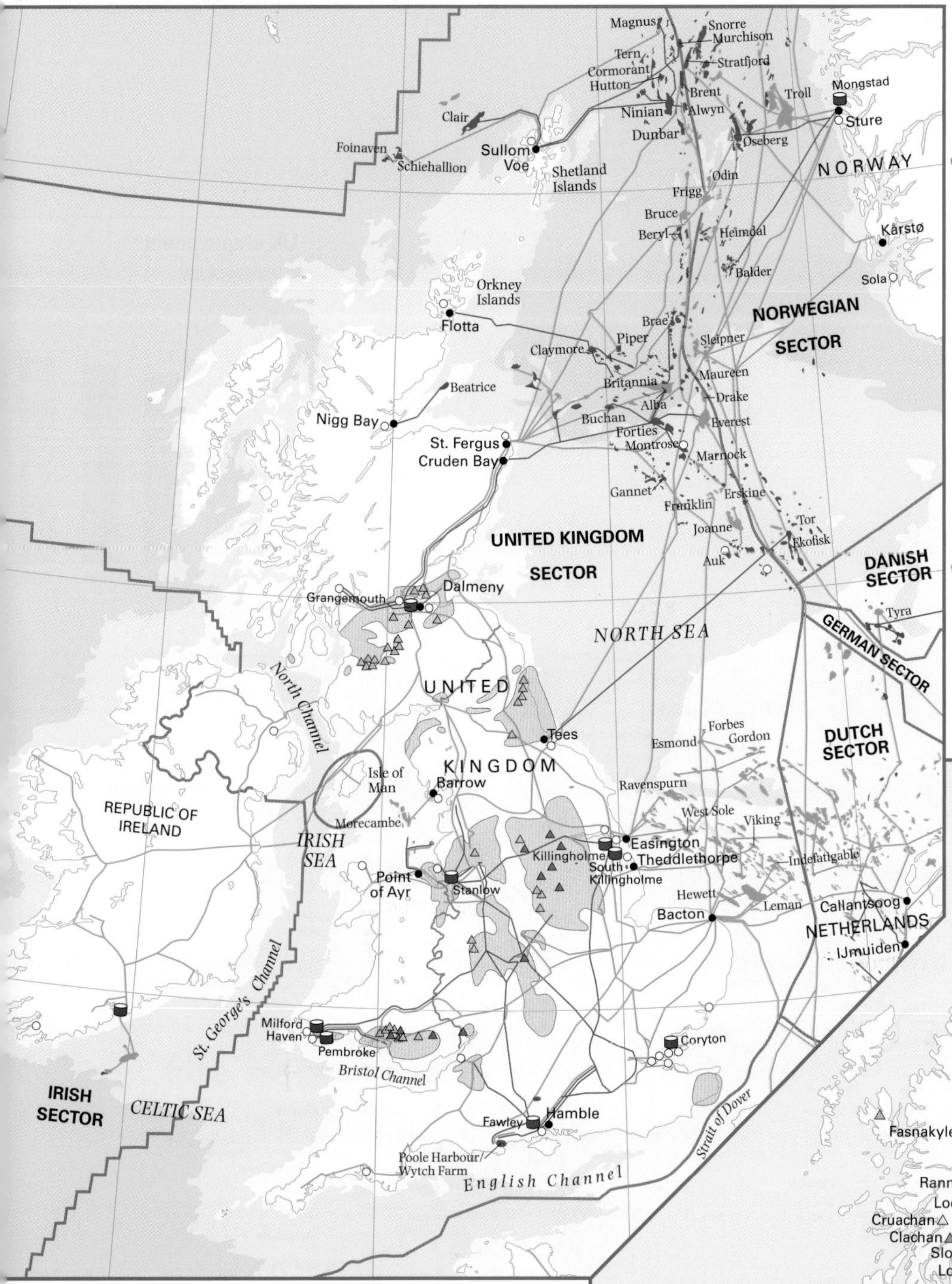

Scale 1: 7 500 000 (main map)

Map labels (main map)

Magnus, Snorre, Murchison, Tern, Stratfjord, Cormorant, Hutton, Brent, Mongstad, Clair, Ninian, Alwyn, Sture, Foinaven, Schiehallion, Dunbar, Sullom Voe, Shetland Islands, NORWAY, Oseberg, Odin, Frigg, Bruce, Heimdal, Beryl, Balder, Karstø, Orkney Islands, NORWEGIAN SECTOR, Sola, Flotta, Brae, Sleipner, Piper, Claymore, Maureen, Beatrice, Britannia, Drake, Nigg Bay, Buchan, Alba, Everest, St. Fergus, Forties, Montrose, Cruden Bay, Marnock, Gannet, Erskine, Franklin, Tor, Joanne, Ekofisk, UNITED KINGDOM SECTOR, Auk, DANISH SECTOR, NORTH SEA, Tyra, GERMAN SECTOR, Grangemouth, Dalmeny, UNITED KINGDOM, Tees, Esmond, Forbes, Gordon, Isle of Man, Barrow, Ravenspurn, DUTCH SECTOR, Morecambe, West Sole, Viking, REPUBLIC OF IRELAND, IRISH SEA, Killingholme, Easington, South Killingholme, Theddlethorpe, Indefatigable, Point of Ayr, Stanlow, Hewett, Leman, Callantsoog, Bacton, NETHERLANDS, IJmuiden, Milford Haven, Pembroke, Coryton, Bristol Channel, IRISH SECTOR, CELTIC SEA, Fawley, Hamble, Poole Harbour/Wytch Farm, English Channel, Strait of Dover, North Channel, St. George's Channel

Oil and gas

- oilfield
- oil pipeline/terminal ●
- gasfield
- gas pipeline/terminal ●
- international exploration dividing line
- tanker terminal ○
- oil refinery

Coal

- coalfield
- deep coal mine ▲
- open cast mine △

sea depth

0	sea level
50	
200	
metres	

Primary energy consumption, 2010

million tonnes oil equivalent

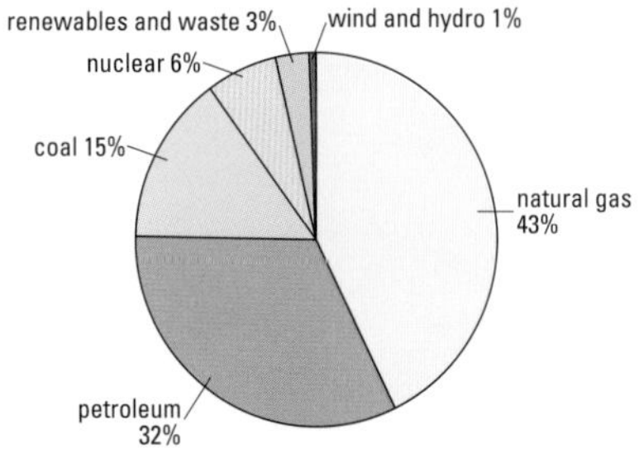

renewables and waste 3%
wind and hydro 1%
nuclear 6%
coal 15%
natural gas 43%
petroleum 32%

Department of Energy and Climate change
www.decc.gov.uk

Energy production

- ■ coal fired over 1000 MW capacity
- ■ oil fired over 1000 MW capacity
- ■ gas fired over 1000 MW capacity
- ■ combined cycle gas turbine over 1000 MW capacity
- ● nuclear
- ▲ hydro electric over 40 MW capacity
- △ pumped storage over 1000 MW capacity
- △ wind over 40 MW capacity
- ■ biomass

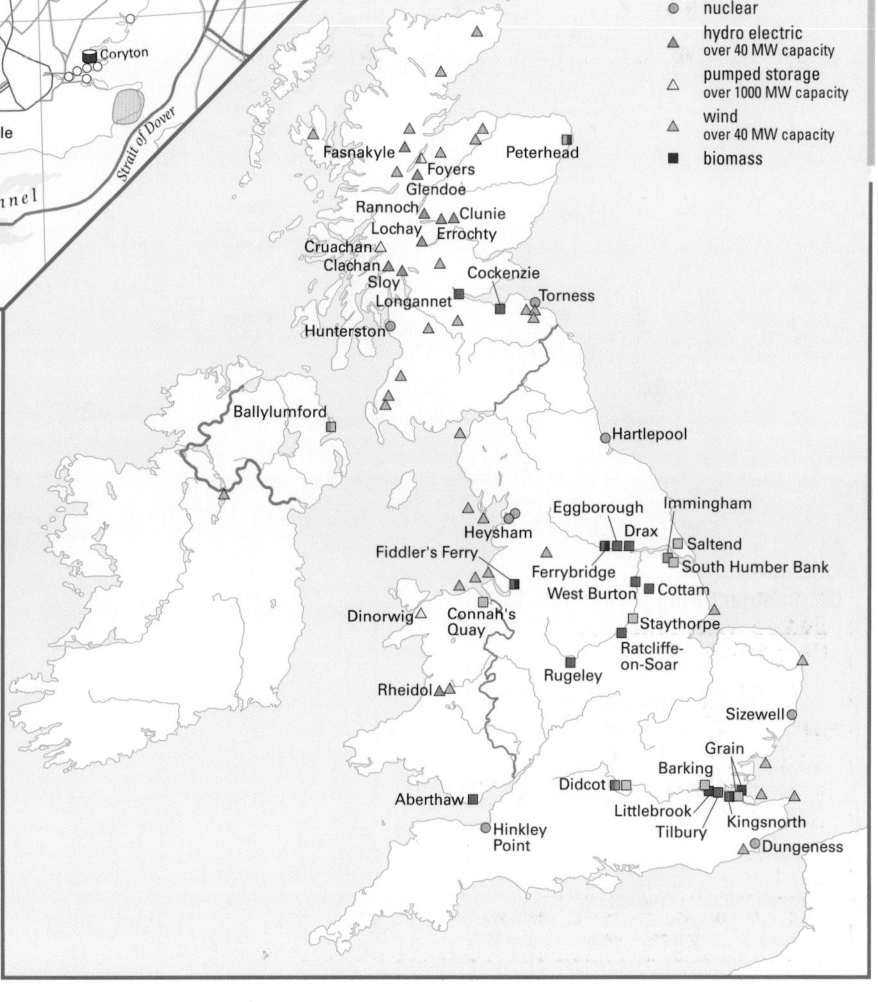

Fasnakyle, Foyers, Glendoe, Peterhead, Rannoch, Clunie, Lochay, Errochty, Cruachan, Clachan, Sloy, Cockenzie, Longannet, Torness, Hunterston, Ballylumford, Hartlepool, Eggborough, Immingham, Heysham, Drax, Saltend, Fiddler's Ferry, South Humber Bank, Ferrybridge, Cottam, West Burton, Dinorwig, Staythorpe, Connah's Quay, Ratcliffe-on-Soar, Rheidol, Rugeley, Sizewell, Grain, Barking, Didcot, Aberthaw, Littlebrook, Kingsnorth, Hinkley Point, Tilbury, Dungeness

Primary fuel consumption

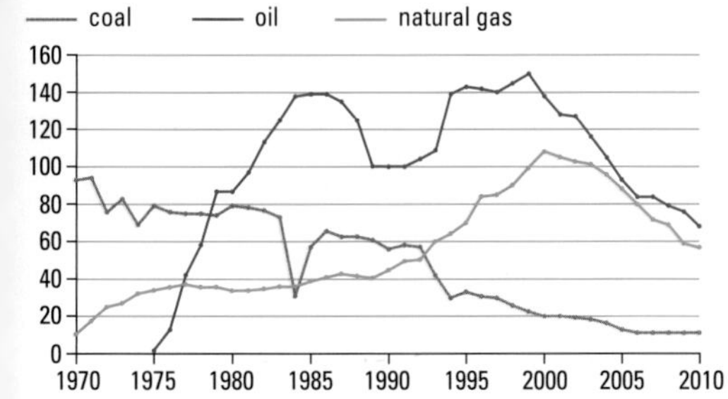

— coal — oil — natural gas

(graph, values 0–160, years 1970 1975 1980 1985 1990 1995 2000 2005 2010)

Electricity generated from renewable sources, 1990–2010

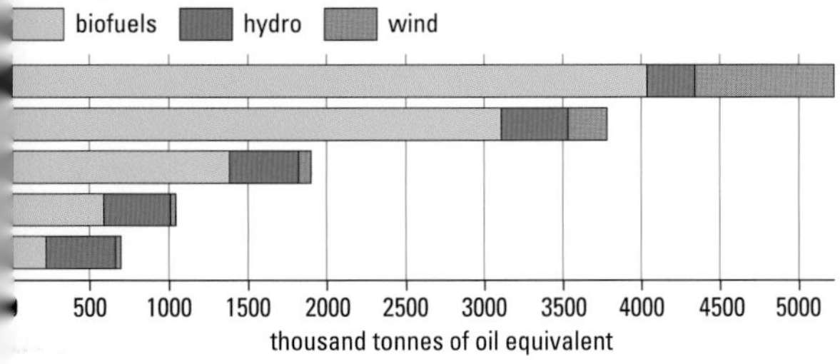

biofuels | hydro | wind

(bar chart axis: 500 1000 1500 2000 2500 3000 3500 4000 4500 5000)
thousand tonnes of oil equivalent

© Oxford University Press — Transverse Mercator Projection

Manufacturing industry

the map shows only the main centres of selected industries

- ▽ chemicals
- ● steel
- ○ non-ferrous metal smelting
- ◉ metal working
- ▢ motor vehicles
- ◼ railway vehicles
- ☐ aircraft and aerospace
- ▣ shipbuilding and repair
- △ mechanical engineering
- ▲ electrical engineering
- △ electronics and computers
- ◆ clothing and footwear
- ◆ textiles and carpets

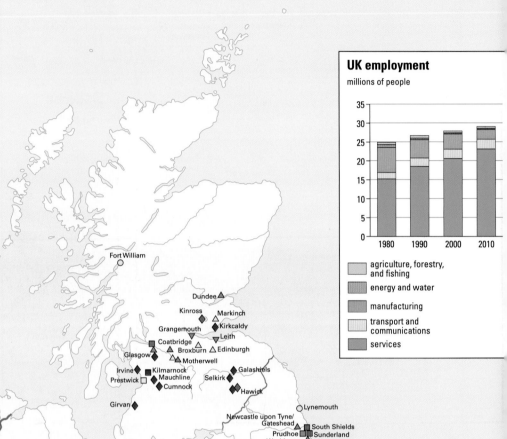

UK employment

millions of people

Legend:
- agriculture, forestry, and fishing
- energy and water
- manufacturing
- transport and communications
- services

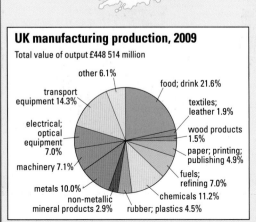

UK manufacturing production, 2009

Total value of output £448 514 million

- food; drink 21.6%
- textiles; leather 1.9%
- wood products 1.5%
- paper; printing; publishing 4.9%
- fuels; refining 7.0%
- chemicals 11.2%
- rubber; plastics 4.5%
- non-metallic mineral products 2.9%
- metals 10.0%
- machinery 7.1%
- electrical; optical equipment 7.0%
- transport equipment 14.3%
- other 6.1%

Department for Business, Innovation and Skills
www.bis.gov.uk

Employment in primary activity, 2010

percentage of the workforce employed
in agriculture, forestry, and fishing,
by administrative area

- over 8%
- 4–8%
- 2–4%
- 1–2%
- under 1%

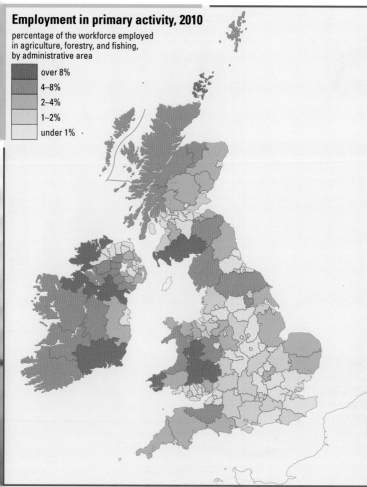

Employment in secondary activity, 2010

percentage of the workforce employed in
mining, manufacturing, construction,
and utilities, by administrative area

- over 24%
- 20–24%
- 16–20%
- 12–16%
- under 12%

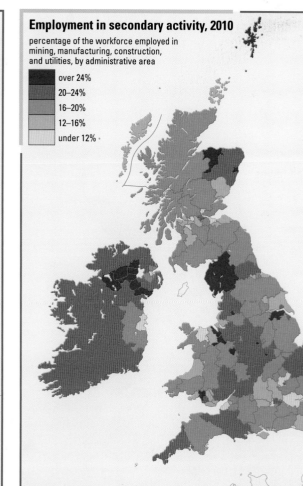

Employment in tertiary activity, 2010

percentage of the workforce employed in services,
transport, finance, and administration,
by administrative area

- over 80%
- 75–80%
- 70–75%
- 65–70%
- under 65%

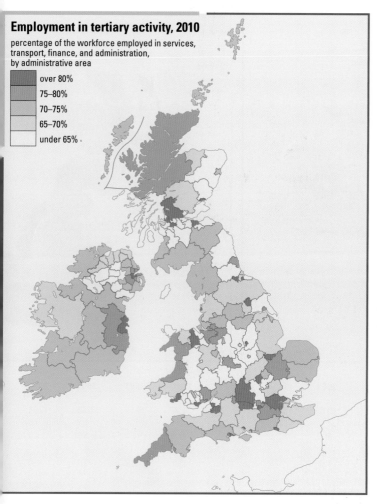

Unemployment, 2010

percentage of the workforce unemployed,
by administrative area

- over 9%
- 8–9%
- 7–8%
- 6–7%
- 5–6%
- under 5%

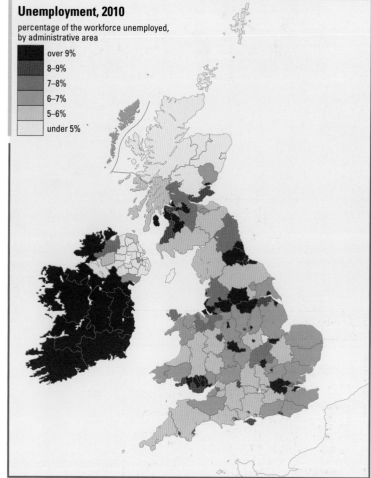

Population density, 2010

Scale 1: 6 000 000

people per square kilometre

- over 1000
- 500–1000
- 250–500
- 100–250
- 50–100
- 10–50
- under 10

Major cities and towns

number of people

- ☐ over 1 000 000
- ○ 400 000–1 000 000
- ◉ 100 000–400 000
- • 25 000–100 000

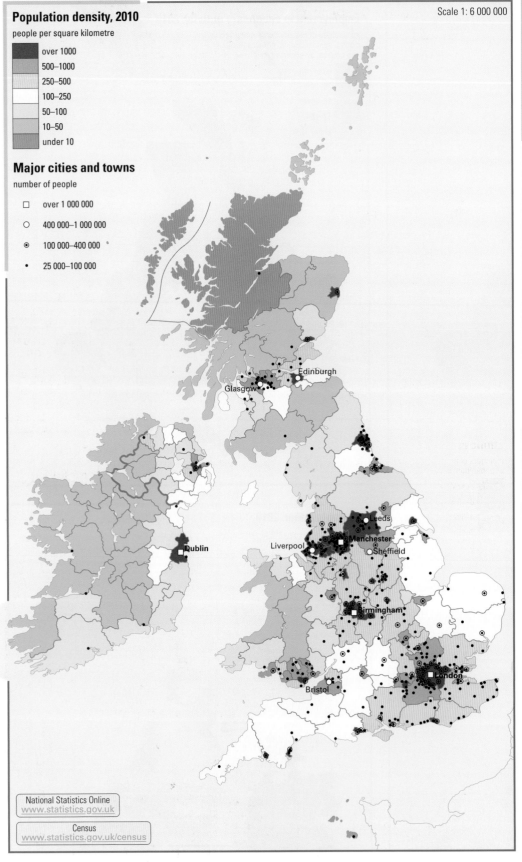

Edinburgh
Glasgow
Dublin
Liverpool
Manchester
Leeds
Sheffield
Birmingham
Bristol
London

Young people, 2010

percentage of the population under 16 years old, by administrative area

- over 22%
- 20–22%
- 19–20%
- 18–19%
- 17–18%
- under 17%

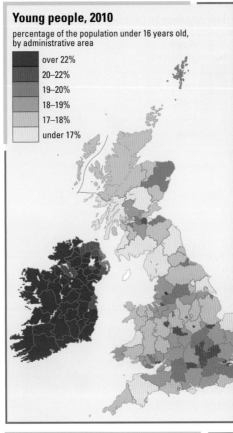

Retired people, 2010

percentage of the population over retirement age*, by administrative area

- over 24%
- 22–24%
- 20–22%
- 18–20%
- 16–18%
- under 16%

*65 for men
60 for women

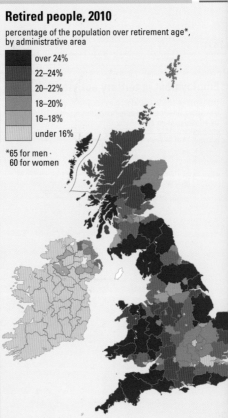

UK population trends	1901	1911	1921	1931	1941	1951	1961	1971	1981	1991	2001	2011
Total population (millions)	38.24	42.08	44.03	46.04	48.22	50.23	52.81	55.93	56.35	57.65	59.62	62.74
Infant mortality (deaths per 1000 live births)	138.0	110.0	76.0	62.0	50.0	27.0	21.0	17.9	11.0	7.4	5.6	4.5
Birth rate (births per 1000 people)	28.6	24.5	22.8	16.3	14.4	15.9	17.9	16.1	13.0	13.8	12.0	13.0
Death rate (deaths per 1000 people)	16.5	14.3	11.9	12.5	13.0	12.6	12.0	11.5	11.6	11.3	10.5	9.0
Life expectancy (years)	47.0	52.2	57.3	60.0	61.0	68.5	70.9	71.9	73.8	76.0	77.5	80.0

Scale 1: 12 500 000 (smallest maps)

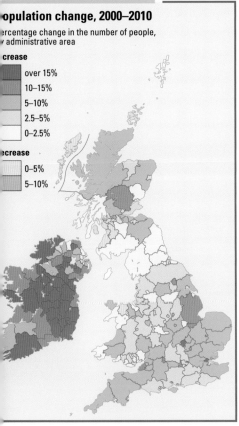

opulation change, 2000–2010

ercentage change in the number of people,
administrative area

crease

- over 15%
- 10–15%
- 5–10%
- 2.5–5%
- 0–2.5%

ecrease

- 0–5%
- 5–10%

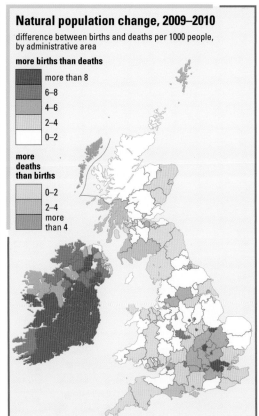

Natural population change, 2009–2010

difference between births and deaths per 1000 people,
by administrative area

more births than deaths

- more than 8
- 6–8
- 4–6
- 2–4
- 0–2

more deaths than births

- 0–2
- 2–4
- more than 4

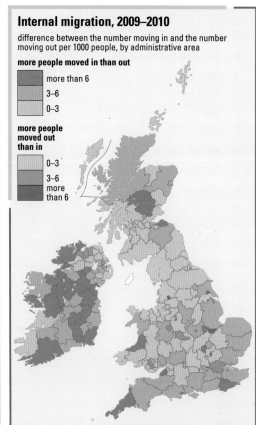

Internal migration, 2009–2010

difference between the number moving in and the number
moving out per 1000 people, by administrative area

more people moved in than out

- more than 6
- 3–6
- 0–3

more people moved out than in

- 0–3
- 3–6
- more than 6

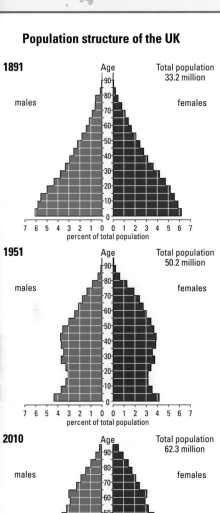

Population structure of the UK

1891

males   Age   females

Total population
33.2 million

percent of total population

1951

males   Age   females

Total population
50.2 million

percent of total population

2010

males   Age   females

Total population
62.3 million

percent of total population

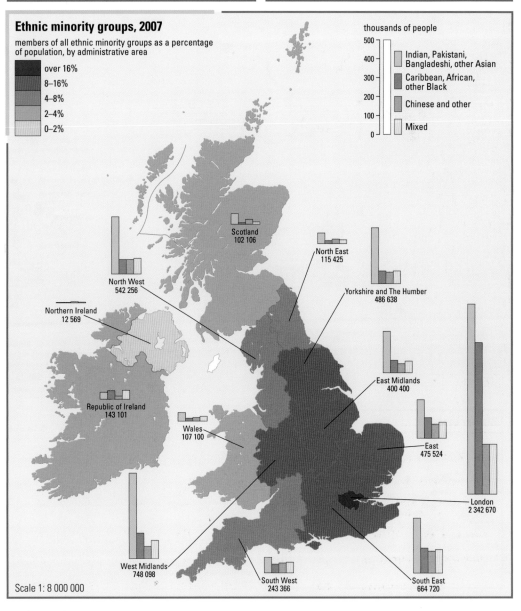

Ethnic minority groups, 2007

members of all ethnic minority groups as a percentage
of population, by administrative area

- over 16%
- 8–16%
- 4–8%
- 2–4%
- 0–2%

thousands of people

- 500
- 400
- 300
- 200
- 100
- 0

Indian, Pakistani,
Bangladeshi, other Asian

Caribbean, African,
other Black

Chinese and other

Mixed

Scotland
102 106

North East
115 425

Yorkshire and The Humber
486 638

North West
542 256

Northern Ireland
12 569

East Midlands
400 400

Republic of Ireland
143 101

Wales
107 100

East
475 524

West Midlands
748 098

London
2 342 670

South West
243 366

South East
664 720

Scale 1: 8 000 000

Transverse Mercator Projection

Scale 1 : 4 500 000

Sports

major sports venues

- Association football (major club)
- Rugby Union (major club)
- Rugby League (major club)
- cricket (first class country club)
- tennis
- golf
- swimming
- athletics
- horse racing
- motor sports
- Gaelic Athletics Association (major grounds)
- international sports stadium/centre

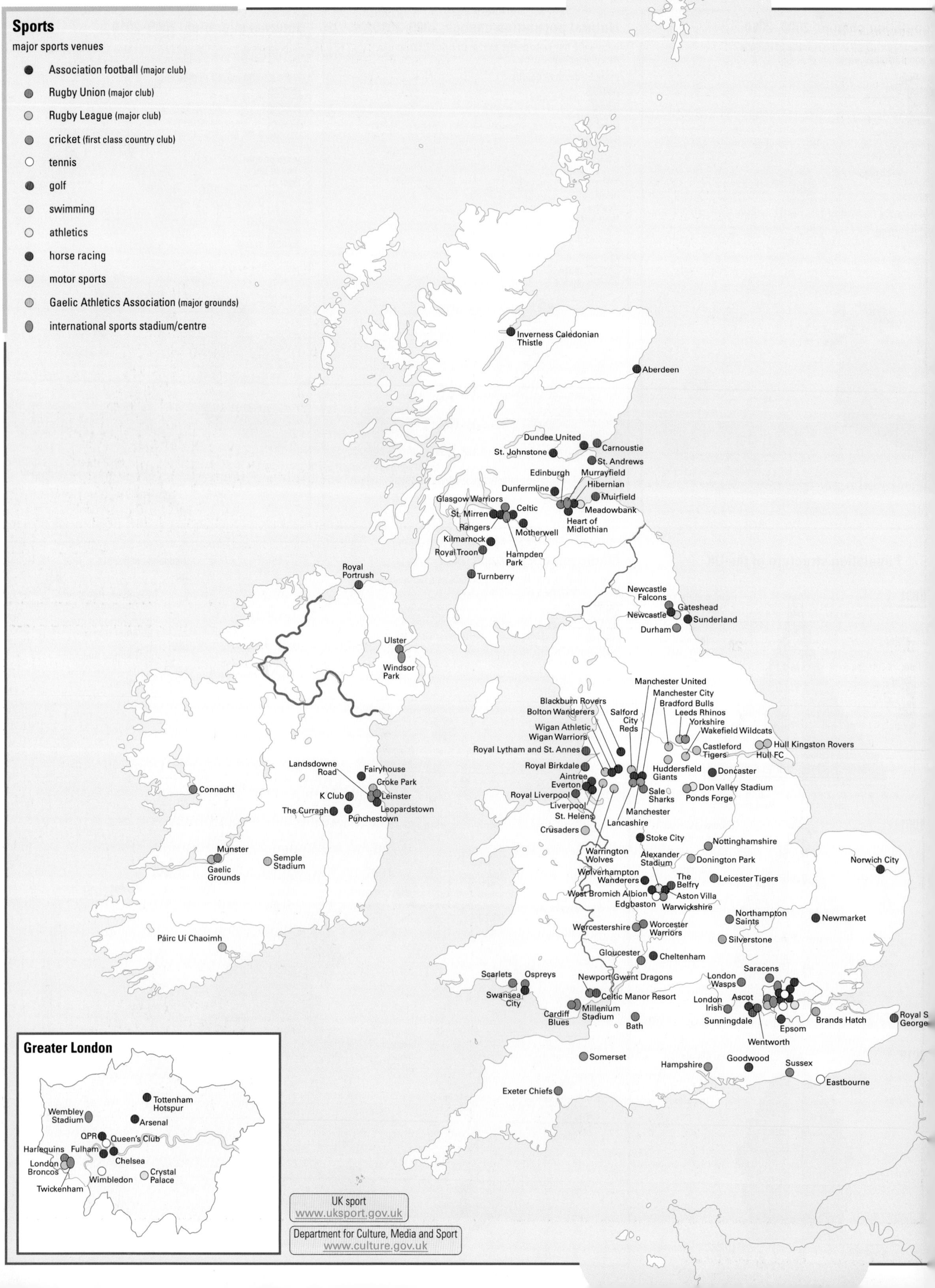

Inverness Caledonian Thistle

Aberdeen

Dundee United
Carnoustie
St. Johnstone
St. Andrews
Edinburgh   Murrayfield
Hibernian
Dunfermline   Muirfield
Glasgow Warriors   Meadowbank
St. Mirren   Celtic
Rangers   Heart of Midlothian
Kilmarnock   Motherwell
Royal Troon
Hampden Park
Turnberry

Royal Portrush

Ulster
Windsor Park

Newcastle Falcons
Gateshead
Newcastle   Sunderland
Durham

Manchester United
Manchester City
Blackburn Rovers   Bradford Bulls
Bolton Wanderers   Leeds Rhinos
Salford City Reds   Yorkshire
Wigan Athletic   Wakefield Wildcats
Wigan Warriors
Castleford Tigers   Hull Kingston Rovers
Royal Lytham and St. Annes   Hull FC
Royal Birkdale   Huddersfield Giants
Aintree   Doncaster
Everton   Sale Sharks   Don Valley Stadium
Royal Liverpool   Ponds Forge
Liverpool
St. Helens   Manchester
Lancashire
Crusaders   Stoke City
Nottinghamshire
Warrington Wolves   Alexander Stadium   Donington Park
Wolverhampton Wanderers   Norwich City
West Bromwich Albion   The Belfry
Aston Villa
Edgbaston   Warwickshire
Leicester Tigers
Worcestershire   Northampton Saints
Worcester Warriors   Newmarket
Silverstone
Gloucester   Cheltenham
Connacht

Landsdowne Road   Fairyhouse
Croke Park
K Club   Leinster
The Curragh   Leopardstown
Punchestown

Munster
Semple Stadium
Gaelic Grounds

Páirc Uí Chaoimh

Scarlets   Ospreys   Saracens
Newport Gwent Dragons   London Wasps
Swansea City   Ascot
Celtic Manor Resort   London Irish
Cardiff Blues   Millenium Stadium   Sunningdale   Epsom   Brands Hatch
Bath   Wentworth   Royal S George

Somerset   Hampshire   Goodwood
Sussex
Exeter Chiefs   Eastbourne

Greater London

Tottenham Hotspur
Wembley Stadium
Arsenal
QPR   Queen's Club
Harlequins   Fulham
London Broncos   Chelsea
Wimbledon   Crystal Palace
Twickenham

UK sport
www.uksport.gov.uk

Department for Culture, Media and Sport
www.culture.gov.uk

Income, 2010

average gross weekly earnings of workers in
full-time employment, by administrative area

- over £675
- £625–£675
- £575–£625
- £525–£575
- £475–£525
- under £475

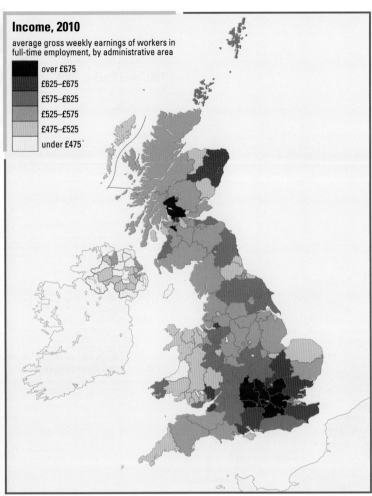

Education, 2009

percentage of 16 year olds entering further
or higher education, by administrative area

- over 90%
- 85–90%
- 80–85%
- 75–80%
- under 75%
- no data

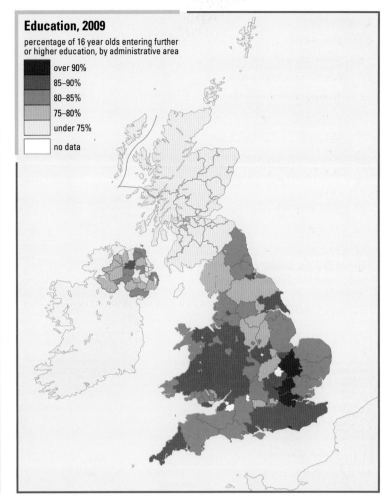

Domestic burglaries, 2010-2011

per 10 000 people, by administrative area

- over 50
- 40–50
- 30–40
- 20–30
- under 20

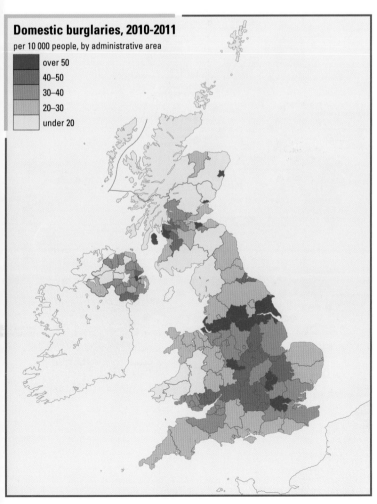

Coronary heart disease, 2006–2008

age-standardised death rates per 100 000 people*,
by administrative area

- over 60
- 50–60
- 40–50
- 30–40
- under 30

*under 65

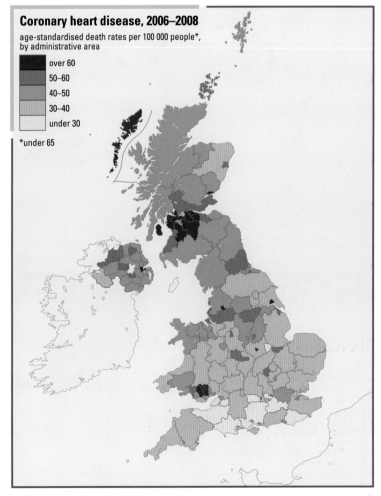

Scale 1: 4 500 000

Conservation

National Parks

Areas of Outstanding Natural Beauty (England, Wales, and Northern Ireland)
National Scenic Areas (Scotland)

Heritage Coast (England and Wales)
Coastal Conservation Zone (Scotland)

△ internationally recognized sites (including Special Protection Areas, 'Ramsar' Sites, and Biosphere Reserves)

✳ World Heritage Sites – Natural

✳ World Heritage Sites – Cultural

● tourist attractions

Great Britain Countryside

percentage of broad habitats, Countryside Survey
one small square represents 1%

improved grassland
neutral grassland
broadleaved, mixed, and yew woodland
arable and horticultural
coniferous woodland
urban and transport
acid grassland
other
dwarf shrub heath
bracken
bog
fen, marsh, and swamp

National Parks, 2009
area and visitor numbers

Scatter plot: area in square kilometres (y-axis, 0–4500) vs visitor days (millions per year) (x-axis, 0–40). Points labelled: Cairngorms, Snowdonia, Lake District, Loch Lomond and The Trossachs, Peak District, Yorkshire Dales, South Downs, North York Moors, Brecon Beacons, Northumberland, Pembrokeshire Coast, Dartmoor, Exmoor, New Forest, The Broads.

Department for Culture, Media and Sport
www.culture.gov.uk

National Parks
www.nationalparks.gov.uk

Visit Britain
www.visitbritain.com

Central London

British Museum
British Library
National Gallery
Somerset House
St. Paul's Cathedral
Tate Modern
Tower of London
London Eye
Imperial War Museum
Royal Naval College
ZSL London Zoo
Madame Tussauds
National Portrait Gallery
Royal Academy of Arts
Westminster Abbey
Science Museum
Natural History Museum
Royal Botanic Gardens, Kew
Victoria & Albert Museum
Tate Britain
Houses of Parliament and Big Ben
Royal Observatory Greenwich
Maritime Greenwich
Old Royal Naval College

Shetland

Hoy and West Mainland
The Heart of Neolithic Orkney

North-west Sutherland
Kyle of Tongue

South Lewis, Harris, and North Uist
Assynt Coigach
Wester Ross

✳ St. Kilda

Trotternish
Kintail
Glen Strathfarrar

South Uist Machair
The Cuillin Hills
Knoydart
Glen Affric
Cairngorms

The Small Isles
Loch Shiel
Ben Nevis / Glen Coe
Loch Tummel

Morar, Moidart, and Ardnamurchan
River Tay
Loch Rannoch/ Glen Lyon
River Earn

Loch na Keal, Isle of Mull
Lynn of Lorn
River Earn

Scarba, Lunga, and the Garvellachs
Knapdale
Loch Lomond and The Trossachs
Royal Botanic Garden
National Museum of Scotland

Jura
Kyles of Bute
Stirling Castle
Gallery of Modern Art
The Falkirk Wheel
Edinburgh Castle
Old and New Towns of Edinburgh

North Arran
Kelvingrove Art Gallery & Museum
New Lanark
Upper Tweeddale
Eildon and Leaderfoot

Glenveagh
Giant's Causeway
Derry Walls
Ulster Museum
Antrim Coast and Glens
East Stewartry Coast
Nith Estuary
Northumberland Coast

Sperrin
Belfast Zoological Gardens
Fleet Valley
Hadrian's Wall
Northumberland

Botanic Gardens Lagan Valley
W5
Stranford Lough
Solway Coast
North Pennines
Durham Cathedral/Castle

Ballycroy
South Armagh
Lecale Coast
Lake District
Yorkshire Dales
North York Moors
Flamingo Land
Howardian Hills

Mourne
Windermere Lake Cruises
Arnside and Silverdale
Nidderdale
Fountain's Abbey/ Studley Royal Park

Connemara
Archaeological Ensemble of the Bend of the Boyne
Forest of Bowland
Blackpool Tower
Saltaire

National Botanic Gardens
Merseyside Maritime Museum
Museums Sheffield: Millennium Gallery
Lincolnshire Wolds

Book of Kells
Dublin Zoo
Liverpool – Maritime Mercantile City
Chester Zoo
Peak District
Holkham National Nature Reserve

National Gallery of Ireland
Guinness Storehouse
Anglesey
Penrhyn Castle
Clwydian Range
Alton Towers
Derwent Valley Mills
Norfolk Coast
The Broads

Cliffs of Moher Visitor Experience
Burren
Castles/Town Walls of King Edward
Portmeirion
Pontcysyllte Aqueduct and Canal
Cannock Chase
Suffolk Coast and Heaths

Lleyn
Erddig
Snowdonia
Ironbridge Gorge
Drayton Manor Park
Dedham Vale

Wicklow Mountains
Shropshire Hills
Malvern Hills

Holy Cross Abbey
Blenheim Palace

Killarney
Blarney Castle
Fota Wildlife Park
Pembrokeshire Coast
St. David's Cathedral
Brecon Beacons
Wye Valley
Cotswolds
Ashmolean Museum
Chilterns
Legoland

Skellig Michael
National Waterfront Museum
Big Pit National Coal Museum
Blaenavon
National Museum
Roman Baths
North Wessex Downs
RHS Garden Wisley
Hampton Court Palace
Canterbury Cathedral
Kent Downs

Gower
St. Fagan's National History Museum
Mendip Hills
Bath
Stonehenge/ Avebury
Surrey Hills
South Downs
High Weald

Exmoor
Quantock Hills
Cranborne Chase and West Wiltshire Downs
Isle of Wight

North Devon
Blackdown Hills
East Devon
New Forest

Cornwall and West Devon Mining Landscape
Dartmoor
Dorset and East Devon Coast
Dorset

Eden Project
Cornwall
Tamar Valley
South Devon

Isles of Scilly

Scale 1: 10 000 000

Acid rain

Environmental damage is more likely where acid deposition is high and soils (particularly those that are already acid) are more sensitive.

areas where potential damage to vegetation from nitrogen in acid rain is

- very high
- high
- moderate
- low

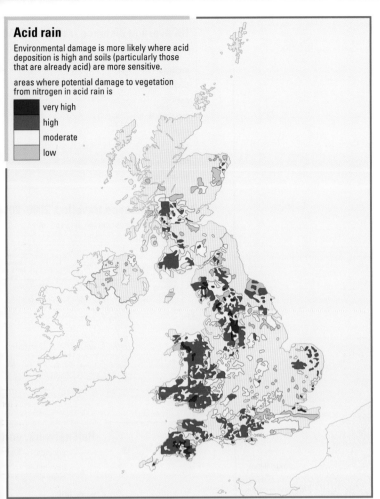

Ozone

Number of days when ozone concentration exceeded 50 parts per billion, used to assess the potential for effects on human health.

days per year

- over 45
- 35–45
- 30–35
- 25–30
- under 25

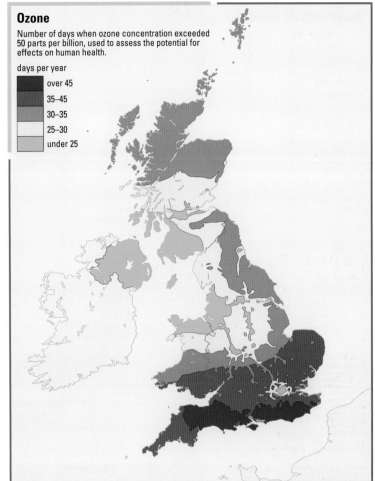

Coastal and offshore pollution

—— bathing beaches heavily polluted by sewage

oil spills within UK waters
tonnes

- over 5000
- 50–5000
- 0–50

Braer 86 248 tonnes
5 January 1993

ATLANTIC OCEAN

NORTH SEA

Sea Empress 72 000 tonnes
15 February 1996

English Channel

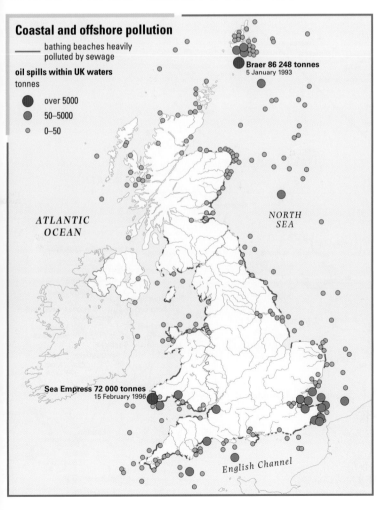

Light pollution

Artificial light, measured by satellite. 0 means the satellite can detect no artificial light. 255 means that the detector is saturated with artificial light.

- 240–255
- 150–240
- 50–150
- 1.7–50
- 0–1.7
- no data

Source: Campaign to Protect Rural England/www.cpre.org.uk

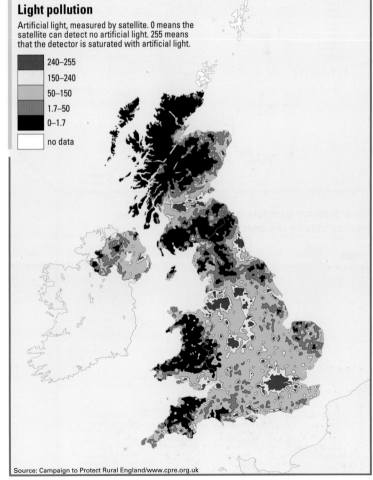

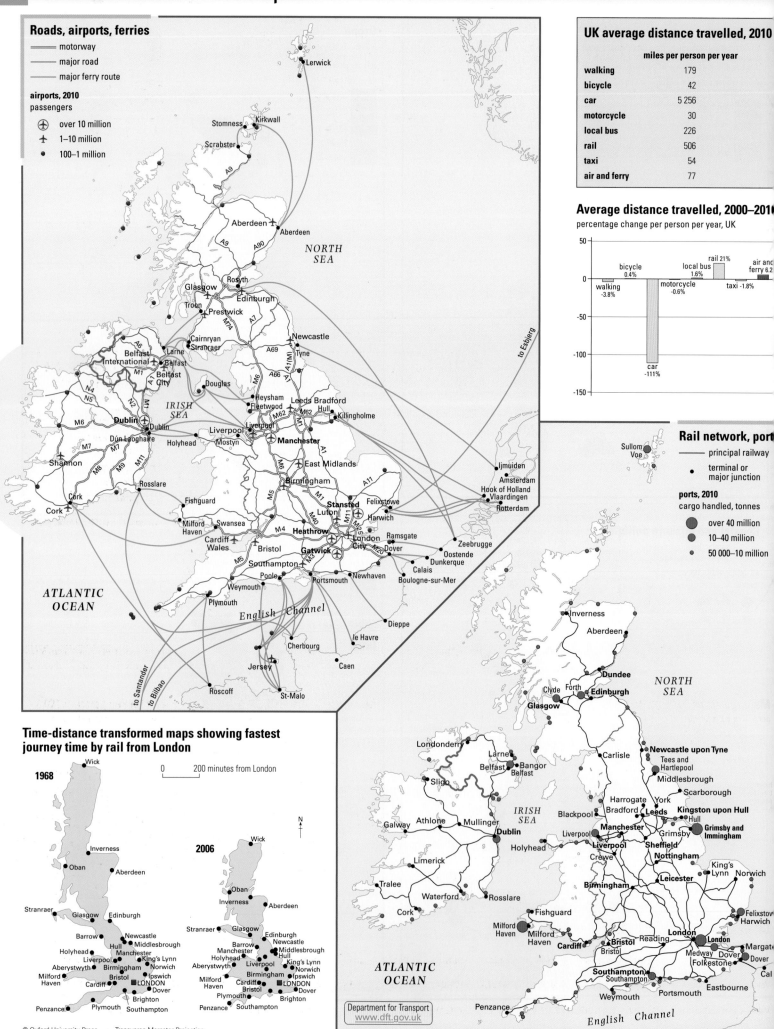

Roads, airports, ferries

— motorway
— major road
— major ferry route

airports, 2010
passengers

⊕ over 10 million
✈ 1–10 million
• 100–1 million

UK average distance travelled, 2010

	miles per person per year
walking	179
bicycle	42
car	5 256
motorcycle	30
local bus	226
rail	506
taxi	54
air and ferry	77

Average distance travelled, 2000–2010

percentage change per person per year, UK

- walking -3.8%
- bicycle 0.4%
- motorcycle -0.6%
- local bus 1.6%
- rail 21%
- taxi -1.8%
- air and ferry 6.2
- car -111%

Rail network, port

— principal railway
• terminal or major junction

ports, 2010
cargo handled, tonnes

⬤ over 40 million
⬤ 10–40 million
• 50 000–10 million

Time-distance transformed maps showing fastest journey time by rail from London

0 — 200 minutes from London

1968

2006

© Oxford University Press   Transverse Mercator Projection

Department for Transport
www.dft.gov.uk

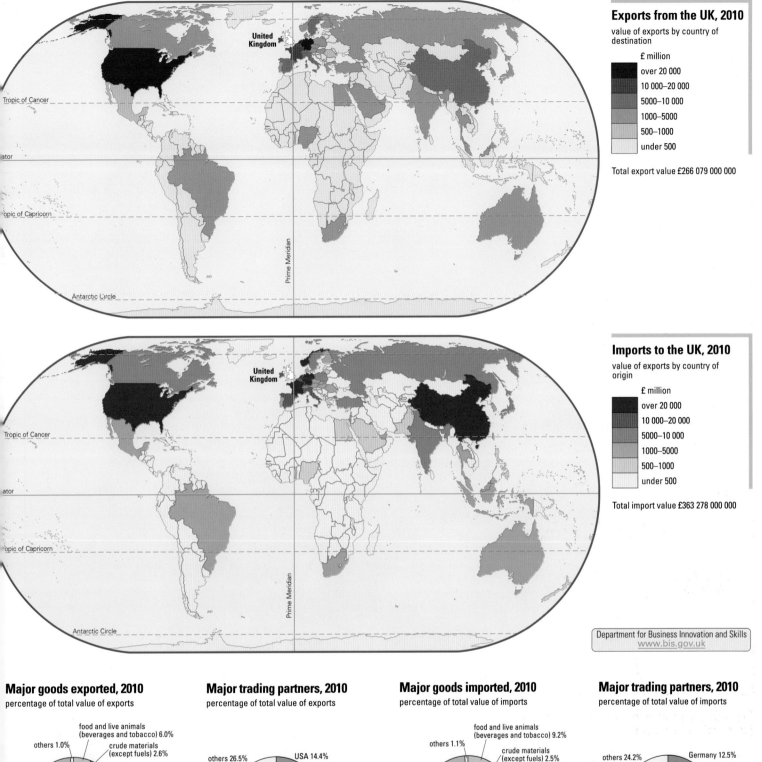

Exports from the UK, 2010

value of exports by country of destination

£ million

- over 20 000
- 10 000–20 000
- 5000–10 000
- 1000–5000
- 500–1000
- under 500

Total export value £266 079 000 000

Imports to the UK, 2010

value of exports by country of origin

£ million

- over 20 000
- 10 000–20 000
- 5000–10 000
- 1000–5000
- 500–1000
- under 500

Total import value £363 278 000 000

Department for Business Innovation and Skills
www.bis.gov.uk

Major goods exported, 2010
percentage of total value of exports

- food and live animals (beverages and tobacco) 6.0%
- crude materials (except fuels) 2.6%
- others 1.0%
- fuels 13.6%
- machinery transport equipment %
- chemicals 19.1%
- manufactured goods 22.7%

Major trading partners, 2010
percentage of total value of exports

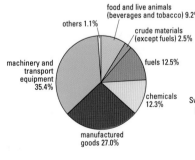

- others 26.5%
- USA 14.4%
- Germany 10.5%
- Netherlands 8.1%
- France 7.2%
- Republic of Ireland 6.4%
- Belgium and Luxembourg 5.1%
- Spain 3.7%
- Italy 3.3%
- China 2.9%
- Sweden 2.1%
- Switzerland 1.9%
- Hong Kong 1.7%
- Japan 1.6%
- Canada 1.6%
- India 1.5%
- UAE 1.5%

Major goods imported, 2010
percentage of total value of imports

- food and live animals (beverages and tobacco) 9.2%
- crude materials (except fuels) 2.5%
- others 1.1%
- fuels 12.5%
- machinery and transport equipment 35.4%
- chemicals 12.3%
- manufactured goods 27.0%

Major trading partners, 2010
percentage of total value of imports

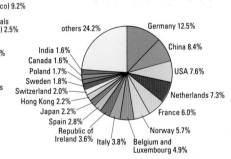

- others 24.2%
- Germany 12.5%
- China 8.4%
- USA 7.6%
- Netherlands 7.3%
- France 6.0%
- Norway 5.7%
- Belgium and Luxembourg 4.9%
- Italy 3.8%
- Republic of Ireland 3.6%
- Spain 2.8%
- Japan 2.2%
- Hong Kong 2.2%
- Switzerland 2.0%
- Sweden 1.8%
- Poland 1.7%
- Canada 1.6%
- India 1.6%

UK Balance of Trade, 1998–2010

the difference in value between exports and imports

	1998	1999	2000	2001	2002	2003	2004	2005	2006	2007	2008	2009	2010
Value of exports (£ million)	164 056	166 166	187 936	189 093	186 524	188 320	190 874	211 608	243 633	220 858	251 643	227 670	266 079
Value of imports (£ million)	185 869	195 217	220 912	230 305	234 229	236 927	251 774	280 197	319 945	310 612	345 024	309 460	363 278

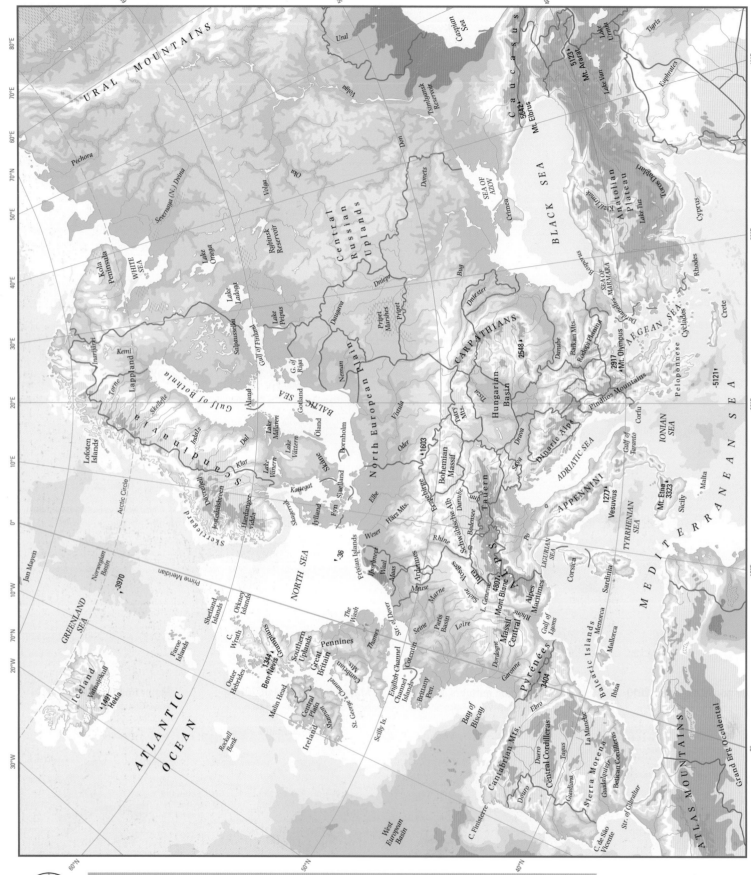

Scale 1: 22 000 000

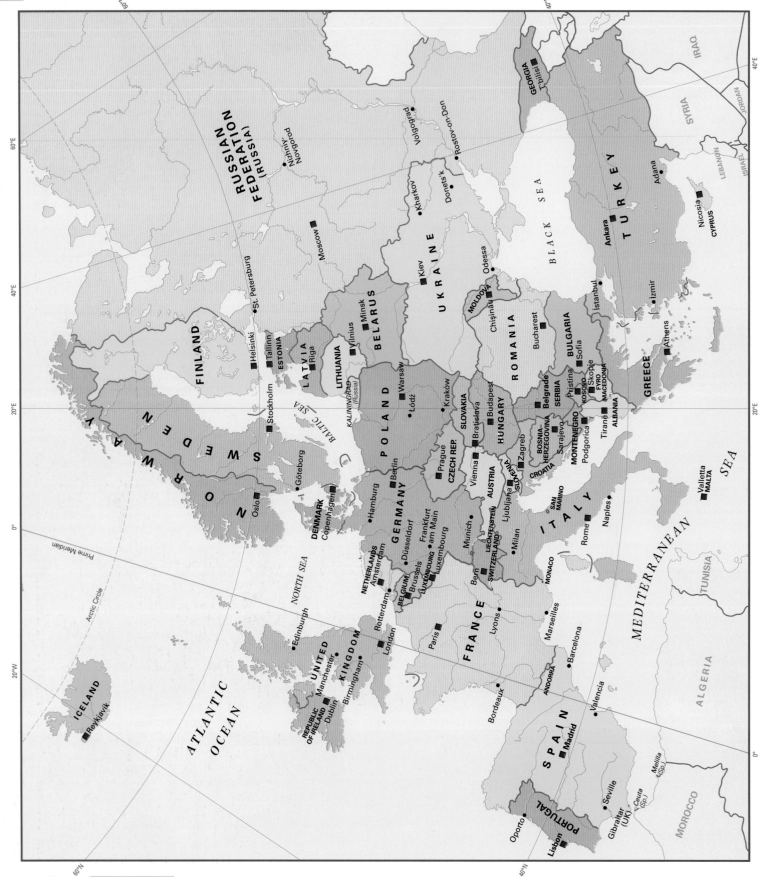

international
disputed
■ capital city
● other important
city

Scale 1 : 22 000 000

© Oxford University Press

Conical Orthomorphic Projection

Population Growth
millions of people

1957	
1973	
1981	
1990	
1995	
2004	
2007	
negotiating	

0 50 100 150 200 250 300 350 400 450 500 550 600

The European Union
date of joining

- 1957
- 1973
- 1981
- 1986
- 1990
- 1995
- 2004
- 2007
- negotiating membership
- ★ headquarters

Brussels: Headquarters

Strasbourg:
European Parliament

Luxembourg:
European Court of Justice

Headquarters of other European and World Organisations

The Hague:
International Court of Justice

Geneva:
World Health Organisation (WHO)

Paris:
United National Education, Scientific and Cultural Organisation (UNESCO)

Organisation for Economic Cooperation and Development (OECD)

Rome:
Food and Agricultural Organisation of the United Nations (FAO)

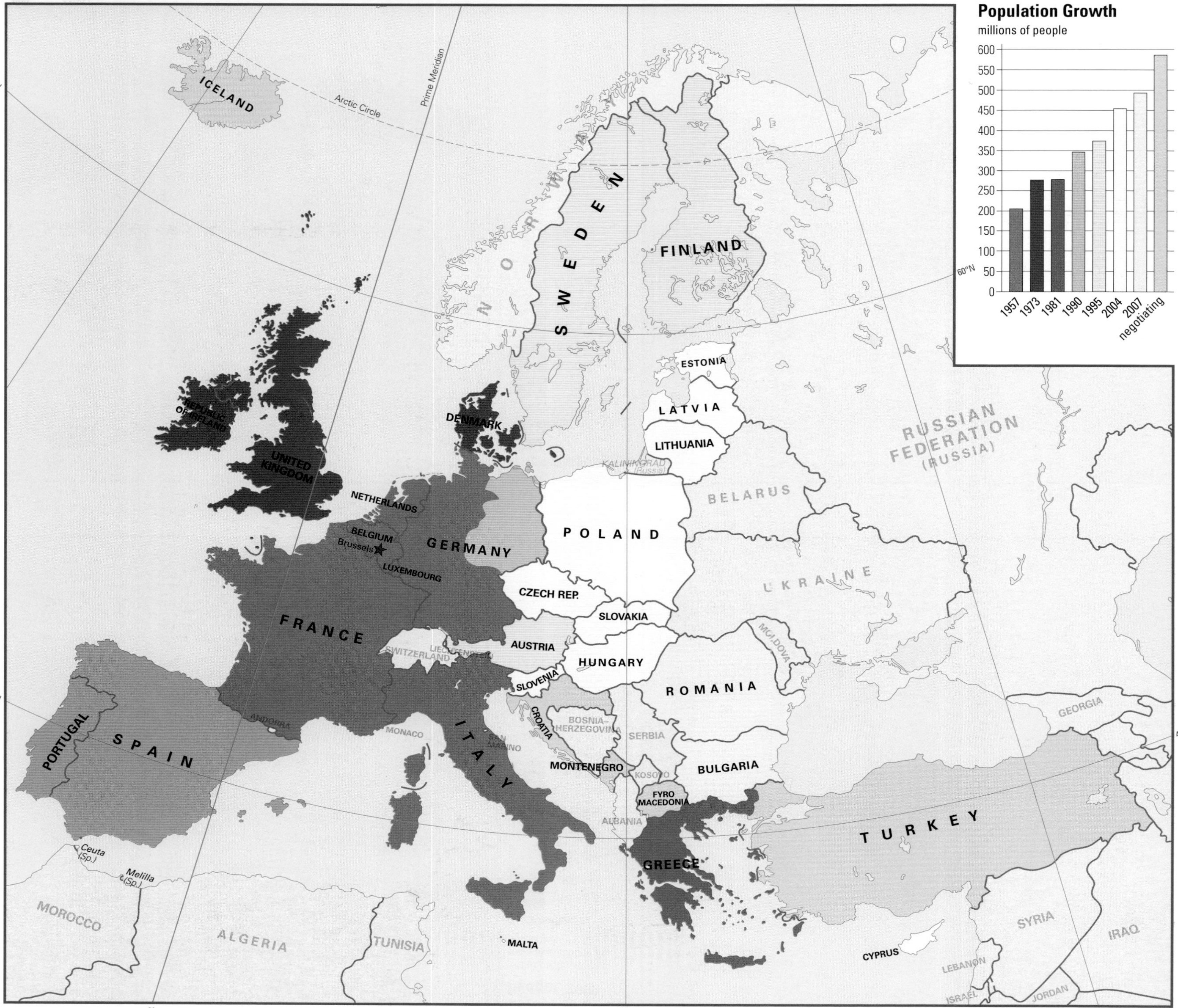

Scale 1: 22 000 000

0 220 440 660 880 1100 km

Map labels

ICELAND

NORWAY

SWEDEN

FINLAND

RUSSIAN FEDERATION (RUSSIA)

ESTONIA

LATVIA

LITHUANIA

KALININGRAD

BELARUS

UKRAINE

MOLDOVA

DENMARK

REPUBLIC OF IRELAND

UNITED KINGDOM

NETHERLANDS

GERMANY

POLAND

CZECH REP.

SLOVAKIA

AUSTRIA

HUNGARY

SLOVENIA

CROATIA

BELGIUM

Brussels ★

LUXEMBOURG

LIECHTENSTEIN

SWITZERLAND

FRANCE

MONACO

ANDORRA

SPAIN

PORTUGAL

ITALY

SAN MARINO

SLOVENIA

BOSNIA–HERZEGOVINA

SERBIA

MONTENEGRO

KOSOVO

ALBANIA

FYRO MACEDONIA

ROMANIA

BULGARIA

GREECE

TURKEY

CYPRUS

MALTA

GEORGIA

IRAQ

SYRIA

LEBANON

ISRAEL

JORDAN

TUNISIA

ALGERIA

MOROCCO

Ceuta (Sp.)

Melilla (Sp.)

Arctic Circle

Prime Meridian

40°N

60°N

0°

20°E

40°E

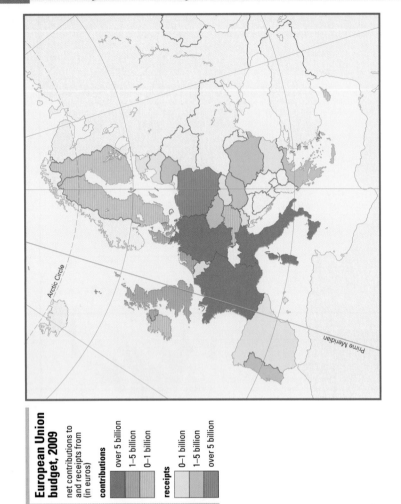

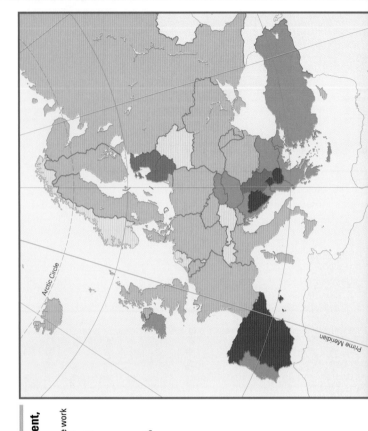

European Union budget, 2009

net contributions to and receipts from (in euros)

contributions
- over 5 billion
- 1–5 billion
- 0–1 billion

receipts
- 0–1 billion
- 1–5 billion
- over 5 billion

Unemployment, 2010

percentage of the work force out of work
- over 20%
- 15–20%
- 10–15%
- 5–10%
- under 5%
- no data

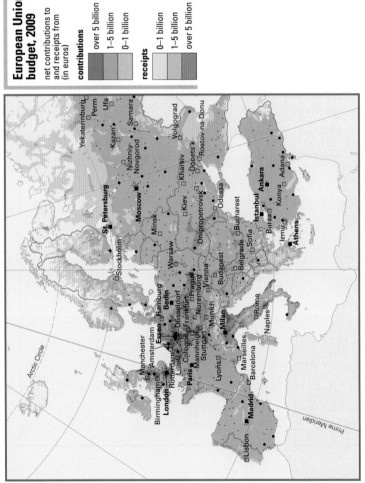

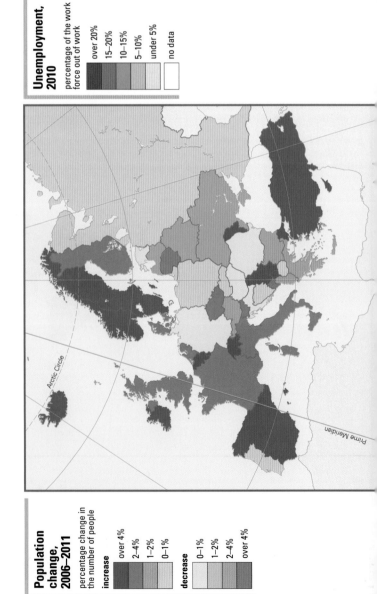

Population density

people per square kilometre
- over 200
- 100–200
- 10–100
- 1–10
- under 1

Major cities

population in millions
- ■ over 3
- □ 1–3
- • 0.5–1
- • 0.1–0.5

Population change, 2006–2011

percentage change in the number of people

increase
- over 4%
- 2–4%
- 1–2%
- 0–1%

decrease
- 0–1%
- 1–2%
- 2–4%
- over 4%

Conical Orthomorphic Projection

Arctic Circle

Prime Meridian

Yekaterinburg
Perm
Ufa
Samara
Nizhniy Novgorod
Kazan
Volgograd
Kharkiv
Rostov-na-Donu
Donets'k
St Petersburg
Moscow
Minsk
Kiev
Dnipropetrovsk
Odessa
Ankara
Adana
Istanbul
Konya
Bursa
Bucharest
Sofia
Belgrade
Izmir
Athens
Stockholm
Warsaw
Budapest
Vienna
Prague
Nuremberg
Berlin
Hamburg
Düsseldorf
Frankfurt
Essen
Munich
Milan
Rome
Naples
Manchester
Amsterdam
Cologne
Mannheim
Stuttgart
Marseilles
Rotterdam
Lille
Lyons
Barcelona
Birmingham
London
Paris
Madrid
Lisbon

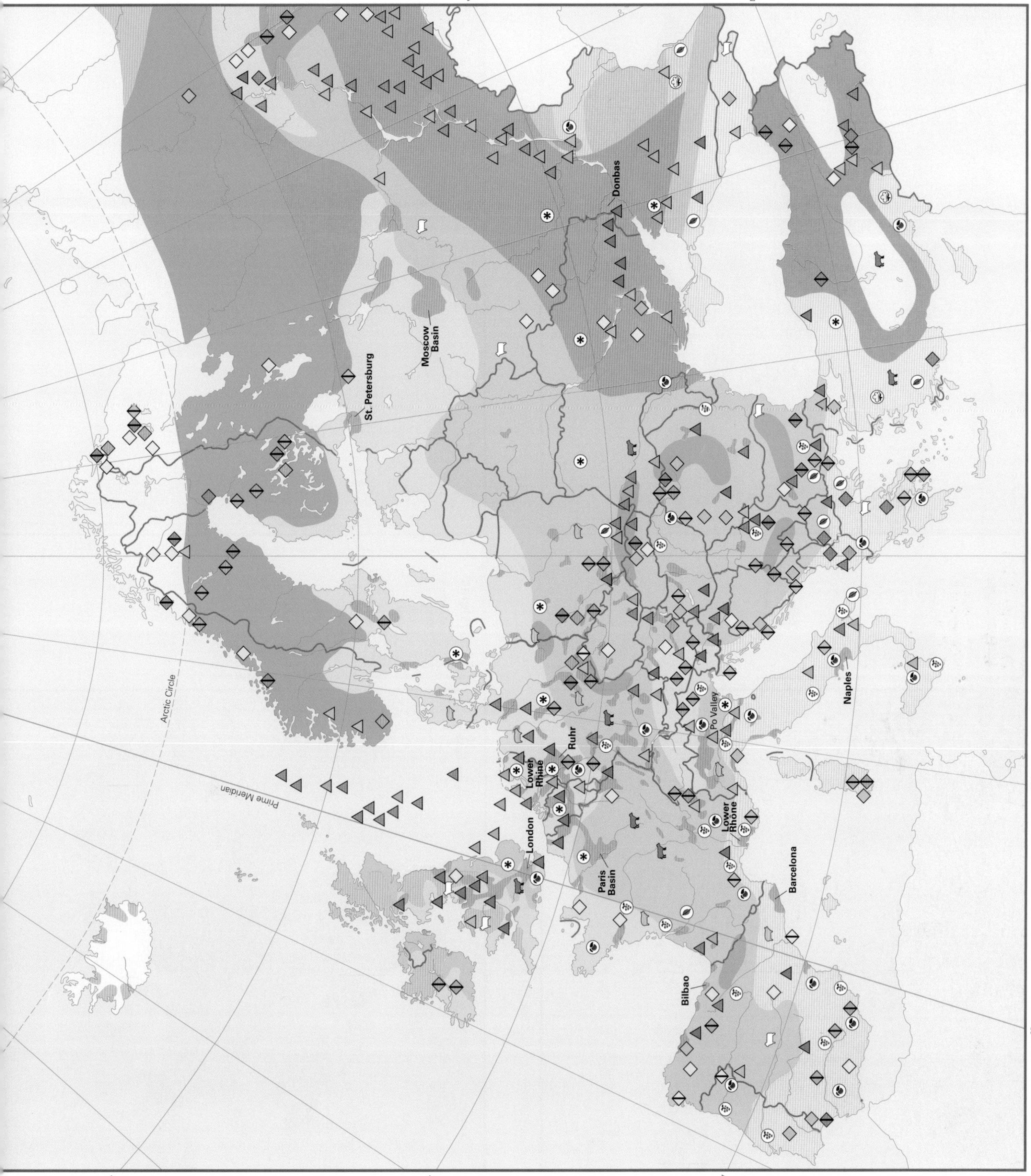

Scale 1: 22 000 000

Map labels

Donbas

Moscow Basin

St. Petersburg

Arctic Circle

Prime Meridian

Ruhr

Lower Rhine

London

Paris Basin

Lower Rhône

Po Valley

Naples

Barcelona

Bilbao

Land use

- rough grazing
- shifting cultivation
- mixed subsistence
- grazing and stock rearing
- mixed farming
- grain farming
- Mediterranean farming
- dairy farming
- specialized horticulture
- forestry
- industrial areas
- unproductive land

Livestock

- sheep
- cattle
- pigs

Crops

- wine grapes
- tobacco
- fruit
- sugar
- cotton

Minerals

- iron ore
- manganese
- chromium
- nickel
- tin
- lead
- zinc
- copper
- bauxite

Energy

- coal
- oil
- gas
- hydro

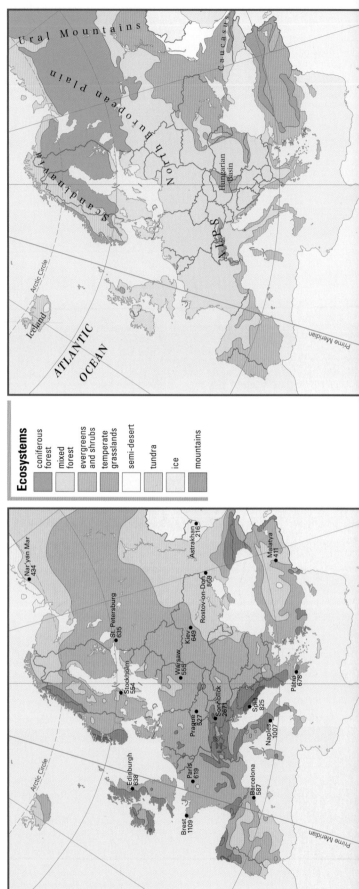

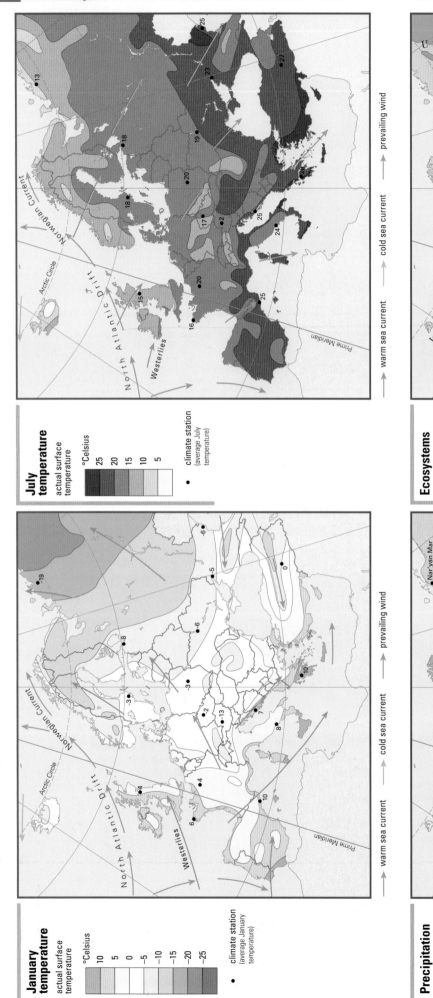

July temperature

actual surface temperature

°Celsius
- 25
- 20
- 15
- 10
- 5

• climate station (average July temperature)

Ecosystems

- coniferous forest
- mixed forest
- evergreens and shrubs
- temperate grasslands
- semi-desert
- tundra
- ice
- mountains

January temperature

actual surface temperature

°Celsius
- 10
- 5
- 0
- -5
- -10
- -15
- -20
- -25

• climate station (average January temperature)

Precipitation

average annual precipitation

mm
- 2000
- 1000
- 500
- 250
- 0

• climate station (average annual precipitation)

Scale 1 : 17 000 000

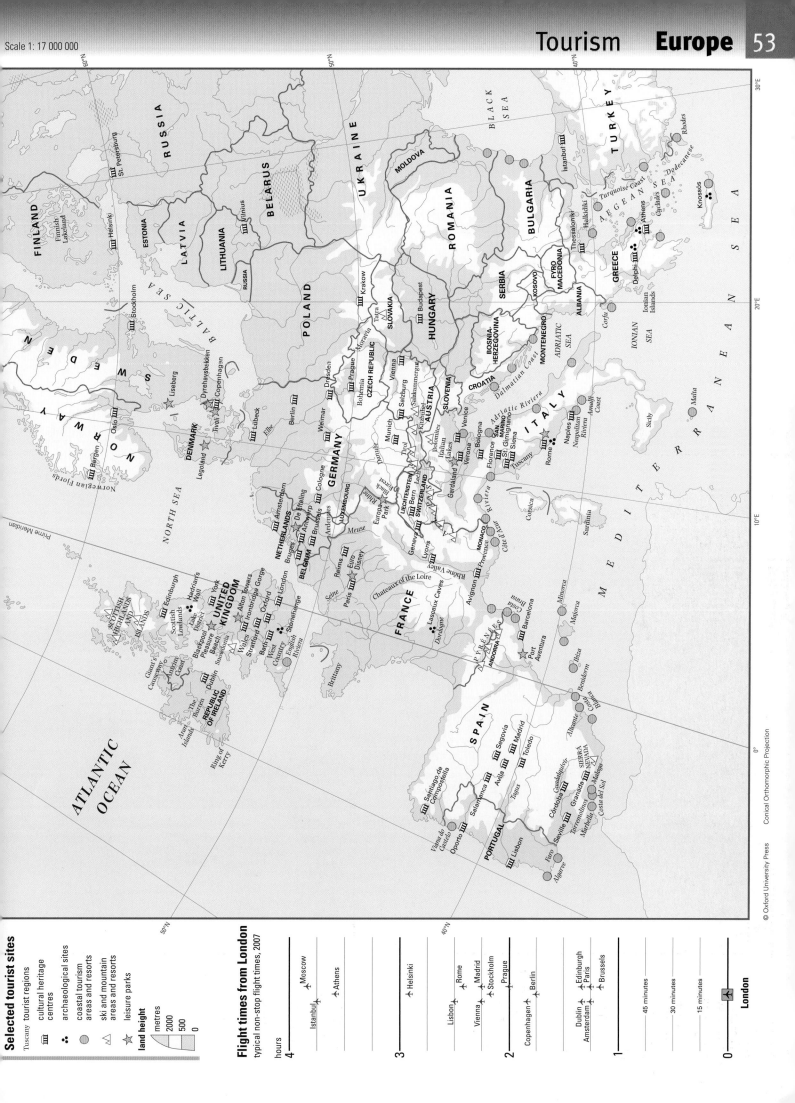

Selected tourist sites

Tuscany tourist regions

- ⅏ cultural heritage centres
- ⁘ archaeological sites
- ◯ coastal tourism areas and resorts
- △ ski and mountain areas and resorts
- ★ leisure parks

land height

metres
2000
500
0

Flight times from London
typical non-stop flight times, 2007

hours

4 ✈ Moscow
  ✈ Athens

  Istanbul ✈

3 ✈ Helsinki

  Lisbon ✈ Rome
  Vienna ✈ Madrid
  ✈ Stockholm
  ✈ Prague

2 Copenhagen ✈ Berlin

  Dublin ✈ Edinburgh
  Amsterdam ✈ Paris
  ✈ Brussels

1

  45 minutes

  30 minutes

  15 minutes

0 ✈ London

Conical Orthomorphic Projection

© Oxford University Press

NORTH SEA

NETHERLANDS

BELGIUM

GERMANY

FRANCE

LUXEMBOURG

Scale 1: 2 500 000

0   25   50   75   100   125 km

Conical Orthomorphic Projection
© Oxford University Press

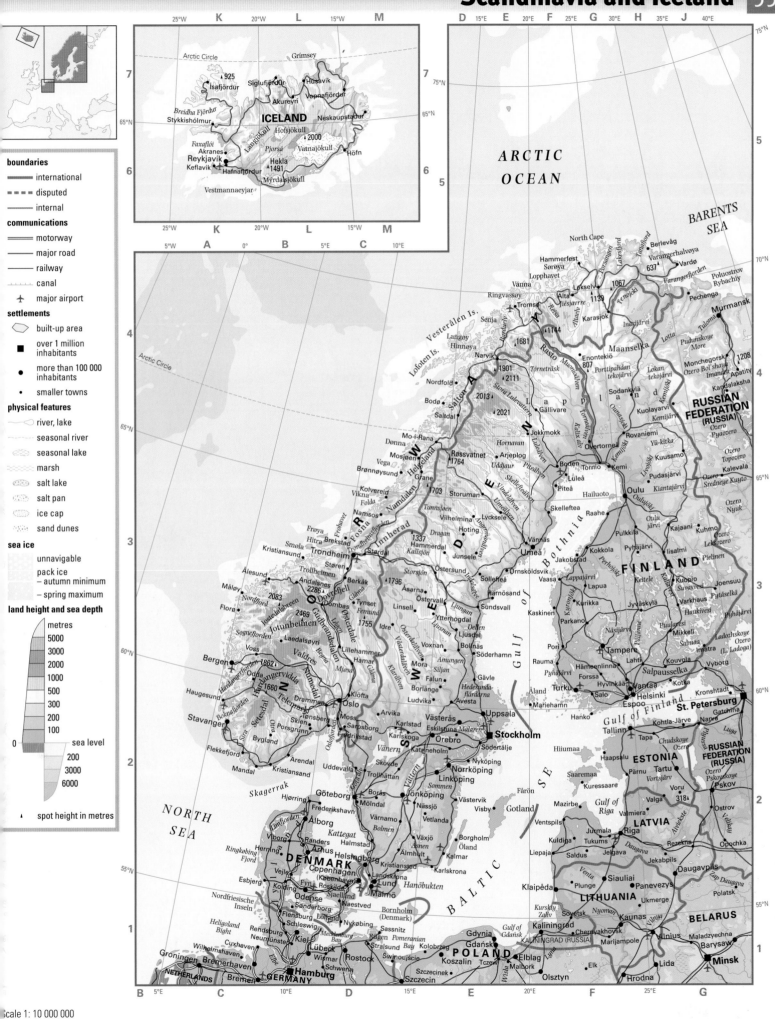

boundaries
— international
--- disputed
— internal

communications
═══ motorway
— major road
— railway
+++ canal
✈ major airport

settlements
⬡ built-up area
■ over 1 million inhabitants
● more than 100 000 inhabitants
• smaller towns

physical features
river, lake
seasonal river
seasonal lake
marsh
salt lake
salt pan
ice cap
sand dunes

sea ice
unnavigable
pack ice
– autumn minimum
– spring maximum

land height and sea depth
metres
5000
3000
2000
1000
500
300
200
100
0 — sea level
200
3000
6000
▲ spot height in metres

ICELAND inset
925
Ísafjördur   Siglufjördur   Húsavik
Breidha Fjördur   Akureyri   Vopnafjördur
Stykkishólmur
ICELAND   Neskaupstadur
Hofsjökull
Faxaflói   Langjökull   2000
Akranes   Pjorsá   Vatnajökull
Reykjavík   Hekla   Höfn
Keflavik   1491
Hafnafjördur
Mýrdalsjökull
Vestmannaeyjar
Grímsey
Arctic Circle

Main map labels
ARCTIC OCEAN
BARENTS SEA
NORTH CAPE
Hammerfest   Sørøya   Tanafjord   Berlevåg
Lopphavet   Varangerhalvøya   Vardø
637   Varangerfjorden
Ringvassøy   Vanna   Lakselv   1067   Poluostrov Rybachiy
Tromsø   Alta   Iesjavrre   1139   Pechenga
Senja   Rensa   Karasjok   Murmansk
Vesterålen Is.   1144   Maanselka
Langøy   Borgefjell   Inarijärvi   Lotta   Pudozhskoye More
Hinnøya   1681   Enontekiö   807   Lokan   Monchegorsk   1208
Lofoten Is.   Narvik   1901   Porttipahdan tekojärvi   Ozero Bol'shaya   Apatity
Nordfold   2111   Stora Lulevatten   Sodankylä   Kandalaksha
Bodø   2013   Lapland   Kemijärvi   RUSSIAN FEDERATION (RUSSIA)
Saltdal   2021   Gällivare   Rovaniemi   Ozero Pyaozero
Mo-i-Rana   Jokkmokk   Overtornea   Yli-kitka   Ozero Topozero
Dønna   Hornavan   Luleälv   Kuusamo   Kalevala
Mosjøen   Arjeplog   Kalix älv   Boden   Pudasjärvi   Ozero Srednye Kuyto
Vega   Uddjaur   Piteälven   Luleå   Ozero Nyuk
Brønnøysund   Rössvatnet   Skellefteälven   Tornio   Kiantajärvi
Grane   1764   Vindelälven   Piteå   Kemi   Oulu   Kuhmo
Kolvereid   1703   Storuman   Umeälven   Hailuoto   Oulujärvi   Ozero Leksozero
Vikna   Namdalen   Skellefteå   Raahe   Kajaani
Folda   Tunnsjøen   Vilhelmina   Angermanälven   Pulkkila   Iisalmi   Pielinen
Namsos   1337   Hammerdal   Vännäs   Kokkola   Pyhäjärvi   Kuopio
Frøya   Prøhavet   Kallsjön   Junsele   Umeå   Jakobstad   FINLAND
Hitra   Brekstad   Dragan   Hoting   Ornsköldsvik   Lappajärvi   Varkaus   Joensuu
Smøla   Innherad   Storsjön   Östersund   Vaasa   Lapua   Jyväskylä   Haukivesi
Kristiansund   Trondheim   1796   Asarna   Sollefteå   Kaskinen   Nasijärvi   Suvasvesi   Pyhäselkä
Ålesund   Støren   Berkåk   Östervall   Härnösand   Parkano   Kurikka   Mikkeli   Pyhäjärvi
Måløy   Andalsnes   2286   Tynset   Linsell   Ljungan   Sundsvall   Pori   Puulavesi   Saimaa   Ladozhskoye Ozero (L. Ladoga)
Nordfjord   2083   Dombås   Femund   Idre   Voxnan   Ljusdal   Rauma   Pyhäjärvi   Tampere   Imatra
Florø   Jostedalsbreen   Dovrefjell   Ljusnan   Dellen   Åland   Lahti   Kouvola   Vyborg
2469   Jotunheimen   Gudbrandsdalen   1755   Mora   Söderhamn   Turku   Hämeenlinna   Salpausselka   Vantaa   Kotka
Sognefjorden   Laedalsøyri   Lillehammer   Amungen   Siljan   Gävle   Forssa   Hyvinkää   Kronstadt
Bergen   Voss   1862   Valdres   Hamar   Falun   Borlänge   Mariehamn   Salo   Helsinki   St. Petersburg
Hardangerfjorden   Odda   Nmndal   Mjøsa   Ludvika   Avesta   Hanko   Espoo   Narva   Gatchina
1660   Hardangervidda   Begna   Klarälven   Hedesunda-   Tallinn   Kohtla-Järve   RUSSIAN FEDERATION (RUSSIA)
Haugesund   Telemark   Drammen   Glåma   flåtdarna   Uppsala   Hiumaa   Tapa   Chudskoye Ozero
Sira   Setesdal   Oslo   Arvika   Västerås   Haapsalu   ESTONIA   Pskov   318
Stavanger   Bøyle   Klofta   Karlstad   Eskilstuna   Mälaren   Stockholm   Saaremaa   Tartu   Ozero Pskovskoye
Flekkefjord   Porsgrunn   Moss   Karlskoga   Örebro   Södertälje   Kuressaare   Vortsjärv   Voru
Mandal   Bygland   Sarpsborg   Örebro   Nyköping   Gulf of Riga   Valga   Ostrov Velikoy
Kristiansand   Skien   Fredrikstad   Vänern   Katrineholm   Mazirbe   Valmiera   Opochka
Arendal   Tønsberg   Norrköping   Fårön   Ventspils   LATVIA   Rezekne
NORTH SEA   Uddevalla   Skövde   Linköping   Gotland   Kuldiga   Riga   Daugava
Skagerrak   Hjørring   Trollhättan   Sommen   Västervik   Jurmala   Tukums   Jekabpils
Frederikshavn   Borås   Jönköping   Visby   Kuressaare   Saldus   Jelgava   Daugavpils
Hjørring   Göteborg   Bolmen   Nässjö   Liepaja   Siauliai   Zap. Daugava
Frederikshavn   Mölndal   Vetlanda   Borgholm   Venta   Plunge   Panevezys   Polatsk
Ålborg   Kattegat   Växjö   Öland   Klaipeda   Ukmerge   LITHUANIA   BELARUS
Viborg   Randers   Älmhult   Kalmar   Kursiu Zaliv   Soyetsk   Nyoman   Vilnius   Barysaw
Limfjorden   Århus   Kristianstad   Karlskrona   Kaliningrad   Marijampole   Maladzyechna
Herning   Helsingborg   DENMARK   Kaliningrad (RUSSIA)   Kaunas   Vilnya   Lida   Minsk
Ringkøbing Fjord   Vejle   Copenhagen (København)   Hanöbukten   Gdynia   Cherryakhovsk   Hrodna
Esbjerg   Kolding   Landskrona   Gulf of Gdansk   KALININGRAD (RUSSIA)   POLAND
Nordfriesische Inseln   Odense   Lund   BALTIC   Gdansk   Koszalin   Elbląg   Elk   Olsztyn
Heligoland Bight   Sønderborg   Malmö   Bornholm (Denmark)   Kolobrzeg   Malbork
Flensburg   Sjaelland   Naestved   Nykøbing   Stralsund   Pomeranian Bay   Szczecinek
Rendsburg   Schleswig   Lolland   Rügen   Swinoujscie   Wisla   Tczew
Neumünster   Kiel   Mecklenburg Bay   Rostock   Szczecin   SEA   Gulf of Gdansk
Groningen   Bremerhaven   Lübeck   Wismar   Schwerin
Wilhelmshaven   Cuxhaven   Elbe   Rostock
NETHERLANDS   Bremen   Hamburg   GERMANY

Seas and regions
ARCTIC OCEAN
BARENTS SEA
NORTH SEA
BALTIC SEA
Gulf of Bothnia
Gulf of Finland
Gulf of Riga
Skagerrak
Kattegat
NORWAY
SWEDEN
FINLAND
DENMARK
LAPLAND

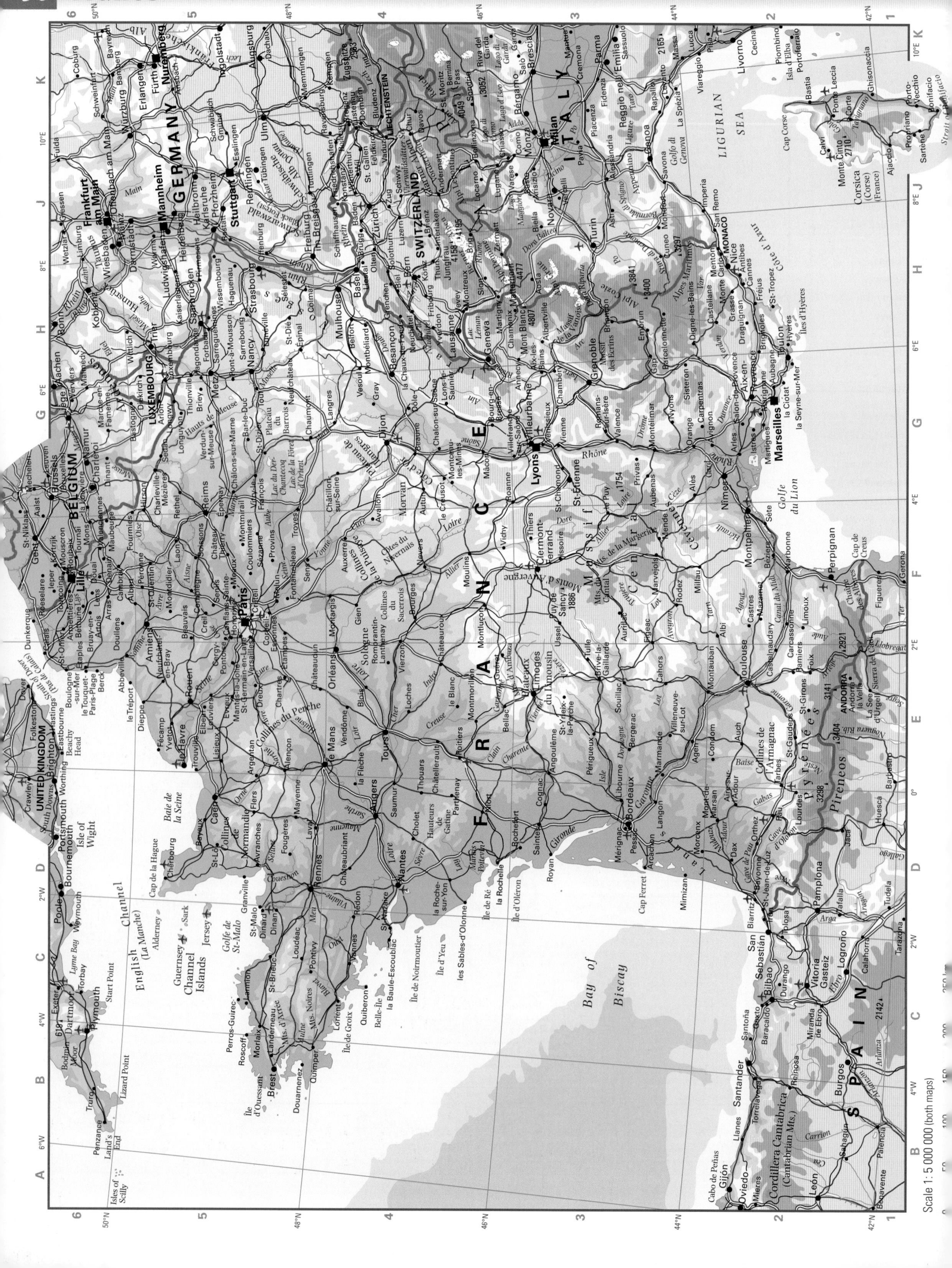

Scale 1 : 5 000 000 (both maps)

GERMANY
LUXEMBOURG
BELGIUM
UNITED KINGDOM
SWITZERLAND
LIECHTENSTEIN
ITALY
F R A N C E
S P A I N
ANDORRA
MONACO

Frankfurt am Main
Mannheim
Stuttgart
Nuremberg
Strasbourg
Mulhouse
Brussels
Lille
Paris
Le Havre
Caen
Rennes
Brest
Nantes
Tours
Angers
Orléans
Bordeaux
Toulouse
Lyons
Grenoble
Marseilles
Nice
Monaco
Milan
Turin
Geneva
Lausanne
Besançon
Dijon
Reims
Metz
Nancy
Clermont-Ferrand
St-Étienne
Limoges
Perpignan
Pamplona
Bilbao
San Sebastián

English Channel (La Manche)
Bay of Biscay
Golfe du Lion
LIGURIAN SEA
Channel Islands
Guernsey
Jersey
Isle of Wight
Corsica (Corse) (France)
Ajaccio
Bastia

Mont Blanc 4807
Pyrenees
Massif Central
Alpes
Rhône
Loire
Seine
Garonne

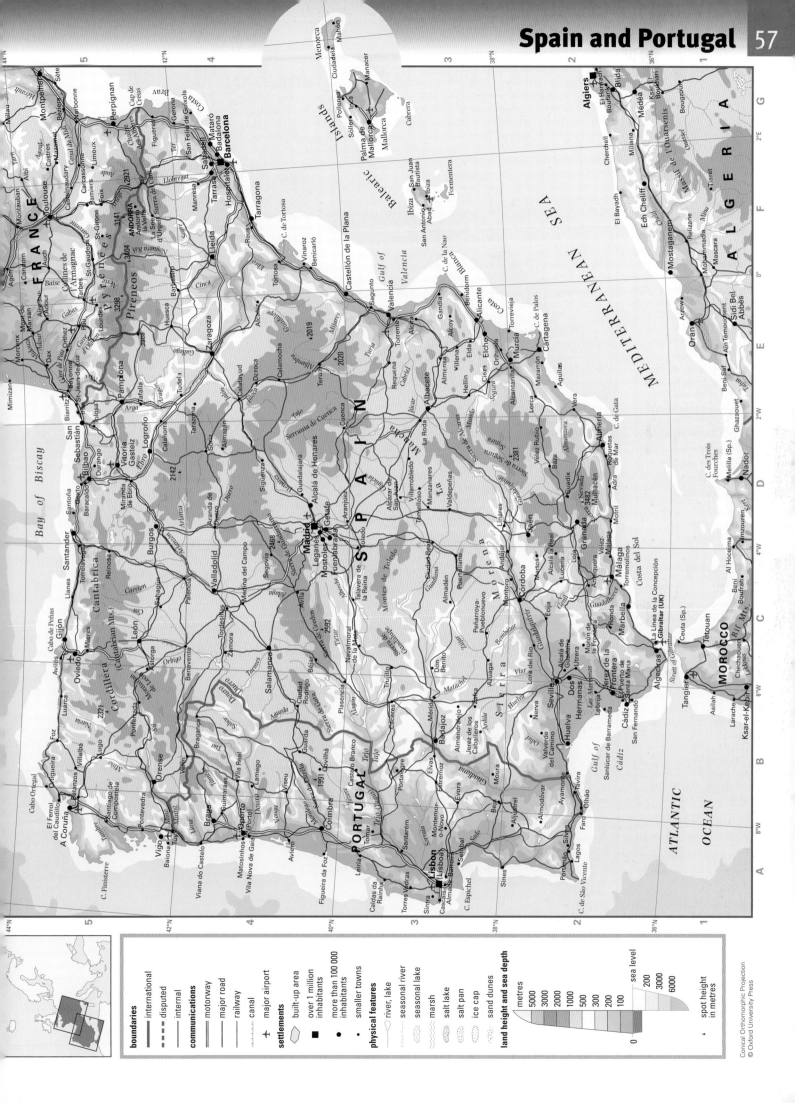

Conical Orthomorphic Projection
© Oxford University Press

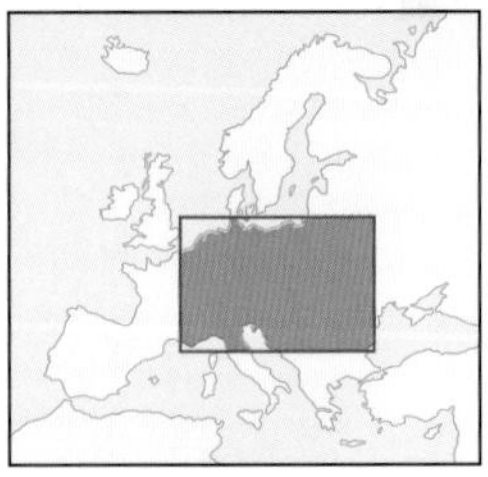

boundaries

- —— international
- - - - disputed
- —— internal

communications

- ═══ motorway
- —— major road
- —— railway
- ···· canal
- ✈ major airport

settlements

- ⬡ built-up area
- ■ over 1 million inhabitants
- ● more than 100 000 inhabitants
- • smaller towns

physical features

- ～ river, lake
- ～ seasonal river
- seasonal lake
- marsh
- salt lake
- salt pan
- ice cap
- sand dunes

sea ice

- unnavigable
- pack ice
  – autumn minimum
  – spring maximum

land height and sea depth

metres
5000
3000
2000
1000
500
300
200
100
0 — sea level
200
3000
6000

▲ spot height in metres

Scale 1: 5 000 000

0   50   100   150   200   250 km

Conical Orthomorphic Projection   © Oxford University Press

NORTH SEA

DENMARK

NETHERLANDS

GERMANY

BELGIUM

LUXEMBOURG

FRANCE

SWITZERLAND

LIECHTENSTEIN

AUSTRIA

ITALY

SLOVENIA

CZECH

Hamburg   Berlin   Bremen   Hannover   Köln   Frankfurt am Main   Mannheim   Nuremberg   Stuttgart   Munich (München)

Amsterdam   Rotterdam   Brussels   Antwerpen   Essen   Düsseldorf   Cologne

Prague (Praha)

Milan   Genoa   Bologna   Florence

Marseilles   Lyons   Geneva   Zürich   Bern

LIGURIAN SEA   ADRIATIC SEA

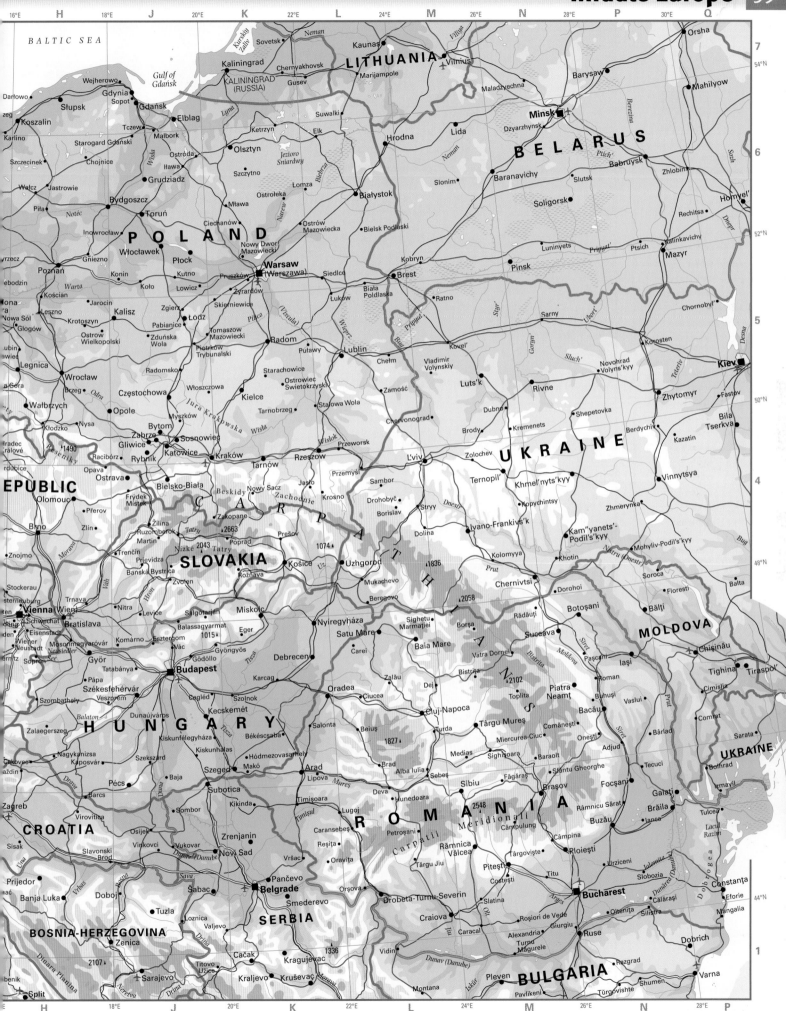

BALTIC SEA

Gulf of Gdańsk

KALININGRAD (RUSSIA)

LITHUANIA

BELARUS

POLAND

Warsaw (Warszawa)

UKRAINE

REPUBLIC

SLOVAKIA

CARPATHIANS

Vienna (Wien)

Bratislava

Budapest

HUNGARY

ROMANIA

MOLDOVA

UKRAINE

Carpaţii Meridionali

CROATIA

SERBIA

Belgrade

Bucharest

BOSNIA-HERZEGOVINA

BULGARIA

boundaries

─── international
- - - disputed
─── internal

communications

═══ motorway
─── major road
─── railway
┼┼┼ canal
✈ major airport

settlements

⬡ built-up area
■ over 1 million inhabitants
● more than 100 000 inhabitants
• smaller towns

physical features

river, lake
seasonal river
seasonal lake
marsh
salt lake
salt pan
ice cap
sand dunes

sea ice

unnavigable
pack ice
— autumn minimum
— spring maximum

land height and sea depth

metres
5000
3000
2000
1000
500
300
200
100
0
sea level
200
3000
6000

▲ spot height in metres

Scale 1: 5 000 000

0 50 100 150 200 250 km

Conical Orthomorphic Projection   © Oxford University Press

SWITZERLAND · AUSTRIA · LIECHTENSTEIN · SLOVENIA · FRANCE · MONACO · ITALY · TUNISIA · MALTA

Geneva · Bern · Lausanne · Grenoble · Turin · Milan · Verona · Padua · Venice · Trieste · Ljubljana · Innsbruck · Graz · Genoa · Bologna · Ravenna · Florence · Rimini · SAN MARINO · Ancona · Pescara · Perugia · Rome (Roma) · Naples · Salerno · Foggia · Caserta

Corsica (Corse) (France) · Ajaccio · Bastia · Sardinia (Sardegna) (Italy) · Sassari · Cágliari · Oristano

LIGURIAN SEA · TYRRHENIAN SEA · ADRIATIC SEA · MEDITERRANEAN SEA · Sicilian Channel

Palermo · Messina · Catania · Siracusa · Sicily · Mt. Etna 3323 · Agrigento · Marsala · Trápani

Bizerte · Tunis · TUNISIA · Annaba · Skikda · Guelma · Souk-Ahras

MALTA · Valletta

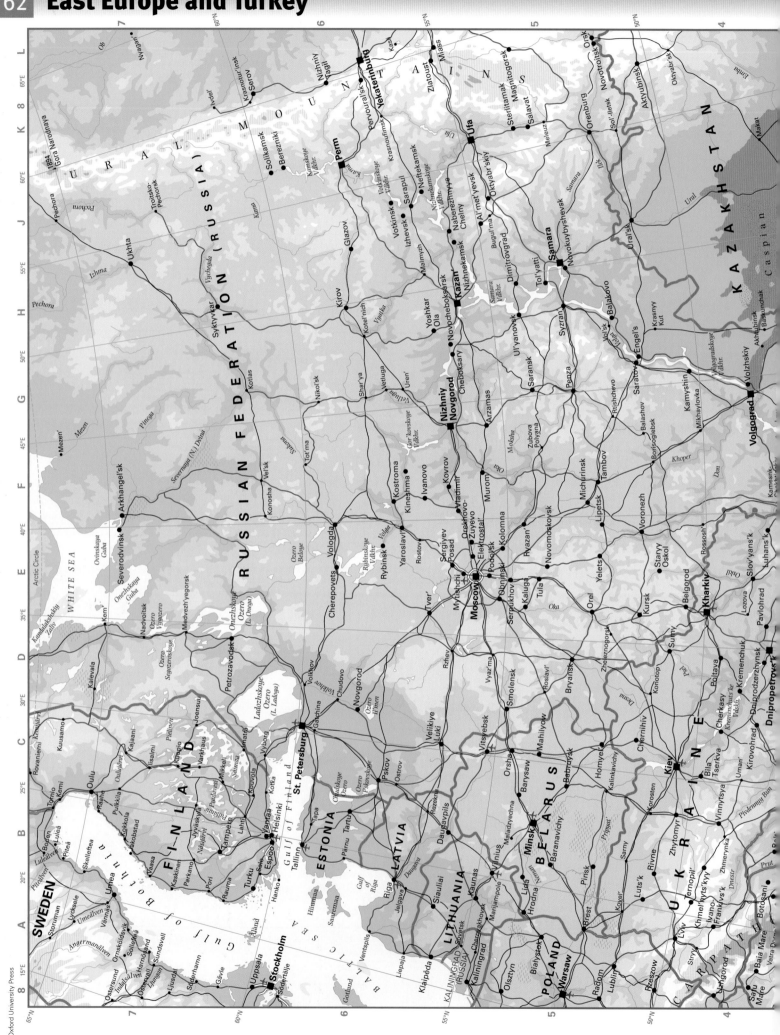

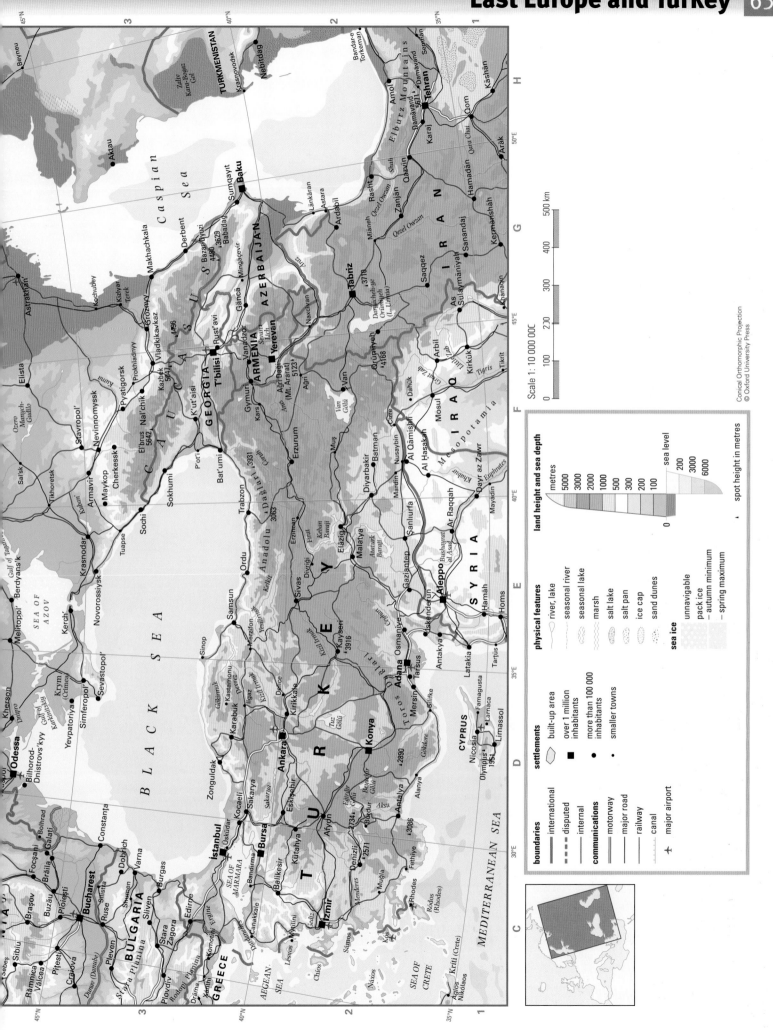

Scale 1: 10 000 000

0   100   200   300   400   500 km

Conical Orthomorphic Projection
© Oxford University Press

boundaries
——— international
- - - disputed
——— internal

communications
——— motorway
——— major road
——— railway
——— canal
✈ major airport

settlements
⬡ built-up area
■ over 1 million inhabitants
■ more than 100 000 inhabitants
• smaller towns

physical features
river, lake
seasonal river
seasonal lake
marsh
salt lake
salt pan
ice cap
sand dunes

sea ice
unnavigable
pack ice
– autumn minimum
– spring maximum

land height and sea depth

metres
5000
3000
2000
1000
500
300
200
100
sea level
200
3000
6000

▲ spot height in metres

Legend

boundaries
— international
--- disputed
.... ceasefire line

physical features
~ river, lake
-- seasonal river
seasonal lake
marsh
salt lake
salt pan
ice cap
sand dunes

sea ice
unnavigable
pack ice
– autumn minimum
– spring maximum

land height and sea depth
metres
5000
3000
2000
1000
500
300
200
100
0 — sea level
200
3000
4000
5000
6000

▲ spot height in metres
▼ sea depth in metres

Scale 1: 55 000 000

0 550 1100 1650 2200 2750 km

Zenithal Equal Area Projection   © Oxford University Press

Map labels

North Pole · ARCTIC OCEAN · Bering Strait · BERING SEA · Franz Josef Land · Svalbard · Severnaya Zemlya · New Siberian Islands · Wrangel · Chukotsk Range · Aleutian Trench · Emperor Seamounts · BARENTS SEA · Novaja Zemlya · LAPTEV SEA · Koryak Range · Kamchatka · Kolyma Lowland · Kolyma · Cherskiy Range · 3147 · Koryak (Gydan) Range · Kuril Islands · Kuril Trench · Sea of Okhotsk · Sakhalin · Northwest Pacific Basin

Ireland · Great Britain · English Channel · NORTH SEA · Scandinavia · Lofoten Islands · Kola Peninsula · WHITE SEA · KARA SEA · Taymyr Peninsula · G. of Ob · Yamal Peninsula · Verkhoyansk Range · Lena · Stanovoy Range · Sikhote Alin · Hokkaido

Bay of Biscay · Loire · Massif Central · ALPS · Rhine · Danube · North European Plain · Russian Uplands · Central Russian Uplands · Ural Mountains · Siberian Lowland · Central Siberian Plateau · Vilyuy · Aldan · Amur (Heilong Jiang) · Honshu · Mt Fuji 3776

Corsica · Sardinia · APENNINES · CARPATHIANS · Hungarian Plain · Dniester · BALTIC SEA · G. of Bothnia · Lake Peipus · Lake Ladoga · Lake Onega · Pechora · Ob · Yenisey · Nizhnyaya (Lower) Tunguska · Angara · Lake Baykal · Eastern Sayan · Yablonovy Range · Greater Khingan Range · Liao · SEA OF JAPAN · Shikoku · Kyushu · Japan Trench

Peloponnese · Crete · Cyprus · MEDITERRANEAN SEA · Nile Delta · BLACK SEA · SEA OF AZOV · Don · Volga · Tobol · Irtysh · Kazakh Upland · Western Sayan · Tannu Ola · Altai Mountains · Gobi Desert · Stanovoy Range

Anatolian Plateau · Toros Daglari · Mt Elbrus 5642 · Caucasus · Mt Ararat 5122 · Caspian Sea · Aral Sea · Syr Darya · Lake Balkhash · Dzungarian Basin · Turfan Depression -154 · Ala Shan · Shandong Peninsula · Bo Hai · YELLOW SEA · Ryukyu Islands

Mt Ararat · Euphrates · Tigris · Syrian Desert · Elburz Mts · Dasht-e-Kavir · Kara Bogaz Gol · Ust Urt Plateau · Kyzyl Kum · Kara Kum · Amu Darya · Tyan Shan · Qullai Garmo 7495 · Tarim Basin · Qilian Shan · Huang He · EAST CHINA SEA · Taiwan Strait · Taiwan

An Nafud · Mesopotamia · The Gulf · Dasht-e-Lut · Helmand · Pamirs · Hindu Kush · 8611 K2 · Karakoram · Kunlun Shan · Altun Shan · Nan Shan · Qaidam Basin · Amne Machin Shan · Xiqing Shan · Sichuan Basin · Chang Jiang (Yangtze) · Dongting Hu · Poyang Hu · Wuyi Shan

Red Sea · Arabian Peninsula · Zagros Mts · Str. of Hormuz · Gulf of Oman · Ladakh Ra. · Gandise Shan · Plateau of Tibet · Bayan Har Shan · Mt Nyainqêntanglha Shan · Tsangpo · Nan Ling · Xi Jiang · Gulf of Tongking · Leizhou Peninsula · Hainan

Asir Mountains · Rub' al Khali · Gulf of Aden · Hadhramaut · Socotra · Thar Desert · Sulaiman Range · Indus · Himalaya · Mt Everest 8848 · Ganga · Brahmaputra · Yamuna · Satpura Ra. · Mahanadi · Mouths of the Ganga · Xarngan Range · Mekong · SOUTH CHINA SEA · Luzon · PHILIPPINE SEA · Challenger Deep -11022

Somali Basin · ARABIAN SEA · Deccan · Western Ghats · Godavari · Eastern Ghats · Bay of Bengal · Irrawaddy · Salween · Song-Koi · Tonle Sap · Mindoro · Panay · Negros · Mindanao · Philippine Trench · -10497

Equator · -5340 · Laccadive Islands · Maldive Coast · Coromandel Coast · Cape Comorin · 2518 Pidurutalagala · Andaman Islands · ANDAMAN SEA · Nicobar Islands · Isthmus of Kra · Gulf of Thailand · Malay Peninsula · 4094 Kinabalu · SULU SEA · CELEBES SEA · Halmahera · West Caroline Basin

Chagos-Laccadive Ridge · Maldive Archipelago · INDIAN OCEAN · Mid-Indian Basin · Ninety East Ridge · Strait of Malacca · Sumatra · Mentawai Islands · 3805 · Cocos Basin · JAVA SEA · Java · Java Trench · Borneo · Sulawesi · Seram · BANDA SEA · Bali · Lesser Sunda Islands · Flores · Timor · TIMOR SEA · ARAFURA SEA · Arnhem Land · New Guinea · PACIFIC OCEAN · Tropic of Capricorn

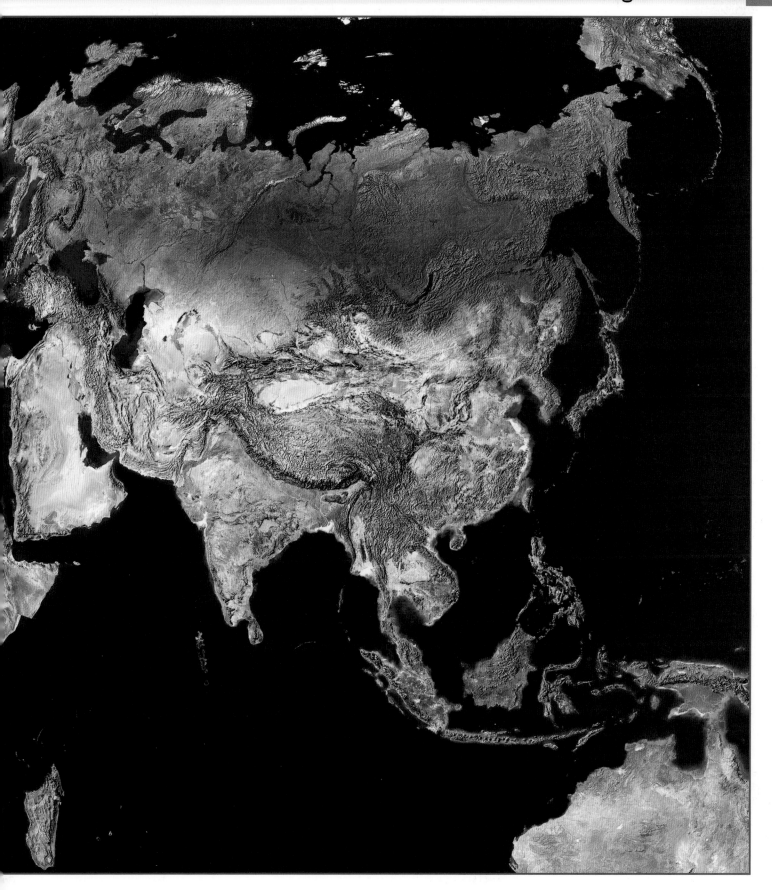

Scale 1: 55 000 000

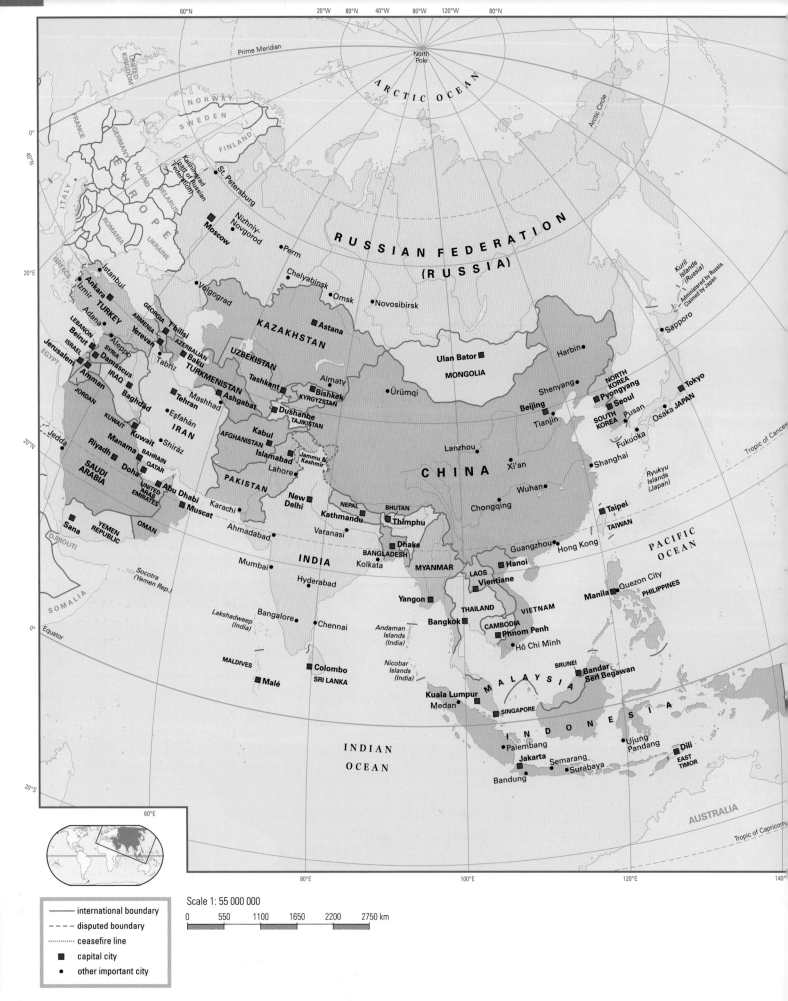

Scale 1: 55 000 000

0 550 1100 1650 2200 2750 km

— international boundary
- - - disputed boundary
······· ceasefire line
■ capital city
• other important city

Zenithal Equal Area Projection   © Oxford University Press

Scale 1: 75 000 000

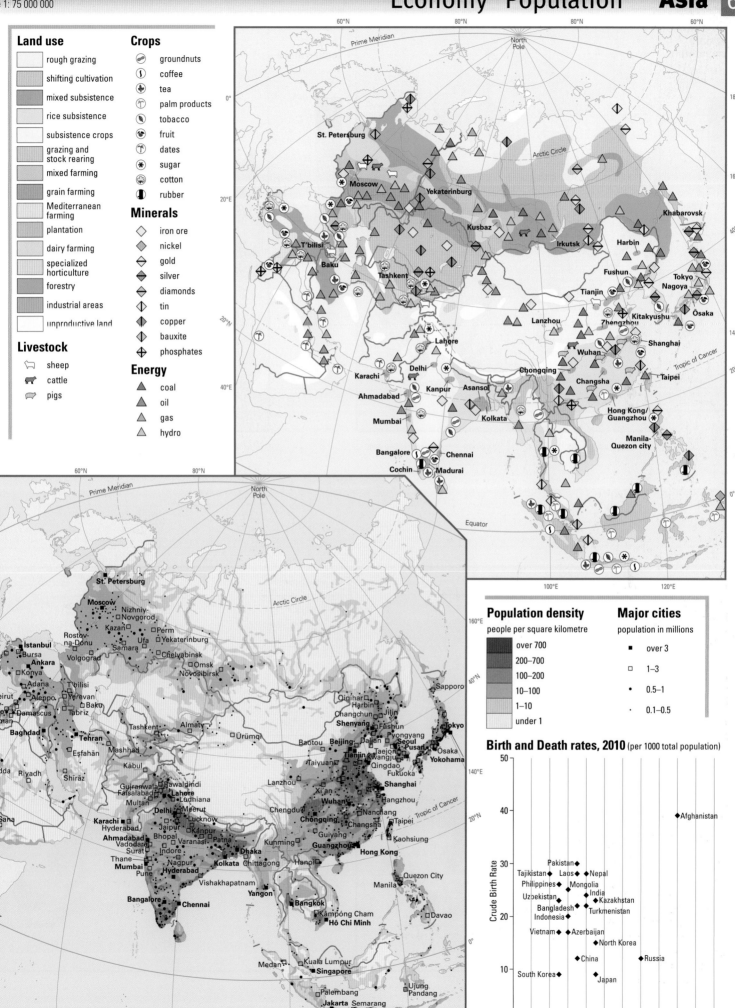

Land use

- rough grazing
- shifting cultivation
- mixed subsistence
- rice subsistence
- subsistence crops
- grazing and stock rearing
- mixed farming
- grain farming
- Mediterranean farming
- plantation
- dairy farming
- specialized horticulture
- forestry
- industrial areas
- unproductive land

Livestock

- sheep
- cattle
- pigs

Crops

- groundnuts
- coffee
- tea
- palm products
- tobacco
- fruit
- dates
- sugar
- cotton
- rubber

Minerals

- iron ore
- nickel
- gold
- silver
- diamonds
- tin
- copper
- bauxite
- phosphates

Energy

- coal
- oil
- gas
- hydro

Population density
people per square kilometre

- over 700
- 200–700
- 100–200
- 10–100
- 1–10
- under 1

Major cities
population in millions

- over 3
- 1–3
- 0.5–1
- 0.1–0.5

Birth and Death rates, 2010 (per 1000 total population)

Crude Birth Rate / Crude Death Rate

Afghanistan, Pakistan, Tajikistan, Laos, Nepal, Philippines, Mongolia, Uzbekistan, India, Kazakhstan, Bangladesh, Turkmenistan, Indonesia, Vietnam, Azerbaijan, North Korea, China, Russia, South Korea, Japan

Zenithal Equal Area Projection

© Oxford University Press

January temperature

actual surface temperature

°Celsius
25
20
15
10
5
0
−10
−20
−30
−40
−50

● climate station
(average January temperature)

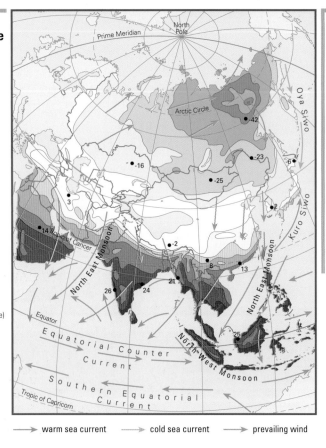

→ warm sea current → cold sea current → prevailing wind

July temperature

actual surface temperature

°Celsius
35
30
25
20
15
10
5
0

● climate station
(average July temperature)

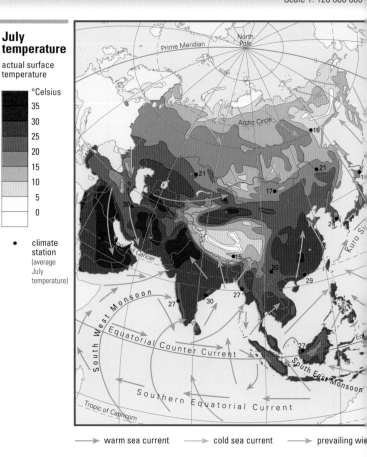

→ warm sea current → cold sea current → prevailing wi

Precipitation

average annual precipitation

mm
3000
2000
1000
500
250
0

● climate station
(average annual precipitation)

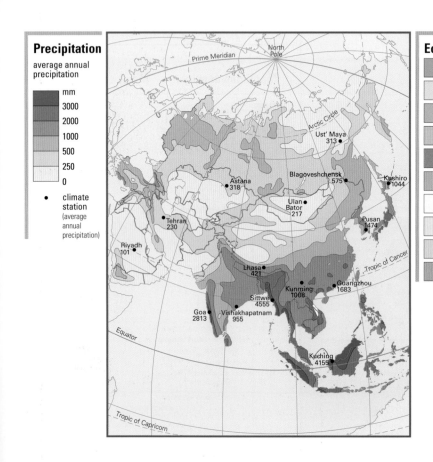

Ecosystems

coniferous forest

mixed forest

tropical rain forest

evergreens and shrubs

thorn forest

temperate grasslands

semi-desert

desert

tundra

mountains

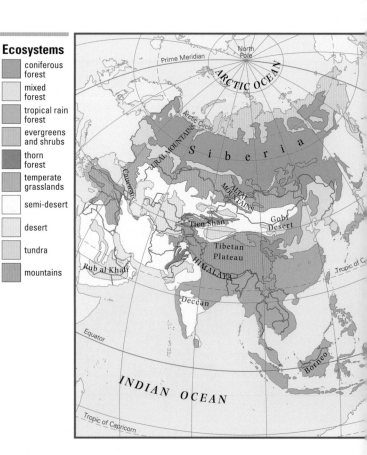

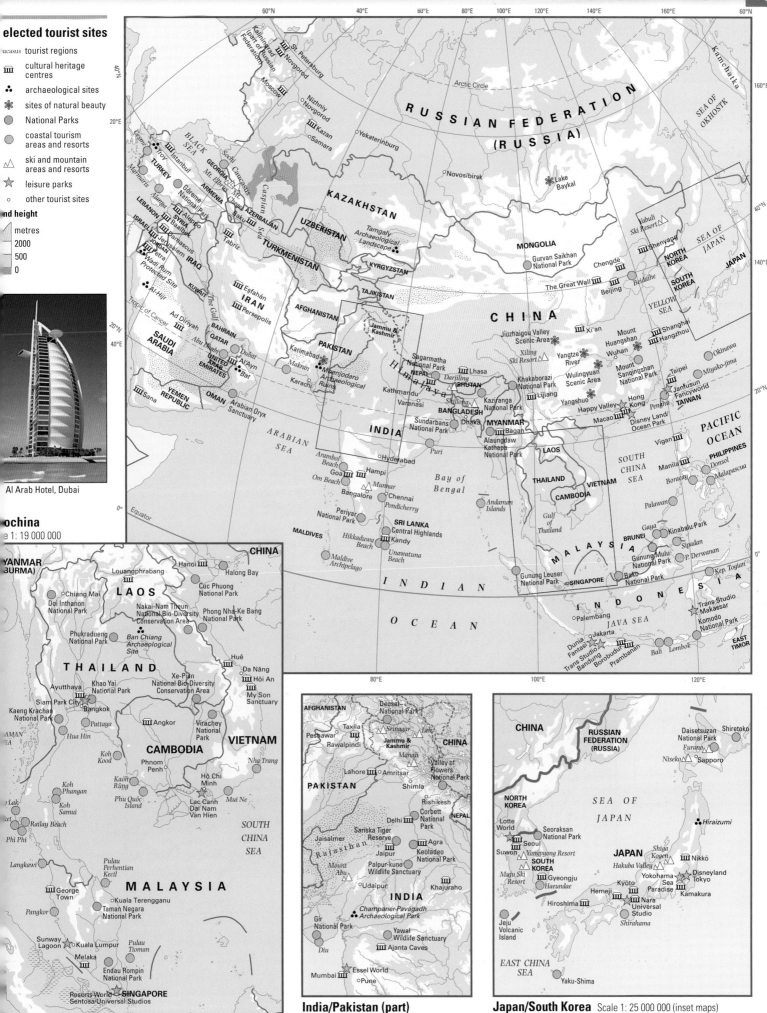

Scale 1: 55 000 000

elected tourist sites

tourist regions
- cultural heritage centres
- archaeological sites
- sites of natural beauty
- National Parks
- coastal tourism areas and resorts
- ski and mountain areas and resorts
- leisure parks
- other tourist sites

nd height
metres
2000
500
0

Al Arab Hotel, Dubai

ochina
e 1: 19 000 000

India/Pakistan (part)

Japan/South Korea Scale 1: 25 000 000 (inset maps)

© Oxford University Press   Zenithal Equal Area Projection

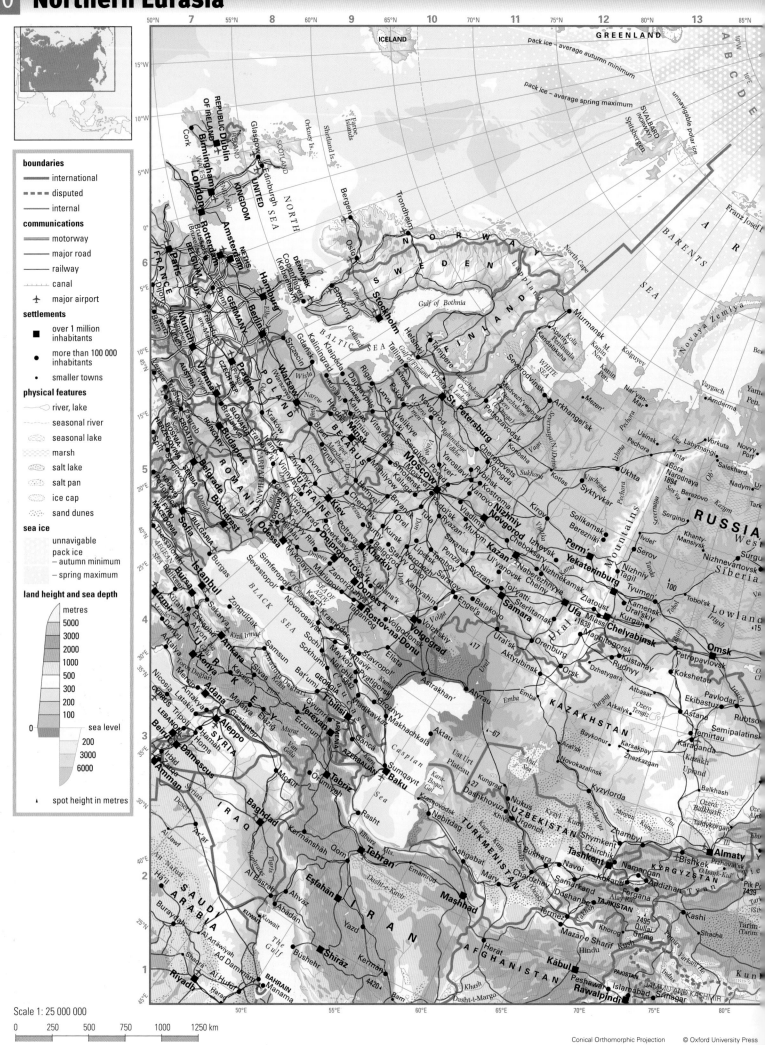

boundaries
— international
--- disputed
— internal

communications
═══ motorway
— major road
— railway
++++ canal
✈ major airport

settlements
■ over 1 million inhabitants
● more than 100 000 inhabitants
• smaller towns

physical features
∿ river, lake
∿ seasonal river
⬡ seasonal lake
⬡ marsh
⬡ salt lake
⬡ salt pan
⬡ ice cap
⬡ sand dunes

sea ice
unnavigable
pack ice
– autumn minimum
– spring maximum

land height and sea depth
metres
5000
3000
2000
1000
500
300
200
100
0 sea level
200
3000
6000
▲ spot height in metres

Scale 1: 25 000 000

0 250 500 750 1000 1250 km

Conical Orthomorphic Projection   © Oxford University Press

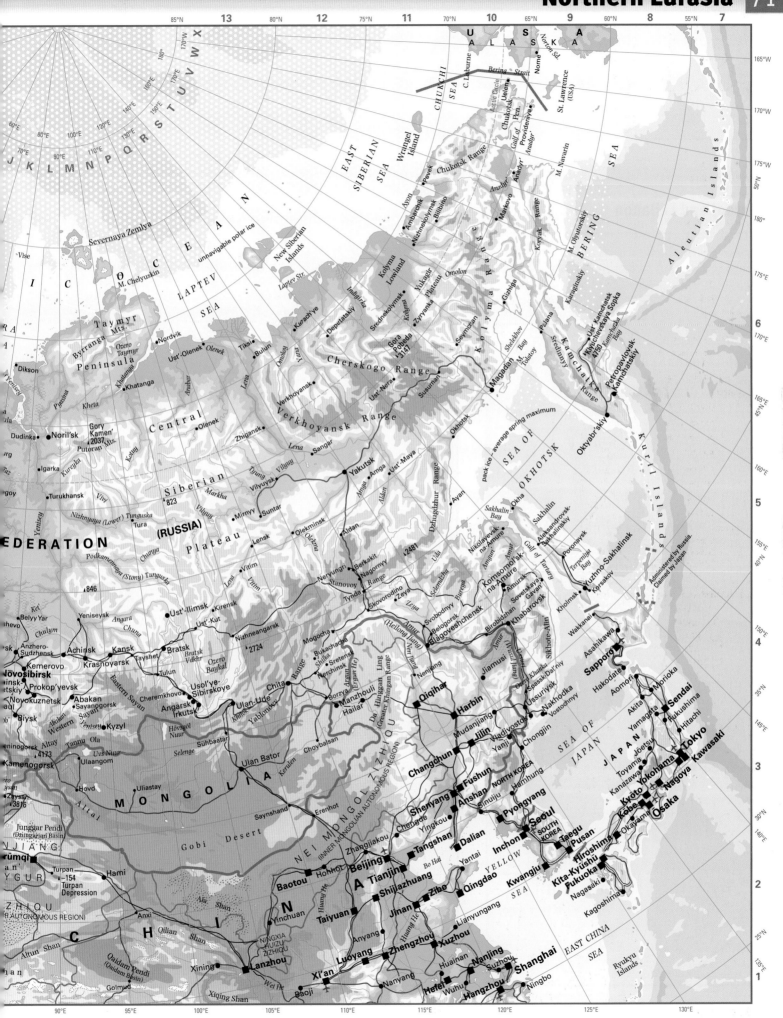

Israel and Lebanon

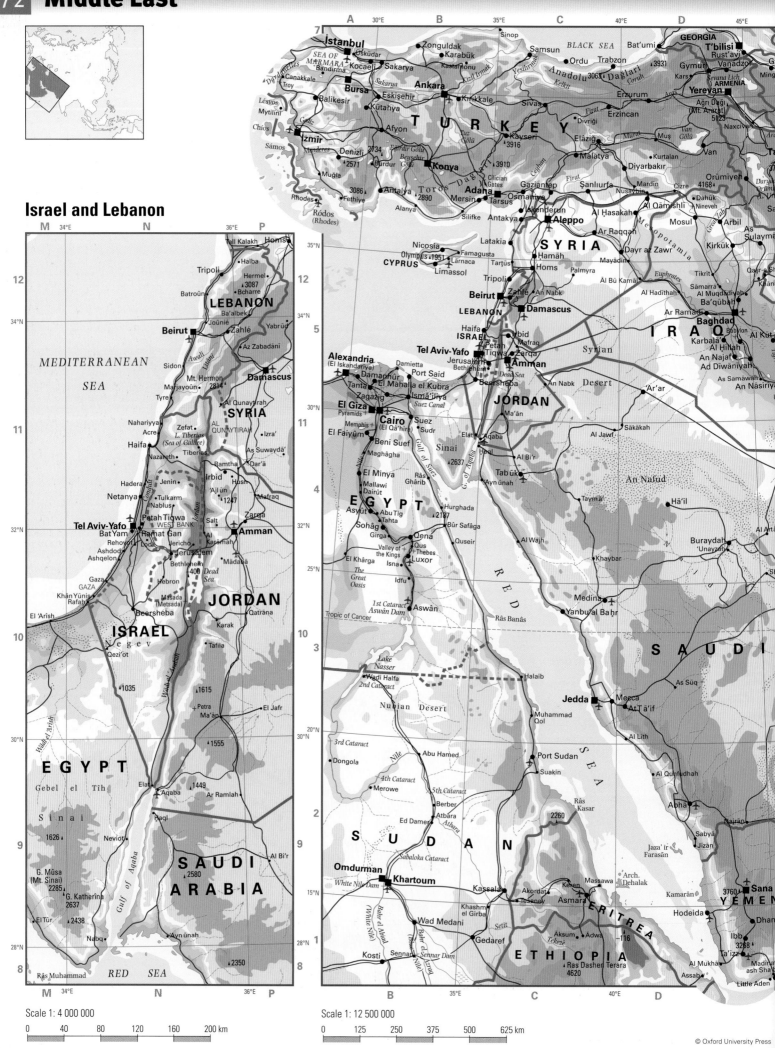

Scale 1: 4 000 000

0 40 80 120 160 200 km

Scale 1: 12 500 000

0 125 250 375 500 625 km

© Oxford University Press

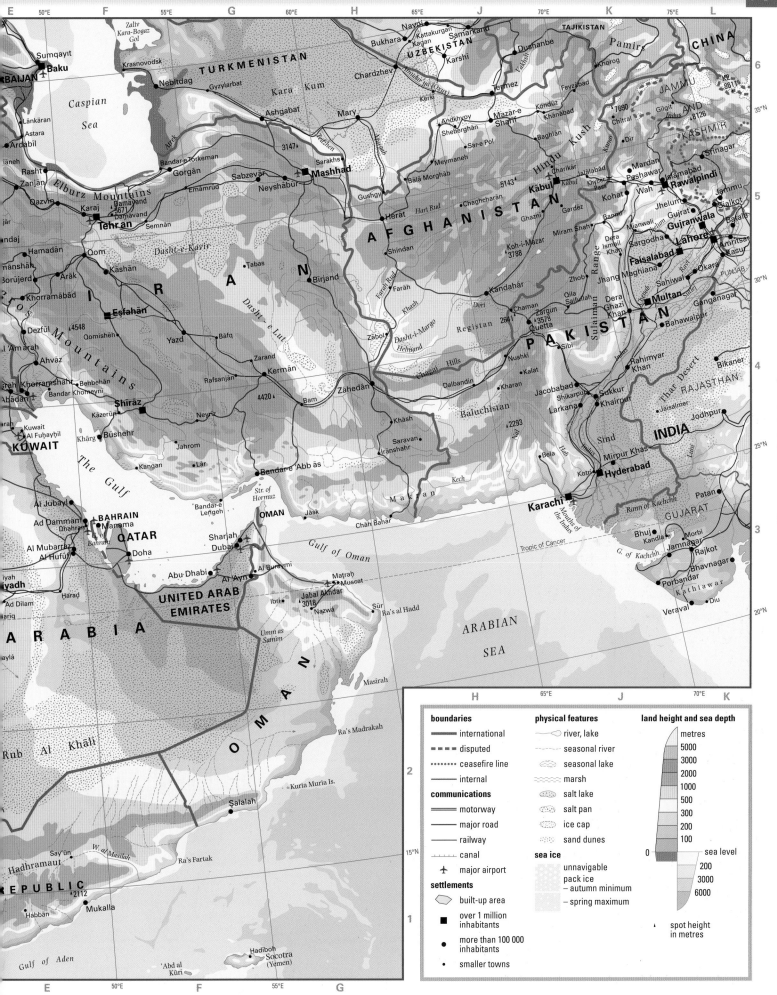

boundaries
— international
- - - disputed
····· ceasefire line
— internal

communications
═══ motorway
— major road
— railway
⊢⊢⊢ canal
✈ major airport

settlements
⬡ built-up area
■ over 1 million inhabitants
● more than 100 000 inhabitants
• smaller towns

physical features
∼ river, lake
⋯ seasonal river
◌ seasonal lake
▥ marsh
▨ salt lake
▦ salt pan
▣ ice cap
⣿ sand dunes

sea ice
▦ unnavigable pack ice
– autumn minimum
– spring maximum

land height and sea depth
metres
5000
3000
2000
1000
500
300
200
100
0 — sea level
200
3000
6000

▲ spot height in metres

© Oxford University Press   Conical Orthomorphic Projection

boundaries

— international
--- disputed
···· ceasefire line
— internal

communications

motorway
major road
railway
canal
✈ major airport

settlements

⬡ built-up area
■ over 1 million inhabitants
● more than 100 000 inhabitants
• smaller towns

physical features

river, lake
seasonal river
seasonal lake
marsh
salt lake
salt pan
ice cap
sand dunes

sea ice

unnavigable
pack ice
– autumn minimum
– spring maximum

land height and sea depth

metres
5000
3000
2000
1000
500
300
200
100
0 sea level
200
3000
6000

▲ spot height in metres

Scale 1: 12 500 000

0   125   250   375   500   625 km

© Oxford University Press

ARABIAN SEA

TAJIKISTAN
AFGHANISTAN
PAKISTAN
INDIA
SRI LANKA

Herat
Shindand
Zābol
Farāh
Kandahār
Chaman
Quetta
Kalat
Kharan
Khāsh
Zāhedān
Saravan
Dalbandin
Nushki
Sibi
Jacobabad
Shikarpur
Larkana
Sukkur
Khairpur
Bela
Kotri
Hyderabad
Karachi
Mirpur Khas

Kerki
Termez
Andkhvoy
Sheberghān
Mazār-e Sharif
Meymaneh
Bālā Morghāb
Sar-e Pol
Kondūz
Khānābad
Baghlān
Feyzābad
Khorog
Chitral
Gilgit
K2 (Qogir Feng, Godwin Austen)
Charikār
Kābul
Jalālābad
Khyber Pass
Peshawar
Kohat
Mardan
Banmi
Miram Shah
Gardēz
Ghazni
Srinagar
Leh
Jammu
Islamabad
Rawalpindi
Jhelum
Gujrat
Sargodha
Mianwali
Sialkot
Pathankot
Jammu
Manali
Shimla
HIMACHAL PRADESH
JAMMU AND KASHMIR
Lahore
Gujranwala
Amritsar
Jalandhar
Batala
Faisalabad
Jhang
Maghiana
Kasur
Ludhiana
Okara
Sahiwal
Bathinda
Patiala
Ambala
Chandigarh
CHANDIGARH
PUNJAB
Multan
Ganganagar
Dera Ghazi Khan
Bahawalpur
Rahimyar Khan
Bikaner
Sikar
Jaipur
Jodhpur
Ajmer
RAJASTHAN
Udaipur
Bhilwara
Kota
Thar Desert
Dehra Dun
UTTARANCHAL
Nanda Devi
Yamunanagar
Saharanpur
HARYANA
Panipat
Hisar
Muzaffarnagar
Meerut
New Delhi
DELHI
Delhi
Faridabad
Ghaziabad
Aligarh
Mathura
Bharatpur
Alwar
Agra
Firozabad
Gwalior
Moradabad
Rampur
Bareilly
Shahjahanpur
Lucknow
Kanpur
UTTAR PRADESH
Varanasi
Allahabad
Faizabad
Bahraich
Gorakhpur

Bhuj
Kandla
GUJARAT
Ahmadabad
Rajkot
Jamnagar
Porbandar
Junagadh
Bhavnagar
Veraval
Diu
Patan
Nadiad
Godhra
Vadodara
Bharuch
Surat
Navsari
Daman
DAMMAN AND DIU
DADRA AND NAGAR HAVELI
Nashik
Thane
Mumbai (Bombay)
Pune
Ulhasnagar
Ahmadnagar
MAHARASHTRA
Ratlam
Ujjain
Indore
Bhopal
MADHYA PRADESH
Khandwa
Burhanpur
Jalgaon
Dhule
Malegaon
Bhusawal
Akola
Amravati
Nagpur
Jabalpur
Satna
Rewa
Murwara
Shahdol
Bilaspur
CHATTISGARH
Durg-Bhilai
Raipur
Gondia
Balaghat
Bhandara
Wardha
Nanded
Chandrapur
Jagdalpur

Aurangabad
Latur
Solapur
Warangal
Nizamabad
Gulbarga
Bijapur
Hyderabad
ANDHRA PRADESH
Khammam
Vijayawada
Vishakhapatnam
Eluru
Rajahmundry
Kakinada
Guntur
Tenali
Kolhapur
Sangli
Ichalkaranji
Bijapur
Raichur
Kurnool
Adoni
Bellary
Hospet
Dharwad
Belgaum
Tungabhadra
Anantapur
Cuddapah
Nellore
Tirupati
Chittoor
KARNATAKA
Shimoga
Bhadravati
Davangere
Tumkur
Bangalore
Kolar Gold Fields
Vellore
Mysore
Chennai (Madras)
PONDICHERRY
Pondicherry
Cuddalore
Mangalore
Kasaragod
Cannanore
Calicut
Nilgiri Hills
Erode
Salem
TAMIL NADU
Tiruppur
Coimbatore
Kumbakonam
Thanjavur
Tiruchchirappalli
Palghat
Trichur
Cochin
Alleppey
Quilon
Trivandrum
Nagercoil
Tuticorin
Tirunelveli
Rajapalaiyam
Dindigul
Madurai
KERALA
Jaffna
Mannar
Trincomalee
Anuradhapura
Puttalam
Negombo
Colombo
Moratuwa
Kandy
Matale
Batticaloa
Galle
Matara
Hambantota

Amindivi Islands
Kavaratti
Cannanore Islands
LAKSHADWEEP
Minicoy Island
Nine Degree Channel
Eight Degree Channel
Ihavandiffulu Atoll
Hanimadu Island

Rann of Kachchh
Mouths of the Indus
Tropic of Cancer

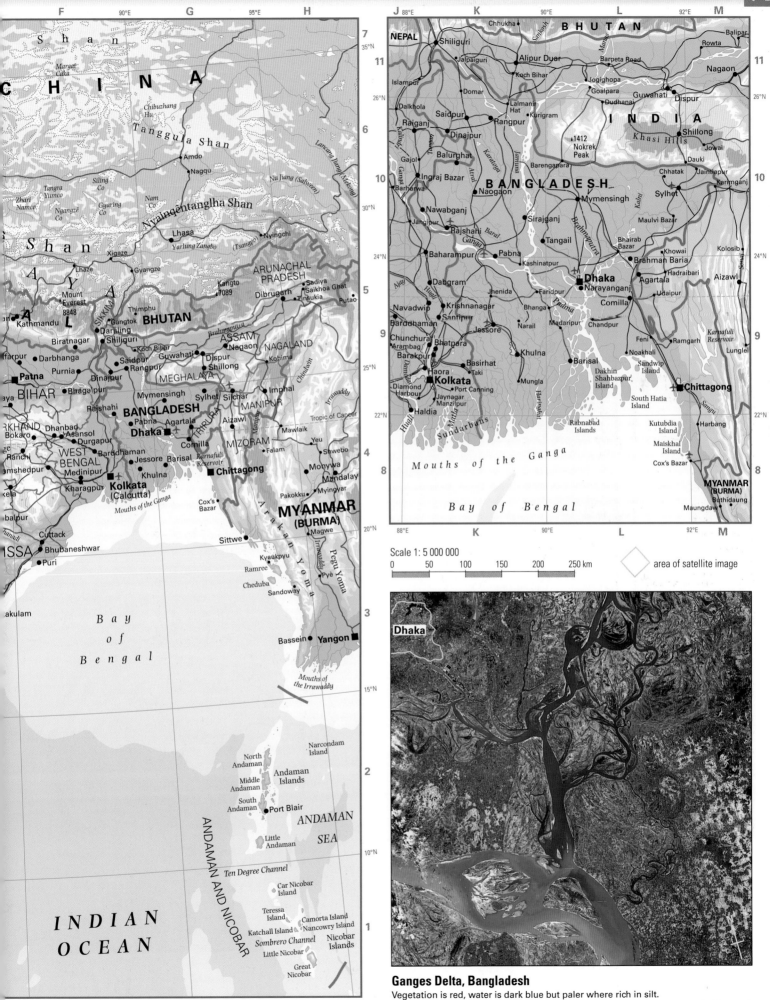

Scale 1 : 5 000 000

0 50 100 150 200 250 km

◇ area of satellite image

Ganges Delta, Bangladesh
Vegetation is red, water is dark blue but paler where rich in silt.

Conical Orthomorphic Projection

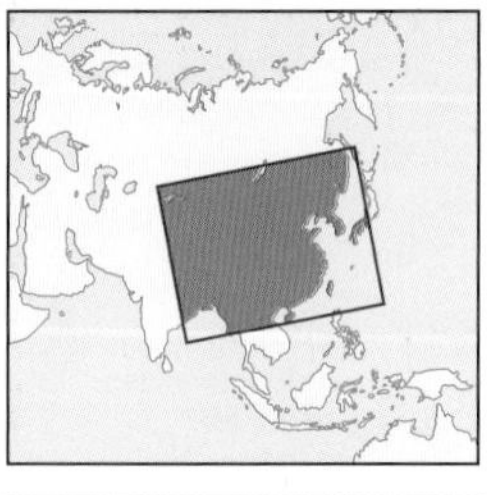

boundaries

— international
--- disputed
···· ceasefire line
— internal

communications

motorway
major road
railway
⊢⊣ canal
✈ major airport

settlements

⬡ built-up area
■ over 1 million inhabitants
● more than 100 000 inhabitants
• smaller towns

physical features

river, lake
seasonal river
seasonal lake
marsh
salt lake
salt pan
ice cap
sand dunes

sea ice

unnavigable pack ice
– autumn minimum
– spring maximum

land height and sea depth

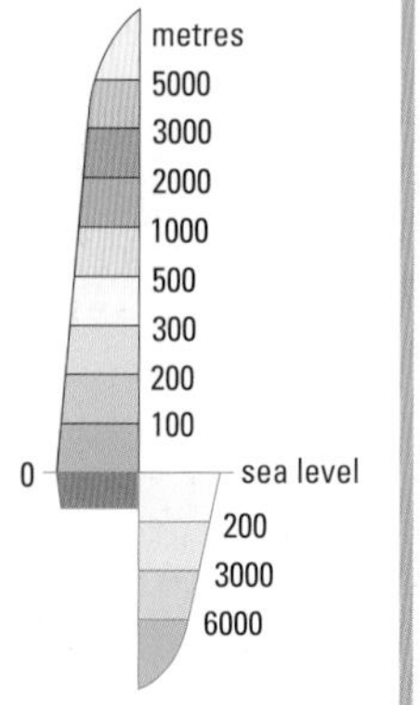

metres
5000
3000
2000
1000
500
300
200
100
0 — sea level
200
3000
6000

▲ spot height in metres

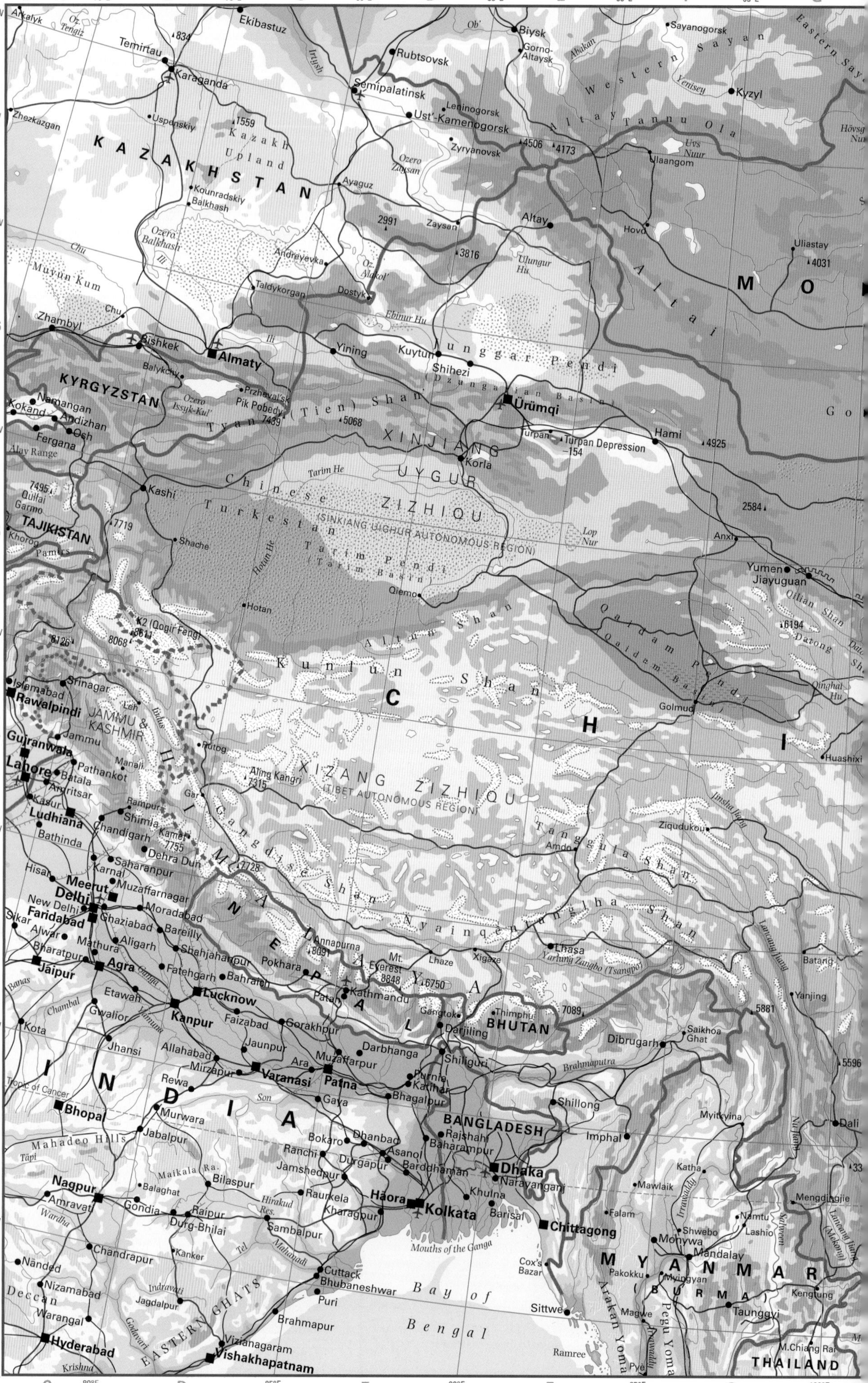

Scale 1: 15 000 000

0 150 300 450 600 750 km

Conical Orthomorphic Projection

© Oxford University Press

KAZAKHSTAN
KYRGYZSTAN
TAJIKISTAN
XINJIANG UYGUR ZIZHIQU (SINKIANG UIGHUR AUTONOMOUS REGION)
Turkestan
Tarim Pendi (Tarim Basin)
Junggar Pendi (Dzungarian Basin)
Tyan' (Tien) Shan
Kunlun Shan
Altun Shan
Qaidam Pendi
XIZANG ZIZHIQU (TIBET AUTONOMOUS REGION)
Gangdise Shan
Nyainqentanglha Shan
Tanggula Shan
HIMALAYA
INDIA
NEPAL
BHUTAN
BANGLADESH
MYANMAR (BURMA)
THAILAND
JAMMU & KASHMIR
M O (MONGOLIA)
Bay of Bengal
Mouths of the Ganga
Tropic of Cancer

Almaty
Bishkek
Ürümqi
Delhi
New Delhi
Faridabad
Lahore
Gujranwala
Rawalpindi
Ludhiana
Meerut
Agra
Jaipur
Lucknow
Kanpur
Varanasi
Patna
Bhopal
Nagpur
Hyderabad
Vishakhapatnam
Kolkata
Haora
Dhaka
Chittagong
Lhasa
Kathmandu
Mandalay

Mt. Everest 8848
K2 (Qogir Feng) 8611

RUSSIAN FEDERATION
(RUSSIA)

MONGOLIA

Ulan Bator

Desert

MONGOL ZIZHIQU
(INNER MONGOLIAN AUTONOMOUS REGION)

Hohhot

Baotou

Datong

Beijing

Tangshan

Tianjin

Shijiazhuang

Taiyuan

Handan

Jinan

Zibo

Qingdao

YELLOW
SEA

Zhengzhou

Luoyang

Xi'an

Xuzhou

Nanjing

Hefei

Wuxi

Shanghai

Hangzhou

Wuhan

Nanchang

Chengdu

Chongqing

Changsha

Guiyang

Kunming

Guangzhou

Hong Kong

Macao

VIETNAM

Hanoi

SOUTH
CHINA
SEA

Hainan Dao

Sanya

TAIWAN

Taipei

Kaohsiung

Qiqihar

Harbin

Changchun

Jilin

Shenyang

Fushun

Anshan

Dalian

NORTH
KOREA

Pyongyang

SOUTH
KOREA

Seoul

Inchon

Taejon

Taegu

Pusan

Kwangju

JAPAN

Kyoto

Kōbe

Osaka

Hiroshima

Fukuoka

Kita-Kyūshū

SEA OF
JAPAN

EAST
CHINA
SEA

Ryukyu Islands
(Nansei-shotō)

NORTH

PACIFIC

OCEAN

Tropic of Cancer

THE
PHILIPPINES

© Oxford University Press

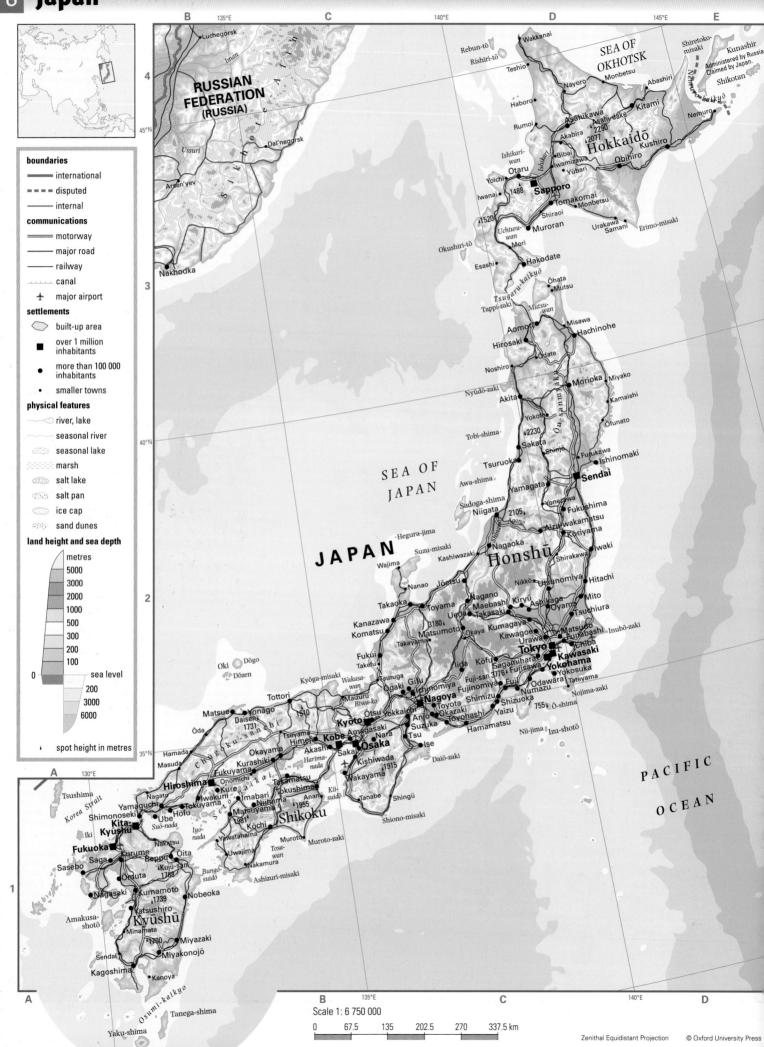

boundaries

━━━	international
╍╍╍	disputed
───	internal

communications

═══	motorway
───	major road
───	railway
┼┼┼	canal
✈	major airport

settlements

⬡	built-up area
■	over 1 million inhabitants
●	more than 100 000 inhabitants
•	smaller towns

physical features

∿	river, lake
∿	seasonal river
⬭	seasonal lake
▦	marsh
▨	salt lake
▨	salt pan
⬭	ice cap
▨	sand dunes

land height and sea depth

metres
5000
3000
2000
1000
500
300
200
100
0 sea level
200
3000
6000

▲ spot height in metres

RUSSIAN FEDERATION (RUSSIA)

Luchegorsk
Innan
Ussuri
Dal'negorsk
Arsen'yev
Nakhodka

Wakkanai
SEA OF OKHOTSK
Shiretoko-misaki
Kunashir
Administered by Russia.
Claimed by Japan.
Shikotan
Rebun-tō
Rishiri-tō
Teshio
Haboro
Nayoro
Monbetsu
Abashiri
Rumoi
Asahikawa
Asahi-dake ▲2290
Akabira
Kitami
Nemuro
Habikyō
Hokkaidō
▲2077
Ishikari-wan
Yoichi
Otaru
Ishikari
Iwamizawa
Yūbari
Kushiro
Obihiro
Iwanai ▲1488 Sapporo
Bibai
Tomakomai
Monbetsu
Shiraoi
Urakawa
▲1520 Uchiura-wan
Muroran
Shiraoi
Samani
Erimo-misaki
Mori
Okushiri-tō
Hakodate
Esashi
Tsugaru-kaikyō
Ōhata
Mutsu
Tappi-zaki
Mutsu-wan
Aomori
Misawa
Hachinohe
Hirosaki
Odate
Noshiro
Morioka
Miyako
Nyūdō-zaki
Akita
Yokote
Kamaishi
▲2230
Ofunato
Tobi-shima
Sakata
Shinjō
Fukukawa
Ishinomaki
Tsuruoka
Yamagata
Sendai
Awa-shima
Yonezawa
SEA OF JAPAN
Sadoga-shima
Niigata
▲2105
Fukushima
Aizuwakamatsu
Kōriyama
JAPAN
Hegura-jima
Nagaoka
Shirakawa
Iwaki
Suzu-misaki
Honshū
Wajima
Kashiwazaki
Nikkō
Utsunomiya
Hitachi
Nanao
Jōetsu
Magano
Mito
Takaoka
Toyama
Maebashi
Ashikaga
Oyama
Tsuchiura
Kanazawa
Ueda
Takasaki
Kiryū
Komatsu
▲3180
Okaya
Kumagaya
Matsumoto
Kawagoe
Matsudo
Fukui
Takayama
Iida
Kōfu
Urawa
Funabashi
Chiba
Takefu
Tokyo
Kawasaki
Tsuruga
Ogaki
Gifu
Fujinomiya
Yokohama
Kyōga-misaki
Wakasa-wan
Ichinomiya
Fuji-san▲3776
Fuji
Yokosuka
Maizuru
Ōtsu
Nagoya
Sagamihara
Fujisawa
Tottori
Biwa-ko
Yokkaichi
Toyota
Shimizu
Odawara
Nojima-zaki
Matsue
Yonago
▲1510
Kyōto
Anjō
Okazaki
Shizuoka
Tateyama
Daisen▲1731
Tsuyama
Kobe
Nara
Suzuka
Toyohashi
▲755
Ō-shima
Ōda
Chūgoku-sanchi
Ōtsu
Amagasaki
Tsu
Hamamatsu
Nii-jima
Izu-shotō
Hamada
Himeji
Osaka
Ise
Daiō-zaki
Masuda
Okayama
Akashi
Sakai
Kishiwada
Kurashiki
Harima-nada
Wakayama
Fukuyama
▲1915
Hiroshima
Onomichi
Takamatsu
Kure
Imabari
Tokushima
Iwakuni
Niihama
Anan
Nagato
Seto-naikai
▲1955
Shingū
Tsushima
Yamaguchi
Tokuyama
Matsuyama
Shikoku
Tanabe
Korea Strait
Shimonoseki
Kōchi
Kii-suidō
Ube
Hofu
▲1981
Kita-Kyūshū
Suō-nada
Iyo-nada
Shiono-misaki
Iki
Fukuoka
Uwajima
Tosa-wan
Nakatsu
Kurume
Beppu
Ōita
Muroto
Saga
Sasebo
Ōruta
Kuju-san▲1788
Bungo-suidō
Muroto-zaki
Nagasaki
Kumamoto
▲1739
Nobeoka
Katsushiro
Ashizuri-misaki
Amakusa-shotō
Kyūshū
Minamata
▲1790
Miyazaki
Sendai
Miyakonojō
Kanoya
Kagoshima
Ōsumi-kaikyō
Yaku-shima
Tanega-shima

PACIFIC OCEAN

Scale 1: 6 750 000

0   67.5   135   202.5   270   337.5 km

Zenithal Equidistant Projection

© Oxford University Press

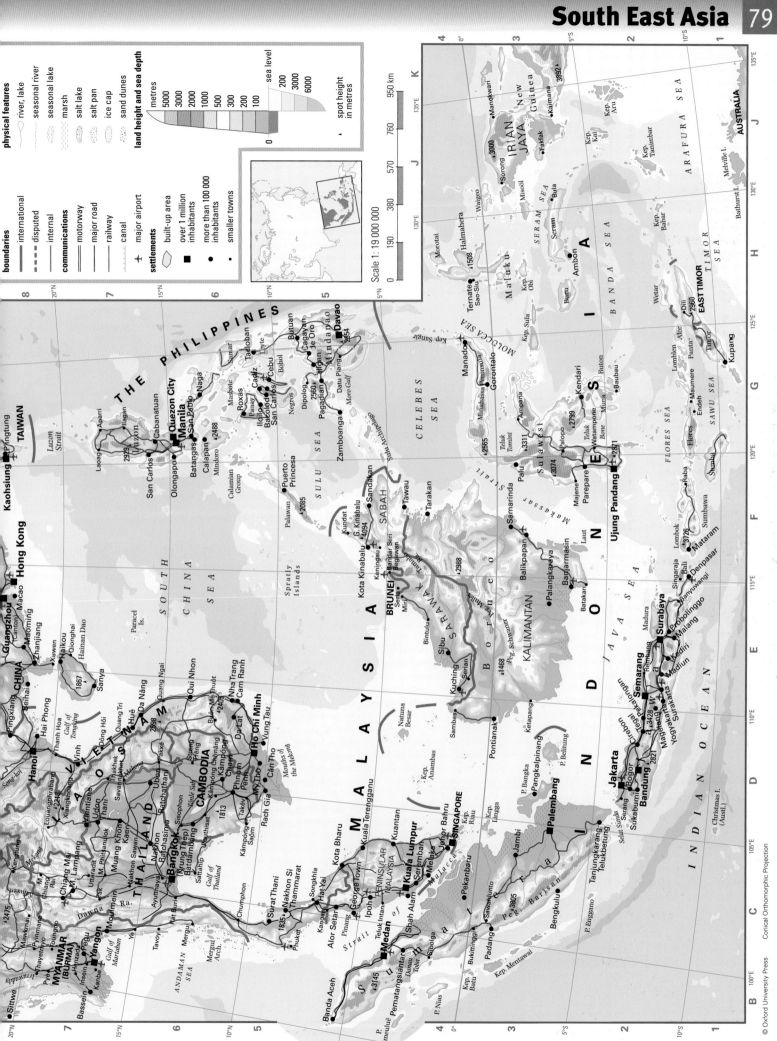

physical features
- river, lake
- seasonal river
- seasonal lake
- marsh
- salt lake
- salt pan
- ice cap
- sand dunes

land height and sea depth

metres
5000
3000
2000
1000
500
300
200
100
sea level
200
3000
6000

metres

spot height in metres

boundaries
- international
- disputed
- internal

communications
- motorway
- major road
- railway
- canal
- + major airport

settlements
- built-up area
- ■ over 1 million inhabitants
- ● more than 100 000 inhabitants
- · smaller towns

Scale 1: 19 000 000

0 190 380 570 760 950 km

© Oxford University Press

Conical Orthomorphic Projection

boundaries
━━━ international
╍╍╍ disputed
─── internal

communications
═══ motorway
─── major road
─── railway
╫╫╫ canal
✈ major airport

settlements
⬡ built-up area
■ over 1 million inhabitants
● more than 100 000 inhabitants
• smaller towns

physical features
～ river, lake
seasonal river
seasonal lake
marsh
salt lake
salt pan
ice cap
sand dunes

sea ice
unnavigable
pack ice
– autumn minimum
– spring maximum

land height and sea depth
metres
5000
3000
2000
1000
500
300
200
100
0 — sea level
200
3000
6000
▲ spot height in metres

Scale 1: 20 000 000

0 200 400 600 800 1000 km

Zenithal Equidistant Projection   © Oxford University Press

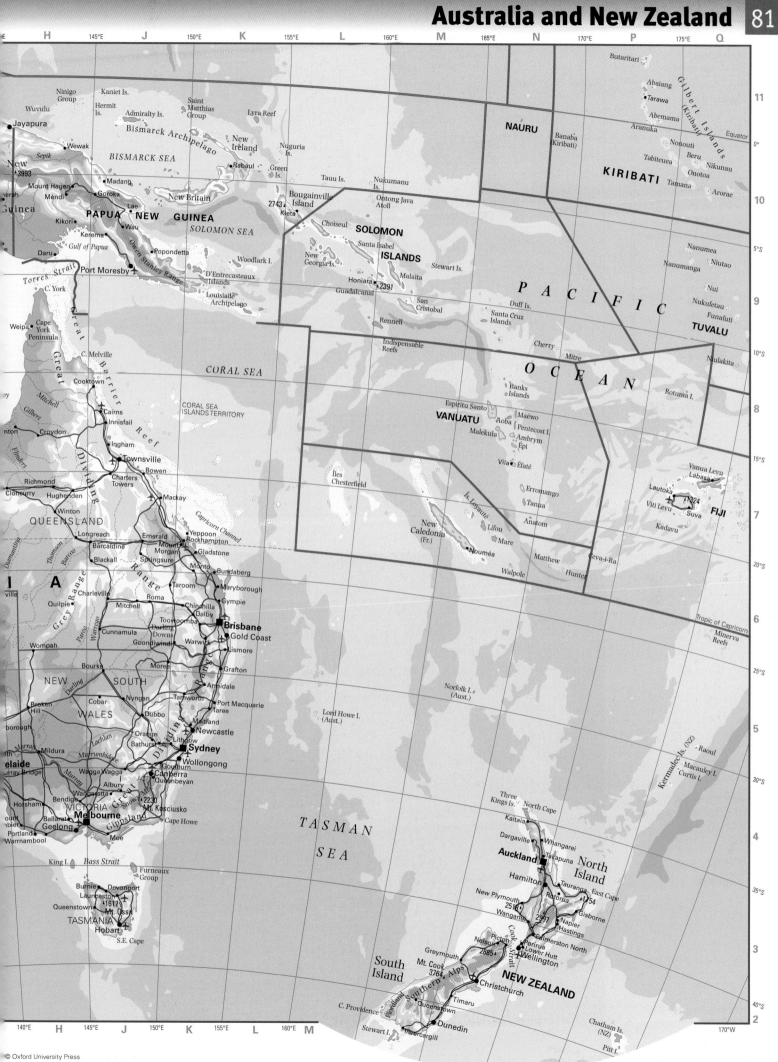

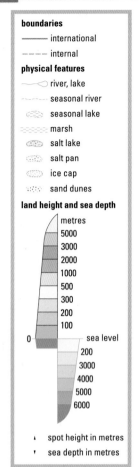

boundaries
— international
-- internal

physical features
river, lake
seasonal river
seasonal lake
marsh
salt lake
salt pan
ice cap
sand dunes

land height and sea depth

metres
5000
3000
2000
1000
500
300
200
100
0 — sea level
200
3000
4000
5000
6000

▲ spot height in metres
▼ sea depth in metres

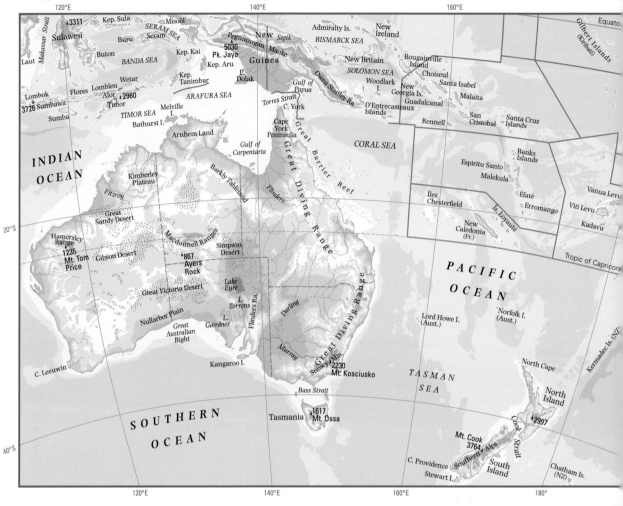

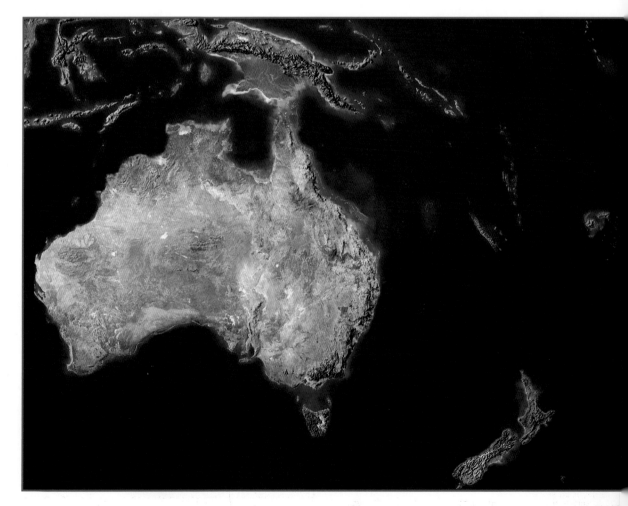

Scale 1 : 75 000 000

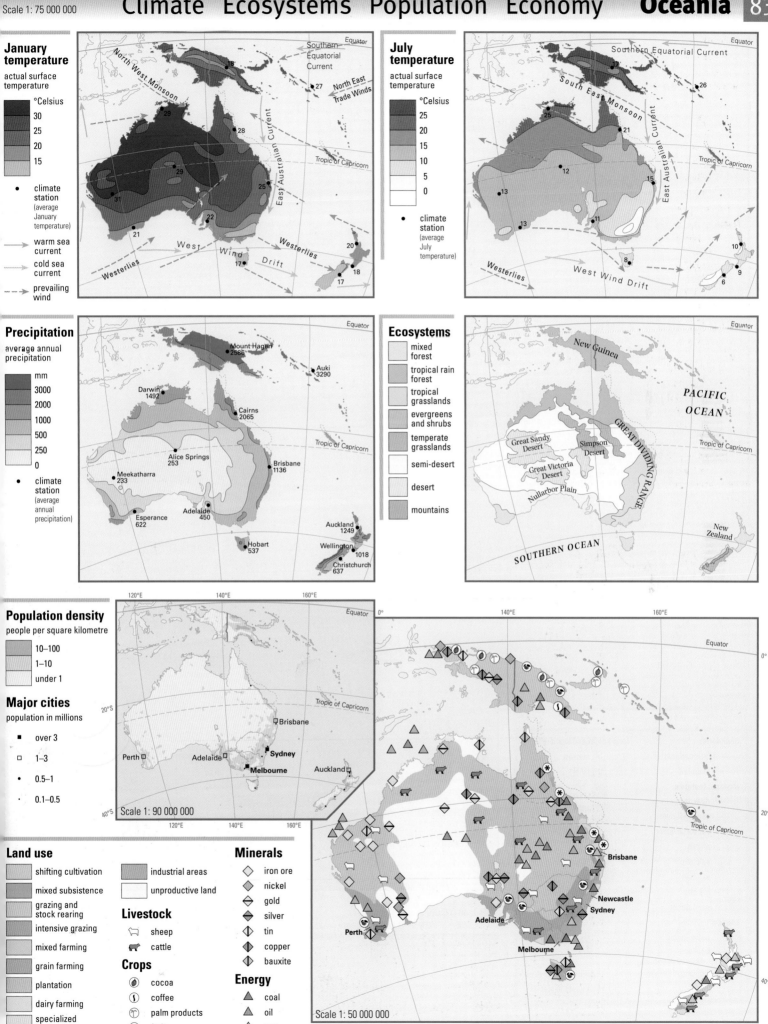

January temperature

actual surface temperature

°Celsius
- 30
- 25
- 20
- 15

• climate station (average January temperature)

→ warm sea current

→ cold sea current

⇢ prevailing wind

Southern Equatorial Current
North West Monsoon
North East Trade Winds
East Australian Current
West Wind Drift
Westerlies
Westerlies
Equator
Tropic of Capricorn

July temperature

actual surface temperature

°Celsius
- 25
- 20
- 15
- 10
- 5
- 0

• climate station (average July temperature)

Southern Equatorial Current
South East Monsoon
East Australian Current
Westerlies
West Wind Drift
Equator
Tropic of Capricorn

Precipitation

average annual precipitation

mm
- 3000
- 2000
- 1000
- 500
- 250
- 0

• climate station (average annual precipitation)

Mount Hagen 2586
Auki 3290
Darwin 1492
Cairns 2065
Alice Springs 253
Brisbane 1136
Meekatharra 233
Adelaide 450
Esperance 622
Hobart 537
Auckland 1249
Wellington 1018
Christchurch 637
Equator
Tropic of Capricorn

Ecosystems

- mixed forest
- tropical rain forest
- tropical grasslands
- evergreens and shrubs
- temperate grasslands
- semi-desert
- desert
- mountains

New Guinea
PACIFIC OCEAN
Great Sandy Desert
Simpson Desert
Great Victoria Desert
Nullarbor Plain
GREAT DIVIDING RANGE
New Zealand
SOUTHERN OCEAN
Equator
Tropic of Capricorn

Population density

people per square kilometre
- 10–100
- 1–10
- under 1

Major cities

population in millions
- ■ over 3
- ▫ 1–3
- • 0.5–1
- · 0.1–0.5

Brisbane
Perth
Adelaide
Sydney
Melbourne
Auckland
Scale 1 : 90 000 000
Tropic of Capricorn

Land use

- shifting cultivation
- mixed subsistence
- grazing and stock rearing
- intensive grazing
- mixed farming
- grain farming
- plantation
- dairy farming
- specialized horticulture
- forestry
- industrial areas
- unproductive land

Livestock

- sheep
- cattle

Crops

- cocoa
- coffee
- palm products
- fruit
- sugar

Minerals

- iron ore
- nickel
- gold
- silver
- tin
- copper
- bauxite

Energy

- coal
- oil
- gas
- hydro

Perth
Adelaide
Melbourne
Brisbane
Newcastle
Sydney
Scale 1 : 50 000 000

Modified Zenithal Equidistant Projection   © Oxford University Press

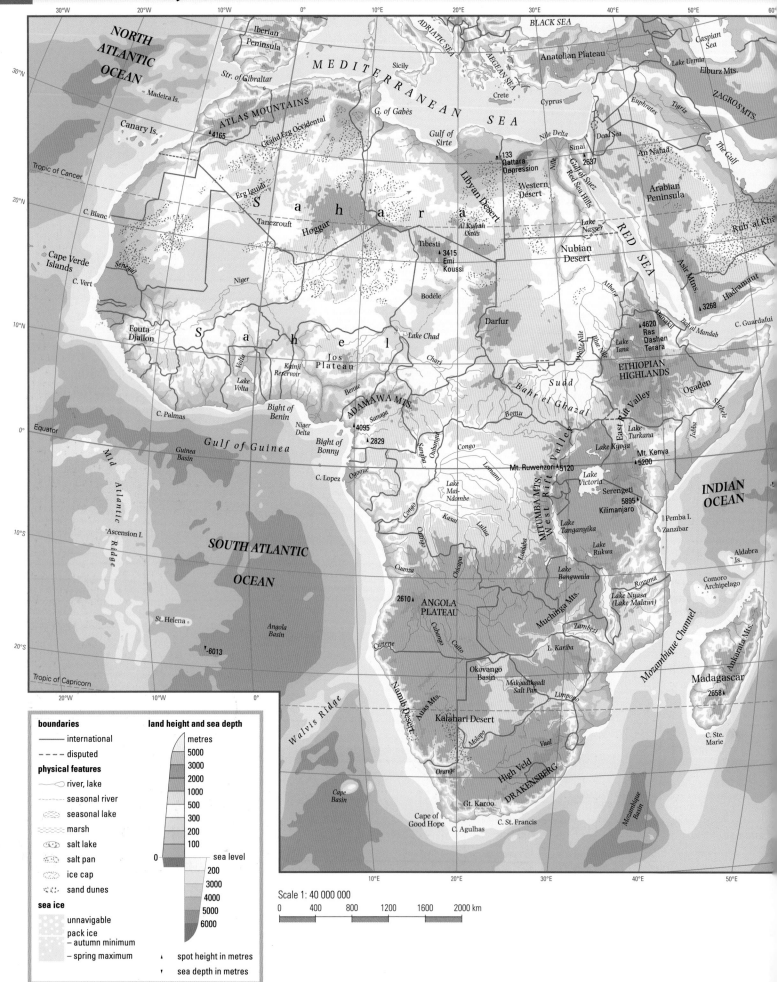

boundaries

— international

-- disputed

physical features

⌒ river, lake

--- seasonal river

⌒ seasonal lake

≋ marsh

⌀ salt lake

⌀ salt pan

⌀ ice cap

⌀ sand dunes

sea ice

unnavigable

pack ice
– autumn minimum

– spring maximum

land height and sea depth

metres

5000
3000
2000
1000
500
300
200
100

0 — sea level

200
3000
4000
5000
6000

▲ spot height in metres

▼ sea depth in metres

Scale 1: 40 000 000

0   400   800   1200   1600   2000 km

Zenithal Equal Area Projection   © Oxford University Press

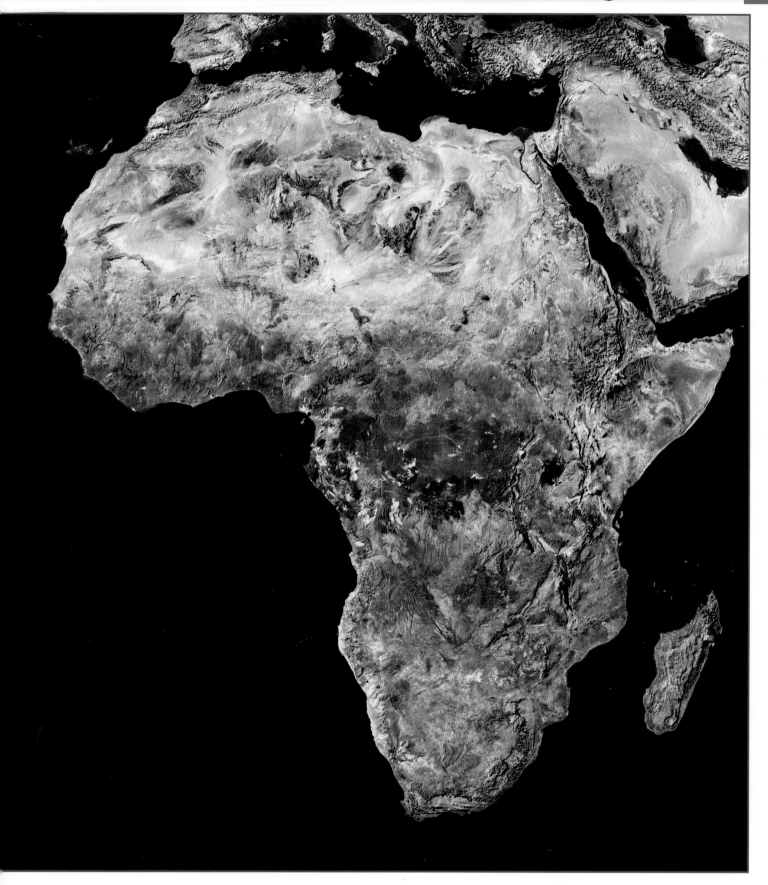

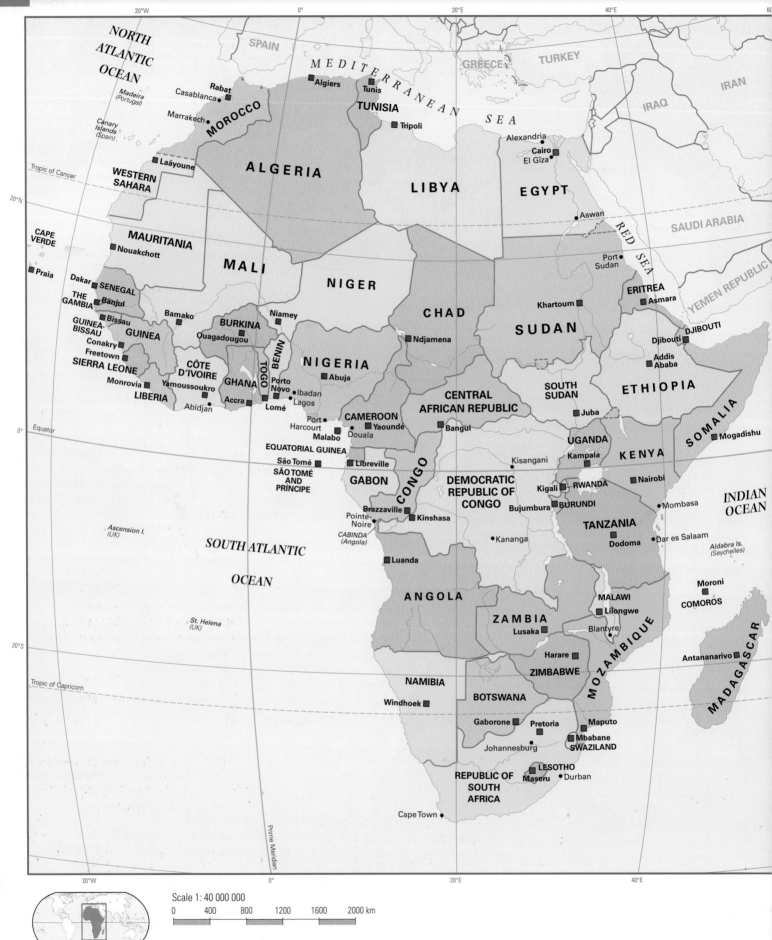

Scale 1: 40 000 000

0   400   800   1200   1600   2000 km

international boundary

disputed boundary

■ capital city

• other important city

Zenithal Equal Area Projection   © Oxford University Press

Scale 1: 55 000 000

Land use

	rough grazing
	shifting cultivation
	mixed subsistence
	rice subsistence
	subsistence crops
	grazing and stock rearing
	mixed farming
	Mediterranean farming
	plantation
	specialized horticulture
	industrial areas
	unproductive land

Livestock

- sheep
- cattle
- camels

Crops

- groundnuts
- cocoa
- coffee
- tea
- palm products
- tobacco
- fruit
- dates
- sugar
- cotton
- rubber

Minerals

- iron ore
- gold
- silver
- diamonds
- tin
- copper
- bauxite
- phosphates

Energy

- coal
- oil
- gas
- hydro

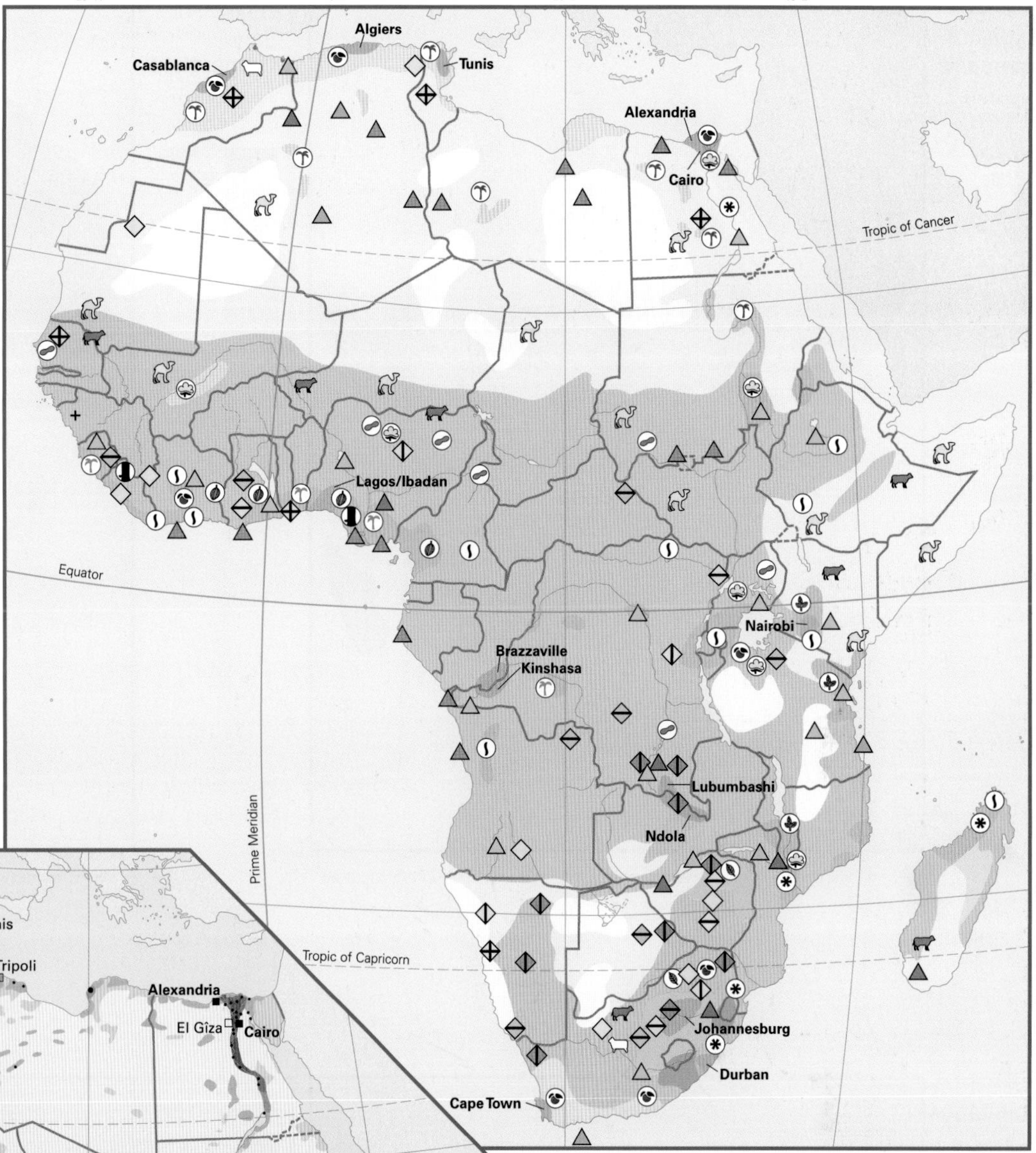

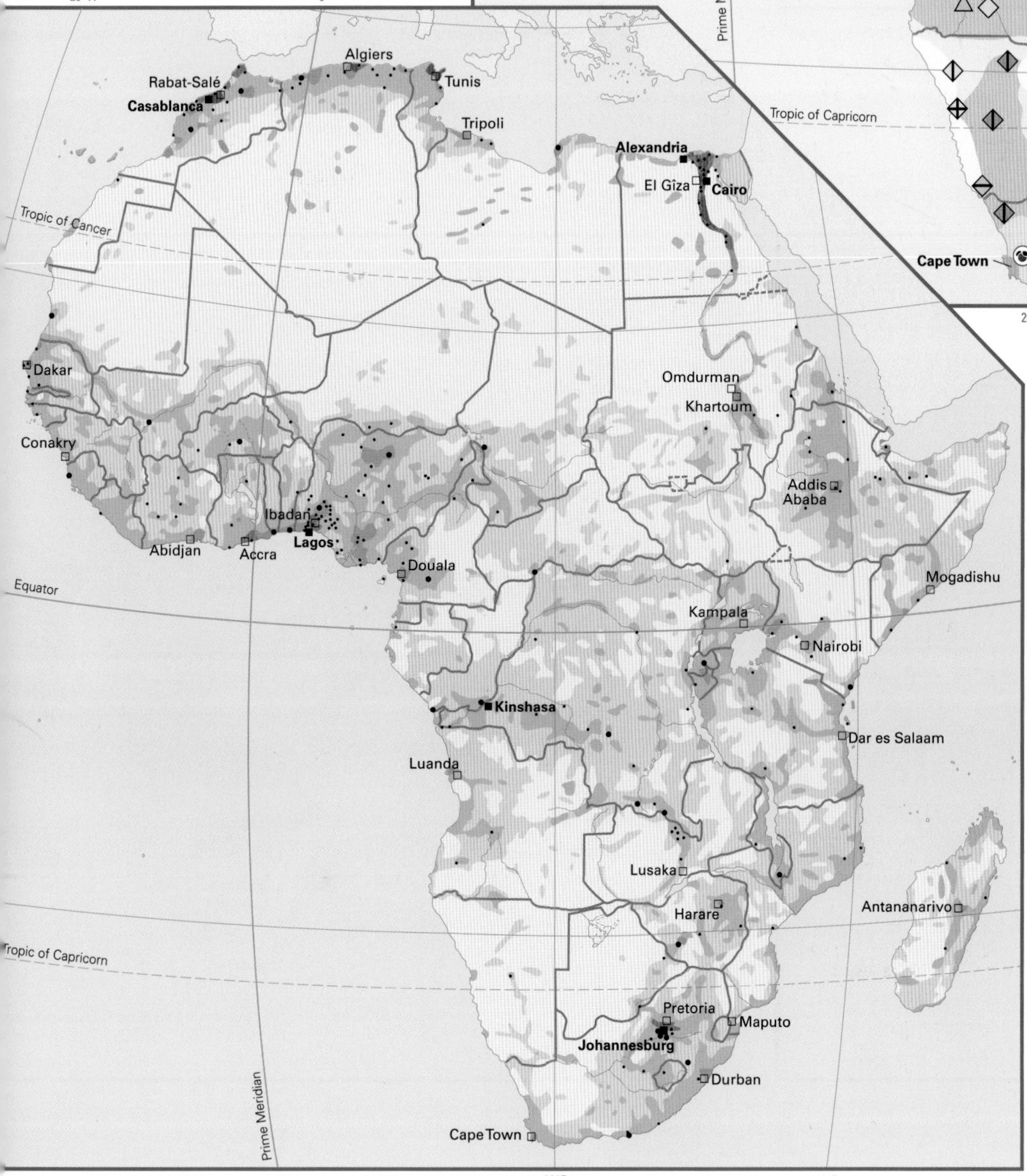

Map labels (economy map)

Casablanca, Algiers, Tunis, Alexandria, Cairo, Lagos/Ibadan, Nairobi, Brazzaville, Kinshasa, Lubumbashi, Ndola, Johannesburg, Durban, Cape Town

Map labels (population density map)

Dakar, Conakry, Abidjan, Accra, Ibadan, Lagos, Douala, Rabat-Salé, Casablanca, Algiers, Tunis, Tripoli, Alexandria, El Gîza, Cairo, Omdurman, Khartoum, Addis Ababa, Mogadishu, Kampala, Nairobi, Dar es Salaam, Kinshasa, Luanda, Lusaka, Harare, Antananarivo, Pretoria, Maputo, Johannesburg, Durban, Cape Town

Population density

people per square kilometre

	over 700
	200–700
	100–200
	10–100
	1–10
	under 1

Major cities

population in millions

- ■ over 3
- ▢ 1–3
- ● 0.5–1
- · 0.1–0.5

Largest urban agglomerations in Africa, 2010

Urban agglomeration is the population contained within a city plus the suburban fringe lying outside of, but adjacent to, the city boundaries.

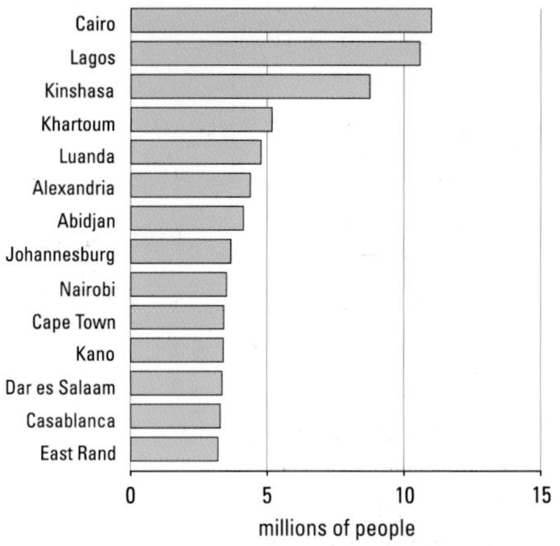

Cairo
Lagos
Kinshasa
Khartoum
Luanda
Alexandria
Abidjan
Johannesburg
Nairobi
Cape Town
Kano
Dar es Salaam
Casablanca
East Rand

0   5   10   15
millions of people

Zenithal Equal Area Projection

© Oxford University Press

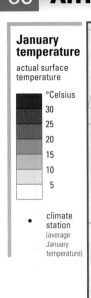

January temperature

actual surface temperature

°Celsius
- 30
- 25
- 20
- 15
- 10
- 5

• climate station (average January temperature)

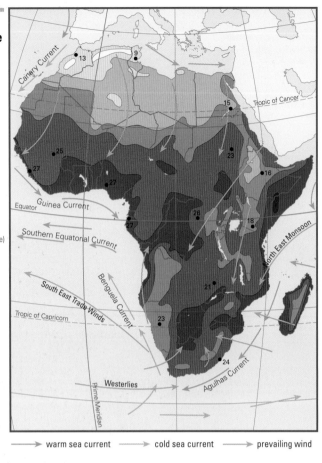

Canary Current

Tropic of Cancer

Guinea Current

Equator

Southern Equatorial Current

South East Trade Winds

Benguela Current

Tropic of Capricorn

North East Monsoon

Westerlies

Agulhas Current

Prime Meridian

→ warm sea current → cold sea current → prevailing wind

July temperature

actual surface temperature

°Celsius
- 35
- 30
- 25
- 20
- 15
- 10
- 5

• climate station (average July temperature)

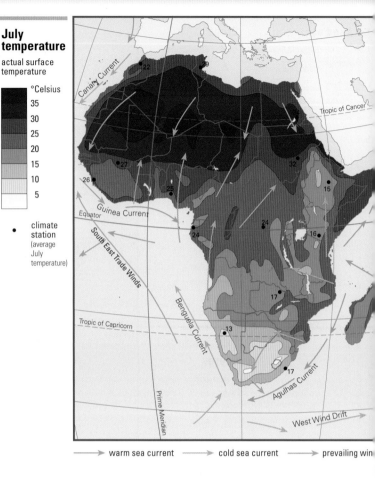

Canary Current

Tropic of Cancer

Guinea Current

Equator

South East Trade Winds

Benguela Current

Tropic of Capricorn

Agulhas Current

West Wind Drift

Prime Meridian

→ warm sea current → cold sea current → prevailing win

Precipitation

average annual precipitation

mm
- 3000
- 2000
- 1000
- 500
- 250
- 0

• climate station (average annual precipitation)

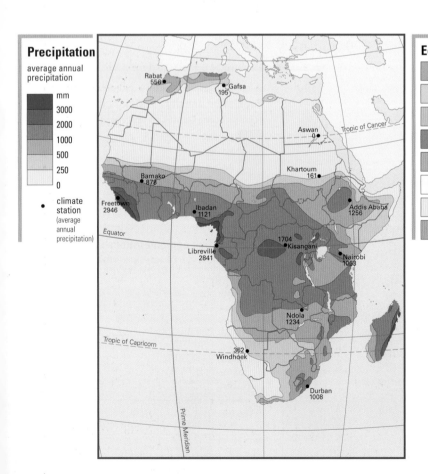

Rabat 556
Gafsa 195
Aswan 0
Tropic of Cancer
Khartoum 161
Bamako 878
Freetown 2946
Ibadan 1121
Addis Ababa 1256
Equator
Libreville 2841
Kisangani 1704
Nairobi 1063
Ndola 1234
Tropic of Capricorn
Windhoek 362
Durban 1008
Prime Meridian

Ecosystems

- tropical rain forest
- tropical grasslands
- evergreens and shrubs
- thorn forest
- temperate grasslands
- semi-desert
- desert
- mountains

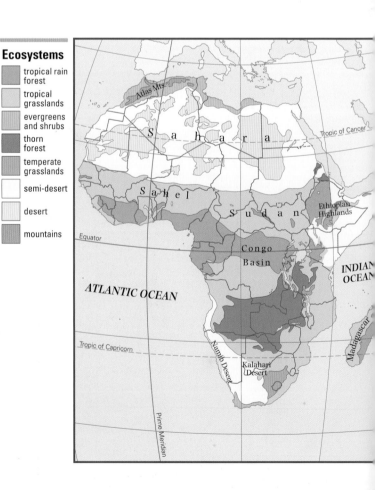

Atlas Mts.

S a h a r a

Tropic of Cancer

S a h e l

S u d a n

Ethiopian Highlands

Equator

Congo Basin

INDIAN OCEAN

ATLANTIC OCEAN

Tropic of Capricorn

Namib Desert

Kalahari Desert

Madagascar

Prime Meridian

Zenithal Equal Area Projection © Oxford University Press

Scale 1: 55 000 000 (main map)

Selected tourist sites

- ▥ cultural heritage centres
- ⁂ archaeological sites
- ✳ sites of natural beauty
- ⬤ National Parks and wildlife reserves
- ⬤ coastal tourism areas and resorts
- ○ other tourist sites

land height

metres
2000
500
0

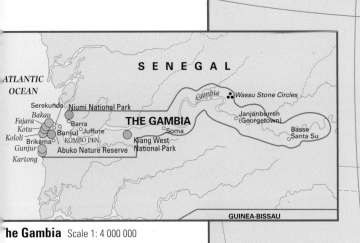

The Gambia Scale 1: 4 000 000

SENEGAL

ATLANTIC OCEAN

Gambia

Wassu Stone Circles

Niumi National Park
THE GAMBIA
Serekunda
Bakau
Barra
Juffure
Janjanburreh (Georgetown)
Fajara
Kotu
Banjul
Soma
Basse Santa Su
Kololi
KOMBO PEN.
Brikama
Kiang West National Park
Gunjur
Abuko Nature Reserve
Kartong

GUINEA-BISSAU

Main map (Africa)

20°W · 0° · 20°E · 40°E

Tropic of Cancer
20°N

MOROCCO · ATLAS MOUNTAINS
Rabat · Fes
Casablanca · Meknes
Marrakesh
Coral Coast · Carthage
TUNISIA
Tripoli · Leptis Magna

ALGERIA
SAHARA DESERT
LIBYA
EGYPT

Parc National du Banc d'Arguin
MAURITANIA
MALI
NIGER
CHAD
SUDAN
Khartoum
Aksum
HORN OF AFRICA

SENEGAL
THE GAMBIA
GUINEA-BISSAU
GUINEA
Timbuktu
DOGON COUNTRY
Agadez
Réserve Naturelle Nationale de l'Aïr et du Ténéré

SIERRA LEONE
LIBERIA
CÔTE D'IVOIRE
Man
GHANA
Kumasi
Mole National Park
BENIN
Parc National de la Pendjari
Kano
Jos
NIGERIA
Abomey
N'Djamena
Parc National de Zakouma
Abeche
CENTRAL AFRICAN REPUBLIC
ETHIOPIA
Bale Mountains National Park
SOMALIA

0° Equator

CAMEROON
GABON
CONGO
DEMOCRATIC REPUBLIC OF CONGO
RWANDA
BURUNDI
Murchison Falls National Park
Bwindi Impenetrable National Park
RIFT VALLEY
SERENGETI
Mombasa
NGORONGORO CRATER
Zanzibar Island

ATLANTIC OCEAN

TANZANIA
INDIAN OCEAN

ANGOLA
ZAMBIA
South Luangwa National Park
Liwonde National Park
MALAWI
MOZAMBIQUE
MADAGASCAR

Tropic of Capricorn

Chobe National Park
VICTORIA FALLS
Hwange National Park
Etosha National Park
TSODILO HILLS
OKAVANGO DELTA
Moremi Wildlife Reserve
Great Zimbabwe Ruins
Parque Nacional de Bazaruto

NAMIB DESERT
NAMIBIA
BOTSWANA
Kruger National Park
20°S

REPUBLIC OF SOUTH AFRICA
KARROO
DRAKENSBERG
Dolphin Coast
Stellenbosch
Wild Coast
Cape Town
Jeffrey's Bay
Garden Route

Nile Valley and Eastern Egypt Scale 1: 10 000 000

MEDITERRANEAN SEA
Tel Aviv-Yafo
Irbid
Rosetta
Damietta
Jerusalem
Alexandria
NILE DELTA
Port Said
Gaza
GAZA STRIP
Damanhûr
El Mansura
Ismâ'iliya
ISRAEL
Dead Sea
JORDAN
El Mahalla
El Giza
Heliopolis
LOWER EGYPT
Pyramids and Sphinx
Cairo
Suez
Saqqara
Memphis
QATTARA DEPRESSION
-133
Dahshur
Lake Qarun
Elat
El Faiyûm
SINAI PENINSULA
Abu Zenîma
Nuweiba
Beni Suef
SAUDI ARABIA
Mount Sinai 2285
Dahab
El Minya
Râs Ghârib
Gulf of Suez
Gulf of Aqaba
Hermopolis
Necropolis of Beni Hasan
EASTERN
Sharm el Sheikh
EGYPT
Tuna el Gabal
Tell el Amarna
DESERT
WESTERN
Asyût
Hurghada
Bûr Safâga
WESTERN DESERT
UPPER EGYPT
Qena
Abydos
Dandara
Karnak
Quseir
Valley of the Kings
Western Thebes
Luxor
RED SEA
Isna
Idfu
Kom Ombo
Aswân
Aswân Dam
Lake Nasser
Amada
Abu Simbel
Qasr Ibrim
SUDAN
Wadi Halfa

Kenya Scale 1: 10 000 000

ETHIOPIA
Lokitaung
RIFT VALLEY
Lake Turkana
Moyale
Moroto
Marsabit
UGANDA
KENYA
SOMALIA
Mount Elgon 4321
Kitale
Tororo
Bungoma
Eldoret
Lake Baringo
Isiolo
Kisumu
Mount Kenya National Park
Meru National Park
Nakuru
Mount Kenya 5200
Crater Lake Game Sanctuary
Aberdare National Park
Garissa
Lake Victoria
Hell's Gate National Park
Lake Naivasha
Thika
Nairobi
Musoma
Masai Mara National Reserve
Nairobi National Park
Mutomo
Serengeti National Park
Amboseli National Park
Tsavo East National Park
Garsen
Namanga
5895 Mount Kilimanjaro
Lamu
Lake Natron
Olduvai Gorge
4565 Mount Meru
Gedi Ruins
Malindi
Tsavo West National Park
Arabuko Sokoke Forest Reserve
Watamu
Arusha
Lake Eyasi
Kilifi
TANZANIA
Mombasa
Shimba Hills National Reserve
INDIAN OCEAN

Zenithal Equal Area Projection
© Oxford University Press

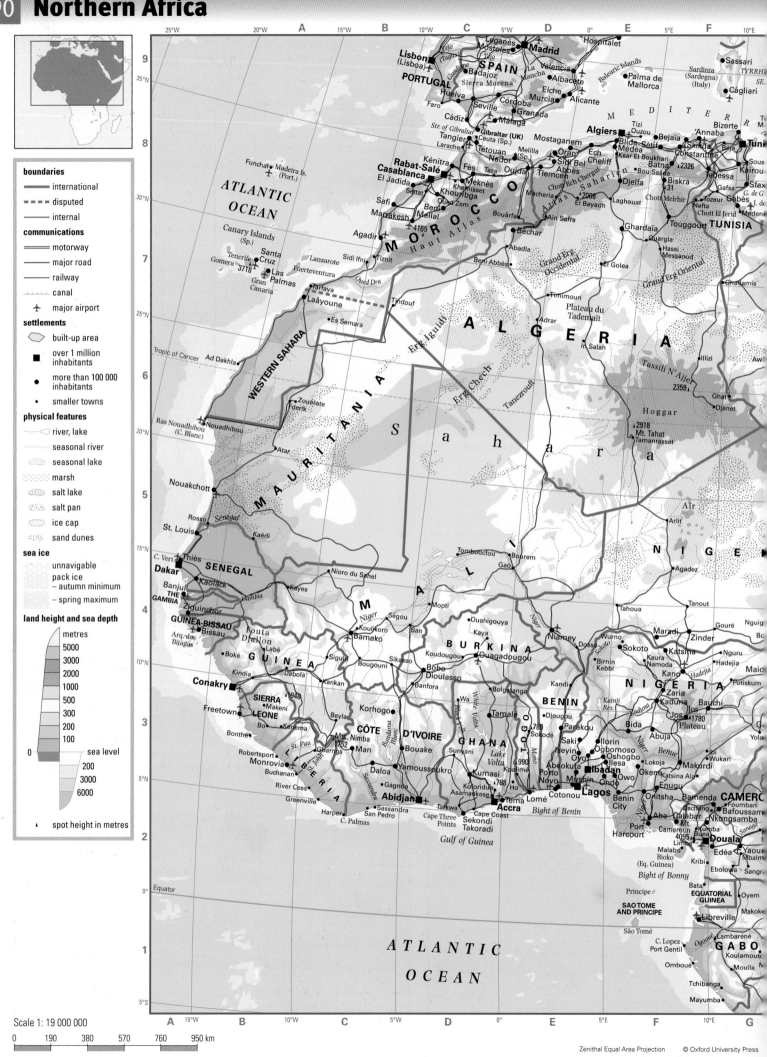

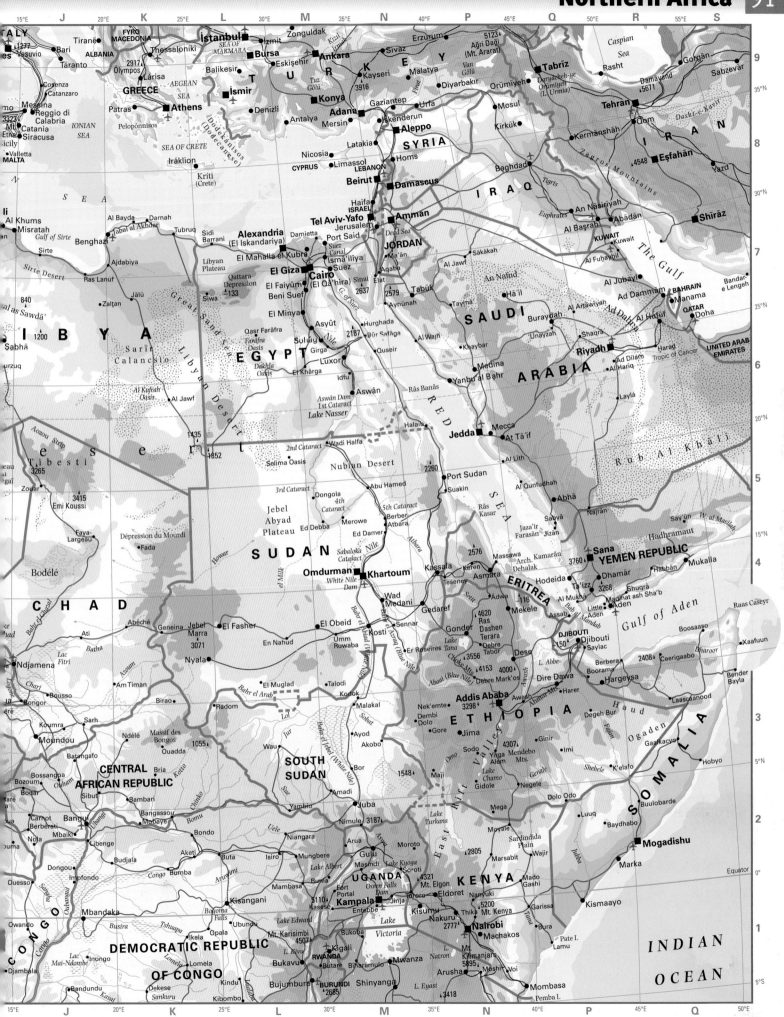

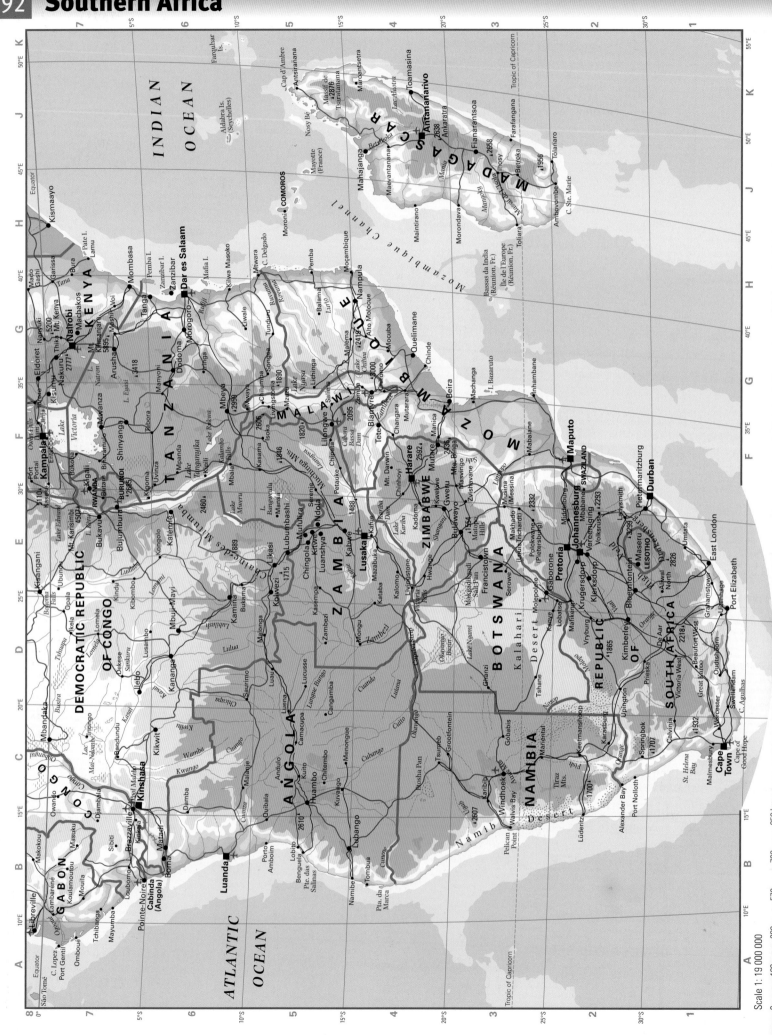

Scale 1: 19 000 000

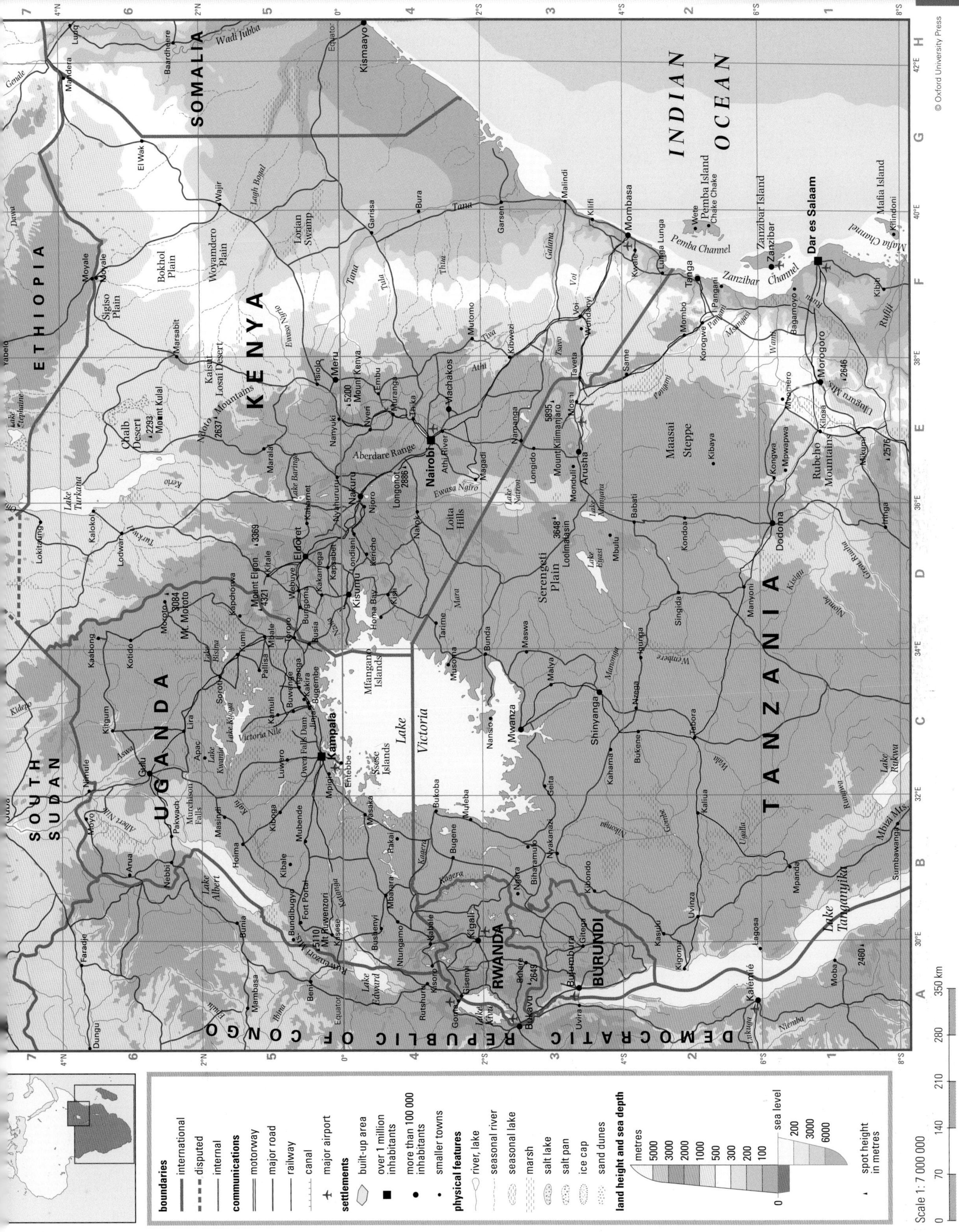

© Oxford University Press

boundaries
— international
--- disputed
— internal

communications
— motorway
— major road
— railway
— canal
+ major airport

settlements
▨ built-up area
■ over 1 million inhabitants
● more than 100 000 inhabitants
• smaller towns

physical features
river, lake
seasonal river
seasonal lake
marsh
salt lake
salt pan
ice cap
sand dunes

land height and sea depth

metres	
5000	
3000	
2000	
1000	
500	
300	
200	
100	
sea level	
200	
3000	
6000	

. spot height in metres

Scale 1: 7 000 000

0   70   140   210   280   350 km

INDIAN OCEAN

SOMALIA
ETHIOPIA
SOUTH SUDAN
UGANDA
KENYA
TANZANIA
RWANDA
BURUNDI
DEMOCRATIC REPUBLIC OF CONGO

Lake Victoria
Lake Tanganyika
Lake Turkana
Lake Albert
Lake Edward
Lake Kivu

Nairobi
Kampala
Dar es Salaam
Mombasa
Dodoma
Zanzibar
Pemba Island
Mafia Island

Mount Kenya 5200
Mount Kilimanjaro 5895
Mount Elgon 4321
Mt Ruwenzori 5110
Mt Moroto 3084

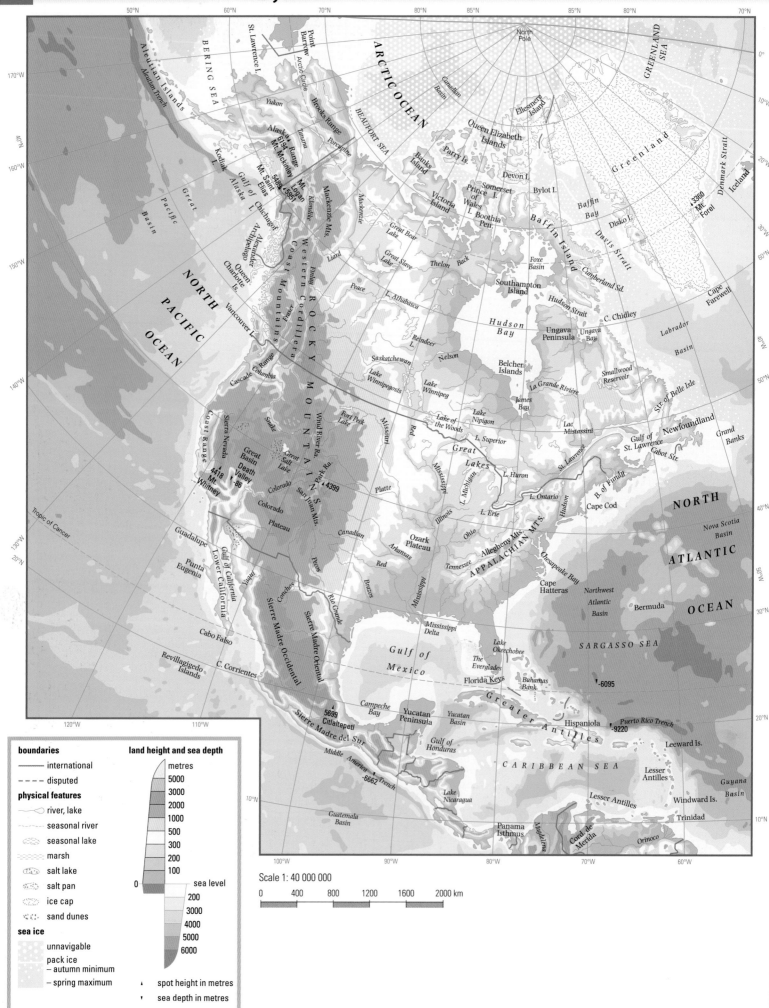

boundaries
— international
--- disputed

physical features
river, lake
seasonal river
seasonal lake
marsh
salt lake
salt pan
ice cap
sand dunes

sea ice
unnavigable
pack ice
– autumn minimum
– spring maximum

land height and sea depth
metres
5000
3000
2000
1000
500
300
200
100
0 — sea level
200
3000
4000
5000
6000

▲ spot height in metres
▼ sea depth in metres

Scale 1: 40 000 000

0   400   800   1200   1600   2000 km

Oblique Mercator Projection   © Oxford University Press

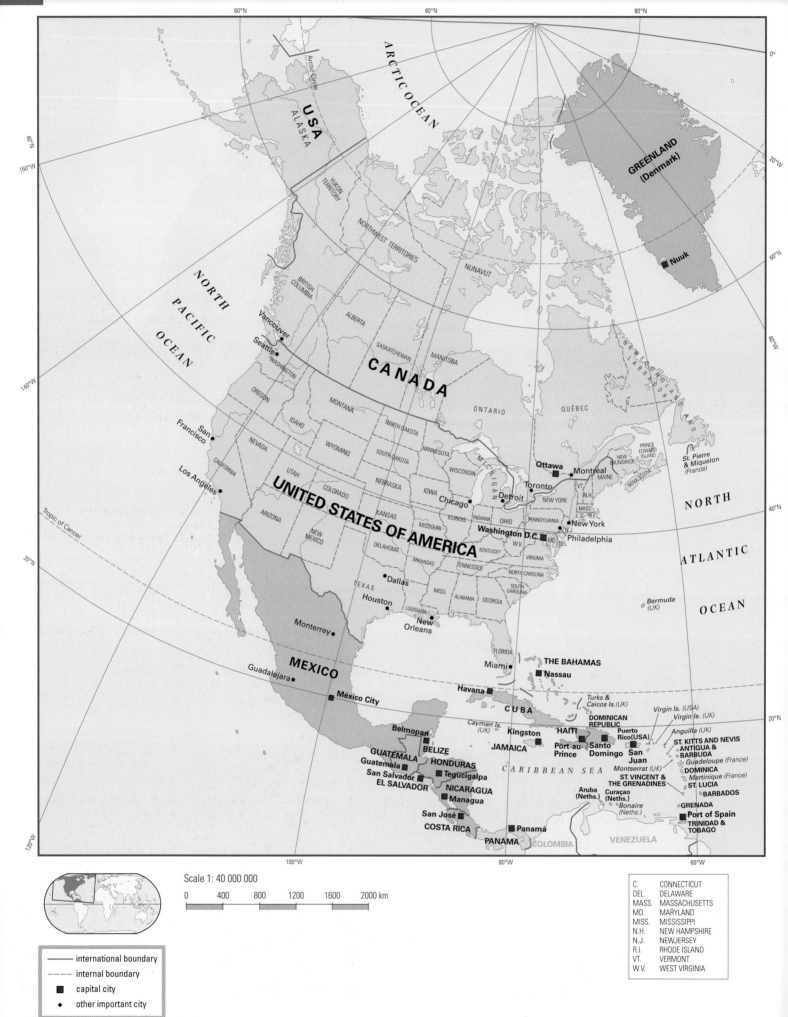

Scale 1: 40 000 000

0 400 800 1200 1600 2000 km

C.	CONNECTICUT	
DEL.	DELAWARE	
MASS.	MASSACHUSETTS	
MD.	MARYLAND	
MISS.	MISSISSIPPI	
N.H.	NEW HAMPSHIRE	
N.J.	NEW JERSEY	
R.I.	RHODE ISLAND	
VT.	VERMONT	
W.V.	WEST VIRGINIA	

— international boundary
--- internal boundary
■ capital city
• other important city

Oblique Mercator Projection   © Oxford University Press

Scale 1: 55 000 000

Land use

- trapping and fishing
- shifting cultivation
- mixed subsistence
- subsistence crops
- grazing and stock rearing
- mixed farming
- grain farming
- Mediterranean farming
- plantation
- dairy farming
- specialized horticulture
- forestry
- industrial areas
- unproductive land

Livestock

- sheep
- cattle
- pigs

Crops

- groundnuts
- cocoa
- coffee
- tobacco
- fruit
- sugar
- cotton

Minerals

- iron ore
- nickel
- gold
- silver
- copper
- bauxite
- phosphates

Energy

- coal
- oil
- gas
- hydro

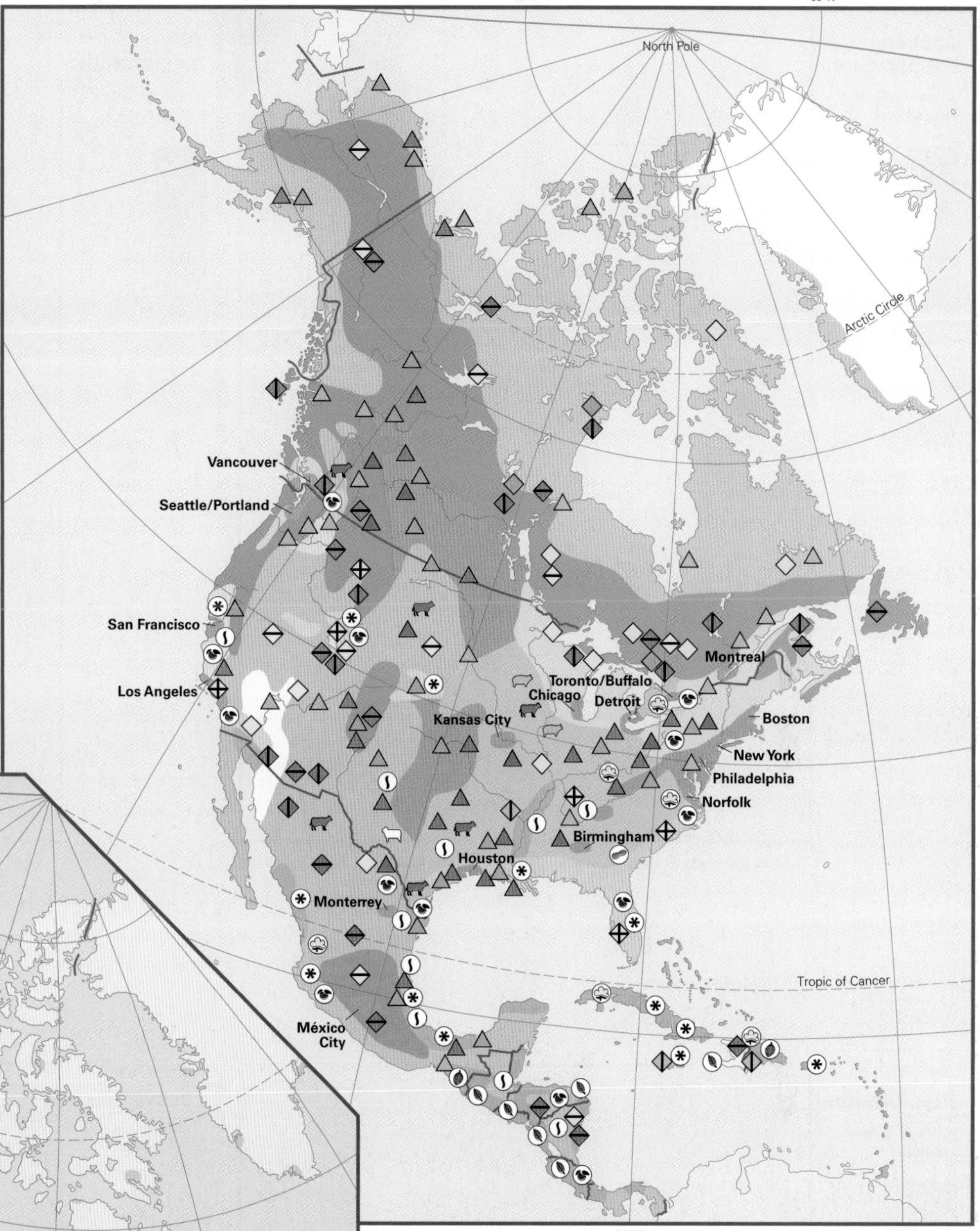

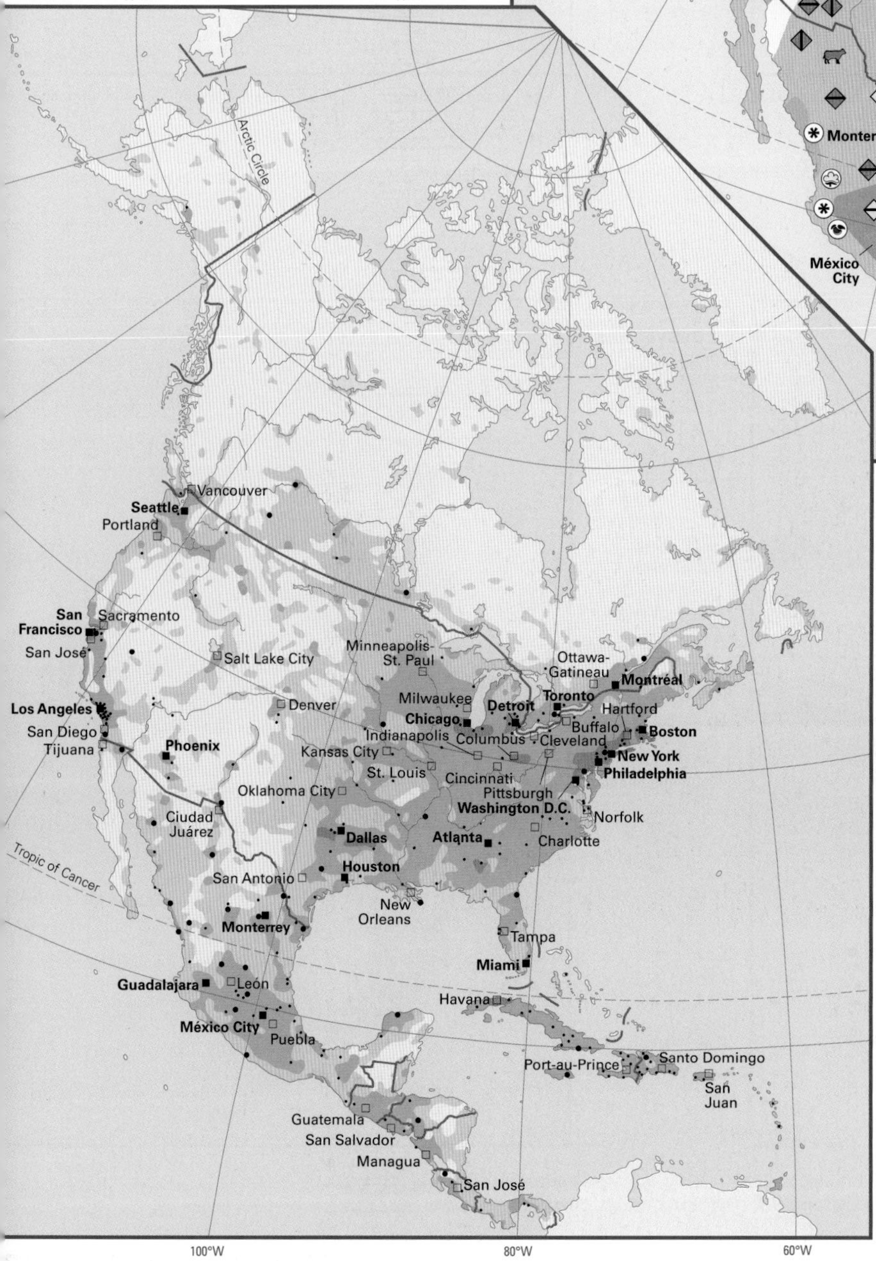

Population density

people per square kilometre

- over 200
- 100–200
- 10–100
- 1–10
- under 1

Major cities

population in millions

- ■ over 3
- ☐ 1–3
- • 0.5–1
- · 0.1–0.5

Largest urban agglomerations in North America, 2010

Urban agglomeration is the population contained within a city plus the suburban fringe lying outside of, but adjacent to, the city boundaries.

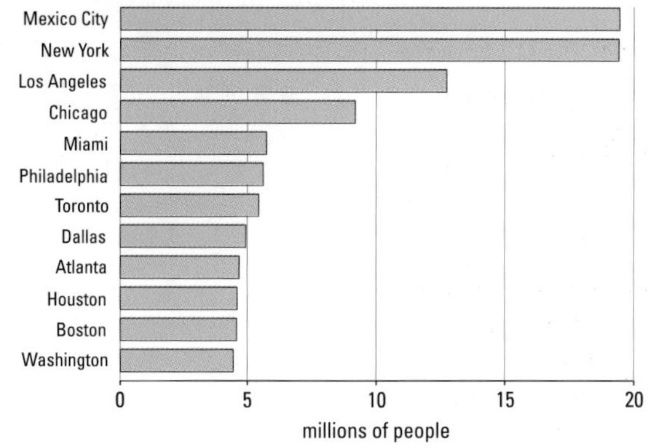

City	millions of people (0–20)
Mexico City	
New York	
Los Angeles	
Chicago	
Miami	
Philadelphia	
Toronto	
Dallas	
Atlanta	
Houston	
Boston	
Washington	

millions of people

Oblique Mercator Projection

© Oxford University Press

January temperature

actual surface temperature

°Celsius
- 25
- 20
- 15
- 10
- 5
- 0
- −10
- −20
- −30

● climate station (average January temperature)

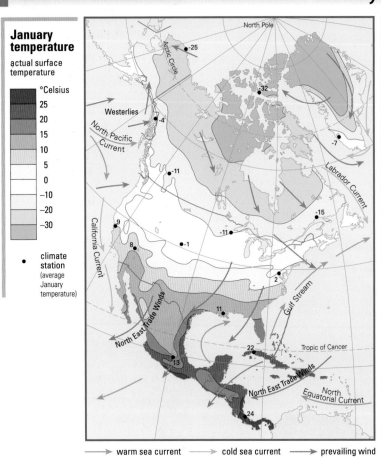

→ warm sea current   → cold sea current   → prevailing wind

July temperature

actual surface temperature

°Celsius
- 30
- 25
- 20
- 15
- 10
- 5
- 0
- −10

● climate station (average July temperature)

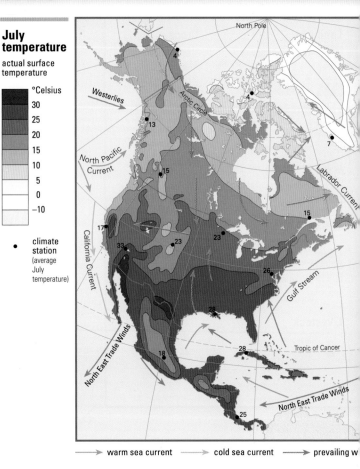

→ warm sea current   → cold sea current   → prevailing w

Precipitation

average annual precipitation

mm
- 3000
- 2000
- 1000
- 500
- 250
- 0

● climate station (average annual precipitation)

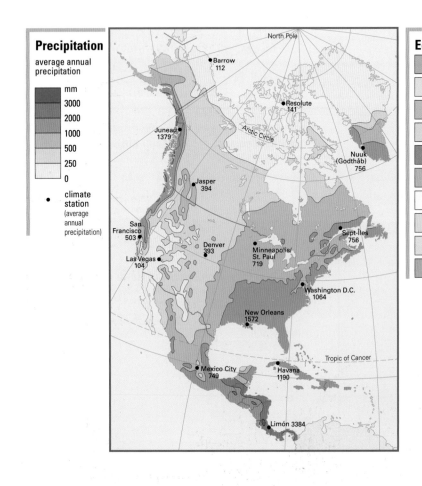

Ecosystems

- coniferous forest
- mixed forest
- tropical rain forest
- tropical grasslands
- thorn forest
- temperate grasslands
- semi-desert
- tundra
- ice
- mountains

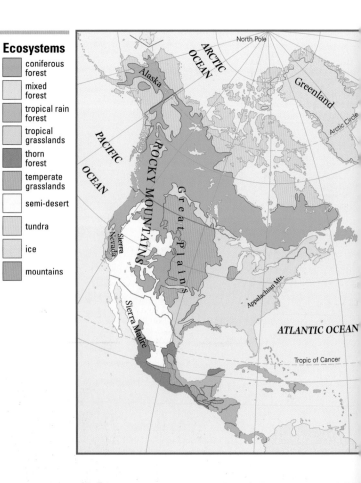

Oblique Mercator Projection   © Oxford University Press

Scale 1: 40 000 000 (main map)

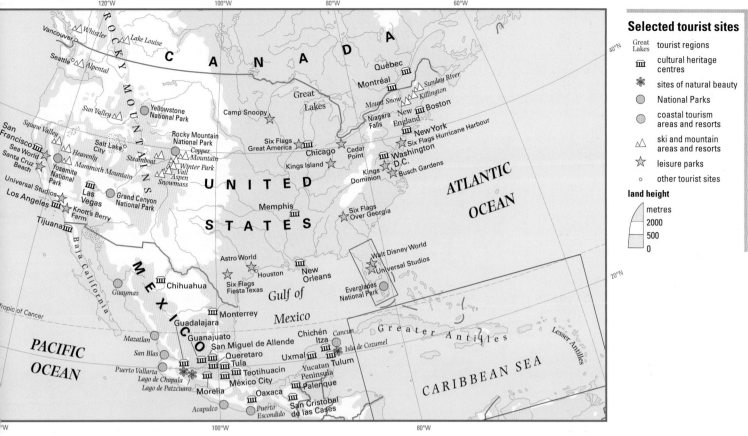

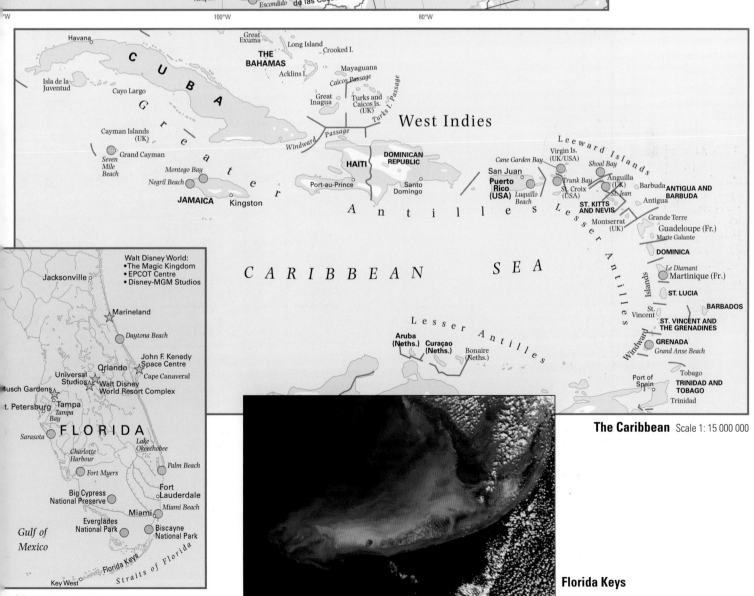

Selected tourist sites

- Great Lakes — tourist regions
- cultural heritage centres
- sites of natural beauty
- National Parks
- coastal tourism areas and resorts
- ski and mountain areas and resorts
- leisure parks
- other tourist sites

land height
metres
2000
500
0

The Caribbean Scale 1: 15 000 000

Florida Keys

Florida Scale 1: 8 000 000

Oblique Mercator Projection   © Oxford University Press

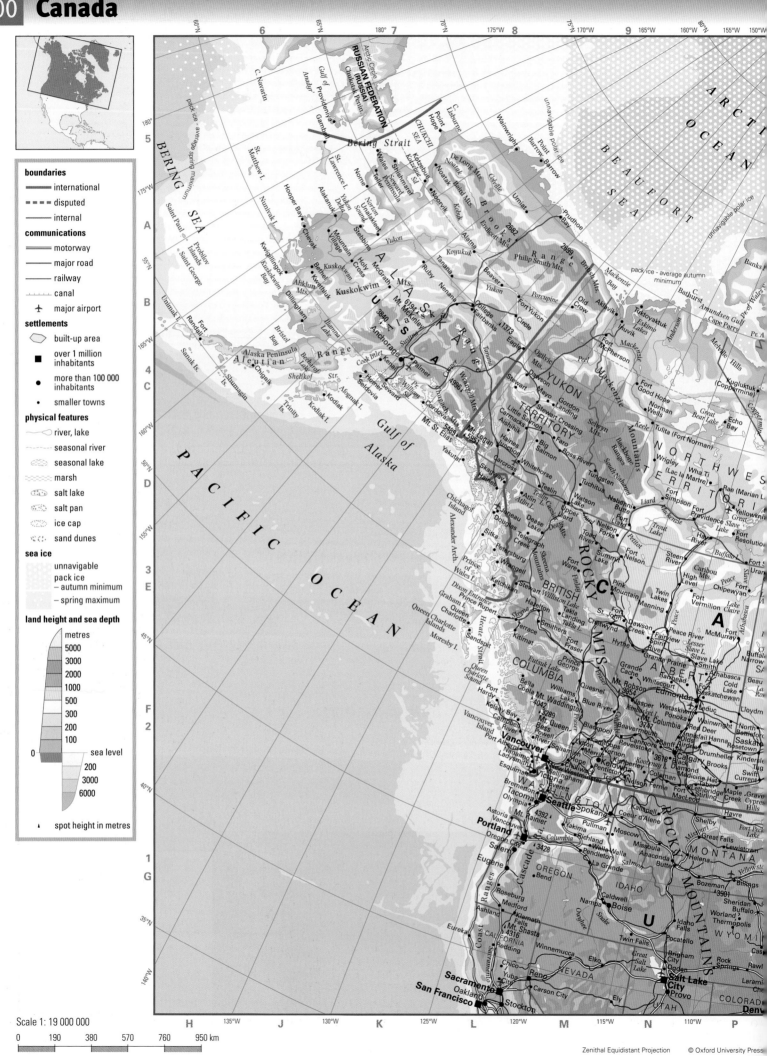

boundaries
— international
--- disputed
— internal

communications
— motorway
— major road
— railway
++++ canal
✈ major airport

settlements
⬡ built-up area
■ over 1 million inhabitants
● more than 100 000 inhabitants
• smaller towns

physical features
river, lake
seasonal river
seasonal lake
marsh
salt lake
salt pan
ice cap
sand dunes

sea ice
unnavigable
pack ice
– autumn minimum
– spring maximum

land height and sea depth
metres
5000
3000
2000
1000
500
300
200
100
0 sea level
200
3000
6000
▲ spot height in metres

Scale 1: 19 000 000

0   190   380   570   760   950 km

Zenithal Equidistant Projection   © Oxford University Press

Greenland
(Denmark)
ICELAND
Reykjavík
Hekla 1491
Ísafjörður
Hafnarfjörður
Vopnafjörður
Akureyri
Arctic Circle
Denmark Strait
pack ice - average autumn minimum
pack ice - average spring maximum
Kong Christian X Land
Kong Oscar Fj.
Jameson Land
Kangertittivaq
Mount Forel 3360
Tasiilaq
Ellesmere Island
Axel Heiberg Island
Nares Strait
Hayes
Qaanaaq
Halvø
Uummannaq
Qimusseriarsuaq
Steenstrup Glacier
Queen Elizabeth Islands
Ellef Ringnes I.
Amund Ringnes I.
Bathurst I.
Parry Islands
Jones Sound
Devon Island
Cornwallis I.
Resolute
Viscount Melville Sound
Lancaster Sound
Bylot Island
Pond Inlet
Somerset Island
Prince of Wales Island
Peel Sound
Prince Regent Inlet
Arctic Bay
Borden Penin.
Brodeur Penin.
McClintock Channel
Victoria Strait
Boothia Penin.
Gulf of Boothia
Cambridge Bay
King William Island
Gjoa Haven
Taloyoak
Kent Peninsula
Queen Maud Gulf
Melville Peninsula
Prince Charles I.
Foxe Basin
Baffin Bay
Baffin Island
Barnes Ice Cap 1250
Clyde River
Home Bay
Upernavik
Uummannaq Fjord
Nuussuaq
Disko
Qeqertarsuaq
Ilulissat
Qeqertarsuup Tunua
Kangerlussuaq
Sisimiut
Davis Strait
Cape Dyer
Maniitsoq
Nuuk
Paamiut
Kangilinnguit
Qaqortoq
Narsarsuaq
Narsaq
Nanortalik
Nunap Isua
Cumberland Penin.
Pangnirtung
Cumberland Sound
Nettilling Lake
Amadjuak L.
Iqaluit (Frobisher Bay)
Hall Penin.
Meta Incognita
Kimmirut
Frobisher Bay
Foxe Penin.
Cape Dorset
Salisbury I.
Nottingham I.
Foxe Channel
Hudson Strait
Pelly Lake
Garry Lake
Back
NUNAVUT
Wager Bay
Roes Welcome Sound
Southampton Island
Coral Harbour
Thelon
Baker Lake
Dubawnt Lake
Fisher Str.
Evans Str.
Coats I.
Mansel I.
Ivujivik
Déception
C. Hopes Advance
Akpatok
C. Chidley
LABRADOR SEA
NORTH ATLANTIC OCEAN
Yathkyed Lake
Rankin Inlet
Eskimo Point
Hudson Bay
Péninsule d'Ungava
Ungava Bay (Baie d'Ungava)
Kuujjuaq
Koksoak
Rivière aux Feuilles
Lac Payne
Puvirnituq
Inukjuak
Ottawa Is.
Lac Minto
George
Torngat Mts
Nutak
Nain
Davis Inlet
Makkovik
Hamilton Inlet
Cartwright
NEWFOUNDLAND AND LABRADOR
Battle Harbour
Nueltin Lake
Stony Rapids
Seal
North River
C. Churchill
Churchill
Wollaston Lake
Reindeer Lake
C. Tatnam
Nelson
York Factory
Southern Indian Lake
Lynn Lake
Hone
Gillam
Hayes
Granville Lake
Thompson
Charles
Sipiwesk
MANITOBA
Flin Flon
Wabowden
Snow Lake
Optic Lake
Sturgeon Landing
The Pas
Cedar Lake
Norway House
Grand Rapids
Gods Lake
Island L.
Lake Winnipeg
Hudson Bay
Winnipegosis
Dauphin
Yorkton
Roblin
Riverton
Russell
Melville
Minnedosa
Rivers
Neepawa
Lake Manitoba
Brandon
Portage la Prairie
Selkirk
Winnipeg
Killarney
Morden
Estevan
Minot
Fort Severn
Severn
Winisk
Big Trout Lake
Winisk L.
Sandy Lake
Pikangikum Lake
Lake St. Joseph
Pickle Lake
Lansdowne House
Fort Hope
Attawapiskat
Albany
Ogoki
Moosonee
ONTARIO
Sioux Lookout
Lac Seul
Dryden
Kenora
Lake of the Woods
Nipigon
Lake Nipigon
Geraldton
Longlac
Nakina
Auden
Hearst
Kapuskasing
Cochrane
Timmins
Thunder Bay
Terrace Bay
White River
Atikokan
Rainy Lake
Fort Frances
Wawa
Michipicoten
Chapleau
Foleyet
Kirkland Lake
New Liskeard
Agawa
Lake Superior
Sudbury
Blind River
Sault Ste. Marie
Manitoulin I.
North Bay
Parry Sound
Georgian Bay
Lake Huron
Owen Sound
Midland
Kincardine
Hanover
Toronto
Guelph
Kitchener
Hamilton
London
Sarnia
Chatham
Windsor
Oshawa
Peterborough
Kingston
Lake Ontario
Pembroke
Renfrew
Ottawa
Smiths Falls
Cornwall
Mattawa
Maniwaki
Gatineau
Les Îles Belcher
Kuujjuarapik
Cape Henrietta Maria
Grande Rivière de la Baleine
Lac à l'Eau Claire
Rés. La Grande 2
La Grande Rivière
Rés. La Grande 3
Chisasibi
Lac Bienville
Lake River
James Bay
Akimiski I.
Eastmain
Waskaganish
Lac Mistassini
Lac Matagami
Matagami
Chibougamau
Harricanaw
Abitibi
Missinaibi
Lac Abitibi
Rouyn-Noranda
Val-d'Or
Réservoir Gouin
Lac St. Jean
Roberval
Dolbeau
Saguenay
Monts Otish 1128
QUÉBEC
Caniapiscau
Réservoir de Caniapiscau
Schefferville (Kawawachikamach)
Labrador City
Wabush
Churchill Falls
Atikonak Lake
Smallwood Reservoir
Labrador
Melville L.
Happy Valley-Goose Bay
Lac Joseph 942
Réservoir Manicouagan
Manicouagan
Baie-Comeau
Betsiamites
Sept-Îles
Mingan
Natashquan
Harrington Harbour
Wolf Bay
Jacques-Cartier Pa.
Île d'Anticosti
Honguedo Pa.
Gulf of St. Lawrence
St. Lawrence
Ste-Anne-des-Monts
Gaspé
Matane
Chandler
Rimouski
Campbellton
Cabano
Bathurst
Îles de la Madeleine
Cabot Strait
Strait of Belle Isle
St. Anthony
White Bay
Notre Dame Bay
Long Ra. Mts 814
Springdale
Deer Lake
Corner Brook
Stephenville
Grand Lake
Newfoundland
Gander
Grand Falls-Windsor
Glovertown
Clarenville
St. John's
Ferryland
Cape Race
Trepassey
Whitbourne
Placentia Bay
Burin
Harbour Breton
Channel-Port aux Basques
Saint-Pierre et Miquelon (Fr.)
Cape Breton I.
Glace Bay
Sydney
Port Hawkesbury
Canso
Sable I.
PRINCE EDWARD I.
Charlottetown
Inverness
NEW BRUNSWICK
Miramichi
Richibucto
Moncton
Amherst
Truro
Dartmouth
Halifax
NOVA SCOTIA
Berwick
Lunenburg
Shelburne
Digby
Yarmouth
Bay of Fundy
Saint John
Fredericton
Woodstock
Grand Falls
Edmundston
Rivière-du-Loup
La Tuque
Québec
Lévis
Montmagny
Presque Isle
Shawinigan
Trois-Rivières
Mont-Laurier
Drummondville
Montreal
Sherbrooke
St. Stephen
Freeport
Clark's Harbour
MAINE
Portland
Portsmouth
Manchester
Boston
Concord
Lewiston
Burlington
VERMONT
N.H.
MASS.
Hartford
Providence
CONN.
New Haven
Bridgeport
New York
NEW JERSEY
Philadelphia
Allentown
Scranton
Catskill Mts
Albany
Glens Falls
Utica
Syracuse
Rochester
Buffalo
Niagara Falls
St. Catharines
Binghamton
Erie
NEW YORK
PENNSYLVANIA
Pittsburgh
Harrisburg
York
Baltimore
MARYLAND
DELAWARE
Washington D.C.
Atlantic City
Newark
Staunton
VIRGINIA
WEST VIRGINIA
Canton
Youngstown
Cleveland
Columbus
OHIO
Dayton
Toledo
Detroit
Lake Erie
Jackson
South Bend
Grand Rapids
Flint
Lake Michigan
Michigan
Milwaukee
Madison
Green Bay
Appleton
Wausau
Eau Claire
WISCONSIN
La Crosse
Rockford
Chicago
Gary
Fort Wayne
INDIANA
Indianapolis
ILLINOIS
Peoria
Springfield
Davenport
Cedar Rapids
Des Moines
Waterloo
IOWA
Council Bluffs
Omaha
Lincoln
Norfolk
Columbus
North Platte
NEBRASKA
Kearney
MISSOURI
Sioux City
Sioux Falls
Yankton
Mitchell
Brookings
Pierre
SOUTH DAKOTA
Watertown
Aberdeen
Minneapolis
St. Paul
Rochester
Mississippi
Minnesota
Willmar
St. Cloud
Brainerd
Duluth
Superior
MINNESOTA
Fergus Falls
Moorhead
Fargo
Grand Forks
Red
Wahpeton
Linton
Jamestown
Bismarck
Dickinson
NORTH DAKOTA
Missouri
CANADA
Hudson Bay
130°W 120°W 110°W 100°W 90°W 80°W 70°W 60°W 55°W 50°W 45°W 40°W 35°W 30°W 25°W 20°W 15°W
75°N 70°N 65°N 60°N 55°N 50°N 45°N 40°N 35°N
100°W 95°W 90°W 85°W 80°W 75°W 70°W 65°W 60°W
Q R S T U V W X Y
HH GG FF EE DD CC BB AA Z
1 2 3 4 5 6 7 8 9

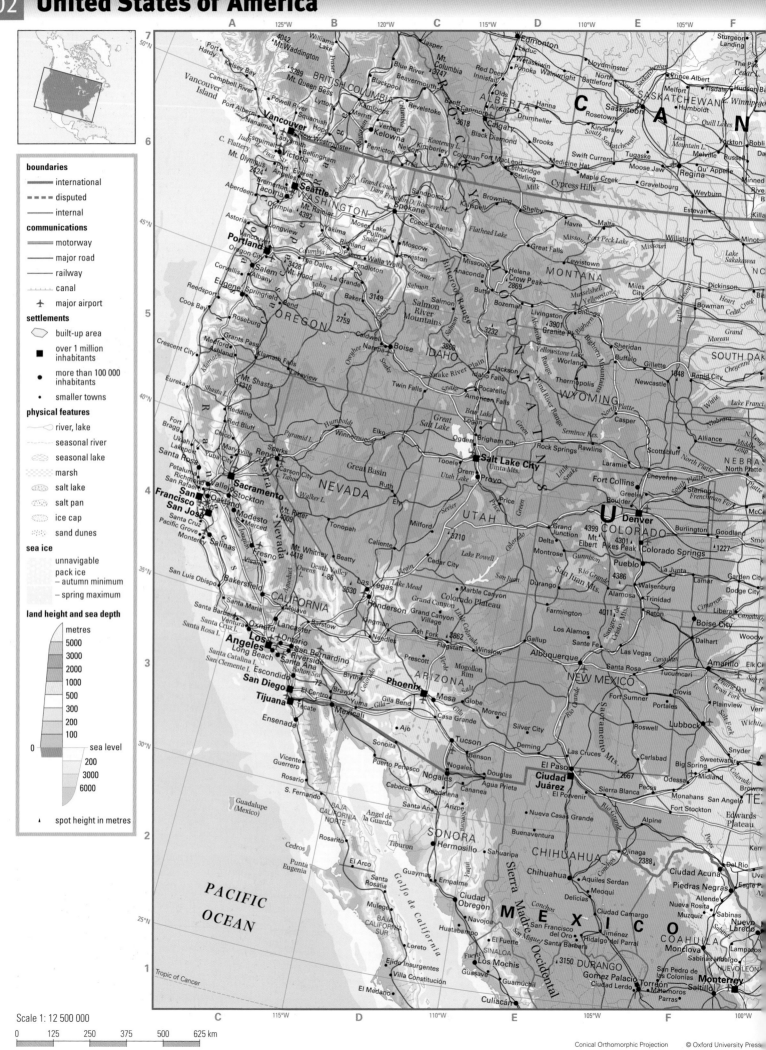

boundaries
— international
--- disputed
— internal

communications
═══ motorway
— major road
— railway
⊥⊥⊥ canal
✈ major airport

settlements
⬡ built-up area
■ over 1 million inhabitants
● more than 100 000 inhabitants
• smaller towns

physical features
river, lake
seasonal river
seasonal lake
marsh
salt lake
salt pan
ice cap
sand dunes

sea ice
unnavigable
pack ice
– autumn minimum
– spring maximum

land height and sea depth
metres
5000
3000
2000
1000
500
300
200
100
0 sea level
200
3000
6000

▲ spot height in metres

Scale 1: 12 500 000

0   125   250   375   500   625 km

Conical Orthomorphic Projection   © Oxford University Press

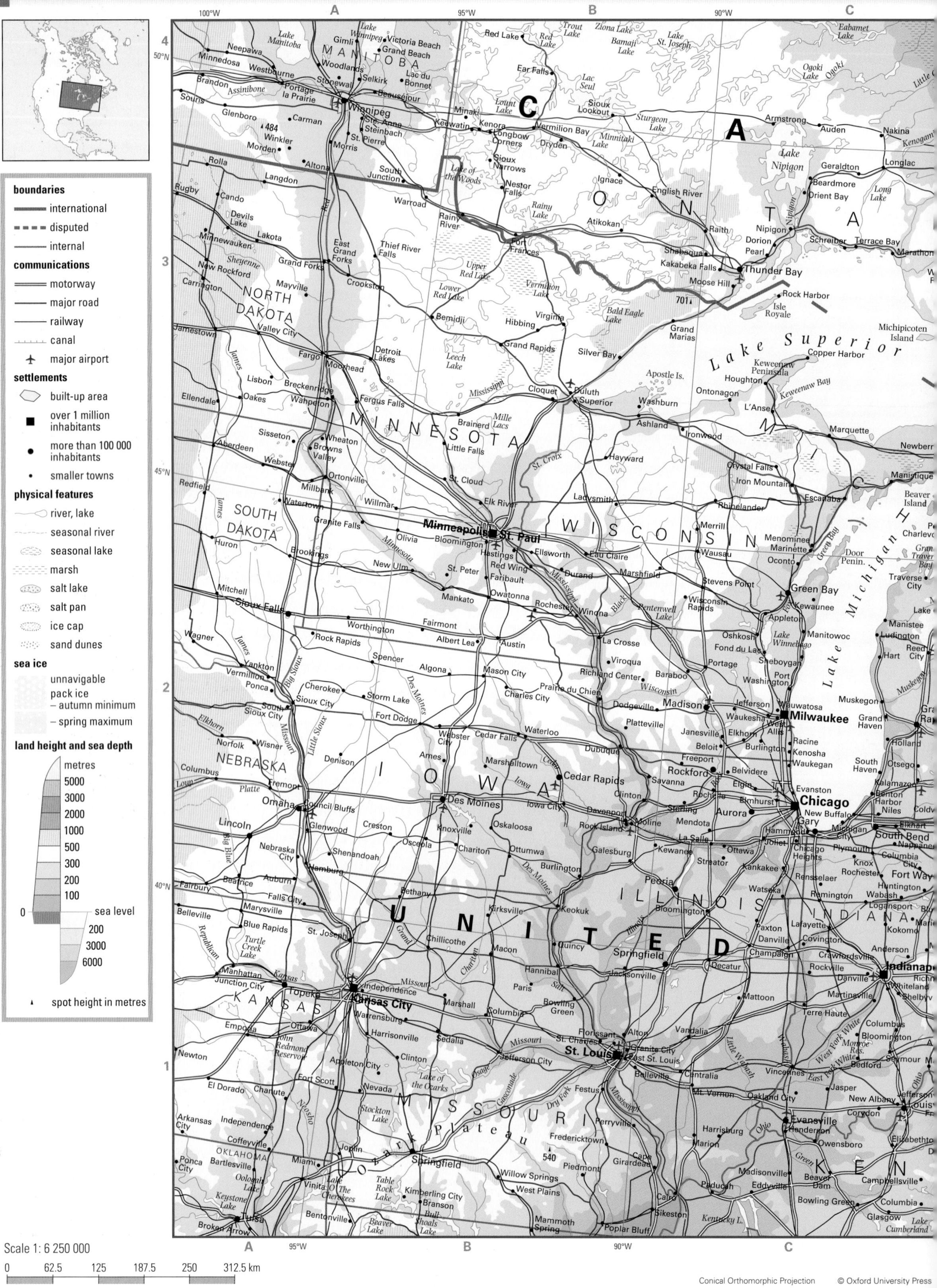
boundaries
international
disputed
internal
communications
motorway
major road
railway
canal
major airport
settlements
built-up area
over 1 million inhabitants
more than 100 000 inhabitants
smaller towns
physical features
river, lake
seasonal river
seasonal lake
marsh
salt lake
salt pan
ice cap
sand dunes
sea ice
unnavigable pack ice – autumn minimum
– spring maximum
land height and sea depth
metres
5000
3000
2000
1000
500
300
200
100
0
sea level
200
3000
6000
spot height in metres
100°W
95°W
90°W
A
B
C
4
3
2
1
50°N
45°N
40°N
CANADA
ONTARIO
MANITOBA
MINNESOTA
WISCONSIN
MICHIGAN
NORTH DAKOTA
SOUTH DAKOTA
NEBRASKA
IOWA
ILLINOIS
INDIANA
KANSAS
MISSOURI
OKLAHOMA
UNITED
Lake Superior
Lake Michigan
Lake Winnipeg
Lake Manitoba
Lake of the Woods
Lake Nipigon
Winnipeg
Thunder Bay
Duluth
Minneapolis
St. Paul
Milwaukee
Chicago
Madison
Green Bay
Des Moines
Cedar Rapids
Omaha
Lincoln
Kansas City
St. Louis
Springfield
Peoria
Rockford
Indianapolis
Evansville
Ozark Plateau
484
701
540
Scale 1: 6 250 000
0
62.5
125
187.5
250
312.5 km
Conical Orthomorphic Projection
© Oxford University Press

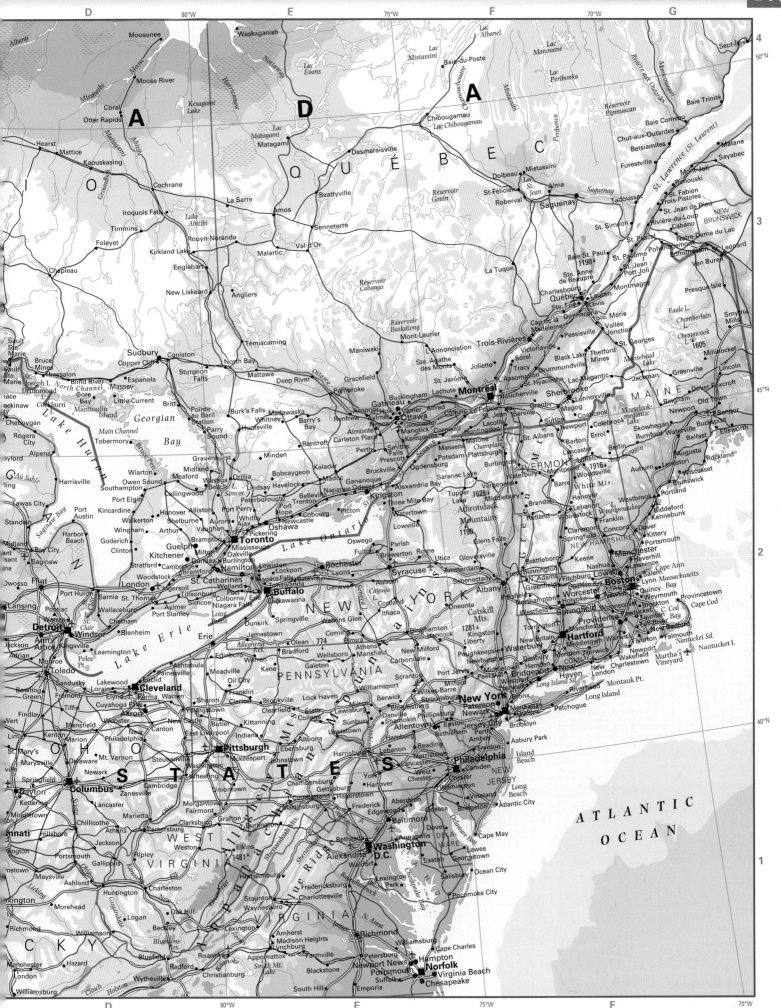

Scale 1: 15 000 000 (main map)

0   150   300   450   600   750 km

Leeward Islands
Scale 1: 5 000 000

Windward Islands
Scale 1: 5 000 000

Zenithal Equidistant Projection   © Oxford University Press

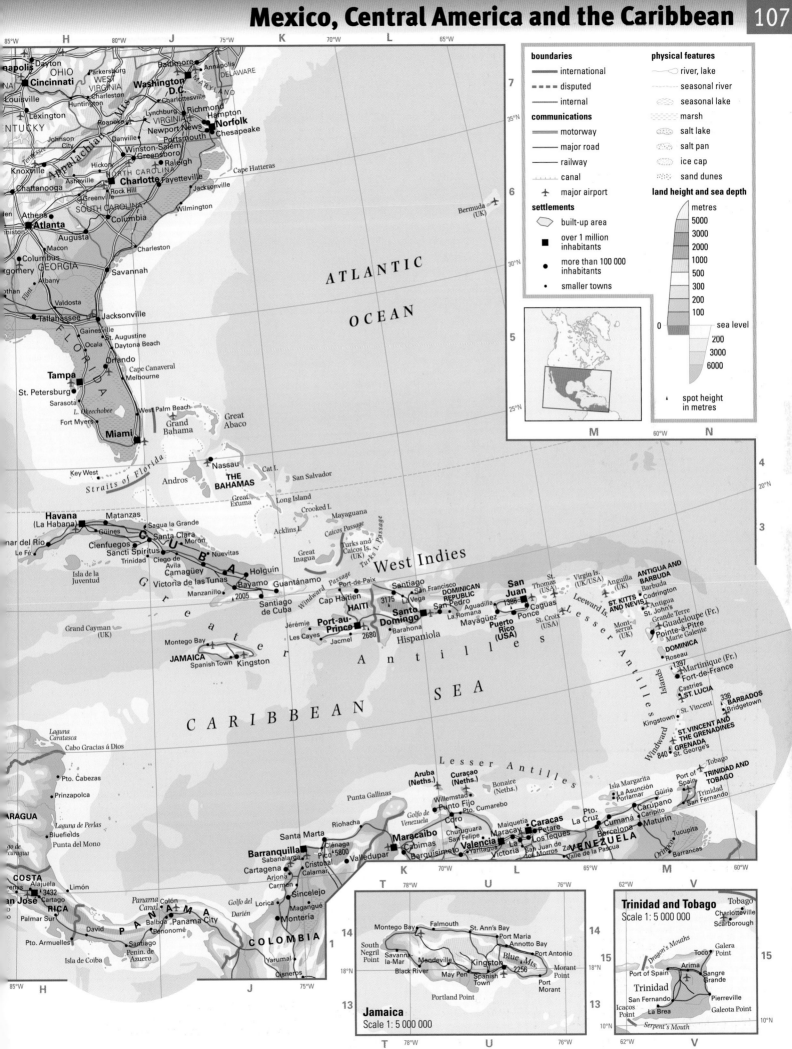

boundaries
- international
- disputed
- internal

communications
- motorway
- major road
- railway
- canal
- major airport

settlements
- built-up area
- over 1 million inhabitants
- more than 100 000 inhabitants
- smaller towns

physical features
- river, lake
- seasonal river
- seasonal lake
- marsh
- salt lake
- salt pan
- ice cap
- sand dunes

land height and sea depth

metres
5000
3000
2000
1000
500
300
200
100
0 sea level
200
3000
6000

spot height in metres

ATLANTIC OCEAN

CARIBBEAN SEA

West Indies

Greater Antilles

Lesser Antilles

Windward Islands

THE BAHAMAS

CUBA

HAITI

JAMAICA

DOMINICAN REPUBLIC

PUERTO RICO (USA)

Hispaniola

VENEZUELA

COLOMBIA

PANAMA

COSTA RICA

NICARAGUA

TRINIDAD AND TOBAGO

ANTIGUA AND BARBUDA

ST KITTS AND NEVIS

DOMINICA

ST LUCIA

BARBADOS

ST VINCENT AND THE GRENADINES

GRENADA

Jamaica
Scale 1: 5 000 000

Trinidad and Tobago
Scale 1: 5 000 000

Trinidad

© Oxford University Press

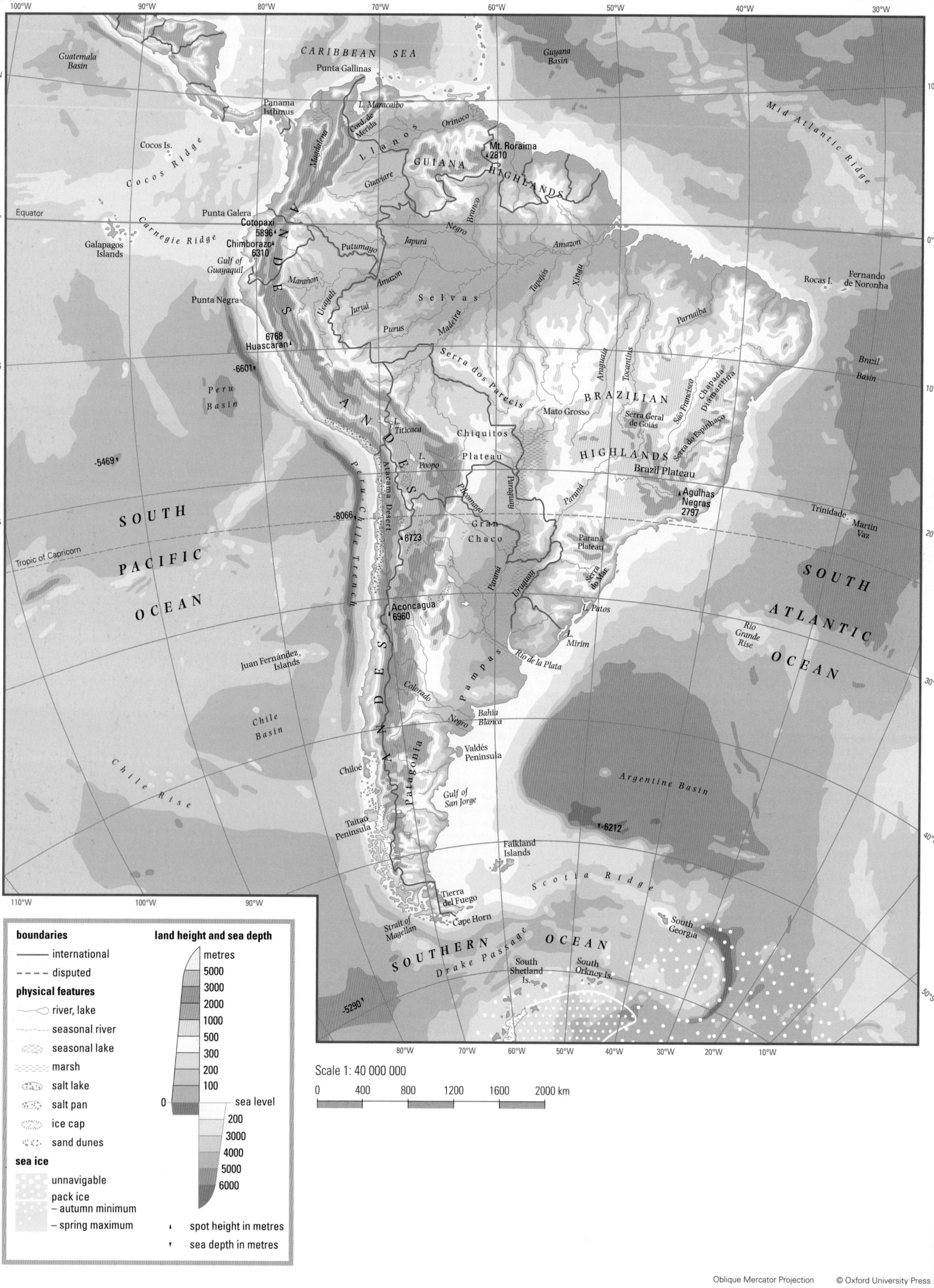

CARIBBEAN SEA
Guatemala Basin
Punta Gallinas
Guyana Basin
Panama Isthmus
L. Maracaibo
Cocos Is.
Cord. de Mérida
Orinoco
Magdalena
Llanos
Mt. Roraima 2810
Cocos Ridge
Guaviare
GUIANA HIGHLANDS
Carnegie Ridge
Punta Galera
Cotopaxi 5896
Chimborazo 6310
Negro
Branco
Amazon
Equator
Galapagos Islands
Gulf of Guayaquil
Putumayo
Japurá
Marañon
Amazon
Tapajós
Xingu
Rocas I.
Fernando de Noronha
Ucayali
Juruá
Selvas
Madeira
Parnaíba
Punta Negra
Purus
Brazil Basin
6768 Huascaran
Serra dos Parecis
Araguaia
Tocantins
BRAZILIAN
São Francisco
Chapada Diamantina
-6601
Peru Basin
L. Titicaca
Chiquitos
Mato Grosso
Serra Geral de Goiás
Serra do Espinhaço
-5469
L. Poopo
Plateau
HIGHLANDS
Brazil Plateau
SOUTH
Pilcomayo
Paraguay
Paraná
Agulhas Negras 2797
Trinidade
Martin Vaz
PACIFIC
Atacama Desert
-8066
Gran Chaco
Paraná Plateau
SOUTH
Tropic of Capricorn
Peru-Chile Trench
6723
Paraná
Serra do Mar
ATLANTIC
OCEAN
L. Patos
Rio Grande Rise
ANDES
Aconcagua 6960
Uruguay
L. Mirim
OCEAN
Juan Fernández Islands
Colorado
Pampas
Rio de la Plata
Chile Basin
Negro
Bahia Blanca
Chiloé
Valdés Peninsula
Chile Rise
Patagonia
Gulf of San Jorge
Argentine Basin
Taitao Peninsula
-6212
Tierra del Fuego
Falkland Islands
Strait of Magellan
Cape Horn
Scotia Ridge
South Georgia
SOUTHERN OCEAN
Drake Passage
South Shetland Is.
South Orkney Is.
-5290

Mid Atlantic Ridge

boundaries
—— international
- - - disputed

physical features
river, lake
seasonal river
seasonal lake
marsh
salt lake
salt pan
ice cap
sand dunes

sea ice
unnavigable
pack ice
– autumn minimum
– spring maximum

land height and sea depth
metres
5000
3000
2000
1000
500
300
200
100
0 — sea level
200
3000
4000
5000
6000

spot height in metres
sea depth in metres

Scale 1 : 40 000 000

0   400   800   1200   1600   2000 km

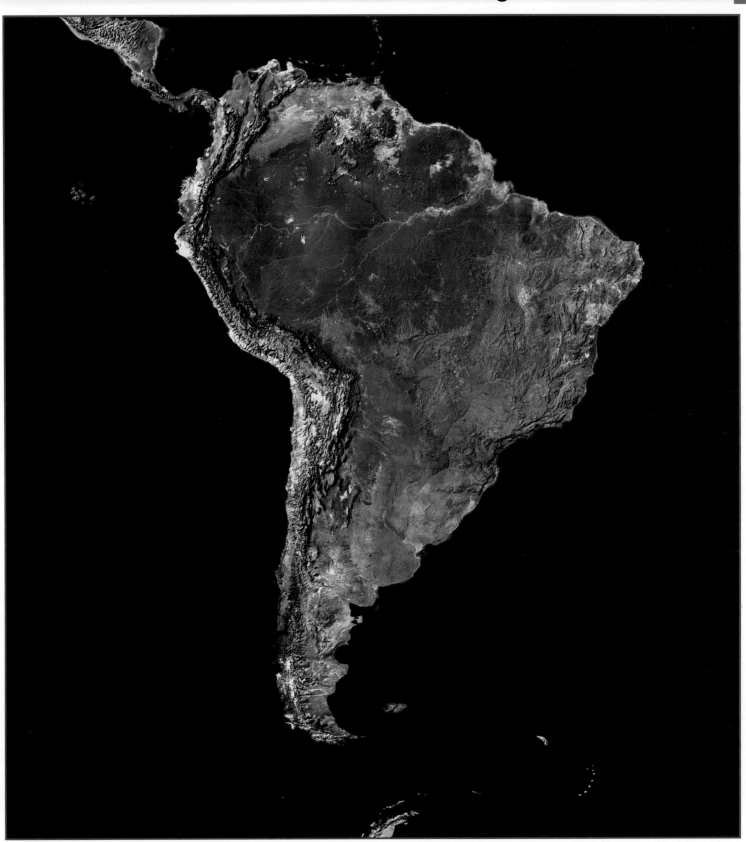

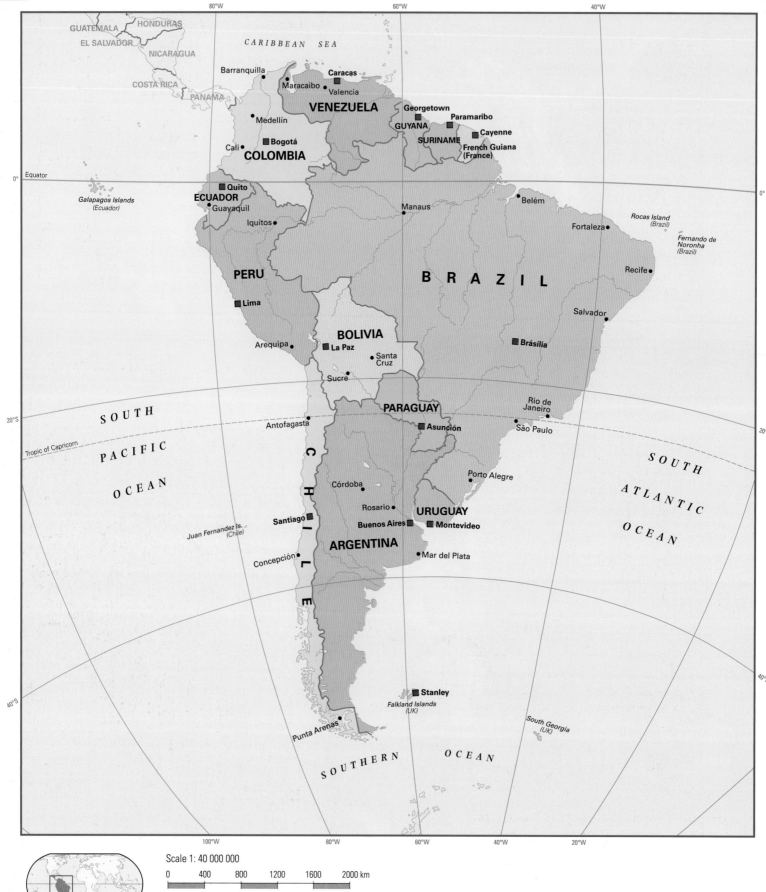

GUATEMALA   HONDURAS
EL SALVADOR
NICARAGUA
COSTA RICA
PANAMA

CARIBBEAN SEA

Barranquilla
• Maracaibo   ■ Caracas
• Valencia
VENEZUELA
• Medellín   Georgetown ■   Paramaribo ■
                              GUYANA   ■ Cayenne
Cali •   ■ Bogotá   **SURINAME**   French Guiana
COLOMBIA   (France)

0° Equator

Galapagos Islands   ■ Quito   Belém •
(Ecuador)   **ECUADOR**   Rocas Island
              • Guayaquil   Manaus •   (Brazil)
              Iquitos •   Fortaleza •   Fernando de
                                                                            Noronha
                                                                            (Brazil)
PERU   B R A Z I L   Recife •

      ■ Lima

                                                          Salvador •
Arequipa •   **BOLIVIA**
              ■ La Paz   ■ Brásília
                    • Santa
                      Cruz
              Sucre •
20°S   **PARAGUAY**   Rio de
                                                           Janeiro •
Antofagasta •   ■ Asunción   São Paulo •
Tropic of Capricorn

SOUTH

PACIFIC   Porto Alegre •   SOUTH

              Córdoba •   ATLANTIC
OCEAN   OCEAN
              Rosario •   **URUGUAY**
Juan Fernandez Is. Santiago ■   Buenos Aires ■ ■ Montevideo
(Chile)
              ARGENTINA
Concepción •   • Mar del Plata

                                                  40°S

                              ■ Stanley
                        Falkland Islands
                        (UK)
                                        South Georgia
              Punta Arenas •   (UK)

        SOUTHERN   OCEAN

Scale 1 : 40 000 000

0   400   800   1200 1600   2000 km

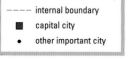

─── international boundary
- - - internal boundary
■ capital city
• other important city

Oblique Mercator Projection   © Oxford University Press

Scale 1: 45 000 000

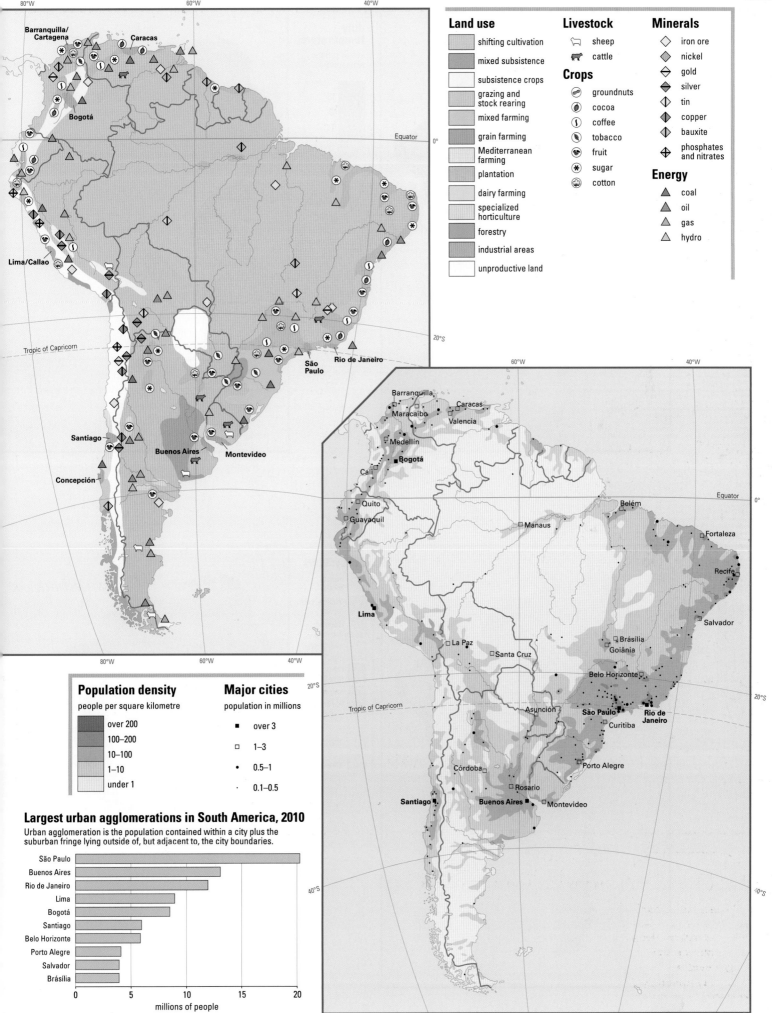

Land use

- shifting cultivation
- mixed subsistence
- subsistence crops
- grazing and stock rearing
- mixed farming
- grain farming
- Mediterranean farming
- plantation
- dairy farming
- specialized horticulture
- forestry
- industrial areas
- unproductive land

Livestock

- sheep
- cattle

Crops

- groundnuts
- cocoa
- coffee
- tobacco
- fruit
- sugar
- cotton

Minerals

- iron ore
- nickel
- gold
- silver
- tin
- copper
- bauxite
- phosphates and nitrates

Energy

- coal
- oil
- gas
- hydro

Population density

people per square kilometre

- over 200
- 100–200
- 10–100
- 1–10
- under 1

Major cities

population in millions

- over 3
- 1–3
- 0.5–1
- 0.1–0.5

Largest urban agglomerations in South America, 2010

Urban agglomeration is the population contained within a city plus the suburban fringe lying outside of, but adjacent to, the city boundaries.

- São Paulo
- Buenos Aires
- Rio de Janeiro
- Lima
- Bogotá
- Santiago
- Belo Horizonte
- Porto Alegre
- Salvador
- Brásília

0   5   10   15   20
millions of people

© Oxford University Press   Oblique Mercator Projection

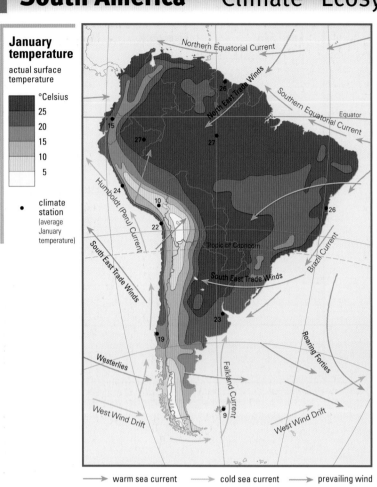

January temperature

actual surface temperature

°Celsius
- 25
- 20
- 15
- 10
- 5

• climate station (average January temperature)

→ warm sea current → cold sea current → prevailing wind

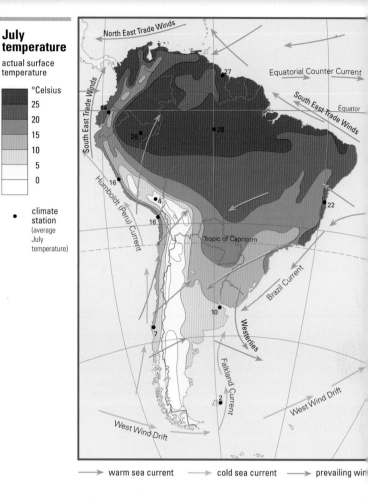

July temperature

actual surface temperature

°Celsius
- 25
- 20
- 15
- 10
- 5
- 0

• climate station (average July temperature)

→ warm sea current → cold sea current → prevailing win

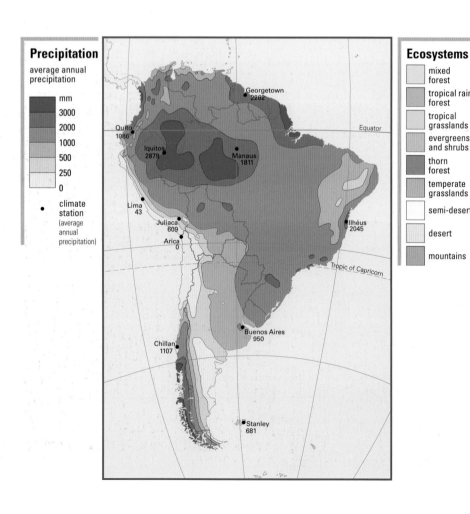

Precipitation

average annual precipitation

mm
- 3000
- 2000
- 1000
- 500
- 250
- 0

• climate station (average annual precipitation)

Ecosystems

- mixed forest
- tropical rain forest
- tropical grasslands
- evergreens and shrubs
- thorn forest
- temperate grasslands
- semi-desert
- desert
- mountains

Oblique Mercator Projection   © Oxford University Press

Scale 1: 40 000 000

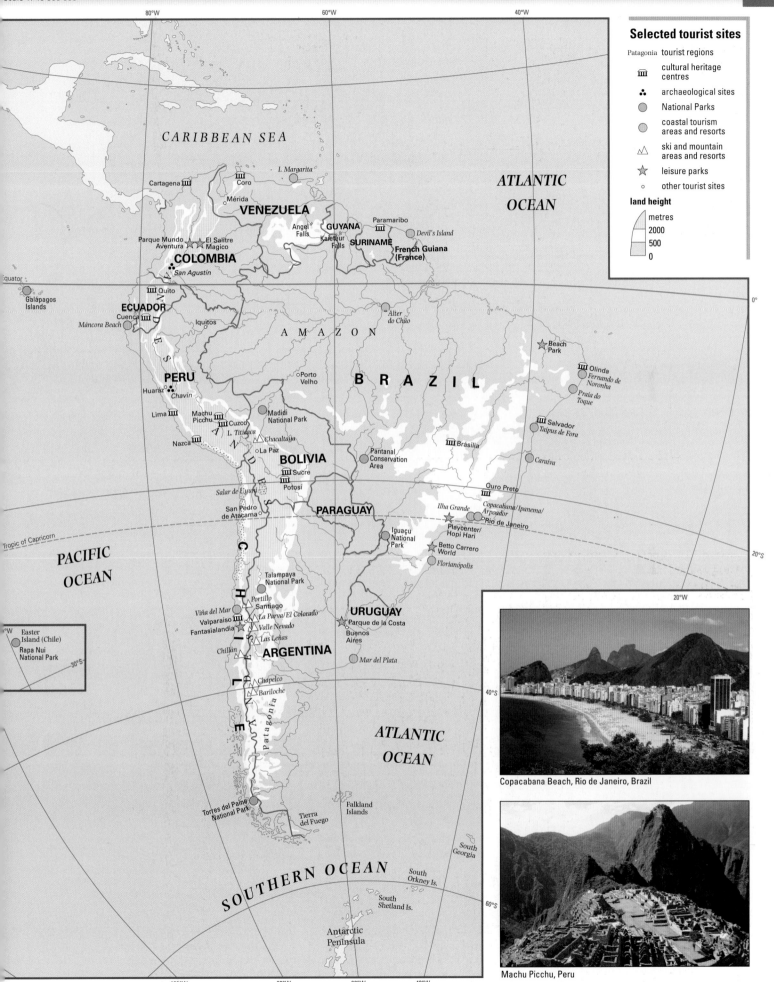

Selected tourist sites

Patagonia   tourist regions

cultural heritage centres

archaeological sites

National Parks

coastal tourism areas and resorts

ski and mountain areas and resorts

leisure parks

other tourist sites

land height

metres
2000
500
0

CARIBBEAN SEA

ATLANTIC OCEAN

Cartagena
Coro
I. Margarita
Mérida
VENEZUELA
Angel Falls
GUYANA
Kaieteur Falls
SURINAME
Paramaribo
Devil's Island
Parque Mundo Aventura
El Salitre Magico
COLOMBIA
San Agustín
French Guiana (France)
Galápagos Islands
Equator
Quito
ECUADOR
Cuenca
Iquitos
Mácora Beach
AMAZON
Alter do Chão
Beach Park
PERU
Porto Velho
B R A Z I L
Olinda
Fernando de Noronha
Huaráz
Chavín
Lima
Machu Picchu
Cuzco
Nazca
L. Titicaca
Chacaltaya
Madidi National Park
Praia do Toque
Salvador
Taipus de Fora
La Paz
BOLIVIA
Sucre
Brasília
Caraíva
Salar de Uyuni
Potosí
Ouro Preto
San Pedro de Atacama
PARAGUAY
Pantanal Conservation Area
Ilha Grande
Copacabana/Ipanema/Arpoador
Rio de Janeiro
Playcenter/Hopi Hari
Iguaçu National Park
Betto Carrero World
Florianópolis
Tropic of Capricorn
PACIFIC OCEAN
Talampaya National Park
Portillo
Viña del Mar
Santiago
Valparaíso
La Parva/El Colorado
Fantasialandia
Valle Nevado
Las Leñas
Chillán
URUGUAY
Parque de la Costa
Buenos Aires
ARGENTINA
Mar del Plata
Easter Island (Chile)
Rapa Nui National Park
Chapelco
Bariloche
Patagonia
ATLANTIC OCEAN
Torres del Paine National Park
Tierra del Fuego
Falkland Islands
South Georgia
SOUTHERN OCEAN
South Orkney Is.
South Shetland Is.
Antarctic Peninsula

80°W   60°W   40°W   20°W   0°   20°S   30°S   40°S   60°S

100°W   80°W   60°W   40°W

Copacabana Beach, Rio de Janeiro, Brazil

Machu Picchu, Peru

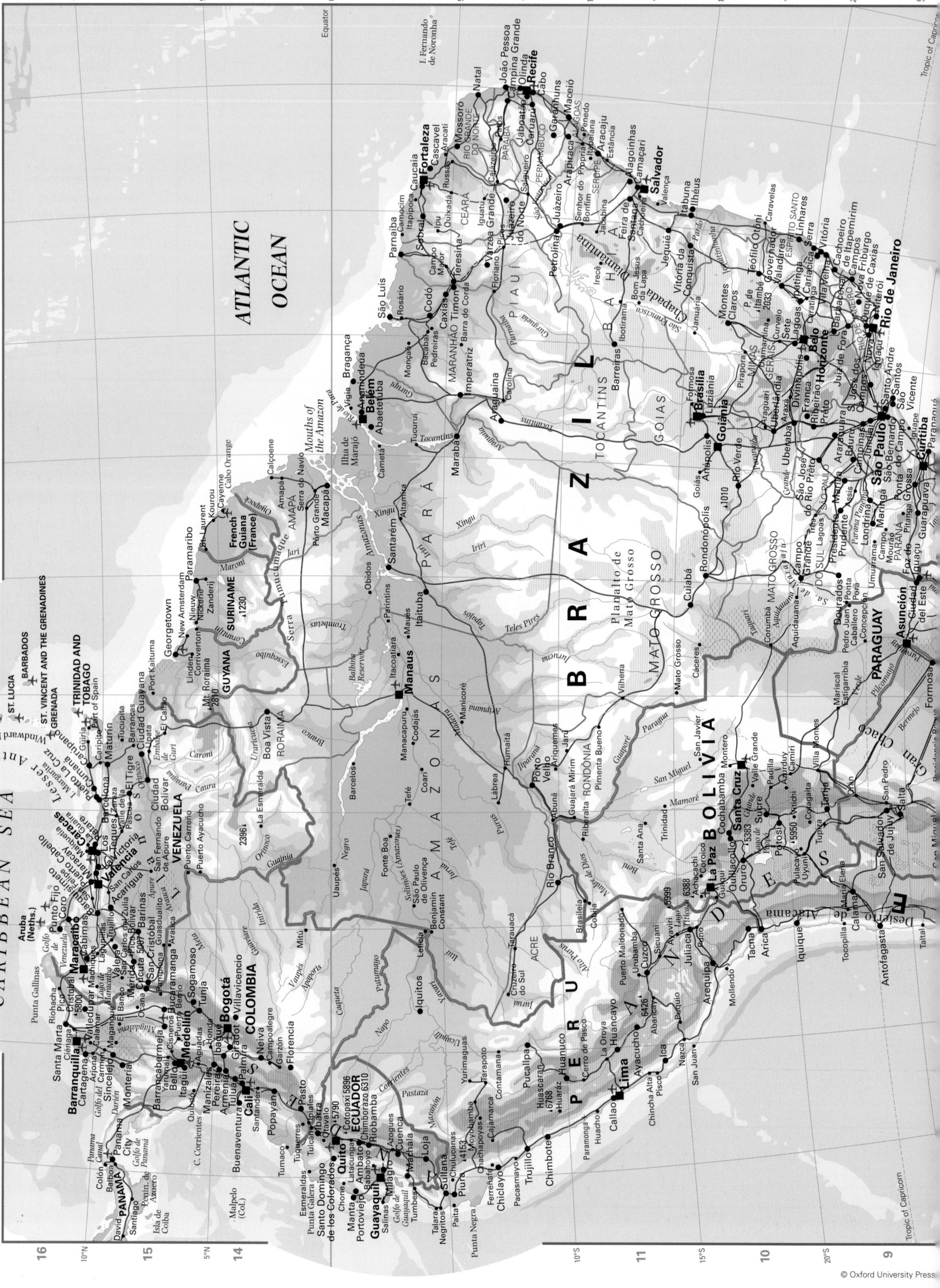

ATLANTIC

OCEAN

CARIBBEAN SEA

Lesser Antilles

DOMINICA
ST. LUCIA
BARBADOS
ST. VINCENT AND THE GRENADINES
GRENADA
TRINIDAD AND TOBAGO

Martinique (Fr.)
Aruba (Neths.)
Windward Islands

PANAMA
VENEZUELA
COLOMBIA
ECUADOR
PERU
BOLIVIA
PARAGUAY

GUYANA
SURINAME
French Guiana (France)

B R A Z I L

AMAZONAS
PARÁ
AMAPÁ
RORAIMA
RONDÔNIA
ACRE
MATO GROSSO
GOIÁS
MARANHÃO
PIAUÍ
CEARÁ
RIO GRANDE DO NORTE
PARAÍBA
PERNAMBUCO
ALAGOAS
SERGIPE
BAHIA
MINAS GERAIS
ESPÍRITO SANTO

Planalto de Mato Grosso
Gran Chaco
Desierto de Atacama

Caracas
Maracaibo
Valencia
Bogotá
Medellín
Cali
Quito
Guayaquil
Lima
Callao
La Paz
Santa Cruz
Sucre
Potosí
Asunción

Georgetown
Paramaribo
Cayenne

Belém
Fortaleza
Recife
Salvador
Manaus
Brasília
Goiânia
Belo Horizonte
Rio de Janeiro
São Paulo
Curitiba
Santos

Amazon
Mouths of the Amazon
Rio Negro
Tocantins
Xingu
Tapajós
São Francisco

Tropic of Capricorn

© Oxford University Press

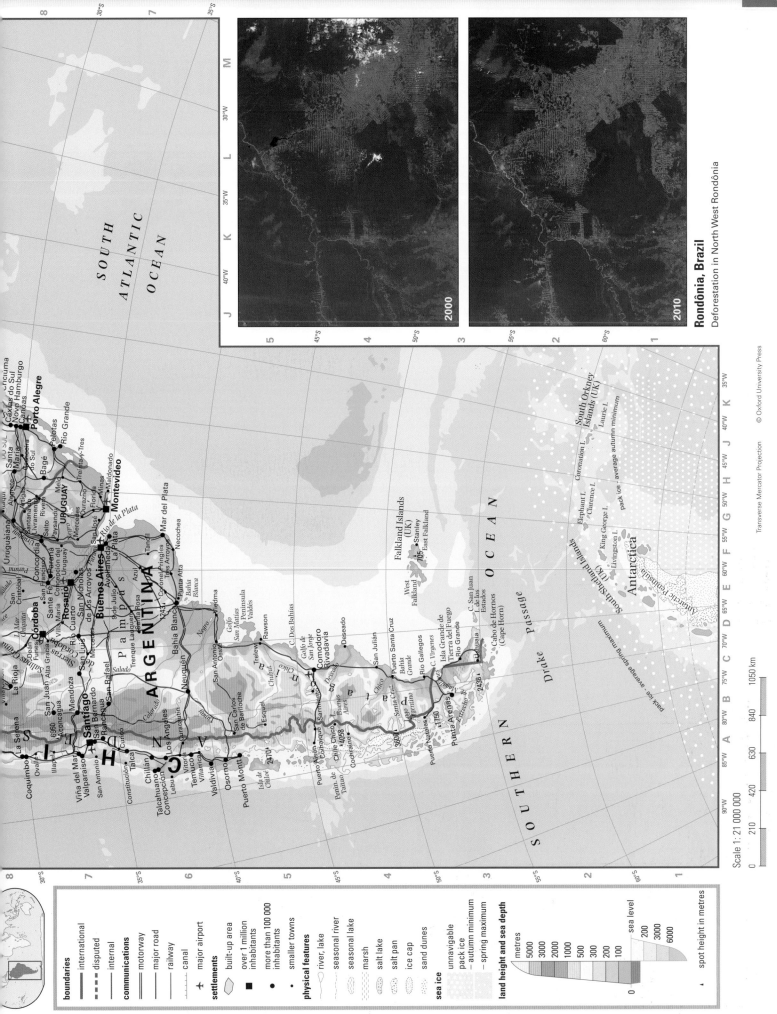

Rondônia, Brazil
Deforestation in North West Rondônia

Scale 1: 21 000 000

Transverse Mercator Projection   © Oxford University Press

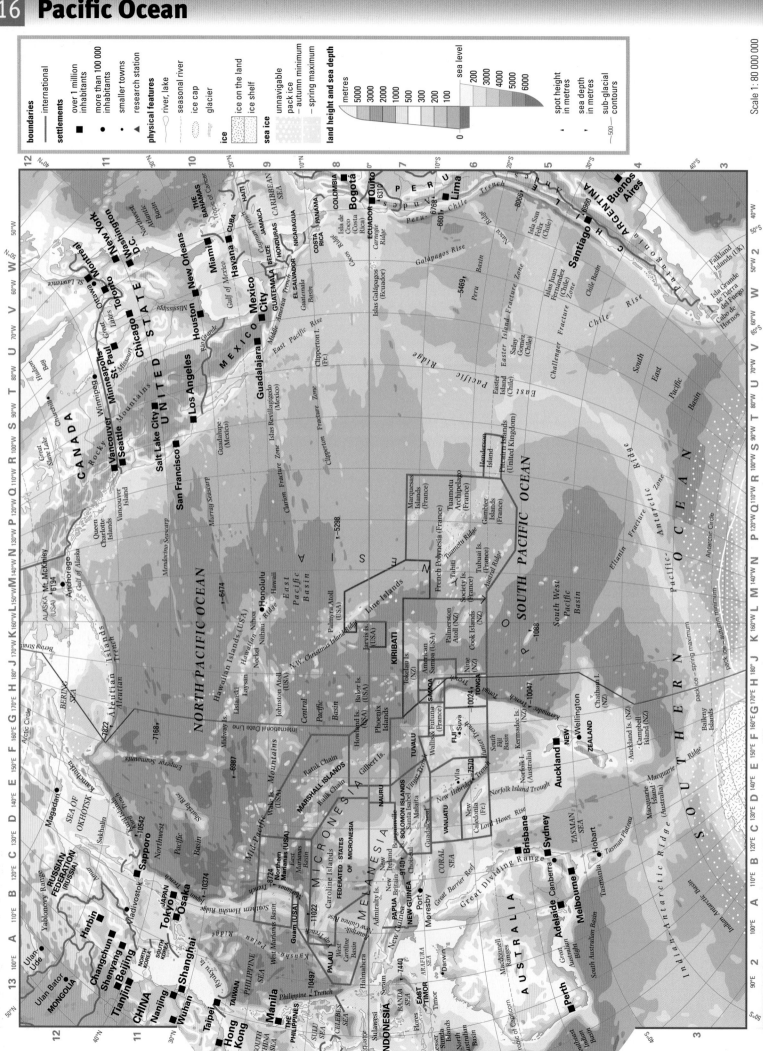

Scale 1 : 80 000 000

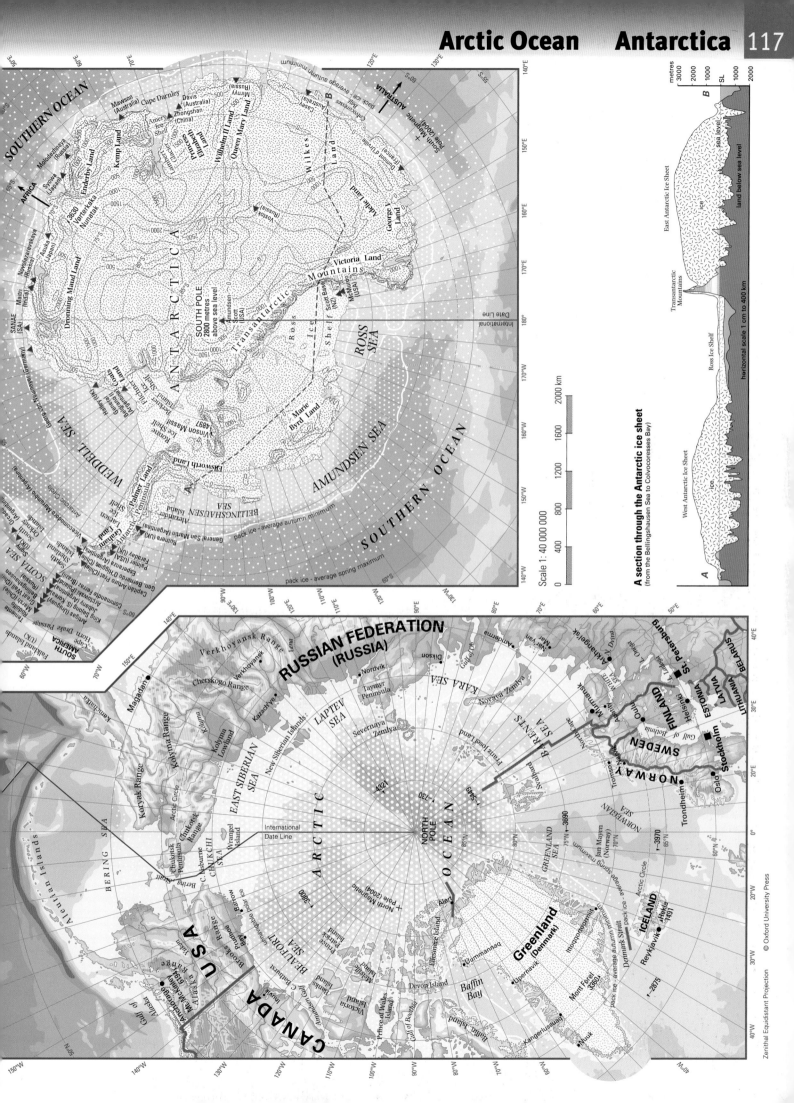

© Oxford University Press

Equatorial scale 1: 95 000 000 (main map)

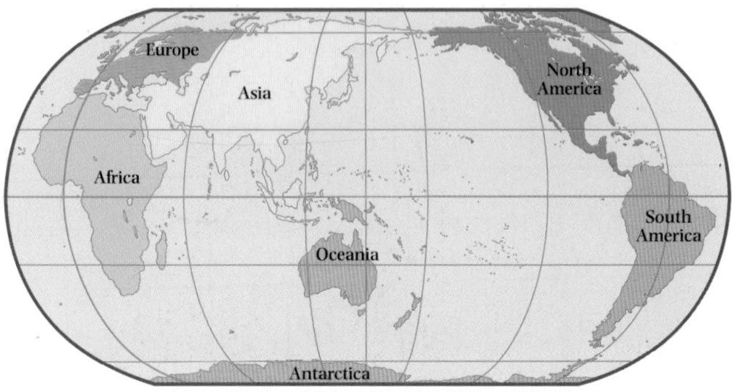

—— international boundary
• capital city

Labels (main map):

10 9 8 7 6 5 4 3

180° A 160°W B 140°W C 120°W D 100°W E 80°W F 60°W G 40°W H 20°W

80°N
Arctic Circle
60°N
40°N
Tropic of Cancer
20°N
Equator 0°
20°S
Tropic of Capricorn
40°S
Antarctic Circle

Greenland (Denmark)
Jan M... (No...

USA
CANADA

Nuuk
Reykjavik • ICELAND
Fae... (De...

REPUBLIC OF IRELAND
Dublin •

Ottawa

UNITED STATES OF AMERICA
Washington D.C.

NORTH ATLANTIC OCEAN

Azores (Portugal)
PORTUGAL
Lisbon •

Madeira (Portugal)
Ra...

Bermuda (UK)
Canary Islands (Spain)
MORO...

MEXICO
THE BAHAMAS
Laayoune
WESTERN SAHARA

Havana
CUBA

Mexico City
JAMAICA
HAITI
DOMINICAN REPUBLIC
MAURITANIA

BELIZE
Belmopan
Kingston
Puerto Rico (USA)
ANTIGUA AND BARBUDA
Nouakchott

GUATEMALA
Guatemala City
ST. KITTS AND NEVIS
DOMINICA
CAPE VERDE
Dakar
SENEGAL

HONDURAS
Tegucigalpa
ST. LUCIA
THE GAMBIA
Bamako

San Salvador
EL SALVADOR
NICARAGUA
ST. VINCENT AND THE GRENADINES
BARBADOS
GUINEA-BISSAU
GUINEA

Managua
GRENADA
Conakry
SIERRA LEONE
C...

COSTA RICA
San José
TRINIDAD AND TOBAGO
Freetown
Ouaga...
Yamous...

PANAMA
Panama City
Caracas
VENEZUELA
Monrovia
LIBERIA

COLOMBIA
Bogotá
Georgetown
GUYANA
SURINAME
Paramaribo
Cayenne
French Guiana (France)

Hawaiian Islands (USA)

PACIFIC OCEAN

Galapagos Islands (Ecuador)
Quito
ECUADOR

KIRIBATI

PERU
Lima

BRAZIL

American Samoa
SAMOA
French Polynesia (France)

Ascension Isla...

Cook Islands (New Zealand)

La Paz
BOLIVIA
Brasilia

St. Helena (...

TONGA
Pitcairn Island (UK)

PARAGUAY
Asunción

CHILE
SOUTH

Easter Island (Chile)
Santiago
URUGUAY
Buenos Aires
Montevideo
ARGENTINA
ATLANTI...

Chatham Islands (NZ)
Tristan da Cunha (UK)
OCEAN

Falkland Islands (UK)
South Georgia (UK)

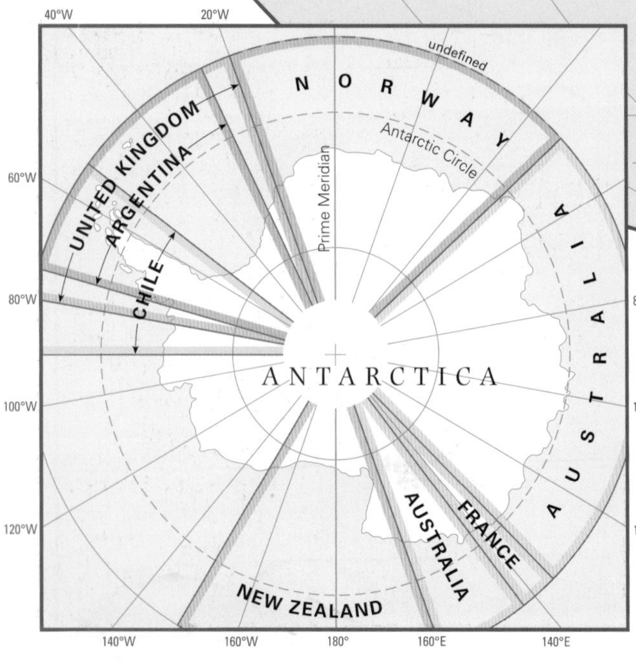

Antarctic Circle

ANTA...

A 160°W B 140°W C 120°W D 100°W E 80°W F 60°W G 40°W H 20°W

Inset map (Antarctica):

40°W 20°W
60°W
80°W
100°W
120°W
140°W 160°W 180° 160°E 140°E

undefined
NORWAY
Antarctic Circle
UNITED KINGDOM
ARGENTINA
CHILE
Prime Meridian
ANTARCTICA
AUSTRALIA
FRANCE
AUSTRALIA
NEW ZEALAND

80°E
100°E
120°E

Inset world map:

Europe
Asia
North America
Africa
Oceania
South America
Antarctica

The main map on this page is centred on the Greenwich meridian. World maps used in Oceania usually have the Pacific Ocean at the centre.

© Oxford University Press

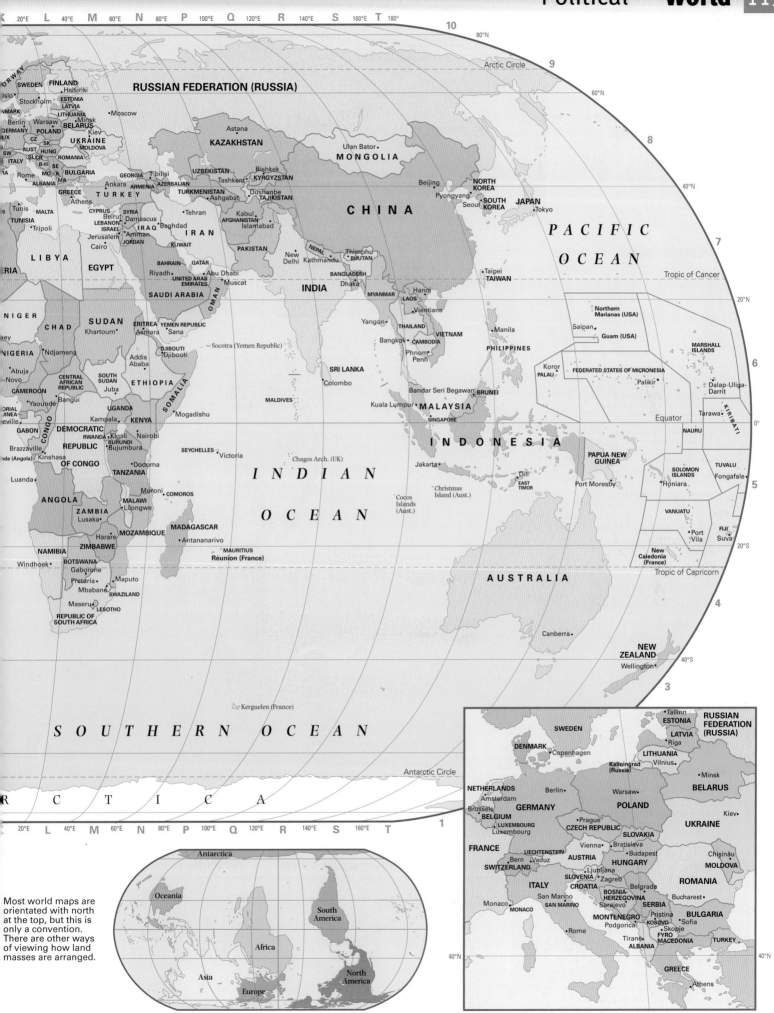

RUSSIAN FEDERATION (RUSSIA)

KAZAKHSTAN

MONGOLIA

CHINA

NORTH KOREA

JAPAN

PACIFIC OCEAN

Tropic of Cancer

LIBYA

EGYPT

SAUDI ARABIA

INDIA

MYANMAR

TAIWAN

LAOS

THAILAND

VIETNAM

CAMBODIA

PHILIPPINES

Northern Marianas (USA)

Guam (USA)

MARSHALL ISLANDS

SRI LANKA

MALDIVES

FEDERATED STATES OF MICRONESIA

KIRIBATI

MALAYSIA

SINGAPORE

INDONESIA

PAPUA NEW GUINEA

NAURU

Equator

SEYCHELLES

BRUNEI

Chagos Arch. (UK)

INDIAN OCEAN

SOLOMON ISLANDS

TUVALU

EAST TIMOR

Christmas Island (Aust.)

Cocos Islands (Aust.)

VANUATU

FIJI

MADAGASCAR

MAURITIUS
Réunion (France)

AUSTRALIA

NEW CALEDONIA (France)

Tropic of Capricorn

NEW ZEALAND

SOUTHERN OCEAN

Kerguelen (France)

Antarctic Circle

A R C T I C A

Most world maps are orientated with north at the top, but this is only a convention. There are other ways of viewing how land masses are arranged.

Antarctica

Oceania

South America

Africa

Asia

Europe

North America

SWEDEN

DENMARK
Copenhagen

ESTONIA
Tallinn

LATVIA
Riga

RUSSIAN FEDERATION (RUSSIA)

LITHUANIA

Kaliningrad (Russia)

Vilnius

Minsk

NETHERLANDS
Amsterdam

Berlin

BELARUS

Brussels
BELGIUM

GERMANY

Warsaw

POLAND

Kiev

UKRAINE

LUXEMBOURG
Luxembourg

Prague
CZECH REPUBLIC

FRANCE

LIECHTENSTEIN

Vienna

Bratislava

SLOVAKIA

Chișinău

MOLDOVA

Bern
SWITZERLAND

Vaduz

AUSTRIA

Budapest

HUNGARY

ROMANIA

SLOVENIA

Ljubljana

Zagreb

Belgrade

Bucharest

ITALY

San Marino
SAN MARINO

CROATIA

BOSNIA-HERZEGOVINA
Sarajevo

SERBIA

BULGARIA

Monaco
MONACO

Rome

MONTENEGRO
Podgorica

KOSOVO
Pristina

Sofia

Tirane

Skopje

FYRO MACEDONIA

TURKEY

ALBANIA

GREECE

Athens

Equatorial scale 1: 95 000 000

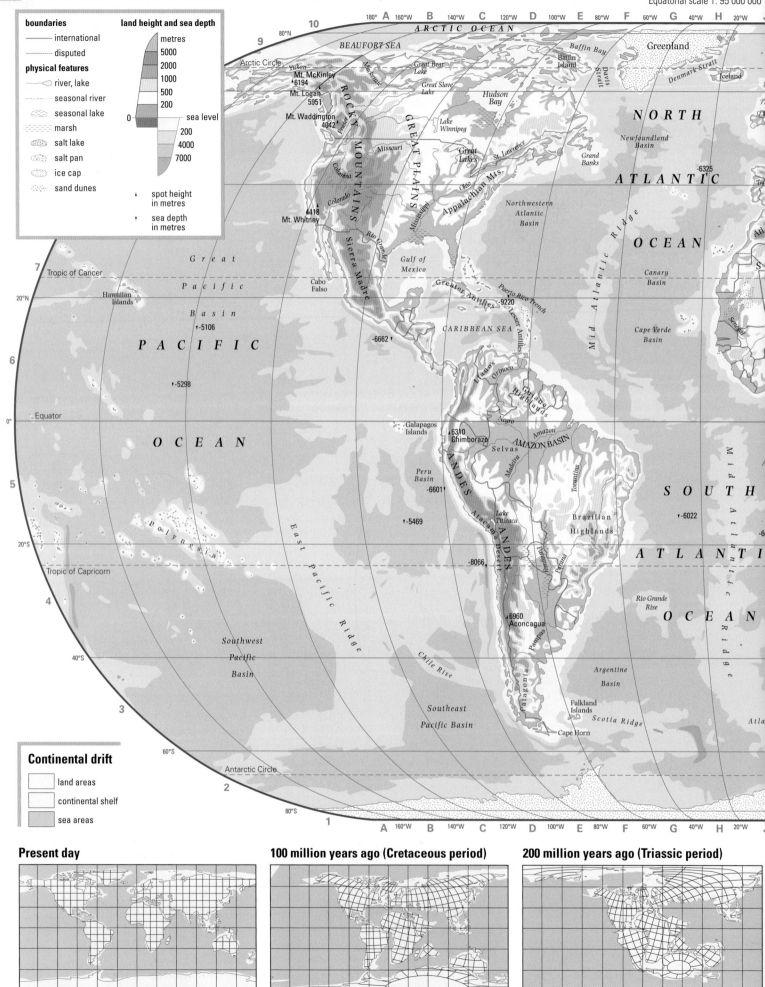

boundaries
—— international
········ disputed

physical features
～ river, lake
––– seasonal river
seasonal lake
marsh
salt lake
salt pan
ice cap
sand dunes

land height and sea depth
metres
5000
2000
1000
500
200
0 — sea level
200
4000
7000

▲ spot height in metres
▼ sea depth in metres

Continental drift
land areas
continental shelf
sea areas

ARCTIC OCEAN
BEAUFORT SEA
Arctic Circle
Yukon
Mt. McKinley 6194
Mt. Logan 5951
Mt. Waddington 4042
Fraser
Columbia
ROCKY MOUNTAINS
Missouri
Mackenzie
Great Bear Lake
Great Slave Lake
Lake Winnipeg
Hudson Bay
Baffin Bay
Baffin Island
Davis Strait
Greenland
Denmark Strait
Iceland
GREAT PLAINS
Great Lakes
St. Lawrence
Ohio
Mississippi
Appalachian Mts.
NORTH
Newfoundland Basin
Grand Banks
ATLANTIC
-6325
OCEAN
4418 Mt. Whitney
Sierra Madre
Rio Grande
Colorado
Gulf of Mexico
Cabo Falso
Northwestern Atlantic Basin
Mid Atlantic Ridge
Canary Basin
Tropic of Cancer
Great
Pacific
Hawaiian Islands
Basin
-5106
Greater Antilles
Lesser Antilles
Puerto Rico Trench
-9220
CARIBBEAN SEA
-6662
Cape Verde Basin
PACIFIC
-5298
OCEAN
Llanos
Orinoco
Guiana Highlands
Negro
Equator
Galapagos Islands
6310 Chimborazo
Selvas
Amazon
AMAZON BASIN
Madeira
ANDES
Tocantins
Mid Atlantic Ridge
SOUTH
-6022
Peru Basin
-6601
-5469
Lake Titicaca
Atacama Desert
Brazilian Highlands
ATLANTIC
Polynesia
Tropic of Capricorn
-8066
Paraguay
Paraná
OCEAN
East Pacific Ridge
Rio Grande Rise
Southwest Pacific Basin
Pampas
6960 Aconcagua
Patagonia
Chile Rise
Argentine Basin
Southeast Pacific Basin
Falkland Islands
Scotia Ridge
Cape Horn
Antarctic Circle

Present day

100 million years ago (Cretaceous period)

200 million years ago (Triassic period)

Eckert IV Projection   © Oxford University Press

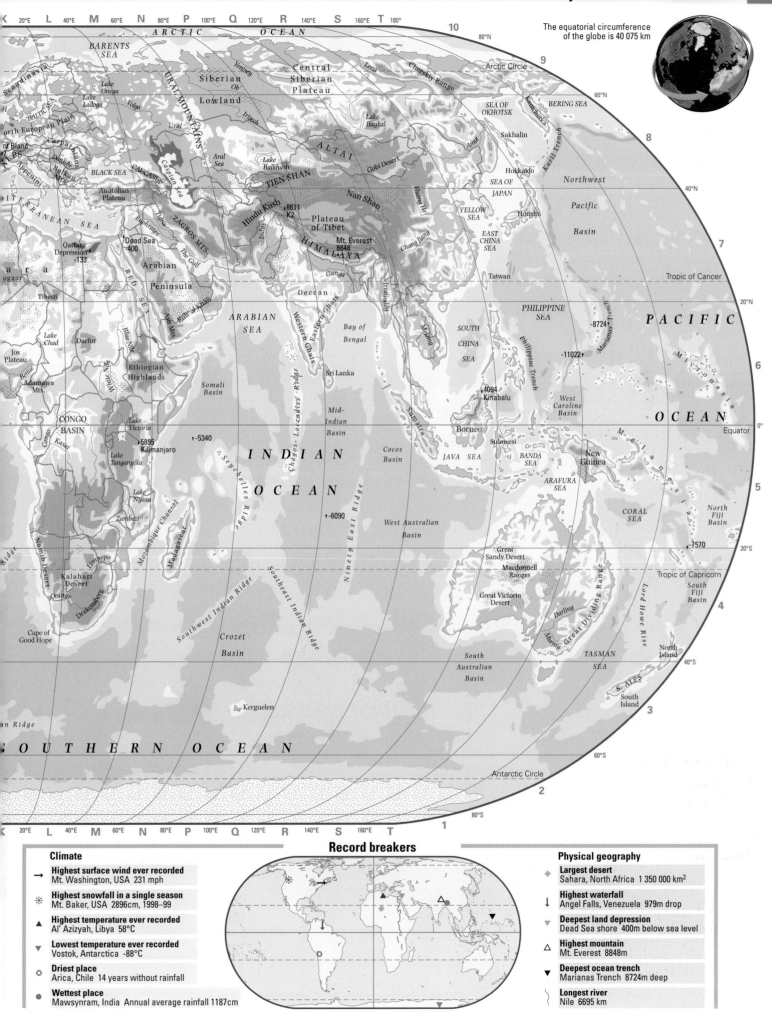

The equatorial circumference of the globe is 40 075 km

Climate

→ **Highest surface wind ever recorded**
Mt. Washington, USA 231 mph

✳ **Highest snowfall in a single season**
Mt. Baker, USA 2896cm, 1998–99

▲ **Highest temperature ever recorded**
Al' Azizyah, Libya 58°C

▼ **Lowest temperature ever recorded**
Vostok, Antarctica -88°C

✷ **Driest place**
Arica, Chile 14 years without rainfall

● **Wettest place**
Mawsynram, India Annual average rainfall 1187cm

Record breakers

Physical geography

◆ **Largest desert**
Sahara, North Africa 1 350 000 km²

↓ **Highest waterfall**
Angel Falls, Venezuela 979m drop

▽ **Deepest land depression**
Dead Sea shore 400m below sea level

△ **Highest mountain**
Mt. Everest 8848m

▼ **Deepest ocean trench**
Marianas Trench 8724m deep

〉 **Longest river**
Nile 6695 km

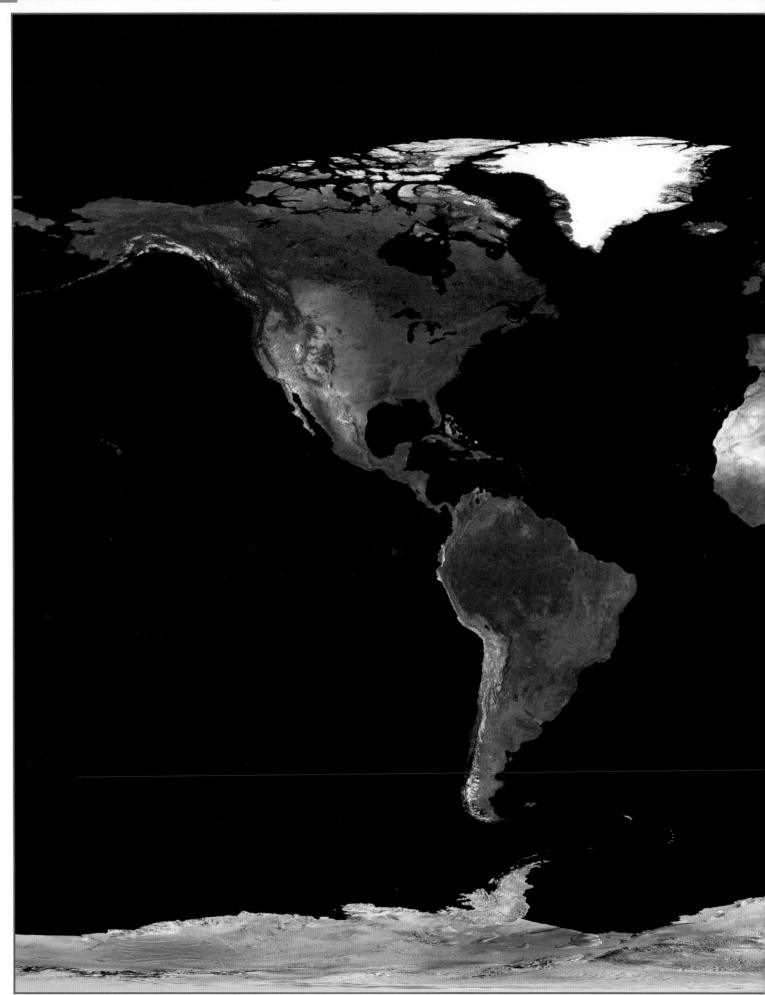

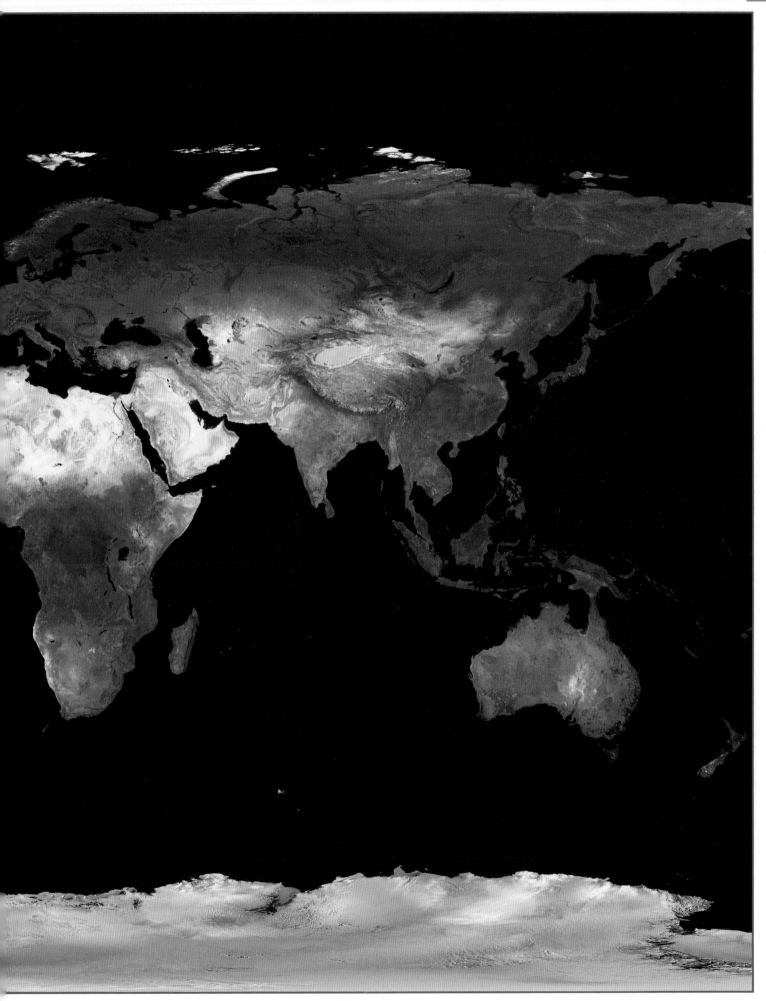

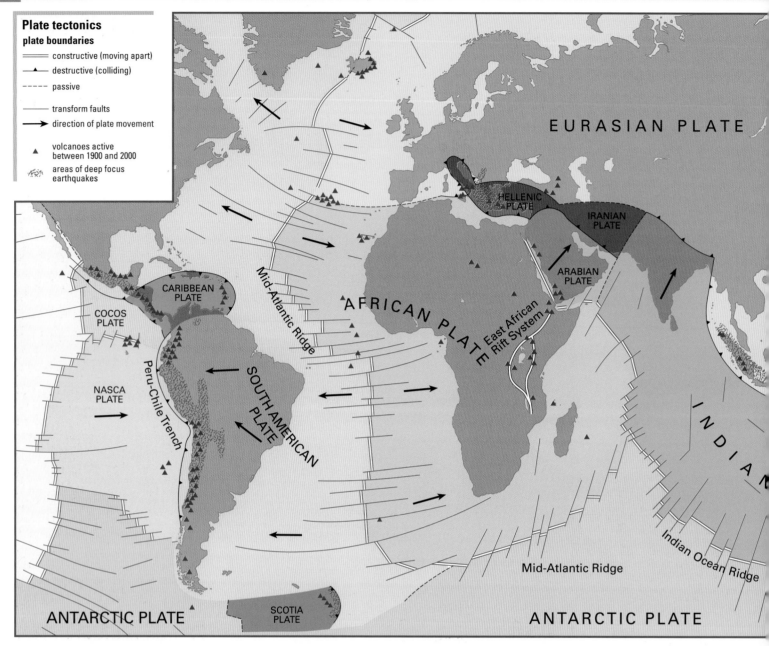

Plate tectonics
plate boundaries

	constructive (moving apart)
▲	destructive (colliding)
- - - -	passive
	transform faults
→	direction of plate movement
▲	volcanoes active between 1900 and 2000
	areas of deep focus earthquakes

EURASIAN PLATE

HELLENIC PLATE

IRANIAN PLATE

ARABIAN PLATE

AFRICAN PLATE

East African Rift System

CARIBBEAN PLATE

COCOS PLATE

NASCA PLATE

Mid-Atlantic Ridge

Peru-Chile Trench

SOUTH AMERICAN PLATE

INDIAN

Indian Ocean Ridge

Mid-Atlantic Ridge

ANTARCTIC PLATE

SCOTIA PLATE

ANTARCTIC PLATE

Mt. Etna, Italy

Deadliest volcanic eruptions, since 1741

Year	Place	Deaths
1741	Oshima, Japan	1475
1772	Papandayan, Indonesia	2957
1783	Asama, Japan	1377
1783	Lakagigar (Laki), Iceland	9350
1792	Unzen, Japan	14 300
1815	Tambora, Indonesia	92 000
1882	Galunggung, Indonesia	4011
1883	Krakatau, Indonesia	36 417
1902	Soufrière, St. Vincent	1680
1902	Mt. Pelée, Martinique	29 025
1911	Taal, Philippines	1335
1919	Kelut, Indonesia	5110
1951	Lamington, PNG	2942
1982	El Chichón, Mexico	2000
1985	Nevado del Ruiz, Colombia	25 000

Latest Volcanoes
http://volcanoes.usgs.gov

Latest Earthquakes
http://earthquakes.usgs.gov

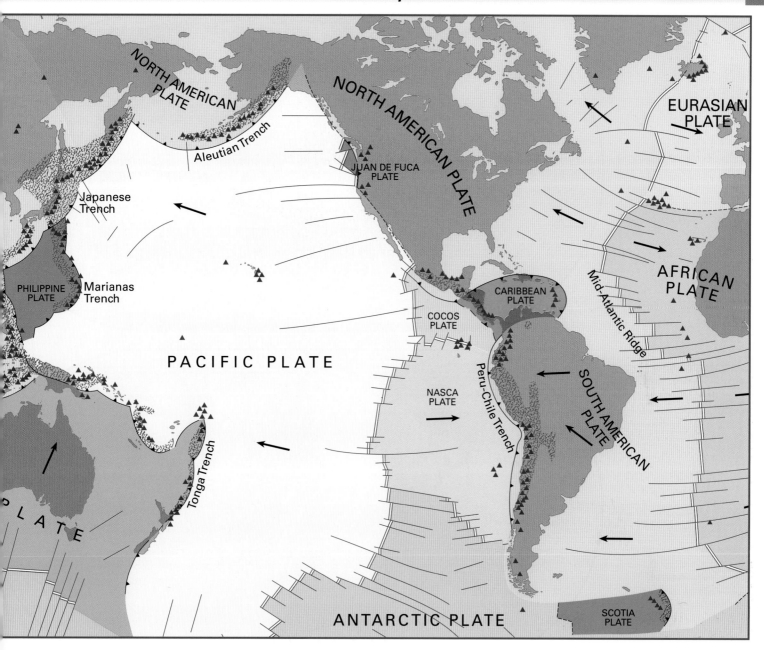

NORTH AMERICAN PLATE

Aleutian Trench

Japanese Trench

JUAN DE FUCA PLATE

PHILIPPINE PLATE

Marianas Trench

PACIFIC PLATE

Tonga Trench

NORTH AMERICAN PLATE

CARIBBEAN PLATE

COCOS PLATE

NASCA PLATE

Peru-Chile Trench

SOUTH AMERICAN PLATE

EURASIAN PLATE

Mid-Atlantic Ridge

AFRICAN PLATE

ANTARCTIC PLATE

SCOTIA PLATE

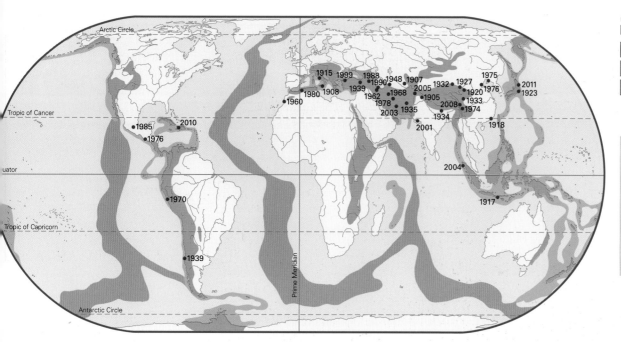

Arctic Circle

1915 1999 1988 1948 1907 1932 1927 1975
1980 1908 1939 1990 2005 1920 1976 2011
Tropic of Cancer 1962 1968 1933 1923
1960 1978 1905 2008 1974
2003 1935 1918
2010 1934
1985 2001
1976
Equator
1970
2004

Tropic of Capricorn

1939 1917

Antarctic Circle

Prime Meridian

Earthquakes

mobile areas (on land)

mobile areas (under sea)

mid-oceanic ridges

• earthquakes causing more than 10 000 deaths, 1900–2011

Earthquakes causing most deaths since 1900
Indonesia (2004) 283 106
China (1976) >255 000
Haiti (2010) 222 570
China (1920) 200 000
Japan (1923) 142 800
Turkmenistan (1948) 110 000
China (2008) 87 587
Pakistan (2005) >86 000
Italy (1908) >72 000
Peru (1970) 70 000
China (1927) 40 900
Turkey (1939) 32 700

Eckert IV Projection

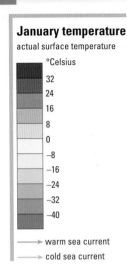

January temperature

actual surface temperature

°Celsius
- 32
- 24
- 16
- 8
- 0
- −8
- −16
- −24
- −32
- −40

→ warm sea current
→ cold sea current

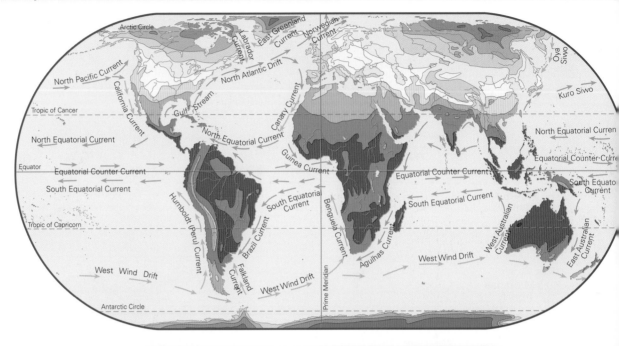

July temperature

actual surface temperature

°Celsius
- 32
- 24
- 16
- 8
- 0
- −8
- −16
- −24
- −32
- −40

→ warm sea current
→ cold sea current

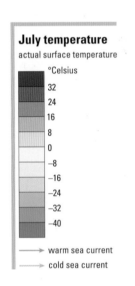

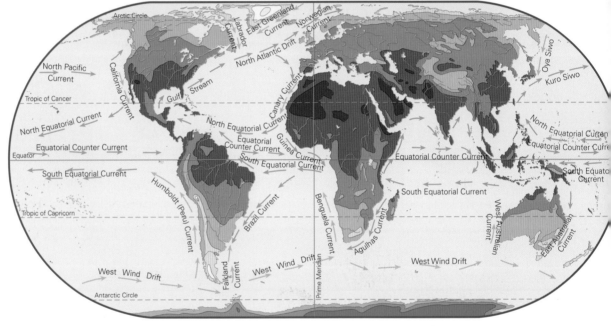

Global warming

predicted annual mean
temperature increase
by 2050

°Celsius
- 4.5
- 4.0
- 3.5
- 3.0
- 2.5
- 2.0
- 1.5
- 1.0

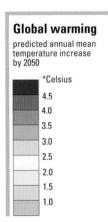

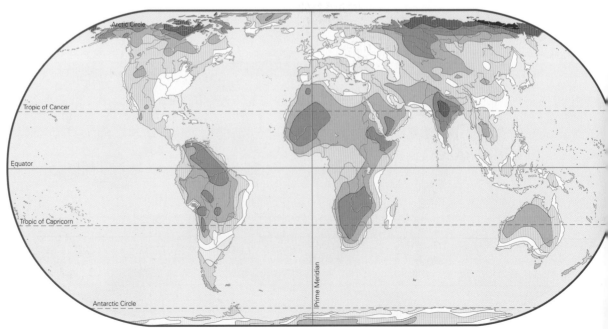

Eckert IV Projection   © Oxford University Press

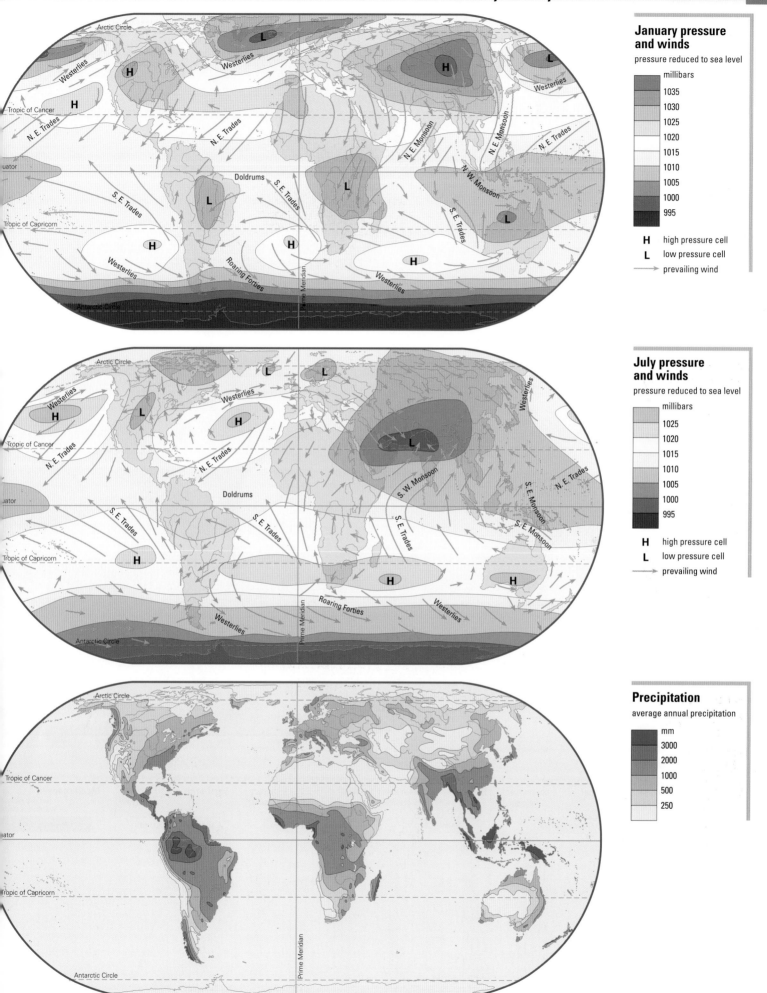

January pressure and winds

pressure reduced to sea level

millibars
- 1035
- 1030
- 1025
- 1020
- 1015
- 1010
- 1005
- 1000
- 995

H high pressure cell
L low pressure cell
→ prevailing wind

July pressure and winds

pressure reduced to sea level

millibars
- 1025
- 1020
- 1015
- 1010
- 1005
- 1000
- 995

H high pressure cell
L low pressure cell
→ prevailing wind

Precipitation

average annual precipitation

mm
- 3000
- 2000
- 1000
- 500
- 250

Equatorial scale 1: 105 000 000

World Meteorological Organization
www.wmo.int

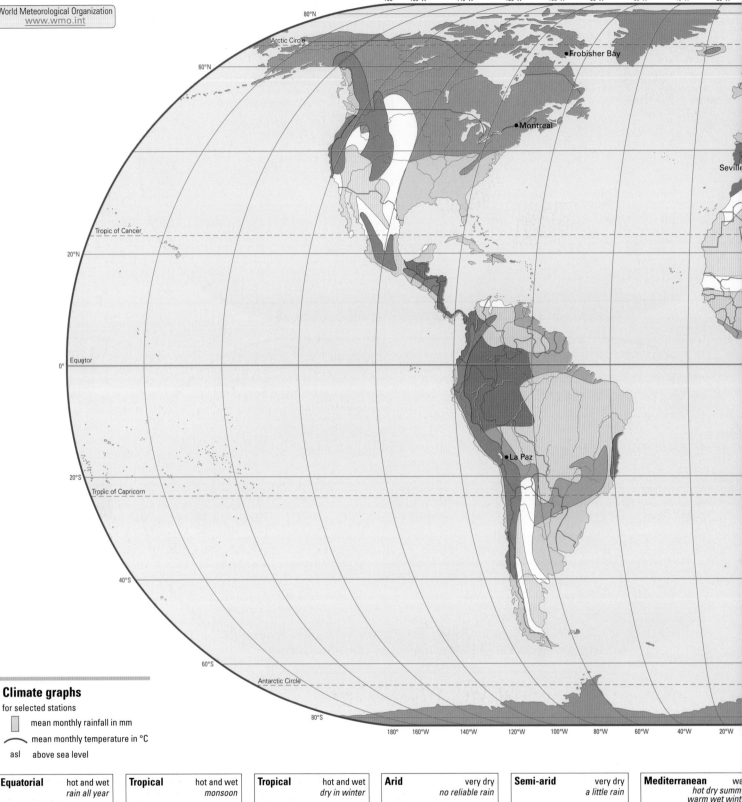

• Frobisher Bay

• Montreal

Seville

Arctic Circle

Tropic of Cancer

Equator

Tropic of Capricorn

• La Paz

Antarctic Circle

Climate graphs

for selected stations

mean monthly rainfall in mm

mean monthly temperature in °C

asl   above sea level

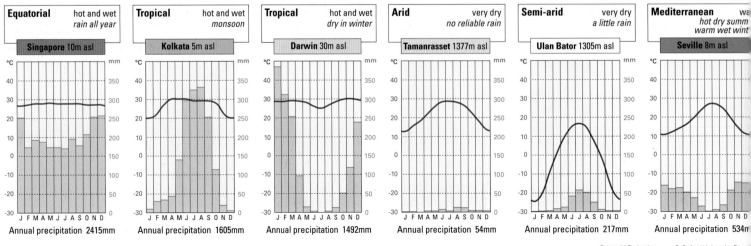

Equatorial	hot and wet rain all year

Singapore 10m asl

Annual precipitation 2415mm

Tropical	hot and wet monsoon

Kolkata 5m asl

Annual precipitation 1605mm

Tropical	hot and wet dry in winter

Darwin 30m asl

Annual precipitation 1492mm

Arid	very dry no reliable rain

Tamanrasset 1377m asl

Annual precipitation 54mm

Semi-arid	very dry a little rain

Ulan Bator 1305m asl

Annual precipitation 217mm

Mediterranean	wa hot dry summ warm wet wint

Seville 8m asl

Annual precipitation 534m

Eckert IV Projection   © Oxford University Press

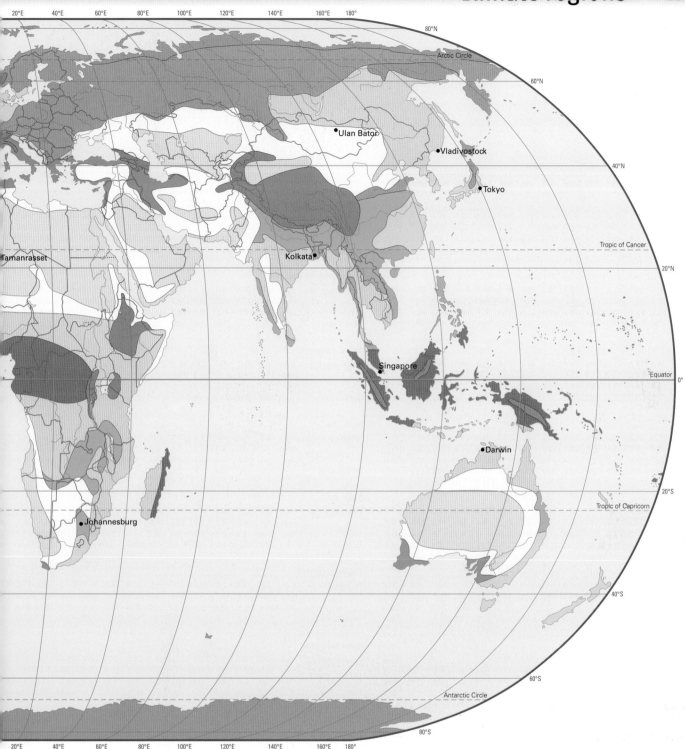

Map labels:
- 80°N
- Arctic Circle
- 60°N
- Ulan Bator
- Vladivostock
- 40°N
- Tokyo
- Tropic of Cancer
- 20°N
- Tamanrasset
- Kolkata
- Singapore
- Equator 0°
- Darwin
- 20°S
- Tropic of Capricorn
- Johannesburg
- 40°S
- 60°S
- Antarctic Circle
- 80°S

Longitude labels: 20°E 40°E 60°E 80°E 100°E 120°E 140°E 160°E 180°

Temperate	mild
warm wet summers	
cool dry winters	

| Johannesburg 1665m asl |

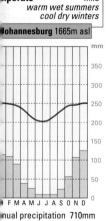

Annual precipitation 710mm

Temperate	mild and wet
warm summers	
no dry season	

| Tokyo 6m asl |

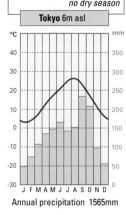

Annual precipitation 1565mm

Continental	cold and wet
warm wet summers	
cold wet winters	

| Montréal 57m asl |

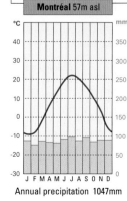

Annual precipitation 1047mm

Continental	cold and wet
warm wet summers	
cold dry winters	

| Vladivostock 29m asl |

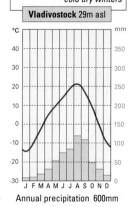

Annual precipitation 600mm

Polar	very cold and dry
no warm season	
fairly dry	

| Frobisher Bay 21m asl |

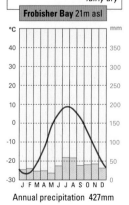

Annual precipitation 427mm

Mountain	height of the land strongly affects the climate
heavy rain or snow	

| La Paz 3632m asl |

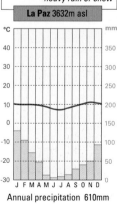

Annual precipitation 610mm

Climate data

Averages are for 1961–1990

Denver 1626m   climate station and its height above sea level

Temperature (°C)
- **high** average daily maximum temperature
- **mean** average monthly temperature
- **low** average daily minimum temperature

Rainfall (mm)   average monthly precipitation

Met Office world weather
www.metoffice.gov.uk/weather/world

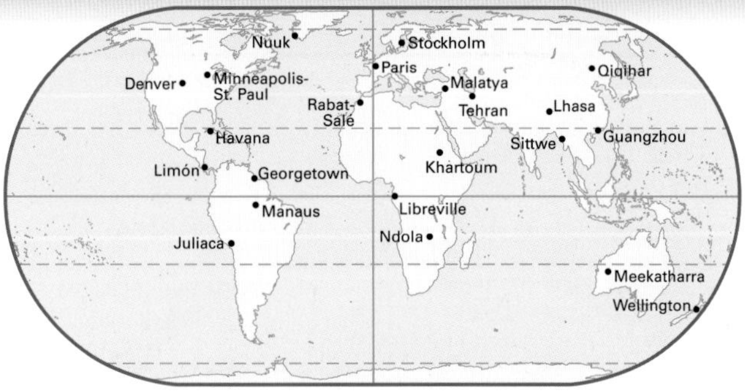

Denver 1626m

	Jan	Feb	Mar	Apr	May	Jun	Jul	Aug	Sep	Oct	Nov	Dec	YEAR
Temperature (°C) high	6.2	8.1	11.2	16.6	21.6	27.4	31.2	29.9	24.9	19.1	11.4	6.9	17.9
mean	-1.3	0.8	3.9	9.0	14.0	19.4	23.1	21.9	16.8	10.8	3.9	-0.6	10.1
low	-8.8	-6.6	-3.4	1.4	6.4	11.3	14.8	13.8	8.7	2.4	-3.7	-8.1	2.4
Rainfall (mm)	13	15	33	43	61	46	49	38	32	25	22	16	393

Georgetown 2m

	Jan	Feb	Mar	Apr	May	Jun	Jul	Aug	Sep	Oct	Nov	Dec	YEAR
Temperature (°C) high	28.6	28.9	29.2	29.5	29.4	29.2	29.6	30.2	30.8	30.8	30.2	29.1	29.6
mean	26.1	26.4	26.7	27.0	26.8	26.5	26.6	27.0	27.5	27.6	27.2	26.4	26.8
low	23.6	23.9	24.2	24.4	24.3	23.8	23.5	23.8	24.2	24.4	24.2	23.8	24.0
Rainfall (mm)	185	89	111	141	286	328	268	201	98	107	186	262	2262

Guangzhou 42m

	Jan	Feb	Mar	Apr	May	Jun	Jul	Aug	Sep	Oct	Nov	Dec	YEAR
Temperature (°C) high	18.3	18.4	21.6	25.5	29.4	31.3	32.7	32.6	31.4	28.6	24.4	20.5	26.2
mean	13.3	14.3	17.7	21.9	25.6	27.3	28.5	28.3	27.1	24.0	19.4	15.0	21.9
low	5.0	6.6	10.7	16.1	20.7	23.5	25.7	25.2	22.6	17.6	11.9	6.5	16.0
Rainfall (mm)	43	65	85	182	284	258	228	221	172	79	42	24	1683

Havana 50m

	Jan	Feb	Mar	Apr	May	Jun	Jul	Aug	Sep	Oct	Nov	Dec	YEAR
Temperature (°C) high	25.8	26.1	27.6	28.6	29.8	30.5	31.3	31.6	31.0	29.2	27.7	26.5	28.8
mean	22.2	22.4	23.7	24.8	26.1	26.9	27.6	27.8	27.4	26.2	24.5	23.0	25.2
low	18.6	18.6	19.7	20.9	22.4	23.4	23.8	24.1	23.8	23.0	21.3	19.5	21.6
Rainfall (mm)	64	69	46	54	98	182	106	100	144	181	88	58	1190

Juliaca 3827m

	Jan	Feb	Mar	Apr	May	Jun	Jul	Aug	Sep	Oct	Nov	Dec	YEAR
Temperature (°C) high	16.7	16.7	16.5	16.8	16.6	16.0	16.0	17.0	17.6	18.6	18.8	17.7	17.1
mean	10.2	10.1	9.9	8.7	6.4	4.5	4.3	5.8	8.1	9.5	10.2	10.4	8.2
low	3.6	3.5	3.2	0.6	-3.8	-7.0	-7.5	-5.4	-1.4	0.3	1.5	3.0	-0.8
Rainfall (mm)	133	109	99	43	10	3	2	6	22	41	55	86	609

Khartoum 380m

	Jan	Feb	Mar	Apr	May	Jun	Jul	Aug	Sep	Oct	Nov	Dec	YEAR
Temperature (°C) high	30.8	33.0	36.8	40.1	41.9	41.3	38.4	37.3	39.1	39.3	35.2	31.8	37.1
mean	23.2	25.0	28.7	31.9	34.5	34.3	32.1	31.5	32.5	32.4	28.1	24.5	29.9
low	15.6	17.0	20.5	23.6	27.1	27.3	25.9	25.3	26.0	25.5	21.0	17.1	22.7
Rainfall (mm)	0	0	0	0.5	4	5	46	75	25	5	1	0	161

Lhasa 3650m

	Jan	Feb	Mar	Apr	May	Jun	Jul	Aug	Sep	Oct	Nov	Dec	YEAR
Temperature (°C) high	6.9	9.0	12.1	15.6	19.3	22.7	22.1	21.1	19.7	16.3	11.2	7.7	15.3
mean	-2.1	1.1	4.6	8.1	11.9	15.5	15.3	14.5	12.8	8.1	2.2	-1.7	7.5
low	-10.1	-6.8	-3.0	0.9	5.0	9.3	10.1	9.4	7.5	1.3	-4.9	-9.0	0.8
Rainfall (mm)	1	1	2	5	27	72	119	123	58	10	2	1	421

Libreville 15m

	Jan	Feb	Mar	Apr	May	Jun	Jul	Aug	Sep	Oct	Nov	Dec	YEAR
Temperature (°C) high	29.5	30.0	30.2	30.1	29.4	27.6	26.4	26.8	27.5	28.0	28.4	29.0	28.6
mean	26.8	27.0	27.1	26.6	26.7	25.4	24.3	24.3	25.4	25.7	25.9	26.2	26.0
low	24.1	24.0	23.9	23.1	24.0	23.2	22.1	21.8	23.4	23.4	23.4	23.4	23.3
Rainfall (mm)	250	243	363	339	247	54	7	14	104	427	490	303	2841

Limón 3m

	Jan	Feb	Mar	Apr	May	Jun	Jul	Aug	Sep	Oct	Nov	Dec	YEAR
Temperature (°C) high	27.9	28.6	29.6	29.6	28.5	27.5	27.7	27.7	27.2	27.0	27.1	27.7	28.0
mean	24.0	24.3	25.0	25.8	26.1	25.9	25.6	25.6	25.7	25.4	25.1	24.3	25.2
low	20.3	20.3	20.9	21.6	22.2	22.3	22.1	22.1	22.2	21.9	21.6	20.9	21.5
Rainfall (mm)	319	201	193	287	281	276	408	289	163	198	367	402	3384

Malatya 849m

	Jan	Feb	Mar	Apr	May	Jun	Jul	Aug	Sep	Oct	Nov	Dec	YEAR
Temperature (°C) high	2.9	5.3	11.1	18.2	23.5	29.2	33.8	33.4	28.9	20.9	11.8	5.7	18.7
mean	-0.4	1.5	6.9	13.0	17.8	22.9	27.0	26.5	22.0	14.8	7.6	2.4	13.5
low	-3.2	-1.7	2.4	7.7	11.8	16.1	19.8	19.4	15.2	9.5	3.7	-0.3	8.4
Rainfall (mm)	42	36	60	61	50	22	3	2	6	40	47	42	411

Manaus 84m

	Jan	Feb	Mar	Apr	May	Jun	Jul	Aug	Sep	Oct	Nov	Dec	YEAR
Temperature (°C) high	30.5	30.4	30.6	30.7	30.8	31.0	31.3	32.6	32.9	32.8	32.1	31.3	31.4
mean	26.1	26.0	26.1	26.3	26.3	26.4	26.5	27.0	27.5	27.6	27.3	26.7	26.7
low	23.1	23.1	23.2	23.3	23.3	23.0	22.7	23.0	23.5	23.7	23.7	23.5	23.3
Rainfall (mm)	260	288	314	300	256	114	88	58	83	126	183	217	2287

Meekatharra 518m

	Jan	Feb	Mar	Apr	May	Jun	Jul	Aug	Sep	Oct	Nov	Dec	YE
Temperature (°C) high	38.1	36.5	34.5	29.2	23.6	19.7	18.9	21.0	25.4	29.4	33.1	36.5	2
mean	31.2	30.1	28.0	23.2	17.8	14.3	13.2	14.8	18.4	22.2	25.9	29.3	2
low	24.3	23.7	21.5	17.1	11.9	8.9	7.5	8.5	11.4	15.0	18.6	22.1	1
Rainfall (mm)	26	30	22	17	27	36	25	12	6	7	14	11	2

Minneapolis-St. Paul 255m

	Jan	Feb	Mar	Apr	May	Jun	Jul	Aug	Sep	Oct	Nov	Dec	YE
Temperature (°C) high	-6.3	-3.0	4.0	13.6	20.8	26.0	28.9	27.1	21.5	14.9	5.0	-3.6	1
mean	-11.2	-7.8	-0.6	8.0	14.7	20.1	23.1	21.4	15.8	9.3	0.7	-7.8	
low	-16.2	-12.7	-5.2	2.3	8.7	14.2	17.3	15.7	10.2	3.8	-3.8	-12.1	
Rainfall (mm)	24	22	49	62	86	103	90	92	69	56	39	27	

Ndola 1270m

	Jan	Feb	Mar	Apr	May	Jun	Jul	Aug	Sep	Oct	Nov	Dec	YE
Temperature (°C) high	26.6	26.9	27.4	27.5	26.6	25.1	25.2	27.5	30.5	31.5	29.4	27.0	1
mean	20.8	20.8	21.0	20.5	18.6	16.5	16.7	19.2	22.5	23.7	22.5	21.0	1
low	17.1	17.1	16.5	14.4	10.8	7.9	7.8	10.2	13.6	16.2	17.1	17.2	1
Rainfall (mm)	29.3	249	170	46	4	1	0	0	3	32	130	306	12

Nuuk 70m

	Jan	Feb	Mar	Apr	May	Jun	Jul	Aug	Sep	Oct	Nov	Dec	YE
Temperature (°C) high	-4.4	-4.5	-4.8	-0.8	3.5	7.7	10.6	9.9	6.3	1.7	-1.0	-3.3	
mean	-7.4	-7.8	-8.0	-3.9	0.6	3.9	6.5	6.1	3.5	-0.6	-3.6	-6.2	
low	-10.1	-10.6	-10.6	-6.1	-1.5	1.3	3.8	3.8	1.6	-2.5	-5.8	-8.7	
Rainfall (mm)	39	47	50	46	55	62	82	89	88	70	74	54	

Paris 65m

	Jan	Feb	Mar	Apr	May	Jun	Jul	Aug	Sep	Oct	Nov	Dec	YE
Temperature (°C) high	6.0	7.6	10.8	14.4	18.2	21.5	24.0	23.8	20.8	16.0	10.1	6.8	1
mean	3.4	4.2	6.6	9.5	13.2	16.4	18.4	18.0	15.3	11.4	6.7	4.2	1
low	0.9	1.3	2.9	5.0	8.3	11.2	12.9	12.7	10.6	7.7	3.8	1.7	
Rainfall (mm)	54	46	54	47	63	58	84	52	54	56	56	56	6

Qiqihar 148m

	Jan	Feb	Mar	Apr	May	Jun	Jul	Aug	Sep	Oct	Nov	Dec	YE
Temperature (°C) high	-12.7	-7.8	2.3	12.9	21.0	26.2	27.8	26.1	20.1	11.1	-1.3	-10.4	
mean	-19.2	-14.8	-4.5	6.1	14.4	20.3	22.8	20.9	14.0	4.8	-7.1	-16.2	
low	-24.5	-20.9	-11.0	-0.9	7.3	14.2	17.9	16.2	8.5	-0.7	-12.0	-21.2	
Rainfall (mm)	1	1	5	15	31	64	138	94	45	19	4	4	4

Rabat Sale 75m

	Jan	Feb	Mar	Apr	May	Jun	Jul	Aug	Sep	Oct	Nov	Dec	YE
Temperature (°C) high	17.2	17.7	19.2	20.0	22.1	24.1	26.8	27.1	26.4	24.0	20.6	17.7	2
mean	12.6	13.1	14.2	15.2	17.4	19.8	22.2	22.4	21.5	19.0	15.9	13.2	
low	8.0	8.6	9.2	10.4	12.7	15.4	17.6	17.7	16.7	14.1	11.1	8.7	1
Rainfall (mm)	77	74	61	62	25	7	1	1	6	44	97	101	5

Sittwe 5m

	Jan	Feb	Mar	Apr	May	Jun	Jul	Aug	Sep	Oct	Nov	Dec	YE
Temperature (°C) high	28.0	29.4	31.4	34.1	31.5	29.5	28.9	28.9	30.1	31.1	30.3	28.5	3
mean	21.4	22.7	24.8	28.9	28.3	27.1	26.8	26.7	27.4	27.6	25.7	22.6	2
low	14.7	15.9	18.2	23.6	25.1	24.6	24.7	24.5	24.6	24.0	21.0	16.6	1
Rainfall (mm)	11	8	5	44	268	1091	1155	1025	537	289	105	17	45

Stockholm 52m

	Jan	Feb	Mar	Apr	May	Jun	Jul	Aug	Sep	Oct	Nov	Dec	YE
Temperature (°C) high	-0.7	-0.6	3.0	8.6	15.7	20.7	21.9	20.4	15.1	9.9	4.5	1.1	1
mean	-2.8	-3.0	0.1	4.6	10.7	15.6	17.2	16.2	11.9	7.5	2.6	-1.0	
low	-5.0	-5.3	-2.7	1.1	6.3	11.3	13.4	12.7	9.0	5.3	0.7	-3.2	
Rainfall (mm)	39	27	26	30	30	45	72	66	55	50	53	46	5

Tehran 1191m

	Jan	Feb	Mar	Apr	May	Jun	Jul	Aug	Sep	Oct	Nov	Dec	YE
Temperature (°C) high	7.2	9.9	15.4	21.9	28.0	34.1	36.8	35.4	31.5	24.0	16.5	9.8	2
mean	3.0	5.3	10.3	16.4	22.1	27.5	30.4	29.2	25.3	18.5	11.6	5.6	
low	-1.1	0.7	5.2	10.9	16.1	20.9	24.0	23.0	19.2	12.9	6.7	1.3	
Rainfall (mm)	37	34	37	28	15	3	3	1	1	14	21	36	2

Wellington 8m

	Jan	Feb	Mar	Apr	May	Jun	Jul	Aug	Sep	Oct	Nov	Dec	YE
Temperature (°C) high	21.3	21.1	19.8	17.3	14.8	12.8	12.0	12.7	14.2	15.9	17.8	19.6	1
mean	17.8	17.7	16.6	14.3	11.9	10.1	9.2	9.8	11.2	12.8	14.5	16.4	1
low	14.4	14.3	13.5	11.3	9.1	7.3	6.4	6.9	8.3	9.7	11.3	13.2	
Rainfall (mm)	67	48	76	87	99	113	111	106	82	81	74	74	1

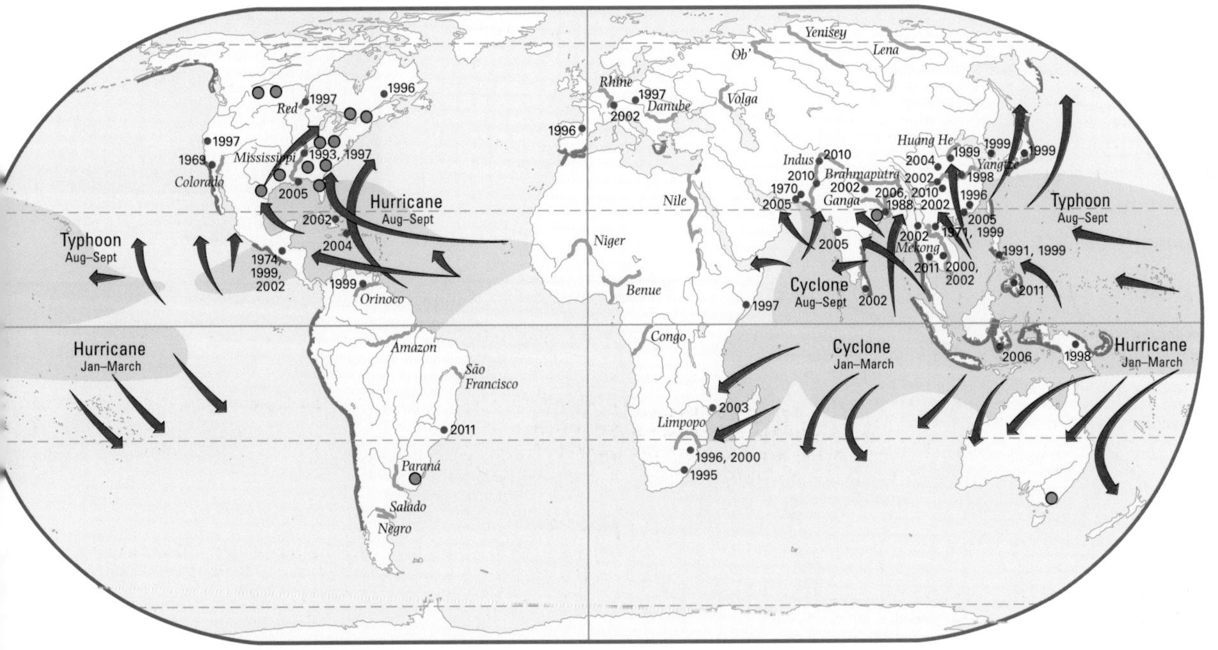
Yenisey
Lena
Ob'
Rhine
1997
Danube
2002
Volga
1996
1996
Red
1997
1997
1969
Mississippi
1993, 1997
Colorado
2005
Hurricane
Aug–Sept
2002
2004
Typhoon
Aug–Sept
1974, 1999, 2002
1999
Orinoco
Nile
Niger
Benue
1997
Congo
Amazon
São Francisco
2003
Limpopo
2011
1996, 2000
1995
Paraná
Salado
Negro
Indus
2010
Brahmaputra
1970
2005
Ganga
Huang He
Yangtze
Mekong
Cyclone
Aug–Sept
Typhoon
Aug–Sept
1991, 1999
2011
Cyclone
Jan–March
Hurricane
Jan–March
2006
1998
Hurricane
Jan–March

Storms and floods

- paths of revolving tropical storms
- areas affected by tropical storms
- coasts vulnerable to tsunamis (seismic sea waves)
- major river flood plains susceptible to flooding
- major floods
- areas affected by tornadoes

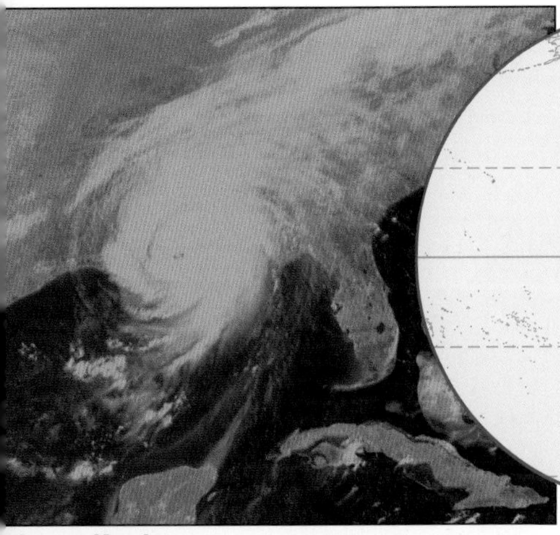

[Hu]rricane Katrina

[Win]ds in this hurricane reached 280km per hour [and] caused 1836 deaths. 29 August, 2005.

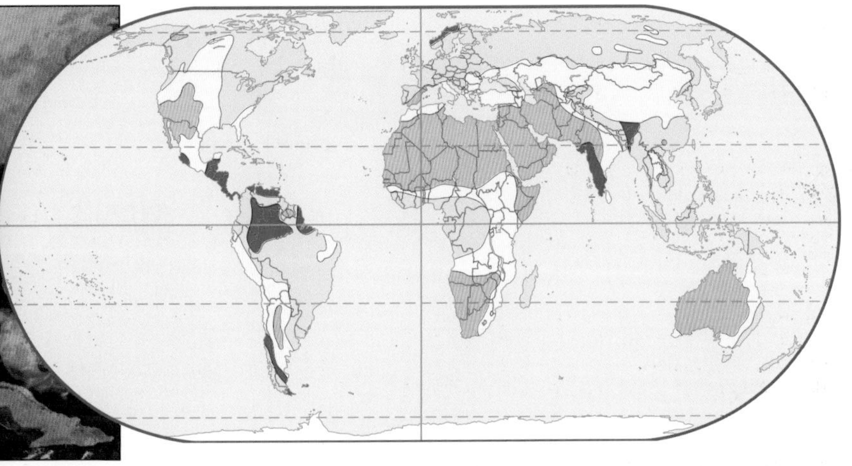

Water

Surplus

Enough water to support vegetation and crops without irrigation.

- large surplus
- surplus

Deficiency

Not enough water to support vegetation and crops without irrigation. After long periods of deficiency these areas may lose their natural vegetation.

- deficiency
- chronic deficiency

[El] Niño and La Niña

[Ch]anges to normal climatic conditions [as] a result of El Niño and La Niña

- dryer and warmer
- dryer
- dryer and cooler
- warmer
- cooler
- wetter and warmer
- wetter
- wetter and cooler

- air circulation
- trade winds
- sea movements

El Niño

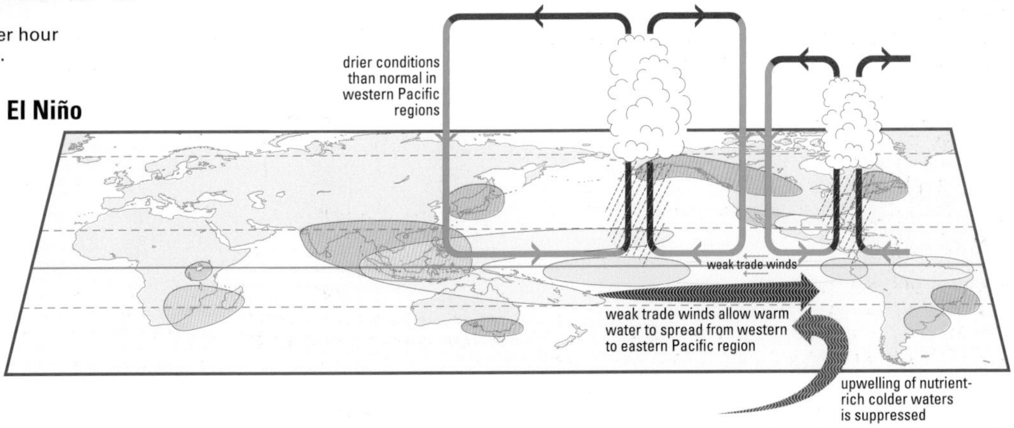
drier conditions than normal in western Pacific regions
weak trade winds
weak trade winds allow warm water to spread from western to eastern Pacific region
upwelling of nutrient-rich colder waters is suppressed

La Niña

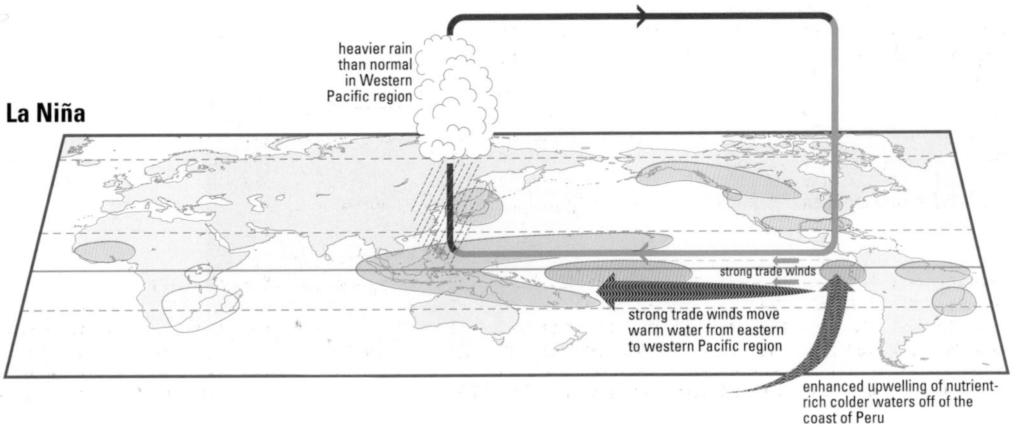
heavier rain than normal in Western Pacific region
strong trade winds
strong trade winds move warm water from eastern to western Pacific region
enhanced upwelling of nutrient-rich colder waters off of the coast of Peru

Equatorial scale 1: 105 000 000

Ecosystems

vegetation types are those which would occur naturally without interference by people

coniferous forest
cone bearing trees

deciduous and mixed forest
leaf shedding and coniferous trees

tropical rain forest
many species of lush, tall trees

tropical grasslands (savannah)
tall grass parkland with scattered trees

evergreen trees and shrubs
plants and small trees with leathery leaves

thorn forest
low trees and shrubs with spines or thorns

temperate grasslands
prairies, steppes, pampas, and veld

semi-desert
short grasses and drought-resistant scrub

desert
sand and stones, very little vegetation

tundra
moss and lichen, with few trees

ice
no vegetation

mountains
thin soils, steep slopes, and high altitude affects type of vegetation

ice
Aerial view of Jameson Land, towards Liverpool Land, Greenland

coniferous forest
MacMillan Provincial Park, British Columbia, Canada

temperate grasslands
Prairie, North Dakota, USA

tropical rain forest
Rain forest near Puerto Viejo, Costa Rica

thorn forest
Acacia shrubs, Tanzania

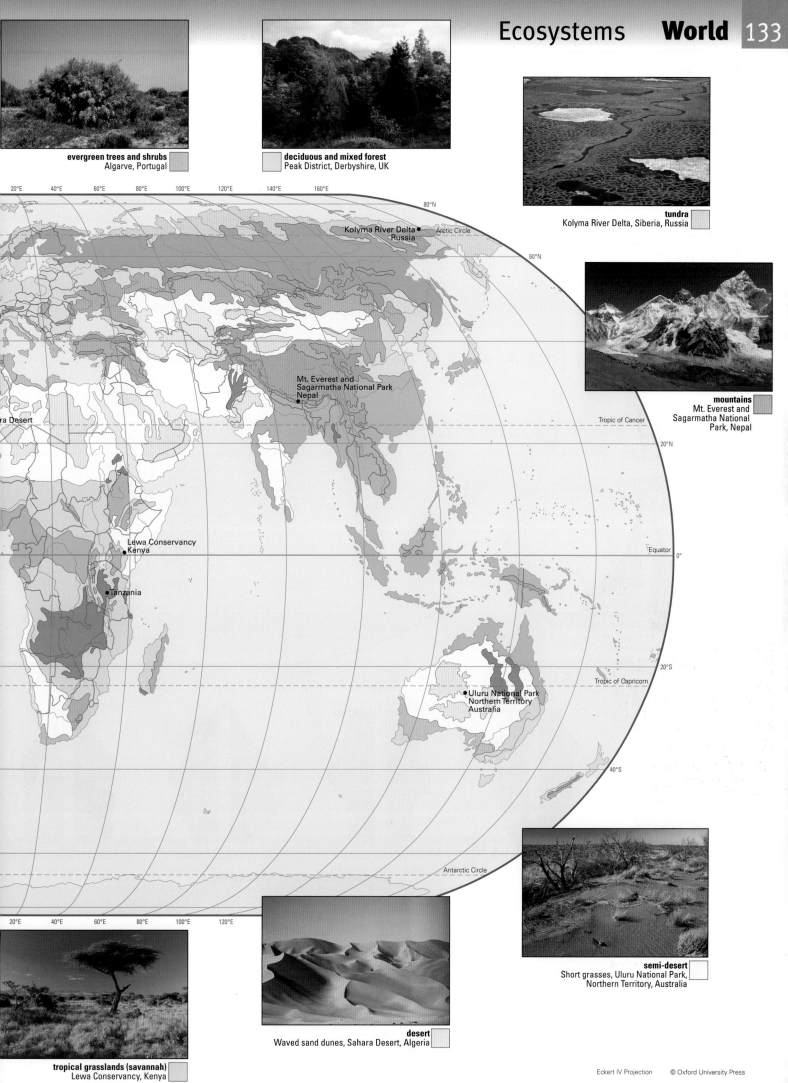

evergreen trees and shrubs
Algarve, Portugal

deciduous and mixed forest
Peak District, Derbyshire, UK

tundra
Kolyma River Delta, Siberia, Russia

mountains
Mt. Everest and Sagarmatha National Park, Nepal

Kolyma River Delta
Russia
Arctic Circle

80°N

60°N

Mt. Everest and
Sagarmatha National Park
Nepal

Tropic of Cancer

20°N

ra Desert

Lewa Conservancy
Kenya

Equator 0°

Tanzania

20°S

Tropic of Capricorn

Uluru National Park
Northern Territory
Australia

40°S

Antarctic Circle

20°E 40°E 60°E 80°E 100°E 120°E 140°E 160°E

20°E 40°E 60°E 80°E 100°E 120°E

semi-desert
Short grasses, Uluru National Park,
Northern Territory, Australia

desert
Waved sand dunes, Sahara Desert, Algeria

tropical grasslands (savannah)
Lewa Conservancy, Kenya

Population density
people per square kilometre

- over 200
- 100–200
- 50–100
- 5–50
- 1–5
- under 1

Major cities
population in millions

- ■ over 10
- ▣ 5–10
- ☐ 1–5

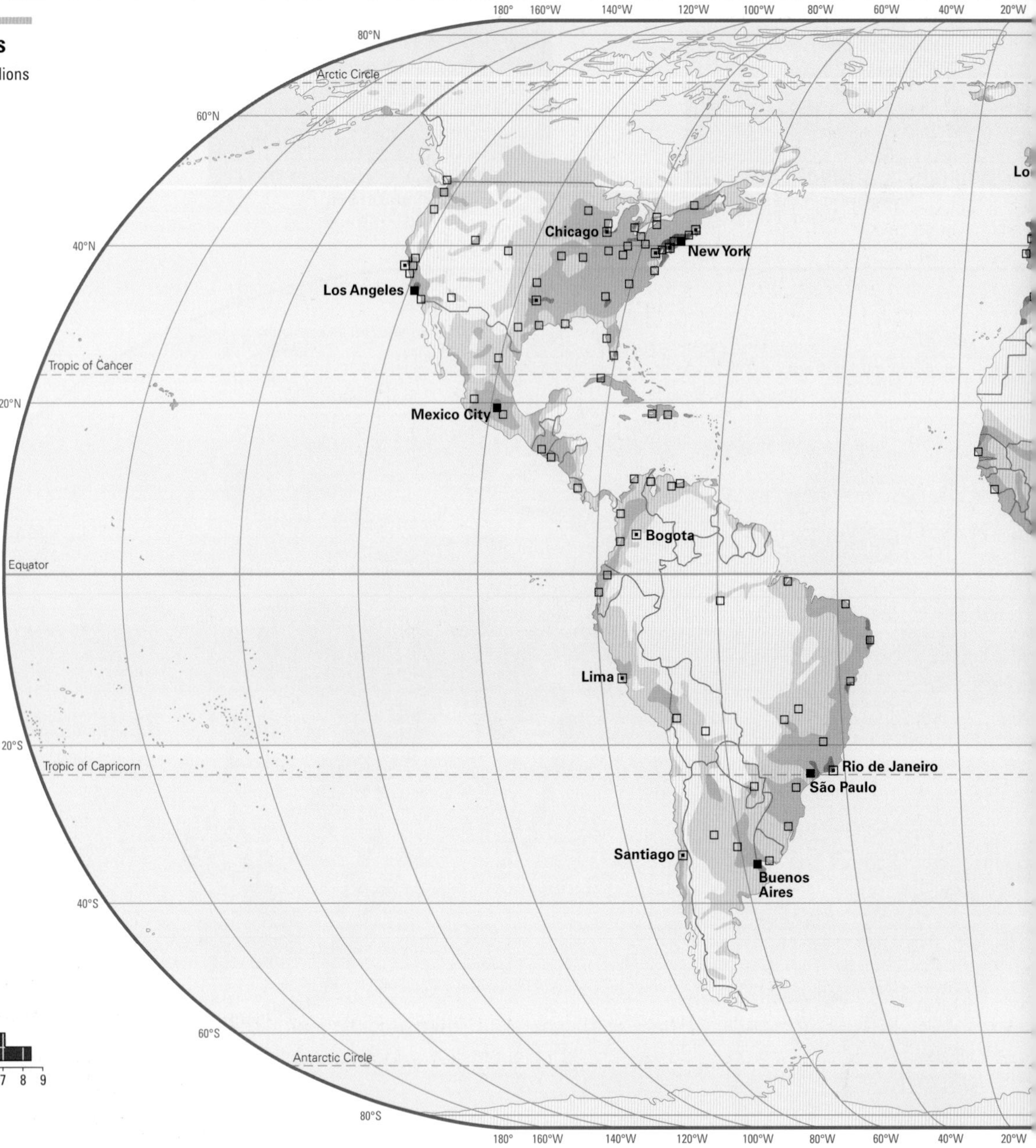

Population structure, 2009

World
males   Age   females

percent of total population

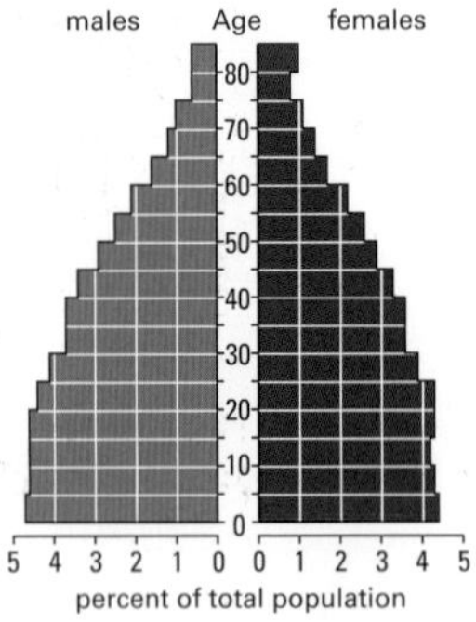

Total population: 6 776 763 237
Land area: 148 940 000km²

Kenya
males   Age   females

percent of total population

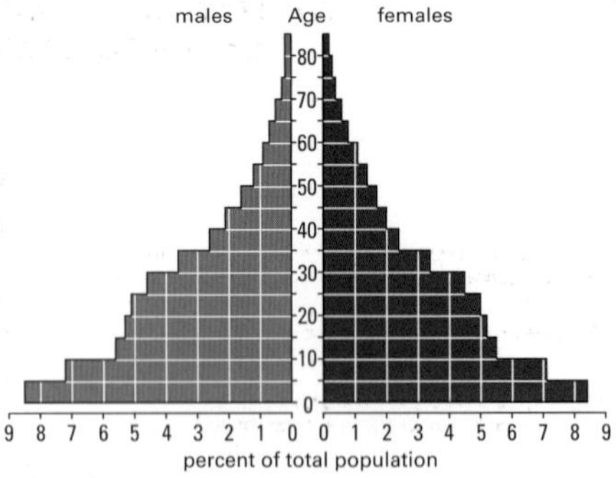

Total population: 39 002 772
Land area: 580 367km²

Brazil
males   Age   females

percent of total population

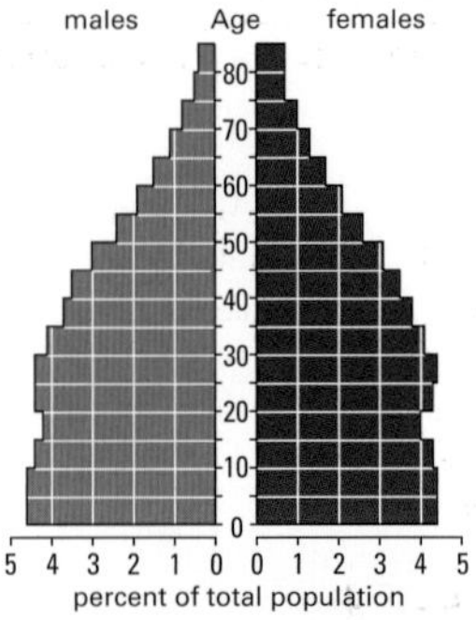

Total population: 198 739 269
Land area: 8 547 403km²

Japan
males   Age   females

percent of total population

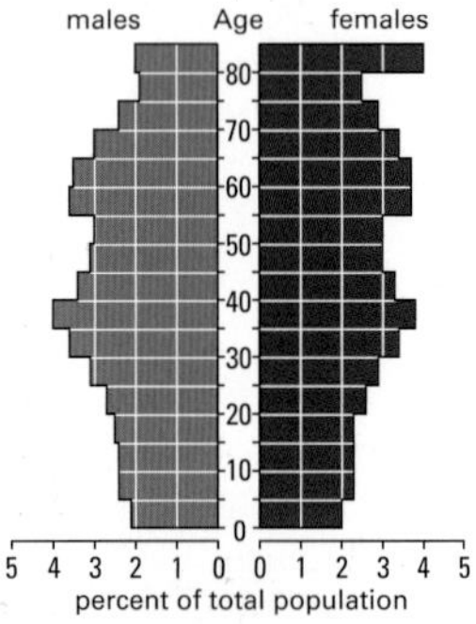

Total population: 127 078 679
Land area: 377 801km²

Italy
males   Age   females

percent of total population

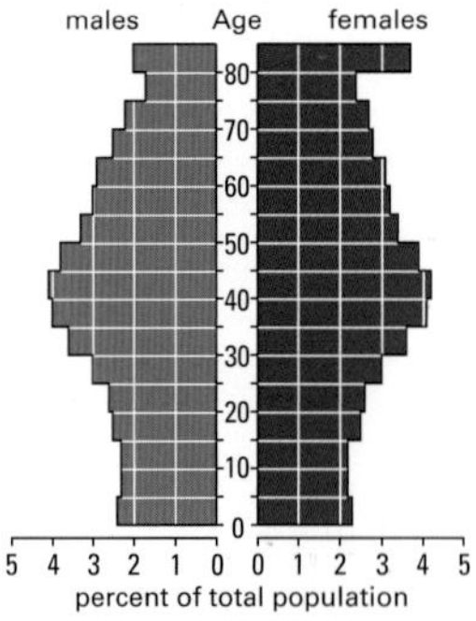

Total population: 60 461 585
Land area: 301 268km²

China
males   Age   females

percent of total population

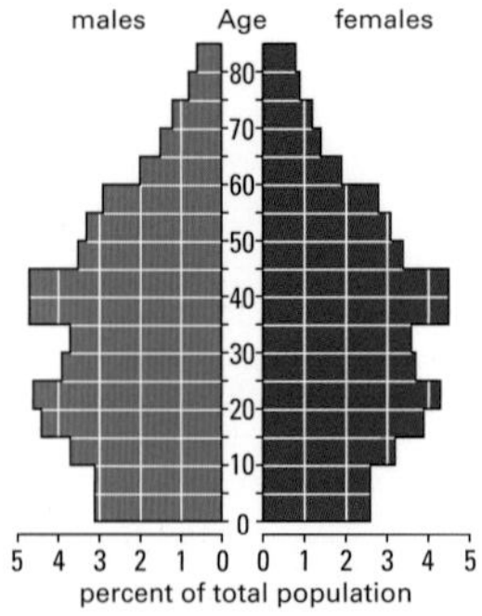

Total population: 1 323 591 583
Land area: 9 596 961km²

USA
males   Age   females

percent of total population

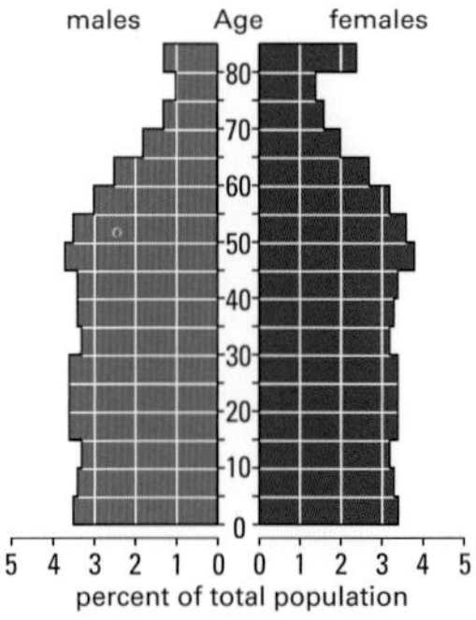

Total population: 307 006 550
Land area: 9 158 960km²

Map labels: Chicago, New York, Los Angeles, Mexico City, Bogota, Lima, Rio de Janeiro, São Paulo, Santiago, Buenos Aires

Arctic Circle, Tropic of Cancer, Equator, Tropic of Capricorn, Antarctic Circle

Population by continent, 2009 millions of people

Europe 738	Asia 4117	Africa 999	North America 534	South America 386	Oceania 36

Land area by continent thousands of square kilometres

Europe 10 498	Asia 44 387	Africa 30 335	Oceania 8503	North America 24 241	South America 17 832	Antarctica 13 340

Eckert IV Projection   © Oxford University Press

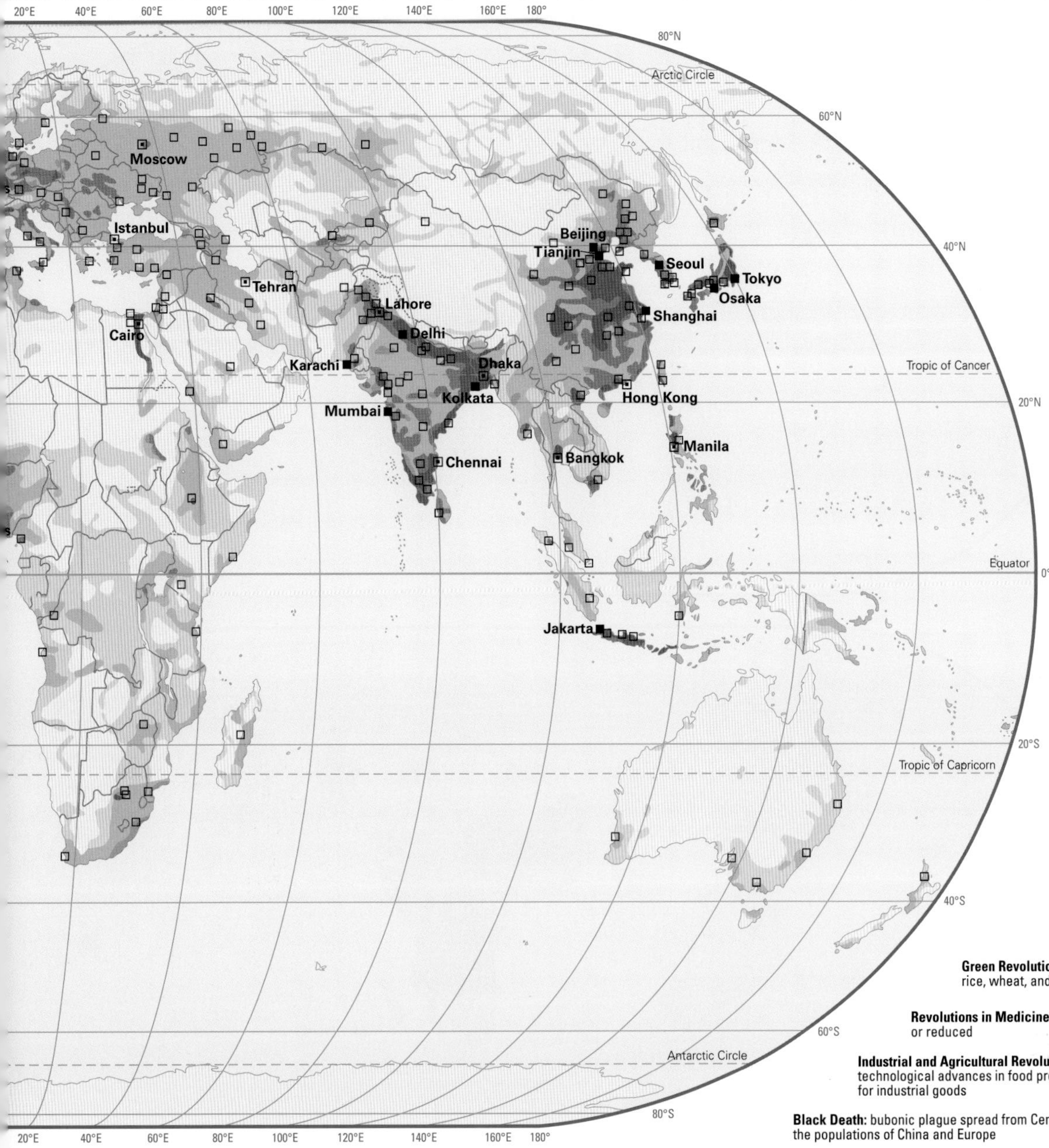

Map labels (left globe map):
Moscow
Istanbul
Tehran
Cairo
Lahore
Delhi
Karachi
Dhaka
Kolkata
Mumbai
Chennai
Bangkok
Beijing
Tianjin
Seoul
Tokyo
Osaka
Shanghai
Hong Kong
Manila
Jakarta

Latitude/longitude labels:
Arctic Circle
80°N
60°N
40°N
Tropic of Cancer
20°N
Equator 0°
20°S
Tropic of Capricorn
40°S
60°S
Antarctic Circle
80°S

20°E 40°E 60°E 80°E 100°E 120°E 140°E 160°E 180°

Urban and rural population, 2009

percentage of
total population

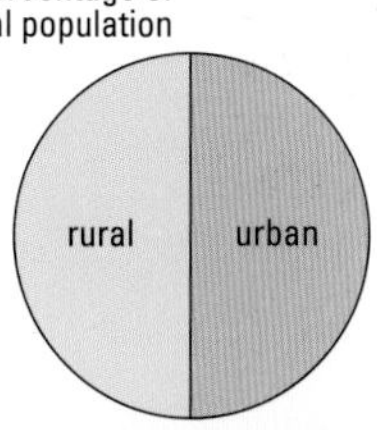

rural | urban

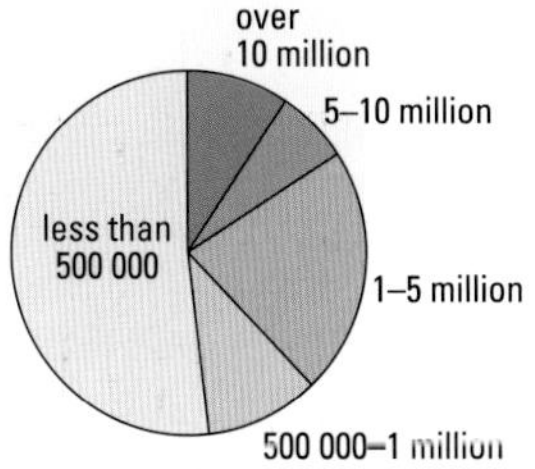

over
10 million
5–10 million
less than
500 000
1–5 million
500 000–1 million

City size as a percent
of urban population, 2009

World population growth
Past growth (1AD to 2000)

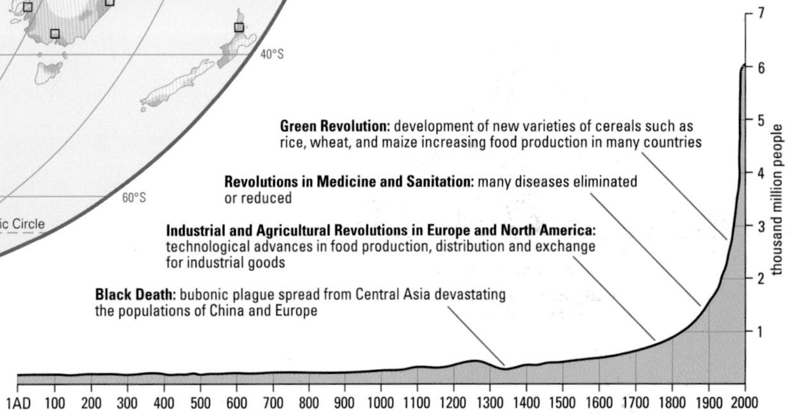

Green Revolution: development of new varieties of cereals such as rice, wheat, and maize increasing food production in many countries

Revolutions in Medicine and Sanitation: many diseases eliminated or reduced

Industrial and Agricultural Revolutions in Europe and North America: technological advances in food production, distribution and exchange for industrial goods

Black Death: bubonic plague spread from Central Asia devastating the populations of China and Europe

thousand million people
7 6 5 4 3 2 1

1AD 100 200 300 400 500 600 700 800 900 1000 1100 1200 1300 1400 1500 1600 1700 1800 1900 2000

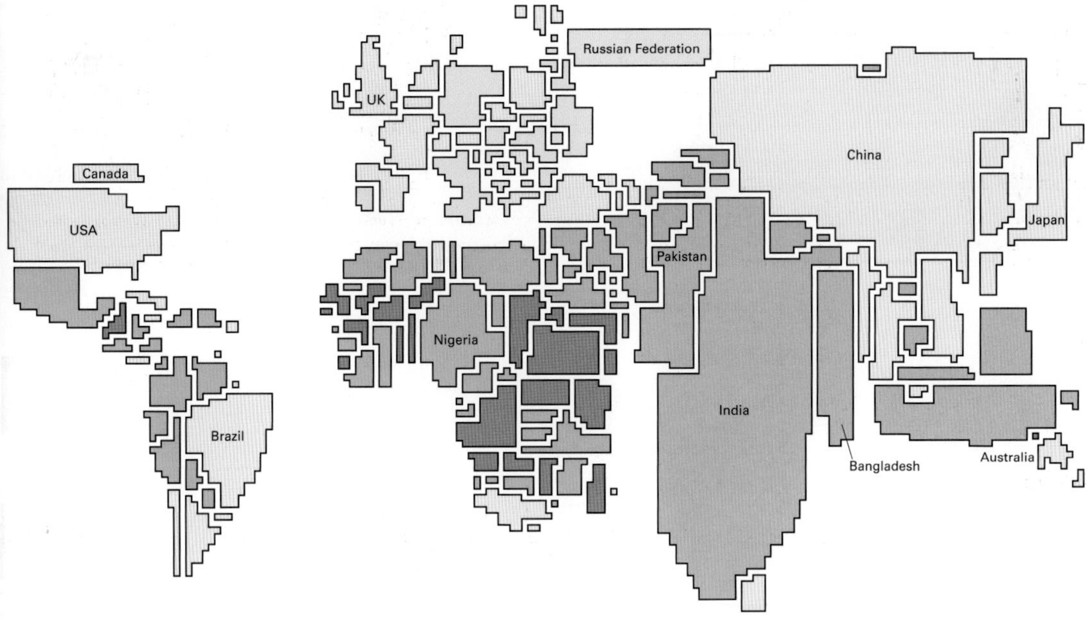

Population cartogram, 2009

the size of each country represents
the number of people living there

100 million
25 million
1 million

Cartogram labels:
Russian Federation
UK
Canada
USA
China
Japan
Pakistan
Nigeria
India
Brazil
Bangladesh
Australia

Population change

average annual increase or decrease

very high increase (over 2.6%)

increase above world average (1.3–2.6%)

increase below world average (0–1.3%)

decrease (by less than 1%)

UN Statistics
http://unstats.un.org

Scale 1: 240 000 000

Population change, 2000–2010

percentage population gain or loss

- over 40% gain
- 30–40% gain
- 20–30% gain
- 10–20% gain
- under 10% gain
- 0–20% loss

Highest population gain
Qatar 183.3%
United Arab Emirates 125.0%
Bahrain 116.7%
Western Sahara 66.7%
Benin 60.7%

United Kingdom 5.8%

Highest population loss
Lithuania -10.8%
Guyana -11.1%
Armenia -11.4%
Lesotho -13.6%
Bhutan -66.7%

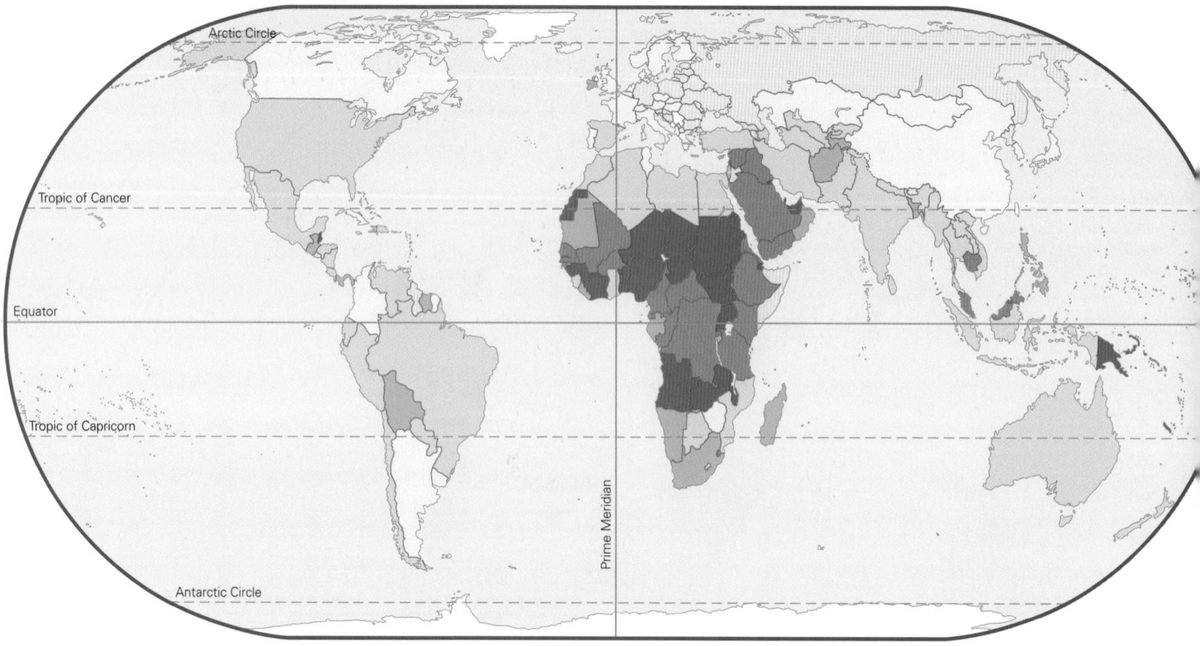

Fertility rate, 2010

average number of children born to childbearing women

- over 6 children
- 5–5.9 children
- 4–4.9 children
- 3–3.9 children
- 2–2.9 children
- 1–1.9 children
- o countries with over 40% of the total population under the age of 15 in 2010

Largest families
Niger 7.4 children
Mali 6.6 children
Somalia 6.5 children
Uganda 6.5 children
Congo, Dem. Rep. 6.4 children

United Kingdom 1.9 children

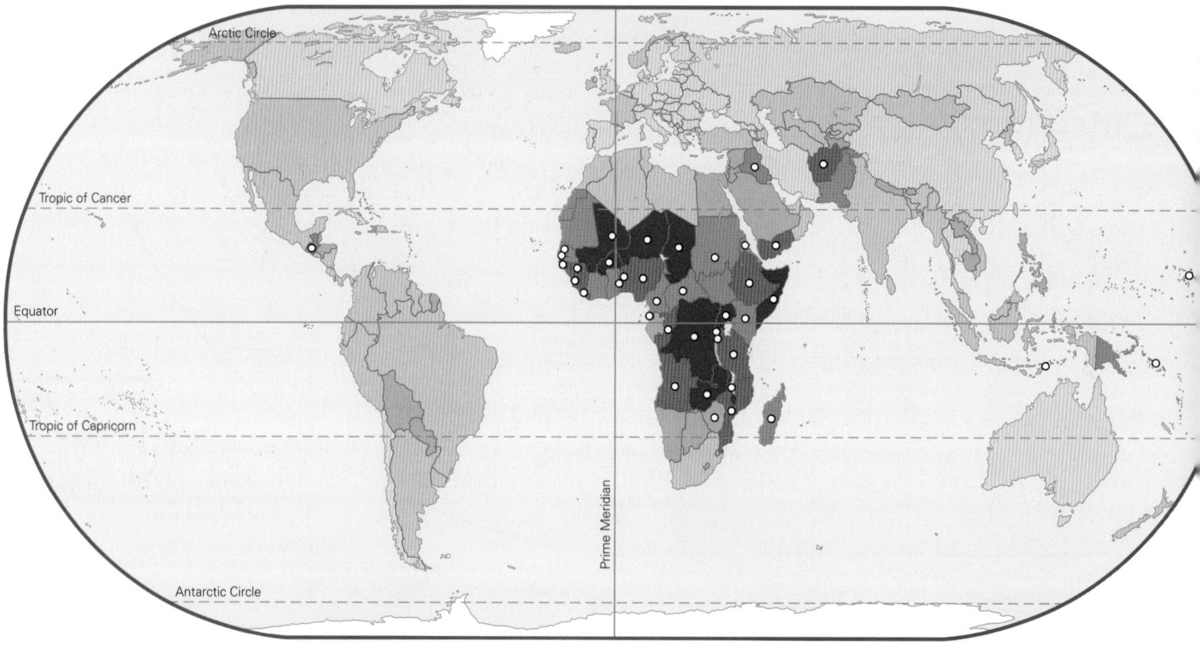

Urban population

percentage of the population living in urban areas

- over 80%
- 60–80%
- 40–60%
- 20–40%
- under 20%
- no data

Most urban in 2010
Singapore 100%
Monaco 100%
Nauru 100%
Kuwait 98%
Belgium 97%

United Kingdom 80%

Least urban in 2010
Liechtenstein 14%
Trinidad & Tobago 14%
Uganda 13%
Papua New Guinea 13%
Burundi 11%

1995

2010

***projected* 2025**

Eckert IV Projection

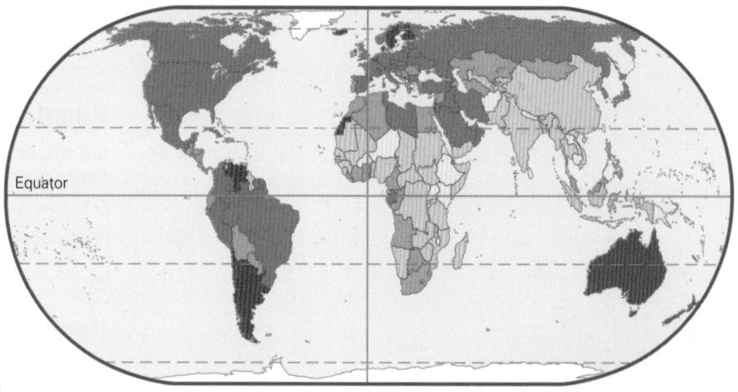

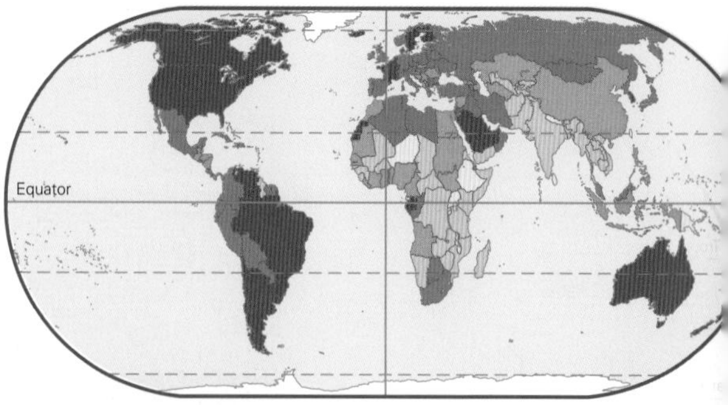

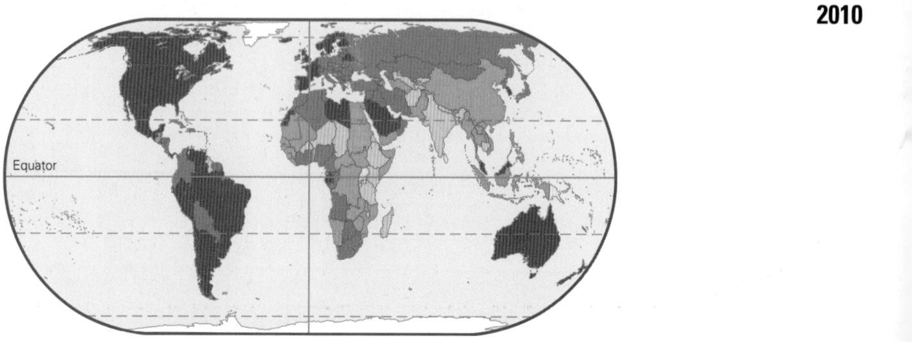

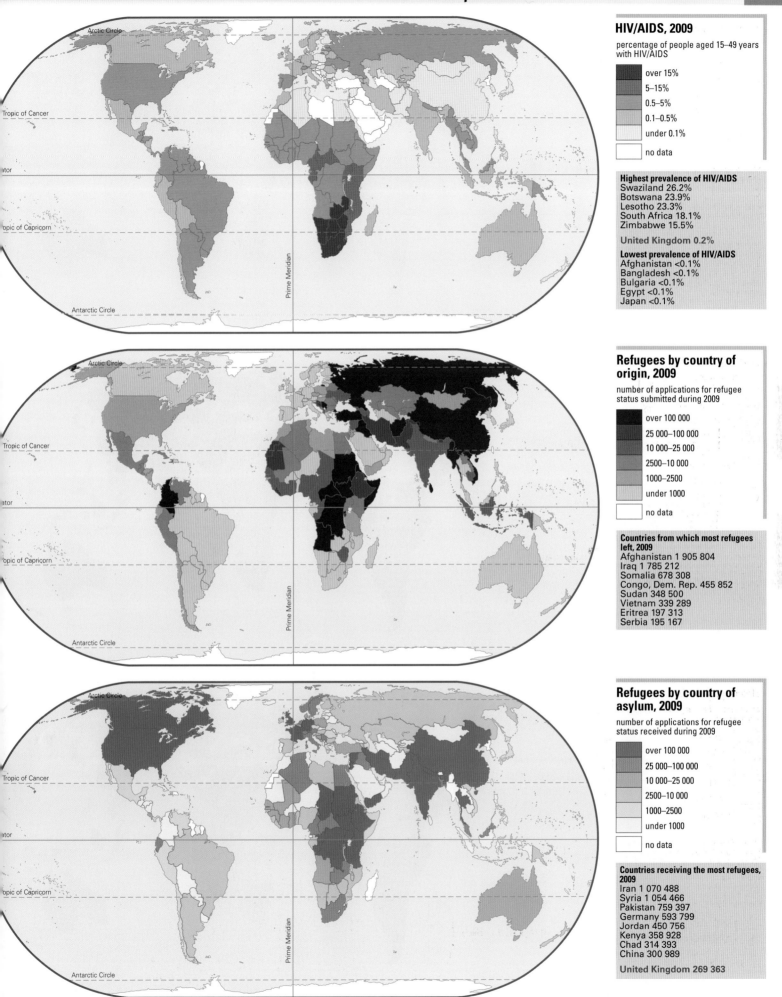

HIV/AIDS, 2009

percentage of people aged 15–49 years with HIV/AIDS

- over 15%
- 5–15%
- 0.5–5%
- 0.1–0.5%
- under 0.1%
- no data

Highest prevalence of HIV/AIDS
Swaziland 26.2%
Botswana 23.9%
Lesotho 23.3%
South Africa 18.1%
Zimbabwe 15.5%

United Kingdom 0.2%

Lowest prevalence of HIV/AIDS
Afghanistan <0.1%
Bangladesh <0.1%
Bulgaria <0.1%
Egypt <0.1%
Japan <0.1%

Refugees by country of origin, 2009

number of applications for refugee status submitted during 2009

- over 100 000
- 25 000–100 000
- 10 000–25 000
- 2500–10 000
- 1000–2500
- under 1000
- no data

Countries from which most refugees left, 2009
Afghanistan 1 905 804
Iraq 1 785 212
Somalia 678 308
Congo, Dem. Rep. 455 852
Sudan 348 500
Vietnam 339 289
Eritrea 197 313
Serbia 195 167

Refugees by country of asylum, 2009

number of applications for refugee status received during 2009

- over 100 000
- 25 000–100 000
- 10 000–25 000
- 2500–10 000
- 1000–2500
- under 1000
- no data

Countries receiving the most refugees, 2009
Iran 1 070 488
Syria 1 054 466
Pakistan 759 397
Germany 593 799
Jordan 450 756
Kenya 358 928
Chad 314 393
China 300 989

United Kingdom 269 363

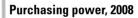

Purchasing power, 2008

Purchasing Power Parity (PPP) in US$
Based on Gross Domestic Product (GDP)
per person, adjusted for the local cost
of living

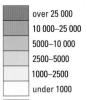

- over 25 000
- 10 000–25 000
- 5000–10 000
- 2500–5000
- 1000–2500
- under 1000
- no data

Highest purchasing power
Luxembourg $64 320
Norway $58 500
Kuwait $52 610
Brunei $50 200
Singapore $47 940

United Kingdom $36 130

Lowest purchasing power
Eritrea $630
Guinea-Bissau $530
Burundi $380
Liberia $300
Congo, Dem. Rep. $290

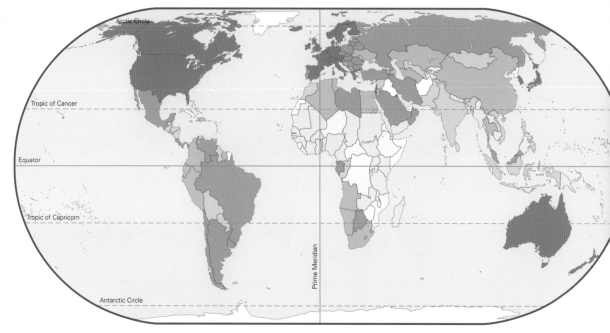

Literacy and schooling, 2010

percentage of people aged 15 and above
who can, with understanding, both read
and write a short, simple statement on
their everyday life

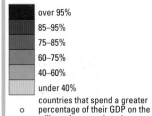

- over 95%
- 85–95%
- 75–85%
- 60–75%
- 40–60%
- under 40%
- ○ countries that spend a greater
  percentage of their GDP on the
  military than on education

Highest literacy levels
Georgia 100%
Belarus 99.8%
Cuba 99.8%
Estonia 99.8%
Latvia 99.8%

United Kingdom 99%

Lowest literacy levels
Guinea 29.5%
Burkina Faso 28.7%
Niger 28.7%
Afghanistan 28%
Mali 26.2%

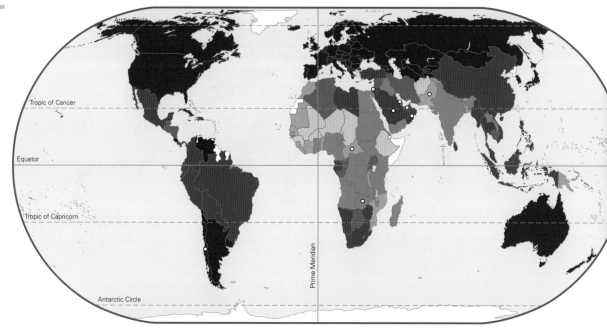

Life expectancy, 2010

average expected lifespan of babies
born in 2010

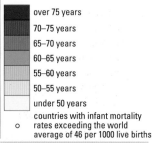

- over 75 years
- 70–75 years
- 65–70 years
- 60–65 years
- 55–60 years
- 50–55 years
- under 50 years
- ○ countries with infant mortality
  rates exceeding the world
  average of 46 per 1000 live births

Highest life expectancy
Japan 83 years
Italy 82 years
Switzerland 82 years
Canada 81 years
Norway 81 years

United Kingdom 80 years

Lowest life expectancy
Guinea-Bissau 46 years
Swaziland 46 years
Zimbabwe 43 years
Zambia 42 years
Lesotho 41 years

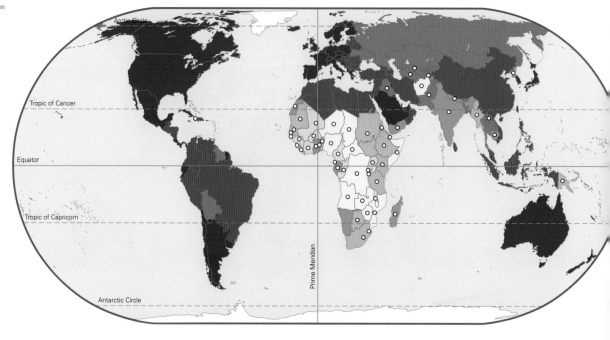

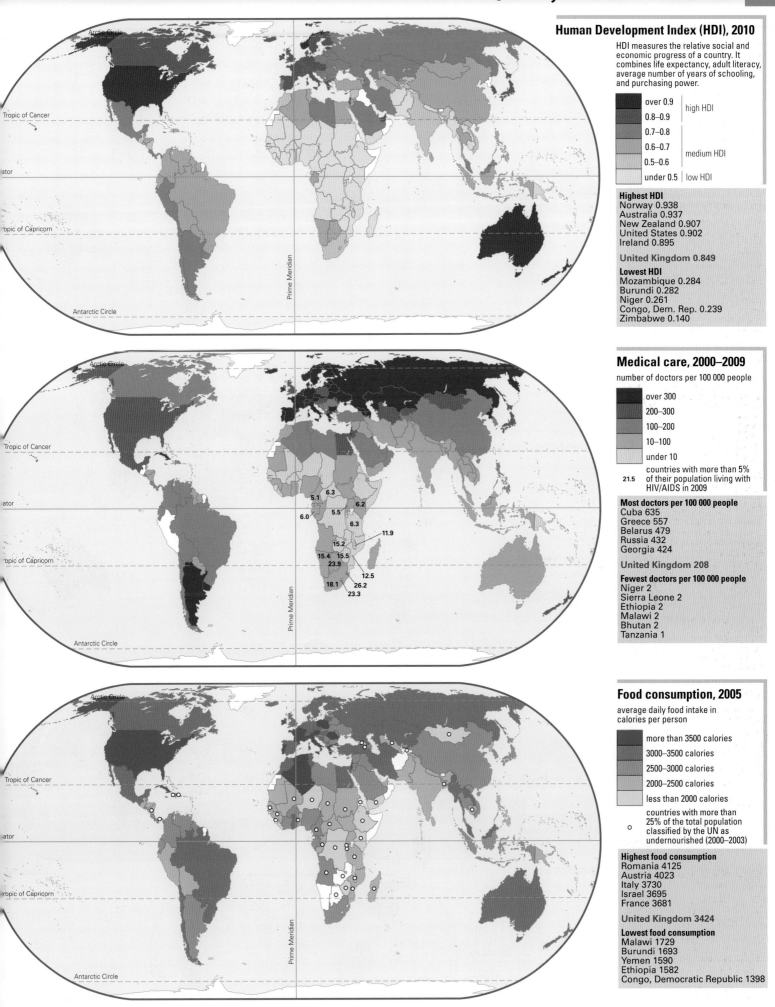

Human Development Index (HDI), 2010

HDI measures the relative social and economic progress of a country. It combines life expectancy, adult literacy, average number of years of schooling, and purchasing power.

over 0.9	high HDI
0.8–0.9	
0.7–0.8	
0.6–0.7	medium HDI
0.5–0.6	
under 0.5	low HDI

Highest HDI
Norway 0.938
Australia 0.937
New Zealand 0.907
United States 0.902
Ireland 0.895

United Kingdom 0.849

Lowest HDI
Mozambique 0.284
Burundi 0.282
Niger 0.261
Congo, Dem. Rep. 0.239
Zimbabwe 0.140

Medical care, 2000–2009

number of doctors per 100 000 people

over 300	
200–300	
100–200	
10–100	
under 10	
21.5	countries with more than 5% of their population living with HIV/AIDS in 2009

Most doctors per 100 000 people
Cuba 635
Greece 557
Belarus 479
Russia 432
Georgia 424

United Kingdom 208

Fewest doctors per 100 000 people
Niger 2
Sierra Leone 2
Ethiopia 2
Malawi 2
Bhutan 2
Tanzania 1

Food consumption, 2005

average daily food intake in calories per person

more than 3500 calories	
3000–3500 calories	
2500–3000 calories	
2000–2500 calories	
less than 2000 calories	
○	countries with more than 25% of the total population classified by the UN as undernourished (2000–2003)

Highest food consumption
Romania 4125
Austria 4023
Italy 3730
Israel 3695
France 3681

United Kingdom 3424

Lowest food consumption
Malawi 1729
Burundi 1693
Yemen 1590
Ethiopia 1582
Congo, Democratic Republic 1398

Industrialization, 2010

Industrialized high income economies
Most people live in cities and have high standards of living based on manufacturing and services. High levels of energy consumption

Industrializing upper-middle income economies
Manufacturing and industrial development are growing alongside traditional economies. Most people have rising incomes.

Industrializing lower-middle income economies
Manufacturing and industrial development are growing alongside traditional economies. Most people have relatively low incomes.

Agricultural low income economies
Most people live in rural areas and depend on agriculture. Little industrial development. Low incomes.

○ more than 40% of the population living below the national poverty line

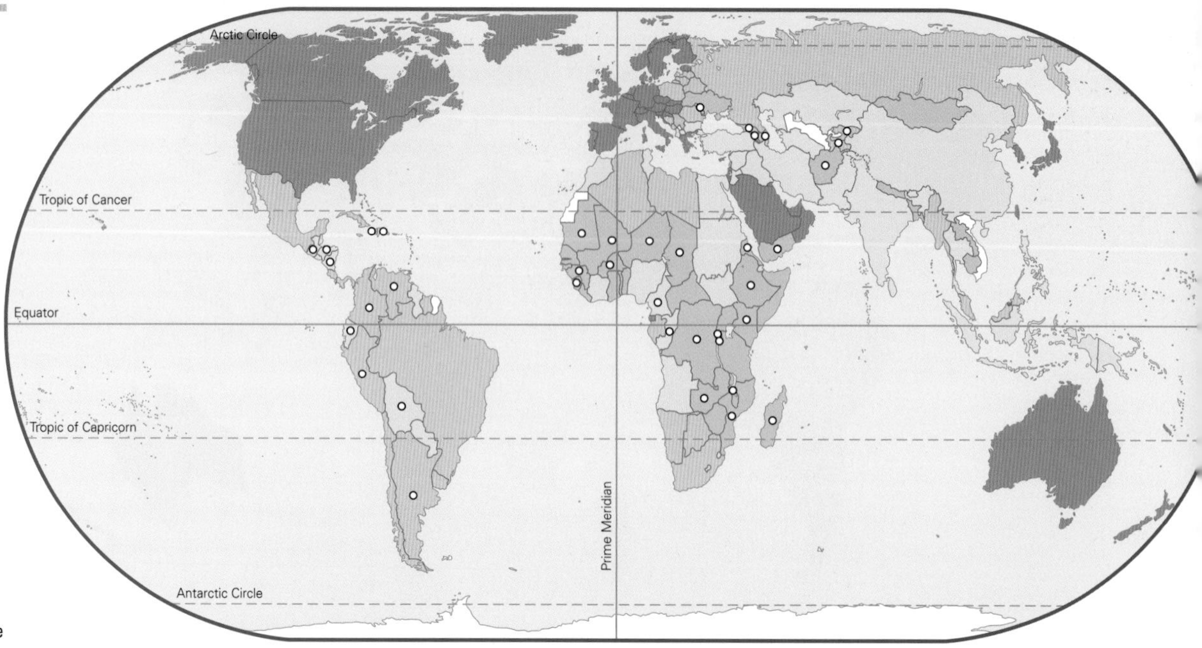

International aid, 2008

Official development assistance (ODA) given or received per person in US$

Countries giving aid

over $100 per person

$50–$100 per person

under $50 per person

Countries receiving aid

under $10 per person

$10–$100 per person

over $100 per person

The economy becomes dependent on financial grants or loans from other, wealthier countries.

Countries giving most aid (total US$)
USA $26 842 000 000
Germany $13 981 000 000
United Kingdom $11 500 000 000
France $10 908 000 000

Countries receiving most aid (total US$)
Iraq $9 326 000 000
Afghanistan $4 672 000 000
Ethiopia $3 196 000 000
Vietnam $2 400 000 000

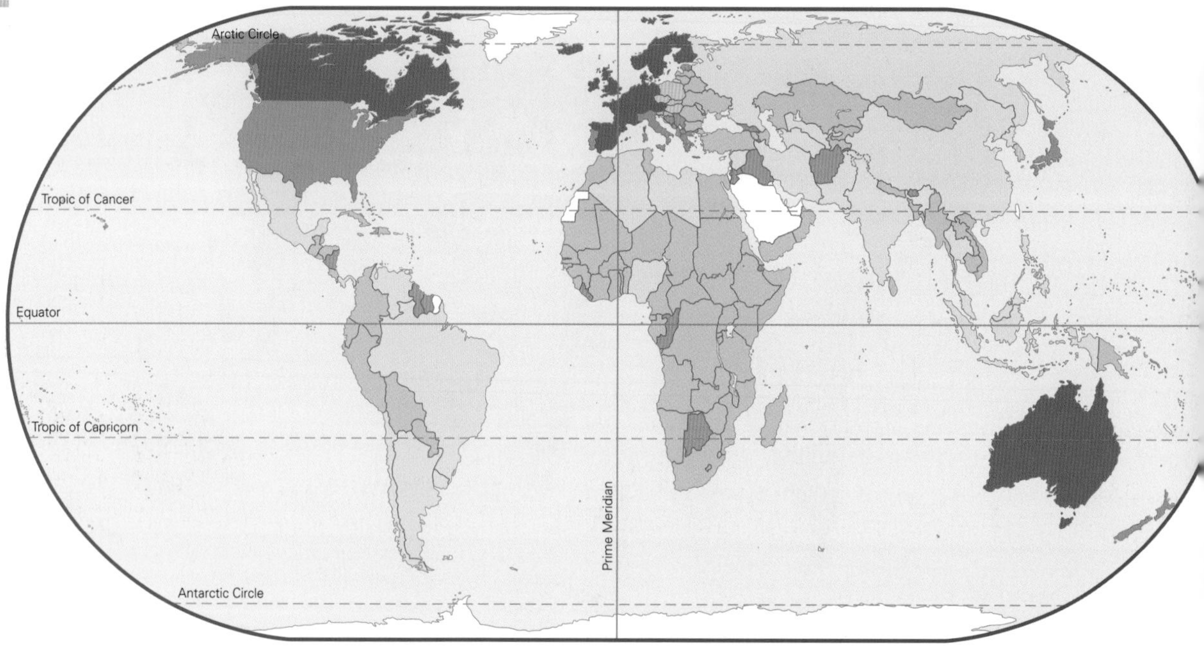

Employment

percentage of the labour force

over 80%

60–80%

30–60%

10–30%

under 10%

no data

Scale 1: 480 000 000

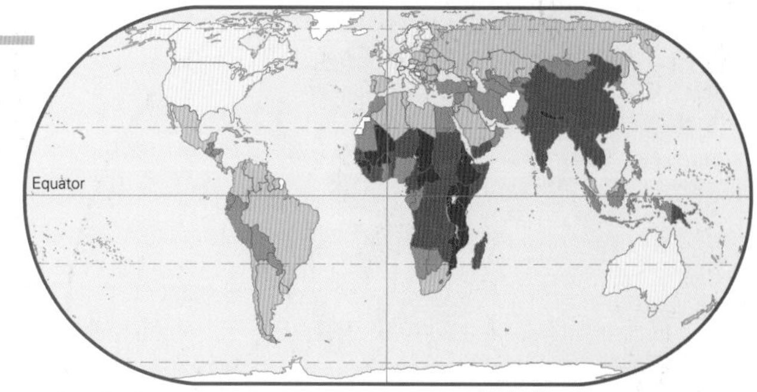

Agriculture

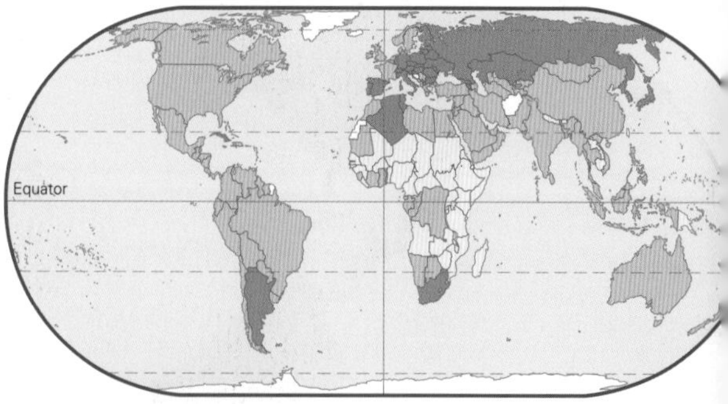

Industry

Services

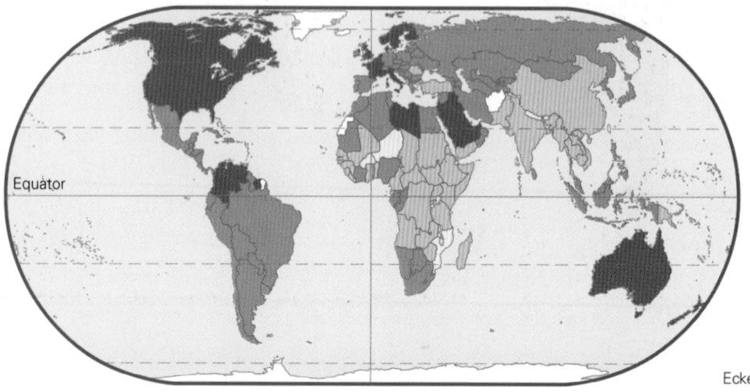

Eckert IV Projection   © Oxford University Press

Employment by economic sector (ternary diagram)

ector	includes
...mary	Farming, fishing, forestry, mining and quarrying
...condary	Manufacturing industry, building and construction
...rtiary	Transport and distribution, wholesale and retail, administration and finance, public services

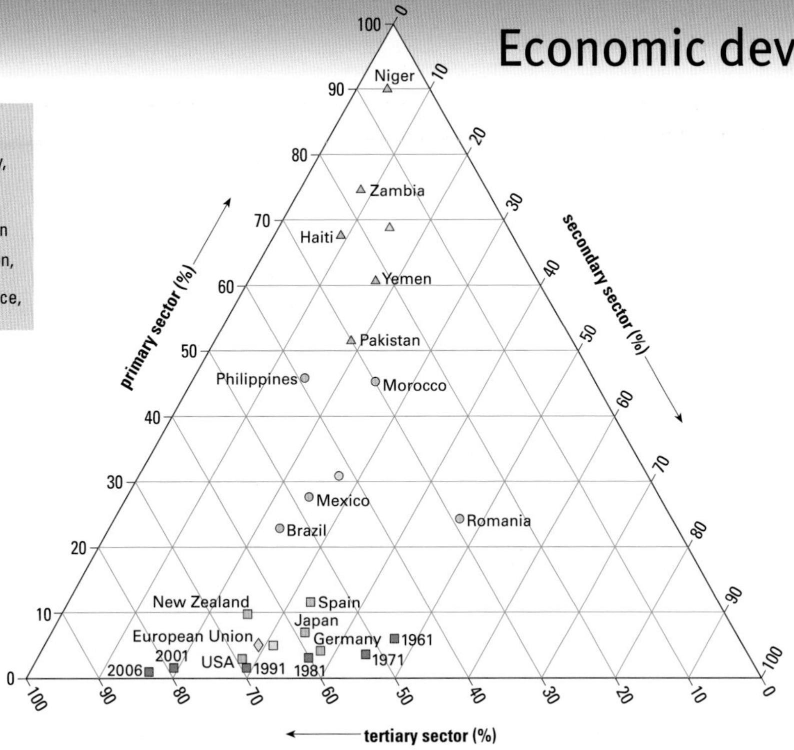

primary sector (%)

secondary sector (%)

tertiary sector (%)

Niger
Zambia
Haiti
Yemen
Pakistan
Philippines
Morocco
Mexico
Brazil
Romania
New Zealand
Spain
Japan
European Union
Germany 1961
2001
USA 1991 1971
2006 1981

Employment by economic sector

△ Low income economies

○ Middle income economies

□ High income economies

◇ European Union

■ UK (selected dates)

average for country categories

selected countries

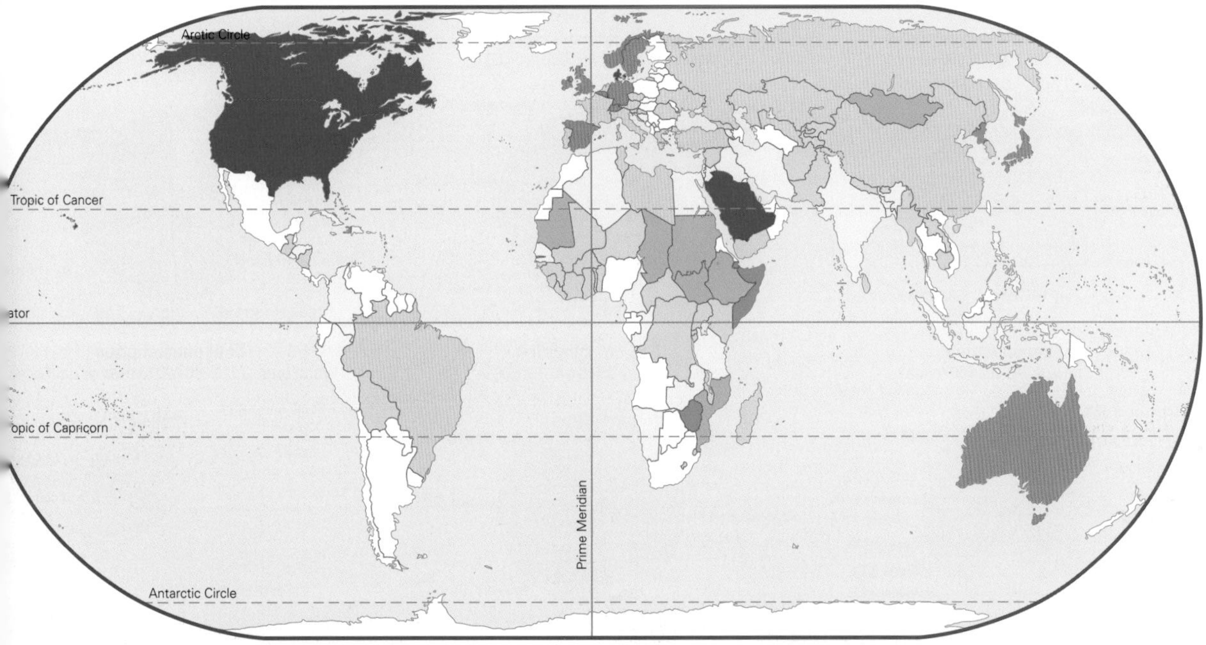

Food aid, 2009

kilograms of cereal per person

Countries giving food aid

over 6kg per person

1–6kg per person

under 1kg per person

Countries receiving food aid

under 1kg per person

1–6kg per person

6–12kg per person

over 12kg per person

no data

Countries giving most food aid (tonnes)
Denmark 413 056 534
United States 2 345 803
Japan 363 364
Canada 211 492

United Kingdom 95 633

Countries receiving most food aid (tonnes)
Ethiopia 904 133
Sudan 427 826
Somalia 281 833
Kenya 216 722

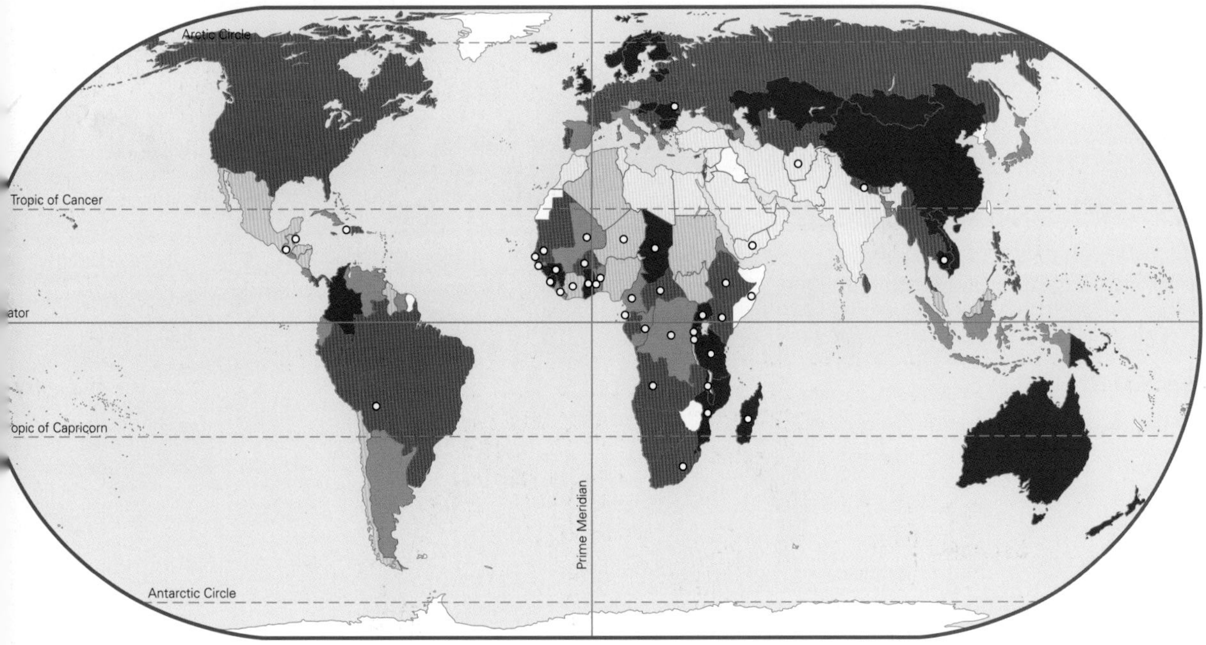

Female income, 2007

percentage of total income earned by females in US$

over 40%

35–40%

30–35%

25–30%

under 25%

○ countries with more than 20% of children aged 5 to 14 years involved in child labour activities

Highest female earned income (US$)
Luxembourg $57 676
Norway $46 576
Brunei $36 838
United States $34 996
Singapore $34 554

United Kingdom $28 421

Lowest female earned income (US$)
Niger $318
Guinea-Bissau $301
Burundi $296
Liberia $240
Congo, Democratic Republic $189

Arctic Circle
Tropic of Cancer
Equator
Tropic of Capricorn
Antarctic Circle
Prime Meridian

Energy production, 2008

kg oil equivalent per person

- over 25 000
- 2500–25 000
- 1000–2500
- 100–1000
- under 100
- no data

Highest energy producers
kg oil equivalent per person

Qatar 134 992
Kuwait 54 928
Norway 49 724
Brunei 48 412
United Arab Emirates 42 573
Equatorial Guinea 36 407
Trinidad & Tobago 31 963
Oman 22 045
Saudi Arabia 21 175
Libya 16 760
Bahrain 16 246
Iceland 15 860
Turkmenistan 13 602
Canada 13 529
Australia 13 264

United Kingdom 2700

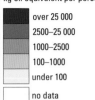
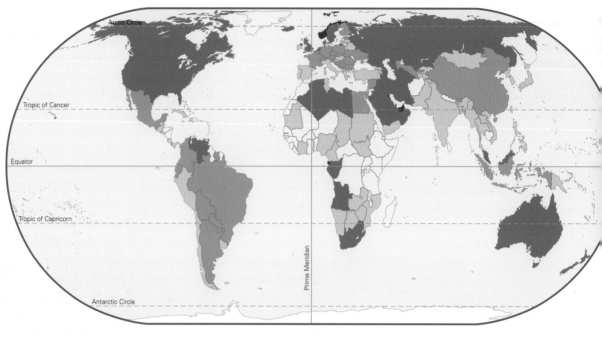

- North America
- Central and South America
- Europe and Eurasia
- Middle East
- Africa
- Asia Pacific

Oil reserves
Proven recoverable reserves
World total: 181 700 000 000 tonnes

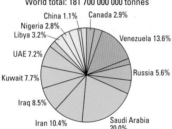

China 1.1%
Canada 2.9%
Nigeria 2.8%
Libya 3.2%
Venezuela 13.6%
UAE 7.2%
Russia 5.6%
Kuwait 7.7%
Iraq 8.5%
Iran 10.4%
Saudi Arabia 20.0%

Gas reserves
Proven recoverable reserves
World total: 187 490 000 000 000 m³

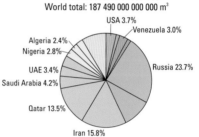

USA 3.7%
Venezuela 3.0%
Algeria 2.4%
Nigeria 2.8%
Russia 23.7%
UAE 3.4%
Saudi Arabia 4.2%
Qatar 13.5%
Iran 15.8%

Coal reserves
Proven recoverable reserves
World total: 826 001 000 000 tonnes

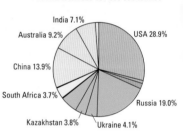

India 7.1%
Australia 9.2%
USA 28.9%
China 13.9%
South Africa 3.7%
Russia 19.0%
Kazakhstan 3.8%
Ukraine 4.1%

Oil consumption
World total: 4 203 900 000 tonnes

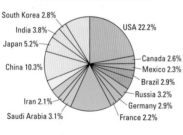

South Korea 2.8%
India 3.8%
USA 22.2%
Japan 5.2%
China 10.3%
Canada 2.6%
Mexico 2.3%
Brazil 2.9%
Russia 3.2%
Iran 2.1%
Germany 2.9%
Saudi Arabia 3.1%
France 2.2%

Gas consumption
World total: 2 940 400 000 000 m³

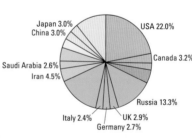

Japan 3.0%
China 3.0%
USA 22.0%
Saudi Arabia 2.6%
Canada 3.2%
Iran 4.5%
Russia 13.3%
Italy 2.4%
UK 2.9%
Germany 2.7%

Coal consumption
World total: 3 278 300 000 tonnes oil equivalent

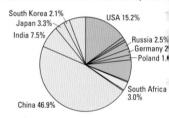

South Korea 2.1%
Japan 3.3%
USA 15.2%
India 7.5%
Russia 2.5%
Germany 2.
Poland 1.
China 46.9%
South Africa 3.0%

Energy consumption, 2008

kg oil equivalent per person

- over 10 000
- 2500–10 000
- 1000–2500
- 250–1000
- under 250
- no data

Highest energy consumers
kg oil equivalent per person

Qatar 26 246
Iceland 19 628
United Arab Emirates 17 062
Bahrain 16 155
Trinidad and Tobago 16 087

United Kingdom 3595

Lowest energy consumers
kg oil equivalent per person

Rwanda 26
Mali 23
Burundi 19
Afghanistan 13
Chad 9

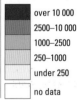
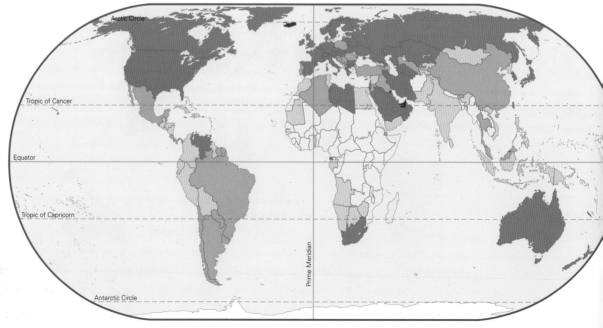

World trade cartogram, 2009

the size of each country represents its share of total world trade

- 1% of world trade
- 0.01% of world trade

Change in share of world trade, 1999–2009

over 50%	growth
5–50%	
0–5% growth or decline	little or no change
5–50	decline
over 50%	

Only those countries with more than 0.01% share in world trade are shown

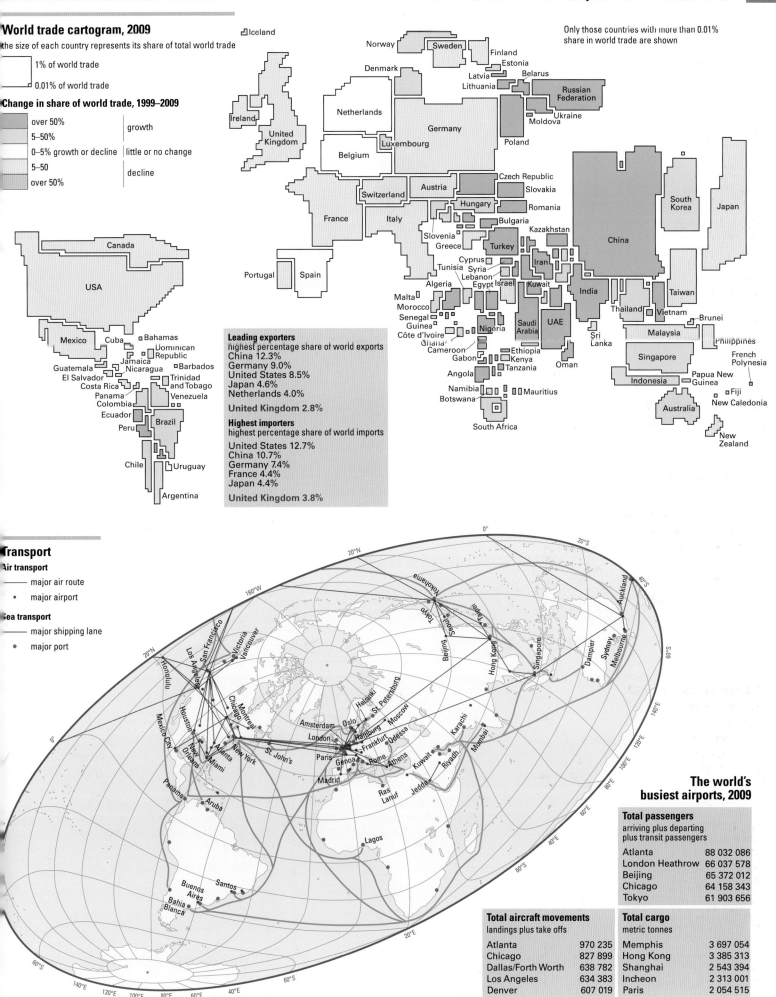

Iceland · Norway · Sweden · Finland · Denmark · Estonia · Latvia · Lithuania · Belarus · Ireland · Netherlands · United Kingdom · Germany · Russian Federation · Ukraine · Moldova · Belgium · Luxembourg · Poland · Czech Republic · Slovakia · Switzerland · Austria · Hungary · Romania · France · Italy · Slovenia · Bulgaria · Kazakhstan · Greece · Turkey · China · South Korea · Japan · Cyprus · Iran · Tunisia · Syria · Lebanon · Israel · Kuwait · India · Taiwan · Portugal · Spain · Algeria · Egypt · Thailand · Vietnam · Malta · Morocco · Saudi Arabia · UAE · Brunei · Senegal · Sri Lanka · Malaysia · Philippines · Guinea · Nigeria · Côte d'Ivoire · Ghana · Cameroon · Ethiopia · Kenya · Singapore · French Polynesia · Gabon · Tanzania · Oman · Indonesia · Papua New Guinea · Angola · Fiji · Namibia · Mauritius · New Caledonia · Botswana · Australia · South Africa · New Zealand

Canada · USA · Mexico · Cuba · Bahamas · Dominican Republic · Jamaica · Barbados · Guatemala · Nicaragua · El Salvador · Trinidad and Tobago · Costa Rica · Venezuela · Panama · Colombia · Ecuador · Brazil · Peru · Chile · Uruguay · Argentina

Leading exporters
highest percentage share of world exports
China 12.3%
Germany 9.0%
United States 8.5%
Japan 4.6%
Netherlands 4.0%

United Kingdom 2.8%

Highest importers
highest percentage share of world imports

United States 12.7%
China 10.7%
Germany 7.4%
France 4.4%
Japan 4.4%

United Kingdom 3.8%

Transport

Air transport
— major air route
• major airport

Sea transport
— major shipping lane
• major port

Oblique Aitoff Projection map showing air routes and shipping lanes with labelled cities: Iceland, Yokohama, Auckland, San Francisco, Victoria, Vancouver, Los Angeles, Honolulu, Seoul, Tokyo, Taipei, Beijing, Hong Kong, Singapore, Dampier, Sydney, Melbourne, Houston, Chicago, Montreal, Helsinki, St. Petersburg, Amsterdam, Oslo, Moscow, Karachi, Mumbai, Mexico City, New Orleans, Atlanta, New York, St. John's, London, Hamburg, Frankfurt, Odessa, Paris, Genoa, Rome, Athens, Kuwait, Riyadh, Miami, Madrid, Ras Lanuf, Jedda, Panama, Aruba, Lagos, Santos, Buenos Aires, Bahia Blanca.

The world's busiest airports, 2009

Total passengers
arriving plus departing
plus transit passengers

Atlanta	88 032 086
London Heathrow	66 037 578
Beijing	65 372 012
Chicago	64 158 343
Tokyo	61 903 656

Total aircraft movements
landings plus take offs

Atlanta	970 235
Chicago	827 899
Dallas/Forth Worth	638 782
Los Angeles	634 383
Denver	607 019

Total cargo
metric tonnes

Memphis	3 697 054
Hong Kong	3 385 313
Shanghai	2 543 394
Incheon	2 313 001
Paris	2 054 515

© Oxford University Press   Oblique Aitoff Projection

Desertification and tropical deforestation

- existing areas of desert
- areas with a high risk of becoming deserts
- areas with a moderate risk of becoming deserts
- existing areas of tropical rain forest
- former areas of tropical rain forest

Countries losing greatest areas of forest ('000 hectares) 2000–2005

Brazil	3103
Indonesia	1871
Sudan	589
Myanmar	466
Zambia	445
Tanzania	412
Nigeria	410
Congo, Dem. Rep.	319
Zimbabwe	313
Venezuela	288

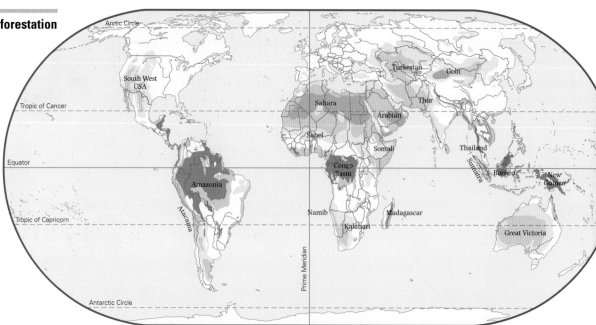

Acid rain

Sulphur and nitrogen emissions

Oxides of sulphur and nitrogen produced by burning fossil fuel react with rain to form dilute sulphuric and nitric acids

- areas with high levels of fossil fuel burning
- cities where sulphur dioxide emissions are recorded and exceed World Health Organization recommended levels

Areas of acid rain deposition

Annual mean values of pH in precipitation

- ▬▬▬ pH less than 4.2 (most acidic)
- ─── pH 4.2–4.6
- ─── pH 4.6–5.0
- ⌒⌒ other areas where acid rain is becoming a problem

Lower pH values are more acidic. 'Clean' rain water is slightly acidic with a pH of 5.6. The pH scale is logarithmic, so that a value of 4.6 is ten times as acidic as normal rain.

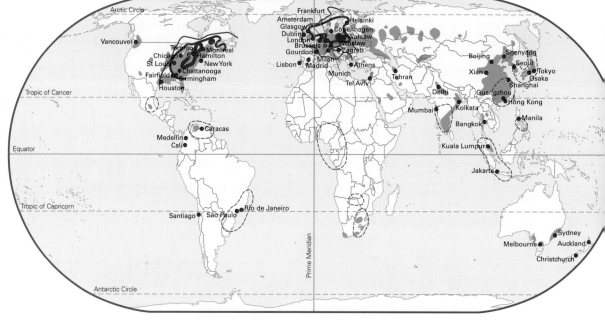

Sea pollution

Major oil spills

- ● over 100 000 tonnes
- · under 100 000 tonnes
- frequent oil slicks from shipping

Other sea pollution

- severe pollution
- moderate pollution
- ▼ deep sea dump sites

Major oil spills ('000 tonnes)

1979	*Ixtoc 1* well blow-out, Gulf of Mexico	467
1979	Collision of *Atlantic Empress* and *Aegean Captain*, off Tobago, Caribbean	138
1983	*Nowruz* well blow-out, The Gulf	267
1989	*Exxon Valdez* spills oil off the coast of Alaska	37
1991	Release of oil by Iraqi troops, *Sea Island* terminal, The Gulf	800
2002	*Prestige* oil tanker sinks off the coast of Spain	63
2010	*Deepwater Horizon* well blow-out, Gulf of Mexico	627

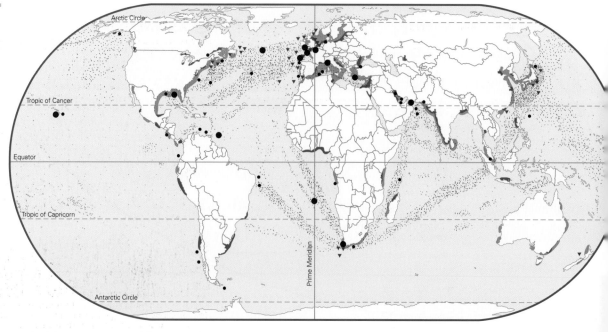

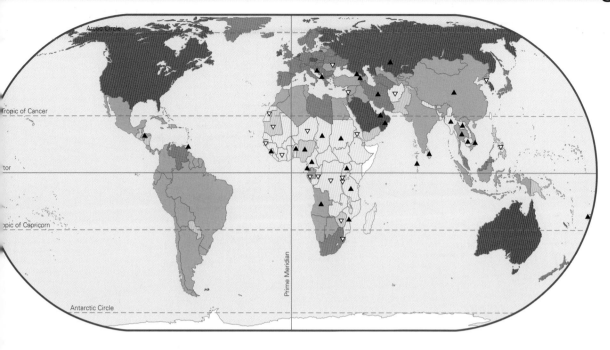

© Oxford University Press

Carbon dioxide emissions, 2007

metric tonnes per person

- over 10
- 5–10
- 1–5
- 0.5–1
- under 0.5

changes in carbon dioxide emissions per person, 1997–2007

- ▲ more than a 50% increase
- ▽ more than a 20% decrease

Highest carbon dioxide emissions
metric tonnes per person

Qatar 55.43
United Arab Emirates 31.06
Kuwait 30.21
Bahrain 29.58
Trinidad and Tobago 27.88

United Kingdom 8.8

Lowest carbon dioxide emissions
metric tonnes per person

Mali 0.05
Congo, Dem. Rep. 0.04
Chad 0.04
Afghanistan 0.03
Burundi 0.02

Global warming

The Earth's climate changes naturally over long periods of time. Scientists now think that these natural cycles of change have been overtaken by a rapid rise in the temperature of the Earth's atmosphere.

Global warming is caused by the **greenhouse effect**. Greenhouses work by trapping heat from the sun. Glass panes let in sunlight but prevent heat from escaping so that plants can survive cold weather. 'Greenhouse gases' in the Earth's atmosphere work in the same way. Without them the Earth would be too cold to sustain life. However, we are now experiencing an enhanced greenhouse effect, widely thought to be the result of large quantities of heat-trapping gases escaping into the atmosphere.

These greenhouse gases include carbon dioxide, methane, nitrogen oxides and chlorofluorocarbons (CFCs) and they are caused by human activities such as burning coal and oil, increasing road and air transport, burning down forests and raising cattle. Even a small increase in temperature can have serious consequences, altering weather patterns and resulting in increased rainfall, storms or drought to different parts of the world. Rising sea levels caused by melting polar ice also threaten low-lying coastal areas.

The natural greenhouse effect

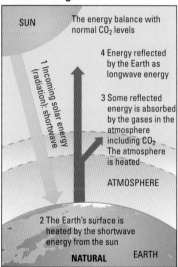

SUN — The energy balance with normal CO_2 levels

1 Incoming solar energy (radiation); shortwave

4 Energy reflected by the Earth as longwave energy

3 Some reflected energy is absorbed by the gases in the atmosphere including CO_2 The atmosphere is heated

ATMOSPHERE

2 The Earth's surface is heated by the shortwave energy from the sun

NATURAL EARTH

How it alters with increased CO_2

SUN — The energy balance with increased CO_2 levels

1 Incoming solar energy (radiation); shortwave

4 Less energy reflected by the Earth (longwave)

3 More reflected energy is absorbed due to the increase in CO_2 and the atmosphere warms – it enhances the greenhouse effect

ATMOSPHERE

2 The Earth's surface is heated by the shortwave energy from the sun

ENHANCED EARTH

Projected change in global warming

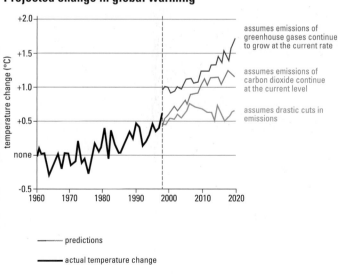

temperature change (°C)

assumes emissions of greenhouse gases continue to grow at the current rate

assumes emissions of carbon dioxide continue at the current level

assumes drastic cuts in emissions

— predictions

— actual temperature change

The Antarctic ozone 'hole'

Three dimensional image of ozone depletion over Antarctica in September, 1998. The lowest ozone concentration is shown in blue.

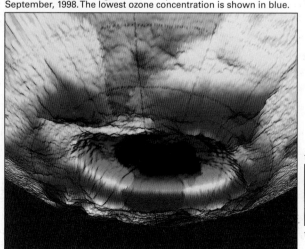
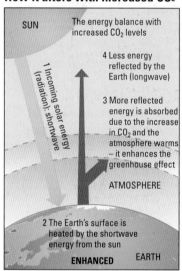

thinnest ozone

thickest ozone

Ozone in the stratosphere absorbs harmful ultra-violet rays. Pollutants in the air destroy ozone, making the ozone layer thinner. Strong winds and intense cold of the Antarctic winter concentrate the effects of pollutants so that ozone is thinnest over Antarctica in spring (September and October).

Selected tourist destinations

The locations shown represent a limited
selection of important tourism sites.

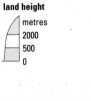

🏛 cultural/historical sites

✳ natural heritage sites

◯ resorts

◯ tourist cities

— main cruise routes

land height

metres
2000
500
0

Top tourist destinations, 2009

	arrivals (000's)	% change 2008–2009
France	74 200	-6.3
USA	54 884	-5.3
Spain	52 231	-8.7
China	50 875	-4.1
Italy	43 239	1.2
United Kingdom	28 033	-7.0
Turkey	25 506	2.0
Germany	24 224	-2.7
Malaysia	23 646	7.2
Mexico	21 454	-5.2

Market share, 2009

percent of all international tourist arrivals

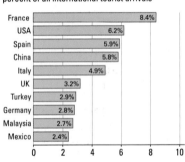

France	8.4%
USA	6.2%
Spain	5.9%
China	5.8%
Italy	4.9%
UK	3.2%
Turkey	2.9%
Germany	2.8%
Malaysia	2.7%
Mexico	2.4%

0 2 4 6 8 10

Earnings from tourism, 2008

tourist receipts in million US$

over 5000
1000–5000
250–1000
100–250
under 100
no data

Highest tourist earnings (millions)
USA $109 976
Spain $61 628
France $56 573
Italy $45 727
China $40 843

United Kingdom $36 028

Scale 1: 125 000 000 (main map

ROUND THE WORLD

TRANSATLANTIC

CARIBBEAN

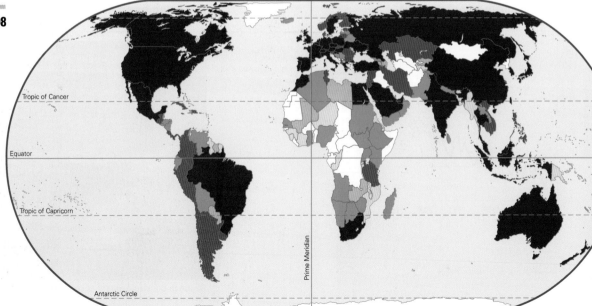

Eckert IV Projection   © Oxford University Press

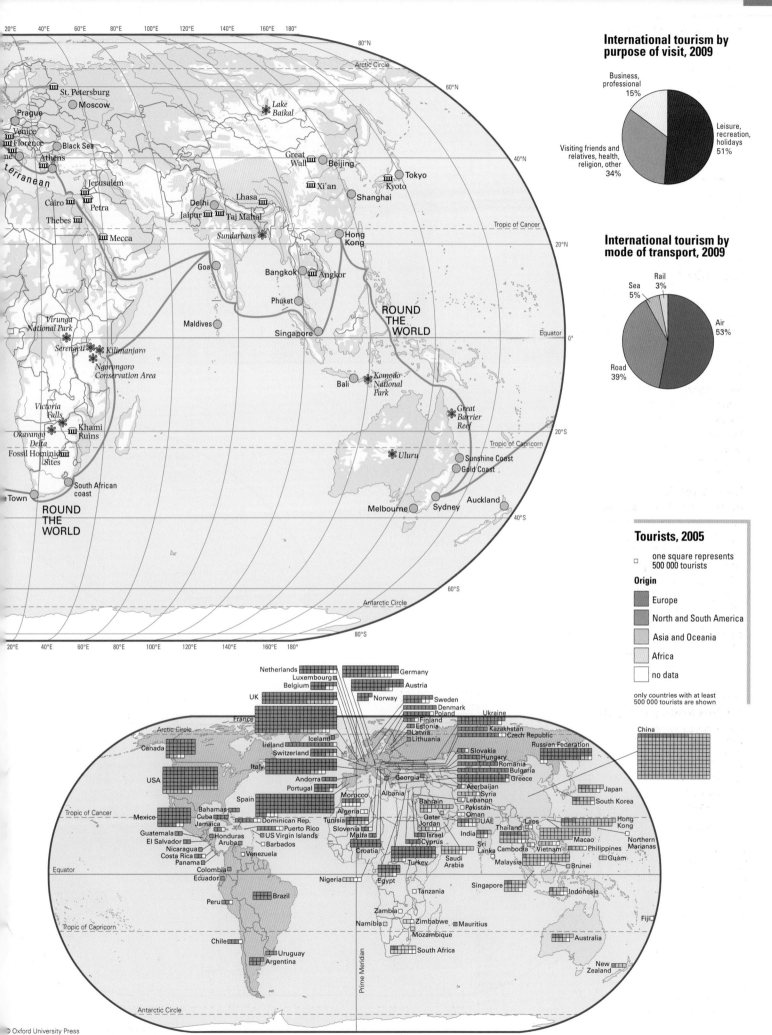

International tourism by purpose of visit, 2009

Business, professional 15%

Leisure, recreation, holidays 51%

Visiting friends and relatives, health, religion, other 34%

International tourism by mode of transport, 2009

Rail 3%

Sea 5%

Air 53%

Road 39%

Tourists, 2005

□ one square represents 500 000 tourists

Origin

- Europe
- North and South America
- Asia and Oceania
- Africa
- no data

only countries with at least 500 000 tourists are shown

ROUND THE WORLD

ROUND THE WORLD

Map labels (top)

St. Petersburg
Moscow
Prague
Venice
Florence
Athens
Mediterranean
Lake Baikal
Black Sea
Jerusalem
Cairo
Petra
Thebes
Mecca
Great Wall
Beijing
Xi'an
Tokyo
Kyoto
Shanghai
Delhi
Lhasa
Jaipur
Taj Mahal
Sundarbans
Hong Kong
Goa
Bangkok
Angkor
Phuket
Maldives
Singapore
Virunga National Park
Serengeti
Kilimanjaro
Ngorongoro Conservation Area
Bali
Komodo National Park
Great Barrier Reef
Victoria Falls
Khami Ruins
Okavango Delta
Fossil Hominid Sites
Uluru
Sunshine Coast
Gold Coast
South African coast
Town
Melbourne
Sydney
Auckland

Map labels (bottom)

Netherlands, Luxembourg, Belgium, Germany, Austria, Norway, Sweden, Denmark, Poland, Finland, Estonia, Latvia, Lithuania, Ukraine, Kazakhstan, Czech Republic, UK, France, Iceland, Ireland, Switzerland, Italy, Andorra, Portugal, Spain, Canada, USA, Mexico, Bahamas, Cuba, Jamaica, Guatemala, El Salvador, Honduras, Nicaragua, Costa Rica, Panama, Colombia, Ecuador, Peru, Chile, Uruguay, Argentina, Brazil, Venezuela, Barbados, Aruba, US Virgin Islands, Puerto Rico, Dominican Rep., Slovakia, Hungary, Romania, Bulgaria, Greece, Russian Federation, China, Japan, South Korea, Georgia, Albania, Azerbaijan, Syria, Bahrain, Lebanon, Pakistan, Oman, Qatar, Jordan, UAE, Israel, Cyprus, India, Sri Lanka, Thailand, Laos, Cambodia, Vietnam, Macao, Hong Kong, Northern Marianas, Malaysia, Guam, Brunei, Morocco, Algeria, Tunisia, Slovenia, Malta, Croatia, Turkey, Saudi Arabia, Nigeria, Egypt, Tanzania, Zambia, Zimbabwe, Mauritius, Namibia, Mozambique, South Africa, Singapore, Indonesia, Fiji, Australia, New Zealand, Philippines

© Oxford University Press

Time zones

Minus numbers show hours behind
Greenwich Mean Time (GMT).
Plus numbers show hours ahead of GMT.

- even numbers of hours difference from GMT
- odd numbers of hours difference from GMT
- half an hour difference from adjacent zone
- less than half an hour difference from adjacent zone

Longitude is measured from the **prime meridian**, which passes through Greenwich. There are 24 standard time zones, each spanning 15° of longitude. Many of the boundaries of these time zones have been adjusted to follow political borders.

The **international date line** marks the point where one calendar day ends and another begins. A traveller crossing from east to west moves forward one day. Crossing from west to east, the calendar goes back one day.

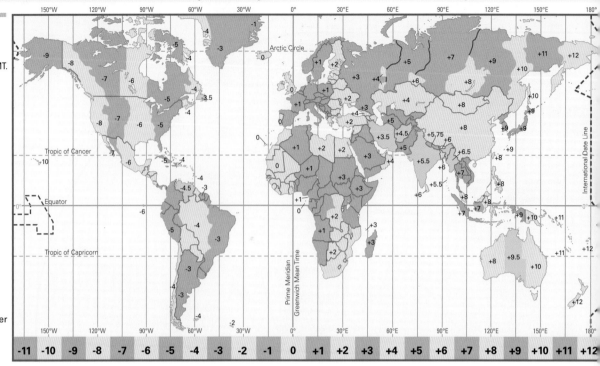

| -11 | -10 | -9 | -8 | -7 | -6 | -5 | -4 | -3 | -2 | -1 | 0 | +1 | +2 | +3 | +4 | +5 | +6 | +7 | +8 | +9 | +10 | +11 | +12 |

Distance

Flight distance between cities in kilometres.
To convert kilometres to miles multiply by 0.62

Beijing

Beijing											
19 307	**Buenos Aires**										
1983	18 484	**Hong Kong**									
11 710	8088	10 732	**Johannesburg**								
8145	11 161	9645	9071	**London**							
10 081	9871	11 678	16 676	8774	**Los Angeles**						
12 468	7468	14 162	14 585	8936	2484	**Mexico City**					
4774	14 952	4306	8274	7193	14 033	15 678	**Mumbai**				
11 000	8548	12 984	12 841	5580	3951	3371	12 565	**New York**			
8226	11 097	9613	8732	338	9032	9210	7032	5839	**Paris**		
4468	15 904	2661	8860	10 871	14 146	16 630	3919	15 533	10 758	**Singapore**	
8949	11 800	7374	11 040	16 992	12 073	12 969	9839	15 989	16 962	6300	**Sydney**
2113	18 388	2903	13 547	9581	8823	11 355	6758	10 871	9726	5322	7823	**Tokyo**

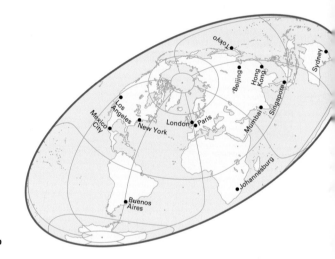

Internet users, 2010

per 100 people

- over 70
- 50–70
- 30–50
- 10–30
- 5–10
- under 5

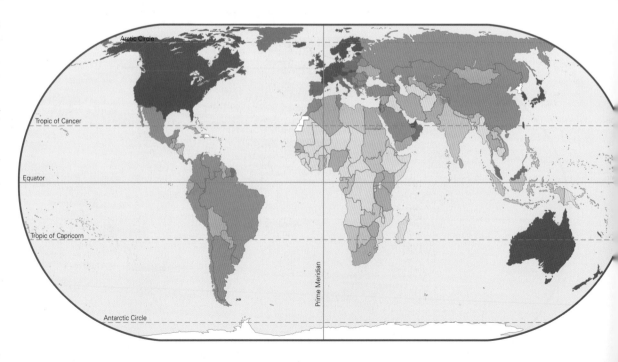

Gall Projection (Timezones)   Oblique Aitoff Projection   © Oxford University Press

Motor vehicle Trans National Corporations (TNCs), 2006

Trans National Corporations (TNCs) are businesses with a parent company in one country and subsidiary operations in other countries. TNC foreign production accounts for about one fifth of world output.

☐ headquarters

○ major manufacturing plant

Corporation

	Ford
	General Motors
	Toyota
	Volkswagen

Globalisation index, 2006

The Globalisation index measures the extent to which countries are globally connected. The index combines country data on trade, foreign investment, international travel, international telephone traffic, internet use and membership of international organisations. The map shows only the top 50 countries.

Ranking

	1–10 (most globalised)
	11–20
	21–30
	31–40
	41–50

○ most rapidly globalising countries

Source: A. T. Kearney/Foreign Policy magazine

World economy

	economic core (countries dominant in the world economy)
	semi-periphery (countries partially dependent on the core)
	periphery (countries highly dependent on the core)

Global cities

Some geographers have identified a network of global cities arranged in a hierarchy according to the power they exert on the global economy. The map shows one view of this hierarchy. The position of each city in the hierarchy can change rapidly through time.

● cities dominating global financial markets

● cities dominating international and national economies

● cities dominating subnational and regional economies

City population

◯	10–25 million
○	5–10 million
○	1–5 million

Source: Friedmann, 1995

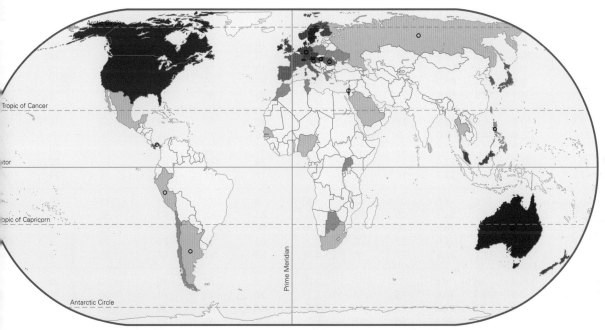

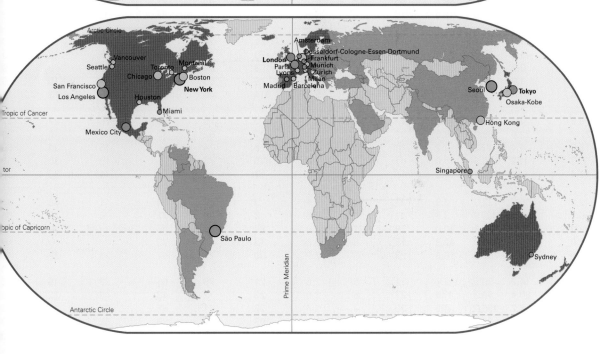

	Land		Population									Employment		
	Area	Arable and permanent crops	Total	Density	Change	Births	Deaths	Fertility	Infant mortality	Life expectancy	Urban	Agriculture	Industry	Servic
		2008	2010	2010	2000–2010	2010	2010	2010	2010	2010	2010			
	thousand km²	% of total	millions	persons per km²	%	births per 1000	deaths per 1000	children per mother	per 1000 live births	years	%	%	%	%
Afghanistan	652	12.1	29.1	44.6	28.2	39	18	5.7	155	44	22	ooo	ooo	ooo
Albania	29	25.4	3.2	110.3	3.2	10	5	1.6	18	75	49	55	23	22
Algeria	2382	3.5	36.0	15.1	14.3	23	5	2.3	28	72	63	26	31	43
Andorra	0.5	2.1	0.1	200.0	25.0	10	3	1.2	3	ooo	90	ooo	ooo	ooo
Angola	1247	3.0	19.0	15.2	47.3	42	17	5.8	118	47	57	75	8	17
Antigua and Barbuda	0.4	20.5	0.1	250.0	42.9	14	6	1.9	16	75	31	ooo	ooo	ooo
Argentina	2780	12.1	40.5	14.6	9.5	18	8	2.3	13	75	91	12	32	56
Armenia	30	17.7	3.1	103.3	-11.4	15	10	1.7	25	72	64	18	43	39
Australia	7741	5.8	22.4	2.9	18.5	14	6	1.9	4	81	82	6	26	68
Austria	84	17.5	8.4	100.0	2.4	9	9	1.4	4	80	67	8	38	54
Azerbaijan	87	25.3	9.0	103.4	16.9	17	6	2.2	11	72	54	31	29	40
Bahamas, The	14	1.1	0.3	21.4	0.0	15	6	1.9	14	74	83	5	16	79
Bahrain	0.7	5.8	1.3	1857.0	116.7	15	2	1.9	8	75	100	2	30	68
Bangladesh	144	66.8	164.4	1141.7	27.2	22	7	2.4	45	66	25	65	16	19
Barbados	0.4	39.5	0.3	750.0	0.0	13	8	1.7	9	74	38	14	30	56
Belarus	208	27.8	9.5	45.7	-6.9	12	14	1.4	5	70	74	20	40	40
Belgium	33	28.7	10.8	327.3	5.9	11	9	1.7	3	80	99	3	28	69
Belize	23	4.5	0.3	13.0	50.0	27	4	3.1	18	73	51	33	19	48
Benin	113	25.7	9.8	86.7	60.7	40	10	5.6	89	59	41	63	8	29
Bhutan	47	4.1	0.7	14.9	-66.7	25	8	3.1	40	68	32	94	2	4
Bolivia	1099	3.5	10.4	9.5	25.3	27	7	3.5	45	66	65	47	18	35
Bosnia-Herzegovina	51	21.4	3.8	74.5	-5.0	9	9	1.2	5	75	46	ooo	ooo	ooo
Botswana	582	0.4	1.8	3.1	12.5	30	11	3.2	48	55	60	46	20	34
Brazil	8547	8.1	193.3	22.6	13.6	17	6	2.0	24	73	84	23	23	54
Brunei	6	1.5	0.4	66.7	33.3	16	3	1.7	7	77	72	2	24	74
Bulgaria	111	29.9	7.5	67.6	-8.5	11	14	1.6	9	73	71	13	48	39
Burkina	274	23.2	16.2	59.1	36.1	46	12	6.0	81	53	23	92	2	6
Burundi	28	50.2	8.5	303.6	26.9	36	15	5.4	98	50	10	92	3	5
Cambodia	181	23.0	15.1	83.4	34.8	25	8	3.3	62	61	20	74	8	18
Cameroon	475	15.2	20.0	42.1	32.5	37	14	4.7	87	51	53	70	9	21
Canada	9971	5.7	34.1	3.4	9.6	11	7	2.0	5	81	80	3	25	72
Cape Verde	4	16.9	0.5	125.0	25.0	25	6	2.9	25	73	61	30	30	40
Central African Republic	623	3.2	4.8	7.7	33.3	38	16	4.8	106	49	38	80	3	17
Chad	1284	3.4	11.5	9.0	49.4	46	17	6.2	130	49	27	83	4	13
Chile	757	2.3	17.1	22.6	12.5	15	6	1.9	8	79	87	19	25	56
China	9598	13.1	1345.6	140.2	4.7	12	7	1.5	21	74	47	72	15	13
Colombia	1139	3.1	45.5	39.9	7.6	20	6	2.4	20	74	75	27	23	50
Comoros	2	72.5	0.7	350.0	0.0	33	7	4.1	53	64	28	78	9	13
Congo	342	1.6	3.9	11.4	34.5	38	13	5.0	79	53	60	49	15	36
Congo, Dem. Rep.	2345	3.3	67.8	28.9	31.1	47	17	6.4	114	48	33	68	13	19
Costa Rica	51	9.8	4.6	90.2	15.0	17	4	1.9	9	79	59	26	27	47
Côte d'Ivoire	322	22.2	22.0	68.3	48.6	37	14	4.9	97	52	50	60	10	30
Croatia	57	16.9	4.4	77.2	-2.2	10	12	1.5	6	76	56	16	34	50
Cuba	111	37.3	11.2	100.9	0.0	11	8	1.6	5	78	75	19	30	51
Cyprus	9	12.4	1.1	122.2	37.5	13	7	1.5	7	79	62	14	30	56
Czech Republic	79	42.3	10.5	132.9	2.9	11	10	1.5	3	77	74	11	45	44
Denmark	43	56.7	5.5	127.9	3.8	11	10	1.8	3	79	72	6	28	66
Djibouti	23	0.04	0.9	39.1	50.0	29	11	4.0	67	55	76	ooo	ooo	ooo
Dominica	0.8	28.0	0.1	125.0	42.9	15	8	2.0	12	75	73	ooo	ooo	ooo
Dominican Republic	49	26.9	9.9	202.0	16.5	23	6	2.7	30	72	67	25	29	46
Ecuador	284	10.1	14.2	50.0	12.7	21	5	2.6	21	75	65	33	19	48
Egypt	1001	3.6	80.4	80.3	17.4	27	6	3.0	28	72	43	40	22	38
El Salvador	21	44.2	6.2	295.2	-1.6	20	7	2.4	22	71	63	36	21	43
Equatorial Guinea	28	7.3	0.7	25.0	40.0	39	16	5.5	103	49	39	66	11	23
Eritrea	118	6.7	5.2	44.1	33.3	37	9	4.7	54	59	21	80	5	15

ooo no data

per capita for each person

Wealth · Energy and trade · Quality of life

[G]NI 2008 [billion] US$	Purchasing power 2008 US$	Growth of PP 2007–2008 annual %	Energy consumption 2008 kg oil equivalent per capita	Imports 2009 US$ per capita	Exports 2009 US$ per capita	Aid received (given) 2008 million US$	Human Development Index 2010	Health care 2000–2009 doctors per 100 000 people	Food consumption 2005 daily calories per capita	Safe water 2008 % access	Illiteracy male 2005–2008 %	Illiteracy female 2005–2008 %	Higher education 2005–2010 students per 1000 people	Cars 2008 per 1000 people	
9.8	ooo	ooo	13	140	20	4672	0.349	19	ooo	48	ooo	ooo	ooo	1	Afghanistan
2.1	7950	5.6	820	1421	340	359	0.719	101	2918	97	1	1	ooo	35	Albania
6.4	7940	1.5	1161	1110	1277	294	0.677	124	3510	83	19	36	1150	109	Algeria
ooo	ooo	ooo	ooo	ooo	ooo	ooo	0.824	356	ooo	100	ooo	ooo	1	ooo	Andorra
2.1	5020	11.8	280	994	2344	352	0.403	10	2518	50	17	43	49	4	Angola
ooo	20 570	ooo	2194	6520	720	8	ooo	ooo	2045	91	ooo	ooo	3	302	Antigua and Barbuda
37.2	14 020	6.0	1956	962	1381	122	0.775	307	2985	97	2	2	2208	239	Argentina
0.3	6310	6.6	1641	1066	225	286	0.695	370	2380	96	0	1	155	ooo	Armenia
2.5	34 040	1.9	6365	7556	7043	(2954)	0.937	97	3330	100	ooo	ooo	1281	619	Australia
6.0	37 680	1.5	4262	17 069	16 390	(1714)	0.851	380	4023	100	ooo	ooo	360	558	Austria
3.2	7770	9.6	1839	740	2397	222	0.713	400	2744	80	0	1	219	51	Azerbaijan
ooo	ooo	ooo	5368	8467	2220	ooo	0.784	ooo	2521	96	ooo	ooo	ooo	289	Bahamas, The
ooo	ooo	ooo	10 155	6083	9895	ooo	0.801	318	ooo	ooo	8	11	22	322	Bahrain
2.6	1440	4.7	140	135	93	1984	0.469	29	2309	80	40	50	1429	2	Bangladesh
ooo	ooo	ooo	1585	4830	1263	5	0.788	ooo	2988	100	ooo	ooo	15	188	Barbados
2.1	12 150	10.2	2816	2945	2194	102	0.732	479	2885	100	0	0	688	87	Belarus
4.5	34 760	0.4	6416	32 588	34 246	(2386)	0.867	424	3109	100	ooo	ooo	429	486	Belgium
ooo	6040	ooo	1317	2227	833	24	0.694	84	2921	99	ooo	ooo	6	10	Belize
6.0	1460	1.8	124	229	112	600	0.435	7	2437	75	46	72	43	2	Benin
ooo	4880	ooo	1849	756	709	80	ooo	2	ooo	92	35	61	5	ooo	Bhutan
4.1	4140	4.3	593	445	490	591	0.643	115	2128	86	4	14	403	46	Bolivia
17	8620	6.2	1839	2309	1034	450	0.710	123	3068	99	1	4	105	193	Bosnia-Herzegovina
ooo	13 100	ooo	812	2364	1729	680	0.633	45	ooo	95	17	16	16	57	Botswana
1.2	10 070	4.1	1284	698	799	427	0.699	170	3244	97	10	10	5958	156	Brazil
ooo	50 200	ooo	10 967	6250	17 250	ooo	0.805	100	2610	ooo	3	7	6	ooo	Brunei
1.8	11 950	6.5	2585	3070	2165	ooo	0.743	377	2839	100	1	2	268	333	Bulgaria
7.3	1160	1.5	33	132	54	936	0.305	7	2593	76	63	78	66	6	Burkina
1.1	380	1.4	19	48	8	479	0.282	2	1693	72	28	40	24	5	Burundi
8.9	1820	3.4	106	419	284	708	0.494	15	2370	61	15	29	138	ooo	Cambodia
1.8	2180	1.9	126	225	159	492	0.460	18	2634	74	16	32	181	8	Cameroon
0.0	36 220	-0.6	9930	9789	9398	(4795)	0.888	188	3486	100	ooo	ooo	ooo	563	Canada
ooo	3450	ooo	219	1418	70	205	0.534	78	2875	84	10	21	9	30	Cape Verde
1.8	730	0.9	32	67	27	242	0.315	8	2105	67	31	59	10	4	Central African Republic
5.9	1160	-3.1	9	189	272	391	0.295	3	2190	50	56	78	20	3	Chad
57.5	13 270	2.2	1705	2496	3161	68	0.783	107	3079	96	1	1	805	97	Chile
9.3	6020	8.4	1513	755	902	1405	0.663	141	2951	89	3	9	27 267	128	China
7.4	8510	1.3	729	729	728	936	0.689	135	2745	92	7	7	1570	67	Colombia
ooo	1170	ooo	56	214	19	35	0.428	16	1766	95	21	32	3	ooo	Comoros
7.1	3090	3.7	235	784	1514	469	0.489	11	2026	71	ooo	ooo	ooo	ooo	Congo
9.8	290	3.2	37	52	45	1543	0.239	9	1398	46	22	44	380	19	Congo, Dem. Rep.
27.5	10 950	1.5	1036	2532	1953	62	0.725	127	2618	97	4	4	111	ooo	Costa Rica
0.3	1580	-0.1	142	283	416	583	0.397	16	2268	80	36	56	157	12	Côte d'Ivoire
0.2	18 420	2.4	2186	4819	2380	369	0.767	262	2811	99	0	2	143	233	Croatia
ooo	ooo	ooo	874	859	278	119	ooo	635	3547	94	0	0	972	ooo	Cuba
ooo	24 040	ooo	2844	7075	1135	ooo	0.810	244	3295	100	1	3	26	450	Cyprus
3.2	22 790	2.3	3659	10 017	10 804	(249)	0.841	361	3303	100	ooo	ooo	413	399	Czech Republic
5.1	37 280	-1.8	3584	15 081	16 972	(2803)	0.866	313	3494	100	ooo	ooo	232	408	Denmark
ooo	2330	ooo	707	456	83	113	0.402	28	2674	92	ooo	ooo	3	28	Djibouti
ooo	8300	ooo	500	2150	340	20	ooo	ooo	3083	95	ooo	ooo	0.2	163	Dominica
3.2	7890	4.1	707	1216	541	146	0.663	170	2673	86	12	12	ooo	62	Dominican Republic
9.1	7760	5.4	849	1110	1015	216	0.695	136	2770	94	13	18	535	44	Ecuador
6.9	5460	5.1	997	572	293	1282	0.620	228	3274	99	25	42	2488	30	Egypt
1.4	6670	2.1	446	994	520	217	0.659	117	2680	87	13	19	139	57	El Salvador
ooo	21 700	ooo	2352	7429	13 000	35	0.538	31	ooo	43	3	11	ooo	ooo	Equatorial Guinea
1.5	630	-1.2	48	106	3	135	ooo	4	ooo	61	23	45	15	ooo	Eritrea

The datasets below are explained on pages 156

	Land		Population									Employment		
	Area	Arable and permanent crops	Total	Density	Change	Births	Deaths	Fertility	Infant mortality	Life expectancy	Urban	Agriculture	Industry	Services
		2008	2010	2010	2000–2010	2010	2010	2010	2010	2010	2010			
	thousand km²	% of total	millions	persons per km²	%	births per 1000	deaths per 1000	children per mother	per 1000 live births	years	%	%	%	%
Estonia	45	14.3	1.3	28.9	-7.1	12	12	1.6	4	74	69	14	41	45
Ethiopia	1104	14.5	85.0	77.0	35.8	39	12	5.4	77	55	16	86	2	12
Fiji	18	13.8	0.9	50.0	12.5	24	7	2.6	18	68	51	46	15	39
Finland	338	7.4	5.4	16.0	3.8	11	9	1.9	3	80	65	8	31	61
France	552	35.3	63.0	114.1	6.6	13	9	2.0	4	81	77	5	29	66
French Guiana	91	0.2	0.2	2.2	0.0	28	3	3.6	14	78	81	○○○	○○○	○○○
Gabon	268	1.8	1.5	5.6	25.0	29	10	3.6	55	60	84	51	16	33
Gambia, The	11	39.5	1.8	163.6	38.5	38	12	5.3	81	55	54	82	8	10
Georgia	70	8.4	4.6	65.7	-8.0	13	10	1.7	17	74	53	26	31	43
Germany	357	34.8	81.6	228.6	-0.7	8	10	1.3	4	80	73	4	38	58
Ghana	239	31.9	24.0	100.4	18.8	31	9	4.0	50	60	48	59	13	28
Greece	132	25.0	11.3	85.6	6.6	11	10	1.5	3	80	73	23	27	50
Greenland	342	○○○	0.1	0.2	○○○	○○○	○○○	○○○	○○○	○○○	○○○	○○○	○○○	○○○
Grenada	0.3	32.4	0.1	333.3	11.1	17	9	2.2	20	70	31	○○○	○○○	○○○
Guatemala	109	21.2	14.4	132.1	26.3	34	6	4.4	34	70	47	52	17	31
Guinea	246	12.6	10.8	43.9	45.9	41	11	5.7	91	57	28	87	2	11
Guinea-Bissau	36	19.6	1.6	44.4	33.3	43	18	5.8	121	46	30	85	2	13
Guyana	215	2.3	0.8	3.7	-11.1	23	7	2.8	38	66	28	22	25	53
Haiti	28	47.2	9.8	350.0	19.5	28	9	3.5	49	61	48	68	9	23
Honduras	112	12.8	7.6	67.9	16.9	28	5	3.3	23	72	50	41	20	39
Hungary	93	53.2	10.0	107.5	0.0	10	13	1.3	5	74	67	15	38	47
Iceland	103	0.07	0.3	2.9	0.0	15	6	2.1	3	81	93	○○○	○○○	○○○
India	3288	56.9	1188.8	361.6	17.3	23	7	2.6	53	64	29	64	16	20
Indonesia	1905	20.5	235.5	123.6	11.0	20	6	2.4	30	71	43	55	14	31
Iran	1633	11.5	75.1	46.0	10.9	19	6	1.8	29	71	69	39	23	38
Iraq	438	12.5	31.5	71.9	36.4	32	6	4.1	84	67	67	16	18	66
Ireland	70	16.0	4.5	64.3	21.6	17	6	2.1	4	79	60	14	29	57
Israel	21	17.5	7.6	361.9	22.6	22	5	3.0	4	81	92	4	29	67
Italy	301	33.2	60.5	201.0	5.6	10	10	1.4	4	82	68	9	31	60
Jamaica	11	21.7	2.7	245.5	3.8	20	7	2.4	26	72	52	25	23	52
Japan	378	12.7	127.4	337.0	0.6	9	9	1.4	3	83	86	7	34	59
Jordan	89	2.6	6.5	73.0	-3.0	31	4	3.8	23	73	83	15	23	62
Kazakhstan	2717	8.4	16.3	6.0	0.6	23	9	2.7	26	69	54	22	32	46
Kenya	580	10.2	40.0	69.0	32.9	37	10	4.6	52	57	18	80	7	13
Kiribati	0.7	42.0	0.1	142.9	25.0	27	9	3.5	52	61	44	○○○	○○○	○○○
Kuwait	18	0.8	3.1	172.2	55.0	22	2	2.2	9	78	98	1	25	74
Kyrgyzstan	199	7.1	5.3	26.6	12.8	24	7	2.8	31	68	35	32	27	41
Laos	237	5.8	6.4	27.0	18.5	28	7	3.5	60	65	27	78	6	16
Latvia	65	18.9	2.2	33.8	-8.3	10	13	1.3	7	73	68	16	40	44
Lebanon	10	28.0	4.3	430.0	30.3	20	5	2.3	19	72	87	7	31	62
Lesotho	30	11.8	1.9	63.3	-13.6	28	19	3.2	94	41	23	40	28	32
Liberia	111	6.4	4.1	36.9	28.1	43	11	5.9	95	56	58	○○○	○○○	○○○
Libya	1760	1.2	6.5	3.7	16.1	23	4	2.7	18	74	77	11	23	66
Liechtenstein	0.2	25.0	0.04	200.0	33.3	10	6	1.4	3	80	15	○○○	○○○	○○○
Lithuania	65	30.1	3.3	50.8	-10.8	11	12	1.5	5	72	67	18	41	41
Luxembourg	3	24.3	0.5	166.7	25.0	11	7	1.6	2	80	83	○○○	○○○	○○○
Macedonia, FYRO*	26	18.5	2.1	80.8	5.0	12	9	1.5	11	74	65	21	40	39
Madagascar	587	6.1	20.1	34.2	26.4	37	9	4.8	48	60	31	78	7	15
Malawi	118	38.5	15.4	130.5	41.3	44	15	6.0	80	49	14	87	5	8
Malaysia	330	23.1	28.9	87.6	30.2	21	5	2.6	9	74	63	27	23	50
Maldives	0.3	26.7	0.3	1000.0	0.0	22	3	2.5	12	73	35	32	31	37
Mali	1240	4.1	15.2	12.3	35.7	46	15	6.6	116	51	33	86	2	12
Malta	0.3	31.3	0.4	1333.3	0.0	10	8	1.4	6	79	94	○○○	○○○	○○○
Marshall Islands	0.2	55.6	0.1	500.0	66.7	34	6	4.3	21	66	68	○○○	○○○	○○○
Mauritania	1026	0.4	3.4	3.3	25.9	34	11	4.5	73	57	40	55	10	35

Key:
- ○○○ no data
- per capita for each person

* Former Yugoslav Republic of Macedonia

© Oxford University Press

Wealth | Energy and trade | Quality of life

NI	Purchasing power	Growth of PP	Energy consumption	Imports	Exports	Aid received (given)	Human Development Index	Health care	Food consumption	Safe water	Illiteracy male	Illiteracy female	Higher education	Cars	
008	2008	2007–2008	2008	2009	2009	2008	2010	2000–2009	2005	2008	2005–2008	2005–2008	2005–2010	2008	
llion US$	US$	annual %	kg oil equivalent per capita	US$ per capita	US$ per capita	million US$		doctors per 100 000 people	daily calories per capita	% access	%	%	students per 1000 people	per 1000 people	
ooo	19 280	ooo	4425	7786	6947	ooo	0.812	340	2744	98	0	0	77	410	Estonia
22.7	870	8.5	36	96	19	3196	0.328	2	1582	38	50	77	296	1	Ethiopia
ooo	4270	ooo	1046	1838	813	43	0.669	42	3197	ooo	ooo	ooo	13	129	Fiji
55.7	35 660	0.4	5745	11 463	11 849	(1166)	0.871	337	3387	100	ooo	ooo	310	543	Finland
02.2	34 400	-0.2	4292	8943	7743	(10 908)	0.872	374	3681	100	ooo	ooo	2198	494	France
ooo	ooo	ooo	1672	ooo	ooo	ooo	ooo	ooo	ooo	84	ooo	ooo	ooo	ooo	French Guiana
ooo	12 270	ooo	802	1467	3400	51	0.648	28	2705	87	9	17	ooo	ooo	Gabon
ooo	1280	ooo	77	190	9	90	0.390	4	2537	92	43	66	6	ooo	Gambia, The
10.8	4850	2.8	858	952	247	849	0.698	424	1797	98	0	0	109	ooo	Georgia
85.7	35 940	1.5	4117	11 443	13 736	(13 981)	0.885	350	3472	100	ooo	ooo	ooo	558	Germany
15.7	1430	4.0	162	342	231	1237	0.467	11	3098	82	28	41	169	ooo	Ghana
22.0	28 470	2.5	3093	5297	1778	(703)	0.855	557	3706	100	2	4	642	455	Greece
nnn	nnn	nnn	nnn	nnn	nnn	nnn	ooo	ooo	ooo	ooo	ooo	ooo	ooo	ooo	Greenland
ooo	8060	ooo	976	2820	290	31	ooo	ooo	2310	94	ooo	ooo	9	ooo	Grenada
36.6	4690	1.5	355	824	515	501	0.560	ooo	2239	94	20	31	234	19	Guatemala
3.7	1190	6.0	53	139	100	300	0.340	10	2428	71	50	74	80	5	Guinea
ooo	530	ooo	87	144	72	123	0.289	6	1949	61	34	63	4	6	Guinea-Bissau
ooo	2510	ooo	615	1451	954	157	0.611	46	2853	94	ooo	ooo	8	41	Guyana
6.5	1180	-0.5	77	223	63	870	0.404	ooo	1945	63	ooo	ooo	ooo	12	Haiti
13.0	3870	2.2	430	1038	693	533	0.604	50	2435	86	16	17	ooo	11	Honduras
28.6	17 790	0.8	2607	7818	8378	(107)	0.805	280	3272	100	1	1	469	301	Hungary
ooo	25 220	ooo	19 628	11 993	13 420	(48)	0.869	373	3189	100	ooo	ooo	17	658	Iceland
15.5	2960	5.7	409	213	139	2034	0.519	58	2417	88	25	49	15 788	12	India
58.2	3830	4.9	572	377	491	1202	0.600	13	2893	80	5	11	4420	21	Indonesia
51.5	10 840	4.2	2651	688	1067	93	0.702	95	3082	93	13	23	3350	133	Iran
ooo	ooo	ooo	1086	1233	1317	9326	ooo	60	ooo	79	14	31	425	50	Iraq
21.2	37 350	-4.4	3612	13 890	25 464	(1328)	0.895	321	3679	100	ooo	ooo	239	542	Ireland
80.5	27 450	2.3	2701	6484	6307	ooo	0.872	396	3695	100	ooo	ooo	337	263	Israel
09.1	30 250	-1.8	3107	6844	6729	(4861)	0.854	370	3730	100	1	1	2041	571	Italy
ooo	7360	ooo	1498	1876	487	75	0.688	80	2826	94	19	9	184	85	Jamaica
79.2	35 220	-0.7	4036	4326	4551	(9579)	0.884	212	2679	100	ooo	ooo	3952	543	Japan
19.5	5530	2.3	1240	2386	1079	717	0.681	259	2741	96	5	11	255	47	Jordan
96.2	9690	1.9	3257	1787	2717	315	0.714	378	3200	95	0	0	1105	170	Kazakhstan
29.5	1580	0.9	129	261	113	1308	0.470	13	1881	59	10	17	243	ooo	Kenya
ooo	3660	ooo	144	680	150	25	ooo	20	2333	64	ooo	ooo	ooo	ooo	Kiribati
ooo	52 610	ooo	10 414	5973	16 776	ooo	0.771	202	ooo	99	5	7	75	ooo	Kuwait
3.9	2130	6.2	833	573	272	340	0.598	238	3052	90	0	1	302	ooo	Kyrgyzstan
4.7	2060	5.6	170	200	149	468	0.497	31	3064	57	18	37	111	ooo	Laos
ooo	16 740	ooo	1669	4246	3343	ooo	0.769	302	2586	99	0	0	131	372	Latvia
26.3	10 880	6.9	1206	4250	1074	1012	ooo	302	3009	100	7	14	200	434	Lebanon
ooo	2000	ooo	75	929	357	136	0.427	4	ooo	85	17	5	9	ooo	Lesotho
0.6	300	2.4	58	138	38	1189	0.300	2	1943	68	37	47	ooo	13	Liberia
72.7	15 630	5.0	2933	1611	5651	57	0.755	120	2892	54	5	19	ooo	234	Libya
39.9	18 210	3.6	2727	5525	4985	ooo	0.783	381	3196	ooo	0	0	214	453	Lithuania
ooo	ooo	ooo	ooo	ooo	ooo	ooo	0.891	ooo	ooo	ooo	ooo	ooo	1	ooo	Liechtenstein
ooo	64 320	ooo	9208	48 760	41 600	(415)	0.852	265	ooo	100	ooo	ooo	4	697	Luxembourg
ooo	9950	ooo	1469	2522	1346	205	0.701	247	2631	100	1	5	66	157	Macedonia, FYRO*
7.8	1040	4.1	58	167	58	794	0.435	17	2148	41	23	35	68	1	Madagascar
4.1	830	7.0	55	120	65	882	0.385	2	1729	80	20	34	6	1	Malawi
88.1	13 740	2.9	2087	4376	5563	145	0.744	70	3013	100	6	10	945	273	Malaysia
ooo	5280	ooo	957	3223	563	51	0.602	76	2791	91	2	2	ooo	ooo	Maldives
7.4	1090	1.9	23	203	162	907	0.309	9	2306	56	65	82	77	1	Mali
ooo	22 460	ooo	2495	9015	5245	ooo	0.815	339	3451	100	9	6	10	539	Malta
ooo	ooo	ooo	ooo	900	210	52	ooo	40	ooo	94	ooo	ooo	ooo	ooo	Marshall Islands
2.6	2000	-0.6	291	433	415	291	0.433	14	2371	49	36	50	12	5	Mauritania

The datasets below are explained on pages 156/

	ooo	no data
	per capita	for each person

	Land		Population									Employment		
	Area	Arable and permanent crops	Total	Density	Change	Births	Deaths	Fertility	Infant mortality	Life expectancy	Urban	Agriculture	Industry	Service
		2008	2010	2010	2000–2010	2010	2010	2010	2010	2010	2010			
	thousand km²	% of total	millions	persons per km²	%	births per 1000	deaths per 1000	children per mother	per 1000 live births	years	%	%	%	%
Mauritius	2	44.8	1.3	650.0	8.3	12	7	1.5	13	73	42	17	43	40
Mexico	1958	14.1	110.6	56.5	11.8	19	5	2.2	17	76	77	28	24	48
Micronesia, Fed. States	0.7	27.9	0.1	142.9	0.0	25	6	3.9	38	68	22	ooo	ooo	ooo
Moldova	34	64.6	4.1	120.6	-4.7	11	12	1.3	12	70	41	33	30	37
Mongolia	1567	0.5	2.8	1.8	3.7	25	6	2.7	41	67	61	32	22	46
Montenegro	14	14.1	0.6	42.9	ooo	13	9	1.8	8	74	64	ooo	ooo	ooo
Morocco	447	20.1	31.9	71.4	12.3	21	6	2.4	31	71	57	45	25	30
Mozambique	802	6.0	23.4	29.2	18.8	40	16	5.1	90	48	31	83	8	9
Myanmar	677	17.9	53.4	78.9	17.1	20	11	2.4	56	58	31	73	10	17
Namibia	824	1.0	2.2	2.7	29.4	28	9	3.4	35	61	35	49	15	36
Nauru	0.02	20.0	0.01	500.0	0.0	28	10	3.2	38	56	100	ooo	ooo	ooo
Nepal	147	17.3	28.0	190.5	17.2	28	8	3.0	48	64	17	94	0	6
Netherlands	41	32.6	16.6	404.9	5.1	11	8	1.7	4	80	66	5	26	69
New Zealand	271	2.0	4.4	16.2	12.8	14	7	2.1	5	80	86	10	25	65
Nicaragua	130	17.7	6.0	46.2	17.6	23	4	2.5	24	71	56	28	26	46
Niger	1267	11.5	15.9	12.5	48.6	52	17	7.4	108	48	20	90	4	6
Nigeria	924	44.5	158.3	171.3	42.0	42	17	5.7	75	47	47	43	7	50
Northern Marianas	0.5	4.3	0.1	180.0	ooo	ooo	ooo	ooo	ooo	ooo	ooo	ooo	ooo	ooo
North Korea	121	24.1	22.8	188.4	-5.0	15	10	2.0	53	63	60	38	32	30
Norway	324	2.8	4.9	15.1	8.9	13	9	2.0	3	81	80	6	25	69
Oman	213	0.3	3.1	14.6	24.0	20	3	2.6	9	72	72	44	24	32
Pakistan	796	27.5	184.8	232.2	18.1	30	7	4.0	64	66	35	52	19	29
Palau	0.5	6.5	0.02	40.0	0.0	13	7	2.0	20	69	78	ooo	ooo	ooo
Panama	76	9.3	3.5	46.1	20.7	20	5	2.5	13	76	64	26	16	58
Papua New Guinea	463	2.0	6.8	14.7	41.7	31	10	4.1	51	59	13	79	7	14
Paraguay	407	10.8	6.5	16.0	18.2	25	6	3.1	32	72	58	39	22	39
Peru	1285	3.5	29.5	23.0	14.8	21	6	2.6	20	73	76	36	18	46
Philippines	300	34.5	94.0	313.3	23.7	26	5	3.2	23	72	63	46	15	39
Poland	323	42.6	38.2	118.3	-1.5	11	10	1.4	6	76	61	27	36	37
Portugal	92	17.9	10.7	116.3	8.1	9	10	1.3	4	79	55	18	34	48
Qatar	11	1.4	1.7	154.5	183.3	9	1	1.8	8	76	100	3	32	65
Romania	238	39.6	21.5	90.3	-3.6	10	12	1.3	10	73	55	24	47	29
Russian Federation	17 075	7.5	141.9	8.3	-3.4	12	14	1.5	8	68	73	14	42	44
Rwanda	26	63.6	10.4	400.0	35.1	42	14	5.4	102	51	17	92	3	5
St. Kitts and Nevis	0.4	15.8	0.1	250.0	150.0	14	7	1.8	11	74	32	ooo	ooo	ooo
St. Lucia	0.6	16.4	0.2	333.3	0.0	14	7	1.7	20	73	28	ooo	ooo	ooo
St. Vincent & the Grenadines	0.4	20.5	0.1	250.0	0.0	17	8	2.1	18	72	40	ooo	ooo	ooo
Samoa	3.0	22.3	0.2	66.7	185.7	26	5	4.2	20	73	22	ooo	ooo	ooo
San Marino	0.06	16.7	0.03	500.0	0.0	10	7	1.2	3	83	84	ooo	ooo	ooo
Sao Tome and Principe	1.0	56.3	0.2	200.0	100.0	37	7	4.9	45	66	58	ooo	ooo	ooo
Saudi Arabia	2150	1.7	29.2	13.6	35.2	28	2	3.8	18	76	81	19	20	61
Senegal	197	18.5	12.5	63.5	31.6	39	11	4.9	58	55	41	77	8	15
Serbia	88	40.8	7.3	83.0	ooo	9	14	1.4	7	74	58	ooo	ooo	ooo
Seychelles	0.5	8.7	0.1	200.0	25.0	18	7	2.3	12	73	53	ooo	ooo	ooo
Sierra Leone	72	26.9	5.8	80.6	18.4	40	16	5.1	89	47	36	68	15	17
Singapore	1	1.0	5.1	5100.0	41.7	10	4	1.2	2	81	100	0	36	64
Slovakia	49	29.2	5.4	110.2	0.0	11	10	1.4	6	75	55	12	32	56
Slovenia	20	10.3	2.1	105.0	5.0	11	9	1.5	2	79	50	6	46	48
Solomon Islands	29	2.7	0.5	17.2	25.0	33	8	4.4	24	62	17	77	7	16
Somalia	638	1.6	9.4	14.7	-6.9	46	16	6.5	111	49	34	ooo	ooo	ooo
South Africa	1221	12.7	49.9	40.9	23.5	21	12	2.4	46	55	52	14	32	54
South Korea	99	18.0	48.9	493.9	4.5	9	5	1.2	3	80	82	18	35	47
Spain	506	34.7	47.1	93.1	18.9	11	8	1.4	4	81	77	12	33	55
Sri Lanka	66	35.1	20.7	313.6	10.1	19	7	2.4	15	74	15	48	21	31
Sudan	2506	8.8	43.2	17.2	46.4	33	11	4.5	81	58	38	70	8	22

Wealth Energy and trade Quality of life

GNI	Purchasing power	Growth of PP	Energy consumption	Imports	Exports	Aid received (given)	Human Development Index	Health care	Food consumption	Safe water	Illiteracy male	Illiteracy female	Higher education	Cars	
2008	2008	2007–2008	2008	2009	2009	2008	2010	2000–2009	2005	2008	2005–2008	2005–2008	2005–2010	2008	
billion US$	US$	annual %	kg oil equivalent per capita	US$ per capita	US$ per capita	million US$		doctors per 100 000 people	daily calories per capita	% access	%	%	students per 1000 people	per 1000 people	
°°°	12 480	°°°	1126	2868	1494	102	0.701	109	3097	99	10	15	30	88	Mauritius
061.4	14 270	0.8	1600	2204	2095	148	0.750	283	3117	94	5	9	2623	209	Mexico
°°°	3000	°°°	°°°	1550	270	91	0.614	60	°°°	94	°°°	°°°	°°°	°°°	Micronesia, Fed. States
5.3	3210	8.2	793	800	314	280	0.623	260	2953	90	1	2	137	49	Moldova
°°°	3480	°°°	774	789	705	232	0.622	240	1995	76	3	2	174	°°°	Mongolia
°°°	13 920	°°°	1410	3117	975	99	0.769	176	2679	98	°°°	°°°	°°°	°°°	Montenegro
80.5	4330	4.6	422	1044	440	1129	0.567	55	3256	81	31	56	419	53	Morocco
8.1	770	4.5	194	171	98	1907	0.284	3	2392	47	30	60	28	2	Mozambique
°°°	1290	11.7	127	86	134	513	0.451	38	3305	71	5	11	508	6	Myanmar
°°°	6270	°°°	836	2327	1615	197	0.606	30	°°°	92	11	12	23	°°°	Namibia
°°°	°°°	°°°	5704	°°°	°°°	30	°°°	100	°°°	°°°	°°°	°°°	°°°	156	Nauru
11.5	1120	3.6	66	160	30	687	0.428	19	2341	88	29	55	289	9	Nepal
324.6	41 670	1.7	5946	27 000	30 202	(6993)	0.890	390	3427	100	°°°	°°°	609	467	Netherlands
119.3	25 090	-2.5	4835	5941	5798	(348)	0.907	200	3337	100	°°°	°°°	302	560	New Zealand
6.1	2620	2.2	313	610	244	698	0.565	37	2402	85	22	22	°°°	33	Nicaragua
4.8	680	6.0	29	98	59	569	0.261	2	1897	48	57	85	17	4	Niger
175.6	1940	3.0	173	256	344	1234	0.423	42	2848	58	28	51	1392	1	Nigeria
°°°	°°°	°°°	°°°	°°°	°°°	°°°	°°°	°°°	°°°	98	°°°	°°°	°°°	°°°	Northern Marianas
°°°	°°°	°°°	888	92	68	210	°°°	323	2291	100	0	0	°°°	°°°	North Korea
415.3	58 500	0.7	9541	14 436	25 183	(3963)	0.938	394	3366	100	°°°	°°°	220	494	Norway
°°°	20 650	°°°	6223	5813	8920	30	°°°	158	°°°	88	10	19	84	150	Oman
162.9	2700	3.7	338	175	98	1493	0.490	77	2446	90	33	60	1239	8	Pakistan
0.2	°°°	°°°	°°°	6000	300	41	°°°	150	°°°	84	°°°	°°°	°°°	°°°	Palau
21.0	11 650	7.5	1655	2229	271	27	0.755	138	2681	93	6	7	145	167	Panama
6.5	2000	3.7	263	485	656	298	0.431	5	°°°	40	36	44	°°°	13	Papua New Guinea
13.6	4820	4.0	1665	1102	503	125	0.640	98	3101	86	4	7	182	63	Paraguay
115.0	7980	8.6	586	743	921	437	0.723	°°°	2411	82	5	15	952	41	Peru
170.4	3900	2.0	337	498	417	80	0.638	101	2497	91	7	6	3535	31	Philippines
453.0	17 310	4.8	2405	3848	3529	(372)	0.795	201	3596	100	0	1	2202	382	Poland
218.4	22 080	-0.2	2358	6589	4090	(620)	0.795	341	3547	99	3	7	382	374	Portugal
°°°	°°°	°°°	26 246	16 429	28 929	°°°	0.803	257	°°°	100	6	10	13	378	Qatar
170.6	13 500	9.4	1838	2523	1890	°°°	0.767	186	4125	°°°	2	3	1102	246	Romania
364.5	15 630	7.5	5054	1353	2140	°°°	0.719	432	3005	96	0	1	9604	213	Russian Federation
4.0	1010	8.2	26	124	19	893	0.385	2	1980	65	25	34	55	2	Rwanda
°°°	15 170	°°°	1768	5620	780	42	°°°	115	2798	99	°°°	°°°	1	223	St. Kitts and Nevis
°°°	9190	°°°	715	2695	765	18	°°°	°°°	2159	98	°°°	°°°	5	166	St. Lucia
°°°	8770	°°°	849	3330	490	25	°°°	89	°°°	°°°	°°°	°°°	°°°	100	St. Vincent & the Grenadines
°°°	4340	°°°	344	1020	60	38	°°°	25	3093	88	1	1	°°°	41	Samoa
°°°	°°°	°°°	°°°	°°°	°°°	°°°	°°°	°°°	°°°	°°°	°°°	°°°	1	°°°	San Marino
°°°	1780	°°°	231	570	45	44	0.488	41	°°°	89	6	17	1	°°°	Sao Tome and Principe
374.3	22 950	2.1	5643	3330	6700	°°°	0.752	155	2631	90	10	20	758	336	Saudi Arabia
11.8	1760	-0.2	164	377	174	998	0.411	6	2228	69	48	67	94	18	Senegal
41.9	11 150	6.1	2320	2135	1143	975	0.735	198	2679	99	1	4	238	°°°	Serbia
°°°	19 770	°°°	3305	8110	4310	11	°°°	121	2992	°°°	9	8	°°°	118	Seychelles
1.8	750	2.4	77	91	41	358	0.317	2	°°°	49	48	71	°°°	11	Sierra Leone
168.2	47 940	-4.1	11 667	48 193	52 908	°°°	0.846	142	°°°	100	3	8	305	158	Singapore
78.6	21 300	6.2	3501	10 241	10 367	(92)	0.818	312	2615	100	°°°	°°°	231	261	Slovakia
°°°	26 910	°°°	3857	13 232	13 185	°°°	0.828	238	3087	99	0	0	117	488	Slovenia
°°°	2580	°°°	154	540	326	216	0.494	10	2262	70	16	31	°°°	°°°	Solomon Islands
°°°	°°°	°°°	32	°°°	°°°	727	°°°	3	°°°	30	°°°	°°°	°°°	3	Somalia
283.3	9780	1.3	2788	1443	1235	1083	0.597	79	2874	91	10	12	°°°	146	South Africa
046.3	28 120	1.9	4795	6634	7465	(802)	0.877	168	2969	98	°°°	°°°	3204	338	South Korea
456.5	31 130	-0.3	3297	6131	4659	(6867)	0.863	405	3285	100	2	3	1781	479	Spain
35.9	4480	5.8	250	498	358	689	0.658	51	2200	90	8	11	°°°	25	Sri Lanka
46.5	1930	5.9	113	229	185	2289	0.379	27	2444	57	21	40	°°°	3	Sudan

	○○○	no data
	per capita	for each person

	Land		Population									Employment		
	Area	Arable and permanent crops	Total	Density	Change	Births	Deaths	Fertility	Infant mortality	Life expectancy	Urban	Agriculture	Industry	Service
		2008	2010	2010	2000–2010	2010	2010	2010	2010	2010	2010			
	thousand km²	% of total	millions	persons per km²	%	births per 1000	deaths per 1000	children per mother	per 1000 live births	years	%	%	%	%
Suriname	163	0.4	0.5	3.1	25.0	19	7	2.4	22	69	67	21	18	61
Swaziland	17	11.2	1.2	70.6	20.0	31	16	3.7	74	46	22	40	22	38
Sweden	450	6.4	9.4	20.9	5.6	12	10	1.9	2	81	84	○○○	○○○	○○○
Switzerland	41	10.8	7.8	190.2	5.4	10	8	1.5	4	82	73	6	35	59
Syria	185	30.9	22.5	121.6	39.8	28	3	3.3	16	74	54	33	24	43
Taiwan	36	○○○	23.2	644.4	○○○	8	6	1.0	5	79	78	○○○	○○○	○○○
Tajikistan	143	6.2	7.6	53.1	22.6	28	4	3.4	60	67	26	41	23	36
Tanzania	945	12.4	45.0	47.6	34.3	42	12	5.6	58	55	25	84	5	11
Thailand	513	36.9	68.1	132.7	10.9	15	9	1.8	7	69	31	64	14	22
Togo	57	48.4	6.8	119.3	47.8	33	8	4.8	81	61	40	66	10	24
Tonga	0.8	37.5	0.1	125.0	0.0	29	7	4.2	19	70	23	○○○	○○○	○○○
Trinidad and Tobago	5	9.2	1.3	260.0	0.0	14	8	1.6	26	69	12	11	31	58
Tunisia	164	32.4	10.5	64.0	9.4	18	6	2.1	18	74	66	28	33	39
Turkey	775	31.8	73.6	95.0	10.5	18	6	2.1	28	72	76	53	18	29
Turkmenistan	488	4.1	5.2	10.7	15.6	22	8	2.5	51	65	47	37	23	40
Tuvalu	0.02	60.0	0.01	500.0	0.0	23	9	3.7	35	64	47	○○○	○○○	○○○
Uganda	241	40.1	33.8	140.2	55.0	47	13	6.5	76	52	13	85	5	10
Ukraine	604	57.6	45.9	76.0	-9.1	11	15	1.5	9	68	69	20	40	40
United Arab Emirates	84	3.2	5.4	64.3	125.0	15	2	2.0	7	77	83	8	27	65
United Kingdom	245	25.0	62.2	253.9	5.8	13	9	1.9	5	80	80	2	29	69
United States of America	9364	18.9	309.6	33.1	11.2	14	8	2.0	6	78	79	3	28	69
Uruguay	177	9.6	3.4	19.2	3.0	14	9	2.0	11	76	94	14	27	59
Uzbekistan	447	10.9	28.1	62.9	15.6	23	5	2.8	48	68	36	34	25	41
Vanuatu	12	11.9	0.2	16.7	0.0	31	6	4.0	25	67	24	○○○	○○○	○○○
Venezuela	912	3.8	28.8	31.6	19.0	21	5	2.6	16	74	88	12	27	61
Vietnam	332	30.4	88.9	267.8	11.4	17	5	2.1	15	74	28	71	14	15
Western Sahara	252	0.02	0.5	2.0	66.7	34	9	4.5	63	60	81	○○○	○○○	○○○
Yemen	528	3.0	23.6	44.7	30.4	38	8	5.5	59	63	29	61	17	22
Zambia	753	3.2	13.3	17.7	44.6	45	20	6.2	70	42	37	75	8	17
Zimbabwe	391	10.0	12.6	32.2	7.7	30	17	3.7	60	43	37	68	8	24

Explanation of datasets

Land

Area does not include areas of lakes and seas.

Arable and permanent crops percentage of total land area used for arable and permanent crops.

Population

Total estimate for mid 2010.

Density the total population of a country divided by its land area.

Change percentage change in population between 2000 and 2010. Negative numbers indicate a decrease.

Births number of births per one thousand people in one year.

Deaths number of deaths per one thousand people in one year.

Fertility average number of children born to child bearing women.

Infant mortality number of deaths of children under one year per 1000 live births.

Life expectancy number of years a baby born now can expect to live.

Urban percentage of the population living in towns and cities.

Employment

Agriculture percentage of the labour force employed in agriculture.

Industry percentage of the labour force employed in industry.

Services percentage of the labour force employed in services.

Wealth | Energy and trade | Quality of life

GNI	Purchasing power	Growth of PP	Energy consumption	Imports	Exports	Aid received (given)	Human Development Index	Health care	Food consumption	Safe water	Illiteracy male	Illiteracy female	Higher education	Cars	
2008	2008	2007–2008	2008	2009	2009	2008	2010	2000–2009	2005	2008	2005–2008	2005–2008	2005–2010	2008	
million US$	US$	annual %	kg oil equivalent per capita	US$ per capita	US$ per capita	million US$		doctors per 100 000 people	daily calories per capita	% access	%	%	students per 1000 people	per 1000 people	
ooo	7130	ooo	1660	2320	2900	94	0.646	38	3424	93	7	12	ooo	172	Suriname
ooo	5010	ooo	417	1333	1250	64	0.498	16	ooo	69	13	14	6	ooo	Swaziland
9.7	38 180	-1.0	5684	12 886	14 112	(4732)	0.885	361	3108	100	ooo	ooo	427	475	Sweden
8.5	46 460	0.5	4090	19 962	22 160	(2038)	0.874	384	3306	100	ooo	ooo	239	539	Switzerland
4.4	4350	0.6	990	744	475	130	0.589	55	2906	89	10	23	ooo	ooo	Syria
ooo	ooo	ooo	4673	ooo	ooo	ooo	ooo	ooo	ooo	ooo	ooo	ooo	ooo	ooo	Taiwan
4.1	1860	6.2	825	343	135	276	0.580	192	ooo	70	0	0	191	ooo	Tajikistan
18.4	1230	4.4	68	145	71	2233	0.398	1	2131	54	21	34	55	ooo	Tanzania
91.7	5990	2.0	1411	1973	2249	-542	0.654	29	2657	98	4	8	2428	ooo	Thailand
2.6	820	-1.4	141	227	121	310	0.428	6	1895	60	23	46	33	ooo	Togo
ooo	3880	ooo	641	1500	90	25	0.677	30	ooo	100	1	1	ooo	174	Tonga
ooo	23 950	ooo	16 087	5350	7020	11	0.736	140	2805	94	1	2	25	151	Trinidad and Tobago
34.0	7070	4.1	799	1836	1389	442	0.683	131	3484	94	14	29	351	110	Tunisia
90.7	13 770	2.5	1357	1884	1365	1866	0.679	157	3212	99	4	19	2533	235	Turkey
14.3	6210	8.4	4511	1324	1293	16	0.669	242	3112	84	0	1	ooo	ooo	Turkmenistan
ooo	ooo	ooo	ooo	3300	0	16	ooo	100	ooo	97	ooo	ooo	ooo	ooo	Tuvalu
13.3	1140	6.0	35	140	81	1575	0.422	12	2392	67	18	33	108	4	Uganda
48.6	7210	2.7	3215	988	863	579	0.710	308	2865	98	0	0	3020	98	Ukraine
ooo	ooo	5.7	17 062	27 451	34 314	ooo	0.815	150	2446	100	11	9	77	193	United Arab Emirates
87.2	36 130	0.1	3595	7795	5704	(11 500)	0.849	208	3424	100	ooo	ooo	2334	458	United Kingdom
56.1	46 970	0.2	7694	5232	3442	(26 842)	0.902	266	3637	99	ooo	ooo	18 671	842	United States of America
27.5	12 540	8.6	1188	2031	1584	31	0.765	364	3066	100	2	2	163	174	Uruguay
24.7	2660	7.2	2039	327	389	175	0.617	262	2074	87	0	1	301	ooo	Uzbekistan
ooo	3940	ooo	196	1470	290	88	ooo	15	2187	83	17	20	ooo	54	Vanuatu
57.8	12 830	3.1	2697	1429	2028	55	0.696	187	2509	93	5	5	2109	110	Venezuela
77.0	2700	4.7	439	801	654	2400	0.572	53	2762	94	5	10	1774	ooo	Vietnam
ooo	ooo	ooo	200	ooo	ooo	ooo	ooo	ooo	ooo	ooo	ooo	ooo	ooo	ooo	Western Sahara
21.9	2210	0.9	334	371	244	291	0.439	31	1590	62	21	57	237	ooo	Yemen
12.0	1230	3.4	244	301	342	1035	0.395	6	ooo	60	19	39	ooo	ooo	Zambia
ooo	ooo	ooo	286	232	182	594	0.140	17	1870	82	6	11	74	ooo	Zimbabwe

Explanation of datasets

Wealth

GNI Gross National Income (GNI) is the total value of goods and services produced in a country plus income from abroad.

Purchasing power Gross Domestic Product (GDP) is the total value of goods and services produced in a country. Purchasing power parity (PPP) is GDP per person, adjusted for the local cost of living.

Growth of PP average annual growth (or decline, shown as a negative value in the table) in purchasing power. This figure shows whether people are becoming better or worse off.

Energy and trade

Energy consumption consumption of commercial energy per person shown as the equivalent in kilograms of oil.

Imports total value of imports per person shown in US dollars.

Exports total value of exports per person shown in US dollars.

Aid received (given) amount of economic aid a country has received. Negative values indicate that the repayment of loans exceeds the amount of aid received. Figures in brackets show aid given.

Quality of life

HDI Human Development Index (HDI) measures the relative social and economic progress of a country. It combines life expectancy, adult literacy, average number of years of schooling, and purchasing power. Economically more developed countries have an HDI approaching 1.0. Economically less developed countries have an HDI approaching 0.

Health care number of doctors in each country per 100 000 people. Latest figure during the period 2000-2009.

Food consumption average number of calories consumed by each person each day.

Safe water percentage of the population with access to safe drinking water.

Illiteracy percentage of men and women who are unable to read and write. Latest available figure during the period 2005-2008.

Higher education number of students in post-secondary or tertiary education per 1000 people. Latest figure during the period 2005-2010.

Cars the number of cars per 1000 people.

How to use the index

To find a place on an atlas map use either the grid code or latitude and longitude.

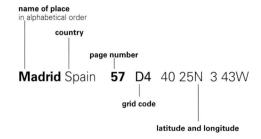

name of place
in alphabetical order

country

page number

Madrid Spain **57** D4 40 25N 3 43W

grid code

latitude and longitude

Grid code

Madrid Spain **57** D4 40 25N 3 43W

Madrid is in grid square D4

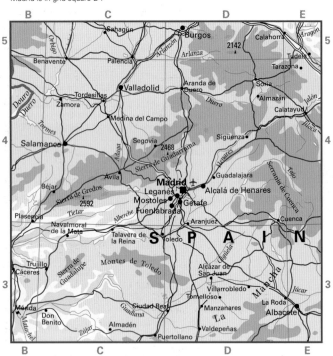

Latitude and longitude

Madrid Spain **57** D4 40 25N 3 43W

Madrid is at latitude 40 degrees, 25 minutes north and 3 degrees, 43 minutes west

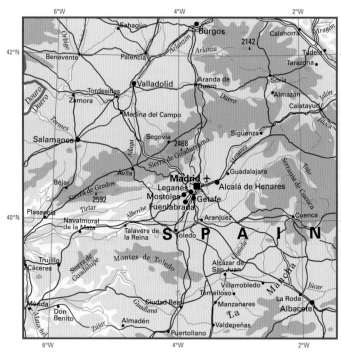

Geographical abbreviations

admin	administrative area
Arch.	Archipelago
b.	bay or harbour
c.	cape, point, or headland
can.	canal
co.	county
d.	desert
fj.	fjord
G.	Gunung; Gebel
g.	gulf
geog. reg.	geographical region
i.	island
is.	islands
Kep.	Kepulauan
l.	lake, lakes, lagoon
mt.	mountain, peak, or spot height
mts.	mountains
NP	National Park
P.	Pulau
p; pen	peninsula
Peg	Pegunungan
plat.	plateau
prov.	province
Pt.	Point
Pta.	Punta
Pte.	Pointe
Pto.	Porto; Puerto
r.	river
Ra.	Range
res.	reservoir
salt l.	salt lake
sd.	sound, strait, or channel
St.	Saint
Ste.	Sainte

Str.	Strait
sum.	summit
tn.	town or other populated place
ua.	unitary authority
v.	valley
vol.	volcano

Political abbreviations

Aust.	Australia
Bahamas	The Bahamas
CAR	Central African Republic
Col.	Columbia
CDR	Congo Democratic Republic
Czech Rep.	Czech Republic
Dom. Rep.	Dominican Republic
Eq. Guinea	Equatorial Guinea
Fr.	France
Med. Sea	Mediterranean Sea
Neths	Netherlands
NI	Northern Ireland
NZ	New Zealand
Philippines	The Philippines
PNG	Papua New Guinea
Port.	Portugal
RoI	Republic of Ireland
RSA	Republic of South Africa
Sp.	Spain
Switz.	Switzerland
UAE	United Arab Emirates
UK	United Kingom
USA	United States of America
W. Indies	West Indies
Yemen	Yemen Republic

A

Aachen Germany 58 C5 50 46N 6 06E
Aalten Belgium 54 B4 51 56N 6 35E
Abādān Iran 73 C5 30 20N 48 15E
Abbeville France 56 E6 50 06N 1 51E
Abbey RoI 25 C3 53 06N 8 24W
Abbeyfeale RoI 25 B2 52 24N 9 18W
Abbeyleix RoI 25 D2 52 55N 7 20W
Abbeytown England 16 C3 54 51N 3 17W
Abbotsbury England 23 E2 50 40N 2 36W
Aberaeron Wales 18 B2 52 49N 44 43W
Abercarn Wales 18 C1 51 39N 3 08W
Aberchirder Scotland 13 G2 57 33N 2 38W
Aberdare Wales 18 C1 51 43N 3 27W
Aberdaron Wales 18 B2 52 49N 44 43W
Aberdeen Scotland 13 G2 57 10N 2 04W
Aberdeen USA 103 G6 45 28N 98 30W
Aberdeen City *u.a.* Scotland 13 G2 57 10N 2 00W
Aberdeenshire *u.a.* Scotland 13 G2 57 10N 2 50W
Aberdyfi Wales 18 B2 52 33N 4 02W
Aberfeldy Scotland 13 F1 56 37N 3 54W
Aberffraw Wales 18 B3 53 12N 4 28W
Aberfoyle Scotland 15 E3 56 11N 4 23W
Abergavenny Wales 18 C1 51 50N 3 00W
Abergele Wales 18 C3 53 17N 3 34W
Aberlady Scotland 15 G3 56 01N 2 51W
Aberporth Wales 18 B2 52 08N 4 34W
Abersoch Wales 18 B2 52 50N 4 31W
Abertillery Wales 18 C1 51 45N 3 09W
Aberystwyth Wales 18 B2 52 25N 4 05W
Abidjan Côte d'Ivoire 90 D3 5 19N 4 01W
Abilene USA 102 G3 32 27N 99 45W
Abingdon England 20 B2 51 41N 1 17W
Abington Scotland 15 F2 55 29N 3 42W
Aboyne Scotland 13 G2 57 05N 2 50W
Abu Dhabi UAE 73 F3 24 28N 54 25E
Abuja Nigeria 90 F3 9 10N 7 11E
Acapulco Mexico 106 E3 16 51N 99 56W
Accra Ghana 90 D3 5 33N 0 15W
Accrington England 16 D2 53 46N 2 21W
Achill Head RoI 24 A3 53 59N 10 13W
Achill Island RoI 24 A3 53 55N 10 05W
Achill Sound *tn.* RoI 24 B3 53 56N 9 54W
Achnacroish Scotland 12 D1 56 32N 5 30W
Achnasheen Scotland 13 D2 57 35N 5 06W
Ackworth Moor Top England 17 E2 53 39N 1 20W
Aclare RoI 24 C4 54 02N 8 54W
Acle England 21 E3 52 38N 1 33E
A Coruña Spain 57 A5 43 22N 8 24W
Adana Turkey 63 E2 37 00N 35 19E
Adare RoI 25 C2 52 34N 8 48W
Ad Dammām Saudi Arabia 73 F4 26 25N 50 06E
Addis Ababa Ethiopia 91 N3 9 03N 38 42E
Addlestone England 20 C2 51 22N 0 31W
Adelaide Australia 81 G4 34 56S 138 36E
Aden Yemen 72 E1 12 50N 45 03E
Aden, Gulf of Indian Ocean 73 E1 12 30N 47 30E
Adriatic Sea Med. Sea 60 F5 43 00N 15 00E
Adrigole RoI 25 B1 51 44N 9 42W
Adur *r.* England 20 C1 50 55N 0 20W
Adwick le Street England 17 E2 53 34N 1 11W
Aegean Sea Med. Sea 61 L3 39 00N 24 00E
AFGHANISTAN 74 A6/B6
Agen France 56 E3 44 12N 0 38E
Aghaville RoI 25 B1 51 39N 9 21W
Agra India 74 D5 27 09N 78 00E
Ağri Daği *mt.* Turkey 63 F2 39 44N 44 15E
Agropoli Italy 60 F4 40 21N 14 59E
Ahascragh RoI 24 C3 53 24N 8 20W
Ahmadabad India 74 C4 23 03N 72 40E
Ahoghill NI 14 C1 54 51N 6 22W
Ailsa Craig *i.* Scotland 14 D2 55 16N 5 07W
Airdrie Scotland 15 F2 55 52N 3 59W
Aire *r.* England 17 E2 53 40N 1 00W
Aire-sur-l'Adour France 56 D2 43 42N 0 15W
Aix-en-Provence France 56 G2 43 31N 5 27E
Aix-les-Bains France 56 G3 45 41N 5 55E
Ajaccio France 56 J1 41 55N 8 43E
Ajmer India 74 C5 26 29N 74 40E
Akron USA 103 K5 41 04N 81 31W
Alabama *state* USA 103 J3 32 00N 87 00W
Åland *is.* Finland 55 E3 60 15N 20 00E
Alaska *state* USA 100 D6/F6 63 10N 157 30W
Alaska, Gulf of USA 100 F5/G5 58 00N 147 00W
Alaska Range USA 100 E6/G6 62 30N 152 30W
Albacete Spain 57 E3 39 00N 1 52W
ALBANIA 61 H4/J4
Al Başrah Iraq 73 E5 30 30N 47 50E
Albert France 56 F6 50 00N 2 40E
Alberta *prov.* Canada 100 M4/N4 54 00N 117 30W
Albertville France 56 H3 45 40N 6 24E
Albi France 56 F2 43 56N 2 08E
Ålborg Denmark 55 C2 57 05N 9 50E
Albrighton England 19 D2 52 38N 2 16W
Albuquerque USA 102 E4 35 05N 106 38W
Alcalá de Henares Spain 57 D4 40 28N 3 22W
Alcantarilla Spain 57 E2 37 59N 1 12W
Alcázar de San Juan Spain 57 D3 39 24N 3 12W
Alcester England 19 E2 52 13N 1 52W
Alcira Spain 57 E3 39 10N 0 27W
Aldbourne England 20 B2 51 30N 1 37W
Aldbrough England 17 F2 53 50N 0 06W
Alde *r.* England 21 E3 52 10N 1 30E
Aldeburgh England 21 E3 52 09N 1 35E
Alderley Edge *tn.* England 16 D2 53 18N 2 15W
Alderney *i.* Channel Islands 23 E1 49 43N 2 12W
Aldershot England 20 C2 51 15N 0 47W
Aldridge England 19 E2 52 36N 1 55W
Aldsworth England 19 E1 51 48N 1 46W
Alençon France 56 E5 48 25N 0 05E
Aleppo Syria 72 C6 36 14N 37 10E
Alès France 56 G3 44 08N 4 05E
Alessándria Italy 60 C6 44 55N 8 37E
Ålesund Norway 55 C3 62 28N 6 11E
Aleutian Range USA 100 D5 56 30N 159 00W
Alexandria Egypt 91 L8 31 13N 29 55E
Alexandria Scotland 15 E2 55 59N 4 36W
Alexandroúpoli Greece 61 L4 40 51N 25 53E
Alford England 17 G2 53 17N 0 11E
Alford Scotland 13 G2 57 13N 2 42W
Alfreton England 17 E2 53 06N 1 23W
Algeciras Spain 57 C2 36 08N 5 27W
ALGERIA 90 D7/F7
Algiers Algeria 90 E9 36 50N 3 00E
Alicante Spain 57 E3 38 21N 0 29W
Alice USA 103 G2 27 45N 98 06W
Alice Springs *tn.* Australia 80 F6 23 42S 133 52E
Alkmaar Neths 54 C5 52 38N 4 44E
Allahabad India 74 E5 25 27N 81 50E
Allegheny Mountains USA 105 E1/2 40 00N 79 00W
Allen *r.* England 16 D3 54 50N 2 20W
Allendale Town England 16 D3 54 54N 2 15W
Allentown USA 103 L5 40 37N 75 30W
Alloa Scotland 15 F3 56 07N 3 49W
Alma USA 105 D2 43 23N 84 40W
Almadén Spain 57 C3 38 47N 4 50W
Almansa Spain 57 E3 38 52N 1 06W
Almaty Kazakhstan 70 K5 43 19N 76 55E
Almería Spain 57 D2 36 50N 2 26W
Älmhult Sweden 55 D2 56 32N 14 10E
Aln *r.* England 15 H2 55 25N 1 45W
Alness Scotland 13 E2 57 41N 4 15W
Alnwick England 15 H2 55 25N 1 42W
Alpes Maritimes *mts.* France/Italy 56 H2 44 15N 6 45E
Alpi Dolomitiche *mts.* Italy 60 D7 46 00N 12 00E
Alpi Pennine *mts.* Italy/Switz. 58 C3 45 55N 7 30E
Alps *mts.* Europe 58 D3 46 00N 7 30E
Alsager England 16 D2 53 06N 2 19W
Alston England 16 D3 54 49N 2 26W
Altai *mts.* Mongolia 76 F7 47 00N 92 30E
Altamira Brazil 114 G13 3 13S 52 15W
Altnaharra Scotland 13 E3 58 16N 4 27W
Alton England 20 C2 51 09N 0 59W
Altrincham England 16 D2 53 24N 2 21W
Alyth Scotland 13 F1 56 37N 3 13W
Amarillo USA 102 F4 35 14N 101 50W
Amazonas *r.* Brazil 114 G13 2 00S 53 00W
Amble England 15 H2 55 20N 1 34W
Ambleside England 16 D3 54 26N 2 58W
Ambon Indonesia 79 H3 3 41S 128 10E
Amersfoort Neths 54 D5 52 09N 5 23E
Amersham England 20 C2 51 40N 0 38W
Amesbury England 20 B2 51 10N 1 47W
Amfípoli Greece 61 K4 40 48N 23 52E
Amiens France 56 F5 49 54N 2 18E
Amlwch Wales 18 B3 53 25N 4 20W
Amman Jordan 72 C5 31 04N 46 17E
Ammanford Wales 18 B1 51 48N 3 58W
Ampthill England 20 C3 52 02N 0 30W
Amritsar India 74 C6 31 35N 74 56E
Amsterdam Neths 54 C5 52 22N 4 54E
Amstetten Austria 58 G4 48 08N 14 52E
Amur *r.* Asia 77 N8 52 30N 126 30E
Anascaul RoI 25 A2 52 09N 10 04W
Anchorage USA 100 F6 61 10N 150 00W
Ancona Italy 60 E5 43 37N 13 31E
Ancroft England 15 G2 55 42N 2 00W
Andalsnes Norway 55 C3 62 33N 7 43E
Andaman Islands India 75 G2 12 00N 94 00E
Anderlecht Belgium 54 C3 50 50N 4 20E
Andermatt Switz. 58 D3 46 38N 8 36E
Andes *mts.* S. America 114/115 B14/C6 10 00S 77 00W
ANDORRA 56 E2
Andorra la Vella Andorra 56 E2 42 30N 1 30E
Andover England 20 B2 51 13N 1 28W
Andreas Isle of Man 16 B3 54 22N 4 26W
Ándros *i.* Greece 61 L2 37 49N 24 54E
Andújar Spain 57 C3 38 02N 4 03W
Angara *r.* Russia 71 M8 58 00N 97 30E
Angers France 56 D4 47 29N 0 32W
Angle Wales 18 A1 51 41N 5 06W
Anglesey *i.* Wales 18 B3 53 18N 4 25W
Anglesey, Isle of *u.a.* Wales 18 B3 53 18N 4 25W
ANGOLA 92 C5
Angoulême France 56 E3 45 40N 0 10E
Anguilla *i.* Leeward Islands 106 P10 18 14N 63 05W
Angus *u.a.* Scotland 13 G1 56 45N 3 00W
Ankara Turkey 63 D2 39 56N 32 50E
'Annaba Algeria 90 F9 36 55N 7 47E
Annalong NI 14 D1 54 06N 5 55W
Annan *r.* Scotland 15 F2 55 05N 3 20W
Annan Scotland 15 F1 54 59N 3 16W
Annapolis USA 103 L4 38 59N 76 30W
Annapurna *mt.* Nepal 74 E5 28 34N 83 50E
Annbank Scotland 15 E2 55 28N 4 30W
Annecy France 56 H3 45 54N 6 07E
Annfield Plain England 17 E3 54 52N 1 45W
Ansbach Germany 58 E4 49 18N 10 36E
Anshan China 77 M6 41 05N 122 58E
Anstey England 19 E2 52 40N 1 10W
Anston England 17 E2 53 22N 1 13W
Anstruther Scotland 15 G3 56 14N 2 42W
Antalya Turkey 63 D2 36 53N 30 42E
Antananarivo Madagascar 92 J4 18 52S 47 30E
Antarctica 117
Antequera Spain 57 C2 37 01N 4 34W
Antibes France 56 H2 43 35N 7 07E
ANTIGUA & BARBUDA 106 Q9
Antofagasta Chile 114 C9 23 40S 70 23W
Antrim NI 14 C1 54 43N 6 13W
Antrim *district* NI 14 C1 54 40N 6 10W
Antrim Mountains NI 14 C2 55 00N 6 10W
Antwerpen Belgium 54 C4 51 13N 4 25W
Aosta Italy 60 B6 45 43N 7 19E
Apeldoorn Neths 54 D5 52 13N 5 57E
Appalachian Mountains USA 103 K4 37 00N 82 00W
Appennini *mts.* Italy 60 C6/F4 43 00N 12 30E
Appleby-in-Westmorland England 16 D3 53 36N 2 29W
Appledore England 22 C3 51 03N 4 12W
Appleton USA 103 J5 44 17N 88 24W
'Aqaba, Gulf of Middle East 72 D4 28 40N 34 40E
Arabian Sea Indian Ocean 73 H3 22 00N 63 00E
Araguaína Brazil 114 H12 7 16S 48 18W
Aral Sea Asia 70 H5/J6 45 00N 60 00E
Aranda de Duero Spain 57 D4 41 40N 3 41W
Aran Fawddwy *mt.* Wales 18 C2 52 47N 3 41W
Aran Island RoI 24 C4 55 00N 8 40W
Aran Islands RoI 25 B3 53 10N 9 50W
Aranjuez Spain 57 D4 40 02N 3 37W
Arbil Iraq 72 D6 36 12N 44 01E
Arbroath Scotland 13 G1 56 34N 2 35W
Arcachon France 56 D3 44 40N 1 11W
Arctic Ocean 117
Ardara RoI 24 C4 54 46N 8 25W
Ardbeg Scotland 14 C2 55 39N 6 05W
Ardee RoI 24 E3 53 52N 6 33W
Ardennes *mts.* Belgium 54 D3 50 10N 5 45E
Ardfert RoI 25 B2 52 20N 9 47W
Ardglass NI 14 D1 54 16N 5 37W
Ardle *r.* Scotland 13 F1 56 40N 3 30W
Ardminish Scotland 14 D2 55 42N 5 44W
Ardmore RoI 25 D1 51 57N 7 43W
Ardmore Point Scotland 14 C2 55 41N 6 01W
Ardnamurchan, Point of Scotland 12 C1 56 44N 6 14W
Ardrossan Scotland 15 E2 55 39N 4 49W
Ards *district* NI 14 D1 54 35N 5 35W
Ards Peninsula NI 14 D1 54 25N 5 30W
Ardvasar Scotland 12 D2 57 03N 5 55W
Arendal Norway 55 C2 58 27N 8 56E
Arequipa Peru 114 C10 16 25S 71 32W
Arezzo Italy 60 D5 43 28N 11 53E
Argentan France 56 D5 48 45N 0 01W
ARGENTINA 115 D5
Argyll and Bute *u.a.* Scotland 14 D3 56 10N 5 00W
Århus Denmark 55 D2 56 15N 10 10E
Arica Chile 114 C10 18 30S 70 20W
Arinagour Scotland 12 C1 56 37N 6 31W
Ariquemes Brazil 114 E12 9 55S 63 06W
Arisaig Scotland 12 D1 56 51N 5 51W
Arisaig, Sound of Scotland 12 D1 56 50N 5 50W
Arizona *state* USA 102 D3 34 00N 112 00W
Arkansas *state* USA 103 H3 34 00N 93 00W
Arkansas *r.* USA 102 G4 36 00N 99 00W
Arkansas City USA 103 G4 37 03N 97 02W
Arkhangel'sk Russia 70 G9 64 32N 40 40E
Arklow RoI 25 E2 52 48N 6 09W
Arles France 56 G2 43 41N 4 38E
Arlon Belgium 54 D2 49 41N 5 49E
Armadale Highland Scotland 12 D2 57 05N 5 54W
Armadale West Lothian Scotland 15 F2 55 54N 3 41W
Armagh NI 14 C1 54 21N 6 39W
Armagh *district* NI 14 C1 54 20N 6 40W
ARMENIA 63 F3
Armentières France 56 F6 50 41N 2 53E
Armthorpe England 17 E2 53 32N 1 03W
Arnhem Neths 54 D4 52 00N 5 53E
Arnold England 19 E2 53 00N 1 09W
Arran *i.* Scotland 14 D2 55 35N 5 15W
Arras France 56 F6 50 17N 2 46E
Artane RoI 24 E3 53 23N 6 12W
Arthur's Seat *sum.* Scotland 15 F2 55 57N 3 11W
Arthurstown RoI 25 E2 52 15N 6 57W
Aruba *i.* Neths 114 C16 12 30N 70 00W
Arun *r.* England 20 C2 51 00N 0 30W
Arundel England 20 C1 50 51N 0 34W
Arvika Sweden 55 D2 59 41N 12 38E
Ascoli Piceno Italy 60 E5 42 52N 13 35E
Ascot England 20 C2 51 25N 0 41W
Ash England 21 E2 51 17N 1 16E
Ashbourne England 17 E2 53 01N 1 43W
Ashbourne RoI 24 E3 53 31N 6 24W
Ashburton England 22 D2 50 31N 3 45W
Ashby-de-la-Zouch England 19 E2 52 46N 1 28W
Ashford England 21 D2 51 09N 0 53E
Ash Fork USA 102 D4 35 13N 112 29W
Ashgabat Turkmenistan 70 H4 37 58N 58 24E
Ashington England 17 E4 55 11N 1 34W
Ashkirk Scotland 15 G2 55 29N 2 50W
Ashton-in-Makerfield England 16 D2 53 29N 2 39W
Ashton-under-Lyne England 16 D2 53 29N 2 06W
Ashwell England 20 C3 52 03N 0 09W
Askeaton RoI 25 C2 52 36N 8 58W
Askern England 17 E2 53 37N 1 09W
Askrigg England 16 D3 54 19N 2 04W
Asmara Eritrea 91 N5 15 20N 38 58E
Aspatria England 16 C3 54 46N 3 20W
Assisi Italy 60 E5 43 04N 12 37E
Astana Kazakhstan 70 K7 51 10N 71 28E
Astee RoI 25 B2 52 33N 9 34W
Asti Italy 60 C6 44 54N 8 13E
Astorga Spain 57 B5 42 27N 6 04W
Astoria USA 102 B6 46 12N 123 50W
Astrakhan' Russia 70 G6 46 22N 48 04E
Asunción Paraguay 114 F7 25 15S 57 40W
Aswân Egypt 91 M6 24 05N 32 56E
Asyût Egypt 91 M7 27 14N 31 07E
Athabasca Canada 100 N4 54 44N 113 15W
Athabasca, Lake Canada 100 P5 59 10N 109 30W
Athboy RoI 24 E3 53 37N 6 55W
Athenry RoI 24 C3 53 18N 8 45W
Athens Greece 61 K2 38 00N 23 44E
Atherstone England 19 E2 52 35N 1 31W
Athleague RoI 24 C3 53 34N 8 15W
Athlone RoI 24 D3 53 25N 7 56W
Áthos *mt.* Greece 61 L4 40 10N 24 19E
Athy RoI 25 E2 52 59N 6 59W
Atlanta USA 103 K3 33 45N 84 23W
Atlantic City USA 103 M4 39 23N 74 27W
Atlantic Ocean 120
Attleborough England 21 E3 52 31N 1 01E
Attymass RoI 24 B4 54 03N 9 04W
Aubagne France 56 G2 43 17N 5 35E
Aubenas France 56 G3 44 37N 4 24E
Auch France 56 E2 43 40N 0 36E
Auchencairn Scotland 15 F1 54 51N 3 53W
Auchterarder Scotland 15 F3 56 18N 3 43W
Auchtermuchty Scotland 15 F3 56 17N 3 15W
Auckland NZ 81 P3 36 51S 174 46E
Audley England 16 D2 53 03N 2 20W
Augher NI 14 B1 54 26N 7 08W
Aughnacloy NI 14 C1 54 25N 6 59W
Aughrim RoI 25 E2 52 52N 6 20W
Aughton England 17 E2 53 22N 1 19W
Augsburg Germany 58 E4 48 21N 10 54E
Augusta USA 103 K3 33 29N 82 00W
Auldgirth Scotland 15 F2 55 12N 3 43W
Aurillac France 56 F3 44 56N 2 26E
Austin USA 103 G3 30 18N 97 47W
AUSTRALIA 80/81
AUSTRIA 58 E3/G3
Autun France 56 G4 46 58N 4 18E
Auxerre France 56 F4 47 48N 3 35E
Avallon France 56 F4 47 30N 3 54E
Avebury England 20 B2 51 27N 1 51W
Aveiro Portugal 57 A4 40 38N 8 40W
Aveley England 21 D2 51 30N 0 15E
Avesta Sweden 55 E3 60 09N 16 10E
Avezzano Italy 60 E5 42 02N 13 26E
Aviemore Scotland 13 F2 57 12N 3 50W
Avignon France 56 G2 43 56N 4 48E
Avila Spain 57 C4 40 39N 4 42W
Avoca RoI 25 E2 52 52N 6 13W
Avon *r.* Warwickshire England 19 E2 52 10N 1 55W
Avon *r.* Hampshire England 20 B1 51 05N 1 55W
Avon *r.* Wiltshire England 20 A2 51 25N 2 05W
Avon *r.* Devon England 22 D2 50 20N 3 48W
Avon *r.* Scotland 13 F2 51 71N 1 40W
Avonmouth England 23 E3 51 31N 2 42W
Avranches France 56 D5 48 42N 1 21W
Axbridge England 23 E3 51 18N 2 49W

Axe *r.* Somerset England 23 E3 51 11N 2 43W
Axe *r.* Dorset England 23 E2 50 50N 2 50W
Axminster England 23 E2 50 47N 3 00W
Ayamonte Spain 57 B2 37 13N 7 24W
Ayers Rock *mt.* Australia 80 F5 25 18S 131 18E
Aylesbury England 20 C2 51 50N 0 50W
Aylesford England 21 D2 51 18N 0 30E
Aylesham England 21 E2 51 12N 1 11E
Aylsham England 21 E3 52 49N 1 15E
Ayr *r.* Scotland 15 E2 55 30N 4 10W
Ayr Scotland 15 E2 55 28N 4 38W
Ayre, Point of Isle of Man 16 B3 54 25N 4 22W
Aysgarth England 16 E3 54 17N 2 00W
AZERBAIJAN 63 G3
Azov, Sea of Asia 63 E4 46 00N 36 00E
Azuaga Spain 57 C3 38 16N 5 40W

B

Babbacombe Bay England 22 D2 50 30N 3 30W
Bacup England 16 D2 53 42N 2 12W
Badajoz Spain 57 B3 38 53N 6 58W
Badalona Spain 57 G4 41 27N 2 15E
Baden Switz. 58 D3 47 28N 8 19E
Bad Ischl Austria 58 F3 47 43N 13 38E
Baffin Bay Canada/Greenland 101 X8/Z8 72 00N 65 00W
Baffin Island Canada 101 U8/W7 68 30N 70 00W
Baggy Point England 22 C3 51 09N 4 16W
Baghdad Iraq 72 D5 33 20N 44 26E
BAHAMAS, THE 107 J4
Bahía Blanca Argentina 115 E6 38 45S 62 15W
Bahia de Campeche Mexico 106 E4/F4 20 00N 95 00W
BAHRAIN 73 F4
Bahrain, Gulf of The Gulf 73 F4 25 55N 50 30E
Bahr el Abiad *r.* South Sudan/Sudan 91 M4 14 00N 32 20E
Bahr el Azraq *r.* Sudan 91 M4 13 30N 33 45E
Baia Mare Romania 59 L3 47 39N 23 36E
Baie de la Seine France 56 D5 49 40N 0 30W
Baildon England 17 E2 53 52N 1 46W
Bailieborough RoI 24 E3 53 54N 6 59W
Baja California *p.* Mexico 106 B5 27 30N 113 00W
Bakersfield USA 102 C4 35 25N 119 00W
Bakewell England 17 E2 53 13N 1 40W
Baku Azerbaijan 63 G3 40 22N 49 53E
Bala Wales 18 C2 52 54N 3 35W
Balaton *l.* Hungary 59 H3 47 00N 17 30E
Balbriggan RoI 24 E3 53 37N 6 11W
Balcombe England 20 C2 51 04N 0 08W
Baldock England 20 C2 51 59N 0 12W
Balearic Islands Med. Sea 57 F3/H3 40 00N 2 00E
Baleshare *i.* Scotland 12 B2 57 32N 7 22W
Bali *i.* Indonesia 79 E2/F2 8 30S 115 00E
Ballachulish Scotland 12 D1 56 40N 5 10W
Ballagan Point RoI 24 E4 54 00N 6 06W
Ballaghaderreen RoI 24 C3 53 55N 8 36W
Ballantrae Scotland 14 D2 55 06N 5 00W
Ballater Scotland 13 F2 57 03N 3 03W
Ballaugh Isle of Man 16 B3 54 18N 4 32W
Ballina RoI 24 B4 54 07N 9 09W
Ballinafad RoI 24 C4 54 02N 8 20W
Ballinagleragh RoI 24 C4 54 09N 8 01W
Ballinalack RoI 24 D3 53 38N 7 28W
Ballinalee RoI 24 D3 53 46N 7 39W
Ballinamore RoI 24 D4 54 03N 7 47W
Ballinasloe RoI 24 C3 53 20N 8 13W
Ballincollig RoI 25 C1 51 54N 8 35W
Ballindine RoI 24 C3 53 40N 8 57W
Ballingry Scotland 15 F3 56 11N 3 20W
Ballinhassig RoI 25 C1 51 49N 8 32W
Ballinrobe RoI 24 B3 53 37N 9 13W
Ballinskelligs Bay RoI 25 A1 51 46N 10 17W
Ballintra RoI 24 C4 54 35N 8 07W
Ballon RoI 25 E2 52 44N 6 46W
Ballybay RoI 24 E4 54 08N 6 54W
Ballybofey RoI 24 D4 54 48N 7 47W
Ballybunnion RoI 25 B2 52 31N 9 40W
Ballycanew RoI 25 E2 52 36N 6 18W
Ballycastle NI 14 C2 55 12N 6 15W
Ballycastle RoI 24 B4 54 17N 9 22W
Ballyclare NI 14 C1 54 45N 6 00W
Ballycolla RoI 25 D2 52 52N 7 26W
Ballyconnell RoI 24 D4 54 07N 7 35W
Ballycotton RoI 25 C1 51 50N 8 01W
Ballycotton Bay RoI 25 D1 51 51N 7 57W
Ballycroy RoI 24 B4 54 02N 9 49W
Ballydavid Head RoI 25 A2 52 14N 10 21W
Ballydehob RoI 25 B1 51 34N 9 28W
Ballydesmond RoI 25 B2 52 10N 9 13W
Ballydonegan RoI 25 A1 51 37N 10 12W
Ballydonegan Bay RoI 25 A1 51 29N 10 09W
Ballygalley Head NI 14 D1 54 54N 5 51W
Ballygowan NI 14 D1 54 30N 5 47W
Ballyhaunis RoI 24 C3 53 46N 8 46W
Ballyheige RoI 25 B2 52 24N 9 50W
Ballyheige Bay RoI 25 B2 52 23N 9 52W
Ballyhoura Mountains RoI 25 C2 52 17N 8 33W
Ballyjamesduff RoI 24 D3 53 52N 7 12W
Ballykinler NI 14 D1 54 17N 5 47W
Ballylanders RoI 25 C2 52 23N 8 21W
Ballylongford RoI 25 B2 52 33N 9 28W
Ballymacarbry RoI 25 D2 52 16N 7 12W
Ballymahon RoI 24 D3 53 34N 7 45W
Ballymena NI 14 C1 54 52N 6 17W
Ballymena *district* NI 14 C1 54 55N 6 20W
Ballymoe RoI 24 C3 53 42N 8 28W
Ballymoney NI 14 C2 55 04N 6 31W
Ballymoney *district* NI 14 C2 55 00N 6 30W
Ballymore Donegal RoI 24 D5 55 09N 7 56W
Ballymore Westmeath RoI 24 D3 53 29N 7 40W
Ballymote RoI 24 C4 54 06N 8 31W
Ballynahinch NI 14 D1 54 24N 5 54W
Ballynamona RoI 25 C2 52 05N 8 39W
Ballynamult RoI 25 D2 52 13N 7 40W
Ballyquintin Point NI 14 D1 54 19N 5 30W
Ballyragget RoI 25 D2 52 47N 7 20W
Ballyshannon RoI 24 C4 54 30N 8 11W
Ballyteige Bay RoI 25 E2 52 12N 6 45W
Ballyvaghan RoI 25 B3 53 07N 9 09W
Ballyvourney RoI 25 B1 51 56N 9 10W
Ballywalter NI 14 D1 54 33N 5 30W
Balmaclellan Scotland 15 E2 55 05N 4 07W
Balmoral Scotland 13 F2 57 02N 3 13W
Balrath RoI 24 E3 53 37N 6 29W
Baltic Sea Europe 55 E2/F2 55 15N 17 00E
Baltimore RoI 25 B1 51 29N 9 22W
Baltimore USA 103 L4 39 18N 76 38W
Baltinglass RoI 25 E2 52 55N 6 41W
Baltray RoI 24 E3 53 44N 6 16W
Bamako Mali 90 C4 12 40N 7 59W
Bamberg Germany 58 E4 49 54N 10 54E
Bamburgh England 15 H2 55 36N 1 42W
Bampton England 22 D2 51 00N 3 29W
Banagher RoI 25 D3 53 11N 7 59W
Banbridge NI 14 C1 54 21N 6 16W
Banbridge *district* NI 14 C1 54 15N 6 20W
Banbury England 20 B3 52 04N 1 20W
Banchory Scotland 13 G2 57 30N 2 30W
Bandar Seri Begawan Brunei 79 F4 4 53N 115 00E
Bandon RoI 25 C1 51 45N 8 45W
Bandung Indonesia 79 D2 6 57S 107 34E
Banff Canada 100 M4 51 10N 115 34W
Banff Scotland 13 G2 57 40N 2 33W
Bangalore India 74 D2 12 58N 77 35E
Bangkok Thailand 79 C6 13 44N 100 30E
BANGLADESH 75 F4/G4
Bangor NI 14 D1 54 40N 5 40W
Bangor RoI 24 B4 54 09N 9 44W
Bangor Wales 18 B3 53 13N 4 08W
Bangui CAR 91 J2 4 23N 18 37E
Banja Luka Bosnia-Herzegovina 61 G6 44 47N 17 11E
Banjul The Gambia 90 A4 13 28N 16 39W
Bann *r.* Coleraine NI 14 C2 55 05N 6 40W
Bann *r.* Banbridge NI 14 C1 54 20N 6 11W
Bann *r.* RoI 25 E2 52 39W 6 24W
Bannockburn Scotland 15 F3 56 05N 3 56W
Bannow Bay RoI 25 E2 52 13N 6 48W
Bansha RoI 25 C2 52 28N 8 04W
Banstead England 20 C2 51 19N 0 12W
Banteer RoI 25 C2 52 08N 8 54W
Bantry RoI 25 B1 51 41N 9 27W
Bantry Bay RoI 25 B1 51 35N 9 40W
Baotou China 77 J6 40 38N 109 59E
Baracaldo Spain 57 D5 43 17N 2 59W
Baranavichy Belarus 59 N6 53 09N 26 00E
BARBADOS 106 S11
Barbastro Spain 57 F5 42 02N 0 07E
Barcelona Spain 57 G4 41 25N 2 10E
Barcs Hungary 59 H2 45 58N 17 30E
Bardsey Island Wales 18 B2 52 46N 4 48W
Barents Sea Arctic Ocean 117 75 00N 40 00E
Bargoed Wales 18 C1 51 43N 3 15W
Bari Italy 61 G4 41 07N 16 52E
Barisal Bangladesh 75 G4 22 41N 90 20E
Barking England 21 D2 51 33N 0 06E
Barle *r.* England 22 D3 51 05N 3 36W
Bar-le-Duc France 56 G5 48 46N 5 10E
Barletta Italy 60 G4 41 20N 16 17E
Barmouth Wales 18 B2 52 43N 4 03W
Barnard Castle England 17 E3 54 33N 1 55W
Barnatra RoI 24 B4 54 13N 9 50W
Barnet England 20 C2 51 39N 0 12W
Barnoldswick England 16 D2 53 56N 2 16W
Barnsley England 17 E2 53 34N 1 28W
Barnstaple England 22 C3 51 05N 4 04W
Barnstaple or Bideford Bay England 22 C3 51 05N 4 25W
Barquisimeto Venezuela 114 D16 10 03N 69 18W
Barra *i.* Scotland 12 B1/B2 57 00N 7 25W
Barra Head Scotland 12 B1 56 47N 7 36W
Barranquilla Colombia 114 C16 11 10N 74 50W
Barra, Sound of Scotland 12 B2 57 06N 7 22W
Barre USA 103 M5 44 13N 72 31W
Barreiras Brazil 114 J11 12 09S 44 58W
Barreiro Portugal 57 A3 38 40N 9 05W
Barrhead Scotland 15 E2 55 48N 4 24W
Barrow *r.* RoI 25 E2 52 38N 6 58W
Barrow-in-Furness England 16 C3 54 07N 3 14W
Barry Wales 18 C1 51 24N 3 18W
Barton-upon-Humber England 17 F2 53 41N 0 27W
Barvas Scotland 12 C3 58 22N 6 32W
Barysaw Belarus 59 P7 54 09N 28 30E
Basel Switz. 58 C3 47 33N 7 36E
Basildon England 21 D2 51 34N 0 25W
Basingstoke England 20 B2 51 16N 1 05W
Bassenthwaite Lake England 16 C3 54 40N 3 13W
Bastia France 56 J2 42 14N 9 26E
Bastogne Belgium 54 D3 50 00N 5 43E
Bath England 23 E3 51 23N 2 22W
Bath and North East Somerset *u.a.* England 23 E3 51 25N 2 30W
Bathgate Scotland 15 F2 55 55N 3 39W
Bathurst Canada 101 X3 47 37N 65 40W
Batley England 17 E2 53 44N 1 37W
Baton Rouge USA 103 H3 30 30N 91 10W
Battle England 21 D1 50 55N 0 29E
Bat Yam Israel 72 N10 31 59N 34 45E
Bawdsey England 21 E3 52 01N 1 25E
Bawtry England 17 E2 53 26N 1 01W
Bayeux France 56 D5 49 16N 0 42W
Bayonne France 56 D2 43 30N 1 28W
Bayreuth Germany 58 E4 49 27N 11 35E
Bayston Hill *tn.* England 18 D2 52 40N 2 48W
Beachy Head England 21 D1 50 44N 0 16E
Beaconsfield England 20 C2 51 37N 0 39W
Beadnell Bay England 15 H2 55 32N 1 30W
Beaminster England 23 E2 50 49N 2 45W
Bear Island RoI 25 B1 51 40N 9 48W
Bearsden Scotland 15 E2 55 56N 4 20W
Bearsted England 21 D2 51 17N 0 35E
Beatrice USA 103 G5 40 17N 96 45W
Beaulieu England 20 B1 50 49N 1 27W
Beauly Scotland 13 E2 57 29N 4 29W
Beauly *r.* Scotland 13 E2 57 25N 4 33W
Beauly Firth Scotland 13 E2 57 30N 4 20W
Beaumaris Wales 18 B3 53 16N 4 05W
Beaune France 56 G4 47 02N 4 50E
Beauvais France 56 F5 49 26N 2 05E
Bebington England 16 D2 53 20N 2 59W
Beccles England 21 E3 52 28N 1 34E
Béchar Algeria 90 D8 31 35N 2 17W
Bedale England 17 E3 54 17N 1 35W
Bedford England 20 C3 52 08N 0 29W
Bedford *u.a.* England 20 C3 52 10N 0 30W
Bedlington England 17 E4 55 08N 1 25W
Bedwas Wales 18 C1 51 35N 3 12W
Bedworth England 19 E2 52 29N 1 28W
Beeston England 19 E2 52 56N 1 12W
Beighton England 17 E2 53 21N 1 21W
Beijing China 77 L5 39 55N 116 26E
Beinn Dearg *mt.* Scotland 13 E2 57 47N 4 56W
Beira Mozambique 92 F4 19 49S 34 52E
Beirut Lebanon 72 C5 33 52N 35 30E
Beith Scotland 15 E2 55 45N 4 38W
Beja Portugal 57 B3 38 01N 7 52W
Bejaïa Algeria 90 F9 36 49N 5 03E
Béjar Spain 57 C4 40 24N 5 45W
BELARUS 62 B5/6
Belderg RoI 24 B4 54 18N 9 33W
Belém Brazil 114 H12 1 27S 48 29W
Belfast NI 14 D1 54 35N 5 55W
Belfast *district* NI 14 C1/D1 54 40N 6 05W
Belfast Lough *est.* NI 14 D1 54 40N 5 50W
Belford England 15 H2 55 36N 1 49W
Belfort France 56 H4 47 38N 6 52E
BELGIUM 54 B3/D3
Belgrade Serbia 61 J6 44 50N 20 30E
BELIZE 106 G3
Bellac France 56 E4 46 07N 1 04E
Bellacorick RoI 24 B4 54 07N 9 34W
Bellanagh RoI 24 C3 53 56N 7 24W
Bellavary RoI 24 B3 53 53N 9 12W
Bellingham England 16 D4 55 09N 2 16W
Bellsbank Scotland 15 E2 55 19N 4 24W
Bellshill Scotland 15 E2 55 49N 4 02W
Belmont Scotland 11 D3 60 41N 0 58W
Belmopan Belize 106 G3 17 13N 88 48W
Belmullet RoI 24 B4 54 14N 10 00W
Belo Horizonte Brazil 114 J10 19 54S 43 54W
Belper England 17 E2 53 01N 1 29W
Belton England 21 E3 52 34N 1 40E
Beltra Lough RoI 24 B3 53 55N 9 25W
Belturbet RoI 24 D4 54 06N 7 28W
Belvoir, Vale of England 19 F2 52 58N 0 55W
Bembridge England 20 B1 50 41N 1 05W
Ben Alder *mt.* Scotland 13 E1 56 49N 4 28W
Benavente Spain 57 C4 42 00N 5 40W
Benbane Head NI 14 C2 55 14N 6 29W
Benbecula *i.* Scotland 12 B2 57 25N 7 20W
Ben Cleuch *mt.* Scotland 15 F3 56 11N 3 47W
Ben Cruachan *mt.* Scotland 12 D1 56 26N 5 09W
Benevento Italy 60 F4 41 08N 14 46E
Bengal, Bay of Indian Ocean 75 F3 17 00N 88 00E
Benghazi Libya 91 K8 32 07N 20 04E
Benguela Angola 92 B5 12 34S 13 24E
Ben Hope *mt.* Scotland 13 E3 58 24N 4 37W
Benicarló Spain 57 F4 40 25N 0 25E
Benidorm Spain 57 E3 38 33N 0 09W
BENIN 90 E4
Benin City Nigeria 90 F3 6 19N 5 41E
Ben Klibreck *mt.* Scotland 13 E3 58 14N 4 22W
Ben Lawers *mt.* Scotland 13 E1 56 33N 4 15W
Benllech Wales 18 B3 53 19N 4 15W
Ben Lomond *mt.* Scotland 15 E3 56 12N 4 38W
Ben Loyal *mt.* Scotland 13 E3 58 24N 4 26W
Ben Macdui *mt.* Scotland 13 F2 57 04N 3 40W
Ben More *mt.* Highland Scotland 12 C1 56 25N 6 02W
Ben More *mt.* Stirling Scotland 13 E1 56 23N 4 31W
Ben More Assynt *mt.* Scotland 13 E3 58 07N 4 52W
Bennettsbridge RoI 25 D2 52 35N 7 10W
Ben Nevis *mt.* Scotland 13 E1 56 40N 5 00W
Benson USA 102 D3 31 58N 110 19W
Bentley England 17 E2 53 33N 1 09W
Benwee Head RoI 24 B4 54 21N 9 48W
Ben Wyvis *mt.* Scotland 13 E2 57 40N 4 35W
Beppu Japan 78 B1 33 18N 131 30E
Bérgamo Italy 60 C6 45 42N 9 40E
Bergen Norway 55 C3 60 23N 5 20E
Bergerac France 56 E3 44 50N 0 29E
Bergisch Gladbach Germany 58 C5 50 59N 7 10E
Bering Sea Pacific Ocean 116 H12/J13 60 00N 175 00W
Bering Strait Russia/USA 100 B7 69 00N 169 00W
Berkeley England 19 D1 51 42N 2 27W
Berkhamsted England 20 C2 51 46N 0 35W
Berkshire Downs England 20 B2 51 30N 1 25W
Berlin Germany 58 F6 52 32N 13 25E
Bern Switz. 58 C3 46 57N 7 26E
Bernalda Italy 61 G4 40 24N 16 443
Berner Alpen *mts.* Switz. 58 C3/D3 46 25N 7 30E
Berneray *i.* Scotland 12 B2 57 45N 7 10W
Bernina Pass Switz. 58 E3 46 25N 10 02E
Berriedale Scotland 13 F3 58 11N 3 33W
Berry Head England 22 D2 50 24N 3 29W
Berwick-upon-Tweed England 15 G2 55 46N 2 00W
Besançon France 56 G4 47 14N 6 02E
Bessacarr England 17 E2 53 30N 1 05W
Bessbrook NI 14 C1 54 12N 6 24W
Betanzos Spain 57 A5 43 17N 8 13W
Bethersden England 21 D2 51 07N 0 45W
Bethesda Wales 18 B3 53 11N 4 03W
Bethlehem Middle East 72 C5 31 42N 35 12E
Béthune France 56 F6 50 32N 2 38E
Bettyhill Scotland 13 E3 58 32N 4 14W
Betws-y-Coed Wales 18 C3 53 05N 3 48W
Beverley England 17 F2 53 51N 0 26W
Bewdley England 19 D2 52 22N 2 19W
Bewl Water *l.* England 21 D2 51 02N 0 23E
Bexhill England 21 D1 50 50N 0 29E
Bexley England 21 D2 51 27N 0 09E
Béziers France 56 F2 43 21N 3 13E
Bharatpur India 74 D5 27 14N 77 29E
Bhopal India 74 D4 23 17N 77 28E
Bhubaneshwar India 75 F4 20 13N 85 50E
BHUTAN 75 G5
Białystok Poland 59 L6 53 09N 23 10E
Biarritz France 56 D2 43 29N 1 33W
Bicester England 20 B2 51 54N 1 09W
Biddeford USA 103 M5 43 29N 70 27W
Biddulph England 16 D2 53 08N 2 10W
Bideford England 22 C3 51 01N 4 13W
Biel Switz. 58 C3 46 27N 8 13E
Bielefeld Germany 58 D6 52 02N 8 32E
Bielsko-Biała Poland 59 J4 49 50N 19 00E
Bigbury Bay England 22 D2 50 17N 4 00W
Biggar Scotland 15 F2 55 38N 3 32W
Biggleswade England 20 C3 52 05N 0 17W
Bihać Bosnia-Herzegovina 60 F6 44 49N 15 53E
Bikaner India 74 C5 28 01N 73 22E
Bila Tserkva Ukraine 59 Q4 49 49N 30 10E
Bilbao Spain 57 D5 43 15N 2 56W
Billericay England 21 D2 51 38N 0 25E
Billinge England 16 D2 53 30N 2 42W
Billingham England 17 E3 54 36N 1 17W
Billingshurst England 20 C2 51 01N 0 28W
Bill of Portland *c.* England 23 E2 50 31N 2 27W
Bingham England 19 F2 52 57N 0 57W
Bingley England 17 E2 53 51N 1 50W
Birchwood *tn.* England 17 F2 53 14N 0 33W
Birkenhead England 16 D2 53 24N 3 02W
Birmingham England 19 E2 52 30N 1 50W
Birmingham USA 103 J3 33 30N 86 55W
Birr RoI 25 D3 53 05N 7 54W
Birstall England 19 E2 52 40N 1 08W
Biscay, Bay of Atlantic Ocean 56 C3 45 30N 2 50W

Bishkek Kyrgyzstan 70 K5 42 53N 74 46E
Bishop Auckland England 17 E3 54 40N 1 40W
Bishopbriggs Scotland 15 E2 55 54N 4 14W
Bishop's Castle *tn.* England 18 C2 52 29N 3 00W
Bishop's Cleeve England 19 D1 51 57N 2 04W
Bishop's Lydeard England 23 D3 51 04N 3 12W
Bishop's Stortford England 21 D2 51 53N 0 09E
Bishopston Wales 18 B1 51 35N 4 03W
Bishop's Waltham England 20 B1 50 58N 1 12W
Bishopton Scotland 15 E2 55 54N 4 31W
Bissau Guinea-Bissau 90 A4 11 52N 15 39W
Blaby England 19 E2 52 35N 1 09W
Black *r.* RoI 24 D3 53 55N 7 42W
Blackburn England 16 D2 53 45N 2 29W
Blackdown Hills England 23 D2 50 55N 3 10W
Blackhall Colliery *tn.* England 17 E3 54 43N 1 20W
Black Head RoI 25 B3 53 09N 9 16W
Blackhope Scar *mt.* Scotland 15 F2 55 58N 3 07W
Black Isle Scotland 13 E2 57 35N 4 15W
Blackmoor Vale England 23 E2 50 56N 2 19W
Black Mountains Wales 18 C1 51 55N 3 10W
Black Mountain Wales 18 C1 51 50N 3 55W
Blackpool England 16 C2 53 50N 3 03W
Black Sea Europe 63 D3/E3 43 00N 35 00E
Blacksod Bay RoI 24 A3/A4 54 05N 10 00W
Blackstairs Mountains RoI 25 E2 52 33N 6 49W
Blackwater *r.* Hampshire England 20 C2 51 22N 0 54W
Blackwater *r.* Essex England 21 D2 51 45N 0 50E
Blackwater *r.* Waterford RoI 25 D2 52 02N 7 51W
Blackwater *r.* Meath RoI 24 E3 53 41N 6 44W
Blackwaterfoot Scotland 14 D2 55 30N 5 19W
Blackwater *r.* NI 14 C1 54 20N 6 50W
Blackwood Wales 18 C1 51 41N 3 13W
Blaenau Ffestiniog Wales 18 C2 52 59N 3 56W
Blaenau Gwent *u.a.* Wales 18 C1 51 45N 3 10W
Blaenavon Wales 18 C1 51 48N 3 05W
Blagoveshchensk Russia 71 Q7 50 19N 127 30E
Blaina Wales 18 C1 51 48N 3 11W
Blair Atholl Scotland 13 F1 56 46N 3 51W
Blairgowrie Scotland 13 F1 56 36N 3 21W
Blakeney Point England 21 E3 52 58N 1 00E
Blandford Forum England 23 E2 50 52N 2 11W
Blantyre Malawi 92 F4 15 46S 35 00E
Blantyre Scotland 15 E2 55 47N 4 06W
Blarney RoI 25 C1 51 56N 8 34W
Blennerville RoI 25 B2 52 15N 9 43W
Blessington RoI 25 E3 53 10N 6 32W
Bletchley England 20 C3 52 00N 0 46W
Blidworth England 17 E2 53 09N 1 11W
Blithe *r.* England 19 E2 52 45N 1 50W
Blois France 56 E4 47 36N 1 20E
Bloody Foreland RoI 24 C5 55 10N 8 15W
Bludenz Austria 58 D3 47 10N 9 50E
Blue Stack Mountains RoI 24 C4 54 44N 8 03W
Blyth Nottinghamshire England 17 E2 53 23N 1 03W
Blyth Northumberland England 17 E4 55 07N 1 30W
Blyth *r.* England 17 E4 55 00N 1 45W
Blyth *r.* England 21 E3 52 28N 1 30E
Boa Vista Brazil 114 E14 3 23S 55 30W
Bocholt Germany 58 C5 51 49N 6 37E
Bochum Germany 58 C5 51 28N 7 11E
Boddam Scotland 13 H2 57 28N 1 48W
Boden Sweden 55 F4 65 50N 21 44E
Bodensee *l.* Switz. 58 D3 47 40N 9 30E
Bodmin England 22 C2 50 29N 4 43W
Bodmin Moor England 22 C2 50 35N 4 40W
Boggeragh Mountains RoI 25 B2/C2 52 00N 8 50W
Bogie *r.* Scotland 13 G2 57 25N 2 50W
Bognor Regis England 20 C1 50 47N 0 41W
Bogotá Colombia 114 C14 4 38N 74 05W
Böhmer Wald *mts.* Germany 58 F4 49 00N 13 00E
Boise City USA 102 F4 36 44N 102 31W
Boldon England 17 E3 54 57N 1 27W
BOLIVIA 114 D10/E10
Bollington England 16 D2 53 18N 2 06W
Bologna Italy 60 E6 44 30N 11 20E
Bolsover England 17 E2 53 15N 1 17W
Bolton England 16 D2 53 35N 2 26W
Bolus Head RoI 25 A1 51 45N 10 10W
Bolzano Italy 60 D7 46 30N 11 22E
Bonar Bridge *tn.* Scotland 13 E2 57 53N 4 21W
Bo'ness Scotland 15 F3 56 01N 3 37W
Bonifacio France 56 J1 41 23N 9 10E
Bonifacio, Strait of France/Italy 56 J1 41 20N 8 45E
Bonn Germany 58 C5 50 44N 7 06E
Bonnybridge Scotland 15 F2 55 59N 3 54W
Bonnyrigg Scotland 15 F2 55 52N 3 08W
Boolakennedy RoI 25 C2 52 20N 8 03W
Bootle Cumbria England 16 C3 54 17N 3 23W
Bootle Merseyside England 16 C2 53 28N 3 00W
Bordeaux France 56 D3 44 50N 0 34W
Bordon Camp England 20 C2 51 07N 0 53W
Borneo *i.* Indonesia/Malaysia 79 D3/F5 1 00N 113 00E
Bornholm *i.* Denmark 55 D2 55 02N 15 00E
Boroughbridge England 17 E3 54 05N 1 24W
Borris in Ossory RoI 25 D2 52 57N 7 37W
Borrisokane RoI 25 C2 53 00N 8 08W
Borrisoleigh RoI 25 D2 52 45N 8 00W
Borrowash England 19 E2 52 55N 1 24W
Borth Wales 18 B2 52 29N 4 03W
Boscastle England 22 C2 50 41N 4 42W
BOSNIA-HERZEGOVINA 61 G6/H6
Boston England 17 F1 52 29N 0 01W
Boston USA 103 M5 42 20N 71 05W
Boston Spa England 17 E2 53 54N 1 21W
Bothnia, Gulf of Finland/Sweden 55 E3/F3 61 00N 19 10E
Botoşani Romania 59 N3 47 44N 26 41E
BOTSWANA 92 D3/E3
Bottrop Germany 58 C5 51 31N 6 55E
Boulder USA 102 E5 40 02N 105 16W
Boulogne-sur-Mer France 56 E6 50 43N 1 37E
Bourg-en-Bresse France 56 G4 46 12N 5 13E
Bourges France 56 F4 47 05N 2 23E
Bourne England 19 F2 52 46N 0 23W
Bourne End England 20 C2 51 34N 0 42W
Bournemouth England 23 F2 50 43N 1 54W
Bournemouth *u.a.* England 23 F2 50 43N 1 54W
Bourton-on-the-Water England 19 E1 51 53N 1 46W
Bovey *r.* England 22 D2 50 40N 3 50W
Bovey Tracey England 22 D2 50 36N 3 40W
Bowes England 16 D3 54 30N 2 01W
Bowland, Forest of England 16 D2/D3 54 00N 2 40W
Bowmore Scotland 14 C2 55 45N 6 17W
Bowness-on-Windermere England 16 D3 54 22N 2 55W
Boxtel Neths 54 D4 51 36N 5 20E
Boyle RoI 24 C3 53 58N 8 18W
Boyne *r.* RoI 24 E3 53 45N 6 25W
Bozeman USA 102 D6 45 40N 111 00W
Brabourne Lees England 21 D2 51 08N 1 00E
Brackley England 19 E2 52 02N 1 09W
Bracknell England 20 C2 51 26N 0 46W
Bracknell Forest *u.a.* England 20 C1 50 25N 0 50W
Bradford England 17 E2 53 48N 1 45W
Bradford-on-Avon England 20 A2 51 22N 2 15W
Bradwell-on-Sea England 21 D2 51 44N 0 54E
Bradworthy England 22 C2 50 54N 4 24W
Braemar Scotland 13 F2 57 01N 3 23W
Braga Portugal 57 A4 41 32N 8 26W
Bragança Portugal 57 B4 41 47N 6 46W
Brahmaputra *r.* India/Bangladesh 75 G5 26 40N 93 00E
Brăila Romania 59 N2 45 17N 27 58E
Brailsford England 19 E2 52 59N 1 36W
Braintree England 21 D2 51 53N 0 32E
Brampton England 16 D3 54 57N 2 43W
Brandenburg Germany 58 F6 52 25N 12 34E
Brandon Durham England 17 E3 54 46N 1 38W
Brandon Suffolk England 21 D3 52 27N 0 37E
Brandon Bay RoI 25 A2 52 15N 10 05W
Brandon Mountain RoI 25 A2 52 10N 10 10W
Brandon Point RoI 25 A2 52 15N 10 05W
Brant *r.* England 17 F2 53 05N 0 35W
Brásilia Brazil 114 H10 15 45S 47 57W
Braşov Romania 59 M2 45 39N 25 35E
Bratislava Slovakia 59 H4 48 10N 17 10E
Braunau Austria 58 F4 48 16N 13 03E
Braunschweig Germany 58 E6 52 15N 10 30E
Braunton England 22 C3 51 07N 4 10W
Bray RoI 24 E3 53 12N 6 06W
Bray Head RoI 25 A1 53 12N 6 05W
BRAZIL 114 F11/H11
Brazzaville Congo 92 C7 4 14S 15 14E
Breaston England 19 E2 52 56N 1 12W
Brechin Scotland 13 G1 56 44N 2 40W
Brecon Wales 18 C1 51 57N 3 24W
Breda Neths 54 C4 51 35N 4 46E
Bregenz Austria 58 D3 47 31N 9 46E
Bremen Germany 58 D6 53 05N 8 48E
Bremerhaven Germany 58 D6 53 33N 8 35E
Brent England 20 C2 51 34N 0 17W
Brentwood England 21 D2 51 38N 0 18E
Brescia Italy 60 D6 45 33N 10 13E
Bressay *i.* Scotland 11 C3 60 08N 1 05W
Brest Belarus 62 B5 52 08N 23 40E
Brest France 56 B5 48 23N 4 30W
Briançon France 56 H3 44 53N 6 39E
Bridgend Wales 18 C1 51 31N 3 35W
Bridgend *u.a.* Wales 18 C1 51 32N 3 35W
Bridge of Dee *tn.* Scotland 13 F1 56 59N 3 20W
Bridge of Don *tn.* Scotland 13 G2 57 11N 2 05W
Bridge of Ericht *tn.* Scotland 13 E1 56 44N 4 23W
Bridge of Orchy *tn.* Scotland 13 E1 56 30N 4 46W
Bridge of Weir *tn.* Scotland 15 E2 55 52N 4 35W
Bridgeport USA 103 M5 41 12N 73 12W
Bridgetown RoI 25 E2 52 14N 6 33W
Bridgnorth England 19 D2 52 33N 2 25W
Bridgwater England 23 D3 51 08N 3 00W
Bridgwater Bay England 23 D3 51 15N 3 20W
Bridlington England 17 F3 54 05N 0 12W
Bridlington Bay England 17 F3 54 03N 0 10W
Bridport England 23 E2 50 44N 2 46W
Brierfield England 16 D2 53 50N 2 14W
Brig Switz. 58 C3 46 19N 8 00E
Brigg England 17 F2 53 34N 0 30W
Brighouse England 17 E2 53 42N 1 47W
Brightlingsea England 21 E2 51 49N 1 02E
Brighton England 20 C1 50 50N 0 10W
Brighton and Hove *u.a.* England 20 C1 50 51N 0 09W
Brignoles France 56 H2 43 25N 6 03E
Bríndisi Italy 61 G4 40 37N 17 57E
Brisbane Australia 81 K5 27 30S 153 00E
Bristol England 23 E3 51 27N 2 35W
Bristol *u.a.* England 23 E3 51 30N 2 38W
Bristol Channel UK 22 C1/D1 51 20N 4 00W
British Columbia *prov.* Canada 100 K4/K5 56 50N 125 30W
British Isles Europe 10
Briton Ferry *tn.* Wales 18 C1 51 38N 3 49W
Brittas RoI 24 E3 53 14N 6 27W
Brive-la-Gaillarde France 56 E3 45 09N 1 32E
Brixham England 22 D2 50 23N 3 30W
Brno Czech Rep. 59 H4 49 13N 16 40E
Broad Bay Scotland 12 C3 58 15N 6 10W
Broadford RoI 25 C2 52 48N 8 38W
Broadford Scotland 12 D2 57 14N 5 54W
Broad Haven *b.* RoI 24 B4 54 18N 9 55W
Broadstairs England 21 E2 51 22N 1 27E
Broadstone England 23 E2 50 45N 2 00W
Broadway England 19 E2 52 02N 1 50W
Brockenhurst England 20 B1 50 49N 1 34W
Brodick Scotland 14 D2 55 35N 5 09W
Bromley England 20 D2 51 31N 0 01E
Bromsgrove England 19 D2 50 20N 2 03W
Bromyard England 19 D2 52 11N 2 30W
Brora Scotland 13 F3 58 01N 3 51W
Brora *r.* Scotland 13 E3 58 05N 4 00W
Broseley England 19 D2 52 37N 2 29W
Brotton England 17 F3 54 34N 0 56W
Brough East Riding of Yorkshire England 17 F2 53 44N 0 35W
Brough Cumbria England 16 D3 54 32N 2 19W
Brough Head Scotland 11 A2 59 09N 3 19W
Broughshane NI 14 C1 54 54N 6 12W
Broughton Wales 18 D3 53 10N 3 00W
Broughton in Furness England 16 C3 54 17N 3 13W
Broughty Ferry *tn.* Scotland 13 G1 56 28N 2 53W
Brownhills *tn.* England 19 E2 52 39N 1 55W
Broxburn Scotland 15 F2 55 57N 3 29W
Bruay-en-Artois France 56 F6 50 29N 2 33E
Brue *r.* England 23 E3 51 10N 2 50W
Brugg Switz. 58 D3 47 29N 8 13E
Brugge Belgium 54 B4 51 13N 3 14E
BRUNEI 79 E4/F4
Brunico Italy 60 D7 46 47N 11 57E
Brunswick USA 103 K3 31 09N 81 30W
Brussels Belgium 54 C3 50 50N 4 21E
Bruton England 23 E3 51 07N 2 27W
Bryher *i.* England 22 A1 49 57N 6 21W
Brymbo Wales 18 C3 53 05N 3 03W
Brynamman Wales 18 C1 51 49N 3 52W
Brynmawr Wales 18 C1 51 49N 3 11W
Bucharest Romania 59 N2 44 25N 26 07E
Buchan Ness Scotland 13 H2 57 28N 1 47W
Buckfastleigh England 22 D2 50 29N 3 46W
Buckhaven Scotland 15 F3 56 11N 3 03W
Buckie Scotland 13 G2 57 40N 2 58W
Buckingham England 20 C2 52 00N 1 00W
Buckinghamshire *co.* England 20 C2 51 50N 0 50W
Buckley Wales 18 C3 53 10N 3 05W
Budapest Hungary 59 J3 47 30N 19 03E
Buddon Ness Scotland 13 G1 56 28N 2 45W
Bude England 22 C2 50 50N 4 33W
Bude Bay England 22 C2 50 50N 4 40W
Budleigh Salterton England 23 D2 50 38N 3 20W
Buenaventura Colombia 114 B14 3 54N 77 02W
Buenos Aires Argentina 115 F7 34 40S 58 30W
Buffalo USA 103 L5 42 52N 78 55W
Builth Wells Wales 18 C2 52 09N 3 24W
Bujumbura Burundi 93 A3 3 22S 29 19E
Bukavu CDR 91 L1 2 30S 28 50E
Bulawayo Zimbabwe 92 E3 20 10S 28 43E
Bulford England 20 B2 51 12N 1 46W
BULGARIA 61 K5/M5
Bulkington England 19 E2 52 28N 1 25W
Bull Point NI 14 C2 55 18N 6 16W
Bunclody RoI 25 E2 52 38N 6 40W
Buncrana RoI 24 D5 55 08N 7 27W
Bundoran RoI 24 C4 54 28N 8 17W
Bungay England 21 E3 52 28N 1 26E
Bunmahon RoI 25 D2 52 08N 7 23W
Bunnahown RoI 24 B3 53 24N 9 47W
Bunnyconnellan RoI 24 B4 54 06N 9 01W
Buraydah Saudi Arabia 72 D4 26 20N 43 59E
Bure *r.* England 21 E3 52 47N 1 20E
Burgas Bulgaria 61 M5 42 30N 27 29E
Burgess Hill *tn.* England 20 C1 50 58N 0 08W
Burghead *tn.* Scotland 13 F2 57 42N 3 30W
Burghead Bay Scotland 13 F2 57 41N 3 31W
Burgh le Marsh England 17 G2 53 10N 0 15E
Burgos Spain 57 D5 42 21N 3 41W
BURKINA 90 D4
Burley-in-Wharfedale England 17 E2 53 55N 1 45W
Burnham Market England 21 D3 52 57N 0 44E
Burnham-on-Crouch England 21 D2 51 38N 0 49E
Burnham-on-Sea England 23 D3 51 15N 3 00W
Burnley England 16 D2 53 48N 2 14W
Burnmouth Scotland 15 G2 55 50N 2 04W
Burnsall England 16 E3 54 03N 1 57W
Burntisland *tn.* Scotland 15 F3 56 03N 3 15W
Burntwood England 19 E2 52 40N 1 56W
Burray *i.* Scotland 11 B1 58 51N 2 54W
Burrow Head Scotland 15 E1 54 41N 4 24W
Burry Port Wales 18 B1 51 42N 4 15W
Bursa Turkey 63 C3 40 12N 29 04E
Burscough Bridge *tn.* England 16 D2 53 37N 2 51W
Burton Agnes England 17 F3 54 03N 0 19W
Burton Latimer England 19 F2 52 22N 0 40W
Burton upon Trent England 19 E2 52 48N 1 36W
BURUNDI 93 A3/B3
Burwell England 21 D3 52 16N 0 19E
Bury England 16 D2 53 36N 2 17W
Bury St. Edmunds England 21 D3 52 15N 0 43E
Bush *r.* NI 14 C2 55 10N 6 30W
Bushey England 20 C2 51 39N 0 22W
Bushmills NI 14 C2 55 12N 6 32W
Bute *i.* Scotland 14 D2 55 50N 5 05W
Bute, Sound of Scotland 14 D2 55 45N 5 10W
Butler's Bridge RoI 24 D4 54 03N 7 22W
Buttermere *l.* England 16 C3 54 32N 3 16W
Buttevant RoI 25 C2 52 14N 8 40W
Butt of Lewis *c.* Scotland 12 C3 58 30N 6 20W
Buxton England 17 E2 53 15N 1 55W
Bydgoszcz Poland 59 H6 53 16N 18 00E
Byfield England 19 E2 52 11N 1 14W
Bytom Poland 59 J5 50 21N 18 51E

C

Cabo de Hornos Chile 115 D2 56 00S 67 15W
Cabo Finisterre Spain 57 A5 42 52N 9 16W
Cabrera *i.* Spain 57 G3 39 00N 2 59E
Cáceres Spain 57 B3 39 29N 6 23W
Cadair Idris *mt.* Wales 18 C2 52 42N 3 54W
Cádiz Spain 57 B2 36 32N 6 18W
Cádiz, Gulf of Spain 57 B2 36 30N 7 15W
Caen France 56 D5 49 11N 0 22W
Caerleon Wales 18 D1 51 37N 2 57W
Caernarfon Wales 18 B3 53 08N 4 16W
Caernarfon Bay Wales 18 B3 53 05N 4 30W
Caerphilly Wales 18 C1 51 35N 3 14W
Caerphilly *u.a.* Wales 18 C1 51 37N 3 5W
Caersws Wales 18 C2 52 31N 3 26W
Cágliari Italy 60 C3 39 13N 9 08E
Caha Mountains RoI 25 B1 51 40N 9 40W
Caher RoI 25 D2 52 21N 7 56W
Caher Island RoI 24 A3 53 43N 10 01W
Cahersiveen RoI 25 A1 51 57N 10 13W
Cahore Point RoI 25 E2 52 34N 6 11W
Cahors France 56 E3 44 28N 0 26E
Cairn Gorm *mt.* Scotland 13 F2 57 07N 3 40W

Cairngorms *mts.* Scotland 13 F2 57 10N 3 30W
Cairnryan Scotland 14 D2 54 58N 5 02W
Cairns Australia 81 J7 16 51S 145 43E
Cairo Egypt 91 M7 30 00N 31 15E
Caister-on-Sea England 21 E3 52 39N 1 44E
Caistor England 17 F2 53 30N 0 20W
Calahorra Spain 57 E5 46 19N 1 58W
Calais France 56 E6 50 57N 1 52E
Calamocha Spain 57 E4 40 54N 1 18W
Calatayud Spain 57 E4 41 21N 1 39W
Caldew *r.* England 16 C3 54 45N 3 00W
Caldey Island Wales 18 B1 51 38N 4 42W
Caldicot Wales 18 D1 51 36N 2 45W
Caldwell USA 102 C5 43 39N 116 40W
Calgary Canada 100 N4 51 05N 11 05W
Cali Colombia 114 B14 3 24N 76 30W
California *state* USA 102 C4 35 00N 119 00W
Callan RoI 25 D2 52 33N 7 23W
Callander Scotland 15 E3 56 15N 4 13W
Callao Peru 114 B11 12 05S 77 08W
Calligarry Scotland 12 D2 57 02N 5 58E
Callington England 22 C2 50 30N 4 18W
Calne England 20 A2 51 27N 2 00W
Calverton England 17 E2 53 03N 1 05W
Calvi France 56 J2 42 34N 8 44E
Cam *r.* England 21 D3 52 15N 0 11E
Camberley England 20 C2 51 21N 0 45W
CAMBODIA 79 C6/D6
Camborne England 22 B2 50 12N 5 19W
Cambrai France 56 F6 50 10N 3 14E
Cambrian Mountains Wales 18 C2 52 15N 3 45W
Cambridge England 21 D3 52 12N 0 07E
Cambridge USA 103 L4 38 34N 76 04W
Cambridgeshire *co.* England 20 C3 52 30N 0 00
Camel *r.* England 22 C2 50 31N 4 44W
Camelford England 22 C2C 50 37N 4 41W
CAMEROON 90 G3
Campbeltown Scotland 14 D2 55 26N 5 36W
Campina Grande Brazil 114 K12 7 15S 35 50W
Campinas Brazil 114 H9 22 54S 47 06W
Campobasso Italy 60 F4 41 33N 14 39E
Campo Grande Brazil 114 G9 20 24S 54 35W
Campos Brazil 114 J9 21 46S 41 21W
Campsie Fells Scotland 15 E3 56 00N 4 15W
CANADA 100/101
Canadian *r.* USA 102 F4 35 00N 104 00W
Canary Islands Spain 90 A7/B7 28 30N 15 10W
Canaveral, Cape USA 103 K2 28 28N 80 28W
Canberra Australia 81 J3 35 18S 149 08E
Cancún Mexico 106 G4 21 09N 86 45W
Canisp *mt.* Scotland 13 D3 58 07N 5 03W
Canna *i.* Scotland 12 C2 57 05N 6 35W
Canna, Sound of Scotland 12 C2 57 00N 6 30W
Cannes France 56 H2 43 33N 7 00E
Cannich Scotland 13 E2 57 12N 4 46W
Cannington England 23 D3 51 09N 3 04E
Cannock England 19 D2 52 42N 2 01W
Cannock Chase England 19 D2/E2 52 45N 2 04W
Canonbie Scotland 15 G2 55 05N 2 57W
Canterbury England 21 E2 51 17N 1 05E
Canvey Island England 21 D2 51 32N 0 33E
Cap de la Hague France 56 D5 49 44N 1 56W
Cape Clear RoI 25 B1 51 30N 9 30W
Cape Cornwall England 22 B2 50 07N 5 44W
Capel England 20 C2 51 10N 0 20W
Cape Town RSA 92 C1 33 56S 18 28E
CAPE VERDE 118
Cape York Peninsula Australia 81 H8 12 30S 142 30E
Cap Ferret *c.* France 56 D3 44 42N 1 16W
Cappagh White RoI 25 C2 52 40N 8 10W
Cappamore RoI 25 C2 52 37N 8 20W
Cappoquin RoI 25 D2 52 08N 7 50W
Capri *i.* Italy 60 F4 40 33N 14 15E
Caprivi Strip Namibia 92 D4 17 30S 27 50E
Caracas Venezuela 114 D16 10 35N 66 56W
Carcassonne France 56 F2 43 13N 2 21E
Cardiff Wales 18 C1 51 30N 3 13W
Cardiff *u.a.* Wales 18 C1 51 32N 3 14W
Cardigan Wales 18 B2 52 06N 4 40W
Cardigan Bay Wales 18 B2 52 30N 4 30W
Cargenbridge Scotland 15 F2 55 05N 3 41W
Caribbean Sea Central America 107 J3/L3 15 00N 75 00W
Carlingford RoI 24 E4 54 02N 6 11W
Carlingford Lough NI/RoI 14 C1 54 05N 6 10W
Carlisle England 16 D3 54 54N 2 55W
Carlow RoI 25 E2 52 50N 6 55W
Carlow *co.* RoI 25 E2 52 40N 6 55W
Carloway Scotland 12 C3 58 17N 6 48W
Carlton in Lindrick England 17 E2 53 22N 1 06W
Carlton-on-Trent England 17 F2 53 10N 0 48W
Carluke Scotland 15 F2 55 45N 3 51W
Carmarthen Wales 18 B1 51 51N 4 20W
Carmarthen Bay Wales 18 B1 51 40N 4 30W
Carmarthenshire *u.a.* Wales 18 B1 51 55N 4 00W
Carmel Head Wales 18 B3 53 24N 4 34W
Carndonagh RoI 24 D5 55 15N 7 15W
Carn Eige *mt.* Scotland 13 D2 57 22N 5 07W
Carnforth England 16 D3 54 08N 2 46W
Carnlough NI 14 D1 54 59N 5 59W
Carnlough Bay NI 14 D1 54 59N 5 57W
Carnoustie Scotland 13 G1 56 30N 2 44W
Carnsore Point RoI 25 E2 52 10N 6 22W
Carpathians *mts.* Europe 59 J4/M3 49 00N 22 00E
Carpentras France 56 G3 44 03N 5 03E
Carradale Scotland 14 D2 55 35N 5 28E
Carrauntoohil *mt.* RoI 25 B2 52 00N 9 45W
Carrbridge Scotland 13 F2 57 17N 3 49W
Carrick RoI 24 C4 54 39N 8 38W
Carrickboy RoI 24 D3 53 37N 7 41W
Carrickfergus NI 14 D1 54 43N 5 49W
Carrickfergus *district* NI 14 D1 54 45N 5 50W
Carrickmacross RoI 24 E3 53 58N 5 49W
Carrick-on-Shannon RoI 24 C3 53 57N 8 05W
Carrick-on-Suir RoI 25 D2 52 21N 7 25W
Carrigaline RoI 25 C1 51 48N 8 24W
Carriganimmy RoI 25 B1 51 57N 9 02W
Carrigtohill RoI 25 C1 51 55N 8 16W
Carron *r.* Scotland 13 E2 57 53N 4 30W
Carronbridge Scotland 15 F2 55 16N 3 48W
Carrutherstown Scotland 15 F2 55 04N 3 24W
Carryduff NI 14 D1 54 31N 5 53W
Carsethorn Scotland 15 F1 54 55N 3 35W
Carsphairn Scotland 15 E2 55 13N 4 16W
Cartagena Colombia 114 B16 10 24N 75 33W
Cartagena Spain 57 E2 37 36N 0 59W
Carterton England 20 B2 51 45N 1 35W
Casablanca Morocco 90 C8 33 39N 7 35W
Cascade Range N. America 102 B5/6 48 00N 121 00W
Caserta Italy 60 F4 41 04N 14 20E
Cashel RoI 25 D2 52 31N 7 53W
Casper USA 102 E5 42 50N 106 20W
Caspian Sea Asia 63 G3/H3 41 00N 50 00E
Cassino Italy 60 E4 41 29N 13 50E
Castellane France 56 H2 43 50N 6 30E
Castellón de la Plana Spain 57 E3 39 59N 0 03W
Castelnaudary France 56 E2 43 18N 1 57E
Castelo Branco Portugal 57 B3 39 50N 7 30W
Castelvetrano Italy 60 E2 37 41N 12 47E
Castlebar RoI 24 B3 53 52N 9 17W
Castlebay Scotland 12 B1 56 57N 7 28W
Castleblaney RoI 24 E4 54 07N 6 44W
Castle Cary England 23 E3 51 06N 2 31W
Castlecomer RoI 25 D2 52 48N 7 12W
Castleconnell RoI 25 C2 52 43N 8 30W
Castledawson NI 14 C1 54 47N 6 33W
Castlederg NI 14 B1 54 42N 7 36W
Castledermot RoI 25 E2 52 55N 6 50W
Castle Donington England 19 E2 52 51N 1 19W
Castle Douglas Scotland 15 F1 54 57N 3 56W
Castlefin RoI 24 D4 54 47N 7 35W
Castleford England 17 E2 43 44N 1 21W
Castleisland RoI 25 B2 52 14N 9 27W
Castle Kennedy Scotland 14 E1 54 54N 4 57W
Castlemaine Harbour RoI 25 B2 52 08N 9 33W
Castlepollard RoI 24 D3 53 41N 7 17W
Castlerea RoI 24 C3 53 46N 8 29W
Castlereagh *district* NI 14 D1 54 35N 5 55W
Castletown Isle of Man 16 B3 54 04N 4 38W
Castletown Scotland 13 F3 58 35N 3 23W
Castletown Bearhaven RoI 25 B2 51 39N 9 55W
Castletownroche RoI 25 C2 52 10N 8 28W
Castlewellan NI 14 D1 54 16N 5 57W
Castres France 56 F2 43 36N 2 14E
Castrovillari Italy 60 G3 39 48N 16 12E
Catánia Italy 60 F2 37 31N 15 06E
Catanzaro Italy 61 G3 38 54N 16 36E
Caterham England 20 C2 51 17N 0 04W
Catlemartyr RoI 25 C1 51 55N 8 03W
Catrine Scotland 15 E2 55 30N 4 20W
Catshill *tn.* England 19 D2 52 22N 2 03W
Catterick Garrison England 17 E3 54 23N 1 40W
Caucasus *mts.* Asia 63 F3/G3 43 00N 43 00E
Cavan RoI 24 D3 53 58N 7 21W
Cavan *co.* RoI 24 D3/4 54 02N 7 10W
Cawood England 17 E2 53 50N 1 07W
Caxias Brazil 114 J13 4 53N 43 20W
Caxias do Sul Brazil 115 G8 29 14S 51 10W
Cayenne French Guiana 114 G14 4 55N 52 18W
Cedar Rapids *tn.* USA 103 H5 41 59N 91 39W
Cefalù Italy 60 F3 38 03N 14 03E
Cefn-mawr Wales 18 C2 52 59N 3 02W
Cellar Head Scotland 12 C3 58 25N 6 11W
Celle Germany 58 E6 52 37N 10 05E
Cemaes Wales 18 B3 53 24N 4 27W
Cemaes Head Wales 18 B2 53 10N 4 50W
CENTRAL AFRICAN REPUBLIC 91 J3/K3
Central Bedfordshire *u.a.* England 20 C2/C3 51 55N 0 35W
Ceredigion *u.a.* Wales 18 B2/C2 52 14N 4 00W
Cergy-Pontoise France 56 F5 49 02N 2 04E
Cerignola Italy 60 F4 41 16N 15 54E
Cerne Abbas England 23 E2 50 49N 2 29W
Cesena Italy 60 E6 44 09N 12 15E
České Budějovice Czech Rep. 58 G4 48 58N 14 29E
Ceuta *territory* Spain 57 C1 35 53N 5 19W
Cévennes *mts.* France 56 F3 44 20N 3 30E
CHAD 91 J4/K4
Chadderton England 16 D2 53 33N 2 08W
Chad, Lake West Africa 91 G4 13 50N 14 00E
Chagford England 22 D2 50 41N 3 50W
Chalfont St. Giles England 20 C2 51 39N 0 35W
Chalkída Greece 61 K3 38 28N 23 36E
Chalkidikí *p.* Greece 61 K4 40 30N 23 00E
Chalmer *r.* England 21 D2 51 54N 0 21E
Châlons-sur-Marne France 56 G5 48 58N 4 22E
Chalon-sur-Saône France 56 G4 46 47N 4 51E
Chambéry France 56 G3 45 34N 5 55E
Chamonix France 56 H3 45 55N 6 52E
Champlain, Lake USA 105 F2 45 00N 73 00W
Chandigarh India 74 D6 30 44N 76 54E
Changchun China 77 N6 43 53N 125 20E
Chang Jiang *r.* China 77 J4 31 00N 110 00E
Changsha China 77 K3 28 10N 113 00E
Chaniá Greece 61 L1 35 31N 24 01E
Channel Islands British Isles 23 E1 49 30N 2 30W
Chapel-en-le-Frith England 17 E2 53 20N 1 54W
Chapel St. Leonards England 17 G2 53 14N 0 20E
Chapeltown England 17 E2 53 28N 1 27W
Chard England 23 E2 50 53N 2 58W
Charing England 21 D2 51 13N 0 48E
Charlbury England 20 B2 51 53N 1 29W
Charleroi Belgium 54 C3 50 25N 4 27E
Charleston USA 103 K4 38 23N 81 40W
Charlestown RoI 24 C3 53 58N 8 47W
Charlestown of Aberlour Scotland 13 F2 57 28N 3 14W
Charleville-Mézières France 56 G5 49 46N 4 43E
Charlotte USA 103 K4 35 03N 80 50W
Charlottesville USA 103 L4 38 02N 78 29W
Charlton Kings England 19 D2 51 53N 2 03W
Chartres France 56 E5 48 27N 1 30E
Châteaubriant France 56 D4 47 43N 1 22W
Châteaudun France 56 E5 48 04N 1 20E
Châteauroux France 56 E4 46 49N 1 41E
Château-Thierry France 56 F5 49 03N 3 24E
Châtellerault France 56 E4 46 49N 0 33E
Chatham England 21 D2 51 23N 0 32E
Chatham Canada 101 U2 42 24N 82 11W
Châtillon-sur-Seine France 56 G4 47 52N 4 35E
Chattanooga USA 103 J4 35 02N 85 18W
Chatteris England 20 D3 52 27N 0 03E
Chaumont France 56 G3 48 07N 5 08E
Cheadle Greater Manchester England 16 D2 53 24N 2 13W
Cheadle Staffordshire England 19 E2 52 59N 1 59W
Cheddar England 23 E3 51 17N 2 46W
Chelmsford England 21 D2 51 44N 0 28E
Cheltenham England 19 D2 51 54N 2 04W
Chelyabinsk Russia 70 J8 55 12N 61 25E
Chemnitz Germany 58 F5 50 50N 12 55E
Chengdu China 77 H4 30 37N 104 06E
Chennai India 74 E2 13 05N 80 18E
Chepstow Wales 19 D1 51 39N 2 41W
Cherbourg France 56 D5 49 38N 1 37W
Cherkasy Ukraine 62 D4 49 27N 32 04E
Chernivtsi Ukraine 59 M4 48 19N 25 52E
Chertsey England 20 C2 51 23N 0 30W
Cherwell *r.* England 20 B2 51 55N 1 18W
Chesapeake USA 103 L4 36 45N 76 15W
Chesham England 20 C2 51 43N 0 38W
Cheshire East *u.a.* England 16 D2 53 15N 2 15W
Cheshire Plain England 16 D2 53 12N 2 50W
Cheshire West and Chester *u.a.* England 16 D2 53 15N 2 40W
Cheshunt England 20 C2 51 43N 0 02W
Chesil Beach England 23 E2 50 38N 2 50W
Chester England 16 D2 53 12N 2 54W
Chesterfield England 17 E2 53 15N 1 25W
Chester-le-Street England 17 E3 54 52N 1 34W
Cheviot Hills England/Scotland 15 G2 55 25N 2 30W
Cheviot, The *mt.* England 15 G2 55 29N 2 20W
Chew *r.* England 23 E3 51 21N 2 40W
Chiba Japan 78 D2 35 38N 140 07E
Chicago USA 103 J5 41 50N 87 45W
Chichester England 20 C1 50 50N 0 48W
Chiclayo Peru 114 B12 6 47S 79 47W
Chieti Italy 60 F5 42 21N 14 10E
Chigwell England 20 D2 51 37N 0 05E
CHILE 114/115 C5/C8
Chillán Chile 115 C6 36 37S 72 10W
Chiltern Hills England 20 B2/C2 51 40N 1 00W
Chimborazo *mt.* Ecuador 114 B13 1 29S 78 52W
Chimbote Peru 114 B12 9 04S 78 34W
CHINA 76/77
Chinnor England 20 C2 51 43N 0 56W
Chioggia Italy 60 E6 45 13N 12 17E
Chíos *i.* Greece 61 E3 38 00N 26 00E
Chippenham England 20 A2 51 28N 2 07W
Chipping Campden England 19 E2 52 03N 1 46W
Chipping Norton England 20 B2 51 56N 1 32W
Chipping Ongar England 21 D2 51 43N 0 15E
Chipping Sodbury England 19 D1 51 33N 2 24W
Chirk Wales 18 C2 52 66N 3 03W
Chisinău Moldova 59 P3 47 00N 28 50E
Chita Russia 71 P7 52 03N 113 35E
Chittagong Bangladesh 75 G4 22 20N 91 48E
Chitterne England 20 A2 51 11N 2 02W
Chobham England 20 C2 51 21N 0 37W
Cholet France 56 D4 47 04N 0 53W
Chongqing China 77 J3 29 30N 106 35E
Chorley England 16 D2 53 40N 2 38W
Chorleywood England 20 C2 51 40N 0 29W
Chornobyl Ukraine 59 Q5 51 17N 30 15E
Christchurch England 23 F2 50 44N 1 45W
Christchurch NZ 81 P2 43 32S 172 38E
Chudleigh England 22 D2 50 36N 3 45W
Chudskoye Ozero *l.* Russia/Estonia 62 C6 58 40N 27 30E
Chulmleigh England 22 D2 50 55N 3 52W
Chum *r.* England 19 D1 51 46N 1 58W
Chur Switz. 58 D3 46 52N 9 32E
Churchill Canada 101 S5 58 45N 94 00W
Church Stoke Wales 18 C2 52 32N 3 05W
Church Stretton England 18 D2 52 32N 2 49W
Chute-aux-Outardes Canada 105 G3 49 17N 67 57W
Cincinnati USA 103 K4 39 10N 83 30W
Cinderford England 19 D1 51 50N 2 29W
Cirencester England 19 E1 51 44N 1 59W
Citlaltépetl *mt.* Mexico 106 E3 19 00N 97 18W
City of Edinburgh *u.a.* Scotland 15 F2 55 55N 3 15W
Ciudad Bolívar Venezuela 114 E15 8 06N 63 36W
Ciudadela Spain 57 G3 40 00N 3 50E
Ciudad Guayana Venezuela 114 E15 8 22N 62 37W
Ciudad Juárez Mexico 106 C6 31 42N 106 29W
Ciudad Obregón Mexico 106 C5 27 28N 109 59W
Ciudad Real Spain 57 D3 38 59N 3 55W
Ciudad Rodrigo Spain 57 B4 40 36N 6 33W
Civitavecchia Italy 60 D5 42 05N 11 47E
Clachan Scotland 14 D2 55 45N 5 34W
Clackmannan Scotland 15 F3 56 05N 3 46W
Clackmannanshire *u.a.* Scotland 15 F3 56 10N 3 40W
Clacton on Sea England 21 E2 51 48N 1 09E
Clane RoI 24 E3 53 18N 6 41W
Claonaig Scotland 14 D2 55 46N 5 22W
Clara RoI 24 D3 53 20N 7 36W
Clare *r.* RoI 24 C3 53 20N 9 00W
Clare *co.* RoI 25 B2/C2 52 45N 9 00W
Clarecastle RoI 25 C2 52 49N 8 57W
Claregalway RoI 24 C3 53 21N 8 57W
Clare Island RoI 24 A3/B3 53 49N 10 00W
Claremorris RoI 24 C3 53 44N 9 00W
Clarksville USA 103 J4 36 31N 87 21W
Clashmore RoI 25 D2 52 00N 7 49W
Clay Cross England 17 E2 53 10N 1 24W
Claydon England 21 E3 52 06N 1 07E
Clay Head Isle of Man 16 B3 54 11N 4 25W
Clayton-le-Moors England 16 D2 53 47N 2 23W
Clayton West England 17 E2 53 36N 1 37W
Clear Island RoI 25 B1 51 26N 9 30W
Clearwater USA 103 K2 27 57N 82 48W
Cleator Moor England 16 C3 54 31N 3 30W
Cleckheaton England 17 E2 53 44N 1 43W
Cleethorpes England 17 F2 53 34N 0 02W
Cleobury Mortimer England 19 D2 52 23N 2 29W
Clermont-Ferrand France 56 F3 45 47N 3 05E
Clevedon England 23 E3 51 27N 2 51W
Cleveland USA 103 K5 43 15N 75 50W
Cleveland Hills England 17 E3 54 25N 1 15W
Cleveleys England 16 C2 53 53N 3 03W
Clew Bay RoI 24 B3 53 50N 9 50W
Clifden RoI 24 A3 53 29N 10 00W
Clinton USA 103 H5 41 51N 90 12W
Clisham *mt.* Scotland 12 C2 57 58N 6 50W
Clitheroe England 16 D2 53 53N 2 23W
Cloghan RoI 24 D3 53 13N 7 53W
Clogheen RoI 25 D2 52 17N 8 00W
Clogher NI 14 B1 54 25N 7 10W
Clogherhead RoI 24 E3 53 45N 6 15W
Clogher Head RoI 24 E3 53 48N 6 13W
Cloghjordan RoI 25 C2 52 57N 8 02W
Clonakilty RoI 25 C1 51 37N 8 54W
Clonakilty Bay RoI 25 C1 51 33N 8 50W

Clonaslee RoI 25 D3 53 09N 7 31W
Clondalkin RoI 24 E3 53 19N 6 24W
Clonee RoI 24 E3 53 25N 6 26W
Clones RoI 24 D4 54 11N 7 15W
Clonmany RoI 24 D5 55 16N 7 25W
Clonmel RoI 25 D2 52 21N 7 42W
Clonroche RoI 25 E2 52 27N 6 43W
Clontarf RoI 24 E3 53 22N 6 12W
Cloondara RoI 24 D3 53 43N 7 54W
Cloppenburg Germany 58 D6 52 52N 8 02E
Cloughton England 17 F3 54 20N 0 27W
Clovelly England 22 C2 51 00N 4 24W
Clowne England 17 E2 53 17N 1 15W
Cluj-Napoca Romania 59 L3 46 47N 23 37E
Clwydian Range Wales 18 C3 53 12N 3 20W
Clydach Wales 18 C1 51 42N 3 56W
Clyde *r.* Scotland 15 F2 55 40N 3 50W
Clydebank Scotland 15 E2 55 54N 4 24W
Clyde River *tn.* Canada 101 X8 70 30N 68 30W
Coachford RoI 25 C1 51 55N 8 47W
Coalisland NI 14 C1 54 32N 6 42W
Coalville England 19 E2 52 44N 1 20W
Coast Ranges USA 102 B4/6 41 00N 123 00W
Coatbridge Scotland 15 E2 55 52N 4 01W
Cobh RoI 25 C1 51 51N 8 17W
Coburg Germany 58 E5 50 15N 10 58E
Cochin India 74 D1 9 56N 76 15E
Cockburnspath Scotland 15 G2 55 56N 2 21W
Cockenzie Scotland 15 G2 55 58N 2 58W
Cockermouth England 16 C3 54 40N 3 21W
Codó Brazil 114 J13 4 28S 43 51W
Codsall England 19 D2 52 37N 2 12W
Coggeshall England 21 D2 51 52N 0 41E
Cognac France 56 D3 45 42N 0 19W
Coimbra Portugal 57 A4 40 12N 8 25W
Colchester England 21 D2 51 54N 0 54E
Coldingham Scotland 15 G2 55 53N 2 10W
Coldstream Scotland 15 G2 55 39N 2 15W
Coleford England 19 D1 51 48N 2 37W
Coleraine NI 14 C2 55 08N 6 40W
Coleraine *district* NI 14 C2 55 00N 6 40W
Coleshill England 19 E2 52 30N 1 42W
Colgrave Sound Scotland 11 D3 60 35N 0 55W
Colintraive Scotland 14 D2 55 56N 5 09W
Coll *i.* Scotland 12 C1 56 40N 6 35W
Collin Scotland 15 F2 55 04N 3 32W
Collon RoI 24 E3 53 47N 6 29W
Collooney RoI 24 C4 54 11N 8 29W
Colmar France 56 H5 48 05N 7 21E
Colmonell Scotland 14 E2 55 08N 4 55W
Coln *r.* England 19 E1 51 46N 1 50W
Colne England 16 D2 53 32N 2 09W
Colne *r.* England 21 D2 51 53N 0 45E
Cologne Germany 58 C5 50 56N 6 57E
COLOMBIA 114 C14
Colombo Sri Lanka 74 D1 6 55N 79 52E
Colonsay *i.* Scotland 14 C3 56 05N 6 15W
Colorado *r.* N. America 102 D3 33 00N 114 00W
Colorado *state* USA 102 E4/F4 39 00N 106 00W
Colorado Springs USA 102 F4 38 50N 104 50W
Colsterworth England 19 F2 52 48N 0 37W
Coltishall England 21 E3 52 44N 1 22E
Columbia *r.* N. America 102 B6 46 00N 120 00W
Columbus USA 103 K5 39 59N 83 03W
Colwyn Bay *tn.* Wales 18 C3 53 18N 3 43W
Comacchio Italy 60 E6 44 42N 12 11E
Combe Martin England 22 C3 51 13N 4 02W
Comber NI 14 D1 54 33N 5 45W
Comeragh Mountains RoI 25 D2 52 19N 7 40W
Como Italy 60 C6 45 48N 9 05E
Comodoro Rivadavia Argentina 115 D4 45 56S 67 30W
COMOROS 92 H5
Compiègne France 56 F5 49 25N 2 50E
Comrie Scotland 15 F1 56 23N 4 00W
Conakry Guinea 90 B3 9 30N 13 43W
Concepción Chile 115 C6 36 50S 73 03W
Concordia USA 103 G4 39 35N 97 39W
Condom France 56 E2 43 58N 0 23E
Conflans-Ste. Honorine France 56 F5 49 01N 2 09E
Cong RoI 24 B3 53 33N 9 16W
Congleton England 16 D2 53 10N 2 13W
CONGO 92 C7
Congo *r.* Congo/CDR 92 J2 2 00S 17 00E
CONGO DEMOCRATIC REPUBLIC 92 D7/E7
Congresbury England 23 E3 51 23N 2 48W
Conisbrough England 17 E2 53 29N 1 13W
Coniston England 16 C3 54 22N 3 05W
Coniston Water England 16 C3 54 20N 3 05W
Connah's Quay Wales 18 C3 53 13N 3 03W
Connecticut *state* USA 103 M5 41 00N 73 00W
Conon Bridge Scotland 13 E2 57 33N 4 26W
Consett England 17 E3 54 51N 1 49W
Constanța Romania 59 P2 44 12N 28 40E
Constantine Algeria 90 F9 36 22N 6 40W
Conwy Wales 18 C3 53 17N 3 50W
Conwy *r.* Wales 18 C3 53 10N 3 49W
Conwy *u.a.* Wales 18 C3 53 10N 3 40W
Cookham England 20 C2 51 34N 0 43W
Cook, Mount NZ 81 P2 43 36S 170 09E
Cookstown *district* NI 14 C1 54 35N 6 55W
Coolgrange RoI 25 D2 53 38N 7 08W
Cootehill RoI 24 D4 54 04N 7 05W
Copeland Island NI 14 D1 54 40N 5 31W
Copenhagen Denmark 55 D2 55 43N 12 34E
Copiapo Chile 115 C8 27 20S 70 23W
Copper Harbor USA 103 J6 47 28N 87 54W
Coppull England 16 D2 53 37N 2 40W
Coquet *r.* England 15 G2 55 20N 2 05W
Coquimbo Chile 115 C8 29 57S 71 25W
Corbally RoI 24 B4 54 10N 9 03W
Corbeil-Essonnes France 56 F5 48 36N 2 29E
Corbridge England 16 D3 54 58N 2 01W
Corby England 19 F2 52 49N 0 32W
Cordillera Cantabrica *mts.* Spain 57 B5/C5 43 00N 5 30W
Córdoba Argentina 115 E7 31 25S 64 11W
Córdoba Mexico 106 E3 18 55N 96 55W
Córdoba Spain 57 C2 37 53N 4 46W
Corfe Castle England 23 E2 50 38N 2 04W
Corfu Greece 61 H3 39 38N 19 55E
Corinth USA 103 J3 34 58N 88 30W
Cork RoI 25 C1 51 54N 8 28W
Cork *co.* RoI 25 C1 51 58N 8 40W
Cork Harbour RoI 25 C1 51 50N 8 10W
Corraun Peninsula RoI 24 B3 53 54N 9 51W
Corrientes Argentina 115 F8 27 30S 58 48W
Corsewall Point Scotland 14 D2 55 00N 5 10W
Corsham England 20 A2 51 26N 2 11W
Corsica *i.* France 56 J1/J2 42 00N 9 00E
Corwen Wales 18 C2 52 59N 3 22W
Cosenza Italy 60 G3 39 17N 16 16E
COSTA RICA 107 H1/2
CÔTE D'IVOIRE 90 C3/D3
Cotgrave England 19 E3 52 54N 1 03W
Cotopaxi *mt.* Ecuador 114 B13 0 40S 78 28W
Cotswold Hills England 19 D1/E1 51 40N 2 10W
Cottbus Germany 58 G5 51 43N 14 21E
Cottenham England 21 D3 52 18N 0 09E
Coulommiers France 56 F5 48 49N 3 05E
Countesthorpe England 19 E2 52 33N 1 09W
Coupar Angus Scotland 13 F1 56 33N 3 17W
Courtown RoI 25 E2 52 38N 6 13W
Cove Bay *tn.* Scotland 13 G2 57 05N 2 05W
Coventry England 19 E2 52 25N 1 30W
Coverack England 22 B2 50 01N 5 05W
Cowbridge Wales 18 C1 51 28N 3 27W
Cowdenbeath Scotland 15 F3 56 07N 3 21W
Cowes England 20 B1 50 45N 1 18W
Cox's Bazar Bangladesh 75 G4 21 25N 91 59E
Craigavon NI 14 C1 54 28N 6 25W
Craigavon *district* NI 14 C1 54 30N 6 30W
Craigellachie Scotland 13 F2 57 29N 3 12W
Craighouse Scotland 14 D2 55 51N 5 57W
Craignure Scotland 12 D1 56 28N 5 42W
Crail Scotland 15 G3 56 16N 2 38W
Craiova Romania 59 L2 44 18N 23 47E
Cramlington England 17 E4 55 05N 1 35W
Cranleigh England 20 C2 51 09N 0 30W
Crathie Scotland 13 F2 57 02N 3 12W
Craughwell RoI 24 C3 53 14N 8 44W
Craven Arms England 18 D2 52 26N 2 50W
Crawford Scotland 15 F2 55 28N 3 40W
Crawley England 20 C2 51 07N 0 12W
Credenhill England 18 D2 52 05N 2 48W
Crediton England 22 D2 50 47N 3 39W
Cree *r.* Scotland 15 E2 55 00N 4 30W
Creeslough RoI 24 D5 55 07N 7 55W
Creetown Scotland 15 E1 54 54N 4 23W
Cregganbaun RoI 24 B3 53 42N 9 51W
Cremona Italy 60 D6 45 08N 10 01E
Creswell England 17 E2 53 16N 1 12W
Crêteil France 56 F5 48 47N 2 28E
Crewe England 16 D2 53 05N 2 27W
Crewkerne England 23 E2 50 53N 2 48W
Crianlarich Scotland 13 E1 56 23N 4 37W
Criccieth Wales 18 B2 52 55N 4 14W
Crickhowell Wales 18 C1 51 53N 3 09W
Cricklade England 20 B2 51 39N 1 51W
Crieff Scotland 13 F1 56 23N 3 52W
Crinan Scotland 14 D3 56 06N 5 35W
CROATIA 61 G6
Crofton England 17 E2 53 39N 1 26W
Cromarty Scotland 13 E2 57 40N 4 02W
Cromarty Firth Scotland 13 E2 57 40N 4 20W
Cromer England 21 E3 52 56N 1 18E
Crook England 17 E3 54 43N 1 44W
Crookhaven RoI 25 B1 51 28N 9 43W
Crookstown RoI 25 C1 51 50N 8 50W
Croom RoI 25 C2 52 31N 8 43W
Crosby England 16 C2 53 30N 3 02W
Cross Fell *mt.* England 16 D3 54 43N 2 29W
Crossgar NI 14 D1 54 24N 5 45W
Cross Hands Wales 18 B1 51 48N 4 05W
Crosshaven RoI 25 C1 51 48N 8 17W
Crossmaglen NI 14 C1 54 05N 6 37W
Crossmolina RoI 24 B4 54 06N 9 20W
Crouch *r.* England 21 D2 51 38N 0 42E
Crowborough England 21 D2 51 03N 0 09E
Crowland England 20 C3 52 41N 0 11W
Crowle England 17 F2 53 37N 0 49W
Crowthorne England 20 C2 51 23N 0 49W
Croyde England 22 C3 51 08N 4 15W
Croydon England 20 C2 51 23N 0 06W
Crumlin NI 14 C1 54 37N 6 14W
Crummock Water England 16 C3 54 34N 3 18W
Crusheen RoI 25 C2 52 56N 8 53W
Cruzeiro do Sul Brazil 114 C12 7 40S 72 39W
Crymych Wales 18 B1 51 59N 4 40W
CUBA 107 J4
Cuckfield England 20 C2 51 00N 0 09W
Cúcuta Colombia 114 C15 7 55N 73 31W
Cudworth England 17 E2 53 35N 1 25W
Cuenca Ecuador 114 B13 2 54S 79 00W
Cuenca Spain 57 D4 40 04N 2 07W
Cuiabá Brazil 114 F10 15 32S 56 05W
Cuillin Hills Scotland 12 C2 57 15N 6 15W
Culdaff RoI 24 D5 55 17N 7 10W
Cullen Scotland 13 G2 57 41N 2 49W
Cullompton England 22 D2 50 52N 3 24W
Cullybackey NI 14 C1 54 53N 6 21W
Culm *r.* England 23 D2 50 55N 3 13W
Culross Scotland 15 F3 56 03N 3 35W
Cumana Venezuela 114 E16 10 29N 64 12W
Cumbernauld Scotland 15 E2 55 57N 4 00W
Cumbria *co.* England 16 C3/D3 54 35N 3 00W
Cumbrian Mountains England 16 C3/D3 54 30N 3 00W
Cumnock Scotland 15 E2 55 27N 4 16W
Cuneo Italy 60 B6 44 24N 7 33E
Cupar Scotland 13 F1 56 19N 3 01W
Curitiba Brazil 114 H8 25 25S 49 25W
Cushendall NI 14 C2 55 04N 6 04W
Cushendun NI 14 C2 55 07N 6 03W
Cuxhaven Germany 58 D6 53 52N 8 42E
Cuzco Peru 114 C11 13 32S 1 57W
Cwmbran Wales 18 C1 51 39N 3 00W
CYPRUS 63 D1/D2
CZECH REPUBLIC 58/59 G4/H4
Częstochowa Poland 59 J5 50 49N 19 07E

D

Dachau Germany 58 E4 48 15N 11 26E
Daingean RoI 24 D3 53 17N 7 17W
Dakar Senegal 90 A4 14 38N 17 27W
Dalbeattie Scotland 15 F1 54 56N 3 49W
Dalby Isle of Man 16 B3 54 10N 4 44W
Dalgety Bay *tn.* Scotland 15 F3 56 03N 3 18W
Dalian China 77 M5 38 53N 121 37E
Dalkeith Scotland 15 F2 55 51N 3 04W
Dallas USA 103 G3 32 47N 96 48W
Dalmally Scotland 13 E1 56 24N 4 58W
Dalmellington Scotland 15 E2 55 19N 4 24W
Dalry Scotland 15 E2 55 43N 4 44W
Dalton USA 103 K3 34 46N 84 59W
Dalton-in-Furness England 16 C3 54 09N 3 11W
Dalwhinnie Scotland 13 E1 56 56N 4 14W
Damascus Syria 72 C5 33 30N 36 19E
Danbury England 21 E2 51 44N 0 33E
Danville USA 103 J5 40 09N 87 37W
Dardanelles *sd.* Turkey 63 C3 40 08N 26 10E
Dar es Salaam Tanzania 93 F1 6 51S 39 18E
Darfield England 17 E2 53 34N 1 22W
Darjiling India 75 F5 27 02N 88 20E
Darling *r.* Australia 81 H4 30 30S 144 00E
Darlington England 17 E3 54 31N 1 34W
Darlington *u.a.* England 17 E3 54 30N 1 30W
Darmstadt Germany 58 D4 49 52N 8 39E
Dart *r.* England 22 D2 50 30N 3 50W
Dartford England 21 D2 51 27N 0 13E
Dartmouth England 22 D2 50 21N 3 35W
Darton England 17 E2 53 36N 1 32W
Darvel Scotland 15 E2 55 37N 4 18W
Darwen England 16 D2 53 42N 2 28W
Darwin Australia 80 F8 12 23S 130 44E
Daugava *r.* Europe 55 F2 56 45N 24 30E
Daugavpils Latvia 55 G2 55 52N 26 31E
Davao Philippines 79 H5 7 05N 125 38E
Davenport USA 103 H5 41 32N 90 36W
Daventry England 19 E2 52 16N 1 09W
Davis Strait Canada/Greenland 101 Y7/Z6 69 00N 60 00W
Davos Switz. 58 D3 46 47N 9 50E
Dawley England 19 D2 52 40N 2 28W
Dawlish England 22 D2 50 35N 3 28W
Dawros Head RoI 24 C4 54 49N 8 34W
Dead Sea Israel/Jordan 72 C5 31 35N 35 30E
Deal England 21 E2 51 14N 1 24E
Deel *r.* RoI 25 C2 52 32N 8 57W
Death Valley USA 102 C4 36 00N 117 00W
Deben *r.* England 21 E3 52 02N 1 25E
Debenham England 21 E3 52 13N 1 11E
Debrecen Hungary 59 K3 47 30N 21 37E
Decatur USA 103 J4 39 51N 88 57W
Deccan *plat.* India 74 D3 18 00N 78 00E
Deddington England 20 B2 51 59N 1 19W
Dee *r.* England/Wales 18 C3 53 15N 3 10W
Dee *r.* RoI 24 E3 53 49N 6 38W
Dee *r.* Aberdeenshire Scotland 13 G2 57 05N 2 10W
Dee *r.* Dumfries and Galloway Scotland 15 E1 54 50N 4 00W
Deel *r.* RoI 24 D3 53 33N 7 07W
Deer Sound Scotland 11 B1 58 57N 2 47W
Delaware *state* USA 103 L4 39 00N 75 00W
Delft Neths 54 C5 52 00N 4 22E
Delfzijl Neths 54 E6 53 19N 6 56E
Delhi India 74 D5 28 40N 77 14E
Delvin RoI 24 D3 53 37N 7 05W
Denbigh Wales 18 C3 53 11N 3 25W
Denbighshire *u.a.* Wales 18 C3 53 05N 3 30W
Denby Dale *tn.* England 17 E2 53 35N 1 38W
Den Helder Neths 54 C5 52 58N 4 46E
Denholme England 17 E2 53 47N 1 53W
Denison USA 103 G3 33 47N 96 34W
Denizli Turkey 63 C2 37 46N 29 05E
DENMARK 55 C2/D2
Denny Scotland 15 F3 56 02N 3 55W
Denpasar Indonesia 79 F2 8 40S 115 14E
Denton England 16 D2 53 27N 2 07W
Denver USA 102 E4 39 45N 105 00W
De Panne Belgium 54 A4 51 06N 2 35E
Derby England 19 E2 52 55N 1 30W
Derby *u.a.* England 19 E2 52 50N 1 30W
Derbyshire *co.* England 17 E2 52 55N 1 30W
Derg *r.* NI 14 B1 54 45N 7 30E
Derriana Lough RoI 25 A1/B1 51 54N 10 01W
Derrybrien RoI 25 C3 53 04N 8 37W
Dersingham England 21 D3 52 51N 0 30E
Derwent *r.* North Yorkshire England 17 F3 54 10N 0 35W
Derwent *r.* Cumbria England 16 C3 54 40N 3 30W
Derwent *r.* Derbyshire England 17 E2 53 15N 1 40W
Derwent *r.* Durham England 16 D3 54 50N 2 05W
Derwent Reservoir England 17 E2 53 25N 1 45W
Derwent Water England 16 C3 54 35N 3 09W
Desborough England 19 F2 52 27N 0 49W
Desierto de Atacama Chile 114 C9/D10 22 30S 70 00W
Des Moines USA 103 H5 41 35N 93 35W
Dessau Germany 58 F5 51 51N 12 15E
Detroit USA 103 K5 42 23N 83 05W
Deveron *r.* Scotland 13 G2 57 35N 2 35W
Devil's Bridge Wales 18 C2 52 23N 3 51W
Devil's Lake *tn.* USA 103 G6 48 03N 98 57W
Devizes England 20 B2 51 22N 1 59W
Devon *co.* England 22 D2 50 45N 3 50W
Dewsbury England 17 E2 53 42N 1 37W
Dezfūl Iran 73 E5 32 23N 48 28E
Dhaka Bangladesh 75 G4 23 42N 90 22E
Didcot England 20 B2 51 37N 1 15W
Dieppe France 56 E5 49 55N 1 05E
Digby Canada 101 X2 44 37N 65 47W
Digne-les-Bains France 56 H3 44 05N 6 14E
Dijon France 56 G4 47 20N 5 02E
Dili East Timor 79 H2 8 33S 125 34E
Dinan France 56 C5 48 27N 2 02W
Dinara Planina *mts.* Europe 61 G5 44 00N 17 00E
Dinard France 56 C5 48 38N 2 03W
Dinas-Mawddwy Wales 18 C2 52 43N 3 41W
Dinas Powys Wales 18 C1 51 25N 3 14W
Dingle RoI 25 A2 52 08N 10 15W
Dingle Bay RoI 25 A2 52 05N 10 15W
Dingle Peninsula RoI 25 A2 52 12N 10 15W
Dingwall Scotland 13 E2 57 35N 4 29W
Dinnington England 17 E2 53 22N 1 12W
Dire Dawa Ethiopia 91 P3 9 35N 41 50E
Diss England 21 E3 52 23N 1 06W
DJIBOUTI 91 P4
Djibouti Djibouti 91 P4 11 35N 43 11E
Dnestr *r.* Ukraine 62 C4 48 00N 27 30E
Dnipro *r.* Europe 63 D4 47 30N 33 00E
Dnipropetrovs'k Ukraine 62 D4 48 29N 35 00E
Dobrich Bulgaria 61 M5 43 34N 27 51E
Dochart *r.* Scotland 13 E1 56 25N 4 25W
Docking England 21 D3 52 55N 0 38E
Dodekánisos *is.* Greece 61 M2 37 00N 26 00E
Dodman Point England 22 C2 50 13N 4 48W
Dodoma Tanzania 93 D1 6 10S 35 40E
Doha Qatar 73 F4 25 15N 51 36E
Dôle France 56 G4 47 05N 5 30E
Dolgellau Wales 18 C2 52 44N 3 53W
Dollar Scotland 15 F3 56 09N 3 41W
Dombas Norway 55 C3 62 05N 9 07E
DOMINICA 106 Q8
DOMINICAN REPUBLIC 107 L3
Don *r.* England 17 E2 53 37N 1 02W
Don *r.* Russia 70 G7 50 00N 41 00E
Don *r.* Scotland 13 F2 57 15N 2 40W
Donabate RoI 24 E3 53 30N 6 09W
Donaghadee NI 14 D1 54 39N 5 33W
Donau *r.* Europe 58 D4 48 00N 16 00E
Doncaster England 17 E2 53 32N 1 07W
Donegal RoI 24 C4 54 39N 8 07W
Donegal *co.* RoI 24 C4/D4 54 55N 8 00W
Donegal Bay RoI 24 C4 54 30N 8 30W
Donegal Point RoI 25 B2 52 44N 9 38W
Donets'k Ukraine 62 E4 48 00N 37 50E
Donnington England 19 D2 52 43N 2 25W
Donoughmore RoI 25 C1 51 57N 8 45W

Dooagh RoI 24 A3 53 58N 10 07W
Doon *r.* Scotland 15 E2 55 20N 4 30W
Doonbeg RoI 25 B2 52 44N 9 32W
Dorchester England 23 E2 50 43N 2 26W
Dorchester England 20 B2 51 39N 1 10W
Dordogne *r.* France 56 E3 44 55N 0 30E
Dordrecht Neths 54 C4 51 48N 4 40E
Dorking England 20 C2 51 14N 0 20W
Dornie Scotland 12 D2 57 17N 5 31W
Dornoch Scotland 13 E2 57 52N 4 02W
Dornoch Firth Scotland 13 E2/F2 57 55N 3 55W
Dorset *co.* England 23 E2 50 50N 2 20W
Dortmund Germany 58 C5 51 32N 7 27E
Douai France 56 F6 50 22N 3 05E
Douala Cameroon 90 F2 4 04N 9 43E
Douglas Isle of Man 16 B3 54 09N 4 29W
Douglas Scotland 15 F2 55 33N 3 51W
Douglas *r.* England 16 D2 53 38N 2 48W
Doulus Head RoI 25 A1 51 57N 10 19W
Doune Scotland 15 E3 56 11N 4 04W
Douro *r.* Portugal/Spain 57 B4 41 00N 8 30W
Dove *r.* England 17 E2 53 05N 1 55W
Dove Dale *v.* England 17 E2 53 10N 1 45W
Dover England 21 E2 51 08N 1 19E
Dover USA 103 L4 39 10N 75 32W
Dover, Strait of English Channel 21 E1/E2 51 00N 1 20W
Dovrefjell *mts.* Norway 55 C3 62 15N 9 10E
Down *district* NI 14 D1 54 25N 5 55W
Downham Market England 21 D3 52 36N 0 23E
Downpatrick NI 14 D1 54 20N 5 43W
Downpatrick Head RoI 24 B4 54 20N 9 15W
Downton England 20 B2 51 00N 1 44W
Dowra RoI 24 C4 54 11N 8 02W
Draguignan France 56 H2 43 32N 6 28E
Drakensberg *mts.* RSA 92 E1/2 30 00S 28 00E
Drammen Norway 55 D2 59 45N 10 15E
Draperstown NI 14 C1 54 48N 6 47W
Drava *r.* Europe 59 H3 46 00N 18 00E
Dreghorn Scotland 15 E2 55 37N 4 37W
Dresden Germany 58 F5 51 03N 13 45E
Drimoleague RoI 25 B1 51 40N 9 15W
Drobeta-Turnu-Severin Romania 59 L2 44 36N 22 39E
Drogheda RoI 24 E3 53 43N 6 21W
Droichead Nua RoI 24 E3 53 11N 6 45W
Droitwich England 19 D2 52 16N 2 09W
Dromcolliher RoI 25 C2 52 20N 8 55W
Dromore NI 14 B1 54 31N 7 28W
Dromore NI 14 C1 54 25N 6 09W
Dromore West RoI 24 C4 54 15N 8 53W
Dronfield England 17 E2 53 19N 1 27W
Drongan Scotland 15 E2 55 29N 4 30W
Drumkeeran RoI 24 C4 54 10N 8 08W
Drummore Scotland 14 E1 54 42N 4 54W
Drumnadrochit Scotland 13 E2 57 20N 4 30W
Drumshanbo RoI 24 C4 54 03N 8 02W
Drumsna RoI 24 D3 53 56N 8 00W
Dryden Canada 101 S3 49 48N 92 48W
Dubai UAE 73 G4 25 14N 55 17E
Dublin RoI 24 E3 53 20N 6 15W
Dublin City *co.* RoI 24 E3 53 25N 6 10W
Dublin USA 103 K3 32 31N 82 54W
Dublin Bay RoI 24 E3 53 20N 6 05W
Dubrovnik Croatia 61 H5 42 40N 18 07E
Duddon *r.* England 16 C3 54 20N 3 20W
Dudley England 19 D2 52 30N 2 05W
Dudley England 17 E4 55 10N 1 20W
Duero *r.* Spain/Portugal 57 B4 41 25N 6 30W
Duffield England 19 E2 52 59N 1 29W
Dufftown Scotland 13 F2 57 26N 3 08W
Duisburg Germany 58 C5 51 26N 6 45E
Duleek RoI 24 E3 53 39N 6 25W
Dulnain *r.* Scotland 13 F2 57 20N 3 57W
Duluth USA 103 H6 46 45N 92 10W
Dulverton England 22 D3 51 03N 3 33W
Dumbarton Scotland 15 E2 55 57N 4 35W
Dumfries Scotland 15 F2 55 04N 3 37W
Dumfries and Galloway *u.a.* Scotland 15 E2/F2 55 10N 4 10W
Duna *r.* Hungary 59 J2/J3 46 00N 19 00E
Dunaff Head RoI 24 D5 55 17N 7 31W
Dunany Point RoI 24 E3 53 51N 6 14W
Dunav *r.* Europe 61 K5 45 00N 20 00E
Dunbar Scotland 15 G2 56 00N 2 31W
Dunbeath Scotland 13 F3 58 15N 3 25W
Dunblane Scotland 15 F3 56 12N 3 59W
Dunboyne RoI 24 E3 53 25N 6 29W
Duncannon RoI 25 E2 51 13N 6 55W
Duncansby Head Scotland 13 F3 58 39N 3 01W
Dunchurch England 19 E2 52 20N 1 16W
Dundalk RoI 24 E4 54 01N 6 25W
Dundalk Bay RoI 24 E3 53 55N 6 15W
Dundee Scotland 13 G1 56 28N 3 00W
Dundee City *u.a.* Scotland 13 F1/G1 56 30N 2 55W
Dundonald NI 14 D1 54 36N 5 48W
Dundrennan Scotland 15 F1 54 49N 3 57W
Dundrum RoI 24 E3 53 17N 6 15W
Dundrum Bay NI 14 D1 54 13N 5 45W
Dunedin NZ 81 P1 45 53S 170 30E
Dunfermline Scotland 15 F3 56 04N 3 29W
Dungannon NI 14 C1 54 31N 6 46W
Dungannon and South Tyrone *district* NI 14 B1/C1 54 30N 7 05W
Dungarvan RoI 25 D2 52 05N 7 37W
Dungarvan Harbour RoI 25 D2 52 04N 7 35W
Dungeness *c.* England 21 D1 50 55N 0 58E
Dungiven NI 14 C1 54 55N 6 55W
Dunglow RoI 24 C4 54 57N 8 22W
Dungourney RoI 25 C1 51 58N 8 05W
Dunholme England 17 F2 53 18N 0 29W
Dunkeld Scotland 13 F1 56 34N 3 35W
Dunkerque France 56 F6 51 02N 2 23E
Dunkery Beacon *sum.* England 22 D3 51 11N 3 35W
Dún Laoghaire RoI 24 E3 53 17N 6 08W
Dún Laoghaire-Rathdown *co.* RoI 24 E3 53 20N 6 10W
Dunleer RoI 24 E3 53 50N 6 24W
Dunmanus Bay RoI 25 B1 51 30N 9 50W
Dunmanway RoI 25 B1 51 43N 9 06W
Dunmore RoI 24 C3 53 37N 8 44W
Dunmurry NI 14 C1 54 33N 6 00W
Dunnamaggan RoI 25 D2 52 29N 7 17W
Dunnet Scotland 13 F3 58 37N 3 21W
Dunnet Bay Scotland 13 F3 58 36N 3 21W
Dunnett Head Scotland 13 F3 58 40N 3 25W
Dunoon Scotland 14 E2 55 57N 4 56W
Duns Scotland 15 G2 55 47N 2 20W
Dunshaughlin RoI 24 E3 53 31N 6 33W
Dunstable England 20 C2 51 53N 0 32W
Dunvegan Scotland 12 C2 57 26N 6 35W
Dunvegan Head Scotland 12 C2 57 30N 6 42W
Durban RSA 92 F2 29 53S 31 00E
Durham England 17 E3 54 47N 1 34W
Durham USA 103 L4 36 00N 78 54W
Durlston Head England 23 E2 50 35N 1 57W
Durness Scotland 13 E3 58 33N 4 45W
Durrington England 20 B2 51 12N 1 48W
Durrow RoI 25 D2 52 51N 7 23W
Dursey Head RoI 25 A1 51 20N 10 10W
Dursey Island RoI 25 A1 51 36N 10 12W
Dursley England 19 D1 51 42N 2 21W
Dushanbe Tajikistan 70 J4 38 38N 68 51E
Düsseldorf Germany 58 C5 51 13N 6 47E
Dyce Scotland 13 G2 57 12N 2 11W
Dyfi *r.* Wales 18 C2 52 38N 3 50W
Dyke *r.* Scotland 13 F3 58 25N 4 00W
Dymchurch England 21 D2 51 02N 1 00E
Dysart Scotland 15 F3 56 08N 3 08W

E

Eaglescliffe England 17 E3 54 31N 1 22W
Eaglesfield Scotland 15 F2 55 04N 3 12W
Ealing England 20 C2 51 31N 0 18W
Earby England 16 D2 53 56N 2 08W
Earls Colne England 21 D2 51 56N 0 42E
Earl Shilton England 19 E2 52 35N 1 18W
Earlston Scotland 15 G2 55 39N 2 40W
Earn *r.* Scotland 13 F1 56 20N 3 40W
Easington England 17 E3 54 47N 1 21W
Easington England 17 G2 53 40N 0 07E
Easingwold England 17 E3 54 07N 1 11W
Easky RoI 24 C4 54 17N 8 58W
East Ayrshire *u.a.* Scotland 15 E2 55 30N 4 30W
Eastbourne England 21 D1 50 46N 0 17E
East Burra *i.* Scotland 11 C3 60 04N 1 19W
East Cowes England 20 B1 50 45N 1 16W
East Dean England 21 D1 50 45N 0 13E
East Dereham England 21 D3 52 41N 0 56E
East Dunbartonshire *u.a.* Scotland 15 E2 55 55N 4 15W
Eastern Ghats *mts.* India 74 D2/E3 15 00N 80 00E
Eastfield England 17 F3 54 15N 0 25W
East Grand Forks USA 104 A3 47 56N 96 59W
East Ilsley England 20 B2 51 32N 1 17W
Eastington England 19 D1 51 45N 2 20W
East Kilbride Scotland 15 E2 55 46N 4 10W
East Leake England 19 E3 52 50N 1 11W
Eastleigh England 20 B1 50 58N 1 22W
East Linton Scotland 15 G2 55 59N 2 39W
East Loch Tarbert Scotland 12 C2 57 53N 6 48W
East London RSA 92 E1 33 00S 27 54E
East Lothian *u.a.* Scotland 15 G2 55 56N 2 42W
Eastmain Canada 101 V4 52 10N 78 30W
East Markham England 17 F2 53 15N 0 54W
Easton England 23 E2 50 32N 2 26W
East Renfrewshire *u.a.* Scotland 15 E2 55 45N 4 25E
East Riding of Yorkshire *u.a.* England 17 F2 53 54N 0 40W
Eastriggs Scotland 15 F1 54 59N 3 10W
East Suisnish Scotland 12 C2 57 21N 6 03W
East Sussex *co.* England 21 D1 50 55N 0 10E
EAST TIMOR 79 H2
East Wittering England 20 C1 50 41N 0 53W
Eastwood England 17 E2 53 01N 1 18W
Eaton Socon England 20 C3 52 13N 0 18W
Ebbw Vale Wales 18 C1 51 47N 3 12W
Ebro *r.* Spain 57 D5 43 00N 4 30W
Ecclefechan Scotland 15 F2 55 03N 3 17W
Eccles England 16 D2 53 29N 2 21W
Eccleshall England 19 D2 52 52N 2 15W
Eckington England 17 E2 53 19N 1 21W
ECUADOR 114 B13
Eday *i.* Scotland 7 B2 59 11N 2 47W
Eday Sound Scotland 7 B2 59 10N 2 43W
Ede Neths 54 D5 52 03N 5 40E
Eden *r.* Cumbria England 16 D3 54 50N 2 45W
Eden *r.* Kent England 21 D2 51 12N 0 06E
Eden *r.* Scotland 15 F3 56 20N 3 15W
Eden USA 103 L4 36 30N 79 46W
Edenbridge England 20 D2 51 12N 0 04E
Edenderry RoI 24 D3 53 21N 7 35W
Eden Mouth Scotland 13 G1 56 20N 2 36W
Edessa Greece 61 K4 40 48N 22 03E
Edgeworthstown RoI 24 D3 53 42N 7 36W
Edinburgh Scotland 15 F2 55 57N 3 13W
Edmonton Canada 100 N4 53 34N 113 25W
Eeklo Belgium 54 B4 51 11N 3 34E
Eems *r.* Neths/Germany 54 E6 53 25N 6 55E
Efyrnwy *r.* Wales 18 C2 52 40N 3 15W
Egham England 20 C2 51 26N 0 34W
Egilsay *i.* Scotland 11 B2 59 09N 2 56W
Eglinton NI 14 B2 55 01N 7 11W
Egremont England 16 C3 54 29N 3 33W
EGYPT 91 L7/M7
Eigg *i.* Scotland 12 C1 56 55N 6 10W
Eindhoven Neths 54 D4 51 26N 5 30E
Elat Israel 72 B4 29 33N 34 57E
Elâziğ Turkey 63 E2 38 41N 39 14E
Elbe *est.* Europe 58 E6 54 00N 9 00E
Elbeuf France 56 E5 49 17N 1 01E
Elbląg Poland 59 J7 54 10N 19 25E
El'brus *mt.* Russia 63 F3 43 21N 42 29E
Elburg Neths 54 D5 52 27N 5 50E
Elburz Mountains Iran 73 F6 36 15N 51 00E
Elche Spain 57 E3 38 16N 0 41W
El Dorado USA 103 H3 33 12N 92 40W
Elgin Scotland 13 F2 57 39N 3 20W
El Gîza Egypt 91 M7 30 01N 31 12E
Elgol Scotland 12 C2 57 09N 6 06W
Elie Scotland 15 G3 56 12N 2 50W
Elland England 17 E2 53 41N 1 50W
Ellen *r.* England 16 C3 54 45N 3 25W
Ellesmere England 18 D2 52 54N 2 54W
Ellesmere Island Canada 101 U9/X10 77 30N 82 30W
Ellesmere Port England 16 D2 53 17N 2 54W
Ellon Scotland 13 G2 57 22N 2 05W
El Minya Egypt 91 M7 28 06N 30 45E
Elmira USA 103 L5 42 06N 76 50W
El Obeid Sudan 91 M4 13 11N 30 10W
El Paso USA 102 E3 31 45N 106 30W
EL SALVADOR 106 G2
Ely England 21 D3 52 24N 0 16E
Elyria USA 103 K5 41 22N 82 06W
Embleton England 15 H2 55 30N 1 37W
Emden Germany 58 C6 53 23N 7 13E
Emmeloord Neths 54 D5 52 43N 5 46E
Emmen Neths 54 E5 52 47N 6 55E
Emsworth England 20 C1 50 51N 0 56W
Emyvale RoI 24 E4 54 21N 6 58W
Enard Bay Scotland 12 D3 58 10N 5 25W
Enfield England 20 C2 51 39N 0 05W
England *country* UK 10 53 00N 2 00W
English Channel UK/France 10 50 00N 2 00W
Enid USA 103 G4 36 24N 97 54W
Ennis RoI 25 C2 52 50N 8 59W
Enniscorthy RoI 25 E2 52 30N 6 34W
Enniskean RoI 25 C1 51 44N 8 56W
Enniskerry RoI 24 E3 53 12N 6 10W
Enniskillen NI 14 B1 54 21N 7 38W
Ennistimon RoI 25 B2 52 57N 9 15W
Enschede Neths 54 E5 52 13N 6 55E
Entebbe Uganda 93 C5 0 04N 32 27E
Épernay France 56 F5 49 02N 3 58E
Épinal France 56 H5 48 10N 6 28E
Epping England 21 D2 51 42N 0 08E
Epsom England 20 C2 51 20N 0 16W
Epworth England 17 F2 53 31N 0 50W
EQUATORIAL GUINEA 90 F2/G2
Erfurt Germany 58 E5 50 58N 11 02E
Erie USA 103 K5 42 07N 80 05W
Erie, Lake Canada/USA 105 D2 42 15N 81 00W
Eriskay *i.* Scotland 12 B2 57 05N 7 10W
ERITREA 91 P4 14 40N 40 15E
Erlangen Germany 58 E4 49 36N 11 02E
Errigal Mountain RoI 24 C5 55 02N 8 07W
Errill RoI 25 D2 52 52N 7 40W
Erris Head RoI 24 A4 54 20N 10 00W
Erzgebirge *mts.* Europe 58 F5 50 00N 13 00E
Erzurum Turkey 63 F2 39 57N 41 17E
Esbjerg Denmark 55 C2 55 20N 8 20E
Escondido USA 102 C3 33 07N 117 05W
Eşfahān Iran 73 F5 32 41N 51 41E
Esha Ness *c.* Scotland 11 C3 60 29N 1 37W
Esher England 20 C2 51 22N 0 22W
Esk *r.* North Yorkshire England 17 F3 54 25N 0 40W
Esk *r.* Cumbria England 16 C3 54 25N 3 20W
Esk *r.* Scotland/England 15 F2 55 10N 3 05W
Eskişehir Turkey 63 D2 39 46N 30 30E
Espoo Finland 55 F3 60 10N 24 40E
Esquel Argentina 115 C5 42 55S 71 20W
Essen Germany 58 C5 51 27N 6 57E
Essex *co.* England 21 D2 51 46N 0 30E
Eston England 17 E3 54 34N 1 07W
ESTONIA 55 G2
Estremoz Portugal 57 B3 38 50N 7 35W
Étampes France 56 F5 48 26N 2 10E
ETHIOPIA 91 N3/P3
Etna, Mount Italy 60 F2 37 45N 15 00E
Eton England 20 C2 51 31N 0 37W
Ettrick Scotland 15 F2 55 25N 3 05W
Ettrickbridge Scotland 15 G2 55 30N 2 58W
Eugene USA 102 B5 44 03N 123 04W
Euphrates *r.* Asia 72 D5 34 40N 42 00E
Europoort Neths 54 C4 51 55N 4 10E
Evanton Scotland 13 E2 57 40N 4 20W
Evercreech England 23 E3 51 09N 2 30W
Everest, Mount China/Nepal 75 F5 27 59N 86 56E
Evesham England 19 E2 52 06N 1 56W
Evora Portugal 57 B3 38 46N 7 41W
Evreux France 56 E5 49 03N 1 11E
Evvoia *i.* Greece 61 L3 38 00N 24 00E
Exe *r.* England 22 D3 51 08N 3 36
Exeter England 22 D2 50 43N 3 31W
Exmouth England 22 D2 50 37N 3 25W
Eyam England 17 E2 53 24N 1 42W
Eye England 21 E3 52 19N 1 09E
Eyemouth Scotland 15 G2 55 25N 2 06W
Eye Peninsula Scotland 12 C3 58 10N 6 10W
Eyeries RoI 25 B1 51 41N 9 57W
Eynsham England 20 B2 51 46N 1 28W

F

Fairbourne Wales 18 B2 52 41N 4 03W
Fair Head NI 14 C2 55 15N 6 10W
Fair Isle Scotland 11 C2 59 32N 1 38W
Fairlight England 21 D1 50 52N 0 38E
Fairmont USA 103 K4 39 28N 80 08W
Faisalabad Pakistan 74 C6 31 25N 73 09E
Fakenham England 21 D3 52 50N 0 51E
Fal *r.* England 22 C2 50 16N 4 56W
Falcarragh RoI 24 C5 55 08N 8 06W
Falfurrias USA 103 G2 27 17N 98 10W
Falkirk Scotland 15 F2 55 59N 3 48W
Falkirk *u.a.* Scotland 15 F2 55 55N 3 45W
Falkland Scotland 15 F3 56 15N 3 13W
Falkland Islands S Atlantic Ocean 115 E2/F2 52 30S 60 00W
Falmouth England 22 B2 50 08N 5 04W
Fanad Head RoI 24 D5 55 17N 7 38W
Fane *r.* RoI 24 E3 53 58N 6 28W
Fano Italy 60 E5 43 51N 13 01E
Fareham England 20 B1 50 51N 1 10W
Fargo USA 103 G6 46 52N 96 49W
Faringdon England 20 B2 51 40N 1 35W
Farnborough England 20 C2 51 17N 0 46W
Farne Islands England 15 H2 55 38N 1 38W
Farnham England 20 C2 51 13N 0 49W
Farnham Royal England 20 C2 51 33N 0 38W
Farnworth England 16 D2 53 33N 2 24W
Faro Portugal 57 B2 37 01N 7 56W
Farranfore RoI 25 B2 52 10N 9 33W
Farrar *r.* Scotland 13 E2 57 15N 4 41W
Faughan *r.* NI 14 B1 54 54N 7 09W
Faversham England 21 D2 51 20N 0 53E
Fawley England 20 B1 50 49N 1 20W
Feale *r.* RoI 25 B2 52 26N 9 22W
Featherstone England 17 E2 53 41N 1 21W
Fécamp France 56 E5 49 45N 0 23E
FEDERATED STATES OF MICRONESIA 116 F8
Feira de Santana Brazil 114 K11 12 17S 38 53W
Feldkirch Austria 58 D3 47 15N 9 38E
Felixstowe England 21 E2 51 58N 1 20E
Felling *tn.* England 17 E3 54 57N 1 33W
Felton England 15 H2 55 18N 1 42W
Feltwell England 21 D3 52 29N 0 33E
Fens, The England 20 C3/D3 52 45N 0 05E
Feolin Ferry *tn.* Scotland 14 C2 55 51N 6 06W
Ferbane RoI 24 D3 53 15N 7 49W
Fermanagh *district* NI 14 B1 54 25N 7 45W
Fermo Italy 60 E5 43 09N 13 44E
Fermoy RoI 25 C2 52 08N 8 16W
Ferndown England 23 F2 50 48N 1 55W
Ferns RoI 25 E2 52 35N 6 30W
Ferrara Italy 60 E6 44 50N 11 38E
Ferryhill *tn.* England 17 E3 54 41N 1 33W
Fès Morocco 90 C8 34 05N 5 00W
Fethaland, Point of Scotland 11 C3 60 35N 1 18W
Fethard RoI 25 D2 52 27N 7 41W
Fethard RoI 25 E2 52 11N 6 50W
Fetlar *i.* Scotland 11 D3 60 37N 0 52W
Fettercairn Scotland 13 G1 56 51N 2 34W
Ffestiniog Wales 18 C2 52 58N 3 55W
Fforest Fawr Wales 18 C1 51 50N 3 40W
Ffostrasol Wales 18 B2 52 06N 4 23W
Fianarantsoa Madagascar 92 J3 21 27S 47 05E
Fiddown RoI 25 D2 52 20N 7 19W
Fife *u.a.* Scotland 15 G3 56 10N 3 00W
Fife Ness *c.* Scotland 15 G3 56 17N 2 35W
Figeac France 56 F3 44 32N 2 01E
Figueira da Foz Portugal 57 A4 40 09N 8 51W
Figueres Spain 57 G5 42 16N 2 57E
FIJI 116 H6

Filey England 17 F3 54 12N 0 17W
Filton England 19 D1 51 31N 2 35W
Findhorn *r.* Scotland 13 F2 57 25N 3 55W
Findhorn Scotland 13 F2 57 39N 3 36W
Findhorn Bay Scotland 13 F2 57 39N 3 36W
Findochty Scotland 13 G2 57 42N 2 55W
Fingal *co.* RoI 24 E3 53 30N 6 15W
Finglas RoI 24 E3 53 24N 6 18W
FINLAND 55 G3
Finland, Gulf of Finland 55 F2/G2 59 40N 23 30E
Finnea RoI 24 D3 53 47N 7 23W
Fintagh Bay RoI 24 C4 54 35N 8 33W
Fintona RoI 14 B1 54 30N 7 19W
Fintown RoI 24 C4 54 52N 8 07W
Fionn Loch Scotland 12 D2 57 45N 5 25W
Fionnphort Scotland 12 C1 56 19N 6 23W
Firat *r.* Asia 63 E2 37 30N 38 00E
Firth of Clyde Scotland 14 D2/E2 55 30N 5 00W
Firth of Forth Scotland 15 F3/G3 56 05N 3 00W
Firth of Lorn Scotland 14 D3 56 15N 6 00W
Firth of Tay Scotland 13 F1 56 25N 3 00W
Fishbourne England 20 B1 50 44N 1 12W
Fishguard Wales 18 B1 51 59N 4 59W
Flagstaff USA 102 D4 35 12N 111 38W
Flamborough England 17 F3 54 07N 0 07W
Flamborough Head
England 17 F3 54 06N 0 04W
Fleet England 20 C2 51 16N 0 50W
Fleetwood England 16 C2 53 56N 3 01W
Flekkefjord Norway 55 C2 58 17N 6 40E
Flimby England 16 C3 54 41N 3 31W
Flint Wales 18 C3 53 15N 3 07W
Flintshire *u.a.* Wales 18 C3 53 15N 3 10W
Flitwick England 20 C3 52 00N 0 29W
Florence Italy 60 D5 43 47N 11 15E
Florianópolis Brazil 115 H8 27 35S 48 31W
Florida *state* USA 103 K2 28 00N 82 00W
Florida Keys *is.* USA 103 K1 25 00N 80 00W
Flotta *i.* Scotland 11 A1 58 49N 3 07W
Fochabers Scotland 13 F2 57 37N 3 05W
Focşani Romania 59 N2 45 41N 27 12E
Fóggia Italy 61 F4 41 28N 15 33E
Folkestone England 21 E2 51 05N 1 11E
Folkingham England 19 F2 52 54N 0 24W
Fontainebleau France 56 F5 48 24N 2 42E
Fontstown RoI 25 E3 53 03N 6 53W
Fordham England 21 D3 52 19N 0 24E
Fordingbridge England 20 B1 50 56N 1 47W
Foreland *p.* England 20 B1 50 41N 1 04W
Foreland Point England 22 D3 51 16N 3 47W
Foreness Point England 21 E2 51 25N 1 27E
Forest Channel Islands 23 E1 49 25N 2 35W
Forest Row England 20 D2 51 06N 0 02E
Forfar Scotland 13 G1 56 38N 2 54W
Forlì Italy 60 E6 44 13N 12 02E
Formby England 16 C2 53 34N 3 05W
Formentera *i.* Spain 57 F3 38 41N 1 30E
FORMER YUGOSLAV REPUBLIC OF MACEDONIA
(FYROM) 61 J4/K4
Formosa Argentina 114 F8 26 07S 58 14W
Forres Scotland 13 F2 57 37N 3 38W
Fortaleza Brazil 114 K13 3 45S 38 35W
Fort Augustus Scotland 13 E2 57 09N 4 41W
Fort George Scotland 13 E2 57 35N 4 05W
Forth *r.* Scotland 15 E3 56 05N 4 05W
Fort Lauderdale USA 103 K2 26 08N 80 08W
Fort Liard Canada 100 L6 60 14N 123 28W
Fortrose Scotland 13 E2 57 34N 4 09W
Fort Saskatchewan
Canada 100 N4 53 42N 113 12W
Fortuneswell England 23 E2 50 33N 2 27W
Fort William Scotland 13 D1 56 49N 5 07W
Fort Worth USA 103 G3 32 45N 97 20W
Foula *i.* Scotland 11 B3 60 08N 2 05W
Foulness Island
England 21 D2 51 35N 0 57E
Foulness Point England 21 D2 51 37N 0 57E
Fowey England 22 C2 50 20N 4 38W
Fowey *r.* England 22 C2 50 27N 4 38W
Foxford RoI 24 B3 53 58N 9 08W
Foyle *r.* NI/RoI 24 D4 54 55N 7 25W
Foynes RoI 25 B2 52 37N 9 06W
Foz Spain 57 B5 43 34N 7 15W
Framlingham England 21 E3 52 13N 1 21E
Frampton Cotterell
England 19 D1 51 32N 2 30W
FRANCE 56
Francistown Botswana 92 E3 21 11S 27 32E
Frankfurt am Main
Germany 58 D5 50 06N 8 41E
Frankfurt an der Oder
Germany 58 G6 52 20N 14 32E
Fraser *r.* Canada 100 L4 52 00N 122 00W
Fraserburgh Scotland 13 G2 57 42N 2 00W
Freckleton England 16 D2 53 46N 2 52W
Frederick USA 105 E1 39 25N 77 25W
Fredericksburg USA 103 L4 38 18N 77 30W
Frederikshavn
Denmark 55 D2 57 28N 10 33E
Fredrikstad Norway 55 D2 59 20N 10 50E
Freemount RoI 25 C2 52 17N 8 53W
Freeport Canada 101 X2 44 17N 66 19W
Freetown Sierra Leone 90 B3 8 30N 13 17W
Freiburg im Breisgau
Germany 58 C3 48 00N 7 52E
Fréjus France 56 H2 43 26N 6 44E
French Guiana *territory*
France 114 G14 5 00N 53 00W
Frenchpark RoI 24 C3 53 53N 8 24W
Freshwater England 20 B1 50 40N 1 30E
Fresno USA 102 C4 36 41N 119 47W
Fribourg Switz. 58 C3 46 50N 7 10E
Friedrichshafen
Germany 58 D3 47 39N 9 29E
Frinton on Sea England 21 E2 51 50N 1 14E
Frodsham England 16 D2 53 18N 2 44W
Frogmore England 20 C2 51 20N 0 50W
Frome England 23 E 51 14N 2 20W
Frome *r.* Herefordshire
England 19 D2 52 05N 2 30W
Frome *r.* Somerset
England 23 E3 51 10N 2 20W
Frome *r.* Dorset
England 23 E2 50 42N 2 16W
Fuday *i.* Scotland 12 B2 57 05N 7 20W
Fuenlabrada Spain 57 D4 40 16N 3 49W
Fuertaventura *i.* Spain 90 B7 28 25N 14 00W
Fuji Japan 78 C2 35 10N 138 37E
Fuji-san *mt.* Japan 78 C2 35 23N 138 42E
Fukuoka Japan 78 B1 33 39N 130 21E
Furnace Scotland 14 D3 56 09N 5 12W
Fürth Germany 58 E4 49 28N 11 00E
Fushun China 77 M6 41 50N 123 54E
Fuzhou China 77 L3 26 09N 119 17E

G

GABON 92 B7
Gaborone Botswana 92 E3 24 45S 25 55E
Gadsden USA 103 J3 34 00N 86 00W
Gaeta Italy 60 E4 41 13N 13 36E
Gainsborough England 17 F2 53 24N 0 48W
Gairloch *tn.* Scotland 12 D2 57 42N 5 40W
Gairsay *i.* Scotland 11 B2 59 05N 2 58W
Galashiels Scotland 15 G2 55 37N 2 49W
Galaţi Romania 59 P2 45 27N 28 02E
Gallan Head Scotland 12 B3 58 14N 7 01W
Galley Head RoI 25 C1 51 35N 8 55W
Gallipoli Italy 61 H4 40 03N 17 59E
Gallup USA 102 E4 32 32N 108 46W
Galston Scotland 15 E2 55 36N 4 24W
Galveston USA 103 H2 29 17N 94 48W
Galway *co.* RoI 24 B3/C3 53 25N 8 45W
Galway RoI 24 B3 53 16N 9 03W
Galway Bay RoI 24 B3 53 15N 9 15W
Gambia *r.*
Senegal/The Gambia 90 B4 13 45N 13 15W
GAMBIA, THE 90 A4
Gandía Spain 57 E3 38 59N 0 11W
Ganga *r.* India 74 E5 25 00N 83 30E
Gangdisê Shan *mts.*
China 76 D4 31 00N 82 30E
Gap France 56 H3 44 33N 6 05E
Garda Italy 60 D6 45 34N 10 43E
Garden City USA 102 F4 37 57N 100 54W
Gardenstown Scotland 13 G2 57 40N 2 20W
Gare Loch Scotland 15 E3 56 03N 4 39W
Garelochhead Scotland 15 E3 56 05N 4 50W
Garforth England 17 E2 53 48N 1 22W
Garlieston Scotland 15 E1 54 48N 4 22W
Garonne *r.* France 56 D3 44 45N 0 15E
Garrison NI 14 A1 54 25N 8 05W
Garron Point NI 14 D2 55 05N 6 00W
Garstang England 16 D2 53 55N 2 47W
Garth Wales 18 C2 52 08N 3 32W
Garthorpe England 17 F2 53 40N 0 42W
Garve Scotland 13 E2 57 37N 4 42W
Gaspé Canada 101 Y3 48 50N 64 30W
Gastonia USA 103 K4 35 14N 81 12W
Gatehouse of Fleet
Scotland 15 E1 54 53N 4 11W
Gateshead England 17 E3 54 58N 1 35W
Gatineau Canada 105 E3 45 29N 75 40W
Gatty Mountains RoI 25 C2 52 21N 8 11W
Gaydon England 19 E2 52 45N 0 34E
Gaza Middle East 72 N10 31 30N 34 28E
Gaziantep Turkey 63 E2 37 04N 37 21E
Gdańsk Poland 59 J7 54 22N 18 41E
Gdynia Poland 59 J7 54 31N 18 30E
Geleen Neths 54 D3 50 58N 5 45E
Gelligaer Wales 18 C1 51 39N 3 15W
Gelsenkirchen
Germany 58 C5 51 30N 7 05E
Geneva Switz. 58 C3 46 13N 6 09E
Genk Belgium 54 D3 50 58N 5 30E
Genova Italy 60 C6 44 24N 8 56E
Gent Belgium 54 B4 51 02N 3 42E
Georgetown Guyana 114 F15 6 46N 58 10W
George Town Malaysia 79 C5 5 25N 100 20E
GEORGIA 63 F3
Georgia *state* USA 103 K3 33 00N 83 00W
Gera Germany 58 F5 50 51N 12 11E
GERMANY 58
Gerona Spain 57 G4 41 59N 2 49E
Gerrards Cross
England 20 C2 51 35N 0 34W
Getafe Spain 57 D4 40 18N 3 44W
GHANA 90 D3
Giant's Causeway NI 14 C2 55 10N 6 30W
Gibraltar *territory* U.K. 57 C2 36 09N 5 21W
Gigha *i.* Scotland 14 D2 55 40N 5 45W
Gijón Spain 57 C5 43 32N 5 40W
Gila Bend USA 102 D3 32 56N 112 42W
Gilfach Goch Wales 18 C1 51 38N 3 30W
Gilford NI 14 C1 54 23N 6 22W
Gillingham Medway
England 21 D2 51 24N 0 33E
Gillingham Dorset
England 23 E3 51 02N 2 17W
Gilsland England 16 D3 55 00N 2 35W
Gironde *r.* France 56 D3 45 30N 0 45W
Girvan Scotland 14 E2 55 15N 4 51W
Givet Belgium 54 C3 50 08N 4 49E
Glanaman Wales 18 C1 51 47N 3 55W
Glanton England 15 H2 55 26N 1 54W
Glasgow Scotland 15 E2 55 53N 4 15W
Glasgow City *u.a.*
Scotland 15 E2 55 52N 4 16W
Glass *r.* Scotland 13 E2 57 15N 4 40W
Glassan RoI 24 D3 53 28N 7 52W
Glasson England 16 D2 54 00N 2 51W
Glastonbury England 23 E3 51 09N 2 43W
Glenaffric *r.* Scotland 12 D2 57 15N 5 15W
Glenbeigh RoI 25 B2 52 03N 9 56W
Glencoe Scotland 13 D1 56 40N 5 04W
Glencolumbkille RoI 24 C4 54 42N 8 44W
Glenfinnan Scotland 12 D1 56 53N 5 27W
Glengad Head RoI 24 D5 55 20N 7 11W
Glengarriff RoI 25 B1 51 45N 9 33W
Glenluce Scotland 15 E1 54 53N 4 49W
Glenamaddy RoI 24 C3 53 37N 8 35W
Glenridding England 16 D3 54 33N 2 58W
Glenrothes Scotland 15 F3 56 12N 3 10W
Glen Shee *r.* Scotland 13 F1 46 45N 3 25W
Glenties RoI 24 C4 54 47N 8 17W
Glin RoI 25 B2 52 34N 9 17W
Glossop England 17 E2 53 27N 1 57W
Gloucester England 19 D1 51 53N 2 14W
Gloucestershire *co.*
England 19 D1/E1 51 50N 2 20W
Glusburn England 16 D2 53 55N 2 01W
Glydar Fawr *mt.* Wales 18 B3 53 05N 4 03W
Glyncorrwg Wales 18 C1 51 41N 3 38W
Glyn-neath Wales 18 C1 51 46N 3 38W
Gniezno Poland 59 H6 52 32N 17 32E
Goat Fell *mt.* Scotland 14 D2 55 39N 5 11W
Gobi Desert Mongolia
76/77 G6/J6 48 30N 100 00E
Godalming England 20 C2 51 11N 0 37W
Godmanchester
England 20 C3 52 19N 0 11W
Goiânia Brazil 114 H10 16 43S 49 18W
Goiás Brazil 114 G10 15 57S 50 07W
Golam Head RoI 24 B3 53 14N 9 44W
Golfo de California
Mexico 106 B5 27 00N 111 00W
Golfo di Genova Italy 60 C6 44 00N 9 00E
Golfo di Táranto Italy 61 G3/G4 40 00N 17 00E
Golfo di Venézia Italy 60 E6 45 00N 13 00E
Golspie Scotland 13 F2 57 58N 3 58W
Gomera *i.* Spain 90 A7 28 08N 17 14W
Good Hope, Cape of RSA 92 C1 34 30S 19 00E
Goodland USA 102 F4 39 20N 101 43W
Goodwick Wales 18 B1 52 00N 5 00W
Goole England 17 F2 53 42N 0 52W
Gorebridge Scotland 15 F2 55 51N 3 02W
Gorey RoI 25 E2 52 40N 6 18W
Gorinchem Neths 54 C4 51 50N 4 59E
Goring England 20 B2 51 32N 1 09W
Gorizia Italy 60 E6 45 57N 13 37E
Gorseinon Wales 18 B1 51 41N 4 02W
Gort RoI 25 C3 53 04N 8 50W
Gorteen RoI 24 C3 53 22N 8 35W
Gortmore RoI 24 B3 53 36N 9 36W
Gorumna Island RoI 24 B3 53 15N 9 55W
Gosforth England 17 E4 55 01N 1 37W
Gosport England 20 B1 50 48N 1 08W
Göteborg Sweden 55 D2 57 45N 12 00E
Gotha Germany 58 E5 50 57N 10 43E
Gotland *i.* Sweden 55 E2 57 30N 18 40E
Göttingen Germany 58 D5 51 32N 9 57E
Gouda Neths 54 C5 52 00N 4 42E
Gourock Scotland 15 E2 55 58N 4 49W
Governador Valadares
Brazil 114 J10 18 49S 41 57W
Gower *p.* Wales 18 B1 51 35N 4 10W
Gowran RoI 25 D2 52 38N 7 04W
Graemsay *i.* Scotland 11 A1 58 56N 3 17W
Grafham Water
England 20 C3 52 18N 0 20W
Graiguenamanagh RoI 25 E2 52 32N 6 56W
Grain England 21 D2 51 28N 0 43E
Grampian Mountains
Scotland 13 E1/F1 56 45N 4 00W
Granada Spain 57 D2 37 10N 3 35W
Granard RoI 24 D3 53 47N 7 30W
Gran Canaria *i.* Spain 90 A7 28 00N 15 35W
Grand Canal RoI 24 D3 53 18N 7 15W
Grand Canyon USA 102 D4 36 04N 112 07W
Grand Cayman *i.*
Caribbean Sea 107 H3 19 20N 81 15W
Grand Rapids *tn.* USA 103 J5 42 57N 86 40W
Grange RoI 24 C4 54 24N 8 31W
Grangemouth
Scotland 15 F3 56 01N 3 44W
Grange-over-Sands *tn.*
England 16 D3 54 33N 3 09W
Grantham England 19 F2 52 55N 0 39W
Grantown-on-Spey
Scotland 13 F2 57 20N 3 58W
Granville France 56 D5 48 50N 1 35W
Grasmere England 16 C3 54 28N 3 02W
Grasse France 56 H2 43 40N 5 56E
Grassington England 16 E3 54 04N 1 59W
Gravelines France 54 A3 50 59N 2 08E
Gravesend England 21 D2 51 27N 0 24E
Gray France 56 G4 47 27N 5 35E
Grays England 21 D2 51 29N 0 20E
Graz Austria 58 G3 47 05N 15 22E
Greasby England 16 C2 53 23N 3 10W
Great Bardfield
England 21 D2 51 57N 0 26E
Great Bear Lake
Canada 100 L7/M7 66 00N 120 00W
Great Broughton
England 17 E3 54 27N 1 110W
Great Chesterford
England 21 D3 52 04N 0 11E
Great Coates England 17 F2 53 35N 0 08W
Great Cumbrae *i.*
Scotland 14 E2 55 46N 4 55W
Great Dividing Range
Australia 81 H8/J3 35 00N 148 00E
Great Driffield England 17 F3 54 01N 0 26W
Great Dunmow
England 21 D2 51 53N 0 22E
Great Eccleston
England 16 D2 53 51N 2 53W
Greater Antilles *is.*
West Indies 107 H4/L3 19 00N 78 00W
Greater London *co.*
England 20 C2 51 30N 0 10W
Greater Manchester
co. England 10 D2 53 30N 2 15W
Great Harwood
England 16 D2 53 48N 2 24W
Great Malvern England 19 D2 52 07N 2 19W
Great Missenden
England 20 C2 51 43N 0 43W
Great Ormes Head
Wales 18 C3 53 21N 3 53W
Great Ouse *r.* England 21 D3 52 40N 0 20E
Great Salt Lake USA 102 D5 41 10N 112 40W
Great Shelford England 21 D3 52 08N 0 09E
Great Slave Lake
Canada 100 N6 62 00N 114 00W
Great Torrington
England 22 C2 51 57N 4 09W
Great Victoria Desert
Australia 80 E5/F5 28 00S 130 00E
Great Whernside *sum.*
England 16 E3 54 10N 1 59W
Great Wyrley England 19 D2 52 27N 2 02W
Great Yarmouth
England 21 E3 52 37N 1 44E
GREECE 61 J3/K3
Greencastle NI 14 C1 54 02N 6 06W
Greenisland *tn.* NI 14 D1 54 42N 5 52W
GREENLAND 101 BB8/EE8
Greenlaw Scotland 15 G2 55 43N 2 28W
Greenock Scotland 15 E2 55 57N 4 45W
Greenore RoI 24 E4 54 02N 6 08W
Greenore Point RoI 25 E2 52 15N 6 18W
Greenstone Point
Scotland 12 D2 57 55N 5 37W
GRENADA 106 R11
Grenoble France 56 G3 45 11N 5 43E
Greta *r.* England 16 D3 54 10N 2 30W
Gretna Scotland 15 F1 54 59N 3 04W
Gretna Green Scotland 15 F1 55 00N 3 04W
Greystones RoI 25 E3 53 09N 6 04W
Grimethorpe England 17 E2 53 34N 1 23W
Grimsby England 17 F2 53 35N 0 05W
Groningen Neths 54 E6 53 13N 6 35E
Grosseto Italy 60 D5 42 46N 11 07E
Grove England 20 B2 51 37N 1 26W
Groznyy Russia 70 G5 43 21N 45 42E
Gruinard Bay Scotland 12 D2 57 55N 5 30W
Guadalajara Mexico 106 D4 20 40N 103 20W
Guadalajara Spain 57 D4 40 37N 3 10W
Guadalquivir *r.* Spain 57 C2 37 45N 5 30W
Guadeloupe *i.*
Lesser Antilles 106 Q9 16 30N 61 30W
Guadiana *r.*
Spain/Portugal 57 B3 38 30N 7 30W
GUAM 116 E9
Guangzhou China 77 K2 23 08N 113 20E
Guantánamo Cuba 107 J4 20 09N 75 14W
Guarda Portugal 57 B4 40 32N 7 17W
GUATEMALA 106 F3
Guatemala City
Guatemala 106 F2 14 38N 90 22W
Guayaquil Ecuador 114 A13 2 13S 79 54W
Guéret France 56 E4 46 10N 1 52E
Guernsey *i.*
Channel Islands 23 E1 46 27N 2 35W
Guide Post England 17 E4 55 10N 1 36W
Guildford England 20 C2 51 14N 0 35W
Guimarães Portugal 57 A4 41 26N 8 19W
GUINEA 90 B4
GUINEA-BISSAU 90 A4/B4
Guisborough England 17 E3 54 32N 1 04W
Guiseley England 17 E2 53 53N 1 42W
Guiyang China 77 J3 26 35N 106 40E
Gujranwala Pakistan 74 C6 32 06N 74 11E
Gulf, The Middle East 73 F4 27 20N 51 00E
Gullane Scotland 15 G3 56 02N 2 50W

Gunnislake England 22 C2 50 31N 4 12W
Gutcher Scotland 11 C3 60 40N 1 00W
Guthrie USA 103 G4 35 53N 97 26W
GUYANA 114 F14
Gweebarra Bay RoI 24 C4 54 55N 8 30W
Gweedore RoI 24 C5 55 03N 8 14W
Gwynedd *u.a.* Wales 18 C2 52 45N 3 55W
Györ Hungary 59 H3 47 41N 17 40E

H

Haarlem Neths 54 C5 52 23N 4 39E
Hacketstown RoI 25 E2 52 52N 6 33W
Haddington Scotland 15 G2 55 58N 2 47W
Hadleigh England 21 D3 52 02N 0 57E
Hadleigh England 21 D2 51 34N 0 36E
Hadley England 19 D2 52 43N 2 28W
Hagen Germany 58 C5 51 22N 7 27E
Hagley England 19 D2 52 26N 2 08W
Hagondange France 56 H5 49 16N 6 11E
Hags Head RoI 25 B2 52 56N 9 30W
Haguenau France 56 H5 48 49N 7 47E
Haifa Israel 72 B5 32 49N 34 59E
Hailsham England 21 D1 50 52N 0 16E
Hainan Dao *i.* China 77 J1/K1 18 50N 109 50E
Hai Phong Vietnam 77 J2 20 50N 106 41E
HAITI 107 K3
Hakodate Japan 78 D3 41 46N 140 44E
Hale England 16 D2 53 22N 2 20W
Halesowen England 19 D2 52 26N 2 05W
Halesworth England 21 E3 52 21N 1 30E
Halifax England 17 E2 53 44N 1 52W
Halifax Canada 101 Y2 44 38N 63 35W
Halkirk Scotland 13 F3 58 30N 3 30W
Halladale *r.* Scotland 13 F3 58 30N 3 55W
Halle Germany 58 E5 51 28N 11 58E
Hallein Austria 58 F3 47 41N 13 06E
Halmstad Sweden 55 D2 56 41N 12 55E
Halstead England 21 D2 51 57N 0 38E
Haltwhistle England 16 D3 54 58N 2 27W
Ḩamāh Syria 72 C6 35 10N 36 45E
Hamamatsu Japan 78 C1 34 42N 137 42E
Hamble-le-Rice England 20 B1 50 52N 1 19W
Hambleton Hills England 17 E3 54 15N 1 15W
Hamburg Germany 58 E6 53 33N 10 00E
Hämeenlinna Finland 55 F3 61 00N 24 25E
Hamilton Canada 101 U2 43 15N 79 50W
Hamilton NZ 81 Q3 37 47S 175 17E
Hamilton Scotland 15 E2 55 47N 4 03W
Hamm Germany 58 C5 51 40N 7 49E
Hammerfest Norway 55 F5 70 40N 23 44E
Hampshire *co.* England 20 B2 51 10N 1 15W
Hampshire Downs England 20 B2 51 15N 1 10W
Hamstreet England 21 D2 51 05N 0 52E
Hangzhou China 77 M4 30 18N 120 07E
Hanko Finland 55 F2 50 50N 23 00E
Hanley England 16 D2 53 01N 2 10W
Hannover Germany 58 D6 52 23N 9 44E
Hanoi Vietnam 77 J2 21 01N 105 52E
Harare Zimbabwe 92 F4 17 50S 31 03E
Harbin China 77 N7 45 45N 126 41E
Hargeysa Somalia 91 P3 9 31N 44 02E
Harlech Wales 18 B2 52 52N 4 07W
Harleston England 21 E3 52 24N 1 18E
Harlingen Neths 54 D6 53 10N 5 25E
Harlow England 21 D2 51 47N 0 08E
Haroldswick Scotland 11 D3 60 47N 0 50W
Harpenden England 20 C2 51 49N 0 22W
Harris *i.* Scotland 12 C2 57 50N 6 55W
Harris, Sound of Scotland 12 B2 57 40N 9 12W
Harrogate England 17 E2 54 00N 1 33W
Harrow England 20 C2 51 34N 0 20W
Hartford USA 103 M5 41 00N 72 00W
Hartington England 17 E2 53 09N 1 48W
Hartland England 22 C2 50 59N 4 29W
Hartland Point England 22 C3 51 02N 4 31W
Hartlepool England 17 E3 54 41N 1 13W
Hartlepool *u.a.* England 17 E3 54 41N 1 13W
Hartshill England 19 E2 52 33N 1 30W
Harwell England 20 B2 51 37N 1 18W
Harwich England 21 E2 51 57N 1 17E
Harworth England 17 E2 53 26N 1 04W
Harz *mts.* Europe 58 E5 52 00N 10 00E
Hascosay *i.* Scotland 11 D3 60 36N 1 00W
Haslemere England 20 C2 51 06N 0 43W
Haslingden England 16 D2 53 43N 2 18W
Hasselt Belgium 54 D3 50 56N 5 20E
Hastings England 21 D1 50 51N 0 36E
Hatfield South Yorkshire England 17 F2 53 36N 0 59W
Hatfield Hertfordshire England 20 C2 51 46N 0 13W
Hatherleigh England 22 C2 50 49N 4 04W
Hathersage England 17 E2 53 19N 1 38W
Hatton Scotland 13 H2 57 25N 1 55W
Haugesund Norway 55 C2 59 25N 5 16E
Haut Atlas *mts.* Morocco 90 C8 30 45N 6 50W
Havana Cuba 107 H4 23 07N 82 25W
Havant England 20 C1 50 51N 0 59W
Haverfordwest Wales 18 B1 51 49N 4 58W
Haverhill England 21 D3 52 05N 0 26E
Havering England 21 D2 51 34N 0 14E
Hawaiian Islands Pacific Ocean 116 J10/L9 25 00N 166 00W
Hawarden Wales 18 C3 53 11N 3 02W
Hawes England 16 D3 54 18N 2 12W
Hawick Scotland 15 G2 55 25N 2 47W
Hawkesbury Canada 101 W3 45 36N 74 38W
Hawkhurst England 21 D2 51 02N 0 30E
Haworth England 17 E2 53 50N 1 57W
Haxby England 17 E3 54 01N 1 05W
Haydon Bridge *tn.* England 16 D3 54 58N 2 14W
Hayle England 22 B2 50 10N 5 25W
Hay-on-Wye Wales 18 C2 52 04N 3 07W
Haywards Heath England 20 C2 51 00N 0 06W
Hazel Grove England 16 D2 53 23N 2 08W
Hazelmere England 20 C2 51 38N 0 44W
Heacham England 21 D3 52 55N 0 30E
Headford RoI 24 B3 53 28N 9 06W
Heanor England 17 E2 53 01N 1 22W
Heathfield England 21 D1 50 58N 0 15E
Hebden Bridge England 16 D2 53 45N 2 00W
Hebi China 77 K5 35 57N 114 08E
Heckington England 19 F2 52 59N 0 18W
Heckmondwike England 17 E2 53 43N 1 45W
Hedge End England 20 B1 50 55N 1 18W
Hednesford England 19 D2 52 43N 2 00W
Hedon England 17 F2 53 44N 0 12W
Heerenveen Neths 54 D5 52 57N 5 55E
Heerlen Neths 54 D3 50 53N 5 59E
Hefei China 77 L4 31 55N 117 18E
Heidelberg Germany 58 D4 49 25N 8 42E
Heighington England 17 F2 54 36N 1 37W
Heilbronn Germany 58 D4 49 08N 9 14E
Heisker *is.* Scotland 12 B2 57 30N 7 40W
Hekla *mt.* Iceland 55 L6 64 00N 19 41W
Helchteren Belgium 54 D4 51 03N 5 23E
Helena USA 102 D6 46 35N 112 00W
Helen's Bay *tn.* NI 14 D1 54 41N 5 50W
Helensburgh Scotland 15 E3 56 01N 4 44W
Hellifield England 16 D3 54 01N 2 12W
Helmsdale *r.* Scotland 13 F3 58 10N 3 50W
Helmsdale Scotland 13 F3 58 07N 3 40W
Helmsley England 17 E3 54 14N 1 04W
Helsingborg Sweden 55 D2 56 03N 12 43E
Helsinki Finland 55 F3 60 08N 25 00E
Helston England 22 B2 50 05N 5 16W
Helvellyn *mt.* England 16 C3 54 32N 3 02W
Hemel Hempstead England 20 C2 51 46N 0 28W
Hemsworth England 17 E2 53 38N 1 21W
Henfield England 20 C1 50 56N 0 17W
Hengelo Neths 54 E5 52 16N 6 46E
Henley-in-Arden England 19 E2 52 17N 1 46W
Henley-on-Thames England 20 C2 51 32N 0 56W
Herbertstown RoI 25 C2 52 32N 8 28W
Hereford England 18 D2 52 04N 2 43W
Herefordshire *co.* England 18/19 D2 52 10N 2 45W
Herentals Belgium 54 C4 51 11N 4 50E
Herm *i.* Channel Islands 23 E1 49 28N 2 27W
Herne Germany 54 F4 51 32N 7 12E
Herne Bay *tn.* England 21 E2 51 23N 1 08E
Herning Denmark 55 C2 56 08N 8 59E
Hertfordshire *co.* England 20 C2 51 50N 0 05W
Hessle England 17 F2 53 44N 0 26W
Hetton-le-Hole England 17 E3 54 50N 1 27W
Hexham England 16 D3 54 58N 2 06W
Heysham England 16 D3 54 02N 2 54W
Heywood England 16 D2 53 36N 2 13W
Higham Ferrers England 19 F2 52 18N 0 36W
High Bentham England 16 D3 54 08N 2 30W
Higher Walton England 16 D2 53 45N 2 37W
Highland *u.a.* Scotland 12/13 D2/E2 57 00N 5 00W
Highworth England 20 B2 51 38N 1 43W
High Wycombe England 20 C2 51 38N 0 46W
Hildesheim Germany 58 D6 52 09N 9 58E
Hillingdon England 20 C2 51 32N 0 27W
Hillsborough NI 14 C1 54 28N 6 05W
Hilversum Neths 54 D5 52 14N 5 10E
Himalaya *mts.* Asia 74/75 D6/G5 28 00N 85 00E
Hinckley England 19 E2 52 33N 1 21W
Hindhead England 20 C2 51 07N 0 44W
Hindley England 16 D2 53 32N 2 35W
Hindu Kush *mts.* Afghanistan 74 B7/C7 35 00N 70 00E
Hiroshima Japan 78 B1 34 23N 132 27E
Hirwaun Wales 18 C1 51 45N 3 30W
Histon England 21 D3 52 15N 0 06E
Hitachi Japan 78 D2 36 35N 140 40E
Hitchin England 20 C2 51 57N 0 17W
Hobart Australia 81 J2 42 54S 147 18E
Hô Chi Minh Vietnam 79 D6 10 46N 106 43E
Hockley England 21 D2 51 35N 0 39E
Hodder *r.* England 16 D2 53 55N 2 30W
Hoddesdon England 20 C2 51 46N 0 01W
Hodnet England 19 D2 52 51N 2 35W
Hoek van Holland Neths 54 C5 51 59N 4 08E
Hohhot China 77 K6 40 49N 117 37E
Hokkaidō *i.* Japan 78 D3 43 30N 143 00E
Holbeach England 20 D3 52 49N 0 01E
Holderness *p.* England 17 F2 53 45N 0 05W
Hollyford RoI 25 C2 52 38N 8 06W
Hollywood RoI 25 E3 53 06N 6 35W
Holmes Chapel *tn.* England 16 D2 53 12N 2 22W
Holme-on-Spalding-Moor England 17 F2 53 49N 0 46W
Holmfirth England 17 E2 53 35N 1 46W
Holmhead Scotland 15 E2 55 29N 4 17W
Holsworthy England 22 C2 50 49N 4 21W
Holt England 21 E3 52 55N 1 05E
Holycross Limerick RoI 25 C2 52 38N 7 52W
Holycross Tipperary RoI 25 D2 52 38N 7 52W
Holyhead Wales 18 B3 53 19N 4 38W
Holy Island England 15 H2 55 41N 1 48W
Holy Island Wales 18 B3 53 16N 4 39W
Holywell Wales 18 C3 53 17N 3 13W
Holywood NI 14 D1 54 38N 5 50W
Homs Syria 72 C5 34 42N 36 40E
Homyel' Belarus 59 Q6 52 25N 31 00E
Honddu *r.* Wales 18 C1 51 50N 2 50W
HONDURAS 106 G2
Hong Kong China 77 K2 23 00N 114 00E
Honiton England 23 D2 50 48N 3 13W
Honshū *i.* Japan 78 C2 37 15N 139 00E
Hoo England 21 D2 51 26N 0 34E
Hoogeveen Neths 54 E5 52 43N 6 29E
Hook England 20 C2 51 17N 0 58W
Hook Head RoI 25 E2 52 10N 6 55W
Hope Wales 18 C3 53 07N 3 03W
Hopton on Sea England 21 E3 52 33N 1 43E
Horbury England 17 E2 53 41N 1 33W
Horley England 20 C2 51 11N 0 11W
Horncastle England 17 F2 53 13N 0 07W
Horn Head RoI 24 D5 55 13N 7 59W
Hornsea England 17 F2 53 55N 0 10W
Horsforth England 17 E2 53 51N 1 39W
Horsham England 20 C2 51 04N 0 21W
Horwich England 16 D2 53 37N 2 33W
Hospital RoI 25 C2 52 29N 8 25W
Hospitalet Spain 57 G4 41 21N 2 06E
Houghton-le-Spring England 17 E3 54 51N 1 28W
Hounslow England 20 C2 51 28N 0 21W
Houston USA 103 G2 29 45N 95 25W
Hove England 20 C1 50 49N 0 11W
Hovingham England 17 F3 54 10N 0 59W
Howden England 17 F2 53 45N 0 52W
Howth RoI 24 E3 53 23N 6 04W
Hoy *i.* Scotland 11 A1 58 48N 3 20W
Hoylake England 16 C2 53 23N 3 11W
Hoyland England 17 E2 53 30N 1 27W
Hoy Sound Scotland 11 A1 58 56N 3 20W
Hrodna Belarus 59 L6 53 40N 23 50E
Huambo Angola 92 C5 12 44S 15 47E
Huancayo Peru 114 B11 12 05S 75 12W
Huang He *r.* China 77 K5 38 00N 111 00E
Hucknall England 17 E2 53 02N 1 11W
Huddersfield England 17 E2 53 39N 1 47W
Hudson Bay Canada 101 T5/T6 60 00N 89 00W
Huelva Spain 57 C2 37 15N 6 56W
Huesca Spain 57 E5 42 08N 0 25W
Hugh Town England 22 A1 49 55N 6 19W
Hull *r.* England 17 F2 53 55N 0 20W
Hullbridge England 21 D2 51 37N 0 37E
Humaitá Brazil 114 E12 7 33S 63 01W
Humberston England 17 F2 53 32N 0 02W
HUNGARY 59 H3/K3
Hungerford England 20 B2 51 26N 1 30W
Hunmanby England 17 F3 54 11N 0 19W
Hunstanton England 21 D3 52 57N 0 30E
Huntford Scotland 15 G2 55 22N 2 28W
Huntingdon England 20 C3 52 20N 0 12W
Huntington USA 103 K4 38 24N 82 26W
Huntly Scotland 13 G2 57 27N 2 47W
Huntsville USA 103 J3 34 44N 86 35W
Huron, Lake Canada/USA 105 D2/3 45 00N 83 00W
Hurstpierpoint England 20 C1 50 56N 0 11W
Husbands Bosworth England 19 E2 52 27N 1 03W
Husum Germany 58 D7 54 29N 9 04E
Hutton Cranswick England 17 F2 53 57N 0 27W
Hyde England 16 D2 53 27N 2 04W
Hyderabad India 74 D3 17 22N 78 26E
Hyderabad Pakistan 74 B5 25 23N 68 24E
Hythe Hampshire England 20 B1 50 51N 1 24W
Hythe Kent England 21 E2 51 05N 1 05E

I

Iaşi Romania 59 N3 47 09N 27 38E
Ibadan Nigeria 90 E3 7 23N 3 56E
Ibagué Colombia 114 B14 4 25N 75 20W
Ibiza *i.* Spain 57 F3 39 00N 1 20E
Ibstock England 19 E2 52 42N 1 23W
Ica Peru 114 B11 14 02S 75 48W
ICELAND 55 L7
Idaho *state* USA 102 D5 44 00N 115 00W
Idrigill Point Scotland 12 C2 57 21N 6 35W
Ieper Belgium 54 A3 50 51N 2 53E
Iglesias Italy 60 C3 39 19N 8 32E
IJsselmeer *l.* Neths 54 D5 52 50N 5 15E
Ilam England 17 E2 53 04N 1 49W
Ilchester England 23 E2 51 00N 2 41W
Ilebo CDR 92 D7 4 20S 20 35E
Îles Loyauté *is.* Pacific Ocean 81 N6/N7 21 00S 167 00E
Ilfracombe England 22 C3 51 13N 4 08W
Ilhéus Brazil 114 K11 14 50S 39 06W
Ilkeston England 19 E2 52 59N 1 18W
Ilkley England 17 E2 53 55N 1 50W
Illinois *state* USA 103 J5 40 00N 89 00W
Ilminster England 23 E2 50 56N 2 55W
Immingham England 17 F2 53 36N 0 11W
Imola Italy 60 E6 44 22N 11 43E
Imperatriz Brazil 114 H12 5 32S 47 28W
Imperia Italy 60 C5 43 53N 8 03E
Imphal India 75 G4 24 47N 93 55E
Inch Island *i.* RoI 24 D5 55 04N 7 30W
Inchon S. Korea 77 N5 37 30N 126 38E
Independence USA 103 G4 37 13N 95 43W
INDIA 74/75
Indiana *state* USA 103 J5 40 00N 86 00W
Indianapolis USA 103 J4 39 45N 86 10W
Indian Ocean 121
INDONESIA 79 C3/H3
Indore India 74 D4 22 42N 75 54E
Indus *r.* Pakistan 74 B5 28 00N 69 00E
Ingatestone England 21 D2 51 41N 0 22E
Ingleborough *sum.* England 16 D3 54 10N 2 23W
Ingleton England 16 D3 54 10N 2 27W
Ingolstadt Germany 58 E4 48 46N 11 27E
Inishannon RoI 25 C1 51 45N 8 38W
Inishbofin *i.* RoI 24 A3 53 38N 10 12W
Inishcrone RoI 24 B4 54 13N 9 05W
Inisheer *i.* RoI 25 B3 53 03N 9 30W
Inishkea North *i.* RoI 24 A4 54 08N 10 11W
Inishkea South *i.* RoI 24 A4 54 08N 10 11W
Inishmaan *i.* RoI 25 B3 53 05N 9 35W
Inishmore *i.* RoI 25 B3 53 07N 9 45W
Inishmurray *i.* RoI 24 C4 54 25N 8 35W
Inishowen Peninsula RoI 24 D5 55 15N 7 15W
Inishshark *i.* RoI 24 A3 53 37N 10 16W
Inishturk *i.* RoI 24 A3 53 43N 10 05W
Inn *r.* Europe 58 E3 48 00N 12 00E
Inner Hebrides *is.* Scotland 12 C1/C2 56 45N 6 45W
Innerleithen Scotland 15 F2 55 38N 3 05W
Inner Sound Scotland 12 D2 57 25N 5 55W
Innfield RoI 24 E3 53 25N 6 50W
Innsbruck Austria 58 E3 47 17N 11 25E
Inny *r.* RoI 25 A1 51 54N 10 06W
Interlaken Switz. 58 C3 46 42N 7 52E
Inuvik Canada 100 J7 68 16N 133 40W
Inverary Scotland 14 D3 56 13N 5 05W
Inver Bay RoI 24 C4 54 36N 8 20W
Inverbervie Scotland 13 G1 56 51N 2 17W
Invercargill NZ 81 N1 46 25S 168 22E
Inverclyde *u.a.* Scotland 15 E2 55 50N 4 45W
Invergarry Scotland 13 E2 57 02N 4 47W
Invergordon Scotland 13 E2 57 42N 4 10W
Inverkeithing Scotland 15 F3 56 02N 3 25W
Invermoriston Scotland 13 E2 57 13N 4 38W
Inverness Scotland 13 E2 57 27N 4 15W
Inverquharity Scotland 13 G1 56 44N 2 59W
Inverurie Scotland 13 G2 57 17N 2 23W
Ioánnina Greece 61 J3 39 40N 20 51E
Iona *i.* Scotland 12 C1 56 19N 6 25W
Iónia Nisiá Greece 61 H3 39 00N 20 00E
Íos *i.* Greece 61 L2 36 00N 25 00E
Iowa *state* USA 103 H5 42 00N 94 00W
Iowa City USA 103 H5 41 39N 91 31W
Ipswich England 21 E3 52 04N 1 10E
Iquique Chile 114 C9 20 14S 70 07W
Iquitos Peru 114 C13 3 51S 73 13W
IRAN 73 F5/G5
IRAQ 72 D5
Irbid Jordan 72 C5 32 33N 35 51E
Irfon *r.* Wales 18 C2 52 10N 3 25W
Irish Sea British Isles 10 53 30N 5 30W
Irkutsk Russia 71 N7 52 18N 104 15E
Ironbridge England 19 D2 52 38N 2 30W
Irrawaddy *r.* Myanmar 79 A8 20 00N 95 00E
Irthing *r.* England 16 D3 55 00N 2 40W
Irthlingborough England 19 F2 52 20N 0 37W
Irtysh *r.* Asia 70 K8 57 30N 72 30E
Irún Spain 57 E5 43 20N 1 48W
Irvine Scotland 15 E2 55 37N 4 40W
Irvinestown NI 14 B1 54 29N 7 38W
Irving USA 103 G3 32 49N 96 57W
Ise *r.* England 19 F2 52 25N 00 50W
Isernia Italy 60 F4 41 35N 14 14E
Iskenderun Turkey 63 E2 36 37N 36 08E
Isla *r.* Scotland 13 F1 56 35N 3 10W
Isla d'Elba Italy 60 D5 42 00N 10 00E
Isla Grande de Tierra del Fuego Chile/Argentina 115 D2 54 00S 67 30W
Islamabad Pakistan 74 C6 33 40N 73 08E
Island Magee NI 14 D1 54 45N 5 40W
Islay *i.* Scotland 14 C2 55 48N 6 12W
Isleham England 21 D3 52 21N 0 25E
Isle of Man British Isles 16 B3 54 15N 4 15W
Isle of Portland England 23 E2 50 33N 2 27W
Isle of Purbeck England 23 E2 50 38N 2 05W
Isle of Whithorn *tn.* Scotland 15 E1 54 42N 4 22W
Isle of Wight *u.a.* England 20 B1 50 40N 1 20W

ISRAEL 72 B5/C5
Istanbul Turkey 63 C3 41 02N 28 57E
Itabuna Brazil 114 K11 14 48S 39 18W
ITALY 60 D5/E5
Itchen *r.* England 20 B2 51 05N 1 15W
Ithon *r.* Wales 18 C2 52 20N 3 25W
Itzehoe Germany 58 D6 53 56N 9 32E
Ivybridge England 22 D2 50 23N 3 56W
Ixworth England 21 D3 52 18N 0 50E
Izhevsk Russia 70 H8 56 49N 53 11E
Izmir Turkey 63 C2 38 25N 27 10E

J

Jackson USA 103 H3 32 20N 90 11W
Jacksonville USA 103 K3 30 20N 81 40W
Jaén Spain 57 D2 37 46N 3 48W
Jaipur India 74 D5 26 53N 75 50E
Jakarta Indonesia 79 D2 6 08S 106 45E
Jakobstad Finland 55 F3 63 40N 22 42E
JAMAICA 107 J3
James Bay Canada 101 U4 53 45N 81 00W
Jamestown USA 103 G6 46 54N 98 42W
Jammu India 74 C6 32 43N 74 54E
JAPAN 78
Jarrow England 17 E3 54 59N 1 29W
Jasper Canada 100 M4 52 55N 118 05W
Jastrowie Poland 59 H6 53 25N 16 50E
Jawa *i.* Indonesia 79 D2/E2 7 00S 110 00E
Jedburgh Scotland 15 G2 55 29N 2 34W
Jedda Saudi Arabia 72 C3 21 30N 39 10E
Jefferson City USA 103 H4 38 33N 92 10W
Jena Germany 58 E5 50 56N 11 35E
Jerez de la Frontera Spain 57 C2 36 41N 6 08W
Jericho Middle East 72 N10 31 51N 35 27E
Jersey *i.* Channel Islands 23 E1 49 13N 2 07W
Jerusalem Israel/Jordan 72 C5 31 47N 35 13E
Jilin China 77 N6 43 53N 126 35E
Jinan China 77 L5 36 41N 117 00E
Jinja Uganda 93 C5 0 27N 33 14E
João Pessoa Brazil 114 K12 7 06S 34 53W
Jodhpur India 74 C5 26 18N 73 08E
Joensuu Finland 55 G3 62 35N 29 46E
Johannesburg RSA 92 E2 26 10S 28 02E
John o'Groats Scotland 13 F3 58 38N 3 05W
Johnstone Scotland 15 E2 55 50N 4 31W
Joinville Brazil 114 H8 26 20S 48 55W
Jönköping Sweden 55 D2 57 45N 14 10E
Jonquière Canada 101 W3 48 25N 71 16W
JORDAN 72 C5
Jordan *r.* Middle East 72 N11 32 15N 32 10E
Joyce Country RoI 24 B3 53 32N 9 33W
Juàzeiro Brazil 114 J12 9 25S 40 30W
Juba South Sudan 91 M2 4 50N 31 35E
Juliaca Peru 114 C10 15 29S 70 09W
Juneau USA 100 J5 58 20N 134 20W
Jungfrau *mt.* Switz. 58 C3 46 33N 7 58E
Junsele Sweden 55 E3 63 40N 16 55E
Jura *mts.* France/Switz. 56 G4/H4 46 30N 6 00E
Jura *i.* Scotland 14 D2/D3 55 55N 6 00W
Jura, Sound of Scotland 14 D2 55 45N 5 55W
Jylland *p.* Denmark 55 C2 55 00N 9 00E
Jyväskylä Finland 55 G3 62 16N 25 50E

K

K2 *mt.* China/India 76 C5 35 47N 76 30E
Kābul Afghanistan 74 B6 34 30N 69 10E
Kagoshima Japan 78 B1 31 37N 130 32E
Kaiserslautern Germany 58 C4 49 27N 7 47E
Kajaani Finland 55 G3 64 14N 27 37E
Kalahari Desert Southern Africa 92 D3 23 30S 23 00E
Kalamáta Greece 61 K2 37 02N 22 07E
Kalémié CDR 92 E6 5 57S 29 10E
Kaliavesi *l.* Finland 55 G3 63 00N 27 20E
Kaliningrad Russia 55 F1 54 40N 20 30E
Kalmar Sweden 55 E2 56 39N 16 20E
Kalmthout Belgium 54 C4 51 23N 4 29E
Kamchatka *p.* Russia 71 T8 57 30N 160 00E
Kames Scotland 14 D2 55 54N 5 15W
Kamina CDR 92 E6 8 46S 25 00E
Kamloops Canada 100 L4 50 39N 120 24W
Kampala Uganda 93 C5 0 19N 32 35E
Kâmpóng Cham Cambodia 79 D6 11 59N 105 26E
Kananga CDR 92 D6 5 53S 22 26E
Kankakee USA 103 J5 41 08N 87 52W
Kannapolis USA 103 K4 35 30N 80 36W
Kano Nigeria 90 F4 12 00N 8 31E
Kanpur India 74 E5 26 27N 80 14E
Kansas *state* USA 102/103 G4 38 00N 98 00W
Kansas City USA 103 H4 39 02N 94 33W
Kanturk RoI 25 C2 52 10N 8 55W
Kaohsiung Taiwan 77 M2 22 36N 120 17E
Kapuskasing Canada 101 U3 49 25N 82 26W
Karachi Pakistan 74 B4 24 51N 67 02E
Kara Sea Russia 117 75 00N 70 00E
Karasjok Norway 55 G4 69 27N 25 30E
Karcag Hungary 59 K3 47 19N 20 53E
Karlovac Croatia 60 F6 45 30N 15 34E
Karlskoga Sweden 55 D2 59 19N 14 33E
Karlskrona Sweden 55 E2 56 10N 15 35E
Karlsruhe Germany 58 D4 49 00N 8 24E
Karlstad Sweden 55 D2 59 24N 13 32E
Kaskinen Finland 55 F3 62 23N 21 10E
Kassala Sudan 91 N5 15 24N 36 30E
Kassel Germany 58 D5 51 18N 9 30E
Kathmandu Nepal 75 F5 27 42N 85 19E
Katowice Poland 59 J5 50 15N 18 59E
Katrineholm Sweden 55 E2 58 59N 16 15E
Kattegat *sd.* Denmark/Sweden 55 D2 57 00N 11 00E
Kaunas Lithuania 55 F1 54 52N 23 55E
Kawasaki Japan 78 C2 35 30N 139 45E
Kayseri Turkey 63 E2 38 42N 35 28E
KAZAKHSTAN 70 H6/J6
Kazan' Russia 70 G8 55 45N 49 10E
Keady NI 14 C1 54 15N 6 42W
Kealkill RoI 25 B1 51 45N 9 20W
Kecskemét Hungary 59 J3 46 56N 19 43E
Kefallonia *i.* Greece 61 J3 38 00N 20 00E
Keighley England 17 E2 53 52N 1 54W
Keith Scotland 13 G2 57 32N 2 57W
Kells RoI 24 E3 53 44N 6 53W
Kelowna Canada 100 M3 49 50N 119 29W
Kelso Scotland 15 G2 55 36N 2 25W
Kelvedon England 21 D2 51 51N 0 42E
Kemnay Scotland 13 G2 57 14N 2 27W
Kempston England 20 C3 52 07N 0 30W
Kempten Germany 58 E3 47 44N 10 19E
Kendal England 16 D3 54 20N 2 45W
Kenilworth England 19 E2 52 21N 1 34W
Kenmare RoI 25 B1 51 53N 9 35W
Kennacraig Scotland 14 D2 55 50N 5 27W
Kennet *r.* England 20 B2 51 30N 1 45W
Kennington England 21 D2 51 09N 0 55E
Kennoway Scotland 15 F3 56 12N 3 03W
Kenora Canada 101 S3 49 47N 94 26W
Kent *co.* England 21 D2 51 10N 0 45E
Kentford England 21 D3 52 16N 0 30E
Kentucky *state* USA 103 J4 37 00N 85 00W
KENYA 93 E5/F5
Kerkrade Neths 54 E3 50 52N 6 04E
Kérkyra *i.* Greece 61 H3 39 00N 19 00E
Kerpen Germany 54 E3 50 52N 6 42E
Kerrera *i.* Scotland 12 D1 56 25N 5 34W
Kerry *co.* RoI 25 B2 52 10N 9 30W
Kerry Head RoI 25 B2 52 25N 9 55W
Kesh NI 14 B1 54 31N 7 43W
Kessingland England 21 E3 52 25N 1 42E
Keswick England 16 C3 54 37N 3 08W
Kettering England 19 F2 52 24N 0 44W
Keynsham England 23 E3 51 26N 2 30W
Key West USA 103 K1 24 34N 81 48W
Keyworth England 19 E2 52 52N 1 05W
Khabarovsk Russia 71 R6 48 32N 135 08E
Kharkiv Ukraine 62 E4 50 00N 36 15E
Khartoum Sudan 91 M5 15 33N 32 35E
Kherson Ukraine 63 D4 46 39N 32 38E
Khmel'nyts'kyy Ukraine 59 N4 49 25N 26 59E
Khulna Bangladesh 75 F4 22 49N 89 34E
Khyber Pass Afghanistan/Pakistan 74 C6 34 06N 71 05E
Kidderminster England 19 D2 52 23N 2 14W
Kidlington England 20 B2 51 50N 1 17W
Kidsgrove England 16 D2 53 05N 2 14W
Kidwelly Wales 18 B1 51 45N 4 18W
Kiel Germany 58 E7 54 20N 10 08E
Kielce Poland 59 K5 50 51N 20 39E
Kielder Water England 16 D4 55 10N 2 30W
Kiev Ukraine 59 Q5 50 25N 30 30E
Kigali Rwanda 93 B4 1 56S 30 04E
Kigoma Tanzania 93 A2 4 52S 29 36E
Kilbaha RoI 25 B2 52 35N 9 52W
Kilbeggan RoI 24 D3 53 22N 7 30W
Kilberry RoI 24 E3 53 42N 6 41W
Kilbirnie Scotland 15 E2 55 46N 4 41W
Kilbrannan Sound Scotland 14 D2 55 30N 5 30W
Kilcavan RoI 24 D3 53 11N 7 21W
Kilchoan Scotland 12 C1 56 43N 6 06W
Kilcock RoI 24 E3 53 24N 6 40W
Kilcormac RoI 25 D3 53 10N 7 43W
Kilcreggan Scotland 15 E2 56 01N 4 48W
Kilcullen RoI 25 E3 53 08N 6 45W
Kildare RoI 25 E3 53 10N 6 55W
Kildare *co.* RoI 25 E3 53 10N 6 55W
Kildorrery RoI 25 C2 52 15N 8 20W
Kilfinnane RoI 25 C2 52 22N 8 28W
Kilgetty Wales 18 B1 51 45N 4 44W
Kinglass Lough RoI 24 C3 53 50N 8 01W
Kilimanjaro *mt.* Tanzania 93 E3 3 04S 37 22E
Kilkeary RoI 25 C2 52 50N 8 07W
Kilkee RoI 25 B2 52 41N 9 38W
Kilkeel NI 14 C1 54 04N 6 00W
Kilkelly RoI 24 C3 53 53N 8 51W
Kilkenny *co.* RoI 25 D2 52 30N 7 10W
Kilkenny RoI 25 D2 52 39N 7 15W
Kilkhampton England 22 C2 50 53N 4 29W
Kilkieran Bay RoI 24 B3 53 18N 9 41W
Kilkishen RoI 25 C2 52 48N 8 45W
Kill RoI 24 E3 53 15N 6 35W
Killala RoI 24 B4 54 13N 9 13W
Killaloe RoI 25 C2 52 48N 8 27W
Killamarsh England 17 E2 53 20N 1 20W
Killarney RoI 25 B2 52 03N 9 30W
Killary Harbour RoI 24 B3 53 38N 9 55W
Killeigh RoI 24 D3 53 13N 7 27W
Killenaule RoI 25 D2 52 34N 7 40W
Killimer RoI 25 B2 52 37N 9 24W
Killimor RoI 25 C3 53 10N 8 17W
Killin Scotland 13 E1 56 28N 4 19W
Killorglin RoI 25 B2 52 06N 9 47W
Killybegs RoI 24 C4 54 38N 8 27W
Killyleagh NI 14 D1 54 24N 5 39W
Kilmacolm Scotland 15 E2 55 54N 4 38W
Kilmacrenan RoI 24 D5 55 02N 7 47W
Kilmacthomas RoI 25 D2 52 12N 7 25W
Kilmallock RoI 25 C2 52 23N 8 34W
Kilmaluag Scotland 12 C2 57 41N 6 17W
Kilmarnock Scotland 15 E2 55 36N 4 30W
Kilmona RoI 25 C1 51 58N 8 33W
Kilmory Scotland 14 D2 55 55N 5 41W
Kilrea NI 14 C1 54 57N 6 33W
Kilrenny Scotland 15 G3 56 15N 2 41W
Kilrush RoI 25 B2 52 39N 9 30W
Kilsheelan RoI 25 D2 52 22N 7 35W
Kilsyth Scotland 15 E2 55 59N 4 04W
Kiltamagh RoI 24 B3 53 51N 9 00W
Kiltealy RoI 25 E2 52 34N 6 45W
Kiltullagh RoI 24 C3 53 35N 8 35W
Kilwinning Scotland 15 E2 55 40N 4 42W
Kimberley Canada 100 M3 49 40N 115 58W
Kimberley England 19 E2 53 00N 1 17W
Kimberley England 19 E2 53 00N 1 17W
Kimbolton RSA 92 D2 28 45S 24 46E
Kinbrace Scotland 13 F3 58 15N 3 56W
Kineton England 19 E2 52 10N 1 30W
Kingsbridge England 22 D2 50 17N 3 46W
Kingsclere England 20 B2 51 20N 1 14W
Kingscourt RoI 24 E3 53 53N 6 48W
Kingskerswell England 22 D2 50 30N 3 37W
Kings Langley England 20 C2 51 43N 0 28W
King's Lynn England 21 D3 52 45N 0 24E
Kings Muir Scotland 15 F2 55 40N 3 12W
Kingsport USA 103 K4 36 33N 82 34W
Kingsteignton England 22 D2 50 33N 3 35W
Kingston Jamaica 107 U13 17 58N 76 48W
Kingston upon Hull England 17 F2 53 45N 0 20W
Kingston upon Hull *u.a.* England 17 F2 53 45N 0 25W
Kingston-upon-Thames England 20 C2 51 25N 0 18W
Kingswood England 19 D1 51 28N 2 30W
Kington England 18 C2 52 12N 3 01W
Kingussie Scotland 13 E2 57 05N 4 03W
Kinloch Scotland 12 C2 57 01N 6 17W
Kinlocheil Scotland 12 D1 56 51N 5 20W
Kinlochewe Scotland 12 D2 57 36N 5 20W
Kinlochleven Scotland 13 E1 56 42N 4 58W
Kinloch Rannoch Scotland 13 E1 56 42N 4 11W
Kinloss Scotland 13 F2 57 38N 3 33W
Kinlough RoI 24 C4 54 27N 8 17W
Kinnaird Head Scotland 13 G2 57 40N 2 00W
Kinnegad RoI 24 D3 53 27N 7 05W
Kinnitty RoI 25 D3 53 06N 7 43W
Kinross Scotland 15 F3 56 13N 3 27W
Kinsale RoI 25 C1 51 42N 8 32W
Kinsale Harbour RoI 25 C1 51 40N 8 30W
Kinshasa CDR 92 C7 4 18S 15 18E
Kintore Scotland 13 G2 57 13N 2 21W
Kintyre *p.* Scotland 14 D2 55 30N 5 35W
Kinvarra RoI 25 C3 53 08N 8 56W
Kippax England 17 E2 53 46N 1 22W
Kippford Scotland 15 F1 54 52N 3 49W
Kirby Muxloe England 19 E2 52 38N 1 14W
Kircubbin NI 14 D1 55 24N 5 28W
KIRIBATI 116 K7
Kirikkale Turkey 63 D2 39 51N 33 32E
Kirkbean Scotland 15 F1 54 55N 3 36W
Kirkburton England 17 E2 53 37N 1 42W
Kirkby England 16 D2 53 29N 2 54W
Kirkby in Ashfield England 17 E2 53 13N 1 15W
Kirkby Londsale England 16 D3 54 13N 2 36W
Kirkbymoorside England 17 F3 54 16N 0 55W
Kirkby Stephen England 16 D3 54 28N 2 20W
Kirkcaldy Scotland 15 F3 56 07N 3 10W
Kirkcolm Scotland 14 D1 54 58N 5 04W
Kirkconnel Scotland 15 F2 55 23N 4 00W
Kirkcowan Scotland 15 E1 54 55N 4 36W
Kirkcudbright Scotland 15 E1 54 50N 4 03W
Kirkgunzeon Scotland 15 F1 54 58N 3 46W
Kirkham England 16 D2 53 47N 2 53W
Kirkintilloch Scotland 15 E2 55 57N 4 10W
Kirkmuirhill Scotland 15 F2 55 39N 3 55W
Kirkpatrick Durham Scotland 15 F2 55 01N 3 54W
Kirk Sandall England 17 E2 53 34N 1 04W
Kirkwall Scotland 11 B1 58 59N 2 58W
Kirov Russia 70 G8 58 00N 49 38E
Kirovohrad Ukraine 62 D4 48 31N 32 15E
Kirriemuir Scotland 13 F1 56 41N 3 01W
Kirton England 20 C3 52 56N 0 04W
Kisangani CDR 91 L2 0 33N 25 14E
Kismaayo Somalia 91 P1 0 25S 42 31E
Kisumu Kenya 93 D4 0 08S 34 47E
Kita-Kyūshu Japan 78 B1 33 52N 130 49E
Kitami Japan 78 D3 43 51N 143 54E
Kitchener Canada 101 U2 43 27N 80 30W
Kitimat Canada 100 K4 54 05N 128 38W
Kitwe Zambia 92 E5 0 08S 30 30E
Kitzbühel Austria 58 F3 47 27N 12 23E
Klaipėda Lithuania 55 F2 55 43N 21 07E
Klamath Falls *tn.* USA 102 B5 42 14N 121 47W
Klöfta Norway 55 D3 60 04N 11 06E
Knapdale Scotland 14 D2 55 52N 5 31W
Knaresborough England 17 E3 54 00N 1 27W
Knighton England 18 C2 52 21N 3 03W
Knock RoI 24 C3 53 47N 8 55W
Knockadoon Head RoI 25 D1 51 50N 7 50W
Knockanevin RoI 25 C2 52 17N 8 21W
Knockdrislagh RoI 25 C2 52 03N 8 41W
Knocktopher RoI 25 D2 52 29N 7 13W
Knokke-Heist Belgium 54 B4 51 21N 3 19E
Knottingley England 17 E2 53 43N 1 14W
Knowle England 19 E2 52 23N 1 43W
Knoxville USA 103 K4 36 00N 83 57W
Knutsford England 16 D2 53 18N 2 23W
Kōbe Japan 78 C1 34 40N 135 12E
Koblenz Germany 58 C5 50 21N 7 36E
Kōfu Japan 78 C2 35 42N 138 34E
Kokkola Finland 55 F3 62 45N 30 06E
Kolhapur India 74 C3 16 40N 74 20E
Kolkata India 75 F4 22 30N 88 20E
Komatsu Japan 78 C2 36 25N 136 27E
Komotiní Greece 61 L4 41 06N 25 25E
Köniz Switz. 58 C3 46 56N 7 25E
Konstanz Germany 58 D3 47 40N 9 10E
Konya Turkey 63 D2 37 51N 32 30E
Konz Germany 54 E2 49 42N 6 35E
Koper Slovenia 60 E6 45 31N 13 44E
Korbach Germany 58 D5 51 16N 8 53E
Korinthiakós Kólpos *g.* Greece 61 K3 38 00N 22 00E
Kórinthos Greece 61 K2 37 56N 22 55E
Kortrijk Belgium 54 B3 50 50N 3 17E
Kós *i.* Greece 61 M2 36 45N 27 10E
Košice Slovakia 59 K4 48 44N 21 15E
KOSOVO 61 J5
Koszalin Poland 59 H7 54 10N 16 10E
Kotka Finland 55 G3 60 26N 26 55E
Kovrov Russia 62 F6 56 23N 41 21E
Kozáni Greece 61 J4 40 18N 21 48E
Kragujevac Serbia 61 J5 44 01N 20 55E
Kraków Poland 59 J5 50 03N 19 55E
Kranj Slovenia 60 F7 46 15N 14 20E
Krefeld Germany 58 C5 51 20N 6 32E
Krems Austria 58 G4 48 25N 15 36E
Kristiansand Norway 55 C2 58 08N 8 01E
Kristianstad Sweden 55 D2 56 02N 14 10E
Kríti *i.* Greece 61 L1 35 00N 25 00E
Kryvyy Roh Ukraine 62 D4 47 55N 33 24E
Kuala Lumpur Malaysia 79 C4 3 09N 101 42E
Kuching Malaysia 79 E4 1 35N 110 21E
Kufstein Austria 58 F3 47 36N 12 11E
Kumamoto Japan 78 B1 32 50N 130 42E
Kunlun Shan *mts.* China 76 D5/E5 36 30N 85 00E
Kunming China 77 H3 25 04N 102 41E
Kurashiki Japan 78 B1 34 36N 133 43E
Kurgan Russia 70 J8 55 30N 65 20E
Kuril Islands Russia 71 T6 50 00N 155 00E
Kursk Russia 70 F7 51 45N 36 14E
Kushiro Japan 78 D3 42 58N 144 24E
KUWAIT 73 E4
Kuwait Kuwait 73 E4 29 20N 48 00E
Kuytun China 76 D6 44 30N 85 00E
Kwangju S. Korea 77 N5 35 07N 126 52E
Kyleakin Scotland 12 D2 57 16N 5 44W
Kyle of Lochalsh Scotland 12 D2 57 17N 5 43W
Kyles of Bute Scotland 14 D2 55 52N 5 13W
Kylestrome Scotland 13 D3 58 16N 5 02W
Kyōto Japan 78 C2 35 02N 135 45E
KYRGYZSTAN 70 K5
Kythira *i.* Greece 61 K2 36 00N 23 00E
Kýthnos *i.* Greece 61 L2 37 25N 24 25E
Kyūshū *i.* Japan 78 B1 32 20N 131 00E

L

Laâyoune Western Sahara 90 B7 27 10N 13 11W
Labrador *geog. reg.* Canada 101 Y4 54 00N 63 00W
la Chaux-de-Fonds Switz. 58 C3 47 07N 6 51E
la Ciotat France 56 G2 43 10N 5 36E
Lac Léman Switzerland 58 C3 46 20N 6 20E
La Crosse USA 103 H5 43 48N 91 04W
Lacul Razim *l.* Romania 59 P2 45 00N 29 00E
Ladozhskoye Ozero *l.* Russia 70 F9 61 00N 30 00E
Ladybank Scotland 15 F3 56 17N 3 08W
Lagan *r.* NI 14 C1 54 30N 6 05W
Laggan Bay *b.* Scotland 14 C2 55 38N 6 17W
Lago di Como *l.* Italy 60 C6 46 00N 9 00E
Lago di Garda *l.* Italy 60 D6 45 00N 10 00E
Lago Maggiore *l.* Italy 60 C6 46 00N 8 00E
Lagos Nigeria 90 E3 6 27N 3 28E
Lagos Portugal 57 A2 37 05N 8 40W
Lago Titicaca *l.* Peru/Bolivia 114 C10/D10 16 00S 69 30W

La Grande USA 102 C6 45 21N 118 05W
La Grande Rivière Canada 101 W4 54 00N 74 00W
Lahore Pakistan 74 C6 31 34N 74 22E
Lahti Finland 55 G3 61 00N 25 40E
Lairg Scotland 13 E3 58 01N 4 25W
Lakenheath England 21 D3 52 25N 0 31E
La Línea de la Concepción Spain 57 C2 36 10N 5 21W
La Maddalena Italy 60 C4 41 13N 9 25E
Lamar USA 102 F4 38 04N 102 37W
Lambay Island RoI 24 E3 53 29N 6 01W
Lambourn England 20 B2 51 31N 1 31W
Lambourn *r.* England 20 B2 51 27N 1 28W
Lamego Portugal 57 B4 41 05N 7 49W
Lamía Greece 61 K3 38 55N 22 26E
Lamlash Scotland 14 D2 55 32N 5 08W
Lammermuir Hills Scotland 15 G2 55 50N 2 45W
Lampeter Wales 18 B2 52 07N 4 05W
Lanark Scotland 15 F2 55 41N 3 48W
Lancashire *co.* England 16 D2 53 50N 2 30W
Lancaster England 16 D3 54 03N 2 48W
Lanchester England 17 E3 54 50N 1 44W
Lancing England 20 C1 50 50N 0 19W
Landerneau France 56 B5 48 27N 4 16W
Land's End *c.* England 22 B2 50 03N 5 44W
Landshut Germany 58 F4 48 31N 12 10E
Landskrona Sweden 55 D2 55 53N 12 50E
Langdon USA 104 A3 48 46N 98 21W
Langholm Scotland 15 F2 55 09N 3 00W
Langport England 23 E3 51 02N 2 50W
Langres France 56 G4 47 53N 5 20E
Lannion France 56 C5 48 44N 3 27W
L'Anse USA 104 C3 46 45N 88 27W
Lansing USA 103 K5 42 44N 85 34W
Lanzarote *i.* Spain 90 B7 29 00N 13 38W
Lanzhou China 77 H5 36 01N 103 45E
Laois *co.* RoI 25 D2 52 59N 7 25W
Laon France 56 F5 49 34N 3 37E
LAOS 79 C7/D7
La Paz Bolivia 114 D10 16 30S 68 10W
Lapford England 22 D2 50 52N 3 47W
La Plata Argentina 115 F6 34 52S 57 55W
Lappland *geog. reg.* Finland/Sweden 55 F4/G4 67 30N 20 05E
Lapua Finland 55 F3 62 57N 23 00E
L'Aquila Italy 60 E5 42 22N 13 24E
Laragh RoI 25 E3 53 00N 6 18W
Laredo USA 102 G2 27 32N 99 22W
Largs Scotland 14 E2 55 48N 4 52W
Lárisa Greece 61 K3 39 38N 22 25E
Larkhall Scotland 15 F2 55 45N 3 59W
Larne NI 14 D1 54 51N 5 49W
Larne *district* NI 14 D1 54 50N 6 00W
Larne Lough *b.* NI 14 D1 54 49N 5 49W
la Rochelle France 56 D4 46 10N 1 10W
la Roche-sur-Yon France 56 D4 46 40N 1 25W
La Roda Spain 57 D3 39 13N 2 15W
La See d'Urgel Spain 57 F5 42 22N 1 27E
la Seyne-sur-Mer France 56 G2 43 06N 5 53E
Las Palmas Spain 90 A7 28 08N 15 27W
La Spézia Italy 60 C6 44 07N 9 48E
Las Vegas USA 102 C4 36 10N 115 10W
Latakia Syria 72 C6 35 31N 35 47E
Latheron Scotland 13 F3 58 17N 3 22W
Latina Italy 60 E4 41 28N 12 53E
LATVIA 55 G2
Lauder Scotland 15 G2 55 43N 2 45W
Laugharne Wales 18 B1 51 47N 4 28W
Launceston Australia 81 J2 41 25S 147 07E
Launceston England 22 C2 50 38N 4 21W
Lauragh RoI 25 B1 51 45N 9 46W
Laurel USA 103 J3 31 41N 89 09W
Laurencekirk Scotland 13 G1 56 50N 2 29W
Laurencetown RoI 24 C3 53 14N 8 10W
Lauria Italy 60 F4 40 03N 15 50E
Laurieston Scotland 15 E1 54 57N 4 03W
Laurieston Scotland 15 F2 55 59N 3 45W
Lausanne Switz. 58 C3 46 32N 6 39E
Laval France 56 D5 48 04N 0 45W
Lavenham England 21 D3 52 06N 0 47E
Lawrence USA 103 G4 38 58N 95 15W
Lawton USA 103 G3 34 36N 98 25W
Laxey Isle of Man 16 B3 54 14N 4 24W
Laxford Bridge *tn.* Scotland 13 D3 58 22N 5 01W
Lay *r.* France 56 D4 46 32N 1 15W
Lazonby England 16 D3 54 46N 2 41W
Lea *r.* England 20 C2 51 47N 0 17W
Leach *r.* England 19 E1 51 46N 1 44W
Leadhills Scotland 15 F2 55 25N 3 47W
Leadon *r.* England 19 D1 51 57N 2 21W
Leatherhead England 20 C2 51 18N 0 20W
LEBANON 72 C5
Lebanon USA 103 H4 37 40N 92 40W
le Blanc France 56 E4 46 38N 1 04E
Lebrija Spain 57 B2 36 55N 6 10W
Lecarrow RoI 24 C3 53 33N 8 02W
Lecce Italy 61 H4 40 21N 18 11E
Lechlade England 19 E1 51 43N 1 41W
le Creusot France 56 G4 46 48N 4 27E
Ledbury England 19 D2 52 02N 2 25W
Ledmore Scotland 13 E3 58 03N 4 58W
Leeds England 17 E2 53 50N 1 35W
Leek England 16 D2 53 06N 2 01W
Leenaun RoI 24 B3 53 36N 9 41W
Leeuwarden Neths 54 D6 53 12N 5 48E
Leeward Islands Lesser Antilles 107 M3 17 30N 64 00W
Lefkáda *i.* Greece 61 J3 38 45N 20 40E
Leganés Spain 57 D4 40 20N 3 46WE
Legnica Poland 59 H5 51 12N 16 10E
le Havre France 56 E5 49 30N 0 06E
Leicester England 19 E2 52 38N 1 05W
Leicester *u.a.* England 19 E2 52 38N 1 05W
Leicestershire *co.* England 19 E2 52 40N 1 20W
Leiden Neths 54 C5 52 10N 4 30E
Leigh England 16 D2 53 30N 2 33W
Leighton Buzzard England 20 C2 51 55N 0 41W
Leipzig Germany 58 F5 51 20N 12 25E
Leiria Portugal 57 A3 39 45N 8 49W
Leiston England 21 E3 52 13N 1 34E
Leith Hill *tn.* England 20 C2 51 11N 0 23W
Leitrim *co.* RoI 24 C4 54 05N 8 00W
Leivadiá Greece 61 K3 38 26N 22 53E
Leixlip RoI 24 E3 53 22N 6 30W
le Mans France 56 E4 48 00N 0 12E
Lemybrien RoI 25 D2 52 10N 7 31W
Lena *r.* Russia 71 Q10 70 00N 125 00E
Lens France 56 F6 50 26N 2 50E
Leoben Austria 58 G3 47 23N 15 06E
Leominster England 18 D2 52 14N 2 45W
León Mexico 106 D4 21 10N 101 42W
León Spain 57 C5 42 35N 5 34W
Leonding Austria 58 G4 48 19N 14 17E
le Puy France 56 F3 45 03N 3 53E
Lerwick Scotland 11 C3 60 09N 1 09W
Lesmahagow Scotland 15 F2 55 38N 3 54W
LESOTHO 92 E2
les Sables-d'Olonne France 56 D4 46 30N 1 47W
Lesser Antilles *is.* W. Indies 107 M2/M3 18 00N 65 00W
Lesser Slave Lake Canada 100 M5 55 25N 115 30W
Lésvos *i.* Greece 61 M3 39 00N 26 00E
Leswalt Scotland 14 D1 54 46N 5 05W
Letchworth England 20 C2 51 58N 0 14W
le Touquet-Paris-Plage France 56 E6 50 13N 1 36E
le Tréport France 56 E6 50 04N 1 22E
Letterfrack RoI 24 B3 53 33N 9 57W
Letterkenny RoI 24 D4 54 57N 7 44W
Leuchars Scotland 13 G1 56 23N 2 53W
Levanto Italy 60 C6 44 10N 9 37E
Leven England 17 F2 53 54N 0 19W
Leven Scotland 15 G3 56 11N 3 00W
Leverburgh Scotland 12 B2 57 45N 7 00W
Leverkusen Germany 58 C5 51 02N 6 59E
Lewes England 20 D1 50 52N 0 01E
Lewis *i.* Scotland 12 C3 58 15N 6 30W
Lexington USA 103 K4 38 03N 84 30W
Lexington USA 105 E1 37 47N 79 27W
Leyburn England 17 E3 54 19N 1 49W
Leyland England 16 D2 53 42N 2 42W
Leysdown on Sea England 21 D2 51 24N 0 55E
Lhasa China 76 F3 29 41N 91 10E
LIBERIA 90 B3/C3
Libourne France 56 D3 44 55N 0 14W
Libreville Gabon 90 F2 0 30N 9 25E
LIBYA 91 G7/K7
Libyan Desert North Africa 91 K7/L6 25 00N 25 00E
Lichfield England 19 E2 52 42N 1 48W
LIECHTENSTEIN 58 D3
Liège Belgium 54 D3 50 38N 5 35E
Lienz Austria 58 F3 46 51N 12 50E
Liepāja Latvia 55 F2 56 30N 21 00E
Liffey *r.* RoI 24 E3 53 16N 6 37W
Lifford RoI 24 D4 54 50N 7 29W
Likasi CDR 92 E5 10 58S 26 47E
Lille France 56 F6 50 39N 3 05E
Lillehammer Norway 55 D3 61 06N 10 27E
Lilongwe Malawi 92 F5 13 58S 33 49E
Lima Peru 114 B11 12 06S 77 03W
Limavady NI 14 C2 55 03N 6 57W
Limavady *district* NI 14 B1/C1 54 50N 7 00W
Limburg Germany 58 D5 50 23N 8 04E
Limerick RoI 25 C2 52 04N 8 38W
Limerick *co.* RoI 25 C2 52 30N 8 40W
Limoges France 56 E3 45 50N 1 15E
Limoux France 56 F2 43 03N 2 13E
Limpopo *r.* Southern Africa 92 F3 22 30S 32 00E
Linares Spain 57 D3 38 05N 3 38W
Lincoln England 17 F2 53 14N 0 33W
Lincoln USA 103 G5 40 49N 96 41W
Lincolnshire *co.* England 17 F2 53 10N 0 20W
Lincoln Wolds England 17 F2 53 25N 0 05W
Lingen Germany 58 C6 52 32N 7 19E
Lingfield England 20 C2 51 11N 0 01W
Linköping Sweden 55 E2 58 25N 15 35E
Linlithgow Scotland 15 F2 55 59N 3 37W
Linslade England 20 C2 51 55N 0 42W
Linton England 21 D3 52 06N 0 17E
Linz Austria 58 G4 48 19N 14 18E
Liphook England 20 C2 51 05N 0 49W
Lippstadt Germany 58 D5 51 41N 8 20E
Lisbellaw NI 14 B1 54 19N 7 32W
Lisbon Portugal 57 A3 38 44N 9 08W
Lisburn NI 14 C1 54 31N 6 03W
Lisburn *co.* NI 14 C1 54 35N 6 10W
Liscannor Bay RoI 25 B2 52 55N 9 30W
Lisdoonvarna RoI 25 B3 53 02N 9 17W
Lisieux France 56 E5 49 09N 0 14E
Liskeard England 22 C2 50 28N 4 28W
Lismore RoI 25 D2 52 08N 7 55W
Lismore *i.* Scotland 12 D1 56 30N 5 30W
Lisnaskea NI 14 B1 54 15N 7 27W
Liss England 20 C2 51 03N 0 55W
Lisse Neths 54 C5 52 16N 4 34E
Lissycasey RoI 25 B2 52 44N 9 12W
Listowel RoI 25 B2 52 27N 9 29W
Litherland England 16 D2 53 28N 2 59W
LITHUANIA 55 F2
Littleborough England 16 D2 53 39N 2 05W
Littlehampton England 20 C1 50 48N 0 33W
Little Minch *sd.* Scotland 12 C2 57 45N 6 30W
Little Ouse *r.* England 21 D3 52 30N 0 30E
Littleport England 21 D3 52 28N 0 19E
Liverpool England 16 D2 53 25N 2 55W
Liverpool Bay England 16 C2 53 28N 3 15W
Liversedge England 17 E2 53 43N 1 41W
Livingston Scotland 15 F2 55 53N 3 32W
Livorno Italy 60 D5 43 33N 10 18E
Lizard England 22 B1 49 57N 5 13W
Lizard Point England 22 B1 49 56N 5 13W
Ljubljana Slovenia 60 F7 46 04N 14 30E
Ljusdal Sweden 55 E3 61 57N 16 05E
Llanberis Wales 18 B3 53 07N 4 06W
Llanbister Wales 18 C2 52 21N 3 19W
Llandeilo Wales 18 C1 51 53N 3 59W
Llandovery Wales 18 C1 51 59N 3 48W
Llandrindod Wells Wales 18 C2 52 15N 3 23W
Llandudno Wales 18 C3 53 19N 3 49W
Llandysul Wales 18 B2 52 02N 4 19W
Llanelli Wales 18 B1 51 42N 4 10W
Llanerchymedd Wales 18 B3 53 20N 4 22W
Llanes Spain 57 C3 43 25N 4 45W
Llanfair Caereinion Wales 18 C2 52 39N 3 20W
Llanfairfechan Wales 18 C3 53 15N 3 58W
Llanfyllin Wales 18 C2 52 46N 3 17W
Llangadfan Wales 18 C2 52 41N 3 28W
Llangadog Wales 18 C1 51 57N 3 55W
Llangefni Wales 18 B3 53 16N 4 18W
Llangollen Wales 18 C2 52 58N 3 10W
Llangurig Wales 18 C2 52 25N 3 36W
Llangynog Wales 18 C2 52 50N 3 25W
Llanharan Wales 18 C1 51 32N 3 28W
Llanidloes Wales 18 C2 52 27N 3 32W
Llanrhystud Wales 18 B2 52 18N 4 09W
Llanrwst Wales 18 C3 53 08N 3 48W
Llantrisant Wales 18 C1 51 33N 3 23W
Llantwit Major Wales 18 C1 51 25N 3 30W
Llanuwchllyn Wales 18 C2 52 52N 3 41W
Llanwrtyd Wells Wales 18 C2 52 07N 3 38W
Llanybydder Wales 18 B2 52 04N 4 09W
Lleida Spain 57 F4 41 37N 0 38E
Lleyn Peninsula Wales 18 B2 52 53N 4 30W
Llyn Brianne Resevoir Wales 18 C2 52 09N 3 43W
Llyn Celyn Wales 18 C2 53 04N 4 10W
Llyn Efyrnwy Wales 18 C2 52 50N 3 30W
Llyn Tegid Wales 18 C2 52 53N 3 38W
Loanhead Scotland 15 F2 55 53N 3 09W
Loch Affric Scotland 13 D2 57 15N 5 00W
Lochailort *tn.* Scotland 12 D1 56 53N 5 40W
Lochaline *tn.* Scotland 12 D1 56 32N 5 47W
Loch Alsh Scotland 12 D2 57 15N 5 35W
Locharbriggs Scotland 15 F2 55 06N 3 35W
Loch Assynt Scotland 13 D3/E3 58 05N 5 00W
Loch Awe Scotland 14 D3 56 15N 5 17W
Lochboisdale *tn.* Scotland 12 B2 57 09N 7 19W
Loch Bracadale Scotland 12 C2 57 20N 6 30W
Loch Broom Scotland 12 D2 57 52N 5 08W
Loch Caolisport Scotland 14 D2 55 53N 5 38W
Lochcarron *tn.* Scotland 12 D2 57 24N 5 30W
Loch Carron Scotland 12 D2 57 40N 5 45W
Loch Chroisg Scotland 12 D2 57 30N 5 10W
Loch Craignish Scotland 14 D3 56 05N 5 30W
Loch Creran Scotland 12 D1 56 30N 5 20W
Lochdon *tn.* Scotland 12 D1 56 25N 5 35W
Loch Duich Scotland 12 D2 57 15N 5 30W
Loch Earn Scotland 13 F1 56 25N 4 10W
Lochearnhead Scotland 13 E1 56 23N 4 18W
Loch Eil Scotland 12 D1 56 50N 5 25W
Loch Eishort Scotland 12 C2/D2 57 08N 6 00W
Loch Eriboll Scotland 13 E3 58 31N 4 41W
Loch Ericht Scotland 13 E1 56 48N 4 25W
Loch Erisort Scotland 12 C3 58 05N 6 30W
Loches France 56 E4 47 08N 1 00E
Loch Etive Scotland 12 D1 56 30N 5 10W
Loch Ewe Scotland 12 D2 57 50N 5 40W
Loch Eynort Scotland 12 B2 57 10N 7 15W
Loch Fannich Scotland 13 E2 57 40N 5 00W
Loch Fyne Scotland 14 D3 56 00N 5 20W
Loch Gairloch Scotland 12 D2 57 45N 5 45W
Loch Garry Scotland 13 D2 57 05N 5 00W
Lochgelly Scotland 15 F3 56 08N 3 19W
Lochgilphead Scotland 14 D3 56 03N 5 26W
Loch Glass Scotland 13 E2 57 40N 4 30W
Loch Goll Scotland 14 E3 56 05N 4 55W
Loch Gorm Scotland 14 C2 55 49N 6 24W
Loch Gruinart Scotland 14 C2 55 51N 6 21W
Loch Hope Scotland 13 E3 58 25N 4 37W
Loch Indaal Scotland 14 C2 55 45N 6 21W
Lochinver Scotland 12 D3 58 09N 5 15W
Loch Katrine Scotland 15 E3 56 16N 4 30W
Loch Ken Scotland 15 E2 55 02N 4 07W
Loch Laggan Scotland 13 E1 56 55N 4 30W
Loch Langavat Scotland 12 C3 58 05N 6 50W
Loch Leven Scotland 13 D1/E1 56 45N 5 05W
Loch Leven Scotland 13 D1 56 15N 3 23W
Loch Leven Scotland 15 F3 56 15N 3 23W
Loch Linnhe Scotland 12 D1 56 35N 5 25W
Loch Lochy Scotland 13 E1 56 58N 4 55W
Loch Lomond Scotland 15 E3 56 10N 4 35W
Loch Long Scotland 14 E3 56 05N 4 55W
Loch Lyon Scotland 13 E1 56 30N 4 55W
Lochmaben Scotland 15 F2 55 08N 3 27W
Lochmaddy Scotland 12 B2 57 36N 7 08W
Loch Maree Scotland 12 D2 57 40N 5 30W
Loch Meig Scotland 13 E2 57 05N 4 45W
Loch Melfort Scotland 14 D3 56 10N 5 30W
Loch Monar Scotland 13 D2 57 25N 5 02W
Loch Morar Scotland 12 D1 57 55N 5 45W
Loch More Scotland 13 E3 58 15N 4 55W
Loch Mullardoch Scotland 13 D2 57 27N 4 58W
Lochnagar *mt.* Scotland 13 F1 56 57N 3 16W
Loch Nan Clar Scotland 13 E3 58 15N 4 05W
Loch Ness Scotland 13 E2 57 02N 4 30W
Loch Nevis Scotland 12 D1/D2 57 00N 5 40W
Loch of Harray Scotland 11 A2 59 02N 3 14W
Loch Rannoch Scotland 13 E1 56 41N 4 18W
Lochranza *tn.* Scotland 14 D2 55 42N 5 18W
Loch Roag Scotland 12 C3 58 10N 6 50W
Loch Ryan Scotland 14 D2 55 00N 5 05W
Loch Scridain Scotland 12 C1 56 20N 6 05W
Loch Seaforth Scotland 12 C2 58 00N 6 40W
Loch Shell Scotland 12 C2 58 00N 6 25W
Loch Shiel Scotland 12 D1 56 45N 5 35W
Loch Shin Scotland 13 E3 58 05N 4 30W
Loch Snizort Scotland 12 C2 57 30N 6 30W
Loch Striven Scotland 14 D2 55 58N 5 07W
Loch Sunart Scotland 12 D1 56 40N 5 45W
Loch Sween Scotland 14 D2 55 58N 5 38W
Loch Tarbert Scotland 14 D2 55 57N 5 55W
Loch Tay Scotland 13 E1 56 31N 4 10W
Loch Torridon Scotland 12 D2 57 35N 5 46W
Lockerbie Scotland 15 F2 55 07N 3 22W
Lockhart USA 103 G2 29 54N 97 14W
Locks Heath England 20 B1 50 52N 1 17W
Loddon England 21 E3 52 32N 1 29E
Łodz Poland 59 J5 51 49N 19 28E
Lofoten Islands Norway 55 D4 68 30N 15 00E
Lofthouse Gate England 17 E2 53 44N 1 30W
Loftus England 17 F3 54 33N 0 53W
Logan, Mount Canada 100 G6 60 34N 140 25W
Logroño Spain 57 D5 42 28N 2 26W
Loire *r.* France 56 D4 47 20N 1 20W
Loja Spain 57 C2 37 10N 4 09W
Lolland *i.* Denmark 55 D1 54 45N 12 20E
Lomé Togo 90 E3 6 10N 1 21E
London Canada 101 U2 42 58N 81 15W
London England 20 C2 51 30N 0 10W
Londonderry NI 14 B1 54 59N 7 19W
Londonderry *district* NI 14 B1 54 55N 7 20W
Londrina Brazil 114 G9 23 18S 51 13W
Long Beach *tn.* USA 102 C3 33 47N 118 15W
Longbenton England 17 E4 55 02N 1 35W
Long Crendon England 20 C2 51 47N 0 59W
Long Eaton England 19 E2 52 54N 1 15W
Longford RoI 24 D3 53 44N 7 47W
Longford *co.* RoI 24 D3 53 40N 7 50W
Longhorsley England 17 E4 55 15N 1 46W
Longhoughton England 15 H2 55 26N 1 36W
Long Melford England 21 D3 52 05N 0 43E
Longridge England 16 D2 53 51N 2 36W
Long Sutton England 21 D3 52 47N 0 08E
Longuyon France 56 G5 49 27N 5 36E
Longwy France 56 G5 49 32N 5 46E
Lons-le-Saunier France 56 G4 46 41N 5 33E
Looe England 22 C2 51 21N 4 27W
Loop Head RoI 25 B2 52 30N 9 55W
Lora del Rio Spain 57 C2 37 39N 5 32W
Lorca Spain 57 E2 37 40N 1 41W
Loreto Italy 60 E5 43 36N 13 36E
Lorient France 56 C4 47 45N 3 21W
Los Angeles USA 102 C3 34 00N 118 15W
Lossiemouth Scotland 13 F2 57 43N 3 18W
Lostwithiel England 22 C2 50 25N 4 40W
Loudéac France 56 C5 48 11N 2 45W
Lough Allen RoI 24 C4/D4 54 15N 8 00W
Lough Arrow RoI 24 C4 54 05N 8 15W
Lough Beg NI 14 C1 54 48N 6 30W
Loughborough England 19 E2 52 47N 1 11W
Lough Carra RoI 24 B3 53 40N 9 15W
Lough Conn RoI 24 B4 54 05N 9 10W
Lough Corrib RoI 24 B3 53 10N 9 10W
Lough Cullin RoI 24 B3 53 58N 9 10W
Lough Dan RoI 25 E3 53 05N 6 17W
Lough Derg Donegal RoI 24 D4 54 35N 7 55W

Lough Derg Tipperary RoI 25 C2 52 55N 8 15W
Lough Derravaragh RoI 24 D3 53 40N 7 22W
Lough Ennell RoI 24 D3 53 28N 7 24W
Lough Eske RoI 24 C4 54 41N 8 05W
Lough Feeagh RoI 24 B3 53 57N 9 35W
Lough Finn RoI 24 C4 54 51N 8 08W
Lough Graney RoI 25 C2 52 59N 8 40W
Lough Kinale RoI 24 D3 53 46N 7 25W
Lough Leane RoI 25 B2 52 03N 9 33W
Lough Macnean Lower NI 14 B1 54 17N 7 50W
Lough Macnean Upper NI/RoI 14 B1 54 18N 7 55W
Lough Mask RoI 24 B3 53 40N 9 30W
Lough Melvin RoI/NI 24 C4 54 25N 8 05W
Lough Neagh NI 14 C1 54 35N 6 30W
Lough Oughter RoI 24 D4 54 00N 7 30W
Loughrea *tn.* RoI 24 C3 53 12N 8 34W
Lough Rea RoI 24 C3 53 11N 8 35W
Lough Ree RoI 24 D3 53 35N 8 00W
Lough Sheelin RoI 24 D3 53 48N 7 20W
Lough Swilly RoI 24 D5 55 20N 7 35W
Loughton England 20 D2 51 39N 0 03E
Louisburgh RoI 24 B3 53 46N 9 48W
Louisiana *state* USA 103 H3 32 00N 92 00W
Louisville USA 103 J4 38 13N 85 48W
Lourdes France 56 D2 43 06N 0 02W
Louth England 17 F2 53 22N 0 01W
Louth RoI 24 E3 53 57N 6 33W
Louth *co.* RoI 24 E3 53 55N 6 25W
Louviers France 56 E5 49 13N 1 11E
Lower Lough Erne NI 14 B1 54 30N 7 45W
Lowestoft England 21 E3 52 29N 1 45E
Lowick England 15 H2 55 38N 1 58W
Lowther Hills Scotland 15 F2 55 25N 3 45W
Luanda Angola 92 B6 8 50S 13 15E
Luarca Spain 57 B5 43 33N 6 31W
Lubango Angola 92 B5 14 55S 13 30E
Lubbock USA 102 F3 33 35N 101 53W
Lübeck Germany 58 E6 53 52N 10 40E
Lublin Poland 59 L5 51 18N 22 31E
Lubumbashi CDR 92 E5 11 41S 27 29E
Lucan RoI 24 E3 53 22N 6 27W
Lucca Italy 60 D5 43 50N 10 30E
Luce Bay Scotland 15 E1 54 47N 4 50W
Lucena Spain 57 C2 37 25N 4 29W
Luckenwalde Germany 58 F6 52 05N 13 11E
Lucknow India 74 E5 26 50N 80 54E
Lüderitz Namibia 92 C2 26 38S 15 10E
Ludgershall England 20 B2 51 16N 1 37W
Ludhiana India 74 D6 30 56N 75 52E
Ludlow England 18 D2 52 22N 2 43W
Ludwigshafen Germany 58 D4 49 29N 8 27E
Ludwigslust Germany 58 E6 53 20N 11 30E
Lugano Switz. 58 D2 46 01N 8 57E
Lugnaquillia *mt.* RoI 25 E2 52 58N 6 27W
Lugo Spain 57 B5 43 00N 7 33W
Luhans'k Ukraine 62 E4 48 35N 39 20E
Luleå Sweden 55 F4 65 35N 22 10E
Lundy *i.* England 22 C3 51 11N 4 40W
Lüneburg Germany 58 E6 53 15N 10 24E
Lunéville France 56 H5 48 35N 6 30E
Lurgan NI 14 C1 54 28N 6 20W
Lusaka Zambia 92 E4 15 26S 28 20E
Lusk RoI 24 E3 53 32N 6 10W
Lustenau Austria 58 D3 47 26N 9 42E
Luton England 20 C2 51 53N 0 25W
Luton *u.a.* England 20 C2 51 53N 0 25W
Lutterworth England 19 E2 52 28N 1 10W
LUXEMBOURG 54 D2/E2
Luxembourg Luxembourg 54 E2 49 37N 6 08E
Luxor Egypt 91 M7 25 41N 32 24E
Luzern Switz. 58 D3 47 03N 8 17E
Luzhou China 77 J3 28 55N 105 25E
Luzon *i.* Philippines 79 G7 15 00N 122 00E
L'viv Ukraine 59 M4 49 50N 24 00E
Lybster Scotland 13 F3 58 18N 3 13W
Lydd England 21 D1 50 57N 0 55E
Lydham England 18 D2 52 31N 2 59W
Lydney England 19 D1 51 43N 2 32W
Lyme Bay England 23 E2 50 40N 2 55W
Lyme Regis England 23 E2 50 44N 2 57W
Lyminge England 21 E2 51 08N 1 05E
Lymington England 20 B1 50 46N 1 33W
Lymm England 16 D2 53 23N 2 28W
Lyndhurst England 20 B1 50 52N 1 34W
Lynher *r.* England 22 C2 50 33N 4 25W
Lynmouth England 22 D3 51 15N 3 50W
Lynn Lake *tn.* Canada 101 Q5 56 51N 101 01W
Lynton England 22 D3 51 15N 3 50W
Lyons France 56 G3 45 46N 4 50E
Lytham St. Anne's England 16 C2 53 45N 3 01W

M

Maam Cross RoI 24 B3 53 27N 9 33W
Maas *r.* Neths 54 E4 51 50N 5 32E
Maastricht Neths 54 D3 50 51N 5 42E
Mablethorpe England 17 G2 53 21N 0 15E
Macao China 77 K2 22 10N 113 40E
Macapá Brazil 114 G14 0 04N 51 04W
Macarata Italy 60 E5 43 18N 13 27E
Macclesfield England 16 D2 53 16N 2 07W
Macdonnell Ranges Australia 80 F6 24 00S 132 30E
Macduff Scotland 13 G2 57 40N 2 29W
Maceió Brazil 114 K12 9 40S 35 44W
Macgillycuddy's Reeks *mts.* RoI 25 B2 52 00N 9 27W
The Machars Scotland 15 E1 54 49N 4 31W
Machrihanish Scotland 14 D2 55 26N 5 44W
Machynlleth Wales 18 C2 52 35N 3 51W
Mackenzie *r.* Canada 100 J7 67 00N 132 00W
Mackenzie Mountains Canada 100 J7/L6 66 00N 130 00W
McKinley, Mount USA 100 E6 62 02N 151 01W
McKinney USA 103 G3 33 14N 96 37W
Mâcon France 56 G4 46 18N 4 50E
Macon USA 103 K3 32 49N 83 37W
Macroom RoI 25 C1 51 54N 8 57W
MADAGASCAR 92 H2/J5
Madeira *r.* Brazil 114 E12 6 00S 61 30W
Madeira Islands Atlantic Ocean 90 A8 32 45N 17 00W
Madison USA 103 J5 43 04N 89 22W
Madrid Spain 57 D4 40 25N 3 43W
Maesteg Wales 18 C1 51 37N 3 40W
Magadan Russia 71 T8 59 38N 150 50E
Magdeburg Germany 58 E6 52 08N 11 37E
Maghera NI 14 C1 54 51N 6 40W
Magherafelt NI 14 C1 54 45N 6 36W
Magherafelt *district* NI 14 C1 54 45N 6 50W
Maghull England 16 D2 55 32N 2 57W
Mahajanga Madagascar 92 J4 15 40S 46 20E
Mahilyow Belarus 59 Q6 53 54N 30 20E
Mahón Spain 57 H3 39 54N 4 15E
Maidenhead England 20 C2 51 32N 0 44W
Maiden Newton England 23 E2 50 46N 2 35W
Maidstone England 21 D2 51 17N 0 32E
Maiduguri Nigeria 90 G4 11 53N 13 16E
Main *r.* NI 14 C1 54 50N 6 20W
Maine *state* USA 103 N6 45 00N 70 00W
Mainz Germany 58 D4 50 00N 8 16E
Malabo Equatorial Guinea 90 F2 3 45N 8 48E
Málaga Spain 57 C2 36 43N 4 25W
Malahide RoI 24 E3 53 27N 6 09W
Malange Angola 92 C6 9 32S 16 20E
Malatya Turkey 63 E2 38 22N 38 18E
MALAWI 92 F5
MALAYSIA 79 C5/E5
Mal Bay RoI 25 B2 52 40N 9 30W
MALDIVES 119
Maldon England 21 D2 51 45N 0 40E
Malé Maldives 66 4 10N 73 29E
MALI 90 C4/D5
Malin Head RoI 24 D5 55 30N 7 20W
Malin More RoI 24 C4 54 41N 8 46W
Mallaig Scotland 12 D2 57 00N 5 50W
Mallorca *i.* Spain 57 G3 39 50N 2 30E
Mallow RoI 25 C2 52 08N 8 39W
Malmesbury England 20 A2 51 36N 2 06W
Malmö Sweden 55 D2 55 35N 13 00E
Malpas England 16 D2 53 01N 2 46W
MALTA 60 F1
Maltby England 17 E2 53 26N 1 11W
Malton England 17 F3 54 08N 0 48W
Malvern Hills England 19 D2 52 05N 2 22W
Manacor Spain 57 G3 39 35N 3 12E
Managua Nicaragua 106 G2 12 06N 86 18W
Manama Bahrain 73 F4 26 12N 50 38E
Manaus Brazil 114 F13 3 06S 60 00W
Manchester England 16 D2 53 30N 2 15W
Manfredonia Italy 60 F4 41 37N 15 55E
Mangotsfield England 19 D1 51 29N 2 31W
Manhattan USA 105 F2 40 48N 73 58W
Manila Philippines 79 G6 14 37N 120 58E
Manitoba *prov.* Canada 101 R5 55 15N 100 00W
Manitoba, Lake Canada 101 R4 50 30N 98 15W
Manizales Colombia 114 B15 5 03N 75 32W
Mannheim Germany 58 D4 49 30N 8 28E
Manningtree England 21 E2 51 57N 1 04E
Manorhamilton RoI 24 C4 54 18N 8 10W
Manresa Spain 57 F4 41 43N 1 50E
Mansfield England 17 E2 53 09N 1 11W
Mansfield Woodhouse England 17 E2 53 10N 1 11W
Mantes-la-Jolie France 56 E5 48 59N 1 43E
Manuta Italy 60 D6 45 10N 10 47E
Manzanares Spain 57 D3 39 00N 3 23W
Maputo Mozambique 92 F2 25 58S 32 35E
Marabá Brazil 114 H12 5 23S 49 10W
Maracaibo Venezuela 114 C16 10 44N 71 37W
Marbella Spain 57 C2 36 31N 4 53W
Marburg Germany 58 D5 50 49N 8 36E
March England 21 D3 52 33N 0 06E
Mar del Plata Argentina 115 F6 38 00S 57 32W
Marden England 21 D2 51 11N 0 30E
Maresfield England 21 D2 51 00N 0 05E
Margam Wales 18 C1 51 34N 3 44W
Margate England 21 E2 51 24N 1 24E
Maribor Slovenia 60 F7 46 34N 15 38E
Marignane France 56 G2 43 25N 5 12E
Mariscal Estigarribia Paraguay 114 E9 22 04S 60 34W
Mariupol' Ukraine 63 E4 47 05N 37 34E
Market Deeping England 19 F2 52 41N 0 19W
Market Drayton England 19 D2 52 54N 2 29W
Market Harborough England 19 F2 52 29N 0 55W
Markethill NI 14 C1 54 18N 6 31W
Market Rasen England 17 F2 53 24N 0 21W
Market Weighton England 17 F2 53 52N 0 40W
Markinch Scotland 15 F3 56 12N 3 09W
Marlborough England 20 B2 51 26N 1 43W
Marlborough Downs England 20 B2 51 28N 1 50W
Marlow England 20 C2 51 35N 0 48W
Marmande France 56 E3 44 30N 0 10E
Marple England 16 D2 53 24N 2 03W
Marrakesh Morocco 90 C8 31 49N 8 00W
Marsala Italy 60 E2 37 48N 12 27E
Marsden West Yorkshire England 17 E2 53 36N 1 55W
Marsden Tyne and Wear England 17 E3 54 58N 1 21W
Marseilles France 56 G2 43 18N 5 22E
MARSHALL ISLANDS 116 G9/H8
Marshfield England 19 D1 51 28N 2 19W
Marske-by-the-Sea England 17 E3 54 36N 1 01W
Martigny Switz. 58 C3 46 07N 7 05E
Martigues France 56 G2 43 24N 5 03E
Martinique *i.* Lesser Antilles 106 R12 14 30N 61 00W
Martos Spain 57 C2 37 44N 3 58W
Maryland *state* USA 103 L4 39 00N 77 00W
Maryport England 16 C3 54 43N 3 30W
Maryport Scotland 14 E1 54 43N 3 30W
Maseru Lesotho 92 E2 29 19S 27 29E
Masham England 17 E3 54 13N 1 40W
Mashhad Iran 73 G6 36 16N 59 34E
Massa Italy 60 D5 44 02N 10 09E
Massachusetts *state* USA 103 M5 42 00N 72 00W
Massif Central France 56 F3 45 00N 3 30E
Massif de la Vanoise France 56 H3 45 20N 6 20E
Matadi CDR 92 B6 5 50S 13 32E
Mataró Spain 57 G4 41 32N 2 27E
Matera Italy 61 G4 40 40N 16 37E
Matlock England 17 E2 53 08N 1 32W
Matterhorn *mt.* Switz. 58 C2 45 59N 7 39E
Maubeuge France 56 F6 50 17N 3 58E
Mauchline Scotland 15 E2 55 31N 4 24W
MAURITANIA 90 B5/C6
MAURITIUS 119
Maybole Scotland 15 E2 55 21N 4 41W
Mayenne France 56 D5 48 18N 0 37W
Maykop Russia 70 G5 44 37N 40 48E
Maynooth RoI 24 E3 53 23N 6 35W
Mayo RoI 24 B3 54 35N 9 07W
Mayo *co.* RoI 24 B3 53 55N 9 20W
Mazamet France 56 F2 43 29N 2 22E
Mazara del Vallo Italy 60 E2 37 40N 12 34E
Mazarrón Spain 57 E2 37 36N 1 19W
Mazatlán Mexico 106 C4 23 11N 106 25W
Mazirbe Latvia 55 F2 57 40N 22 21E
Mbabane Swaziland 92 F2 26 20S 31 08E
Mbandaka CDR 91 J2 0 03N 18 20E
Mbeya Tanzania 92 F6 8 54S 33 29E
Meath *co.* RoI 24 E3 35 35N 6 30W
Meaux France 56 F5 48 58N 2 54E
Mecca Saudi Arabia 72 C3 21 26N 39 49E
Medan Indonesia 79 B4 3 35N 98 39E
Medellín Colombia 114 B15 6 15N 75 36W
Mediterranean Sea 60 B2/E2 35 00N 15 00E
Medway *r.* England 21 D2 51 24N 0 40E
Medway *u.a.* England 21 D2 51 25N 0 35E
Meerut India 74 D5 29 00N 77 42E
Meig *r.* Scotland 13 E2 57 35N 4 50W
Mekong *r.* Asia 79 C8 16 00N 105 00E
Melbourn England 20 D3 52 05N 0 01E
Melbourne Australia 81 H3 37 45S 144 58E
Melbourne England 19 E2 52 49N 1 25W
Melilla *territory* Spain 57 D1 35 17N 2 57W
Melitopol' Ukraine 63 E4 46 51N 35 22E
Melksham England 20 A2 51 23N 2 09W
Melrose Scotland 15 G2 55 36N 2 44W
Meltham England 17 E2 53 36N 1 52W
Melton Mowbray England 19 F2 52 46N 0 53W
Melun France 56 F5 48 32N 2 40E
Melvich Scotland 13 F3 58 33N 3 55W
Memmingen Germany 58 E3 47 59N 10 11E
Memphis USA 103 J4 35 10N 90 00W
Menai Bridge *tn.* Wales 18 B3 53 14N 4 10W
Menai Strait Wales 18 B3 53 14N 4 10W
Mende France 56 F3 44 32N 3 30E
Mendip Hills England 23 E3 51 18N 2 45W
Mendoza Argentina 115 D7 32 48S 68 52W
Menorca *i.* Spain 57 G4/H3 39 45N 4 15E
Menton France 56 H2 43 47N 7 30E
Meppel Neths 54 E5 52 42N 6 12E
Merano Italy 60 D7 46 41N 11 10E
Mere England 20 A2 51 06N 2 16W
Mérida Mexico 106 G4 20 59N 89 39W
Mérida Spain 57 B3 38 55N 6 20W
Mérignac France 56 D3 44 50N 0 36W
Merrick *mt.* Scotland 15 E2 55 08N 4 29W
Merriott England 23 E2 50 55N 2 49W
Mersea Island England 21 D2 51 46N 0 57E
Mersey *r.* England 16 D2 53 20N 2 53W
Merseyside *co.* England 16 D2 53 30N 3 20W
Merthyr Tydfil Wales 18 C1 51 46N 3 23W
Merthyr Tydfil *u.a.* Wales 18 C1 51 48N 3 20W
Merton England 20 C2 51 25N 0 12W
Messina Italy 60 F3 38 13N 15 33E
Metheringham England 17 F2 53 08N 0 25W
Methil Scotland 15 F3 56 12N 3 01W
Metz France 56 H5 49 07N 6 11E
Meuse *r.* Belgium/France 54 D3 50 03N 4 40E
Mevagissey England 22 C2 50 16N 4 48W
Mexborough England 17 E2 53 30N 1 17W
MEXICO 106 C5/E3
Mexico City Mexico 106 E3 19 25N 99 10W
Mexico, Gulf of Mexico 106 F4/G4 25 00N 90 00W
Miami USA 103 K2 25 45N 80 15W
Michigan *state* USA 103 J5/K5 45 00N 85 00W
Michigan, Lake Canada/USA 104 C2/C3 45 00N 87 00W
Middlesbrough England 17 E3 54 35N 1 14W
Middlesbrough *u.a.* England 17 E3 54 33N 1 04W
Middleton England 16 D2 53 33N 2 12W
Middleton-in-Teesdale England 16 D3 54 38N 2 04W
Middleton-on-the-Wolds England 17 F2 53 56N 0 33W
Middlewich England 16 D2 53 11N 2 27W
Midhurst England 20 C1 50 59N 0 45W
Midleton RoI 25 C1 51 55N 8 10W
Midlothian *u.a.* Scotland 15 F2 55 50N 3 05W
Midsomer Norton England 23 E3 51 17N 2 30W
Mieres Spain 57 C5 43 15N 5 46W
Mikkeli Finland 55 G3 61 44N 27 15E
Milan Italy 60 C6 45 28N 9 12E
Milborne Port England 23 E2 50 58N 2 29W
Mildenhall England 21 D3 52 21N 0 30E
Milestone RoI 25 C2 52 40N 8 05W
Milford RoI 24 D5 55 07N 7 43W
Milford Haven Wales 18 A1 51 44N 5 02W
Millau France 56 F3 44 06N 3 05E
Millisle NI 14 D1 54 37N 5 30W
Millom England 16 C3 54 13N 3 18W
Millport Scotland 14 E2 55 46N 4 55W
Millstreet RoI 25 B2 52 03N 9 04W
Milltown Malbay RoI 25 B2 52 52N 9 23W
Milngavie Scotland 15 E2 55 57N 4 19W
Milnthorpe England 16 D3 54 14N 2 46W
Milton Keynes England 20 C3 52 02N 0 42W
Milton Keynes *u.a.* England 20 C3 52 02N 0 42W
Milverton England 23 D3 51 02N 3 16W
Milwaukee USA 103 J5 43 03N 87 56W
Mimizan France 56 D3 44 12N 1 14W
Minch, The *sd.* Scotland 12 C3/D3 58 00N 6 00W
Mindanao *i.* Philippines 79 G5/H5 8 00N 125 00E
Minden Germany 58 D6 52 18N 8 54E
Mindoro *i.* Philippines 79 G6 13 00N 121 00E
Minehead England 22 D3 51 13N 3 29W
Mine Head RoI 25 D1 52 00N 7 35W
Mingulay *i.* Scotland 12 B1 56 49N 7 38W
Minneapolis USA 103 H5 45 00N 93 15W
Minnedosa Canada 101 R4 50 14N 99 50W
Minnesota *state* USA 103 H6 47 00N 95 00W
Minsk Belarus 62 C5 53 51N 27 30E
Minster England 21 D2 51 26N 0 49E
Minster England 21 E2 51 20N 1 19E
Minsterley England 18 D2 52 39N 2 55W
Mintlaw Scotland 13 G2 57 31N 2 00W
Mirfield England 17 E2 53 41N 1 42W
Miskolc Hungary 59 K4 48 07N 20 47E
Misratah Libya 91 G8 32 23N 15 00E
Mississippi *r.* USA 103 H3 35 00N 90 00W
Mississippi *state* USA 103 H3/J3 32 00N 90 00W
Missouri *r.* USA 103 H4 39 00N 93 00W
Missouri *state* USA 103 H4 38 00N 93 00W
Mitchelstown RoI 25 C2 52 16N 8 16W
Mito Japan 78 D2 36 22N 140 29E
Mizen Head RoI 25 B1 51 30N 9 50W
Moate RoI 24 D3 53 24N 7 58W
Mobile USA 103 J3 30 40N 88 05W
Moçambique Mozambique 92 H4 15 03S 40 45E
Modbury England 22 D2 50 21N 3 53W
Módena Italy 60 D6 44 39N 10 55E
Modesto USA 102 B4 37 37N 121 00W
Mödling Austria 59 H4 48 06N 16 18E
Moelfre Wales 18 B3 53 21N 4 14W
Moffat Scotland 15 F2 55 20N 3 27W
Mogadishu Somalia 91 Q2 2 02N 45 21E
Mohill RoI 24 C3 53 54N 7 52W
Mo-i-Rana Norway 55 D4 66 18N 14 00E
Mold Wales 18 C3 53 10N 3 08W
MOLDOVA 59 P3
Mole *r.* England 20 C2 51 15N 0 20W
Molfetta Italy 61 G4 41 12N 16 36E
Mölndal Sweden 55 D2 57 40N 12 00E
Mombasa Kenya 93 F2 4 04S 39 40E
MONACO 56 H2
Monadhliath Mountains Scotland 13 E2 57 10N 4 00W

Monaghan RoI 24 E4 54 15N 6 58W
Monaghan *co.* RoI 24 D4/E4 54 10N 7 00W
Monasterevin RoI 25 D3 53 07N 7 02W
Mönchengladbach Germany 58 C5 51 12N 6 25E
Moncton Canada 101 Y3 46 04N 64 50W
Mondovì Italy 60 B6 44 23N 7 49E
Moneen RoI 24 C3 53 26N 8 54W
Moneymore NI 14 C1 54 42N 6 40W
Monfalcone Italy 60 E6 45 49N 13 32E
MONGOLIA 76/77 G7/K7
Moniaive Scotland 15 F2 55 12N 3 55W
Monifieth Scotland 13 G1 56 29N 2 49W
Monmouth Wales 18 D1 51 50N 2 43W
Monmouthshire *u.a.* Wales 18 D1 51 47N 2 55W
Monopoli Italy 61 G4 40 57N 17 18E
Monrovia Liberia 90 B3 6 20N 10 46W
Montana Bulgaria 61 K5 43 25N 23 11E
Montana *state* USA 102 E6 47 00N 111 00W
Montargis France 56 F4 48 00N 2 44E
Montauban France 56 E3 44 01N 1 20E
Montbéliard France 56 H4 47 31N 6 48E
Mont Blanc France/Italy 56 H3 45 50N 6 52E
Montceau-les-Mines France 56 G4 46 40N 4 23E
Mont-de-Marsan France 56 D2 43 54N 0 30W
Montdidier France 56 F5 49 39N 2 35E
Monte Carlo Monaco 56 H2 43 44N 7 25E
Montélimar France 56 G3 44 33N 4 45E
MONTENEGRO 61 H5
Montepulciano Italy 60 D5 43 05N 11 46E
Monterrey Mexico 106 D5 25 40N 100 20W
Montes Claros Brazil 114 J10 16 45S 43 52W
Montevideo Uruguay 115 F6 34 55S 56 10W
Montgomery USA 103 J3 32 22N 86 20W
Montgomery Wales 18 C2 52 34N 3 10W
Montluçon France 56 F4 46 20N 2 36E
Montmirail France 56 F5 48 52N 3 34E
Montmorillon France 56 E4 46 26N 0 52E
Montoro Spain 57 C3 38 02N 4 23W
Montpelier RoI 25 C2 52 45N 8 30W
Montpellier France 56 F2 43 36N 3 53E
Montréal Canada 101 W3 45 32N 73 36W
Montreux Switz. 58 C3 46 27N 6 55E
Montrose Scotland 13 G1 56 43N 2 29W
Montserrat *i.* Lesser Antilles 106 P9 16 45N 62 14W
Monza Italy 60 C6 45 35N 9 16E
Mooncoin RoI 25 D2 52 17N 7 15W
Moone RoI 25 E2 52 58N 6 49W
Moorfoot Hills Scotland 15 F2/G2 55 50N 3 00W
Moosonee Canada 101 U4 51 18N 80 39W
Mora Sweden 55 D3 61 00N 14 30E
Moray *u.a.* Scotland 13 F2 57 20N 3 10W
Moray Firth Scotland 13 F2 57 45N 3 45W
Morcenx France 56 D3 44 02N 0 55W
Morecambe England 16 D3 54 04N 2 53W
Morecambe Bay England 16 D3 54 10N 2 55W
Morelia Mexico 106 D3 19 40N 101 11W
Moreton England 16 C2 53 24N 3 07W
Moretonhampstead England 22 D2 50 40N 3 45W
Moreton-in-Marsh England 19 E1 51 59N 1 42W
Morlaix France 56 C5 48 35N 3 50W
Morley England 17 E2 53 46N 1 36W
MOROCCO 90 C8/D8
Morón de la Frontera Spain 57 C2 37 07N 5 27W
Moroni Comoros 92 H5 11 40S 43 16E
Morpeth England 17 E4 55 10N 1 41W
Morte Point England 22 C3 51 10N 4 15W
Mosborough England 17 E2 53 19N 1 22W
Moscow Russia 70 F8 55 45N 37 42E
Mosel *r.* Germany/France 58 C4 50 00N 7 00E
Mossley NI 14 D1 54 42N 5 57W
Mossoró Brazil 114 K12 5 10S 37 18W
Mostar Bosnia-Herzegovina 61 G5 43 20N 17 50E
Móstoles Spain 57 D4 40 19N 3 53W
Mosul Iraq 72 D6 36 21N 43 08E
Motherwell Scotland 15 E2 55 48N 3 59W
Motril Spain 57 D2 36 45N 3 31W
Moulins France 56 F4 47 00N 3 48E
Mountain Ash Wales 18 C1 51 42N 3 24W
Mount Bellew RoI 24 C3 53 28N 8 30W
Mount Leinster RoI 25 E2 52 36N 6 42W
Mountmellick *tn.* RoI 25 D3 53 07N 7 20W
Mountrath RoI 25 D3 53 00N 7 27W
Mounts Bay England 22 B2 50 05N 5 30W
Mountshannon RoI 25 C2 52 56N 8 26W
Mountsorrel England 19 E2 52 44N 1 07W
Moura Portugal 57 B3 38 08N 7 27W
Mourne Mountains NI 14 C1 54 05N 6 05W
Mousehole England 22 B2 50 04N 5 34W
Moville RoI 24 D5 55 11N 7 03W
Moy NI 14 C1 54 27N 6 42W
Moycullen RoI 24 B3 53 20N 9 10W
Moygashel NI 14 C1 54 31N 6 46W
Moyle *district* NI 14 C2 55 10N 6 10W
Moyvore RoI 24 D3 53 22N 7 37W
MOZAMBIQUE 92 F3/G5
Much Wenlock England 19 D2 52 36N 2 34W
Muck *i.* Scotland 12 C1 56 50N 6 15W
Muckross RoI 25 B2 52 01N 9 29W
Muff RoI 24 D5 55 04N 7 16W
Muine Bheag RoI 25 E2 52 41N 6 58W
Muirkirk Scotland 15 E2 55 31N 4 04W
Muir of Ord Scotland 13 E2 57 31N 4 27W
Mulhacén *mt.* Spain 57 D2 37 04N 3 19W
Mülheim an der Ruhr Germany 54 E4 51 25N 6 50E
Mulhouse France 56 H4 47 45N 7 21E
Mulhuddart RoI 24 E3 53 24N 6 24W
Mulkear *r.* RoI 25 C2 52 38N 8 24W
Mull *i.* Scotland 12 D1 56 25N 6 00W
Mullet Peninsula RoI 24 A4 54 07N 10 05W
Mull Head Scotland 11 B2 59 20N 2 58W
Mullinahone RoI 25 D2 52 30N 7 30W
Mullinavat RoI 25 D2 52 22N 7 10W
Mullingar RoI 24 D3 53 32N 7 20W
Mullion England 22 B2 50 01N 5 14W
Mull of Galloway Scotland 14 E1 54 38N 4 55W
Mull of Kintyre Scotland 14 D2 55 17N 5 55W
Mull of Oa Scotland 14 C2 55 35N 6 20W
Mull, Sound of Scotland 12 D1 56 30N 6 00W
Multan Pakistan 74 C6 30 10N 71 36E
Mumbai India 74 C3 18 56N 72 51E
Mundesley England 21 E3 52 53N 1 26E
Munich Germany 58 E4 48 08N 11 35E
Münster Germany 58 C5 51 58N 7 37E
Murcia Spain 57 E2 37 59N 1 08W
Murmansk Russia 70 F10 68 59N 33 08E
Murray *r.* Australia 81 H3 35 30S 144 00E
Murray Bridge Australia 81 G3 35 10S 139 17E
Murton England 17 E3 54 49N 1 23W
Muş Turkey 63 F2 38 45N 41 30E
Muscat Oman 73 G3 23 37N 58 38E
Mushin Nigeria 90 E3 6 30N 3 15E
Musselburgh Scotland 15 F2 55 57N 3 04W
Mutare Zimbabwe 92 F4 18 58N 32 40E
Mutton Island *i.* RoI 25 B2 52 49N 9 31W
Mwanza Tanzania 93 C3 2 31S 32 56E
MYANMAR 79 B7
Mybster Scotland 13 F3 58 27N 3 25W
Mykolayiv Ukraine 63 D4 46 57N 32 00E
Mynydd Eppynt Wales 18 C2 52 02N 3 35W
Mynydd Preseli Wales 18 B1 51 58N 4 45W
Mytilíni Greece 61 M3 39 06N 26 34E
Mytishchi Russia 62 E6 55 54N 37 47E

N

Naas RoI 24 E3 53 13N 6 39W
Naestved Denmark 55 D2 55 14N 11 47E
Náfplio Greece 61 K2 37 34N 22 48E
Nagano Japan 78 C2 36 39N 138 10E
Nagasaki Japan 78 A1 32 45N 129 52E
Nagles Mountains RoI 25 C2 52 10N 8 25W
Nagoya Japan 78 C2 35 08N 136 53E
Nagpur India 74 D4 21 10N 79 12E
Nailsea England 23 E3 51 26N 2 46W
Nailsworth England 19 D1 51 42N 2 14W
Nairn Scotland 13 F2 57 35N 3 53W
Nairobi Kenya 93 E4 1 17S 36 50E
Namib Desert Namibia 92 B3/C2 22 00S 14 00E
NAMIBIA 92 C3
Nampula Mozambique 92 G4 15 09S 39 14E
Namur Belgium 54 C3 50 28N 4 52E
Nanchang China 77 L3 28 33N 115 58E
Nancy France 56 H5 48 42N 6 12E
Nanjing China 77 L4 32 03N 118 47E
Nantes France 56 D4 47 14N 1 35W
Nantwich England 16 D2 53 04N 2 32W
Naples Italy 60 F4 40 50N 14 15E
Naples USA 103 K2 26 09N 81 48W
Narberth Wales 18 B1 51 48N 4 45W
Narbonne France 56 F2 43 11N 3 00E
Narborough England 19 E2 52 35N 1 11W
Narvik Norway 55 E4 68 26N 17 25E
Naseby England 19 F2 52 23N 0 59W
Nashville USA 103 J4 36 10N 86 50W
Nassau Bahamas 107 J5 25 05N 77 20W
Nasser, Lake Egypt 91 M6 22 35N 31 40E
Nässjö Sweden 55 D2 57 40N 14 40E
Natal Brazil 114 K12 5 46S 35 15W
Natchez USA 103 H3 31 32N 91 24W
Naul RoI 24 E3 53 35N 6 17W
NAURU 116 G7
Navan RoI 24 E3 53 39N 6 41W
Navenby England 17 F2 53 06N 0 32W
Naver *r.* Scotland 13 E3 58 30N 4 10W
Ndjamena Chad 91 J4 12 10N 14 59E
Néapoli Greece 61 K2 36 31N 23 03E
Neath Wales 18 C1 51 40N 3 48W
Neath Port Talbot *u.a.* Wales 18 C1 51 37N 3 43W
Nebraska *state* USA 102 F5 42 00N 102 00W
Needham Market England 21 E3 52 09N 1 03E
Needles, The England 20 B1 50 39N 1 35W
Nefyn Wales 18 B2 52 56N 4 32W
Negro *r.* Brazil 114 D13 0 05S 67 00W
Neiva Colombia 114 B14 2 58N 75 15W
Nelson England 16 D2 53 51N 2 13W
Neman *r.* Lithuania/Russia 62 C5 55 00N 22 00E
Nenagh RoI 25 C2 52 52N 8 12W
Nene *r.* England 19 F2 52 25N 0 30W
Nene *r.* England 21 D3 52 45N 0 10E
NEPAL 74/75 E5/F5
Nephin *mt.* RoI 24 B4 54 01N 9 22W
Nephin Beg Range RoI 24 B3/B4 54 00N 9 34W
Nerva Spain 57 B2 37 41N 6 33W
Neston England 16 C2 53 18N 3 03W
NETHERLANDS 54 D5/E5
Nether Stowey England 23 D3 51 09N 3 10W
Netzahualcóyotl Mexico 106 E3 19 24N 99 02W
Neubrandenburg Germany 58 F6 53 33N 13 16E
Neuchâtel Switz. 58 C3 46 55N 6 56E
Neufchâteau France 56 G5 48 21N 5 42E
Neufchâtel-en-Bray France 56 E5 49 44N 1 26E
Neumünster Germany 58 D7 54 05N 9 59E
Neuruppin Germany 58 F6 52 56N 12 49E
Neuss Germany 58 C5 51 12N 6 42E
Neustrelitz Germany 58 F6 53 22N 13 05E
Nevada *state* USA 102 C4 39 00N 118 00W
Nevers France 56 F4 47 00N 3 09E
New Abbey Scotland 15 F1 54 59N 3 38W
New Alresford England 20 B2 51 06N 1 10W
Newark USA 103 M5 40 44N 74 24W
Newark-on-Trent England 17 F2 53 05N 0 49W
New Ash Green England 21 D2 51 21N 0 18E
Newbiggin-by-the-Sea England 17 E4 55 11N 1 30W
Newbridge Wales 18 C1 51 41N 3 09W
Newbridge-on-Wye Wales 18 C2 52 13N 3 27W
New Brunswick *prov.* Canada 101 X3 47 30N 66 00W
New Buildings NI 14 B1 54 56N 7 21W
Newburgh Scotland 13 F1 56 21N 3 15W
Newburn England 17 E3 54 59N 1 43W
Newbury England 20 B2 51 25N 1 20W
New Caledonia *i.* Pacific Ocean 81 M6/N6 22 00S 165 00E
Newcastle NI 14 D1 54 12N 5 54W
Newcastle Emlyn Wales 18 B2 52 02N 4 28W
Newcastle-under-Lyme England 16 D2 53 00N 2 14W
Newcastle upon Tyne England 17 E3 54 59N 1 35W
Newcastle West RoI 25 B2 52 27N 9 03W
New Cumnock Scotland 15 E2 55 24N 4 12W
New Deer Scotland 13 G2 57 30N 2 12W
New Delhi India 74 D5 28 37N 77 14E
Newfoundland *i.* Canada 101 Z3 48 15N 57 00W
Newfoundland and Labrador *prov.* Canada 101 Y5/AA3 52 30N 62 30W
New Galloway Scotland 15 E2 55 05N 4 10W
New Guinea *i.* Pacific Ocean 80/81 F10/J9 5 00S 141 00E
New Hampshire *state* USA 103 M5 43 00N 72 00W
New Haven USA 103 M5 41 18N 72 55W
New Holland England 17 F2 53 42N 0 22W
Newick England 20 D1 50 58N 0 01E
Newinn RoI 25 D2 52 26N 7 53W
New Jersey *state* USA 103 M4 40 00N 75 00W
New Liskeard Canada 101 V3 47 31N 79 41W
Newlyn England 22 B2 50 06N 5 34W
Newmachar Scotland 13 G2 57 16N 2 10W
Newmains Scotland 15 F2 55 47N 3 53W
Newmarket England 21 D3 52 15N 0 25E
Newmarket RoI 25 C2 52 13N 9 00W
Newmarket-on-Fergus RoI 25 C2 52 45N 8 53W
New Mexico *state* USA 102 E3 35 00N 107 00W
New Milton England 20 B1 50 46N 1 40W
New Orleans USA 103 H2 30 00N 90 03W
Newport Telford and Wrekin England 19 D2 52 47N 2 22W
Newport Isle of Wight England 20 B1 50 42N 1 18W
Newport Essex England 21 D2 51 58N 0 13E
Newport Mayo RoI 24 B3 53 53N 9 32W
Newport Tipperary RoI 25 C2 52 43N 8 25W
Newport Pembrokeshire Wales 18 B2 52 01N 4 50W
Newport Newport Wales 18 C1 51 35N 3 00W
Newport *u.a.* Wales 18 C1/D1 51 33N 3 00W
Newport Bay RoI 24 B3 53 51N 9 41W
Newport News USA 103 L4 36 59N 76 26W
Newport-on-Tay Scotland 13 G1 56 27N 2 56W
Newport Pagnell England 20 C3 52 05N 0 44W
Newquay England 22 B2 50 25N 5 05W
New Quay Wales 18 B2 52 13N 4 22W
New Radnor Wales 18 C2 52 15N 3 10W
New Romney England 21 D1 50 59N 0 57E
New Ross RoI 25 E2 52 24N 6 56W
New Rossington England 17 E2 53 29N 1 04W
Newry NI 14 C1 54 11N 6 20W
Newry and Mourne *district* NI 14 C1 54 10N 6 35W
New Sauchie Scotland 15 F3 56 08N 3 41W
New Scone Scotland 13 F1 56 25N 3 25W
Newton Abbot England 22 D2 50 32N 3 36W
Newton Aycliffe England 17 E3 54 37N 1 34W
Newton Mearns Scotland 15 E2 55 45N 4 18W
Newtonmore Scotland 13 E2 57 04N 4 08W
Newton Stewart Scotland 15 E1 54 57N 4 29W
Newtown RoI 25 D2 52 52N 7 07W
Newtown Wales 18 C2 52 32N 3 19W
Newtownabbey NI 14 D1 54 40N 5 54W
Newtownabbey *district* NI 14 C1/D1 54 40N 6 05W
Newtownards NI 14 D1 54 36N 5 41W
Newtown Cunningham RoI 24 D4 54 59N 7 31W
Newtownhamilton NI 14 C1 54 12N 6 35W
Newtownmountkennedy RoI 25 E3 53 06N 6 07W
Newtown St. Boswells Scotland 15 G2 55 34N 2 40W
Newtownstewart NI 14 B1 54 43N 7 24W
New Tredegar Wales 18 C1 51 44N 3 15W
New York USA 103 M5 40 40N 73 50W
New York *state* USA 103 L5 43 00N 76 00W
NEW ZEALAND 81
Neyland Wales 18 B1 51 43N 4 57W
Niagara Falls *tn.* Canada 105 E2 43 05N 79 06W
Niamey Niger 90 E4 13 32N 2 05E
NICARAGUA 107 G2
Nice France 56 H2 43 42N 7 16E
Nicobar Islands India 75 G1 8 30N 94 00E
Nicosia Cyprus 63 D2 35 11N 33 23E
Nienburg Germany 58 D6 52 38N 9 13E
NIGER 90 E5/G5
Niger *r.* West Africa 90 F3 5 30N 6 15E
NIGERIA 90 F4/G4
Nigg Scotland 13 G2 57 08N 2 03W
Nigg Bay Highland Scotland 13 E2 57 42N 4 01W
Nigg Bay Aberdeenshire Scotland 13 G2 57 08N 2 03W
Nijmegen Neths 54 D4 51 50N 5 52E
Nikopol' Ukraine 62 D4 45 34N 34 25E
Nile *r.* North Africa 91 M7 27 30N 31 40E
Nîmes France 56 G2 43 50N 4 21E
Niort France 56 D4 46 19N 0 27W
Niterói Brazil 114 J9 22 54S 43 06W
Nith *r.* Scotland 15 F2 55 20N 3 50W
Nizhniy Novgorod Russia 70 G8 56 20N 44 00E
Nordhausen Germany 58 E5 51 31N 10 48E
North Cape Norway 55 F5 71 11N 25 40E
Norfolk *co.* England 21 D3 52 45N 1 00E
Norfolk USA 103 L4 36 54N 76 18W
Norham England 15 G2 55 43N 2 10W
Normanton England 17 E2 53 42N 1 25W
Norrköping Sweden 55 E2 58 35N 16 10E
Northallerton England 17 E3 54 20N 1 26W
Northam England 22 C3 51 02N 4 14W
Northampton England 19 F2 52 14N 0 54W
Northamptonshire *co.* England 19 E2/F2 52 20N 1 00W
North Ayrshire *u.a.* Scotland 15 E2 55 30N 5 05W
North Baddesley England 20 B1 50 58N 1 27W
North Ballachulish Scotland 12 D1 56 42N 5 11W
North Berwick Scotland 15 G3 56 04N 2 44W
North Carolina *state* USA 103 L4 36 00N 80 00W
North Channel British Isles 14 D1/D2 55 20N 5 50W
North Dakota *state* USA 102/103 F6/G6 47 00N 102 00W
North Dorset Downs England 23 E2 50 40N 2 30W
North Down *co.* NI 14 D1 54 40N 5 40W
North Downs England 20 C2 51 13N 0 30W
North East Lincolnshire *u.a.* England 17 F2 53 30N 0 10W
Northern Ireland UK 14 B1/C1 54 40N 7 00W
NORTHERN MARIANAS 116 F9
North Foreland England 21 E2 51 23N 1 27E
North Hykeham England 17 F2 53 12N 0 34W
Northiam England 21 D1 50 59N 0 36E
North Island NZ 81 P3/Q3 39 00N 176 00E
North Kessock Scotland 13 E2 57 30N 4 15W
NORTH KOREA 77 N5/N6
North Lanarkshire *u.a.* Scotland 15 E2/F2 55 50N 3 55W
Northleach England 19 E1 51 51N 1 50W
North Lincolnshire *u.a.* England 17 F2 53 40N 0 40W

© Oxford University Press

North Petherton England	23	D3	51 06N	3 01W
North Pole Arctic Ocean	321		90 00N	
North Ronaldsay *i.* Scotland	11	B2	59 23N	2 26W
North Shields England	17	E4	55 01N	1 26W
North Somercotes England	17	G2	53 28N	0 08E
North Somerset *u.a.* England	23	E3	51 15N	2 50W
North Sound Rol	25	B3	53 11N	9 43W
North Sound, The Scotland	11	B2	59 17N	2 45W
North Tawton England	22	D2	50 48N	3 53W
North Tidworth England	20	B2	51 16N	1 40W
North Tipperary *co.* Rol	25	C2	52 45N	8 00W
North Uist *i.* Scotland	12	B2	57 04N	7 15W
Northumberland *co.* England	16	D4	55 10N	2 05W
North Walsham England	21	E3	52 50N	1 24E
Northwest Highlands Scotland	12/13	D2/E3	58 00N	5 00W
Northwest Territories *territory* Canada	100	L6/N6	65 15N	115 00W
North Wheatley England	17	F2	53 22N	0 52W
Northwich England	16	D2	53 16N	2 32W
North Wingfield England	17	E2	53 09N	1 24W
North York Moors England	17	F3	55 22N	0 45W
North Yorkshire *co.* England	17	E3/F3	54 10N	2 10W
Norton England	17	F3	54 08N	0 48W
NORWAY	55	C2/F4		
Norwich England	21	E3	52 38N	1 18E
Norwich USA	105	F2	41 32N	72 05W
Noss Head Scotland	13	F3	58 28N	3 04W
Nottingham England	19	E2	52 58N	1 10W
Nottingham *u.a.* England	19	E2	52 55N	1 10W
Nottinghamshire *co.* England	17	E2/F2	53 20N	1 00W
Nouadhibou Mauritania	90	A6	20 54N	17 01W
Nouakchott Mauritania	90	A5	18 09N	15 58W
Novara Italy	60	C6	45 27N	8 37E
Nova Scotia *prov.* Canada	101	Y2/Y3	44 30N	65 00W
Novgorod Russia	70	F8	58 30N	31 20E
Novi Sad Serbia	61	H6	45 15N	19 51E
Novosibirsk Russia	71	L8	55 04N	83 05E
Nubian Desert Sudan	91	M6	21 00N	33 00E
Nullarbor Plain Australia	80	E4	32 00S	128 00E
Nuneaton England	19	E2	52 32N	1 28W
Nuoro Italy	60	C4	40 20N	9 21E
Nuremberg Germany	58	E4	49 27N	11 05E
Nuuk Greenland	101	AA6	64 10N	51 40W
Nyasa, Lake Southern Africa	92	F5	12 00S	35 00E
Nykøbing Denmark	55	D1	54 47N	11 53E
Nyköping Sweden	55	E2	58 45N	17 03E
Nyons France	56	G3	44 22N	5 08E

O

Oadby England	19	E2	52 36N	1 04W
Oakengates England	19	D2	52 42N	2 28W
Oakham England	20	F2	52 40N	00 43W
Oakland USA	102	B4	37 50N	122 15W
Oakley England	20	B2	51 15N	1 11W
Oakley Scotland	15	F3	56 05N	3 35W
Ob' *r.* Russia	70	J10	65 30N	66 00E
Oban Scotland	12	D1	56 25N	5 29W
Oberhausen Germany	58	C5	51 27N	6 50E
Ob', Gulf of Russia	70	K10	68 00N	74 00E
O'Briensbridge Rol	25	C2	52 45N	8 30W
Ochil Hills Scotland	15	F3	56 15N	3 30W
Odda Norway	55	C3	60 03N	6 34E
Oddsta Scotland	11	D3	60 37N	0 59W
Odense Denmark	55	D2	55 24N	10 25E
Oder *r.* Europe	58	G6	52 00N	15 30E
Odessa Ukraine	63	D4	46 30N	30 46E
Offaly *co.* Rol	24	D3	53 15N	7 35W
Offenbach am Main Germany	58	D5	50 06N	8 46E
Offenburg Germany	58	C4	48 29N	7 57E
Ohio *state* USA	103	K5	40 00N	83 00W
Ohio *r.* USA	103	J4	38 00N	86 00W
Oilgate Rol	25	E2	52 25N	6 32W
Ōita Japan	78	B1	33 15N	131 36E
Okehampton England	22	C2	50 44N	4 00W
Oklahoma *state* USA	103	G4	36 00N	98 00W
Oklahoma City USA	103	G4	35 28N	97 33W
Öland *i.* Sweden	55	E2	56 45N	51 50E
Olbia Italy	60	C4	40 56N	9 30E
Oldbury England	19	D2	52 30N	2 00W
Oldcastle Rol	24	D3	53 46N	7 10W
Oldenburg Germany	58	D6	53 08N	8 13E
Old Fletton England	20	C3	52 34N	0 12W
Oldham England	16	D2	53 33N	2 07W
Old Head of Kinsale *c.* Rol	25	C1	51 40N	8 30W
Oldmeldrum Scotland	13	G2	57 20N	2 20W
Olhâo Portugal	57	B2	37 01N	7 50W
Ollerton England	17	E2	53 12N	1 00W
Olney England	20	C3	52 09N	0 43W
Olsztyn Poland	59	K6	53 48N	20 29E
Olten Switz.	58	C3	47 22N	7 55E
Ólympos *mt.* Greece	61	J4	40 05N	22 21E
Omagh NI	14	B1	54 36N	7 18W
Omagh *district* NI	14	B1	54 30N	7 30W
Omaha USA	103	G5	41 15N	96 00W
OMAN	73	F2/G3		
Oman, Gulf of Iran/Oman	73	G3	24 30N	58 30E
Omdurman Sudan	91	M5	15 37N	32 29E
Omeath Rol	24	E4	54 06N	6 17W
Omsk Russia	70	K8	55 00N	73 22E
Ōmuta Japan	78	B1	33 02N	130 26E
Onezhskoye Ozero *l.* Russia	70	F9	62 00N	40 00E
Ontario *prov.* Canada	101	S4/U4	51 00N	91 00W
Ontario, Lake Canada/USA	105	E2	43 45N	78 00W
Oola Rol	25	C2	52 33N	8 16W
Oostende Belgium	54	A4	51 13N	2 55E
Opava Czech Rep.	59	H4	49 58N	17 55E
Opole Poland	59	H5	50 40N	17 56E
Oporto Portugal	57	A4	41 09N	8 37W
Oran Algeria	90	D9	35 45N	0 38W
Orange France	56	G3	44 08N	4 48E
Oranmore Rol	24	C3	53 16N	8 54W
Orbetello Italy	60	D5	42 27N	11 07E
Örebro Sweden	55	E2	59 17N	15 13E
Oregon *state* USA	102	B5/C5	44 00N	120 00W
Oregon City USA	102	B6	45 21N	122 36W
Orel Russia	70	F7	52 58N	36 04E
Orenburg Russia	70	H7	51 50N	55 00E
Orense Spain	57	B5	42 20N	7 52W
Orford England	21	E3	52 06N	1 31E
Orihuela Spain	57	E3	38 05N	0 56W
Orinoco *r.* Venezuela	114	E15	8 00N	64 00W
Oristano Italy	60	C3	39 54N	8 36E
Orkney Islands *u.a.* Scotland	11	A1/B2	59 00N	3 00W
Orlando USA	103	K2	28 33N	81 21W
Orléans France	56	E4	47 54N	1 54E
Ormskirk England	16	D2	53 35N	2 54W
Oronsay *i.* Scotland	14	C3	56 00N	6 15W
Orrell England	16	D2	53 33N	2 45W
Orsha Belarus	62	D5	54 30N	30 23E
Orthez France	56	D2	43 29N	0 46W
Ortigueira Spain	57	B5	43 43N	8 13W
Ortona Italy	60	F5	42 21N	14 24E
Oruro Bolivia	114	D10	17 59S	67 08W
Orvieto Italy	60	E5	42 43N	12 06E
Orwell *r.* England	21	E3	52 00N	1 15E
Ōsaka Japan	78	C1	34 40N	135 30E
Oshawa Canada	101	V2	43 53N	78 51W
Oslo Norway	55	D2	59 56N	10 45E
Osmaniye Turkey	63	E2	37 04N	36 15E
Osnabrück Germany	58	D6	52 17N	8 03E
Osorno Chile	115	C5	40 35S	73 14W
Ossett England	17	E2	53 41N	1 35W
Östersund Sweden	55	D3	63 10N	14 40E
Östervall Sweden	55	E3	62 20N	15 20E
Ostrava Czech Rep.	59	J4	49 50N	18 15E
Oswaldtwistle England	16	D2	53 44N	2 24W
Oswestry England	18	C2	52 52N	3 03W
Otford England	21	D2	51 19N	0 12E
Otley England	17	E2	53 54N	1 41W
Otranto Italy	61	H4	40 08N	18 30E
Ottawa Canada	101	V3	45 24N	75 38W
Otterburn England	16	D4	55 14N	2 10W
Ottery St. Mary England	23	D2	50 45N	3 17W
Ouagadougou Burkina	90	D4	12 20N	1 40W
Oughterard Rol	24	B3	53 26N	9 19W
Oulart Rol	25	E2	53 30N	6 23W
Oulu Finland	55	G4	65 02N	25 27E
Oundle England	19	F2	52 29N	0 29W
Ouse *r.* North Yorkshire England	17	E3	54 05N	1 15W
Ouse *r.* East Sussex England	20	D1	50 55N	0 03E
Outer Hebrides *is.* Scotland	12	B2/B3	58 00N	7 00W
Outwell England	21	D3	52 37N	0 14E
Overton England	20	B2	51 15N	1 15W
Overton Wales	18	D2	52 58N	2 56W
Oviedo Spain	57	C5	43 21N	7 18W
Owen Sound Canada	101	U2	44 3N	80 56W
Oxford England	20	B2	51 46N	1 15W
Oxfordshire *co.* England	20	B2	51 50N	1 25W
Oxted England	20	C2	51 15N	0 01W
Oysterhaven Rol	25	C1	51 41N	8 26W
Ozero Balkhash *l.* Kazakhstan	70	K6	46 00N	75 00E
Ozero Baykal *l.* Russia	71	N7	54 00N	109 00E
Ozieri Italy	60	C4	40 35N	9 01E

P

Pacific Ocean	116			
Padang Indonesia	79	C3	1 00S	100 21E
Paddock Wood *tn.* England	21	D2	51 11N	0 23E
Paderborn Germany	58	D5	51 43N	8 44E
Padiham England	16	D2	53 49N	2 19W
Padstow England	22	C2	50 33N	4 56W
Padua Italy	60	D6	45 24N	11 53E
Paisley Scotland	15	E2	55 50N	4 26W
PAKISTAN	74	B5/C5		
PALAU	116	D8	7 30N	134 30E
Palawan *i.* Philippines	79	F5/F6	10 00N	119 00E
Palembang Indonesia	79	C3	2 59S	104 45E
Palencia Spain	57	C3	41 01N	4 32W
Palermo Italy	60	E3	38 08N	13 23E
Palma de Mallorca Spain	57	G3	39 35N	2 39E
Palmer USA	100	F6	61 35N	149 10W
Palmyra Syria	72	C5	34 40N	38 10E
Pamiers France	56	E2	43 07N	1 36E
Pampas *geog. reg.* Argentina	115	E6	36 00S	63 00W
Pamplona Spain	57	E5	42 49N	1 39W
PANAMA	107	H1/J1		
Panama Canal Panama	107	J1	9 00N	80 00W
Panama City Panama	107	J1	8 57N	19 30W
Pangbourne England	20	B2	51 29N	1 05W
Papa Sound Scotland	11	B2	59 20N	2 54W
Papa, Sound of Scotland	11	C3	60 37N	1 40W
Papa Stour *i.* Scotland	11	C3	60 20N	1 42W
Papa Westray *i.* Scotland	11	B2	59 22N	2 54W
PAPUA NEW GUINEA	81	H9/K9		
PARAGUAY	114	F9		
Paraguay *r.* Paraguay/Argentina	114	F8	26 30S	58 00W
Paramaribo Suriname	114	F15	5 52N	55 14W
Parana Argentina	115	E7	31 45S	60 30W
Paraná *r.* Paraguay/Argentina	114	F7	27 00S	56 00W
Paris France	56	F5	48 52N	2 20E
Parkano Finland	55	F3	62 03N	23 00E
Parma Italy	60	D6	44 48N	10 19E
Parnaíba Brazil	114	J13	2 58S	41 46W
Páros Greece	61	L2	37 04N	25 06E
Parrett *r.* England	23	E3	51 05N	2 54W
Parthenay France	56	D4	46 39N	0 14W
Partry Rol	24	B3	53 42N	9 16W
Partry Mountains Rol	24	B3	53 39N	9 27W
Paşcani Romania	59	N3	47 14N	26 46E
Passage East Rol	25	E2	52 13N	6 59W
Passage West *tn.* Rol	25	C1	51 52N	8 20W
Passau Germany	58	F4	48 35N	13 28E
Pasto Colombia	114	B14	1 12N	77 17W
Patagonia *geog. reg.* Argentina	115	C2/D4	48 00S	70 00W
Pateley Bridge *tn.* England	17	E3	54 05N	1 45W
Patna Scotland	15	E2	55 20N	4 30W
Patna India	75	F5	25 37N	85 12E
Patras Greece	61	J3	38 14N	21 44E
Patrickswell Rol	25	C2	52 36N	8 42W
Patrington England	17	F2	53 41N	0 02W
Pau France	56	D2	43 18N	0 22W
Pavia Italy	60	C6	45 12N	9 09E
Pavullo nel Frignano Italy	60	D6	44 20N	10 49E
Peacehaven England	20	C1	50 47N	0 01E
Peč Kosovo	61	J5	42 40N	20 19E
Pécs Hungary	59	J3	46 04N	18 15E
Peebles Scotland	15	F2	55 39N	3 12W
Peel Isle of Man	16	B3	54 14N	4 42W
Pelopónnisos *geog. reg.* Greece	61	J2/K2	37 00N	22 00E
Pelotas Brazil	115	G7	31 45S	52 20W
Pembridge England	18	D2	52 14N	2 53W
Pembroke Wales	18	B1	51 41N	4 55W
Pembroke Dock Wales	18	B1	51 42N	4 56W
Pembrokeshire *u.a.* Wales	18	A1/B1	51 50N	5 00W
Pembury England	21	D2	51 08N	0 19E
Penarth Wales	18	C1	51 27N	3 11W
Pencoed Wales	18	C1	51 31N	3 30W
Pendine Wales	18	B1	51 34N	4 35W
Penicuik Scotland	15	F2	55 50N	3 14W
Penistone England	17	E2	53 32N	1 37W
Penkridge England	19	D2	52 44N	2 07W
Penmaenmawr Wales	18	C3	53 16N	3 54W
Pennines England	16/17	D3/E2	54 30N	2 10W
Pennsylvania *state* USA	103	L5	41 00N	78 00W
Penrhyndeudraeth Wales	18	B2	52 56N	4 04W
Penrith England	16	D3	54 40N	2 44W
Penryn England	22	B2	50 09N	5 06W
Pensilva England	22	C2	50 30N	4 25W
Pentland Firth Scotland	11	A1	58 45N	3 10W
Pentland Hills Scotland	15	F2	55 45N	3 30W
Pen-y-ghent *sum.* England	16	D3	54 10N	2 14W
Penygroes Wales	18	B3	53 04N	4 17W
Penzance England	22	B2	50 07N	5 33W
Périgueux France	56	E3	45 12N	0 44E
Perm' Russia	70	H8	58 01N	56 10E
Pernik Bulgaria	61	K5	42 36N	23 03E
Péronne France	56	F5	49 56N	2 57E
Perpignan France	56	F2	42 42N	2 54E
Perranporth England	22	B2	50 20N	5 09W
Perth Australia	80	C4	31 58S	115 49E
Perth Scotland	13	F1	56 42N	3 28W
Perth and Kinross *u.a.* Scotland	13	F1	56 45N	3 50W
PERU	114	B11/C11		
Perugia Italy	60	E5	43 07N	12 23E
Pesaro Italy	60	E5	43 54N	12 54E
Pescara Italy	60	F5	42 27N	14 13E
Peshawar Pakistan	74	C6	34 01N	71 40E
Pessac France	56	D3	44 49N	0 37W
Peterborough England	20	C3	52 35N	0 15W
Peterculter Scotland	13	G2	57 05N	2 16W
Peterhead Scotland	13	H2	57 30N	1 46W
Peterlee England	17	E3	54 46N	1 19W
Petersfield England	20	C2	51 00N	0 56W
Petrolina Brazil	114	J12	9 22S	40 30W
Petworth England	20	C1	50 59N	0 38W
Pevensey England	21	D1	50 49N	0 20E
Pewsey England	20	B2	51 21N	1 46W
Pforzheim Germany	58	D4	48 53N	8 41E
Phenix City USA	103	J3	32 28N	85 01W
Philadelphia USA	103	L4	40 00N	75 10W
PHILIPPINES, THE	79	G7/H5		
Phnom Penh Cambodia	79	C6	11 35N	104 55E
Phoenix USA	102	D3	33 30N	112 03W
Piacenza Italy	60	C6	45 03N	9 41E
Pickering England	17	F3	54 14N	0 46W
Píndhos *mts.* Greece	61	J3	40 00N	21 00E
Pinsk Belarus	63	C5	52 08N	26 01E
Pinwherry Scotland	14	E2	55 09N	4 50W
Piombino Italy	60	D5	42 56N	10 32E
Pirineos *mts.* Spain/France	57	E5/F5	42 50N	0 30E
Pirmasens Germany	58	C4	49 12N	7 37E
Pisa Italy	60	D5	43 43N	10 24E
Pistoia Italy	60	D5	43 56N	10 55E
Piteå Sweden	55	F4	65 19N	21 30E
Piteşti Romania	59	M2	44 51N	24 51E
Pitlochry Scotland	13	F1	56 43N	3 45W
Pitmedden Scotland	13	G2	57 19N	2 11W
Pittenweem Scotland	15	G3	56 13N	2 44W
Pittsburgh USA	103	L5	40 26N	80 00W
Piura Peru	114	A12	5 15S	80 38W
Planalto de Mato Grosso *geog. reg.* Brazil	114	F11/G11	13 00S	56 00W
Plasencia Spain	57	B4	40 02N	6 05W
Platte *r.* USA	102	F5	41 00N	100 00W
Plauen Germany	58	F5	50 29N	12 08E
Pleven Bulgaria	61	L5	43 25N	24 04E
Płock Poland	59	J6	52 32N	19 40E
Plockton Scotland	12	D2	57 20N	5 40W
Ploieşti Romania	59	M2	44 57N	26 01E
Plovdiv Bulgaria	61	L5	42 08N	24 45E
Plymouth England	22	C2	50 23N	4 10W
Plympton England	22	C2	50 23N	4 03W
Plymstock England	22	C2	50 21N	4 07W
Plynlimon *mt.* Wales	18	C2	52 28N	3 47W
Plzeň Czech Rep.	58	F4	49 45N	13 25E
Po *r.* Italy	60	D6	45 00N	10 00E
Pocklington England	17	F2	53 56N	0 46W
Podgorica Montenegro	61	H5	42 28N	19 17E
Point-Noire *tn.* Congo	92	B7	4 46S	11 53E
Poitiers France	56	E4	46 35N	0 20E
POLAND	59	J6/K6		
Polegate England	21	D1	50 50N	0 15E
Polesworth England	19	E2	52 44N	1 36W
Policoro Italy	61	G4	40 12N	16 40E
Pollensa Spain	57	G3	39 52N	3 01E
Polperro England	22	C2	50 19N	4 31W
Polýgyros Greece	61	K4	40 23N	23 25E
Pondicherry India	74	D2	11 59N	79 50E
Ponferrada Spain	57	B5	42 33N	6 35W
Pont *r.* England	16	E4	55 02N	1 55W
Ponta Grossa Brazil	114	G8	25 07S	50 09W
Pont-à-Mousson France	56	H5	48 55N	6 03E
Pontardawe Wales	18	C1	51 44N	3 52W
Pontardulais Wales	18	B1	51 43N	4 02W
Pontefract England	17	E2	53 42N	1 18W
Ponteland England	17	E4	55 03N	1 44W
Ponte Leccia France	56	J2	42 28N	9 12E
Ponterwyd Wales	18	C2	52 25N	3 50W
Pontevedra Spain	57	A5	42 25N	8 39W
Pontivy France	56	C5	48 04N	2 58W
Pontrilas England	18	D1	51 57N	2 53W
Pontyclun Wales	18	C1	51 33N	3 23W
Pontycymer Wales	18	C1	51 36N	3 35W
Pontypool Wales	18	C1	51 43N	3 02W
Pontypridd Wales	18	C1	51 37N	3 22W
Poole England	23	F2	50 43N	1 59W
Poole *u.a.* England	23	F2	50 43N	1 59W
Poole Bay *b.* England	23	F3	50 41N	1 52W
Poolewe Scotland	12	D2	57 45N	5 37W
Pooley Bridge *tn.* England	16	D3	54 38N	2 49W
Popacatepetl *mt.* Mexico	106	E3	19 02N	98 38W
Pordenone Italy	60	E6	45 58N	12 39E
Pori Finland	55	F3	61 28N	21 45E
Porlock England	22	D3	51 14N	3 36W
Portadown NI	14	C1	54 26N	6 27W
Portaferry NI	14	D1	54 23N	5 33W
Portalegre Portugal	57	B3	39 17N	7 25W
Portarlington Rol	25	D3	53 10N	7 11W
Port Askaig Scotland	14	C2	55 51N	6 07W
Port-au-Prince Haiti	107	K3	18 33N	72 20W
Portavogie NI	14	D1	54 28N	5 25W
Port Elizabeth RSA	92	E1	33 58S	25 36E
Port Ellen Scotland	14	C2	55 39N	6 12W
Port Erin Isle of Man	16	B3	54 05N	4 45W
Port-Eynon Wales	18	B1	51 28N	4 12W
Port Gentil Gabon	92	A7	0 40S	8 50E
Port Glasgow Scotland	15	E2	55 56N	4 41W

Portglenone NI 14 C1 54 52N 6 29W
Port Harcourt Nigeria 90 F2 4 43N 7 05E
Porthcawl Wales 18 C1 51 29N 3 43W
Porthleven England 22 BB2 50 30N 5 21W
Porthmadog Wales 18 B2 52 55N 4 08W
Portimaõ Portugal 57 A2 37 08N 8 32W
Port Isaac England 22 C2 50 35N 4 49W
Portishead England 23 E3 51 30N 2 46W
Portknockie Scotland 13 G2 57 42N 2 52W
Portland USA 102 B6 45 32N 122 40W
Portlaoise RoI 25 D3 53 02N 7 17W
Portlaw RoI 25 D2 52 17N 7 19W
Portlethen Scotland 13 G2 57 03N 2 07W
Portmahomack Scotland 13 F2 57 49N 3 50W
Port Moresby PNG 81 J9 9 30S 147 07E
Portnaguran Scotland 12 C3 58 17N 6 13W
Portnahaven Scotland 14 C2 55 41N 6 30W
Porto Alegre Brazil 115 G7 30 03S 51 10W
Port of Ness Scotland 12 C3 58 29N 6 13W
Port of Spain Trinidad and Tobago 107 V15 10 38N 61 31W
Porto Novo Benin 90 E3 6 30N 2 47E
Porto Tórres Italy 60 C4 40 51N 8 24E
Porto-Vecchio France 56 J1 41 35N 9 16E
Pôrto Velho Brazil 114 E12 8 45S 63 54W
Portpatrick Scotland 14 D2 54 51N 5 07W
Portreath England 22 B2 50 51N 5 17W
Portree Scotland 12 C2 57 24N 6 12W
Portrush NI 14 C2 55 12N 6 40W
Port Said Egypt 91 M8 31 17N 6 40W
Portskerra Scotland 13 F3 58 33N 3 55W
Portsmouth England 20 B1 50 48N 1 05W
Portsmouth *u.a.* England 20 B1 50 48N 1 05W
Portsmouth USA 103 L4 36 50N 76 20W
Portsoy Scotland 13 G2 57 41N 2 41W
Portstewart NI 14 C2 55 11N 6 43W
Port Sudan Egypt 91 N5 19 38N 37 07E
Port Talbot Wales 18 C1 51 36N 3 47W
PORTUGAL 57 A3/B3
Portumna RoI 25 C3 53 06N 8 13W
Port Wemyss Scotland 14 C2 55 42N 6 29W
Port William Scotland 15 E1 54 46N 4 35W
Potenza Italy 60 F4 40 38N 15 48E
Potomac *r.* USA 103 L4 39 10N 77 30W
Potsdam Germany 58 F6 52 24N 13 04E
Potter's Bar England 20 C2 51 42N 0 11W
Potton England 20 C3 52 08N 0 14W
Poulton-le-Fylde England 16 D2 53 51N 3 00W
Powell River *tn.* Canada 100 L3 49 54N 124 34W
Power Head RoI 25 C1 51 47N 8 10W
Powfoot Scotland 15 F1 54 59N 3 20W
Powys *u.a.* Wales 18 C2 52 10N 3 30W
Poznań Poland 59 H6 52 25N 16 53E
Prague Czech Rep. 58 G5 50 06N 14 26E
Prato Italy 60 D5 43 53N 11 06E
Prawle Point England 22 D2 50 12N 3 44W
Preesall England 16 D2 53 55N 2 57W
Prešov Slovakia 59 K4 49 00N 21 10E
Prestatyn Wales 18 C3 53 20N 3 24W
Presteigne Wales 18 C2 52 17N 3 00W
Preston England 16 D2 53 46N 2 42W
Prestonpans Scotland 15 G2 55 57N 3 00W
Prestwich England 16 D2 53 32N 2 17W
Prestwick Scotland 15 E2 55 30N 4 37W
Pretoria RSA 92 E2 25 45S 28 12E
Příbram Czech Rep. 58 G4 49 42N 14 01E
Prince Albert Canada 101 P4 53 13N 105 45W
Prince Edward Island *prov.* Canada 101 Y3 46 30N 63 00W
Prince Rupert Canada 100 J4 54 09N 130 20W
Princes Risborough England 20 C2 51 44N 0 51W
Princetown England 22 D2 50 33N 3 59W
Pripyats' *r.* Belarus 62 B5/C5 52 30N 27 00E
Priština Kosovo 61 J5 42 39N 21 20E
Privas France 56 G3 44 44N 4 36E
Prokop'yevsk Russia 71 L7 53 55N 86 45E
Providence USA 103 M5 41 50N 71 28W
Provins France 56 F5 48 34N 3 18E
Prudhoe England 17 E3 54 58N 1 51W
Prudhoe Bay *tn.* USA 100 F8 70 05N 148 20W
Pruszków Poland 59 K6 52 10N 20 47E
Prut *r.* Romania 59 P3 47 00N 28 00E
Pskov Russia 70 E8 57 48N 28 26E
Pucallpa Peru 114 C12 8 21S 74 33W
Puddletown England 23 E2 50 45N 2 21W
Pudsey England 17 E2 53 48N 1 40W
Puebla Mexico 106 E3 19 03N 98 10W
Pueblo USA 102 F4 38 17N 104 38W
Puertollano Spain 57 C3 38 41N 4 07W
Puerto Montt Chile 115 C5 41 28S 73 00W
PUERTO RICO 107 L3
Pulborough England 20 C1 50 58N 0 30W
Pumsaint Wales 18 C2 52 03N 3 58W
Pune India 74 C3 18 34N 73 58E
Punta Arenas Chile 115 C3 53 10S 70 56W
Purfleet England 21 D2 51 29N 0 14E
Puri India 75 F3 19 49N 85 54E
Pusan S. Korea 77 N5 35 05N 129 02E
Puulavesi *l.* Finland 55 G3 61 50N 26 40E
Pwllheli Wales 18 B2 52 53N 4 25W
Pyle Wales 18 C1 51 32N 3 42W
Pyongyang N. Korea 77 N5 39 00N 125 47E
Pyrénées *mts.* France/Spain 56 E2 42 50N 0 30E
Pýrgos Greece 61 J2 37 40N 21 27E
Pýrgos Greece 61 L1 35 00N 25 10E

Q

QATAR 73 F4
Qingdao China 77 M5 36 04N 120 22E
Qiqihar China 77 M7 47 23N 124 00E
Quantock Hills England 23 D3 51 10N 3 15W
Québec *prov.* Canada 101 V4/X4 50 00N 75 00W
Québec Canada 101 W3 46 50N 71 15W
Queenborough England 21 D2 51 26N 0 45E
Queen Charlotte Islands Canada 100 J4 53 00N 132 30W
Queen Elizabeth Islands Canada 101 N9/S9 77 30N 105 00W
Queensbury England 17 E2 53 46N 1 50W
Queenstown Australia 81 J2 42 07S 145 33E
Querétaro Mexico 106 D4 20 38N 100 23W
Quetta Pakistan 74 B6 30 15N 67 00E
Quezon City Philippines 79 G6 14 39N 121 02E
Quiberon France 56 C4 47 29N 3 07W
Quigley's Point RoI 24 D5 55 10N 7 08W
Quimper France 56 B4 48 00N 4 06W
Quito Ecuador 114 B13 0 14S 78 30W
Quorn England 19 E2 52 45N 1 10W

R

Raahe Finland 55 F3 64 42N 24 30E
Raasay *i.* Scotland 12 C2 57 25N 6 05W
Rabat-Salé Morocco 90 C8 34 02N 6 51W
Radcliffe England 16 D2 53 34N 2 20W
Radcliffe on Trent England 19 E3 52 57N 1 03W
Radlett England 20 C2 51 41N 0 19W
Radom Poland 59 K5 51 26N 21 10E
Radstadt Austria 58 F3 47 23N 13 28E
Radstock England 23 E3 51 18N 2 28W
Raglan Wales 18 D1 51 47N 2 51W
Ragusa Italy 60 F2 36 56N 14 44E
Rainford England 16 D2 53 30N 2 48W
Rainier, Mount USA 102 B6 46 25N 121 45W
Rainworth England 17 E2 53 08N 1 08W
Raipur India 74 E4 21 16N 81 42E
Rame Head England 22 C2 50 19N 4 13W
Ramore Head NI 14 C2 55 13N 6 39W
Ramsbottom England 16 D2 53 39N 2 19W
Ramsey England 20 C3 52 27N 0 07W
Ramsey Isle of Man 16 B3 54 19N 4 23W
Ramsey Island Wales 18 A1 51 53N 5 20W
Ramsgate England 21 E2 51 20N 1 25E
Randalstown NI 14 C1 54 45N 6 19W
Rangpur Bangladesh 75 F5 25 45N 89 21E
Rannoch Moor Scotland 13 E1 56 35N 4 50W
Rannoch Station Scotland 13 E1 5642N 4 34W
Rapallo Italy 60 C6 44 21N 9 13E
Raphoe RoI 24 D4 54 52N 7 36W
Rastatt Germany 58 D4 48 51N 8 13E
Rathangan RoI 24 E3 53 12N 6 59W
Rathcoole RoI 24 E3 53 17N 6 28W
Rathcormack RoI 25 C2 52 05N 8 17W
Rathdowney RoI 25 D2 52 51N 7 35W
Rathdrum RoI 25 E2 52 56N 6 13W
Rathfriland NI 14 C1 54 14N 6 10W
Rathkeale RoI 25 C2 52 32N 8 56W
Rathlackan RoI 24 B4 54 18N 9 15W
Rathlin Sound NI 14 C2 55 20N 6 25W
Rath Luirc RoI 25 C2 52 21N 8 41W
Rathmelton RoI 24 D5 55 02N 7 38W
Rathmore RoI 25 B2 52 05N 9 13W
Rathnew RoI 25 E2 52 58N 6 05W
Rathvilly RoI 25 E2 52 53N 6 41W
Ratoath RoI 24 E3 53 31N 6 24W
Raton USA 102 F4 36 45N 104 27W
Rattray Scotland 13 F1 56 36N 3 20W
Rattray Head Scotland 13 H2 57 38N 1 45W
Rauma Finland 55 F3 61 09N 21 30E
Raunds England 19 F2 52 21N 0 33W
Ravenglass England 16 C3 54 21N 3 24W
Ravenna Italy 60 E6 44 25N 12 12E
Ravensburg Germany 58 D3 47 47N 9 37E
Ravenshead England 17 E2 53 40N 1 10W
Rawalpindi Pakistan 74 C6 33 40N 73 08E
Rawmarsh England 17 E2 53 27N 1 21W
Rawtenstall England 16 D2 53 42N 2 18W
Rayleigh England 21 D2 51 36N 0 36E
Reading England 20 C2 51 28N 0 59W
Reading *u.a.* England 20 B1/C1 50 25N 1 00W
Reay Forest Scotland 13 E3 58 30N 4 55W
Recife Brazil 114 L12 8 06S 34 53W
Recklinghausen Germany 58 C5 51 37N 7 11E
Red Bay NI 14 C2 55 04N 6 01W
Redbourn England 20 C2 51 48N 0 24W
Redbridge England 20 D2 51 34N 0 05E
Redcar England 17 E3 54 37N 1 04W
Redcar and Cleveland *u.a.* England 17 E3/F3 54 30N 1 00W
Redditch England 19 E2 52 19N 1 56W
Redhill *tn.* England 20 C2 51 14N 0 11W
Redon France 56 C4 47 39N 2 05W
Redruth England 22 B2 50 13N 5 14W
Red Sea Middle East 72 C4/C2 27 00N 35 00E
Reepham England 21 E3 52 46N 1 07E
Regensburg Germany 58 F4 49 01N 12 07E
Reggio di Calabria Italy 60 F3 38 06N 15 39E
Regina Canada 101 Q4 50 30N 104 38W
Reigate England 20 C2 51 14N 0 13W
Reims France 56 G5 49 15N 4 02E
Reinosa Spain 57 C3 43 01N 4 09W
Rendsburg Germany 58 D7 54 19N 9 39E
Renfrew Canada 101 V3 45 28N 76 44W
Renfrew Scotland 15 E2 55 53N 4 24W
Renfrewshire *u.a.* Scotland 15 E2 55 50N 4 40W
Rennes France 56 D5 48 06N 1 40W
Reno USA 102 C4 39 32N 119 49W
REPUBLIC OF IRELAND 24/25
REPUBLIC OF SOUTH AFRICA 92 D1/D2
Requena Spain 57 E3 39 29N 1 08W
Resistencia Argentina 115 F8 27 28S 59 00W
Resolute Canada 101 S8 74 40N 95 00W
Retford England 17 F2 53 19N 0 56W
Rethel France 56 G5 49 31N 4 22E
Reus Spain 57 F4 41 10N 1 06E
Reutlingen Germany 58 D4 48 30N 9 13E
Reykjavík Iceland 55 K6 64 09N 21 58W
Rhayader Wales 18 C2 52 18N 3 30W
Rheden Neths 54 E5 52 01N 6 02E
Rheidol *r.* Wales 18 C2 52 23N 3 55W
Rhein *r.* Germany 58 C4 50 30N 8 00E
Rheine Germany 58 C6 52 17N 7 26E
Rhode Island *state* USA 103 M5 41 00N 71 00W
Rhondda Wales 18 C1 51 40N 3 30W
Rhondda Cynon Taff *u.a.* Wales 18 C1 51 40N 3 30W
Rhône *r.* Switz./France 56 G3 45 00N 4 50E
Rhoose Wales 18 C1 51 26N 3 22W
Rhosllanerchrugog Wales 18 C3 53 01N 3 04W
Rhosneigr Wales 18 B3 53 14N 4 31W
Rhossili Wales 18 B1 51 34N 4 17W
Rhubodach Scotland 14 D2 55 56N 5 09W
Rhum *i.* Scotland 12 C2 57 00N 6 20W
Rhyl Wales 18 C3 53 19N 3 29W
Rhymney Wales 18 C1 51 46N 3 18W
Rhynie Scotland 13 G2 57 19N 2 50W
Ribble *r.* England 16 D2 53 45N 2 30W
Ribeirão Prêto Brazil 114 H9 21 09S 47 48W
Riccall England 17 E2 53 51N 1 04W
Richhill NI 14 C1 54 22N 6 33W
Richmond England 17 E3 54 24N 1 44W
Richmond upon Thames England 20 C2 51 28N 0 19W
Rickmansworth England 20 C2 51 38N 0 29W
Ried Austria 58 F4 48 13N 13 29E
Riesa Germany 58 F5 51 18N 13 18E
Rieti Italy 60 E5 42 24N 12 51E
Riga Latvia 55 F2 56 53N 24 08E
Rimini Italy 60 E6 44 03N 12 34E
Ringabella Bay RoI 25 C1 51 46N 8 13W
Ringaskiddy RoI 25 C1 51 49N 8 18W
Ringwood England 20 B1 50 51N 1 47W
Rio Branco *tn.* Brazil 114 D12 9 59S 67 49W
Rio de Janeiro *tn.* Brazil 114 I8 22 53S 43 17W
Rio de la Plata *est.* Uruquay/Argentina 115 F5 35 00S 57 00W
Rio Grande *tn.* Brazil 115 G7 32 03S 52 08W
Río Grande *r.* Mexico/USA 102 E3/F3 30 00N 105 00W
Ripley England 17 E2 53 03N 1 24W
Ripon England 17 E3 54 08N 1 31W
Risca Wales 18 C1 51 37N 3 07W
Rishton England 16 D2 53 47N 2 24W
Riva del Garda Italy 60 D6 45 53N 10 50E
Riverton Canada 101 R4 51 00N 97 00W
Rivne Ukraine 59 M5 50 39N 26 10E
Riyadh Saudi Arabia 73 E3 24 39N 46 46E
Roanne France 56 G4 46 02N 4 05E
Robin Hood's Bay *tn.* England 17 F3 54 25N 0 33W
Rochdale England 16 D2 53 38N 2 09W
Rochefort France 56 D3 45 57N 0 58W
Rochester Northamptonshire England 16 D4 55 16N 2 16W
Rochester Medway England 21 D2 51 24N 0 30E
Rochester USA 103 L5 43 12N 77 37W
Rochford England 21 D2 51 36N 0 43E
Rochfortbridge RoI 24 D3 53 25N 7 18W
Rockhampton Australia 81 K6 23 22S 150 32E
Rocky Mountains Canada/USA 100 K5/P2 55 00N 125 00W
Rodel Scotland 12 C2 57 41N 7 05W
Rodez France 56 F3 44 21N 2 34E
Roding *r.* England 21 D2 51 45N 0 15E
Roermond Neths 54 D4 51 12N 6 00E
ROMANIA 59 L2/M2
Romans-sur-Isère France 56 G3 45 03N 5 03E
Rome Italy 60 E4 41 53N 12 30E
Romney Marsh England 21 D2 51 03N 0 58E
Romorantin-Lanthenay France 56 E4 47 22N 1 44E
Romsey England 20 B1 50 59N 1 30W
Rona *i.* Scotland 12 D2 57 32N 5 59W
Ronda Spain 57 C2 36 45N 5 10W
Ronse Belgium 54 B3 50 45N 3 36E
Roosendaal Neths 54 C4 51 32N 4 28E
Roosky RoI 24 D3 53 50N 7 55W
Roquetas de Mar Spain 57 D2 36 46N 2 35W
Rora Head Scotland 11 A1 58 52N 3 26W
Rosario Argentina 115 E7 33 00S 60 40W
Rosarno Italy 60 F3 38 29N 15 59E
Roscoff France 56 C5 48 43N 3 59W
Roscommon RoI 24 C3 53 38N 8 11W
Roscommon *co.* RoI 24 C3 53 45N 8 10W
Roscrea RoI 25 D2 52 57N 7 47W
Rosehearty Scotland 13 G2 57 42N 2 07W
Rosenheim Germany 58 F3 47 51N 12 09E
Roskilde Denmark 55 D2 55 39N 12 07E
Rossano Italy 60 G3 39 35N 16 38E
Rossan Point RoI 24 C4 54 40N 8 50W
Ross Carbery RoI 25 B1 51 35N 9 02W
Rosscarbery Bay RoI 25 B1 51 32N 9 00W
Rosslare RoI 25 E2 52 15N 6 22W
Rosslare Harbour *tn.* RoI 25 E2 52 15N 6 22W
Rosslare Point RoI 25 E2 52 19N 6 21W
Ross-on-Wye England 19 D1 51 55N 2 35W
Rostock Germany 58 F7 54 06N 12 09E
Rostov-na-Donu Russia 70 F6 47 15N 39 45E
Rostrevor NI 14 C1 54 06N 6 12W
Rothbury England 15 H2 55 19N 1 55W
Rother *r.* England 20 C1 51 00N 0 50W
Rother *r.* England 21 D2 51 00N 0 17E
Rotherham England 17 E2 53 26N 1 20W
Rothes Scotland 13 F2 57 31N 3 13W
Rothesay Scotland 14 D2 55 51N 5 03W
Rothwell West Yorkshire England 17 E2 53 45N 1 29W
Rothwell Northamptonshire England 19 F2 52 25N 0 48W
Rotterdam Neths 54 C4 51 54N 4 28E
Rottingdean England 20 C1 50 48N 0 04W
Roubaix France 56 F6 50 42N 3 10E
Rouen France 56 E5 49 26N 1 05E
Roundwood RoI 25 E3 53 04N 6 13W
Rousay *i.* Scotland 11 A2 59 10N 3 00W
Rovigo Italy 60 D6 45 04N 11 47E
Rowlands Gill England 17 E3 54 54N 1 45W
Royal Leamington Spa England 19 E2 52 18N 1 31W
Royal Tunbridge Wells England 21 D2 51 08N 0 16E
Royan France 56 D3 45 38N 1 02W
Royston South Yorkshire England 17 E2 53 37N 1 27W
Royston Hertfordshire England 20 C3 52 03N 0 01W
Royton England 16 D2 53 34N 2 08W
Ruabon Wales 18 C2 52 59N 3 02W
Ruddington England 19 E2 52 54N 1 09W
Rufford England 16 D2 53 39N 2 49W
Rugby England 19 E2 52 23N 1 15W
Rugeley England 19 E2 52 46N 1 55W
Ruhr *r.* Germany 58 D5 51 00N 7 00E
Rumney Wales 18 C1 51 30N 3 10W
Runcorn England 16 D2 53 20N 2 44W
Ruse Bulgaria 61 M5 43 50N 25 59E
Rush RoI 24 E3 53 32N 6 06W
Rushden England 19 F2 52 17N 0 36W
RUSSIAN FEDERATION 70/71
Ruthin Wales 18 C3 53 07N 3 18W
Rutland *u.a.* England 19 F2 5241N 00 39W
Rutland Water England 19 F2 52 40N 0 37W
RWANDA 93 A3/B3
Ryazan' Russia 70 F7 54 37N 39 43E
Rybinsk Russia 70 F8 58 03N 38 50E
Rybnik Poland 59 J5 50 07N 18 30E
Ryde England 20 B1 50 44N 1 10W
Rye *r.* England 17 E3 54 15N 1 10W
Rye England 21 D1 50 57N 0 44E
Ryton England 17 E3 54 59N 1 57W
Ryukyu Islands Japan 77 N3 27 30N 127 30E

S

Saalfeld Germany 58 E5 50 39N 11 22E
Saarbrücken Germany 58 C4 49 15N 6 58E
Sabadell Spain 57 G4 41 33N 2 07E
Sacramento USA 102 B4 38 32N 121 30W
Sacriston England 17 E3 54 50N 1 38W
Saffron Walden England 21 D3 52 01N 0 15E
Saga Japan 78 B1 33 16N 130 18E
Sagunto Spain 57 E3 39 40N 0 17W
Sahagún Spain 57 C3 42 23N 5 02W
St. Abbs Scotland 15 G2 55 54N 2 08W
St. Abb's Head Scotland 15 G2 55 55N 2 09W
St. Agnes England 22 B2 50 18N 5 13W
St. Albans England 20 C2 51 46N 0 21W
St Alban's or St Aldheim's Head England 23 E2 50 34N 2 04W
St. Andrews Scotland 13 G1 56 20N 2 48W
St Anne Channel Islands 23 E1 49 43N 2 12W
St. Asaph Wales 18 C3 53 15N 3 26W
St. Austell England 22 C2 50 20N 4 48W
St. Bees England 16 C3 54 29N 3 35W
St. Blazey England 22 C2 50 22N 4 43W
St. Bride's Bay Wales 18 A1 51 50N 5 15W
St-Brieuc France 56 C5 48 31N 2 45W
St. Catharines Canada 101 V2 43 10N 79 15W

St-Chamond France 56 G3 45 29N 4 32E
St. Clears Wales 18 B1 51 50N 4 30W
St. Columb Major England 22 C2 50 26N 4 56W
St. David's Wales 18 A1 51 54N 5 16W
St. David's Head Wales 18 A1 51 55N 5 19W
St.-Dié France 56 H5 48 17N 6 57E
St.-Dizier France 56 G5 48 38N 4 58E
Saintes France 56 D3 45 44N 0 38W
St.-Étienne France 56 G3 45 26N 4 23E
Saintfield NI 14 D1 54 28N 5 50W
St. Finnan's Bay RoI 25 A1 51 50N 10 23W
St. Gallen Switz. 58 D3 47 25N 9 23E
St.-Gaudens France 56 E2 43 07N 0 44E
St. George's Grenada 106 R11 12 04N 61 44W
St. George's Channel British Isles 25 E2 52 00N 6 00W
St.-German en-Laye France 56 F5 48 54N 2 04E
St-Girons France 56 E2 42 59N 1 08E
St. Helens England 16 D2 53 28N 2 44W
St. Helier Channel Islands 23 E1 49 12N 2 07W
St. Ives England 20 C3 52 20N 0 05W
St. Ives England 22 B2 50 12N 5 29W
St. Jean-de-Luz France 56 D2 43 23N 1 39W
Saint John Canada 101 X3 45 16N 66 03W
St. John's Canada 101 AA3 47 34N 52 41W
St. John's Point NI 14 D1 54 15N 5 35W
St Johnstown RoI 24 D4 54 56N 7 28W
St. John's Town of Dalry Scotland 15 E2 55 07N 4 10W
St. Just England 22 B2 50 07N 5 41W
St. Keverne England 22 B2 50 03N 5 06W
St. Kilda *i.* Scotland 12 A2 57 49N 8 34W
ST. KITTS AND NEVIS 106 P9
St. Lawrence *r.* Canada/USA 101 X3 46 55N 55 24W
St. Leonards England 23 F2 50 50N 1 50W
St-Lô France 56 D5 49 07N 1 05W
St. Louis USA 103 H4 38 40N 90 15W
ST. LUCIA 106 R11/R12
St. Malo France 56 C5 48 39N 2 00W
St. Margaret's at Cliffe England 21 E2 51 10N 1 23E
St. Mawes England 22 B2 50 09N 5 01W
St. Monance Scotland 15 G3 56 13N 2 46W
St. Moritz Switz. 58 D3 46 30N 9 51E
St.-Nazaire France 56 C4 47 17N 2 12W
St. Neots England 20 C3 52 14N 0 17W
St.-Omer France 56 F6 50 45N 2 15E
St. Paul USA 103 H5 45 00N 93 10W
St. Peter Port Channel Islands 23 E1 49 27N 3 32W
St. Petersburg Russia 70 F8 59 55N 30 25E
Saint-Pierre & Miquelon *is.* Atlantic Ocean 101 Z3 47 00N 56 20W
St. Pölten Austria 59 G4 48 13N 15 37E
St.-Quentin France 56 F5 49 51N 3 17E
St.-Tropez France 56 H2 43 16N 6 39E
ST. VINCENT AND THE GRENADINES 106 R11
Sakhalin *i.* Russia 71 S7 50 00N 143 00E
Salamanca Spain 57 C4 40 58N 5 40W
Salcombe England 22 D2 50 13N 3 47W
Sale England 16 D2 53 26N 2 19W
Salen Scotland 12 D1 56 43N 5 47W
Salen Scotland 12 D1 56 31N 5 57W
Salerno Italy 60 F4 40 40N 14 46E
Salford England 16 D2 53 30N 2 16W
Salisbury England 20 B2 51 05N 1 48W
Salisbury Plain England 20 B2 51 10N 1 55W
Salmon USA 102 D6 45 11N 113 55W
Salo Finland 55 F3 60 23N 23 10E
Salò Italy 60 D6 45 37N 10 31E
Salon-de-Provence France 56 G2 43 38N 5 06E
Salt Jordan 72 N11 32 03N 35 44E
Salta Argentina 114 D9 24 46S 65 28W
Saltash England 22 C2 50 24N 4 12W
Saltburn-by-the-Sea England 17 F3 54 35N 0 58W
Saltcoats Scotland 15 E2 55 38N 4 47W
Saltdal Norway 55 E4 67 06N 15 25E
Saltdean England 20 C1 50 49N 0 02W
Saltfleet England 17 G2 53 26N 0 10E
Saltillo Mexico 106 D5 25 30N 101 00W
Salt Lake City USA 102 D5 40 45N 111 55W
Salvador Brazil 114 K11 12 58S 38 29W
Salween *r.* China/Myanmar 79 B8 20 00N 103 00E
Salzburg Austria 58 F3 47 48N 13 03E
Salzgitter Germany 58 E6 52 13N 10 20E
Samara Russia 70 H7 53 10N 50 10E
SAMOA 116 J6
Samsun Turkey 63 E3 41 17N 36 22E
Sana Yemen 72 D2 15 23N 44 14E
San Antonio USA 103 G2 29 25N 98 30W
San Cristóbal Venezuela 114 C15 7 46N 72 15W
Sanda Island Scotland 14 D2 55 18N 5 35W
Sanday *i.* Scotland 11 B2 59 15N 2 30W
Sandbach England 16 D2 53 09N 2 22W
Sandhead Scotland 14 E1 54 48N 4 58W
Sandhurst England 20 C2 51 21N 0 48W
San Diego USA 102 C3 32 45N 117 10W
Sandown England 20 B1 50 39N 1 09W
Sandray *i.* Scotland 12 B1 56 53N 7 30W
Sandringham England 21 D3 52 50N 0 31E
Sandwich England 21 E2 51 17N 1 20E
Sandy England 20 C3 52 08N 0 18W
San Fernando Spain 57 B2 36 28N 6 12W
San Francisco USA 102 B4 37 45N 122 27W
San José Costa Rica 107 H1 9 59N 84 04W
San José USA 102 B4 37 20N 121 55W
San Juan Argentina 115 D7 31 33S 68 31W
San Juan Puerto Rico 107 L3 18 29N 66 08W
San Juan Bautista Spain 57 F3 39 05N 1 31E
SAN MARINO 60 E5 44 00N 12 00E
Sanmenxia China 77 K4 34 46N 111 17E
San Miguel de Tucumán Argentina 114 D8 26 48S 65 16W
Sanming China 77 L3 26 16N 117 35E
Sannox Scotland 14 D2 56 41N 5 08W
Sanquhar Scotland 15 F2 55 22N 3 56W
San Remo Italy 60 B5 43 48N 7 46E
San Salvador El Salvador 106 G2 13 40N 89 10W
San Sebastián Spain 57 E5 43 19N 1 59W
San Severo Italy 60 F4 41 41N 15 23E
Santa Barbara USA 102 C3 33 29N 119 01W
Santa Cruz Bolivia 114 E10 17 50S 63 10W
Santa Cruz Spain 90 A7 28 28N 16 15W
Sante Fé Argentina 115 E7 31 35S 60 50W
Santa Fe USA 102 E4 35 41N 105 57W
Santa Maria Brazil 115 G8 29 45S 53 40W
Santa Marta Colombia 114 C16 11 18N 74 10W
Santander Spain 57 D5 43 28N 3 48W
Sant'Antioco Italy 60 C3 39 04N 8 27E
Santarém Brazil 114 G13 2 26S 54 41W
Santarém Portugal 57 A3 39 14N 8 40W
Santa Teresa Gallura Italy 60 C4 41 14N 9 12E
Santiago Chile 115 C6 33 30S 70 40W
Santiago de Compostela Spain 57 A5 42 52N 8 33W
Santiago del Estero Argentina 115 E8 27 45S 64 19W
Santo Andre Brazil 114 H9 23 39S 46 29W
Santo Domingo Dom. Rep. 107 L3 18 30N 69 57W
Santoña Spain 57 D5 43 27N 3 26W
Santos Brazil 114 H9 23 56S 46 22W
São Francisco *r.* Brazil 114 J11 15 00S 44 00W
São Luís Brazil 114 J13 2 34S 44 16W
Saône *r.* France 56 G4 46 28N 4 55E
São Paulo Brazil 114 H9 23 33S 46 39W
SÃO TOMÉ AND PRINCIPE 90 F2
Sapporo Japan 78 D3 43 05N 141 21E
Sarajevo Bosnia-Herzegovina 61 H5 43 52N 18 26E
Saratov Russia 70 G7 51 30N 45 55E
Sardinia *i.* Italy 60 C3/C4 40 00N 9 00E
Sark *i.* Channel Islands 23 E1 49 26N 2 22W
Sarnia Canada 101 U2 42 58N 82 23W
Sarrebourg France 56 H5 48 43N 7 03E
Sarreguemines France 56 H5 49 06N 6 55E
Sartène France 56 J1 41 37N 8 58E
Saskatchewan *prov.* Canada 100/101 P5/Q5 53 50N 109 00W
Saskatoon Canada 100 P4 52 10N 106 40W
Sassari Italy 60 C4 40 43N 8 34E
Sassnitz Germany 58 F7 54 32N 13 40E
Sassuolo Italy 60 D6 44 32N 10 47E
Satu Mare Romania 59 L3 47 48N 22 52E
SAUDI ARABIA 72/73 D3/F3
Sault Ste. Marie Canada 101 U3 46 31N 84 20W
Saumur France 56 D4 47 16N 0 05W
Saundersfoot Wales 18 B1 51 43N 4 43W
Savannah USA 103 K3 32 04N 81 07W
Savona Italy 60 C6 44 18N 8 28E
Sawbridgeworth England 21 D2 51 50N 0 09E
Sawel *mt.* NI 14 B1 54 49N 7 02W
Sawston England 21 D3 52 07N 0 10E
Saxilby England 17 F2 53 17N 0 40W
Saxmundham England 21 E3 52 13N 1 29E
Saxthorpe England 21 E3 52 50N 1 09E
Scafell Pike *mt.* England 16 C3 54 27N 3 14W
Scalasaig Scotland 14 C3 56 04N 6 12W
Scalby England 17 F3 54 18N 0 27W
Scalloway Scotland 11 C3 60 08N 1 17W
Scalpay *i.* Scotland 12 C2 57 52N 6 40W
Scalpay *i.* Scotland 12 D2 57 15N 6 00W
Scapa Scotland 11 B1 58 58N 2 59W
Scapa Flow *sd.* Scotland 11 A1 58 55N 3 00W
Scarborough England 17 F3 54 17N 0 24W
Scarinish Scotland 12 C1 56 29N 6 48W
Scarp *i.* Scotland 12 B3 58 02N 7 08W
Scarriff RoI 25 C2 52 55N 8 37W
Scartaglin RoI 25 B2 52 10N 9 26W
Schaffhausen Switz. 58 D3 47 42N 8 38E
Schefferville Canada 101 X4 54 50N 67 00W
Schleswig Germany 58 D7 54 32N 9 34E
Schwäbisch Gmünd Germany 58 D4 48 49N 9 48E
Schwarzwald *mts.* Germany 58 D4 47 00N 8 00E
Schwaz Austria 58 E3 47 21N 11 44E
Schwechat Austria 59 H4 48 09N 16 27E
Schweinfurt Germany 58 E5 50 03N 10 16E
Schwerin Germany 58 E6 53 38N 11 25E
Schwyz Switz. 58 D3 47 02N 8 34E
Sciacca Italy 60 E2 37 31N 13 05E
Scilly, Isles of England 22 A1 49 56N 6 20W
Sconser Scotland 12 C2 57 18N 6 07W
Scotland UK 10 56 00N 4 00W
Scottish Borders *u.a.* Scotland 15 F2/G2 55 30N 2 55W
Scourie Scotland 12 D3 58 20N 5 08W
Scrabster Scotland 13 F3 58 37N 3 34W
Scunthorpe England 17 F2 53 35N 0 39W
Seaford England 21 D1 50 46N 0 06E
Seaham England 17 E3 54 50N 1 20W
Seahouses England 15 H2 55 35N 1 38W
Seascale England 16 C3 54 24N 3 29W
Seaton Devon England 23 D2 50 43N 3 05W
Seaton Cumbria England 16 C3 54 40N 3 30W
Seaton Delaval England 17 E4 55 04N 1 31W
Seattle USA 102 B6 47 35N 122 20W
Sedan France 56 G5 49 42N 4 57E
Sedbergh England 16 D3 54 20N 2 31W
Segovia Spain 57 C4 40 57N 4 07W
Seine *r.* France 56 E5 49 15N 1 15E
Sekondi Takoradi Ghana 90 D2 4 59N 1 43W
Selborne England 20 C2 51 06N 0 56W
Selby England 17 E2 53 48N 1 04W
Sélestat France 56 H5 48 16N 7 28E
Selkirk Scotland 15 G2 55 33N 2 50W
Selsey England 20 C1 50 44N 0 48W
Selsey Bill *p.* England 20 C1 50 43N 0 48W
Semarang Indonesia 79 E2 6 58S 110 29E
Sendai Japan 78 D2 38 16N 140 52E
SENEGAL 90 A4/B4
Senlis France 56 F5 49 12N 2 35E
Sennen England 22 B2 50 03N 5 42W
Sennybridge Wales 18 C1 51 57N 3 34W
Sens France 56 F5 48 12N 3 18E
Seoul S. Korea 77 N5 37 32N 127 00E
Sept-Îles *tn.* Canada 101 X4 50 10N 66 00W
SERBIA 61 H6/K6
Serov Russia 70 J8 59 42N 60 32E
Serra Brazil 115 J10 20 06S 40 16W
Sérres Greece 61 K4 41 03N 23 33E
Sète France 56 F2 43 25N 3 43E
Settle England 16 D3 54 04N 2 16W
Setúbal Portugal 57 A3 38 31N 8 54W
Sevastopol' Ukraine 63 D3 44 36N 33 31E
Seven Head *c.* RoI 25 C1 51 34N 8 42W
Severn *r.* England/Wales 18 C2 52 30N 3 15W
Severodvinsk Russia 70 F9 64 35N 39 50E
Seville Spain 57 C2 37 24N 5 59W
Seward USA 100 F6 60 05N 149 34W
SEYCHELLES 119
Sézannes France 56 F5 48 44N 3 44E
Sfântu Gheorghe Romania 59 M2 45 51N 25 48E
Sfax Tunisia 90 G8 34 45N 10 43E
Sgurr Mór *mt.* Scotland 13 D2 57 42N 5 03W
Shaftesbury England 23 E3 51 01N 2 12W
Shaldon England 22 D2 51 35N 3 30W
Shanghai China 77 M4 31 06N 121 22E
Shanklin England 20 B1 50 38N 1 10W
Shannon RoI 25 C2 52 41N 8 55W
Shannon *r.* RoI 25 C2/B2 52 45N 8 57W
Shap England 16 D3 54 32N 2 41W
Shapinsay *i.* Scotland 11 B2 59 03N 2 51W
Sheerness England 21 D2 51 27N 0 45E
Sheffield England 17 E2 53 23N 1 30W
Shefford England 20 C3 52 02N 0 20W
Shelburne Canada 101 X2 43 37N 65 20W
Shenandoah USA 103 G5 40 48N 95 22W
Shenyang China 77 M6 41 50N 123 26E
Shepetovka Ukraine 59 N5 50 12N 27 01E
Shepperton England 20 C2 51 23N 0 28W
Sheppey, Isle of England 21 D2 51 25N 0 50E
Shepshed England 19 E2 52 47N 1 18W
Shepton Mallet England 23 E3 51 12N 2 33W
Sherborne England 23 E2 50 57N 2 31W
Sherbrooke Canada 101 W3 45 24N 71 54W
Shercock RoI 24 E3 53 59N 6 54W
Sheringham England 21 E3 52 57N 1 12E
Sherkin Island RoI 25 B1 51 28N 9 25W
's-Hertogenbosch Neths 54 D4 51 41N 5 19E
Shetland Islands *u.a.* Scotland 11 C2/D3 60 00N 1 15W
Shieldaig Scotland 12 D2 57 31N 5 39W
Shifnal England 19 D2 52 41N 2 22W
Shijiazhuang China 77 K5 38 04N 114 28E
Shilbottle England 15 H2 55 23N 1 42W
Shildon England 17 E3 54 38N 1 39W
Shillelagh RoI 25 E2 52 45N 6 32W
Shipley England 17 E2 53 50N 1 47W
Shipston-on-Stour England 19 E2 52 04N 1 37W
Shipton England 17 E3 54 01N 1 09W
Shīrāz Iran 73 F4 29 38N 52 34E
Shirebrook England 17 E2 53 13N 1 13W
Shoeburyness England 21 D2 51 32N 0 48E
Shoreham-by-Sea England 20 C1 50 49N 0 16W
Shotton Wales 18 C3 53 12N 3 02W
Shotts Scotland 15 F2 55 49N 3 48W
Shrewsbury England 18 D2 52 43N 2 45W
Shrewton England 20 B2 51 12N 1 55W
Shropshire *co.* England 18/19 D2 52 35N 2 25W
Shumen Bulgaria 61 M5 43 17N 26 55E
Sible Hedingham England 21 D2 51 58N 0 35E
Sicily *i.* Italy 60 E2/F2 37 00N 14 00E
Siderno Italy 60 G3 38 16N 16 17E
Sidi Bel Abbès Algeria 90 D9 35 15N 0 39W
Sidlaw Hills Scotland 13 F1/G1 56 30N 3 10W
Sidmouth England 23 D2 50 41N 3 15W
Siegen Germany 58 D5 50 52N 8 02E
Siena Italy 60 D5 43 19N 11 19E
SIERRA LEONE 90 B3
Sierra Madre Occidental *mts.* Mexico 106 C5/D4 26 00N 107 00W
Sierra Nevada *mts.* Spain 57 D2 37 00N 3 20W
Sierra Nevada *mts.* USA 102 C4 37 00N 119 00W
Sighişoara Romania 59 M3 46 12N 24 48E
Sigüenza Spain 57 D4 41 04N 2 38W
Sileby England 19 E2 52 44N 1 05W
Silistra Bulgaria 61 M6 44 06N 27 17E
Silloth England 16 C3 54 52N 3 23W
Silverton England 22 D2 50 48N 3 30W
Silves Portugal 57 A2 37 11N 8 26W
Simferopol' Ukraine 63 D3 44 57N 34 05E
Simonsbath England 22 D3 51 09N 3 45W
Sinclair's Bay Scotland 13 F3 58 30N 3 07
Sines Portugal 57 A2 37 58N 8 52W
SINGAPORE 79 C4
Sintra Portugal 57 A3 38 48N 9 22W
Sion Switz. 58 C3 46 14N 7 22E
Sion Mills NI 14 B1 54 47N 7 28W
Siracusa Italy 60 F2 37 04N 15 19E
Sisak Croatia 60 G6 45 30N 16 22E
Sisteron France 56 G3 44 16N 5 56E
Sittingbourne England 21 D2 51 21N 0 44E
Sixmilebridge RoI 25 C2 52 45N 8 46W
Sjaelland *i.* Denmark 55 D2 55 15N 11 30E
Skagerrak *sd.* Denmark/Norway 55 C2 57 30N 8 00E
Skegness England 17 G2 53 10N 0 21E
Skelleftea Sweden 55 F3 64 45N 21 00E
Skellingthorpe England 17 F2 53 14N 0 37W
Skelmanthorpe England 17 E2 53 36N 1 40W
Skelmersdale England 16 D2 53 55N 2 48W
Skelmorlie Scotland 14 E2 55 51N 4 53W
Skelton England 17 F3 54 33N 0 59W
Skerries RoI 24 E3 53 35N 6 07W
Skibbereen RoI 25 B1 51 33N 9 15W
Skiddaw *mt.* England 16 C3 54 40N 3 08W
Skien Norway 55 C2 59 14N 9 37E
Skipton England 16 D2 53 58N 2 01W
Skokholm Island Wales 18 A1 51 42N 5 16W
Skomer Island Wales 18 A1 51 45N 5 18W
Skopje FYROM 61 J4 42 00N 21 28E
Skövde Sweden 55 D2 58 24N 13 52E
Skull RoI 25 B1 51 32N 9 40W
Skye *i.* Scotland 12 C2 57 20N 6 15W
Slaidburn England 16 D2 54 00N 2 26W
Slane RoI 24 E3 54 43N 6 33W
Slaney *r.* RoI 25 E2 52 24W 6 33W
Slatina Romania 59 M2 44 26N 24 22E
Slave *r.* Canada 100 N5 59 20N 111 10W
Slavonski Brod Croatia 61 G6 45 09N 18 02E
Sleaford England 17 F2 53 00N 0 24W
Sleat, Point of Scotland 12 C2 57 01N 6 01W
Sleat, Sound of Scotland 12 D2 57 00N 5 55W
Sledmere England 17 F3 54 04N 0 35W
Sleights England 17 F3 54 26N 0 40W
Slieve Donard *mt.* NI 14 D1 54 11N 5 55W
Slieve Gamph *hills* RoI 24 C4 54 11N 8 53W
Slieve Mish Mountains RoI 25 B2 51 12N 10 00W
Sligo RoI 24 C4 54 17N 8 28W
Sligo *co.* RoI 24 C4 54 10N 8 40W
Sligo Bay *b.* RoI 24 C4 54 15N 8 55W
Sliven Bulgaria 61 M5 42 40N 26 19E
Slough England 20 C2 51 31N 0 36W
Slough *u.a.* England 20 C1 50 25N 0 40W
SLOVAKIA 59 J4/K4
SLOVENIA 60 F6
Smethwick England 19 E2 52 30N 1 58W
Smolensk Russia 70 F7 54 49N 32 04E
Smolyan Bulgaria 61 L4 41 34N 24 42E
Snaefell *mt.* Isle of Man 16 B3 54 16N 4 28W
Snake *r.* USA 102 C5 44 00N 118 00W
Sneek Neths 54 D6 53 02N 5 40E
Sneem RoI 25 B1 51 50N 9 45W
Snodland England 21 D2 51 20N 0 27E
Snowdon *mt.* Wales 18 B3 53 04N 4 05W
Snowy Mountains Australia 81 J3 36 50S 147 00E
Soar *r.* England 19 E2 52 50N 1 15W
Soay *i.* Scotland 12 C2 57 08N 6 14W
Socotra *i.* Yemen 73 F1 12 05N 54 10E
Söderhamn Sweden 55 E3 61 19N 17 10E
Södertälje Sweden 55 E2 59 11N 17 39E
Sofia Bulgaria 61 K5 42 40N 23 18E
Soham England 21 D3 52 20N 0 20E
Soissons France 56 F5 49 23N 3 20E

Index

Solāpur India 74 D3 17 43N 75 56E
Solent, The *sd.* England 20 B1 50 45N 1 25W
Soligorsk Belarus 59 N6 52 50N 27 32E
Solihull England 19 E2 52 25N 1 45W
Sollefteå Sweden 55 E3 63 09N 17 15E
Sóller Spain 57 G3 39 46N 2 42E
SOLOMON ISLANDS 81 L9/M9
Solothurn Switz. 58 C3 47 13N 7 32E
Soltau Germany 58 D6 52 59N 9 50E
Solway Firth Scotland 15 F1 54 45N 3 40W
SOMALIA 91 Q2/Q3
Somerset *co.* England 23 D3/E3 51 10N 3 00W
Somerton England 23 E3 51 03N 2 44W
Sompting England 20 C1 50 50N 0 21W
Sønderborg Denmark 55 C1 54 55N 9 48E
Sondrio Italy 60 C7 46 11N 9 52E
Sonning Common *tn.* England 20 C2 51 31N 0 59W
Sopron Hungary 59 H3 47 40N 16 35E
Sora Italy 60 E4 41 43N 13 37E
Soria Spain 57 D4 41 46N 2 28W
Soroca Moldova 59 P4 48 08N 28 12E
Sosnowiec Poland 59 J5 50 16N 19 07E
Souillac France 56 E3 44 53N 1 29E
Southam England 19 E2 52 15N 1 23W
Southampton England 20 B1 50 55N 1 25W
Southampton *u.a.* England 20 B1 50 55N 1 25W
Southampton Water *sd.* England 20 B1 50 50N 1 20W
South Ayrshire *u.a.* Scotland 15 E2 55 20N 4 40W
South Ballachulish Scotland 12 D1 56 42N 5 09W
South Bank *tn.* England 17 E3 54 35N 1 10W
South Benfleet England 21 D2 51 33N 0 34E
Southborough England 21 D2 51 10N 0 15E
South Brent England 22 D2 50 25N 3 50W
South Carolina *state* USA 103 K3 34 00N 81 00W
South Cave *tn.* England 17 F2 53 46N 0 35W
South Cerney England 19 E1 51 41N 1 57W
South Dakota *state* USA 102 F5 45 00N 102 00W
South Dorset Downs England 23 E2 50 40N 2 30W
South Downs England 20 C1 50 50N 0 30W
South Dublin *co.* RoI 24 E3 53 20N 6 20W
Southend *u.a.* England 21 D2 51 32N 0 50E
Southend Scotland 14 D2 55 20N 5 38W
Southend-on-Sea England 21 D2 51 33N 0 43E
Southerness Point Scotland 15 F1 54 53N 3 37W
Southern Ocean 117
South Esk *r.* Scotland 13 F1 56 50N 3 10W
South Foreland *c.* England 21 E2 51 09N 1 23E
South Gloucestershire *u.a.* England 19 D1 51 30N 2 30W
South Hayling England 20 C1 50 47N 0 59W
South Island NZ 81 N1/P2 42 30S 172 00E
South Kirkby England 17 E2 53 34N 1 20W
SOUTH KOREA 77 N5
South Lanarkshire *u.a.* Scotland 15 E2/F2 55 35N 3 55W
Southminster England 21 D2 51 40N 0 50E
South Molton England 22 D3 51 01N 3 50W
South Normanton England 17 E2 53 06N 1 20W
South Ockendon England 21 D2 51 32N 0 18E
South Petherton England 23 E2 50 58N 2 49W
South Pole Antarctica 117 90 00S
Southport England 16 C2 53 39N 3 01W
South Queensferry Scotland 15 F2 55 59N 3 25W
South Shields England 17 E3 55 00N 1 25W
SOUTH SUDAN 90 L3/M3
South Tipperary *co.* RoI 25 C2/D2 52 30N 7 45W
South Tyne *r.* England 16 D3 54 52N 2 30W
South Uist *i.* Scotland 12 B2 57 20N 7 15W
South Walls *i.* Scotland 11 A1 58 47N 3 11W
Southwick England 20 C1 51 01N 0 14W
Southwold England 21 E3 52 20N 1 40E
South Woodham Ferrers England 21 D2 51 38N 0 38E
South Yorkshire *co.* England 17 E2 53 30N 1 30W
Sowerby Bridge England 17 E2 53 43N 1 54W
SPAIN 57 C3/E3
Spalding England 20 C3 52 47N 0 10W
Spárti Greece 61 K2 37 05N 22 25E
Spean Bridge *tn.* Scotland 13 E1 56 53N 4 54W
Spennymoor England 17 E3 54 42N 1 35W
Sperrin Mountains NI 14 B1 54 49N 7 06W
Spey *r.* Scotland 13 F2 57 15N 3 45W
Spiddle RoI 24 B3 53 15N 9 18W
Spilsby England 17 G2 53 11N 0 05E
Spink RoI 25 D2 52 53N 7 12W
Spithead *sd.* England 20 B1 50 45N 1 10W
Spitsbergen *i.* Arctic Ocean 70 D12 79 00N 15 00E
Spittal an der Drau Austria 58 F3 46 48N 13 30E
Split Croatia 61 G5 43 31N 16 28E
Spokane USA 102 C6 47 40N 117 25W
Spoleto Italy 60 E5 42 44N 12 44E
Springfield Illinois USA 103 J4 39 49N 89 39W
Springfield Massachusetts USA 103 M5 42 07N 72 35W
Spurn Head England 17 G2 53 36N 0 07E
SRI LANKA 74 E1
Srinagar Kashmir 74 C6 34 08N 74 50E
Stacks Mountains RoI 25 B2 52 19N 9 33W
Staffa *i.* Scotland 12 C1 56 30N 6 15W
Stafford England 19 D2 52 48N 2 07W
Staffordshire *co.* England 19 D2/E2 52 50N 2 00W
Staines England 20 C2 51 26N 0 30W
Stainforth England 17 E2 53 36N 1 01W
Stalbridge England 23 E2 50 58N 2 23W
Stalybridge England 19 D3 53 29N 2 04W
Stamford Bridge *tn.* England 17 F2 53 59N 0 55W
Standish USA 105 D2 43 59N 83 58W
Stane Scotland 15 F2 55 50N 3 47W
Stanhope England 16 D3 54 45N 2 01W
Stanley England 17 E2 53 44N 1 28W
Stanley England 17 E3 54 53N 1 42W
Stanley Falkland Islands 115 F3 51 45S 57 56W
Stansted Mountfitchet England 21 D2 51 54N 0 12E
Stapleford England 19 E2 52 56N 1 15W
Staplehurst England 21 D2 51 10N 0 33E
Starachowice Poland 59 K5 51 03N 21 00E
Stara Zagora Bulgaria 61 L5 42 25N 25 37E
Start Bay England 22 D2 50 16N 3 35W
Start Point England 22 D2 50 13N 3 38W
Staunton USA 103 L4 38 10N 79 05W
Stavanger Norway 55 C2 58 58N 5 45E
Staveley England 17 E2 53 16N 1 20W
Stavropol' Russia 70 G6 45 03N 41 59E
Staxton England 17 F3 54 11N 0 26W
Steeping *r.* England 17 G2 53 10N 0 10E
Stendal Germany 58 E6 52 36N 11 52E
Stenhousemuir Scotland 15 F3 56 02N 3 49W
Stevenage England 20 C2 51 55N 0 14W
Stevenston Scotland 15 E2 55 39N 4 45W
Stewart Canada 100 J5 55 56N 130 01W
Stewarton Scotland 15 E2 55 41N 4 31W
Stewartstown NI 14 C1 54 35N 6 41W
Steyning England 20 C1 50 53N 0 20W
Steyr Austria 58 G3 48 04N 14 25E
Stilton England 20 C3 52 29N 0 17W
Stinchar *r.* Scotland 15 E2 55 10N 4 50W
Stirling Canada 100 N3 49 34N 112 30W
Stirling *u.a.* Scotland 15 E3 56 10N 4 15W
Stirling Scotland 15 F3 56 07N 3 57W
Stockbridge England 20 B2 51 07N 1 29W
Stockerau Austria 59 H4 48 24N 16 13E
Stockholm Sweden 55 E2 59 20N 18 05E
Stockport England 16 D2 53 25N 2 10W
Stocksbridge England 17 E2 53 27N 1 34W
Stockton-on-Tees England 17 E3 54 34N 1 19W
Stockton-on-Tees *u.a.* England 17 E3 54 33N 1 24W
Stoer, Point of Scotland 12 D3 58 25N 5 25W
Stoke-on-Trent *u.a.* England 16 D2 53 00N 2 10W
Stokenchurch England 20 C2 51 40N 0 55W
Stoke-on-Trent England 16 D2 53 00N 2 10W
Stoke Poges England 20 C2 51 33N 0 35W
Stokesley England 17 E3 54 28N 1 11W
Stone England 19 D2 52 54N 2 10W
Stonehaven Scotland 13 G1 56 38N 2 13W
Stonehouse Scotland 15 F2 55 43N 3 59W
Stony Stratford England 20 C3 52 04N 0 52W
Størdal Norway 55 D3 63 18N 11 48E
Støren Norway 55 C3 63 03N 10 16E
Stornoway Scotland 12 C3 58 12N 6 23W
Storrington England 20 C1 50 55N 0 28W
Storr, The *mt.* Scotland 12 C2 57 30N 6 11W
Storuman Sweden 55 E4 65 05N 17 10E
Stotfold England 20 C3 52 01N 0 15W
Stour *r.* Warwickshire England 19 E2 52 05N 1 45E
Stour *r.* Suffolk England 21 D3 52 10N 0 30E
Stour *r.* Kent England 21 E2 51 10N 1 10E
Stour *r.* Dorset England 23 E2 50 50N 2 10W
Stourbridge *tn.* England 19 D2 52 27N 2 09W
Stourport-on-Severn England 19 D2 52 21N 2 16W
Stow Scotland 15 G2 55 42N 2 51W
Stowmarket England 21 E3 52 11N 1 00E
Stow-on-the-Wold England 19 E1 51 56N 1 44W
Strabane NI 14 B1 54 49N 7 27W
Strabane *district* NI 14 B1 54 45N 7 30W
Strachur Scotland 14 D3 56 10N 5 04W
Stradbally RoI 25 D3 53 00N 7 08W
Stradone RoI 24 D3 53 59N 7 14W
Stralsund Germany 58 F7 54 18N 13 06E
Strangford Lough NI 14 D1 54 30N 5 35W
Stranorlar RoI 24 D4 54 48N 7 46W
Stranraer Scotland 14 D2 54 55N 5 02W
Strasbourg France 56 H5 48 35N 7 45E
Stratford-upon-Avon England 19 E2 52 12N 1 41W
Strathaven Scotland 15 E2 55 41N 4 05W
Strathcarron Scotland 12 D2 57 26N 5 27W
Strathpeffer Scotland 13 E2 57 35N 4 33W
Strathy Scotland 13 F3 58 33N 3 59W
Strathy *r.* Scotland 13 E3 58 30N 4 00W
Strathy Point Scotland 13 E3 58 35N 4 02W
Stratton England 22 C2 50 50N 4 31W
Straubing Germany 58 F4 48 53N 12 35E
Street England 23 3 51 03N 2 45W
Stretford England 16 D2 53 27N 2 19W
Strímonas *r.* Greece 61 K4 41 00N 23 00E
Strokestown RoI 24 C3 53 47N 8 06W
Stroma *i.* Scotland 11 A1 58 40N 3 08W
Stromboli *mt.* Italy 60 F3 38 48N 15 15E
Stromeferry Scotland 12 D2 57 21N 5 34W
Stromness Scotland 11 A1 58 57N 3 18W
Stronsay *i.* Scotland 11 B2 59 07N 2 37W
Stronsay Firth Scotland 11 B2 59 00N 2 55W
Strontian Scotland 12 D1 56 41N 5 34W
Strood England 21 D2 51 24N 0 28E
Stroud England 19 D1 51 45N 2 12W
Strumble Head Wales 18 A2 52 02N 5 04W
Stryy Ukraine 59 L4 49 16N 23 51E
Stubbington England 20 B1 50 49N 1 13W
Studley England 19 E2 52 16N 1 52W
Sturminster Marshall England 23 E2 50 48N 2 04W
Sturminster Newton England 23 E2 50 55N 2 18W
Stuttgart Germany 58 D4 48 47N 9 12E
Subotica Serbia 61 H7 46 04N 19 41E
Sucre Bolivia 114 D10 19 05S 65 15W
SUDAN 91 L4/M4
Sudbury Canada 101 U3 46 30N 81 01W
Sudbury England 21 E3 52 02N 0 44E
Suffolk *co.* England 21 D3/E3 52 10N 1 00E
Suhl Germany 58 E5 50 37N 10 43E
Sulawesi *i.* Indonesia 79 F3/G3 2 00S 120 00E
Sumatera *i.* Indonesia 79 B4/C3 0 00 100 00E
Sumburgh Head Scotland 11 C2 59 51N 1 16W
Summerhill RoI 24 E3 53 29N 6 44W
Sumy Ukraine 62 D5 50 55N 34 49E
Sunderland England 17 E3 54 55N 1 23W
Sundsvall Sweden 55 E3 62 22N 17 20E
Sunningdale England 20 C2 51 24N 0 37W
Superior, Lake Canada/USA 104 C3 48 00N 88 00W
Surabaya Indonesia 79 E2 7 14S 112 45E
Surat India 74 C4 21 10N 72 54E
SURINAME 114 F14
Surrey *co.* England 20 C2 51 15N 0 30W
Sutton England 20 C2 51 22N 0 12W
Sutton Coldfield England 19 E2 52 34N 1 48W
Sutton in Ashfield England 17 E2 53 08N 1 15W
Sutton on Sea England 17 G2 53 19N 0 17E
Suwałki Poland 59 L7 54 06N 22 56E
Suzhou China 77 M4 31 21N 120 40E
Svilengrad Bulgaria 61 M4 41 45N 26 14E
Swadlincote England 19 E2 52 46N 1 33W
Swaffham England 21 D3 52 39N 0 41E
Swale *r.* England 16 D3 54 20N 2 00W
Swanage England 23 F2 50 37N 1 58W
Swanley England 21 D2 51 24N 0 12E
Swanlinbar RoI 24 D4 54 12N 7 42W
Swanscombe England 21 D2 51 26N 0 18E
Swansea Wales 18 C1 51 38N 3 57W
Swansea Bay Wales 18 C1 51 35N 3 55W
Swansea *u.a.* Wales 18 B1/C1 51 35N 4 10W
SWAZILAND 92 F2
SWEDEN 55 D2/E4
Swiebodzin Poland 59 G6 52 15N 15 31E
Swilly *r.* RoI 24 D4 54 55N 7 45W
Swindon England 20 B2 51 34N 1 47W
Swindon *u.a.* England 20 B2 51 34N 1 47W
Swinford RoI 24 C3 53 57N 8 57W
Swinoujście Poland 58 G6 53 55N 14 18E
Swinton England 17 E2 53 30N 1 19W
SWITZERLAND 58 C3/D3
Swords RoI 24 E3 53 28N 6 13W
Sydney Australia 81 K4 33 55S 151 10E
Sylt Germany 58 D7 54 00N 8 00E
Symbister Scotland 11 C3 60 21N 1 02W
Symington Scotland 15 F2 55 37N 3 35W
Syracuse USA 103 L5 43 03N 76 10W
SYRIA 72 C6
Syzran' Russia 70 G7 53 10N 48 29E
Szczecin Poland 58 G6 53 25N 14 32E
Szeged Hungary 59 K3 46 15N 20 09E
Szombathely Hungary 59 H3 47 14N 16 38E

T

Tábor Czech Rep. 58 G4 49 25N 14 39E
Tabrīz Iran 73 E6 38 05N 46 18E
Tacoma USA 102 B6 47 16N 122 30W
Tadcaster England 17 E2 53 53N 1 16W
Tadley England 20 B2 51 21N 1 08W
Taegu S. Korea 77 N5 35 52N 128 36E
Taejon S. Korea 77 N5 36 20N 127 26E
Tafalla Spain 57 E5 42 32N 1 41W
Taff *r.* Wales 18 C1 51 30N 3 10W
Taghmon RoI 25 E2 52 19N 6 39W
Tain Scotland 13 E2 57 48N 4 04W
Taipei Taiwan 77 M3 25 05N 121 32E
TAIWAN 77 M2
Taiyuan China 77 K5 37 50N 112 30E
TAJIKISTAN 70 J4/K4
Tajo *r.* Spain/Portugal 57 B3 39 00N 7 00W
Takamatsu Japan 78 B1 34 20N 134 01E
Talca Chile 115 C6 35 28S 71 40W
Talcahuano Chile 115 C6 36 40S 73 10W
Talgarth Wales 18 C1 52 00N 3 15W
Tallaght RoI 24 E3 53 17N 6 21W
Tallahassee USA 103 K3 30 26N 84 16W
Tallinn Estonia 55 F2 59 22N 24 48E
Tallow RoI 25 C2 52 05N 8 01W
Tal-y-bont Wales 18 C2 52 29N 3 59W
Tamanrasset Algeria 90 F6 22 50N 5 28E
Tamar *r.* England 22 C2 50 32N 4 13W
Tambov Russia 70 G7 52 44N 41 28E
Tame *r.* England 19 E2 52 40N 1 45W
Tampa USA 103 K2 27 58N 82 38W
Tampere Finland 55 F3 61 32N 23 45E
Tamworth England 19 E2 52 39N 1 40W
Tandragee NI 14 C1 54 22N 6 25W
Tanganyika, Lake East Africa 93 B1 7 00S 30 00E
Tangier Morocco 90 C9 35 48N 5 45W
Tangshan China 77 L5 39 37N 118 05E
TANZANIA 93 B1/D1
Tapachula Mexico 106 F2 14 54N 92 15W
Taransay *i.* Scotland 12 B2 57 55N 7 00W
Táranto Italy 61 G4 40 28N 17 15E
Tarazona Spain 57 E4 41 54N 1 44W
Tarbat Ness *c.* Scotland 13 F2 57 50N 3 45W
Tarbert RoI 25 B2 52 32N 9 23W
Tarbert Western Isles Scotland 12 C2 57 54N 6 49W
Tarbert Argyle and Bute Scotland 14 D2 55 52N 5 26W
Tarbes France 56 E2 43 14N 0 05E
Tarbet Scotland 15 E3 56 12N 4 43W
Tarbolton Scotland 15 E2 55 31N 4 29W
Târgoviște Romania 59 M2 44 56N 25 27E
Târgu Mureș Romania 59 M3 46 33N 24 34E
Tarija Bolivia 114 D9 21 33S 65 02W
Tarleton England 16 D2 53 41N 2 50W
Tarporley England 16 D2 53 10N 2 40W
Tarragona Spain 57 F4 41 07N 1 15E
Tarrasa Spain 57 G4 41 34N 2 00E
Tarsus Turkey 63 D2 26 25N 34 52E
Tartu Estonia 55 G2 58 20N 26 44E
Tashkent Uzbekistan 70 J5 41 16N 69 13E
Taunton England 23 D3 51 01N 3 06W
Taunus *mts.* Germany 58 D5 50 00N 8 00E
Tauranga NZ 81 Q3 37 41S 176 10E
Taverham England 21 E3 52 41N 1 10E
Tavira Portugal 57 B2 37 07N 7 39W
Tavistock England 22 C2 50 33N 4 08W
Tavy *r.* England 22 C2 50 36N 4 04W
Taw *r.* England 22 D2 50 46N 3 55W
Tay *r.* Scotland 13 F1 56 30N 3 25W
Taynuilt Scotland 12 D1 56 25N 5 14W
Tayport Scotland 13 G1 56 27N 2 53W
T'bilisi Georgia 63 F3 41 43N 44 48E
Tczew Poland 59 J7 54 05N 18 46E
Tebay England 16 D3 54 26N 2 35W
Tees *r.* England 16 D3 54 40N 1 20W
Tegucigalpa Honduras 106 G2 14 05N 87 14W
Tehran Iran 73 F6 35 40N 51 26E
Teifi *r.* Wales 18 B2 52 03N 4 30W
Teign *r.* England 22 D2 50 42N 3 48W
Teignmouth England 22 D2 50 33N 3 30W
Teith *r.* Scotland 15 E3 56 10N 4 08W
Tejo *r.* Portugal 57 B3 39 30N 8 15W
Tel Aviv-Yafo Israel 72 B5 32 05N 34 46E
Telford England 19 D2 52 42N 2 28W
Teme *r.* England 19 D2 52 15N 2 25W
Tempio Pausania Italy 60 C4 40 54N 9 07E
Templemore RoI 25 D2 52 48N 7 50W
Templenoe RoI 25 B1 51 51N 9 41W
Temuco Chile 115 C6 38 45S 72 40W
Tenbury Wells England 19 D2 52 19N 2 35W
Tenby Wales 18 B1 51 41N 4 43W
Tenerife *i.* Spain 90 A7 28 15N 16 35W
Tennessee *r.* USA 103 J4 35 00N 88 00W
Tennessee *state* USA 103 J4 35 00N 87 00W
Tenterden England 21 D2 51 05N 0 41E
Teramo Italy 60 E5 42 40N 13 43E
Teresina Brazil 114 J12 5 09S 42 46W
Termini Imerese Italy 60 E2 27 59N 13 42E
Termoli Italy 60 F4 42 00N 15 00E
Terni Italy 60 E5 42 34N 12 39E
Terracina Italy 60 E4 41 17N 13 15E
Terrasini Italy 60 E3 38 09N 13 05E
Terre Haute USA 103 J4 39 27N 87 24W
Teruel Spain 57 E4 40 21N 1 06W
Teslin Canada 100 J6 60 10N 132 42W
Test *r.* England 20 B2 51 05N 1 30W
Tetbury England 19 D1 51 39N 2 10W
Tetney England 17 F2 53 30N 0 01W
Tétouan Morocco 90 C9 35 34N 5 22W
Teviotdale Scotland 15 G2 55 20N 3 00W
Teviothead Scotland 15 G2 55 19N 2 56W
Tewkesbury England 19 D1 51 59N 2 09W
Texas *state* USA 102 G3 31 00N 100 00W
THAILAND 79 B7/C7
Thame *r.* England 20 B2 51 45N 1 05W

Thame England 20 C2 51 45N 0 59W
Thames *r.* England 20 C2 51 32N 0 50W
Thane India 74 C3 19 14N 73 02E
Thar Desert India 74 C5 27 30N 72 00E
Thatcham England 20 B2 51 25N 1 15W
Thaxted England 21 D2 51 57N 0 20E
The Downs *tn.* RoI 24 D3 53 30N 7 14W
The Everglades USA 103 K2 26 00N 81 00W
The Mumbles *tn.* Wales 18 C1 51 35N 3 59W
The Peak *mt.* England 17 E2 53 24N 1 51W
Thermaïkós Kólpos *g.* Greece 61 K3/K4 40 00N 22 50E
The Rower *tn.* RoI 25 E2 52 27N 6 57W
Thessaloníki Greece 61 K4 40 38N 22 58E
Thetford England 21 D3 52 25N 0 45E
Thiers France 56 F3 45 51N 3 33E
Thimphu Bhutan 75 F5 27 32N 89 43E
Thionville France 56 H5 49 22N 6 11E
Thíra *i.* Greece 61 L2 36 00N 25 00E
Thirsk England 17 E3 54 14N 1 20W
Thíva Greece 61 K3 38 19N 23 19E
Thomastown RoI 25 D2 52 31N 7 08W
Thompson Canada 101 R5 55 45N 97 54W
Thornaby-on-Tees England 17 E3 54 34N 1 18W
Thornbury England 19 D1 51 37N 2 32W
Thorne England 17 F2 53 37N 0 58W
Thorney England 20 C3 52 37N 0 07W
Thornhill Scotland 15 F2 55 15N 3 46W
Thornton England 16 D2 53 53N 3 00W
Thorpe-le-Soken England 21 E2 51 52N 1 10E
Thouars France 56 D4 46 59N 0 13W
Thrapston England 19 F2 52 24N 0 32W
Thuin Belgium 54 C3 50 21N 4 18E
Thun Switz. 58 C3 46 46N 7 38E
Thurcroft England 17 E2 53 24N 1 16W
Thurles RoI 25 D2 52 41N 7 49W
Thurrock *u.a.* England 21 D2 51 30N 0 25E
Thursby England 16 C3 54 51N 3 03W
Thurso Scotland 13 F3 58 35N 3 32W
Thurso *r.* Scotland 13 F3 58 20N 3 40W
Thurso Bay Scotland 13 F3 58 37N 3 34W
Tianjin China 77 L5 39 08N 117 12E
Tiberias, Lake Israel 72 N11 32 45N 35 30E
Tibesti *mts.* Chad 91 J6 21 00N 17 00E
Tickhill England 17 E2 53 26N 1 06W
Tighnabruaich Scotland 14 D2 55 56N 5 14W
Tigris *r.* Turkey/Iraq 73 E5 32 00N 46 00E
Tijuana Mexico 106 A6 32 29N 117 10W
Tilburg Neths 54 D4 51 34N 5 05E
Tilbury England 21 D2 51 28N 0 23E
Till *r.* England 15 G2 55 38N 2 08W
Till *r.* England 17 F2 53 20N 0 40W
Tillicoultry Scotland 15 F3 56 09N 2 45W
Tilt *r.* Scotland 13 F1 56 50N 3 45W
Timişoara Romania 59 K2 45 45N 21 15E
Timor *i.* Indonesia 79 G1/H2 9 00S 125 00E
Tinahely RoI 25 E2 52 48N 6 28W
Tingwall Scotland 11 A2 59 04N 3 03W
Tintagel England 22 C2 50 40N 4 45W
Tintagel Head England 22 C2 50 41N 4 46W
Tipperary RoI 25 C2 52 29N 8 10W
Tiptree England 21 D2 51 49N 0 45E
Tiranë Albania 61 H4 41 20N 19 49E
Tiree *i.* Scotland 12 C1 56 30N 6 55W
Titu Romania 59 M2 44 40N 25 32E
Tiverton England 22 D2 50 55N 3 29W
Tivoli Italy 60 E4 41 58N 12 48E
Tlemcen Algeria 90 D8 34 53N 1 21W
Toamasina Madagascar 92 J4 18 10S 49 23E
Tobercurry RoI 24 C4 54 03N 8 43W
Tobermore NI 14 C1 54 48N 6 42W
Tobermory Scotland 12 C1 56 37N 6 05W
Todmorden England 16 D2 53 43N 2 05W
Toe Head RoI 25 B1 51 30N 9 12W
Toe Head Scotland 12 B2 57 50N 7 07W
TOGO 90 E3
Tokelau Islands Pacific Ocean 116 J7 9 00S 168 00W
Tokyo Japan 78 C2 35 40N 139 45E
Toledo Spain 57 C3 39 52N 4 02W
Toledo USA 103 K5 41 40N 83 35W
Toliara Madagascar 92 H3 23 20N 43 41E
Tolmezzo Italy 60 E7 46 24N 13 01E
Tolosa Spain 57 D5 43 09N 2 04W
Tolsta Head Scotland 12 C3 58 20N 6 10W
Toluca Mexico 106 E3 19 20N 99 40W
Tomar Portugal 57 A3 39 36N 8 25W
Tomatin Scotland 13 E2 57 20N 3 59W
Tombouctou Mali 90 D5 16 49N 2 59W
Tomelloso Spain 57 D3 39 09N 3 01W
Tomintoul Scotland 13 F2 57 14N 3 22W
Tomsk Russia 71 L8 56 30N 85 05E
Tonbridge England 21 D2 51 12N 0 16E
TONGA 116 J5
Tongue Scotland 13 E3 58 28N 4 25W
Tønsberg Norway 55 D2 59 16N 10 25E
Tonyrefail Wales 18 C1 51 36N 3 25W
Toomyvara RoI 25 C2 52 51N 8 02W
Topsham England 22 D2 50 42N 3 27W
Tor Bay England 22 D2 50 27N 3 30W
Torbay England 22 D2 50 27N 3 30W
Tordesillas Spain 57 C4 41 30N 5 00W
Tore Scotland 13 E2 57 27N 4 21W
Torfaen *u.a.* Wales 18 C1 51 38N 3 04W
Tornio Finland 55 F4 65 50N 24 10E
Toronto Canada 101 V2 43 42N 79 46W
Torpoint *tn.* England 22 C2 50 22N 4 11W
Torre del Greco Italy 60 F4 40 46N 14 22E
Torrelavega Spain 57 C3 43 21N 4 03W
Torremolinos Spain 57 C2 36 38N 4 30W
Torrente Spain 57 E3 39 27N 0 28W
Torres Vedras Portugal 57 A3 39 05N 9 15W
Torrevieja Spain 57 E2 37 59N 0 40W
Torridge *r.* England 22 C2 50 56N 4 22W
Torridon Scotland 12 D2 57 33N 5 31W
Tortosa Spain 57 F4 40 49N 0 31E
Toruń Poland 59 J6 53 01N 18 35E
Tory Island RoI 24 C5 55 16N 8 14W
Tory Sound RoI 24 C5 55 15N 8 05W
Totland England 20 B1 50 40N 1 32W
Totnes England 22 D2 50 25N 3 41W
Tottington England 16 D2 53 37N 2 20W
Totton England 20 B1 50 56N 1 29W
Touggourt Algeria 90 F8 33 08N 6 04E
Toul France 56 G5 48 41N 5 54E
Toulon France 56 G2 43 07N 5 55E
Toulouse France 56 E2 43 33N 1 24E
Tourcoing France 56 F6 50 44N 310E
Tours France 56 E4 47 23N 0 42E
Toward Scotland 14 E2 55 54N 4 58W
Towcester England 19 F2 52 08N 1 00W
Townsville Australia 81 J7 19 13S 146 48E
Toyama Japan 78 C2 36 42N 137 14E
Toyota Japan 78 C2 35 05N 137 09E
Tralee RoI 25 B2 52 16N 9 42W
Tralee Bay RoI 25 B2 52 20N 9 55W
Tramore RoI 25 D2 52 10N 7 10W
Tramore Bay RoI 25 D2 52 08N 7 08W
Tranent Scotland 15 G2 55 57N 2 57W
Trani Italy 61 G4 41 17N 16 25E
Trápani Italy 60 E3 38 02N 12 32E
Traun Austria 58 G4 48 14N 14 15E
Trawsfynydd Wales 18 C2 52 54N 3 55W
Tredegar Wales 18 C1 51 47N 3 16W
Tregaron Wales 18 C2 52 13N 3 55W
Tregony England 22 C2 50 16N 4 55W
Tremadog Bay Wales 18 B2 52 54N 4 15W
Trent *r.* England 17 F2 53 30N 0 50W
Trento Italy 60 D7 46 04N 11 08E
Tresco *i.* England 22 A1 49 57N 6 20W
Treviso Italy 60 E6 45 40N 12 15E
Trevose Head England 22 B2 50 33N 5 01W
Trier Germany 58 C4 49 45N 6 39E
Trieste Italy 60 E6 45 39N 13 47E
Tríkala Greece 61 J3 39 33N 21 46E
Trim RoI 24 E3 53 34N 6 47W
Tring England 20 C2 51 48N 0 40W
TRINIDAD AND TOBAGO 107 M2
Trípoli Greece 61 K2 37 31N 22 22E
Tripoli Lebanon 72 C5 34 27N 35 50E
Tripoli Libya 91 G8 32 54N 13 11E
Trois-Rivières *tn.* Canada 101 W3 46 21N 72 34W
Trollhätten Sweden 55 D2 58 17N 12 20E
Tromsø Norway 55 E4 69 42N 19 00E
Trondheim Norway 55 D3 63 36N 10 23E
Troon Scotland 15 E2 55 32N 4 40W
Trotternish *p.* Scotland 12 C2 57 00N 6 00W
Troup Head Scotland 13 G2 57 41N 2 19W
Trouville France 56 E5 49 22N 0 05E
Trowbridge England 20 A2 51 20N 2 13W
Troyes France 56 G5 48 18N 4 05E
Trujillo Peru 114 B12 8 06S 79 00W
Trujillo Spain 57 C3 39 28N 5 53W
Truro England 22 B2 50 16N 5 03W
Tuam RoI 24 C3 53 31N 8 50W
Tübingen Germany 58 D4 48 32N 9 04E
Tubruq Libya 91 K8 32 05N 23 59E
Tucson USA 102 D3 32 15N 110 57W
Tudela Spain 57 E5 42 04N 1 37W
Tudweiliog Wales 18 B2 52 55N 4 39W
Tula Russia 70 F7 54 11N 37 38E
Tulcea Romania 59 P2 45 10N 28 50E
Tulla RoI 25 C2 52 52N 8 45W
Tullamore RoI 24 D3 53 16N 7 30W
Tulle France 56 E3 45 16N 1 46E
Tullow RoI 25 E2 52 48N 6 44W
Tulsa USA 103 G4 36 07N 95 58W
Tulsk RoI 24 C3 53 47N 8 15W
Tummel *r.* Scotland 13 E1 56 40N 4 00W
Tummel Bridge Scotland 13 F1 56 43N 3 58W
Tunis Tunisia 90 G9 36 50N 10 13E
TUNISIA 90 F8/G8
Türgovishte Bulgaria 61 M5 43 14N 26 37E
Turgutlu Turkey 61 M3 38 30N 27 43E
Turin Italy 60 B6 45 04N 7 40E
Turkana, Lake Ethiopia/Kenya 93 D6/E6 4 00N 36 00E
TURKEY 63 C2/E2
TURKMENISTAN 70 H4/J4
Turks and Caicos Islands W. Indies 107 K4 21 30N 72 00W
Turku Finland 55 F3 60 27N 22 15E
Turnberry Scotland 14 E2 55 20N 4 50W
Turriff Scotland 13 G2 57 32N 2 28W
Tutbury England 19 E2 52 52N 1 40W
Tuttlingen Germany 58 D4 47 59N 8 49E
TUVALU 116 H7
Túy Spain 57 A5 42 03N 8 39W
Tuz Gölü *l.* Turkey 63 D2 38 40N 33 35E
Tuzla Bosnia-Herzegovina 61 H6 44 33N 18 41E
Tver' Russia 70 F8 56 49N 35 57E
Tweed *r.* Scotland/England 15 G2 55 45N 2 10W
Tweedmouth England 15 G2 55 47N 2 00W
Twin Falls *tn.* USA 102 D5 42 34N 114 30W
Twyford England 20 C2 51 29N 0 53W
Twyford England 20 B2 51 01N 1 19W
Tyldesley England 16 D2 53 32N 2 29W
Tylers Green England 20 C2 51 37N 0 42W
Tyndrum Scotland 13 E1 57 27N 4 44W
Tyne *r.* Scotland 15 G2 55 58N 2 43W
Tyne and Wear *co.* England 17 E3 55 00N 1 10W
Tynemouth *tn.* England 17 E4 55 01N 1 24W
Tynset Norway 55 D3 62 17N 10 47E
Tywi *r.* Wales 18 B1 51 50N 4 25W
Tywyn Wales 18 B2 52 35N 4 05W

U

Uaupés Brazil 114 D13 0 07S 67 05W
Uberaba Brazil 114 H10 19 47S 47 57W
Uberlândia Brazil 114 H10 18 57S 48 17W
Uckfield England 21 D1 50 58N 0 05E
Uddevalla Sweden 55 D2 58 20N 11 56E
Udine Italy 60 E7 46 04N 13 14E
Uelzen Germany 58 E6 52 58N 10 34E
Ufa Russia 70 H7 54 45N 55 58E
Uffculme England 23 D2 50 54N 3 21W
UGANDA 93 B6/C6
Ugie *r.* 13 H2 57 31N 1 55W
Uig Scotland 12 C2 57 35N 6 22W
Uithuizen Neths 54 E6 53 24N 6 41E
Ujung Pandang Indonesia 79 F2 5 09S 119 28E
UKRAINE 62 C4/D4
Ulan Bator Mongolia 77 J7 47 54N 106 52E
Ulan-Ude Russia 71 N7 51 55N 107 40E
Ullapool Scotland 12 D2 57 54N 5 10W
Ullswater *l.* England 16 D3 54 35N 2 55W
Ulm Germany 58 D4 48 24N 10 00E
Ulva *i.* Scotland 12 C1 56 30N 6 15W
Ulverston England 16 C3 54 12N 3 06W
Umeå Sweden 55 F3 63 50N 20 15E
Unapool Scotland 13 D3 58 14N 5 01W
Ungava Bay Canada 101 X5 59 00N 67 30W
Unimak Island USA 100 C4 55 00N 164 00W
UNITED ARAB EMIRATES 73 F3
UNITED KINGDOM 10
UNITED STATES OF AMERICA 102/103
Unst *i.* Scotland 11 D3 60 45N 0 55W
Upavon England 20 B2 51 18N 1 49W
Upper Lough Erne NI 14 B1 54 15N 7 30W
Upper Tean England 19 E2 52 57N 2 00W
Uppingham England 19 F2 52 35N 0 43W
Uppsala Sweden 55 E2 59 55N 17 38E
Upton West Yorkshire England 17 E2 53 37N 1 17W
Upton Dorset England 23 E2 50 42N 2 02W
Ural *r.* Asia 70 H6 48 00N 52 00E
Ural Mountains Russia 70 H7/H9 57 00N 60 00E
Ure *r.* England 17 E3 54 20N 1 55W
Urlingford RoI 25 D2 52 43N 7 35W
Urmston England 16 D2 53 27N 2 21W
Urr *r.* Scotland 15 F2 55 05N 3 57W
URUGUAY 115 F6
Uruguay *r.* Uruguay/Argentina 115 F6 32 00S 57 40W
Ürümqi China 76 E6 43 43N 87 38E
Ushaw Moor *tn.* England 17 E3 54 47N 1 39W
Usk *r.* Wales 18 C1 51 55N 3 40W
Ussel France 56 F3 45 32N 2 18E
Ust'-Ilimsk Russia 71 N8 58 03N 102 39E
Utah *state* USA 102 D4 39 00N 112 00W
Utah Lake USA 102 D5 40 10N 111 50W
Utrecht Neths 54 D5 52 05N 5 07E
Utrera Spain 57 C2 37 10N 5 47W
Uttoxeter England 19 E2 52 54N 1 52W
UZBEKISTAN 70 J5

V

Vác Hungary 59 J3 47 46N 19 08E
Vadodara India 74 C4 22 19N 73 14E
Valdepeñas Spain 57 D3 38 46N 3 24W
Valdivia Chile 115 C6 39 46S 73 15W
Val-d'Or Canada 101 V3 48 07N 77 47W
Valence France 56 G3 44 56N 4 54E
Valencia Spain 57 E3 39 29N 0 24W
Valencia Venezuela 114 D16 10 14N 67 59W
Valencia, Gulf of Spain 57 F3 39 30N 0 20E
Valencia Island *i.* RoI 25 A1 51 52N 10 20W
Valenciennes France 56 F6 50 22N 3 32E
Vale of Glamorgan, The *u.a.* Wales 18 C1 51 30N 3 30W
Valladolid Mexico 106 G4 20 40N 88 11W
Valladolid Spain 57 C4 41 39N 4 45W
Valletta Malta 60 F1 35 54N 14 32E
Valley *tn.* Wales 18 B3 53 17N 4 34W
Valparaíso Chile 115 C7 33 05S 71 40W
Valverde del Camino Spain 57 B2 37 35N 6 45W
Vanadzor Armenia 63 F3 40 49N 44 30E
Vancouver Canada 100 L3 49 13N 123 06W
Vancouver USA 102 B6 45 38N 122 40W
Vänern *l.* Sweden 55 D2 59 00N 13 30E
Van Gölü *l.* Turkey 63 F2 38 33N 42 46E
Vanna *i.* Norway 55 E5 70 05N 19 50E
Vännäs Sweden 55 E3 63 56N 19 50E
Vannes France 56 C4 47 40N 2 44W
Vantaa Finland 55 F3 60 20N 24 50E
VANUATU 81 N7
Varanasi India 74 E5 25 20N 83 00E
Vardø Norway 55 K6 70 22N 31 06E
Varese Italy 60 C6 45 49N 8 49E
Varkhaus Finland 55 G3 62 20N 27 50E
Varna Bulgaria 61 M5 43 12N 27 57E
Värnamo Sweden 55 D2 57 11N 14 03E
Vaslui Romania 59 N3 46 37N 27 46E
Västerås Sweden 55 E2 59 36N 16 32E
Västervik Sweden 55 E2 57 45N 16 40E
Vasto Italy 60 F5 42 07N 14 43E
Vatersay *i.* Scotland 12 B1 56 55N 7 32W
Vatra Dornei Romania 59 M3 47 20N 25 21E
Vättern *l.* Sweden 55 D2 58 20N 14 20E
Växjö Sweden 55 D2 56 52N 14 50E
Vejle Denmark 55 C2 55 43N 9 33E
Velebit *mts.* Croatia 60 F6 44 00N 15 00E
Vélez-Málaga Spain 57 C2 36 47N 4 06W
Vélez Rubio Spain 57 D2 37 39N 2 04W
Vementry *i.* Scotland 11 C3 60 20N 1 28W
Vendôme France 56 E4 47 48N 1 04E
VENEZUELA 114 D15
Venice Italy 60 E6 45 26N 12 20E
Venissieux France 56 G3 45 42N 4 46E
Venlo Netherland 54 E4 51 22N 6 10E
Ventnor England 20 B1 50 36N 1 11W
Ventura USA 102 C3 34 16N 119 18W
Vera Spain 57 E2 37 15N 1 51W
Veracruz Mexico 106 E3 19 11N 96 10W
Vercelli Italy 60 CC6 45 19N 8 26E
Verdun-sur-Meuse France 56 G5 49 10N 5 24E
Verin Spain 57 B4 41 55N 7 26W
Vermont *state* USA 103 M5 44 00N 73 00W
Verona Italy 60 D6 45 26N 11 00E
Versailles France 56 F5 48 48N 2 07E
Verviers Belgium 54 D3 50 36N 5 52E
Verwood England 23 F2 50 53N 1 52W
Vesoul France 56 H4 47 38N 6 09E
Vesuvio *vol.* Italy 60 F4 40 49N 14 26E
Veszprém Hungary 59 H3 47 06N 17 54E
Vetlanda Sweden 55 E2 57 26N 15 05E
Vevey Switz. 58 C3 46 28N 6 51E
Viano do Castelo Portugal 57 A4 41 41N 8 50W
Viareggio Italy 60 D5 43 52N 10 15E
Viborg Denmark 55 C2 56 28N 9 25E
Vibo Valentia Italy 60 G3 38 40N 16 06E
Vicenza Italy 60 D6 45 33N 11 32E
Vichy France 56 F4 46 07N 3 25E
Victoria Canada 100 L3 48 26N 123 20W
Victoria, Lake East Africa 93 C4 2 00S 33 00E
Vienna Austria 59 H4 48 13N 16 22E
Vienne France 56 G3 45 32N 4 54E
Vientiane Laos 79 C7 17 59N 102 38E
Vierzon France 56 F4 47 14N 2 03E
VIETNAM 79 D7
Vigo Spain 57 A5 42 15N 8 44W
Vila Nova de Gaia Portugal 57 A4 41 08N 8 37W
Vila Real Portugal 57 B4 41 17N 7 45W
Vilhelmina Sweden 55 E3 64 38N 16 40E
Villach Austria 58 F3 46 37N 13 51E
Villalba Spain 57 B5 43 17N 7 41W
Villarrobledo Spain 57 D3 39 16N 2 36W
Villefranche-sur-Saône France 56 G3 46 00N 4 43E
Villena Spain 57 E3 38 39N 0 52W
Villeneuve-sur-Lot France 56 E3 44 25N 0 43E
Villeurbanne France 56 G3 45 46N 4 54E
Vilnius Lithuania 55 G1 54 40N 25 19E
Viña del Mar Chile 115 C7 33 02S 71 35W
Vinaroz Spain 57 F4 40 29N 0 28E
Vipiteno Italy 60 D7 46 54N 11 27E
Virginia RoI 24 D3 53 49N 7 04W
Virginia USA 103 H6 47 30N 92 28W
Virginia *state* USA 103 L4 38 00N 77 00W
Virginia Water *tn.* England 20 C2 51 24N 0 34W
Virgin Islands W. Indies 107 M3 18 00N 64 30W
Visby Sweden 55 E2 57 32N 18 15E
Viseu Portugal 57 B4 40 40N 7 55W
Vishakhapatnam India 74 E3 17 42N 83 24E
Viterbo Italy 60 E5 42 24N 12 06E
Vitória Brazil 114 J9 20 20S 40 18W
Vitoria Gasteiz Spain 57 D5 42 51N 2 40W
Vitry-le-François France 56 G5 48 44N 4 36E
Vitsyebsk Belarus 62 D6 55 10N 30 14E
Vittoria Italy 60 F2 36 58N 14 32E
Vladimir Russia 70 G8 56 08N 40 25E
Vladivostok Russia 71 R5 43 09N 131 53E
Vlissingen Neths 54 B4 51 27N 3 35E
Voitsberg Austria 58 G3 47 04N 15 09E
Volga *r.* Russia 70 G6 50 00N 45 00E
Volgograd Russia 70 G6 48 45N 44 30E

Volta, Lake Ghana 90 D3 7 30N 0 30W
Vóreioi Sporádes is. Greece 61 K3/L3 39 00N 24 00E
Vosges mts. France 55 H5 48 10N 6 50E
Voss Norway 55 C3 60 38N 6 25E
Voxnan Sweden 55 E3 61 22N 15 39E
Vukovar Croatia 61 H6 45 19N 19 01E

W

Waal r. Neths 54 D4 51 50N 5 07E
Waalwijk Neths 54 D4 51 42N 5 04E
Waddesdon England 20 C2 51 51N 0 56W
Waddington England 17 F2 53 10N 0 32W
Wadebridge England 22 C2 50 32N 4 50W
Wadhurst England 21 D2 51 04N 0 21E
Wadi Halfa Sudan 91 M6 21 55N 31 20E
Wainfleet All Saints England 17 G2 53 06N 0 15E
Wakefield England 17 E2 53 42N 1 29W
Wales UK 18 C2 52 40N 3 30W
Wallasey England 16 C2 53 26N 3 03W
Wallingford England 20 B2 51 37N 1 08W
Wallis and Futuna is. Pacific Ocean 116 J6 13 16S 176 15W
Walls Scotland 11 C3 60 14N 1 34W
Wallsend England 17 E3 55 00N 1 31W
Walney, Isle of England 16 C3 54 05N 3 10W
Walsall England 19 E2 52 35N 1 58W
Waltham Abbey England 20 D2 51 41N 0 00
Waltham Forest England 20 C2 51 36N 0 00
Waltham on the Wolds England 19 F2 52 49N 0 49W
Walton-le-Dale England 16 D2 53 45N 2 41W
Walton-on-the-Naze England 21 E2 51 51N 1 16E
Walvis Bay tn. Namibia 92 B3 22 59S 14 31E
Wanganui NZ 81 P3 39 56S 175 03E
Wanlockhead Scotland 15 F2 55 24N 3 47W
Wantage England 20 B2 51 36N 1 25W
Warboys England 20 C3 52 24N 0 06W
Ward Hill Scotland 11 A1 58 54N 3 20W
Ware England 20 C2 51 49N 0 02W
Wareham England 23 E2 50 41N 2 07W
Warley England 19 E2 52 30N 1 59W
Warlingham England 20 C2 51 19N 0 04W
Warminster England 23 A2 51 13N 2 12W
Warrenpoint tn. NI 14 C1 54 06N 6 15W
Warrington England 16 D2 53 24N 2 37W
Warsaw Poland 59 K6 52 15N 21 00E
Warsop England 17 E2 53 13N 1 10W
Warton England 16 D2 53 46N 2 54W
Warwick England 19 E2 52 17N 1 34W
Warwickshire co. England 19 E2 52 15N 1 40W
Washingborough England 17 F2 53 14N 0 28W
Washington England 17 E3 54 54N 1 31W
Washington state USA 102 B6/C6 47 00N 120 00W
Washington D.C. USA 103 L4 38 55N 77 00W
Wash, The b. England 21 D3 52 55N 0 10E
Watchet England 23 D3 51 12N 3 20W
Waterbeach England 21 D3 52 16N 0 11E
Waterford Rol 25 D2 52 15N 7 06W
Waterford co. Rol 25 D2 52 10N 7 30W
Waterford Harbour Rol 25 E2 52 10N 7 00W
Watergrasshill Rol 25 C2 52 00N 8 20W
Waterlooville England 20 B1 50 53N 1 02W
Waterville Rol 25 A1 51 50N 10 10W
Watford England 20 C2 51 39N 0 24W
Wath upon Dearne England 17 E2 53 31N 1 21W
Watlington England 20 C2 51 39N 1 00W
Watton England 21 D3 52 34N 0 50E
Waveney r. England 21 E3 52 30N 1 30E
Wavre Belgium 54 C3 50 43N 4 37E
Wear r. England 16 D3 54 45N 2 05W
Weaverham England 16 D2 53 16N 2 35W
Wedmore England 23 E3 51 14N 2 49W
Weedon Bec England 19 E2 52 14N 1 05W
Weiden Germany 58 F4 49 40N 12 10E
Weimar Germany 58 E5 50 59N 11 20E
Weissenfels Germany 58 E5 51 12N 11 58E
Welland r. England 19 E2 52 50N 0 10
Welland r. England 19 F2 52 30N 0 50W
Wellingborough England 19 F2 52 19N 0 42W
Wellington Telford and Wrekin England 19 D2 52 43N 2 31W
Wellington Somerset England 23 D2 50 59N 3 15W
Wellington NZ 81 P2 41 17S 174 46E
Wells England 23 E3 51 13N 2 39W
Wells-next-the-Sea England 21 D3 52 58N 0 51E
Wels Austria 58 F4 48 10N 14 02E
Welshpool Wales 18 C2 52 40N 3 09W
Welton England 17 F2 54 47N 3 00W
Welwyn Garden City England 20 C2 51 48N 0 13W
Wem England 19 D2 52 51N 2 44W
Wemyss Bay Scotland 14 E2 55 55N 4 53W
Wendover England 20 C2 51 46N 0 46W
Wensum r. England 21 D3 52 45N 1 10E
Wenzhou China 77 M3 28 02N 120 40E

West Berkshire u.a. England 20 B2 51 28N 1 00W
West Bridgford England 19 E2 52 56N 1 08W
West Bromwich England 19 E2 52 31N 1 59W
Westbury England 20 A2 51 16N 2 11W
West Dunbartonshire u.a. Scotland 15 E3 56 02N 4 39W
Westerham England 20 D2 51 16N 0 05E
Western Ghats mts. India 74 C3/D2 15 30N 74 00E
Western Isles u.a. Scotland 12 B2/B3 57 45N 7 30W
WESTERN SAHARA 90 B6/B7
Western Sayan mts. Russia 71 M7 52 30N 92 30E
West Felton England 18 D2 52 49N 2 58W
West Haddon England 19 E2 52 20N 1 04W
Westhill Scotland 13 G2 57 11N 2 16W
West Horsley England 20 C2 51 16N 0 26W
West Indies is. Caribbean Sea 107 K4/L4 22 00N 69 00W
West Kilbride Scotland 14 E2 55 42N 4 51W
West Kirby England 16 C2 53 22N 3 10W
West Loch Tarbert Western Isles Scotland 12 B2/C2 57 55N 6 52W
West Loch Tarbert Argyll and Bute Scotland 14 D2 55 48N 5 31W
West Lothian u.a. Scotland 15 F2 55 50N 3 36W
Westmeath co. Rol 24 D3 53 30N 7 30W
West Mersea England 21 D2 51 47N 0 55E
West Midlands co. England 19 D2 52 35N 2 00W
Weston-super-Mare England 23 E3 51 21N 2 59W
Westport Rol 24 B3 53 48N 9 32W
Westport Bay Rol 24 B3 53 49N 9 37W
West Sussex co. England 20 C1 51 00N 0 25W
West Thurrock England 21 D2 51 28N 0 20E
West Virginia state USA 103 K4 39 00N 81 00W
Westward Ho! England 22 C3 51 02N 4 15W
West Wittering England 20 C1 50 47N 0 54W
West Yorkshire co. England 17 E2 53 50N 1 30W
Wetherby England 17 E2 53 56N 1 23W
Wetzlar Germany 58 D5 50 33N 8 30E
Wexford co. Rol 25 E2 52 25N 6 35W
Wexford Rol 25 E2 52 20N 6 27W
Wexford Bay Rol 25 E2 52 25N 6 10W
Wexford Harbour Rol 25 E2 52 20N 6 25W
Wey r. England 20 C2 51 18N 0 30W
Weybridge England 20 C2 51 22N 0 28W
Weyburn Canada 101 Q3 49 39N 103 51W
Weymouth England 23 E2 50 37N 2 25W
Whaley Bridge England 16 E2 53 20N 1 59W
Whalley England 16 D2 53 50N 2 24W
Wharfe r. England 16 D3 54 10N 2 05W
Wharfedale v. England 16 D3 54 05N 2 00W
Wheatley England 20 B2 52 52N 0 52W
Whernside sum. England 16 D3 54 14N 2 23W
Whickham England 17 E3 54 57N 1 40W
Whitburn England 17 E3 54 57N 1 21W
Whitburn Scotland 15 F2 55 52N 3 42W
Whitby England 17 F3 54 29N 0 37W
Whitchurch Shropshire England 19 D2 52 58N 2 41W
Whitchurch Buckinghamshire England 20 C2 51 53N 0 51W
Whitchurch Hampshire England 20 B2 51 14N 1 20W
Whitefield England 16 D2 53 34N 2 18W
Whitegate Rol 25 C1 51 50N 8 14W
Whitehaven England 16 C3 54 33N 3 35W
Whitehead NI 14 D1 54 45N 5 43W
Whitehills Scotland 13 G2 57 40N 2 35W
White Horse, Vale of England 20 B2 51 35N 1 30W
Whiten Head Scotland 13 E3 58 34N 4 32W
Whiteparish England 20 B2 51 01N 1 39W
Whitfield England 21 E2 51 09N 1 17E
Whithorn Scotland 15 E1 54 44N 4 25W
Whitland Wales 18 B1 51 50N 4 37W
Whitley Bay tn. England 17 E4 55 03N 1 25W
Whitney, Mount USA 102 C4 36 35N 118 17W
Whitsand Bay England 22 C2 50 20N 4 25W
Whitstable England 21 E2 51 22N 1 02E
Whittington England 18 C2 52 52N 3 00W
Whittlesey England 20 C3 52 34N 0 08W
Whitton England 17 F2 53 43N 0 38W
Whitworth England 16 D2 53 40N 2 10W
Wichita USA 103 G4 37 43N 97 20W
Wick Scotland 13 F3 58 26N 3 06W
Wick r. Scotland 13 F3 58 26N 3 10W
Wickford England 21 D2 51 38N 0 31E
Wickham England 20 B1 50 54N 1 10W
Wickham Market England 21 E2 52 09N 1 22E
Wicklow Rol 25 E2 52 59N 6 03W
Wicklow co. Rol 25 E2 52 55N 6 25W
Wicklow Mountains Rol 25 E2/E3 53 00N 6 20W
Widnes England 16 D2 53 22N 2 44W

Wiener Neustadt Austria 59 H3 47 49N 16 15E
Wierden Neths 54 E5 52 21N 6 35E
Wiesbaden Germany 58 D5 50 05N 8 15E
Wigan England 16 D2 53 33N 2 38W
Wigston England 19 E2 52 36N 1 05W
Wigton England 16 C3 54 49N 3 09W
Wigtown Scotland 15 E1 54 52N 4 26W
Wigtown Bay Scotland 15 E1 54 45N 4 20W
Wil Switzerland 58 D3 47 28N 9 03E
Wilberfoss England 17 F2 53 57N 0 53W
Wilhelmshaven Germany 58 D6 53 32N 8 07E
Willington England 17 E3 54 43N 1 41W
Williton England 23 D3 51 10N 3 20W
Wilmslow England 16 D2 53 20N 2 15W
Wilton England 20 B2 51 05N 1 52W
Wiltshire co. England 20 A2/B2 51 30N 2 00W
Wimborne Minster England 23 F2 50 48N 1 59W
Wincanton England 23 E3 51 04N 2 25W
Winchelsea England 21 D1 50 55N 0 42E
Winchester England 20 B2 51 04N 1 19W
Windermere tn England 16 D3 54 23N 2 54W
Windermere l. England 16 D3 54 20N 2 56W
Windhoek Namibia 92 C3 22 34S 17 06E
Windsor Canada 101 U2 42 18N 83 00W
Windsor England 20 C2 51 29N 0 38W
Windsor and Maidenhead u.a. England 20 C1 50 25N 0 50W
Windward Islands Lesser Antilles 107 M2 12 30N 62 00W
Wingate England 17 E3 54 55N 1 23W
Wingerworth England 17 E2 53 13N 1 28W
Winkleigh England 22 D2 50 51N 3 56W
Winnipeg Canada 101 R3 49 53N 97 10W
Winnipeg, Lake Canada 101 R4 52 30N 97 30W
Winnipegosis, Lake Canada 101 Q4 52 10N 100 00W
Winschoten Neths 54 F6 53 07N 7 02E
Winscombe England 23 E3 51 28N 2 52W
Winsford England 16 D2 53 11N 2 31W
Winslow England 20 C2 51 57N 0 54W
Winterbourne England 19 D1 51 30N 2 31W
Winterthur Switz. 58 D3 47 30N 8 45E
Winterton-on-Sea England 21 E3 52 43N 1 42E
Wirksworth England 17 E2 53 05N 1 34W
Wisbech England 21 D3 52 40N 0 10E
Wisconsin state USA 103 H6/J6 45 00N 90 00W
Wishaw Scotland 15 F2 55 47N 3 56W
Wisła r. Poland 59 J6 53 00N 19 00E
Wismar Germany 58 E6 53 54N 11 28E
Wissembourg France 56 H5 49 02N 7 57E
Witham r. England 17 F2 53 05N 0 40W
Witham England 21 D2 51 48N 0 38E
Witheridge England 22 D2 50 55N 3 42W
Withernsea England 17 G2 53 44N 0 02E
Witley England 20 C2 51 08N 0 39W
Witney England 20 B2 51 48N 1 29W
Wittenberg Germany 58 F5 51 53N 12 39E
Wittenberge Germany 58 E6 52 59N 11 45E
Wittlich Germany 58 C4 49 59N 6 54E
Wiveliscombe England 23 D3 51 03N 3 19W
Wivenhoe England 21 D2 51 52N 0 58E
Woburn Sands tn. England 20 C3 52 01N 0 39W
Woking England 20 C2 51 20N 0 34W
Wokingham England 20 C2 51 25N 0 51W
Wokingham u.a. England 20 C1 50 25N 0 55W
Wolfsberg Austria 58 G3 46 50N 14 50E
Wolfsburg Germany 58 E6 52 27N 10 49E
Wollaston England 19 F2 52 16N 0 41W
Wollongong Australia 81 K4 34 25S 150 52E
Wolsingham England 17 E3 54 44N 1 52W
Wolverhampton England 19 D2 52 36N 2 08W
Wolverton England 20 C3 52 04N 0 50W
Wombourne England 19 D2 52 32N 2 11W
Wombwell England 17 E2 53 32N 1 24W
Woodbridge England 21 E2 52 06N 1 19E
Woodford Halse England 19 E2 52 10N 1 13W
Woodhall Spa England 17 F2 53 09N 0 14W
Woodlands tn. Canada 104 A4 50 12N 97 40W
Woodstock England 20 B2 51 52N 1 21W
Wool England 23 E2 50 41N 2 14W
Woolacombe England 22 C3 51 10N 4 13W
Wooler England 15 G2 55 33N 2 01W
Wootton Bassett England 20 B2 51 33N 1 54W
Worcester England 19 D2 52 11N 2 13W
Worcester USA 103 M5 42 17N 71 48W
Worcestershire co. England 19 D2 52 15N 2 15W
Workington England 16 C3 54 39N 3 33W
Worksop England 17 E2 53 18N 1 07W
Worms Germany 58 D4 49 38N 8 23E
Worms Head Wales 18 B1 51 34N 4 20W
Worsbrough England 17 E2 53 33N 1 29W
Worthing England 20 C1 50 48N 0 23W
Wotton-under-Edge England 19 D1 51 39N 2 21W
Wragle England 17 G2 53 02N 0 07E
Wrath, Cape Scotland 13 D3/E3 58 37N 5 01W
Wrexham tn Wales 18 C3 53 03N 3 00W

Wrexham u.a. Wales 18 C3/D3 53 00N 3 00W
Writtle England 21 D2 51 44N 0 26E
Wrocław Poland 59 H5 51 05N 17 00E
Wrotham England 21 D2 51 19N 0 19E
Wroughton England 20 B2 51 31N 1 48W
Wroxham England 21 E3 52 42N 1 24E
Wuhan China 77 K4 30 35N 114 19E
Wuppertal Germany 58 C5 51 15N 7 10E
Würtzburg Germany 58 D4 49 48N 9 57E
Wuxi China 77 M4 31 35N 120 19E
Wye England 21 D2 51 11N 0 56E
Wylye England 20 B2 51 08N 2 01W
Wylye r. England 20 A2 51 08N 2 13W
Wymondham England 21 E3 52 34N 1 07E
Wyoming state USA 102 E5 43 00N 108 00W

X

Xi'an China 77 J4 34 16N 108 54E

Y

Yakutsk Russia 71 Q9 62 10N 129 50E
Yamoussoukro Côte d'Ivoire 90 C3 6 50N 5 20W
Yangon Myanmar 79 B7 16 47N 96 10E
Yaoundé Cameroon 90 G2 3 51N 11 31E
Yaroslavl' Russia 70 F8 57 34N 39 52E
Yate England 19 D1 51 32N 2 25W
Yateley England 20 C2 51 20N 0 51W
Yatsushiro Japan 78 B1 32 32N 130 35E
Yatton England 23 E3 51 24N 2 49W
Yaxley England 20 C3 52 31N 0 16W
Yeadon England 17 E2 53 52N 1 41W
Yealmpton England 22 D2 50 21N 3 59W
Yekaterinburg Russia 70 J8 56 52N 60 35E
Yell i. Scotland 11 C3 60 35N 1 10W
Yellowknife Canada 100 N6 62 30N 114 29W
Yelverton England 22 C2 50 30N 4 05W
YEMEN REPUBLIC 72/73 D2/E2
Yeovil England 23 E2 50 57N 2 39W
Yerevan Armenia 63 F3 40 10N 44 31E
Yokohama Japan 78 C2 35 27N 139 38E
York England 17 E2 53 58N 1 05W
York u.a. England 17 E2 53 56N 1 05W
York, Cape Australia 81 H8 10 42S 142 32E
Yorkshire Wolds England 17 F3 54 00N 0 45W
York, Vale of England 17 E3 54 10N 1 20W
Youghal Rol 25 D1 51 51N 7 50W
Youghal Bay Rol 25 D1 51 55N 7 48W
Yoxford England 21 E3 52 16N 1 30E
Ystalyfera Wales 18 C1 51 47N 3 47W
Ystrad Aeron Wales 18 B2 52 10N 4 10W
Ystradgnylais Wales 18 C1 51 47N 3 45W
Ystwyth r. Wales 22 C2 52 20N 3 55W
Ytterhogdal Sweden 55 D3 62 10N 14 55E
Yucatan p. Mexico 106 G3 19 00N 89 00W
Yuci China 77 K5 37 40N 112 44E
Yukon r. Canada/USA 100 D6 63 30N 159 40W
Yukon Territory territory Canada 100 H6/J6 64 15N 135 00W
Yumen China 76 G5 39 54N 97 43E
Yverdon Switz. 58 C3 46 47N 6 38E
Yvetot France 56 E5 49 37N 0 45E

Z

Zaanstad Neths 54 C5 52 27N 4 49E
Zadar Croatia 60 F6 44 07N 15 14E
Zafra Spain 57 B3 38 25N 6 25W
Zagań Poland 58 G5 51 37N 15 20E
Zagreb Croatia 60 F6 45 48N 15 58E
Zagros Mountains Iran 73 E5/F5 32 45N 48 50E
Zakopane Poland 59 J4 49 17N 19 54E
Zákynthos i. Greece 61 J2 37 45N 20 50E
Zambezi r. Zambia/Zimbabwe 92 D4 16 00S 23 00E
ZAMBIA 92 D5/E5
Zamora Spain 57 C4 41 30N 5 45W
Zanzibar Tanzania 93 F1 6 10S 39 12E
Zaragoza Spain 57 E4 41 39N 0 54W
Zaria Nigeria 90 F4 11 01N 7 44E
Zeebrugge Belgium 54 B4 51 20N 3 13E
Zell-am-See tn. Austria 58 F3 47 19N 12 47E
Zenica Bosnia-Herzegovina 61 G6 44 11N 17 53E
Zermatt Switz. 58 C3 46 01N 7 45E
Zhengzhou China 77 K4 34 45N 113 38E
Zhmerynka Ukraine 59 P4 49 00N 28 02E
Zhytomyr Ukraine 59 P5 50 18N 28 40E
Zibo China 77 L5 36 51N 118 01E
Zielona Góra Poland 59 G5 51 57N 15 30E
ZIMBABWE 92 E4/F4
Zinder Niger 90 F4 13 46N 8 58E
Zlín Czech Rep. 59 H4 49 14N 17 40E
Zug Switz. 58 D3 47 10N 8 31E
Zugspitze mt. Austria 58 E3 47 25N 11 00E
Zürich Switz. 58 D3 47 23N 8 33E
Zvolen Slovakia 59 J4 48 34N 19 08E
Zwettl Austria 58 G4 48 37N 15 11E
Zwickau Germany 58 F5 50 43N 12 30E
Zwolle Neths 54 E5 52 31N 6 06E